Bloodsucking Witchcraft

HUGO G. NUTINI & JOHN M. ROBERTS

Bloodsucking Witchcraft

An Epistemological Study of

Anthropomorphic Supernaturalism

in Rural Tlaxcala

The University of Arizona Press

Tucson & London

The University of Arizona Press
Copyright © 1993
Arizona Board of Regents
All Rights Reserved

98 97 96 95 94 93   6 5 4 3 2 1

Library of Congress Cataloging-in-Publication Data

Nutini, Hugo G.
    Bloodsucking witchcraft : an epistemological study of
anthropomorphic supernaturalism in rural Tlaxcala / Hugo G. Nutini
and John M. Roberts.
        p.   cm.
    Includes bibliographical references and index.
    ISBN 0-8165-1197-7 (cloth : acid-free paper)
    1. Nahuas—Religion and mythology.   2. Nahuas—Magic.
3. Witchcraft—Mexico—Tlaxcala (State)   4. Vampires—Mexico—
Tlaxcala (State)   5. Blood—Religious aspects.   6. Tlaxcala (Mexico
: State)—Social life and customs.   I. Roberts, John M. (John
Milton), 1916–1990.   II. Title.   92-34513
F1221.N3N87   1993   CIP

British Library Cataloguing-in-Publication Data
A catalogue record for this book is available from the British Library.

To the Memory of

John M. Roberts:

Friend, Colleague, and

Source of Inspiration

Contents

Maps and Tables

Preface

This book is about culture loss and decay. It analyzes the bloodsucking witch-craft system that affected the great majority of the population of rural Tlaxcala a generation ago, and it chronicles its drastic transformation since then. The relentless process of secularization since World War II has nearly destroyed the traditional fabric of rural Tlaxcalan society, which had resisted modernizing changes since before the turn of the century. The people of the region are on the verge of losing the cultural identity that had maintained them as a distinct ethnic group since the time of the Spanish Conquest. One of the goals of this book is to preserve a complex of beliefs and practices that was an important component of their ideology and overall *imago mundi*. In sociocultural con-figuration, rural Tlaxcalans are emerging from a traditional Indian-peasant seg-ment of pluri-ethnic Mexico into an essentially proletarian, urban-oriented segment of the national culture, and the transition has afforded us an appropri-ate juncture and context for the analysis of the changes in perception and inference that such a fundamental transition entails. Focusing on the problem of bloodsucking witchcraft, this book demonstrates the new *imago mundi* that comes into existence after the sequential and sustained effect of four genera-tions of modernization and secularization. This is the crucial problem of change, which, perceived from the standpoint of evolution and decay, must be fundamentally framed as an exercise in anthropological epistemology, the basic premise underlying the synchronic and diachronic dimensions of this work.

This book has been difficult to write: partly because the original set of data on which it is based was gathered a generation ago, and the traditional system to which it refers has ceased to exist for at least ten years; and partly because, in the absence of a theoretical model to analyze this particular case of witchcraft, we were unable to devise our own before additional comparable data had been gathered for the thorough implementation of the model ultimately devised. As explained in the text, the study lacks an exacting psychological data base, which, insofar as the rapidly changing ethnographic situation permitted, we tried to remedy by gathering additional data as required by the model, and as comparable as possible to the original data set. Despite these inevitable disadvantages, we were able to fashion an approach to the study of witchcraft and other forms of magic supernaturalism that is distinct from any other devised by anthropologists in two generations.

In the prefaces of five previous monographs (Nutini 1968; Nutini and Isaac 1974; Nutini and Bell 1980; Nutini 1984; Nutini 1987), gratitude to the many individuals and institutions who helped make these works possible was expressed. That gratitude remains as warm today. For the generous financial support that enabled Nutini to gather the ethnological and ethnohistorical data on which this book is based, we would like to thank the following institutions: the Social Science Research Council, the National Science Foundation, the Wenner-Gren Foundation for Anthropological Research, the American Philosophical Society, the Pittsburgh Foundation, the University of Pittsburgh Center for International Studies, and the University of Pittsburgh Humanities Research Fund. Without their assistance, Nutini could have completed neither the specific studies on kinship, ritual kinship, and the cult of the dead nor the more general comparative work on Tlaxcala as exemplified by this monograph.

What also remains true today is that it would be impossible to single out every individual or institution who, in one way or another, helped in the writing of this book and in the fieldwork and archival research on which it is based. We would like, however, to express our appreciation to those who made the most significant contributions: to the Instituto Nacional de Anthropología e Historia in general, and to its former directors, the late Dr. Eusebio Dávalos Hurtado, Dr. Ignacio Bernal y García Pimental, and Dr. Guillermo Bonfil Batalla in particular, we are grateful for administrative support. To the authorities of the state of Tlaxcala from 1959 to 1982, and particularly to the former governors Licenciado Don Joaquín Cisneros Molina, the late Licenciado Don Anselmo Cervantes H., the late General Don Antonio Bonilla Vásquez, Dr. Don Luciano Huerta Sánchez, and the late Licenciado Don Emilio Sánchez Piedras, we are grateful for administrative and material support. To the bishop of the diocese of Tlaxcala, Dr. Don Luis Munive y Escobar, we are greatly indebted not only for administrative support but also for the many ways in which he facilitated our research in the local parochial archives and helped create goodwill among parish priests and the local religious hierarchies. To the countless municipal authorities of the Tlaxcalan communities where we have worked during the past generation, we are grateful for the openness and willingness to help and for the time and effort they devoted to establishing the proper conditions of fieldwork.

We are intellectually and professionally indebted to Lisa Moskowitz, Jean F. Nutini, Vinigi L. Grotanelli, María Teresa Cervantes, Douglas R. White, Lilyan Brudner-White, Terrence S. Kaufman, Lola R. Ross, Barry L. Isaac, Alan R. Rogers, Italo Signorini, Allesandro Lupo, James S. Boster, Andrew J. Strathern, Edward J. McCord, John G. Kennedy, Robert B. Edgerton, A. Kimball Romney, and Timothy D. Murphy, who either read parts of the text, made constructive criticisms, and suggested changes in style, presentation, and organization or discussed with us theoretical or methodological matters. To Solange Behocaray de Alberro we owe several ideas concerning the evolution of various Mesoamerican institutions since the time of the Conquest. She has for many years been an invaluable source of inspiration on the history of mentalities in Mexico throughout Colonial times. L. Keith Brown read the entire manuscript and offered many insightful comments and suggestions. For many years Brown has read manuscripts of Nutini's most important publications, and his creative criticisms have resulted in improved works. His generous, always available help is most gratefully acknowledged. We are grateful to Doren L. Slade for suggesting the concept of fugue to explain some aspects of the behavior of mothers after their infants are believed to have died as the result of witchcraft.

Nutini wishes to express his gratitude for the generosity and availability of his chief informants in approximately fifty communities, in which information on witchcraft in particular and magic supernaturalism in general was collected. We owe a special debt to the people of the communities, neighborhoods, and households, where we gathered the cases of bloodsucking witchcraft on which this study is based, for the receptivity, patience, and warmth with which they received the inquiries. We are also very grateful to Nutini's more than 140 ritual kinsmen contracted over the past generation. Many of these ritual kinsmen were highly instrumental in facilitating the intrinsically difficult task of gathering structured and systematic information on bloodsucking witchcraft cases and their aftereffects.

Finally, we are very grateful to the noted Mexican artist Desiderio H. Xochitiotzin and his wife, Lilia Ortega de Xochitiotzin. Throughout Nutini's entire Tlaxcalan experience, Desiderio Xochitiotzin has been a most valuable contact in interpersonal relationships at all levels of Tlaxcalan society, as well as a rich source of ideas and information about ethnographic details and historical sources. For this monograph he contributed magico-religious interpretations, clarified ritual and ceremonial descriptions, and pointed out a number of pre-Hispanic religious and magical survivals.

H.G.N.

Pittsburgh, Pennsylvania

January 1992

John M. Roberts died after submitting the manuscript for publication. I dedicate the book to him as a testimony of his intellectual creativity and in recognition of his influence on my mature analytical development.

Glossary

All the Spanish and Nahuatl terms included in this glossary are used at least twice in the text and explained as they occur, but for the convenience of the reader we have compiled them in one place.

Acompañante	Attendants to the stewards and officers of the local religious hierarchy
Antojoso(a)	A state of hankering in an adult male or female provoked by couvade-like or other psychological disorders
Apellido(s)	Patronymic. Paternal and material first surname
Ataque de espíritus	Attack of spirits. An aggravated case of espanto. Serious psychological disturbance suffered by some mothers during the postsucking period
Atlan teittaqui	Pre-Hispanic sorcerer; he who has the power to return the soul or guardian spirit to the body
Atole	Thick porridgelike drink made of ground corn, wheat, or barley
Ayuntamiento religioso (república, eclesiástica)	Religious government. Body of officials elected on a yearly basis by local communities
Barranca	Ravine
Barrios	Localized or non-localized quasi-socioreligious units into which most rural Tlaxcalan communities are divided

Bilis	Bile, folk disease
Brujo(a) (tlahuelpuchi)	Male or female witch. Male or female bloodsucking witch
Brujos nahualles	The term for witches, as reported by a priest-scholar for the first half of the seventeenth century
Cabecera(s)	Seat of municipal governments. Headtowns
Caliente	Hot. An inherent quality of foodstuffs and human psychological states
Calmecac	Priestly houses in pre-Hispanic times
Capulin	A kind of cherry tree. Prunus capuli
Cargo	Religious office. Religious sponsorship
Chipil	Psychological state experienced by a father after his infant has been sucked by the witch
Chipilería	Psychological aftereffects exhibited by fathers upon the death of infants attributed to the witch
Cihuanotzqui	Pre-Hispanic sorcerer
Cofradía	Sodality. A group of stewardships. The officers of a sodality or group of stewardships
Comadre	Comother; female ritual kinswoman; term of reference for female ritual kinswoman
Comadrita	Diminutive of comother; term of reference for female ritual kinswoman
Compadrazgo	Ritual kinship. The ritual sponsorship of a person, image, object, or occasion, together with a complex of temporary and permanent social, religious, economic, and symbolic attributes binding its personnel (parents, owners, kinsmen, sponsors, and mediating entities)
Compadre	Cofather; male ritual kinsman; term of reference for male ritual kinsman
Compadres	Coparents; ritual kinsmen; term of reference for ritual kin in general
Compadrito	Diminutive of cofather; term of address for male ritual kinsman
Concuña(da)	Co-sisters-in-law; term of reference between sisters-in-law
Copal	Pine resin. Incense

Copalcaxitl	Earthenware incense burner
Cuezcomate	Storage bin
Curandero	Curer; herbalist, medicine man
Desmayo(s)	Fainting spells; generally experienced by parents after infants have been sucked by the witch
El Cuatlapanga	The anthropomorphic supernatural owner of the hill of the same name. Male tutelary mountain owner in the Tlaxcala-Pueblan valley
Enchiladas	Large corn tortillas smeared with red chili sauce
Encomienda	Indians entrusted to individual Spaniards or Creoles throughout the sixteenth and seventeenth centuries
Escalafón religioso	Civil religious hierarchy
Espanto	Fright; a sudden seizure or nightmare. Psychological disturbance suffered by some mothers during the postsucking period
Fiscal(es)	The main officials of the local religious hierarchy. The integrated group of the main officials of the local religious hierarchy and their assistants (attendants, messenger boys, sextons, doormen, and so on)
Frío	Cold. An inherent quality of foodstuffs and human psychological states
Hacienda	Latifundia. The form of land tenure that predominated in Mexico, from the middle to the seventeenth century until the Revolution of 1910
Hechicero(a)	Male or female sorcerer
Hermandad(es)	Brotherhoods. Special kind of stewardships which include among their annual religious functions a pilgrimage to the place where their images are venerated
Hojeada	Ritual cleansing. A succession of eight daily baths given to a woman in the temazcal, starting three days after childbirth
Huexolotl	Turkey
Indios	Indians. A socioethnic category
Insulto	Insult. Folk disease

La Malintzi	The anthropomorphic supernatural center of the mountain of the same name. Female tutelary mountain owner in the Tlaxcala-Pueblan valley
Las Pastorcitas	Stewardship of the little shepardesses
Limpia	Ritual cleansing; hojeada
Macehualtin	Commoners in pre-Hispanic times
Madeja	Skein
Madrina	Godmother; female ritual sponsor; term of reference and address for female ritual sponsor
Mal aire (ehecatl, yeyecatl)	Bad or evil air
Mal de ojo	Evil eye
Manda	A promise to God, the Virgin, or the saints in return for a certain favor
Matlalcihua	Slightly malevolent spirit of the ravines. Apparition
Matlapouhqui	Pre-Hispanic sorcerer; he who counts through the forearms
Mayordoma	The wife of a mayordomo
Mayordomía(s)	The sponsorship of the religious fiesta in honor of a given saint, together with a whole complex of ritual, ceremonial, administrative, and economic functions
Mayordomo	The principal officer in a stewardship; steward
Metepalca (yotlezahuitl)	A person with inherent bad luck; a person of bad omen
Milpa	Cultivated plot of land; crops growing on the plot
Mometzcopinqui	Pre-Hispanic witch; she whose legs are torn off
Moyohualitoani	Pre-Hispanic witch; he who is ready to make love at night
Municipio(s)	Municipality. County. Territorial and administrative subdivisions of the state of Tlaxcala
Nahual(es)	Individuals endowed with the supernatural powers to transform themselves into donkeys, turkeys, and other small animals. Tricksters of sorts
Nahuala	A female nahual
Nahualism	The craft of the nahual

Nahualli	The Nahuatl term for nahual (a hispanicized word). One of the terms for witch in pre-Hispanic times and throughout the sixteenth and seventeenth centuries
Nomotzale	Generic name for a group of pre-Hispanic sorcerers
Nomotzaleque	Pre-Hispanic sorcerer; assassin for hire
Ocoxochitl	Pine flower, a parasite
Octava de cruz	Octave of setting up a cross
Ofrenda	Offerings to the dead elaborately displayed in front of the family altar during the All Saints Day–All Souls Day celebration
Ofrenda (personal)	Institutionalized symmetrical or asymmetrical exchange between individuals and groups for many occasions in the life and annual cycles
Padrino	Godfather; male ritual sponsor; term of reference and address for male ritual sponsor
Paini	A kind of pre-Hispanic sorcerer; the messenger
Paraje	Circumscribed area of land. Circumscribed area of land associated with a non-residential extended family or name group
Perdida del alma	Soul loss
Pesadilla	Nightmare; one of several psychological disturbances affecting mothers during the postsucking period
Petate	Palm or straw mat
Pipiltin	Nobles in pre-Hispanic times
Racha(s)	Bloodsucking witchcraft epidemic
Recibimiento	The acceptance of a bride, image, or any ceremonial object. Introductory round of speeches during important ritual and ceremonial occasions
Repartimiento	Periodic allotment of Indians to individual Spaniards throughout the sixteenth and seventeenth centuries
República de Indios (congregación)	Republic of Indians; indian congregation; indian reserve in Colonial times
República eclesiástica (ayuntamiento religioso)	Ecclesiastic republic. Body of officials elected on a yearly basis by local communities

Rezadores	Prayer leaders
Ruda	Ruda cabruna. One of the plant elements of a cleansing bunch
Sarapes	Woolen blankets of many sizes and designs
Señoró	Principality. Small kingdoms in pre-Hispanic times
Solar	House site; "household." The type of house generally associated with extended-family households
Tamales	Several kinds of steamed cornmeal dough, with or without filling, wrapped in corn husks
Tapete	Woolen rug or rug-like textile
Tecitos	Many varieties of herb teas
Teciuhpeuhque	Term for weatherman in the seventeenth century
Teciuhque	Pre-Hispanic sorcerer
Tecocoliani	Pre-Hispanic sorcerer; he who makes people ill
Tecotzcuani	Pre-Hispanic witch; he who eats the calves of people
Tecuixtliliztli	The childbirth ceremony of blessing the fire in the seventeenth century
Teipitzani	Pre-Hispanic sorcerer; he who blows harmful spells on people
Telpochcalli	Men's house in pre-Hispanic times
Temacpalitoti	Generic name for a group of pre-Hispanic sorcerers
Temazcal	Steam bath
Temicnamictiani	A kind of pre-Hispanic sorcerer; interpreter of dreams
Temiquiximati	Pre-Hispanic sorcerer; he who interprets dreams
Tepan mizoni	Generic name for a group of pre-Hispanic sorcerers
Tetlachihuiani	Pre-Hispanic sorcerer; he who enchants people
Tetlachihuic (tetlachihuique, tetlahuachimic, hechicero)	Sorcerer
Tetlapanquetzqui	Pre-Hispanic sorcerer
Tetonaltiani	Seventeenth-century sorcerer

Texoxqui	Seventeenth-century sorcerer; he who enchants people
Teyollocuani	Pre-Hispanic witch; he who eats the hearts of people
Tezitlazc (*quiatlazc, tezitlazque, conjurador*)	Weatherman; rainmaker
Tiaxcas	Elders. Men who have reached the top of the ladder system. Men who have discharged important civil and religious offices
Tiempero (*tezitlazc*)	Weatherman; rainmaker
Tilma	Woolen cape
Titici	Pre-Hispanic curers; medical practitioners
Tlachihuiane	Seventeenth-century sorcerer
Tlachixqui	Generic name for a large group of pre-Hispanic sorcerers; diviners, astrologers, fortune tellers, weathermen
Tlahuelpochime	Plural of tlahuelpuchi
Tlahuelpuchi (*tlahuelpoche, tlahualpochitzi, brujo, bruja*)	Male or female witch. Male or female bloodsucking witch
Tlahuipuchtli	Pre-Hispanic witch; luminous incensory
Tlamatocani	Pre-Hispanic individuals endowed with certain extraordinary powers: very strong sight, the evil eye, etc.
Tlaolximiani	Seventeenth-century sorcerer
Tlapaltizoliztli	The property of having very strong sight, and the state of being strong in mind, body, and will
Tlatepantil	Symbolic sacred protective fence
Tlatlacatecolo	Generic name for a large group of pre-Hispanic supernatural practitioners
Tlatztini	Pre-Hispanic individuals endowed with certain extraordinary powers: very strong sight, the evil eye, etc.

Tlecuil	Hearth
Tleutlipan moquetzani	Pre-Hispanic "ritual impersonators"
Tonalli	Soul; guardian or companion spirit
Totolli	Turkey
Tonalpouhqui	Pre-Hispanic sorcerer
Tzipitictoc	Psychological aftereffects exhibited by mothers upon the death of infants attributed to the witch
Vahidos	Fainting spells; generally experienced by parents after infants have been sucked by the witch
Vaho	Vapor or mist released by the witch in order to suck the blood of its victims
Xocoyote	Ultimogenit; last-born son
Xoxal	The extraordinary powers associated with twinning
Yotlezahuitl	A person with tlapaltizoliztli
Zacate	Grass
Zoapatl	Pain-deadening plant. Uppricata ingenitus

Bloodsucking Witchcraft

Introduction

THIS BOOK IS concerned with bloodsucking witchcraft in rural Tlax-cala, Mexico, the most prominent, personified complex in the non-Catholic belief system of the region. The primary aim of this book is to analyze the social and psychological contexts of witchcraft and to place it within the framework of rural Tlaxcalan culture. The manifold aspects of bloodsucking witchcraft are complex and ramified, and they are described and analyzed within the overall system of magic and religious supernaturalism as these phenomena are embedded in kinship, ritual kinship, the household, the non-residential extended family, the neighborhood, the community, and the entire region. Theoretically and methodologically, bloodsucking witchcraft is analyzed structurally, ideologically, psychologically, historically, and syncretically. The theoretical approach postulated in this book rests on the assumption that understanding and explaining witchcraft, and most kinds of magic, entail the interaction of normative expectations and physical realization. Under this condition, the ideology and belief system of bloodsucking witchcraft must be positioned historically and syncretically in order to generate the most reliable matrix in which the structure of the phenomenon is physically, socially, and psychologically realized. Or, from a slightly different perspective, the structure of bloodsucking witchcraft is perceived through the screen of its ideology and belief system, and explanations emerge at the level of the actors of the complex in action, that is, as an inferential system of inputs and outputs.

Although the context of analysis is primarily psychological and the bloodsucking witchcraft complex is thoroughly embedded in the social structure of the community and the region, this book is not a sociological (functional) nor a psychological study of witchcraft, as this form of magic supernaturalism has been commonly analyzed by British, and occasionally American, anthropologists. Rather, this study is molded by a perceptual and inferential focus and strategy that is essentially conceived as an epistemological approach. Throughout most of this monograph (particularly Chapters 7 to 12), the analysis is squarely focused on the logic of bloodsucking witchcraft and the perceptions and inferences of actors at the various levels of realization. Ethnographically, the study presents the native, folk theory of knowledge of a witchcraft complex conditioned by an ideology and belief system of long standing and discharged in a structural ambience underlined, and to some extent configurated, by a changing situation in which science, technology, and other external forms of knowledge are beginning to transform irreversibly the traditional framework and efficacy of magic supernaturalism. Ethnologically and comparatively, the study is positioned in the wider framework of all forms of normative supernatural action and expectation, the theoretical aim being to envisage, and to some extent configurate, an approach that is sufficiently dynamic to account for secularism and the incessant effect of alternative forms of knowledge upon the remaining primitive societies and increasing number of folk societies.

In the balance of this introduction we will do three things: place magic supernaturalism within the context of Mesoamerican ethnology and ethnography, and outline the scope and content of the study by chapters; present a synoptic statement of what has been accomplished in the domains of witchcraft, sorcery, and other forms of magic supernaturalism during the past two generations; and briefly discuss the main tenets and implications of the epistemological approach to the study of magic and religion in the changing, contemporary world. The theoretical orientation on which this monograph is based is discussed in Chapter 12, and the sole aim of these introductory remarks is to tell the reader at the outset what he can expect from the study, given the fact that it departs considerably from what anthropologists have come to expect from sociological and psychological analyses of witchcraft.

THE ETHNOGRAPHIC AND ETHNOLOGIC SETTING OF WITCHCRAFT AND SORCERY IN MESOAMERICA: SCOPE AND CONTENT OF THE STUDY

The Context of Magic Supernaturalism in Folk Societies
Witchcraft, sorcery, and all related magical phenomena involving anthropomorphic, personified components (henceforth, anthropomorphic supernaturalism, or magic supernaturalism when contrasted with religious supernaturalism) have seldom been discussed exhaustively within the context of folk, peasant societies. The great majority of descriptive monographs and theoretical interpretations have been on tribal societies, where anthropomorphic supernaturalism is

still an integral part of the cultural fabric and is usually closely interrelated with the social structure and religious system. Thus, the theories, explanations, and methodologies that have been developed by anthropologists since the pioneer work of Evans-Pritchard (1937) among the Azande, to Kluckhohn's (1944) work among the Navaho, to the work of the British in Africa (Forde 1958; Lienhardt 1951; Marwich 1952; Mayer 1954; Nadel 1952; Wilson 1941), and to the more recent work in Africa and other culture areas of the world (Crawford 1967; Faron 1964; Lieban 1967; Mair 1969; Middleton and Winter 1969; Douglas 1970; Simmons 1971), are not entirely adequate for the analytical handling of folk societies, in which anthropomorphic supernaturalism is not always an intrinsic part of the social and religious systems and is sometimes difficult to relate structurally to the rest of the culture or to analyze functionally within the context of religion, kinship, economics, and/or politics. Although this generalization may not necessarily apply to folk societies in all major culture areas of the world, especially in areas such as sub-Saharan Africa or parts of Oceania that are emerging from an immediate tribal past, it does apply to Mesoamerica and all comparable areas of Spanish America.

Under these circumstances, the complexes of witchcraft and sorcery that anthropologists have described for communities and regions of Mesoamerica demand modes of analysis and explanations that are consonant both with the position of anthropomorphic supernaturalism within the total configuration of local culture and society and the syncretic, acculturative, and/or synthetic conception of supernatural forces and personages that have been a permanent feature of the area for more than 300 years. Thus, we visualize the following approach: Functional analysis can be of only limited value in dealing with anthropomorphic supernaturalism in Mesoamerica, given the fact that the manifold structures entail dynamic situations of change. Indeed, no functional analysis or explanation of anthropomorphic supernaturalism is ever fully adequate by itself, much less when this phenomenon is not largely embedded in the prevailing social structure and discharged within the context of the culture as a whole.

The sociological, ideological, psychological, and historical perspectives must not be regarded as separate analytical levels, not at least in the ethnographic and ethnological contexts of well-delineated culture areas. Rather they should be considered as playing some explanatory role at specific junctures; jointly they can generate answers about the efficacy of witchcraft and sorcery, and other forms of anthropomorphic supernaturalism, in the conduct of daily life, about their relative isolation or seeming independence of the social fabric, and, above all, about the dynamic forces that have shaped these phenomena and the changes that are likely to occur in the presence of modernization and strong secularizing pressures from the outside world. These are the main features of anthropomorphic supernaturalism that are to be explained in the folk, peasant setting. This monograph is an effort to exemplify how this analytical framework may be employed.

Briefly, what are the substantive and analytical requirements in the implementation of the foregoing focus and strategy for the conceptualization of anthropomorphic supernaturalism in a clearly bounded culture area, ethnographically and ethnologically? The following are the main interrelated points:

1. The ideology and belief system of the particular anthropomorphic supernatural complex in question must be exactingly specified in terms of basic assumptions (the worldview), general rules and injunctions, and specific constraints and commands in action. This initial step of the approach is one of the two necessary requirements: substantively, in the degree of exactness and completeness with which the ideology and belief systems are configurated; analytically, in properly positioning the normative system vis-à-vis the structural system in operation.

2. The structural realization of the magic supernatural phenomena at hand must be specified in terms of empirical cases of carefully observed incidents, events, and happenings with a certain modicum of control. Probably the single most pervasive deficiency in studies of witchcraft and sorcery is lack of quantitative, hard, and systematic cases. This deficiency is particularly evident in the literature on folk, peasant societies.

3. Passing to the supporting framework of the foregoing points, it is seldom the case that the ideology and belief system can be configurated on the basis of the synchronic situation alone. Rather, they must be elicited and configurated within the diachronic context, and this normative complex may include syncretic, acculturative, and/or diffused elements and components. This step is important to the understanding, positioning, and efficient assessing of the efficacy and domains of action of the ideology and belief system.

4. The anthropomorphic supernatural complex under consideration must be both ideologically and structurally positioned with respect to the wider context of magico-religious supernaturalism in particular, and the global sociocultural worldview in general. Essentially, this operation entails two tasks: placing the normative and structural components of witchcraft and sorcery in a relationship of efficacious interaction and within the context of the magico-religious system; and establishing the extent to which magical, supernatural causation affects the structural discharge of manifold domains of the total sociocultural system.

5. The final point, a consequence of point 4, has to do with placing anthropomorphic supernaturalism and the entire magico-religious system in a dynamic,

changing context. It is assumed, of course, that folk, peasant societies are constantly being influenced by diffusion and contact with the outside world. It is therefore of primary importance to determine how the local worldview in general, and the magic and religious ideology and belief system in particular, are being affected by the internalization of new knowledge, diffused from the greater tradition or directly introduced by local personnel.

The Nature, Position, and Variation of Anthropomorphic Supernaturalism

This monograph was written not only because of the intrinsic significance of the phenomena it describes and analyzes but also because there is surprisingly little written on Mesoamerican anthropomorphic supernaturalism, given the voluminous anthropological literature. Since the beginning of systematic and extensive research in the late 1920s, a substantial number of articles and chapters or parts of chapters in community monographs have described and to some extent analyzed an anthropomorphic supernatural complex that includes several manifestations of the witch, several kinds of sorcerers, the shaman, and a fairly extensive array of magical objects and places associated directly or indirectly with variations of the witch and the sorcerer. There is every indication that this magical complex is more extensive and of greater intensity than has been reported in the literature. But why the study of anthropomorphic supernaturalism has attracted so little interest and has been treated so cavalierly, we are not entirely certain. Three reasons, however, come to mind.

First, the most obvious reason is structural, and it has do to with the anthropological tradition initiated by Redfield (1930) and carried on until the 1960s. This approach to Mesoamerican community studies may be characterized as the little-bit-of-everything-but-nothing-in-detail school of anthropology, which produced more than a hundred monographs on Indian and Mestizo societies in Mexico and Guatemala. Thus, the average community monograph is a conglomerate of ethnographic domains, most of which deserved several chapters and some a separate monograph. The most one can say is that many supernatural personages have been identified, some of which have been reasonably well described and configurated and a few of which have become bywords throughout the cultural area; and many supernatural activities, some of them related to specific anthropomorphic practitioners, have been equally identified and described.

The situation has not changed much since the late 1960s, and since then the main culprit has been the new anthropological orientation that made its appearance at that time and began to flourish in the early 1970s. Its practitioners rightly criticized and reacted against the atomistic, ahistorical nature of community studies and whatever ethnological works had been published by 1970.

The old guard was composed mostly of American anthropologists, a considerable number of Mexican anthropologists, and a sprinkling of European anthropologists. With the onset of the new orientation, many more Mexicans joined the cohort of Mesoamericanists; they rallied against what they considered old-fashioned community studies and kindred enterprises, which they began to refer to deprecatingly as "la escuela de Chicago." There is significant merit in the criticisms of community functionalism and what its practitioners accomplished in forty years of research, which have been duly noted elsewhere (Nutini 1968:4–14; Nutini and Bell 1980:15). Pretty much the same can be said of most young American and European anthropologists who began to work in Mexico and Guatemala in the late 1960s, with whom Mexican anthropologists shared similar beliefs about the role of anthropology in the modern world.

This new fashion of doing anthropology does not have a methodology of its own, nor may it be regarded as a distinct approach. Rather it can be characterized as a somewhat hazy Marxist-oriented endeavor, which is only tangentially concerned with the analysis of concrete corpora of data gathered under acceptably controlled field situations. Indeed, the long-standing tradition of prolonged, intensive fieldwork has nearly vanished, and young and middle-aged anthropologists venture into the field "tarde, mal, o nunca," as the saying goes, and produce almost journalistic interpretations of the data they collect in the few months, or even weeks, that the most dedicated spend in the field. Much the same can be said of their American counterparts, among whom it is now fashionable to write "essay ethnography"—that is, short, superficial accounts for a readership that is no longer interested in those magnificent ethnographies of the past. The picture is not so bleak as the foregoing account may lead the reader to believe. There are exceptions, and the Mesoamerican scene has not lacked those scholars who, impervious to methodological fashions or facile scientism on the one hand, or unwilling to compromise their traditional scientific standards for the sake of illusory ideological commitments on the other, have continued to produce good ethnographies and some ethnology. This is particularly the case among ethnohistorians, that rather unique breed of Mesoamericanists who have successfully managed to combine an essentially anthropological mode of analysis with controlled historical reconstruction.

The second and principal reason for the consistent lack of attention paid to anthropomorphic supernaturalism since the beginnings of Mesoamerican anthropology is that, concentrating on the administrative aspects of the Catholic folk system, ethnographers have regarded the several manifestations of witchcraft, sorcery, and other magical phenomena as survivals of the past, as oddities that may be worth recording for posterity but that do not warrant in-depth investigation; it is assumed a priori that, whatever the composition of the magical complex, it does not play a significant role in the organization of local supernaturalism, much less in the structure of local culture and society. Thus, witchcraft, sorcery, and shamanistic beliefs, practices, and personages are seen as standing in a kind of limbo with respect to religious supernaturalism in particular and to the social structure in general. It is unquestionably true, as we argue throughout this monograph, that anthropomorphic supernaturalism in Mesoamerica is not an integral part of the social structure, as it is in most tribal societies; hence, it has no significant primary social functions. It is also true, however, that, because it entails primary psychological functions, it is worthy of intensive systematic study.

A related aspect is that anthropomorphic supernaturalism, insofar as it is at all anchored to another domain, is viewed through the mantle of folk Catholicism as an ancillary complex which shares certain magical properties with the religious ritualism and ceremonialism of propitiation and entreaty but which entails a different belief system. The folk Catholic system of propitiation, intensification, and entreaty may share similar objectives with whatever other-directed magical activities take place, but they stem from different ontological supernatural domains that no longer have much in common. Thus, results for praying to the saints for good crops may also be achieved by propitiating local pagan supernaturals, but the former and the latter have nothing or very little in common; they constitute separate complexes. On the other hand, anthropomorphic personages (that is, the several manifestations of the witch and sorcerer) and their activities are considered and conceptualized as individual acts and behaviors but not in their proper psychological matrix. Moreover, individual acts of witchcraft and sorcery (and how they and the supernaturals that are supposed to produce them are perceived) are regarded as survivals; no attempt is made to describe, let alone analyze, the complex of ideology and beliefs that *must* sustain such a structural realization. Anthropomorphic supernaturalism in Mexico and Guatemala is deceptively misleading. It is discharged at several levels of the pluri-ethnic continuum. Under various veneers of modernization and/or secularization lie complexes that are sufficiently structured and systematic to have warrantewd many regional monographs. Not even the most detailed descriptions and the few sophisticated analyses (see Chapter 4) can give the reader any appreciation of the richness and diversity of anthropomorphic supernaturalism that sixty years of Mesoamerican anthropology have not been able to unravel. Secularization and urban environments have often been unable to stamp out all aspects of witchcraft and sorcery.

Third, Nutini (1988) has characterized the magico-religious supernaturalism of rural Tlaxcala as a monistic ideology and belief system pluralistically discharged. For long-standing reasons of syncretism and acculturation (see Nutini 1988:Conclusions), the same is probably true in most distinct Mesoamerican regions. Briefly, what this particular ideological-structural articulation entails is the following: For the most part, the structural discharge (the ritualism, ceremonialism, and any other activities of propitiation, intensification, and entreaty) of the folk religion (essentially the cult of the saints, centered in the church and to a significant extent in the household) is kept separate from that of pagan supernatural personages (tutelary mountain owners and other deities of pre-Hispanic origin) and the entire array of witches, sorcerers, and other anthropomorphic figures. What this large and diversified pagan, pre-Hispanic and folk, Catholic system shares is a common ideology and to a large extent a belief complex that makes the total magico-religious system a unitary phenomenon: individuals and the collectivity propitiate and entreat Catholic supernaturals (including the saints, dead souls, and the many manifestations of Jesus Christ and the Virgin Mary) and approach pagan deities or avail themselves of the services of or protect themselves from anthropomorphic supernaturals in different contexts, for different reasons and motivations. But all individual and collective actions, activities, and behaviors are determined by or are the expression of the same normative system. This is the fundamental tenet of magico-religious supernaturalism in rural Tlaxcala, which has been thoroughly demonstrated and exemplified elsewhere (Nutini 1988). It is this state of affairs that may constitute a common denominator of Mesoamerican magic and religion, with variations and different degrees of intensity, to be sure, but manifesting essentially the same operational principles. Thus, the supernatural position of the saints and dead souls, their powers of intercession (*dulia*) and their distinctly pagan powers of granting boons (*latria*), the power and position of tutelary mountain owners, the inexorable proclivities of the bloodsucking witch, and the various powers and attributes of the sorcerer and the weatherman are intelligible as part of a single ideological system and explainable in terms of the same operational principles, specified in slightly different belief complexes at several levels of realization. This monograph and Nutini's monograph on the cult of the dead in rural Tlaxcala may be regarded as complementary studies in which the magical and religious spheres of local and regional supernaturalism, respectively, are described and analyzed as two sides of the same coin. This generalized ideological-structural juncture is explained partly as an expression of the peculiar interaction of pre-Hispanic polytheism and sixteenth-century Spanish Catholicism and partly as the result of the syncretic and acculturative processes that ensued, which ultimately resulted in a monolatrous magico-religious system that has predominated in Tlaxcala for more than two hundred years, and possibly in many other regions of Mesoamerica as well. Failure to grasp the implications of local and regional magico-religious systems, as configured by a monistic ideology pluralistically discharged, has prevented Mesoamericanists from properly conceptualizing anthropomorphic supernaturalism and understanding its more complex and systemic configuration.

Lack of understanding of the syncretic configuration of both the magic and religious systems may underlie the second and third reasons for failure to conceptualize anthropomorphic supernaturalism in Mesoamerica. Lest the reader misunderstand, we are not saying that it is not known that, say, the bloodsucking witch (or other varieties of witches) and the sorcerer, as reported in the ethnographic literature, are of pre-Hispanic or European origin or have elements of both. This much is clear, as the more sophisticated sources have given us an adequate anatomy of the provenance of various anthropomorphic supernatural personages. What is not clear, and what has not been investigated, is how, under what conditions, and due to what agents and external inputs the pre-Hispanic and Spanish-Catholic magico-religious systems have evolved and coalesced into an ideological monistic system pluralistically discharged. This is an essentially syncretic task which has been achieved for the folk religion (Nutini 1988) and anthropomorphic supernaturalism (this study) of rural Tlaxcala but has only been envisaged and to some extent outlined for other contexts and regions of Mesoamerica (see Madsen 1957; Foster 1960; Beals 1950; Carrasco 1952, 1961).

Briefly, three different types of syncretism have been identified and conceptualized. First, guided syncretism is the main diachronic process underlying the contemporary local religious hierarchy (*ayuntamiento religioso, república eclesiástica,* or *escalafón religioso,* as it is variously known) as it developed throughout the sixteenth and seventeenth centuries out of the original confrontation of pre-Hispanic polytheism and Spanish Catholicism under the early guidance of the Franciscan friars (Nutini 1976). Second, spontaneous syncretism characterized the historical development of the cult of the same confrontation, but largely as a free diachronic process, that is, independent from the Franciscan friars in the sixteenth century and from the secular priests in the seventeenth century (Nutini 1988). Third, this monograph characterizes the development of anthropomorphic supernaturalism also as a case of spontaneous syncretism, but with two significant differences: the syncretic process entails not only structural and ideological elements of pre-Hispanic and European origin but also some elements of African origin; and the original blending in the seventeenth century is not only free but sub rosa—that is, it does not entail any inputs from religious authorities (see Chapters 3 and 4).

Content of the Monograph by Chapter

This book is not only a description and analysis of a particular case of witchcraft but a more complex study involving several related topics. The table of contents does not give an accurate impression of the scope of the study, and the following account by chapter is designed to present the reader with a more detailed view of the topics and problems being discussed. Knowing what to expect, the reader may appreciate better the unfolding description and analysis and their relationships.

Chapter 1 presents a general discussion of the basic nature and properties of nahualism, weathermaking, and sorcery, which, together with bloodsucking witchcraft, constitute the core of the magical system and the extent of personalized anthropomorphic supernaturalism.

Chapter 2 describes the ideology and belief system of bloodsucking witchcraft and the structural context in which the phenomenon takes place. The manifold attributes of the witch, its incidence and relationship to the other anthropomorphic supernaturals, its relationship to ordinary men, its physical manifestation, and witchcraft accusations are placed in the social and everyday context of community life.

Chapter 3 constitutes the ethnohistorical, diachronic background to the study. The nature and content of pre-Hispanic anthropomorphic supernaturalism, its syncretic development throughout the sixteenth and seventeenth centuries, its linguistic underpinnings, and the position of the complex within the overall magico-religious system are discussed.

Chapter 4 has the aim of placing bloodsucking witchcraft in particular, and anthropomorphic supernaturalism in general, within the context of Mesoamerican studies. We present a general assessment and critique of what has been done and give a definition of witchcraft and sorcery that is more conducive to the clarification of concepts than has formerly been the case for this culture area.

Chapter 5 is an account of a bloodsucking witchcraft epidemic that afflicted one of the wards of a community in December of 1960. In addition to placing the phenomenon in the context of kinship, the family, and the household, this dramatic event serves to exemplify the psychological ambience and sociophysical milieu in which multiple infant deaths occasionally occurred in traditional times.

Chapter 6 presents the empirical evidence of bloodsucking witchcraft and the methodology of gathering and presenting the data on which this monograph is based. Forty-seven concrete cases of infants believed to have been killed (sucked) by the witch are presented in detail with reference to twenty variables, including the most salient conditions of time, space, physical parameters, social considerations, and psychological states.

Chapter 7 may be regarded as an analysis laying the epistemological foundations of this particular witchcraft study, but with wider application for the study of witchcraft, sorcery, and other magical phenomena.

Chapter 8 presents the diagnostic and etiological analysis of bloodsucking witchcraft; that is, it determines the causes of infant death as attributed to the witch.

Chapter 9 analyzes the social and psychological manipulations engaged in by members of the afflicted household, nonresidential extended family, and the neighborhood when the bloodsucking witch strikes and an infant dies. The distortions, exaggerations, and rationalizations of affected individuals are analyzed in the context and circumstances in which the normative belief system is physically, socially, and psychologically perceived and realized.

Chapter 10 analyzes the aftereffects and the psychological contexts of the household, the nonresidential extended family, and the neighborhood during a period of several days immediately after an infant has died as a result of the action of the bloodsucking witch. The individual and collective contexts of guilt, culpability, responsibility, and the entailment of moral action are analyzed with reference to the maximal extension of actors affected by the sucking and in the framework of the global and magico-religious ideology and belief system.

Chapter 11 presents a social and psychological functional analysis of bloodsucking witchcraft in terms of primary and secondary functions.

Chapter 12 endeavors to present an epistemological approach to the study of magic and religious supernaturalism in order to conceptualize any domain in which there is a direct or indirect interplay between normative expectations and physical realization and in which supernatural inputs are believed to produce natural outcomes or vice versa. A wide range of topics is discussed, but all are centered on the epistemic conditions and requirements for sociopsychological explanations.

The organization of this monograph is unorthodox, but it does have a logic of its own. The ideology and belief system of bloodsucking witchcraft is first embedded in the structure of anthropomorphic supernaturalism within the sociological context of community culture and society. Then, bloodsucking witchcraft is positioned historically and comparatively and in the context of a well-delineated social structure. At midpoint the main conceptual stand (Chapter 7) is discussed, which is followed by the in-depth analysis of the phenomenon in all of its most salient implications. Since the monograph is not based on any of the established approaches to the study of witchcraft, our own analytical approach is discussed last and is based primarily on data presented in the monograph.

A SYNOPTIC ASSESSMENT OF TWO GENERATIONS OF WITCHCRAFT, SORCERY, AND MAGIC STUDIES

It is beyond the scope of the following statement to present an exhaustive, in-depth appreciation and critique of the literature on witchcraft, sorcery, and related magical phenomena that has been published, mostly by British and American anthropologists, for more than fifty years. This task has been accomplished piecemeal with varying degrees of success by several scholars during the past two decades (see Middleton and Winter 1969; Douglas 1970; Marwick 1970; Kennedy 1967; Simmons 1971; Finnegan and Horton 1973). Rather, the aim is to place this monograph in the context of what has been accomplished in the study of anthropomorphic supernaturalism, by itself and with reference to other kinds of supernaturalism.

Social Analysis and Explanations of Witchcraft and Sorcery: The British Contribution

Anthropologists are probably unanimous in recognizing that the first modern study of witchcraft and sorcery is also the most outstanding and comprehensive. We refer, of course, to the Evans-Pritchard (1937) study of witchcraft and sorcery among the Azande. Seven years later Kluckhohn (1944) published his study of witchcraft among the Navaho, which quickly, at least in the United States and continental Europe, became a classic and came to share with Evans-Pritchard's work a place of honor in studies of magic supernaturalism. For the next generation, roughly until the early 1970s, the works of Evans-Pritchard and Kluckhohn were hailed as the "models" for the study of witchcraft and sorcery: the former as the epitome of how to approach the analysis and explanation of magical phenomena sociologically without any reference to psychological considerations; the latter as an insightful approach to the analysis of witchcraft and sorcery psychologically (psychoanalytically) without firm embedment in the social structure. This rather generalized impression and understanding of the work of these scholars is incorrect on two counts. First, Evans-Pritchard's work is by no means an exclusively sociological study of Azande witchcraft and sorcery because he is very much concerned with ideation, motivation, and the logic and psychology of these phenomena; and Kluckhohn's study of Navaho witchcraft is not purely psychological because he takes considerable pains to relate his psychological interpretations to the ongoing social structure. Second, and more significant, neither the work of Evans-Pritchard nor that of Kluckhohn ever became models for the study of magical phenomena, but they remain, in description and sophisticated analysis, the most exhaustive.

It is interesting to note that Evans-Pritchard's monograph on the Azande is the least sociological and the least concerned with functional assignment. There is little emphasis on the principles, functional integration, and the almost compulsive tendency to present a homeostatic vision that characterizes the Nuer studies. This lack of functional rigidity and undue emphasis on the social system makes *Witchcraft, Oracles and Magic Among the Azande* probably the greatest single ethnography to come out of the distinguished school of British anthropology pioneered by Malinowski and Radcliffe-Brown. But what makes this work so significant, and how did it influence forty years of witchcraft and sorcery studies? The first question is easier to answer than the second.

For whatever reasons, not yet constrained by functionalism's excessive concern with integration, Evans-Pritchard described and analyzed Azande witchcraft and sorcery as a cultural system in the American tradition rather than as a social system in the functional mode. Evans-Pritchard was never noted for his systematic presentation, but the meticulous and in-depth description of the beliefs, attributes, events, and conditions of witchcraft and sorcery and related magical phenomena more than compensates for the rather unstructured analysis. From the purely ethnographic viewpoint, Evans-Pritchard's monograph has never been surpassed by subsequent studies of witchcraft and sorcery. But the Azande monograph is, of course, much more than description; the lasting importance and influence of Evans-Pritchard lie in the ideas, viewpoints, and basic attributes of magical thought it contains. From the analytical viewpoint, *Witchcraft, Oracles and Magic* is essentially an epistemological study of Azande magical thought. It is concerned with the logic of witchcraft and sorcery, the ideational framework that configurates it, the "properties" of Azande supernatural thought, and the moral order that supports it. Evans-Pritchard's accomplishment stands in the same line of inquiry initiated by Durkheim, Mauss, and Lévy-Bruhl on the way human groups, at various cultural-evolutionary stages, think and conceptualize the social and physical universes. In fact, Evans-Pritchard, with the exception of Lévi-Strauss, appears to have been the only major figure in anthropology until very recently to have rekindled this aspect of the French sociological school.

In order of inclusiveness, the following ideas and specific analytical notions underlying the approach developed in this monograph are either directly traceable to Evans-Pritchard or are influenced by his work on the Azande.

1. The study of witchcraft, sorcery, and all magical phenomena is essentially an epistemological enterprise that primarily entails psychological explanations

obtaining in well-specified milieux of social interaction. Understanding and explaining magic supernaturalism is tantamount to the comparative task of specifying how human groups perceive and make inferences in this social and physical universe along the entire cultural-evolutionary continuum.

2. In no other domain of culture and society is the normative system (ideology and belief) so efficacious, both in enforcing or molding structural compliance and as a screen through which the social and physical universes are experienced, as in the domain of magic supernaturalism. This is the single, most pervasive principle that operates at every level of realization and discharge. We express this relationship by the statement that a witchcraft or sorcery system in action is understood and explained as a function of the interaction of normative expectations and structural realization.

3. As a corollary of (2), it follows that all effective witchcraft and sorcery systems are self-fulfilling. By a self-fulfilling system it is essentially understood that there is a significant degree of concordance between what the people believe, and expect, and a certain physical realization in a well-delineated domain. Although the degree of concordance may vary from complex to complex, the generating principle is the same: the higher the concordance, the more efficient the witchcraft or sorcery.

4. There is no supernatural system or complex (magical or religious] in which the actors constantly act and behave, in ordinary and extraordinary conditions and situations, as if constrained or motivated by supernatural powers and forces. Rather, there is every indication that, even under the influence of the strongest and most pervasive witchcraft, sorcery, or any other magical complex, most actors in a social system behave and act most of the time, situationally and contexturally, in a common-sense fashion and according to the dictates of "natural" law.

5. In light of (1), (2), and (3), and as a corollary of (4), the main conceptual tool in implementing an epistemic focus and strategy for the study of magic supernaturalism is the specification of the objectivization of causality and the transposition of causation. In a nutshell, they entail, respectively, the specification of the supernatural-natural chain of behaviors and events leading to a magical outcome, and the configuration of psychological factors and conditions under which people perceive and infer magical acts.

6. Irrespective of the emic situation, the comparative study of the core of magic supernaturalism requires the distinction between witchcraft and sorcery, ontologically and epistemically, and with respect to personnel, beliefs, and activities. Had Evans-Pritchard's original distinction been strictly heeded, regardless of whether it is made on the ground by the actors themselves, we would today have a clearer view of these magical phenomena.

7. Evans-Pritchard's most distinct notion, "witchcraft explains unfortunate events," merits to be considered as perhaps the main parameter in the study of witchcraft. In this monograph we have elaborated this notion and made it into a dynamic concept of how systems of witchcraft, and to some extent sorcery, change by the diffusion and internalization of new knowledge—that is, by the acquisition of new modes of perception and inference.

Answering the second question concerning the work of Evans-Pritchard is a more involved and difficult task. Evans-Pritchard is invariably given credit for having molded the study of witchcraft and sorcery for more than a generation of anthropologists. Thus, in the work of British anthropologists throughout the 1940s, 1950s, and 1960s, there are evident such ideas and conceptual notions as witchcraft as an explanation for unfortunate or unforeseen events, the self-fulfilling nature of magical phenomena, the normative effect in the realization of witchcraft and sorcery, the distinction between witchcraft and sorcery, and several others. However, the impact of Evans-Pritchard on the progress of anthropomorphic supernaturalism studies has been rather negligible in the two domains that we consider his most valuable contributions: substantively, his superb description of a witchcraft and sorcery system; conceptually, the epistemological thrust he pioneered in explaining magical phenomena. With respect to the former, there is nothing in the ethnographic literature comparable to the completeness of Evans-Pritchard's work on the Azande. With respect to the latter, no anthropologist, as far as we are aware, has ever picked up the epistemic strands of Evans-Pritchard's work and produced a full-fledged analysis of a witchcraft or sorcery system that aimed at specifying the logic of the phenomenon from a particular perceptual and inferential stand. Not until 1970 did there develop an interest in non-Western modes of thought fairly directly related to Evans-Pritchard's epistemic concerns (see Horton and Finnegan 1973). Why this almost total disregard for Evans-Pritchard's most distinctive and original contribution to the study of magic and supernaturalism, and why the significant disregard of witchcraft and sorcery studies in comparison to other ethnographic domains? Two reasons come to mind, and the task of expounding them affords us the opportunity to assess what has been accomplished since the publication of Evans-Pritchard's work on the Azande.

First, from the beginning of British social anthropology, the almost overwhelming concern has been with kinship and the social structure of tribal and occasionally transitional societies, primarily in Africa and to a lesser degree in Oceania and Southeast Asia—that is, mostly in the vast territories of the British Empire. By the social structure and the glue of kinship, at least Radcliffe-Brown and his followers understand fundamentally how and under what conditions economics, politics, territorial organization, and to some extent religion coalesce into an organic whole: a homeostatic entity occupying a fixed position in space and time. This characterization (some would call it a caricature) is, of course, a model that somewhat changes as functionalism is passed on from parents (Radcliffe-Brown and Malinowski), to children (Evans-Pritchard, Fortes, Firth, Leach, Gluckman, and so on), to grandchildren (Needham, Goody, Lienhardt, Middleton, Beattie, Lewis, Gray, and so on) to name some of the most outstanding members of this anthropological genealogy: the approach becomes less rigid, as it is differentially applied to various sociocultural milieux; it becomes less homeostatic, as attempts, largely unsuccessful, are undertaken to accommodate diachronic dimensions in an increasingly changing world; and it becomes diversified, as the basic tenets of functionalism are variously interpreted by its main exponents (Nadel, Leach, Fortes, Firth). Although it became steadily apparent that the theoretical framework of functionalism did not generate linear explanations, its descriptive integrational properties never waned, confirming functionalism's proven attributes for effective monographic description.

British anthropology after World War II did increase the output of witchcraft and sorcery studies but not nearly to the extent that one might have expected. Many articles were written, and full-fledged monographs on kinship and other aspects of the social structure included descriptions and analyses of various aspects of anthropomorphic supernaturalism. But independent, in-depth monographs on witchcraft and sorcery shine by their absence; those by Reynolds (1963), Marwick (1965), Crawford (1967), and perhaps two or three that escape us are the notable exceptions. Under these conditions, after 1973 or so the output of witchcraft, sorcery, and related magical studies became negligible.

Second, if practical constraints accounted for this failure of British social anthropology to have followed in the substantive footsteps initiated by Evans-Pritchard, theoretical and methodological factors account for its inability to have pursued the epistemological study of magic supernaturalism also initiated by him. Functional analyses and explanations appear to force all operationally discernible domains into patterns of interaction and mutual dependence that may not necessarily be part of the ontological reality at hand. This is the distinct impression that one obtains in reading the pat, institutionally monolithic accounts of the most notable British social anthropologists, in which cultural sharing rests on a social structure that is assumed but never demonstrated. Thus, in such an ambience and ontologically assumed reality, even religious, much less magic, supernaturalism is seldom if ever conceptualized as independent domains, or as entailing sets of independent variables. Rather, magic and religion are regarded as entailing dependent functions or as ancillary aspects of the social structure in operation—that is, as the web of kinship expressed in the primary contexts of economics and politics. More specifically, the functional analysis of magic supernaturalism admits only sociological explanations posited on the putative integration of all the parts of an ongoing system.

Given the foregoing constraints, what has been the achievement of British functionalism since the publication of Evans-Pritchard's magnum opus, and how have studies of witchcraft, sorcery, and related magical phenomena progressed since then? First, the main contribution of British anthropology has been in documenting a fairly wide-ranging array of magical phenomena in specific social settings in a variety of cultural conditions. Even though Evans-Pritchard himself mildly complained (Middleton and Winter 1969:III) about how disappointingly few works on witchcraft and sorcery had been published up to that time, it is nonetheless the case that, from the mid-1950s to the late 1960s, more accounts of these phenomena were published than at any other period before or since, and most of them by British-trained anthropologists. In these publications, best exemplified by the collections of essays edited by Middleton and Winter (1969) and Douglas (1970), a fair range of the incidence of witchcraft and sorcery in manifold settings is presented ethnographically and historically. The reader gets the impression, however, that these studies, elegant and sophisticated as they are, constitute essentially preliminary reports, the hors d'oeuvre for the pièce de résistance to come. Second, the exclusive theoretical contribution of social anthropologists to the study of anthropomorphic supernaturalism is centered on the functional explanation of the phenomena in specific ethnographic and historical settings exhibiting varied sociocultural configurations. Thus, magical phenomena, particularly witchcraft, are explained as having some positive or negative function in the ongoing social structure at given junctures in time and space. From this standpoint, magic supernaturalism is conceived as exhibiting the various dynamic interactions that obtain in the domains of kinship, politics, and economics: mechanisms for social control, especially under conditions of stress and disarray; mechanisms for the resolution of tension affecting various social units of local groups; expressing hostilities in socially acceptable ways, thereby assuaging collective tensions; and so on. Third, the most distinct and valuable contribution of functionalists to the study of magic supernaturalism is to have embedded these phenomena in solid sociological matrices. Their insistence that the ideology and belief systems of witchcraft, sorcery, shamanism, divination, and related phenomena must be placed in concrete social settings is a necessary requirement for the explanation of magic supernaturalism. But this is only the first step. Lest the reader misunderstand, we are not saying that functional explanations of witchcraft and sorcery are wrong or invalid, but only that they are partial explanations.

But can we say that there has been progress in the study of magic supernaturalism since the publication of *Witchcraft, Oracles and Magic Among the Azande?* With the exception that we know now the general outlines of the magical systems of a large number of societies, the answer is no, theoretically and methodologically. By overplaying the functional focus and strategy, very few British social anthropologists rose above general, fuzzy functional explanations, despite the psychological bent in the original model. Methodologically, the single, most damaging drawback in the social analyses and explanations of magic supernaturalism is lack of structural data: hard empirical facts, individually observed cases, and quantitative analysis. All these attributes are virtually absent in the studies of social anthropologists, and their analyses are almost exclusively based on verbalized normative data.

Psychological Analysis and Explanations of Witchcraft and Sorcery:
The American Contribution
Kluckhohn was not as influential as Evans-Pritchard in shaping the course of magic supernaturalism in the following generation. The reasons are twofold. First, Kluckhohn never had much impact in British social anthropology, although occasionally his influence is evident in the psychological statements that social functionalists make as part of their analyses. More often, perhaps, social functionalists did not escape making various kinds of psychological assignments. This mixing of social and psychological facts, which British functionalists tried hard to avoid, is perhaps inevitable, for there is every reason to believe that "all sociological analyses are based upon a set of psychological assumptions" (Kennedy 1967:224). Second, if concern with the study of magic supernaturalism in British functionalism was moderate, that of the several approaches in American anthropology was even less. If we also consider that quite a few American anthropologists during the past two generations have followed in the functionalist footsteps of the British, then Kluckhohn's influence in this particular domain is further diminished. Insofar as Kluckhohn's psychological orientation to the study of magic supernaturalism influenced anthropologists, these studies have been almost entirely an American contribution.

In most ways the positions of Kluckhohn and Evans-Pritchard are similar within their respective orbits of influences: the misguided characterization of their approaches as exclusively psychological and sociological; the mistaken notion that their *magna opera* became, in fact, the models for future research in these putatively antinomous approaches to the study of magic supernaturalism; and the value of their works is descriptively and analytically unsurpassed. It seems that the same substantive constraint is also at work in explaining the lack of interest and limited success of the psychological approach in producing extensive and sophisticated studies of magic supernaturalism: namely, the high investment of time and resources necessary to generate adequate data bases.

Kluckhohn's monograph on Navaho witchcraft strikes one surprisingly as more concerned with function than Evans-Pritchard's work on the Azande. Kluckhohn's functionalism, however, is psychological, perhaps as a result of his interest in descriptive integration. The general framework of his work on Navaho witchcraft may be described as a rather balanced account of psychological and sociological facts, and the allegation that he does not properly embed his analysis sociologically is grossly unfair (Devons and Gluckman 1964:244). Another aspect of Kluckhohn's work that stands out in comparison to Evans-Pritchard is that the former's analysis is more systematic and is concerned not so much with description as with presenting facts within a theoretical perspective that presumably could be replicated (Kennedy 1967:220). This laudable aim, however, is hindered by the fact that Kluckhohn deals exclusively with the normative system of Navaho witchcraft.

The most oustanding contribution of Kluckhohn to magic supernaturalism in general, and to witchcraft in particular, is to have placed in perspective the entailed psychological processes and behavioral conditions within a social structure in operation, or as he puts it explicitly, "What are the relationships between witchcraft and Navaho history, social organization, economy, and value system?" (Kluckhohn 1944:65). This program, of course, is the same as that of most British functionalists' studies of witchcraft and sorcery, with the difference that the latter expected to achieve their goals on the basis of social facts alone. Not that Kluckhohn achieved a dynamic, theoretical synthesis of how social and psychological facts constitute a single explanatory framework, but he did demonstrate that social facts alone yield only partial explanations.

Kluckhohn's psychological functional analysis and explanation of witchcraft have been widely accepted, even implicitly by some British functionalists (see particularly Marwick 1952). It should be noted, however, that in these cases there is a covert functional assignment that almost invariably makes it appear that somehow the social system generates individual psychological states, making the social structure in operation the independent variable and causal agent. Or, as Mair (1969:220) puts it, "But whereas Beattie and most social anthropologists are concerned with situations that society regards as giving cause for anxiety, Kluckhohn is discussing anxiety as a condition of individuals." Be this as it may, Kluckhohn's psychological functional assignment of witchcraft may be summarized as follows:

1. Witchcraft expresses hostilities in socially acceptable ways, thereby relieving psychological tensions—that is, it reduces individual anxiety and societal stress. Or, as Kennedy (1967:221) puts it, witchcraft "beliefs are functional in maintaining the stability of the society and at the same time are adjustive for individuals." This psychological function appears to be the most universal, or at least the ethnographic literature conveys this impression, even though the psychological function may be implicit or reformulated in sociological disguise.

2. Witchcraft resolves ambivalences, thereby keeping personality together; that is, it results in the psychological integration of individuals in circumscribed social settings. This is one of the "functional" aspects of witchcraft that Kluckhohn does not develop adequately—namely, the extension of the concept of personality to small, tightly knit social groups. This dimension of his analysis is explored (see Chapters 9 and 11) in the context of the extended family (household) and non-residential extended family, not as a functional aspect of bloodsucking witchcraft but rather as how and under what conditions the "personality" of the propinquous group is affected when the bloodsucking witch strikes.

3. Witchcraft provides identity for culturally dissatisfied individuals: the alienated, the displaced, and those who do not easily fit into the established norms of the society. If we understand Kluckhohn correctly, this function of witchcraft is one of those junctures in which psychological motivations and states entail ascertainable collective responses in specific situations of anxiety and stress. Moreover, this function of witchcraft must be approached from the standpoint of the society at large which views the alienated and displaced as exhibiting anomalous psychological characteristics, thereby rendering them the prime targets of witchcraft accusations.

4. The last psychological function of witchcraft is essentially a corollary of (3), namely, individual and collective scapegoatism. In this function, individuals and groups (kinship units, neighborhoods, communities) are specifically accused of witchcraft or groups are regarded, latently or manifestly, as being dens of witches or as possessing an extraordinary number of them. At the heart of scapegoatism stands the mechanism of displacement, probably one of the most universal of human proclivities, which neither Kluckhohn nor any anthropologist has yet conceptualized, even in the context of witchcraft accusations.

It should be noted that psychological anthropologists in the United States have tended to describe anthropomorphic supernaturalism within the wider context of religion. This sound strategy was first advocated by Wilson (1957:3). It is not coincidental that this basic epistemic truth in dealing with highly normative systems has been emphasized by psychological anthropologists but not by social functionalists, for whom behavior and action has little to do with individual or collective perceptions and inferences. In theory, but not necessarily in practice, the study of all forms of supernaturalism is more profitably approached from the psychological perspective than from the social-institutional perspective. This is perhaps the most significant attribute that characterizes the contribution of psychological anthropologists to the study of magic and religion supernaturalism. Here again, institutional analysis may be regarded as the first step. The work of Spiro (1967), Wallace (1966), and Levine (1969), to name some of the outstanding anthropologists in this tradition, have assumed that the social system is the necessary receptacle in which magico-religious phenomena are realized in manifold arrangements of personnel in action, but they have refused to regard the social structure as the independent entity in which explanations are generated.

Finally, a conception of witchcraft that may be profitable to pursue should be mentioned. In the psychological tradition discussed above, Kennedy (1969) considers witchcraft as an institutionalized system of psychopathology. He says, "I take the view that witchcraft ideas and practices are largely the products of individual psycho-pathology which have been accepted, systematized and institutionalized by members of many groups. I believe this partly accounts for the extremely wide geographical distribution of many of the common attributes of witchcraft, which must otherwise be accounted for by unbelievable diffusion. This view, as I will indicate, is also consistent with the particular character of witch beliefs and with the level of scientific knowledge in these societies" (Kennedy 1969:167). This view of witchcraft contains two important ideas, both of which are developed in this monograph. First, the nonrelativistic notion that, just as there are mentally ill individuals, there are also sick societies. Kennedy notes that this notion was probably first expressed by Benedict, later reactivated by Fromm, and apparently has recently been receiving renewed attention (see Colby and Colby 1981). After warning the reader that one should be very careful to define terms such as "paranoid" and "megalomaniac" (as describing the Kwakiutl by Benedict and the Dobu by Fortune) when applied to entire societies, Kennedy (1969:167) maintains that, "we should seriously entertain the possibility of the existence of 'sick societies' or pathological institutions and culture patterns, rather than asking the a priori relativistic assumption that all groups automatically find a healthy balanced level of functioning." Kennedy goes on to develop these ideas into a coherent viewpoint within the context of the structure and content of witchcraft systems. The second idea implicitly expressed by Kennedy is that witchcraft systems are not immutable and that they change with the diffusion and internalization of new knowledge, particularly scientific knowledge. In a sense, the second idea is a corollary of the first, for ultimately, it is assumed, all full-fledged witchcraft systems evolve into mechanisms of last resort.

Witchcraft, as an Allegory, as a Manifestation of Moral Evil, and
as an Analogical Mode of Thought

In 1982, when the first seven chapters of this monograph had been written, Vinigi Grottanelli (1981) sent us his article entitled "Witchcraft: An Allegory?" which originally appeared in 1976 and was reprinted in 1981. Grottanelli's conception of witchcraft influenced the formulation of one of the basic concepts of this monograph and stimulated us to bring together several conceptual strands. Before discussing Grottanelli's view on witchcraft, let us first put the problems at hand in some sort of epistemic perspective.

There is no more difficult subject in the social sciences than to conceptualize ideology and belief, that is, the normative system of a functioning social group. It is such a thorny and elusive problem to deal with that often it seems intractable to scientific treatment. Of these interrelated concepts, probably belief is the easiest to pinpoint and, at least in anthropology, the one with the widest usage. Although anthropologists have traditionally regarded ideological and belief systems as ultimate, irreducible data in their ethnographic studis, it is quite within the realm of scientific possibility that methods can be devised to falsify, say, social, political, or economic ideologies and belief complexes, particularly when such complexes are formulated with a certain end in view, as in the case of Marxism, or for that matter in the case of any political and/or economic ism. But this is most definitely not the case with all forms of supernaturalism. It is impossible to falsify the existence of God, gods, witches, or any supernatural personage or force; human reason can only entertain the possibility that they exist, and belief falls largely into the realm of Pascal's wager. From this standpoint, beliefs about the creation of the universe of astronomy by a supreme being and about the lowliest of animistic spirits in the most primitive society are logically and epistemologically the same. They cannot be falsified; either they are believed or they are not, and these are ultimate facts by themselves, not amenable to rational or scientific treatment. But, narrowing down the problem, what does this quandary mean for the conduct of anthropological studies of magic and religion?

First, all supernatural entities and personages (God, gods, witches, spirits, and so on) are epistemologically the same from the standpoint of their study in concrete social settings. That is, just as there are no primitive or advanced languages, all supernatural entities, regardless of extension (size of the ontological domain to which they apply—vocabulary, one would say, in language) and complexity (theology and teleology—variations in grammar), play the same role psychologically and must be treated conceptually in the same fashion. Thus, the almighty God of monotheism and the humble water spirits of an Amazonian Indian tribe, as supernatural beliefs per se, entail the same epistemic properties and cannot in any aspect but extension and complexity, and the consequences that follow from them, be regarded as different. One may therefore scale or rank supernatural beliefs in terms of complexity (often buttressed by elaborate theologies and ritual-ceremonial complexes, almost always the function of techno-cultural complexity), but to say that God is higher than the gods, and that the latter are higher than witches or other assorted spirits, is nothing more than the ethnocentrism that constitutes an invariant aspect of man's "progress" from the hunting and gathering stage to modern civilization. Supernatural beliefs could even be ranked in terms of how beneficial or detrimental they are with respect to the social settings in which they are present (for example, most anthropologists would undoubtedly maintain that a society ridden with witchcraft and sorcery is not as socially and psychologically balanced as one in which the magical system is mild and circumscribed), but such a scale would be based on consequences observable at the level of the social structure in operation and not with the beliefs themselves, which are altogether an entirely different ontological matter. Thus, the study of all forms of supernaturalism must be centered on consequences, for any other conceptual task is scientifically thankless.

Second, what do consequences mean in the study of supernaturalism? Essentially the following, if we are able to make sense of the phenomena scientifically. Once a belief, or an entire coherent system, is isolated, described, and analyzed within a social setting, it becomes a primitive datum. Disregarding any ontological consideration, one must concentrate on the epistemic properties of belief systems, that is, on how and under what conditions they affect the perception and interpretation of the social and physical universe. All belief systems, but particularly magico-religious belief systems, configurate, mold, and/or determine the perceptions of the social and physical universes and the inferences of individuals and the collectivity. This is the conceptual fulcrum that is at the heart of magic and religious studies.

Third, the last consideration is a corollary of the second. Endeavoring to ascertain the existence of supernatural personages and entities falls outside the province of anthropology. What individuals and collectivities believe are acts of faith not amenable to proof, and we must deal exclusively with the social and physical consequences that follow epistemologically from such psychological acts of acceptance. The only legitimate scientific concern is to ascertain and conceptualize the epistemic and psychological reality of the consequences of supernatural beliefs in sociophysical settings that are as controllable and circumscribed as one can possibly establish. This reality and existence may be summarized as follows. Epistemologically, the manifold beliefs in bloodsucking witchcraft determine perceptual and inferential reality to the extent that, when the bloodsucking witch strikes, an infant dies, and for a considerable number of days afterward the "normal" (and this normal must be carefully established) conception of social and physical phenomena is suspended, distorted, and/or bent enough so that the affected actors interpret certain empirical phenomena as they have normatively been conditioned to expect. Ontologically, the reality of bloodsucking witchcraft is manifested in many social and physical things, events, conditions, rites, ceremonies, and paraphernalia that, although given specific meaning by the normative belief system, are firmly anchored to empirical phenomena. Behaviorally, the propinquous group affected by an instance of bloodsucking witchcraft may be considered, albeit temporarily, as a closed system, that is, its personnel act and behave conditioned by the ontological reality being epistemologically perceived according to the specifications of the normative belief system. This is the strongest, self-fulfilling mechanism that maintains the bloodsucking witchcraft system traditionally in place.

Since supernaturalism, whatever its form, does not admit degrees of ultimate reality, it follows that the epistemological and ontological existence of consequences entailed by all supernatural beliefs are subject to the same analysis, in order to ascertain the role these consequences play in the empirical universe of social and physical existence. This probably sounds monstrous to the Christian theologian. However, at least scientifically, there is no other way to conceptualize magic and religious supernaturalism but to assume the existential reality of consequences but not that of ultimate entities, be they the God of monotheism, flesh-eating witches, or the manifold agents of sundry supernatural interventions in the natural, normal world of everyday existence. Functional, symbolic, and even theological approaches to the study of magic and religious supernaturalism are useful at different levels of realization and in conditioning the social and psychological matrix of magic and religion. But the ultimate aim of supernatural studies is essentially an epistemological task: understanding and explaining causation and entailment in the manifold situations in which supernatural inputs are believed to produce natural outcomes, vice versa, and all permutations in which individuals and the collectivity are affected socially, psychologically, and physically by the interaction of natural and supernaturally conceived entities and forces.

Grottanelli's work (1981:178–83) is one of the few studies with a new idea or conception of witchcraft since those of Evans-Pritchard and Kluckhohn. Grottanelli says that Western anthropologists have limited their study of magical phenomena, dismissing a priori the reality of witchcraft. With reference to the Nzema, an Akan society of West Africa that he knows in depth, Grottanelli considers the "reality" and "illusion" of witchcraft. He ponders the existence of flesh-eating witches, the authenticity of magical powers, and fundamentally whether supernatural inputs can, in fact, produce natural outcomes. Laudably, he questions whether the skeptical attitude of Western anthropologists and most of the educated public is nothing more than ethnocentrism reflecting the arrogance of an overly positivistic science. With a good measure of skepticism himself, Grottanelli asks whether there is an ontological reality to witchcraft that has escaped Western anthropology, and whether science has been remiss in approaching the existential reality of witchcraft. But Grottanelli is too much of a hard-headed anthropologist to accept the notion that perhaps there is something to the reality of witchcraft, including some sort of parapsychological, extrasensory reality. He does not pursue several interesting epistemic problems implicit in his analysis; rather, he takes a somewhat traditional but original way out. Capitalizing on the transitional, changing state of witchcraft among the Nzema, Grottanelli defines witchcraft symbolically and metaphorically. As his longitudinal study of the Nzema tells him, Grottanelli is well aware that witchcraft in this society is no longer traditional, that perhaps most people no longer believe that there are such real entities as witches engaged in loathsome activities, and that, as a local philosopher puts it, witchcraft (*ayene*) takes place *"in ayene way"* (that is, "in a Pickwickian sense," as a positivist would say). Because of the transitional stage of Nzema witchcraft, or perhaps for other analytical reasons not made clear in the text, Grottanelli defines witchcraft as *an allegory of social and moral subversion.* He concludes the analysis with the statement that the witch embodies a category of evil that can be cross-culturally translated and that certain universal human proclivities may therefore be expressed by the concept of witchcraft.

We agree with most of Grottanelli's analysis, but not with his concluding definition of witchcraft. Nonetheless, he correctly focuses the conceptualization of witchcraft and envisages some of the epistemological problems involved in a nonfunctional approach to magic supernaturalism. First, he raises the possibility of reality which led us to realize that, although scientifically one cannot entertain the ontological reality of witches, the existential reality of witchcraft's consequences cannot be doubted. Under the rubric of witchcraft's consequences, a rather large corpus of social, psychological, and physical phenomena are included, not forgetting a certain parapsychological, extrasensory component that Grottanelli regards as a possibility. This is significant, for there is a chance that magic phenomena, particularly sorcery, may be associated with what parapsychologists call "psi," referring to a presumed unitary force underlying two types of abilities, extrasensory perception and psychokinesis. Winkelman (1987) discusses this question and concludes that certain practices and practitioners of magic may have such parapsychological components. This is an avenue of research that should not be discussed a priori, and it fits in well with the epistemological focus and strategy.

Second, and more significant, is Grottanelli's conception of witchcraft as an allegory. Whether witchcraft is an allegory of social and moral subversion, we leave to the functionalists turned symbolists to determine. For us, this definition is a symptom that witchcraft is no longer traditional, that it is evolving, owing perhaps to the introduction of other beliefs and elements not present in the traditional setting. The fact that, among the Nzema, witchcraft now (Grottanelli's ethnographic present) takes place *in ayene way* implies that, in a putative, traditional ethnographic present, witchcraft's beliefs were absolute and the people had no caveats for the existence of witches and their doings. Thus, the conception of witchcraft as an allegory is a label for a transitional stage of a traditional system toward that point when witchcraft became a mechanism of last resort. Herein lies the genesis of this concept, which can be made into a comparative category. Although the exercise has not been attempted, there is voluminous information for scholars to test the following sequence: At the beginning of modern European times, theologians asserted and laymen believed in the absolute, ultimate existence of witches as the embodiment of evil and the manifestation of the Christian devil; by the end of the seventeenth century, the *in ayene way* syndrome had set in, and probably lasted until the middle of the nineteenth century; from then on the belief in witchcraft has been quickly diminishing, and nowadays even theologians would regard such belief as superstition. But we still have many spurious witches, there are periodic witch-hunts, and inquisitors of various stripes are periodically busy accusing people of all kinds of dreadful acts.

We read Tambiah's (1973:199–229) article, "Form and Meaning of Magical Acts: A Point of View," shortly after it was originally published. But it was not until several years later that we realized the significance of Tambiah's conception of magic for the analysis of bloodsucking witchcraft. It has influenced the development of the epistemological focus and strategy, both in a positive and negative way. Positively, by making us aware of some of the epistemological concerns that underlie this study; negatively, as an example of what to avoid in conceptualizing several aspects of magic supernaturalism.

Tambiah begins by stating that the analogical mode of thought is a universal attribute of humankind. He then contrasts magic and science as characterized by different forms of analogical thought and action. Magic is "magical acts," as he narrows down the scope of his study. On the one hand, magical acts "constitute 'performative' acts by which a property is imperatively transferred to a recipient object or person on an analogical basis. Magical acts are ritual acts, and ritual acts are in turn performative acts whose positive and creative meaning is missed and whose persuasive validity is misjudged if they are subjected to that kind of empirical verification associated with scientific activity" (Tambiah 1973:199). On the other hand, science also employs the analogical method, but, in contrast, it "consists in making the known or apprehended instance serve as a model for the incompletely known in the phenomenon to be explained. The model serves to generate a prediction concerning the *explicandum*, which is then the subject of observation and verification tests to ascertain the prediction's truth value" (Tambiah 1973:199–200). Tambiah maintains that it is quite likely that science arose out of some forms of magic, but that this does not excuse anthropologists from approaching the study of magic exclusively from the rationalistic, explanatory standpoint. Rather, so-called primitive societies have had their own historical experiences, may not have had the same evolution from magic to science, and therefore must be viewed in their own terms and in their own social settings if we are to make sense of their forms and functions. This is the gist of Tambiah's argument.

Evans-Pritchard's study of Azande witchcraft and sorcery provides Tambiah with most of the empirical matrix for the identification and exemplification of magical analogy and how it is performed and acted out in ritual activity, although examples are also taken from other societies. Ingeniously, Tambiah combs out of these sources the forms, contents, and functions that analogy may serve and their implications for his argument. Based on the work of two historians of the philosophy of science (Lloyd and Hesse), he outlines the various forms of analogy in science, their inception in primitive Greek thought, and tentatively suggests that at the inception of Western civilization (that is, during that period of Greek history from the Homeric epic to Thales) analogical analysis in logic and philosophy evolved from some prevalent form of magic. Lest the reader become overenthusiastic about this linear evolution of analogy from magic to science, Tambiah warns the reader (particularly anthropologists) not to interpret the analogical thought of primitives in terms of scientific analogizing—that is, as subject to empirical verification, falsification, and inductive-deductive reasoning.

Tambiah goes on to examine the various forms of analogy from the standpoint of the logical and epistemological properties that they exhibit and as they are used in science and language. He points out the vital differences between the use of analogy in science and magical rituals, which center on the objectives and criteria that they entail: the former, essentially prediction and verification; the latter, persuasion, expansion of meaning, legitimacy of outcome, and so on.

The weakest part of the analysis, probably because it is the most symbolic, is the section concerned with elucidating how anthropologists should understand ritual magical acts. Starting from the assumption that most magical acts "combine word and deed," Tambiah draws theoretical support from Austin (a philosopher of language) and his classification of speech acts. Adapting Austin's notions, he classifies performing speech acts as follows:

> *Locutionary*—descriptive referential statements that can be proved true or false.
>
> *Illocutionary*—statements laden explicitly with value and emotion and designed to influence people's actions in a variety of ways; these statements cannot be falsified but can be judged as "happy/unhappy," "valid/invalid," and so forth.
>
> *Perlocutionary*—statements laden implicitly with value and emotion and designed to convince with reference to the "intended and unintended *consequences* upon the bearer of words uttered by the speaker"; these utterances also cannot be falsified.

Most magical acts, Tambiah maintains, are illocutionary or perlocutionary, and it is these two forms of analogy that he wants to conceptualize as the main means of understanding this aspect of supernaturalism. He concludes the analysis by stating: "(1) while to particular instances of ritual enactment of the illocutionary or performative type, *normative* judgments of efficacy (legitimacy, defectiveness, propriety, etc.) may be applied, it is inappropriate to judge their efficacy in terms of *verification statements* and inductive rules, and (2) while ritual in general as an institution cannot be declared to be defective, particular instances of it may be so declared, if the proper conditions of performance were not met" (Tambiah 1973:224). Tambiah then takes Evans-Pritchard and Horton to task for having failed to understand these basic properties of magical acts—that is, for having tried to explain magical action in the empirical, inductive, verifying mode of science. He concludes the essay by admonishing those who would label as "magic" a complex of rites that they regard as empirically false, and he warns anthropologists not to impose supernatural categories on observational data that do not have equivalent referents in the observer's own cultural tradition.

There is much in Tambiah's analysis of magic that is useful and to the point. First, his discussion of the use of analogy in science and magic unmistakably indicates that in both domains the entailed logic is the same. His analysis is particularly instructive in demonstrating that it is not a question of whether primitives think differently from scientists. All humans think alike—that is, have the same categories for thinking—and what has recently been rather fashionable to call "different modes of thought" is a misnomer. The differences between primitives and scientists, then, are ones of perception and the inferences they make from perceptions; or, to put it differently, one should not confuse logic with epistemology, and one should concentrate on the specific assumptions that individuals and collectivities make about the world, the screen through which they perceive it, and the inferences that they make, given certain techno-evolutionary constraints.

Second, Tambiah stimulates thought about the evolutionary aspects of the magic-science problem. We have two caveats, though. On the one hand, the magic-science evolutionary sequence is more complex than Tambiah stipulates, even for the Western cultural tradition, from its magic stage in pre-sixth century B.C. to its mature scientific stage beginning with the Industrial Revolution. As an evolutionary sequence of Western society's epistemological outlook, the classic magic-religion-science sequence is only a good start. On the other hand, and with due cognizance of the very careful attention that the problem requires, we are puzzled about Tambiah's reluctance to replicate the magic-science evolutionary sequence in the primitive and folk contexts. Although it is undoubtedly correct to think of the epistemological evolution of non-Western societies in a linear magic-science manner from the long-range perspective (that is, since the Neolithic Revolution), our own experience suggests that, from the short-range perspective, many societies have linearly evolved from a magical stage, to a putative religious stage, and in some cases are on the verge of a scientific stage.

Third, even though we disagree with several of Tambiah's premises, his cautionary remarks—about conceptualizing magic as a science that more often than not fails or as some sort of applied science subject to empirical verification and induction—are well taken, a timely warning to simple-minded empiricists. For us the lesson of this warning is an implicit recognition that, although the logic of scientists and the logic of primitives is the same, perceptually and inferentially the differences that separate them may be vast.

On the debit side, there are three premises in Tambiah's work with which we disagree and which tend rather to diminish his essentially epistemic orientation in the study of magic supernaturalism. First, he overemphasizes the use and significance of analogy in science, at least in contemporary social and physical science. It looks plausible that in the gestating stage of science, as some aspects of magic evolved into a new epistemic tradition, analogic conceptualization was foremost; however, as science began to mature after the Middle Ages, analogy became one of several constructs in conceptualizing the universe. This undue emphasis on analogy does not fit well with the main attributes of science, thereby biasing comparison with non-scientific enterprises. Second, Tambiah also overestimates the presence of analogy in the realm of magic and the role it plays in understanding the nature and form of this type of supernaturalism.

Although it is true that the ritual manipulations of much of supernatural curing and other magical acts that are subsumed under the rubric of sorcery have analogical forms and variations, this is not the case with the beliefs and practices that most anthropologists regard as subsumed under the rubric of witchcraft. The same obtains in other domains of magic supernaturalism in which, as in witchcraft, implicit or explicit outcomes and expectations are achieved and realized by means other than analogy. In the same vein, his insistence that most magical acts are couched in social rites is misplaced; this is also an exaggeration that constrains the plausibility of his analysis. Third, Tambiah's characterization of magical acts as illocutionary acts entailing performative action may be a good metaphor in understanding the form, function, and logic of the phenomena, but it obfuscates the fundamental epistemological issues that underlie the study of magic, or of any other kind of supernaturalism.

There is a fourth assumption in Tambiah's analysis that seriously restricts his approach and renders the study of magic intractable to scientific analysis. Tambiah's conception of magical acts constitutes an object language of the metalanguage of science. His analysis is exclusively centered on the normative system. Lest the reader misunderstand, we are not saying that the logic of magic as illocutionary performance is given at the level of the belief system, but only that understanding is generated at this level, as experience teaches the social group to structure closed normative systems. Explanations, however, are generated by the interaction of normative systems and concrete empirical reality. In other words, one cannot regard illocutionary magical performance as one of the data sets in the scientific task of establishing how normative expectations serve as the screen through which social and physical reality is experienced and at the same time validated. The overriding flaw in Tambiah's argument is that he indiscriminately jumps from the object language of illocutionary performance to the metalanguage of science. This is clearly the case when he says that ". . . this same African thought-system whose aim is explanatory and predictive (just like science) refuses to subject itself (like good science) to falsifiability and other verification tests" (Tambiah 1973:115). No objection here, for one predicts at the level of the object language, while one verifies at the level of the metalanguage. Thus, Tambiah's conclusions are acceptable at the level of the object language of magic, but the anthropologist's main concern should be with the metalanguage of science. Tambiah understands that magical systems are closed systems, but he should also realize that closed systems become open systems, and this is the fundamental problem to grapple with. His repeated assertions that the illocutionary performative structure of magic is not susceptible to scientific analysis is a kind of misplaced relativism counterproductive to good conceptualization.

THE EPISTEMOLOGICAL FOCUS AND STRATEGY IN THE STUDY
OF MAGIC AND RELIGIOUS SUPERNATURALISM

In gauging the pros and cons of the main approaches that have been employed in the study of magic supernaturalism, the content and scope of the epistemological approach of this monograph has also been intimated. In connection with specific junctures of the sociological and psychological approaches, it was necessary to point out how the present focus and strategy depart from the essentially functional orientation of these approaches. The theoretical ideas, basic assumptions, and methodological *modi operandi* that underlie the analysis of bloodsucking witchcraft are discussed in Chapters 7 and 12. The purpose of the following remarks, therefore, is not to describe the epistemological approach in detail for the reader but only to put him in a receptive mood for a different way of looking at magic supernaturalism.

Theoretical Considerations and Analytical Emphasis

Let us begin by stating what this study is and is not. First and foremost, the analysis of bloodsucking witchcraft in rural Tlaxcala is neither a sociological nor a psychological study. Functional assignment per se is not contemplated and the analysis of Chapter 11 is subsidiary, entailing primarily descriptive integrational purposes as a means of demonstrating the dynamics of the phenomena. On the other hand, the study is sociologically and psychologically structured so that the primary analytical thrust of the psychological structure is realized in a well specified context of the sociological structure. This monograph is an endeavor of which the primary concerns are the perceptions and inferences of a social group within a circumscribed domain and under well-specified conditions. The accent is on the theory of knowledge of a magic supernatural complex and how it is embedded in an epistemological and ontological reality: the former normative and the latter sociophysical, but in an intimate state of interaction. Explanation is sought in the realm of how and under what conditions a normative, what-ought-to-be construct conditions the reality of perceptual domains, and at the same time ontological reality validates epistemological reality as a guide to action. The epistemological approach to the study of magic supernaturalism requires the specifications of a normative system (that is, an overall ideology configurated by specific beliefs) discharged in a carefully controlled complex of social and physical reality (that is, well authenticated cases of the phenomena at hand, the ambience in which they take place, and the cultural embedding of happenings and events). So conceived, the study of magic supernaturalism requires that the normative system be thoroughly embedded in an ongoing social structure of long standing, while the observed social and physical realities exhibit the psychological mechanisms that individuals and well bounded groups manifest in perceiving the phenomena at hand in particular, and a significant part of the universe around them in general, as conditioned by what they believe and what they infer from what they observe. The following are the most salient components of the approach.

Probably since as early as the Golden Age of Greece in the fifth and fourth centuries B.C., there have been individuals, perhaps small segments of Western society, for whom the explanation of the social and physical universes was a purely naturalistic matter—that is, there was no appeal to supernaturalism and the proverbial deus ex machina of philosophy. But it was probably not until the eighteenth century, at least for the nascent social sciences, that the French philosophers of the Enlightenment and the Scottish moral philosophers popularized the notion of human evolution from a largely supernaturally dominated worldview to an increasingly naturalistic conception of the universe. This view of humankind's intellectual evolution was conceptualized by Comte several decades later in his famous magic-religion-science evolutionary scheme, still latently (and sometimes manifestly) present in the French sociological school well into the twentieth century. Simplistic as Comte's original scheme was, it does contain significant descriptive validity, and it should not have been abandoned without a fair attempt to make use of it. There is little doubt that society has evolved according to the stipulation of this scheme, and a reasonable attitude on the part of twentieth-century anthropology should have been to test the theory in the light of increasing empirical evidence. That in Western society the rise of naturalism and its ups and downs resulted in the birth, growth, and maturity of science is a foregone conclusion. These are extremely complex matters, and here we wish only to bring to the fore the fundamental notion that underlies the study of magic and religious supernaturalism—namely, the distinction between natural and supernatural causation and the implications that it entails. The distinction pervades most aspects of magic and religion: disentangling what it means for the practice and consequences of every form of supernaturalism is at the heart of the psychological-epistemological approach. Some anthropologists maintain that often no distinction emerges between natural and supernatural domains, and the consequences that follow, both in the realm of magic and religion, regardless of whether these forms of supernaturalism are emically distinct or constitute a single realm. Such assertions seem dubious at best, both behaviorally and as springs to action, although normatively it may be true that no distinction obtains. Witchcraft and sorcery can be conceived as closed systems in which the natural-supernatural distinction is perhaps not relevant, but as soon as a magical system begins to open up, the distinction becomes crucial. Thus, distinguishing between natural and supernatural contexts and domains of efficacy is a necessary condition for explaining how particular magical and religious systems change. It is evident that the study of closed systems constitutes the beginning of research on magic supernaturalism, but the ultimate end is to determine how systems change under the influence of alternative forms of knowledge.

The second component of the epistemological approach is a consequence of the natural-supernatural distinction. Indeed, it may perhaps be regarded as a concept whose implementation brings the magic-religion-science evolutionary sequence to an adequate resolution—namely, that it may be used and eventually acquire theoretical importance. We have in mind, of course, the fact that the sequence is not strictly syntagmatic, exclusive, and unilineal, since magic, religion, and/or science have coexisted in varying proportions at any isolable evolutionary stage. It is clear to the student of Western culture that, at least since the end of the fifteenth century, first magic and then religion, as screens conditioning circumscribed segments of the social and physical universes, have become increasingly marginal. Religion is now normatively only mildly effective; magic remains latent but its consequences have all but disappeared, except that it may occasionally manifest itself in domains that are no longer regarded as belonging to the supernatural realm. Outside the context of Western culture, similar transformations have been recorded in folk and tribal societies. Whatever the trajectory from magic to science, and however it is configurated in particular societies in terms of content and stages, countless tribal and folk societies during the last one hundred years have experienced irreversible transformation in their magico-religious systems: religion is being secularized, and magic is becoming increasingly latent. This particular twist in looking at magic supernaturalism has been characterized as the "elements or mechanisms of last resort" syndrome, or, perhaps ontologically more accurately, as one of the fundamental existential conditions of man. When a magical complex has become a mechanism of last resort, it no longer entails continuous social or physical consequences, nor does it play a role in conditioning the group's perceptions. But the complex may occasionally surface under extraordinary conditions and may even color for some time the actions of the group. Another property of magical behavior and action as a mechanism of last resort is that it is not necessarily realized in what is commonly referred to as a sacred domain, and it may manifest itself in practically any domain of culture.

The analysis of magic supernaturalism from an epistemological standpoint is posited on the assumption that explanations emerge at the level in which the normative system and social and physical realization are viewed as efficaciously interrelated and entailing a feedback effect. Thus, the necessary conditions for the implementation of the epistemological approach are three: first, that the normative system be minutely specified in terms of an underlying ideology expressed in individual beliefs; second, that the consequences of magical beliefs be ascertained socially and physically in terms of concrete cases, events, happenings, and contextual observations; and, third, that the interaction of normative expectations and sociophysical realization be measured as entailing feedback and reinforcement. At this point two caveats are in order. First, it is our empirical claim that there are no entirely projective magical systems. Rather, it is a question of degrees of projection: the less projective the system, the more a sociophysical component can be observed and quantified, and vice versa. Second, harnessing the normative system in terms of an underlying ideology and specific circumscribed beliefs is difficult, and, even though most studies of magic supernaturalism are almost entirely based on normative data bases, it does not mean that anthropologists have achieved a significant degree of qualitative and quantitative exactness in this basic operation.

This monograph and the approach that underlies it may be summarized as a study of folk modes of perception, the inferences that perceptions engender, and the actions and behaviors that perceptions and inferences entail in a circumscribed cultural domain. The focus is on the folk theory of knowledge that configurates bloodsucking witchcraft, and whether the same principles of perception and inference apply to other rural Tlaxcalan cultural domains. The basic question being asked is, do the natural and supernatural inputs and outputs that constitute the perceptual and inferential structure of bloodsucking witchcraft as a closed, albeit temporary and intermittent, system also obtain in other cultural domains, or, to what discernible degree do similar inputs and outputs affect the behavior and action of rural Tlaxcalans? The answer to the basic question is a tentative yes, but the study raises as many questions as it answers, given that some of our assumptions and propositions have not yet been properly tested. What is undoubtedly the case, and most likely to obtain cross-culturally and comparatively, is that in order to establish differences and similarities of perceptual and inferential modes along the sociocultural evolutionary continuum, the problem must be framed by the natural-supernatural dichotomy, causally and contextually. In the broadest perspective, the comparative application of the epistemological focus and strategy aims at answering a number of questions that have preoccupied anthropologists and sociologists since the turn of the century, most of them centered on the problem that we have framed as "different modes of perception and inference."

Finally, let us reiterate the significance of the objectification of causality and the transposition of causation, that are the main analytical tools in the implementation of the epistemological focus and strategy. The former concept may be characterized as establishing the causal parameters for the analysis of single-directed, well-bounded magical phenomena configurated in clearly discernible, self-contained events, happenings, and occurrences. The latter concept, on the other hand, entails essentially epistemic tasks, namely, the specification of individual and collective states in which magical acts take place, establishing the perceptions of magical consequences, and ordering and interpreting the ambience in which consequences unfold.

Substantive and Methodological Considerations

In assessing what has been accomplished by British functionalists, we discussed some of the considerations for the implementation of the epistemological approach. These matters can be disposed of quickly here. The substantive centerpiece is a data base that includes two distinctly separate corpora of facts. On the one hand, the normative system must be precisely collected and spelled out in terms of the magical complex's overall ideology and a set of specific beliefs. On the other hand, the social and physical realization of the magical system at hand, and the consequences of its conditional beliefs, must be quantitatively configurated in terms of observed cases, authenticated events, and circumstantially inferred facts and happenings. Let us elaborate a bit on these data sets and on how they should be handled methodologically.

First, collecting the data base for structuring a magical complex's normative system is easier said than done. Of the two aspects of the normative system, the beliefs on which a magical complex is posited are the easiest to elicit and configurate into meaningful sets and subsets and in some sort of ranking or hierarchical order. Needless to say, the exhaustiveness, ranking, or hierarchical order of beliefs, and their systematic presentation, are of crucial importance for the primary task of causally entailing normative expectations and sociophysical realization. Harnessing the overall ideology in which a magical complex is embedded is a more difficult and time-consuming task. The reason why this aspect of the normative system has generally not been successfully accomplished is probably twofold: lack of systematic concern with magic and religious systems themselves; and, more important, the ideology of a magical complex is almost invariably part of a wider configuration—most often, of course, religion, but also some aspects of kinship and, not infrequently, other cultural domains. Given this common state of affairs, the ideology of witchcraft or sorcery is either glossed over or inadvertently ignored. The ideology should be specified in terms of imperatives and constraints and ranked from more to less inclusive. In the case of bloodsucking witchcraft, its ideology is an integral part of the folk religious system, which constitutes a whole at the normative core of the entire sociocultural system.

Second, what distinguishes this study from most descriptions and analyses of magic supernaturalism is that it is based on a solid structural (social and physical) data base. Like the best studies of witchcraft and sorcery, the action and behavioral components of bloodsucking witchcraft take place and unfold in the controlled ambience of a social group that is well bounded and propinquitous, entailing several levels of realization. Unlike the great majority of witchcraft and sorcery studies, the antecedents, consequences, and effects of bloodsucking witchcraft are physically and psychologically realized and observed or circumstantially inferred in the context of specific cases, repeated events, manifold happenings, and much more additional information. The structural data base of this study includes the careful and systematic observation of forty-seven cases of bloodsucking witchcraft, hundreds of recorded cases, dozens of cases investigated for the purpose of corroboration, and much verbally elicited information throughout a generation. We are well aware, however, that there is room for improvement in generating structural data bases on magic supernaturalism studies. For example, comparatively complete as it is, the data base of this monograph has several gaps, particularly in the psychological components of the complex. The reason for this shortcoming is that the systematic study of cases, and most of the less structured data, were gathered when we had not yet conceived the epistemological approach and most of the analytical tools employed in this monograph.

Third, and finally, a methodological note. In several aspects this is a tentative study, both in the theoretical framework it employs and the methodology for handling the data base and the analysis. We have taken ideas from several anthropologists, but fashioning the epistemological focus and strategy is our achievement. It has taken a long time to complete this study, but in the process we have learned a certain methodological orientation. Substantively, the gathering of the various data bases is best undertaken in the context of longitudinal studies, namely, in field situations having well-bounded cultural domains, with an easily accessible diachronic dimension, and involving continuous fieldwork for at least four or five years. There are a significant number of societies in most culture areas of the world that are still traditional, and these environments are probably the most propitious for the kind of study envisaged here. Indeed, it would be very valuable to restudy many of the classic studies of witchcraft and sorcery, particularly in Africa, to determine how these systems have changed since traditional times. It has been our experience that it is best to begin with the gathering of the normative system, and then go on to the systematic investigation of cases, although this was not exactly the procedure that was serendipitously forced upon us in investigating the forty-seven–case sample. This modus operandi is more efficient and provides greater insight with which to approach the social and physical realization of a magical system

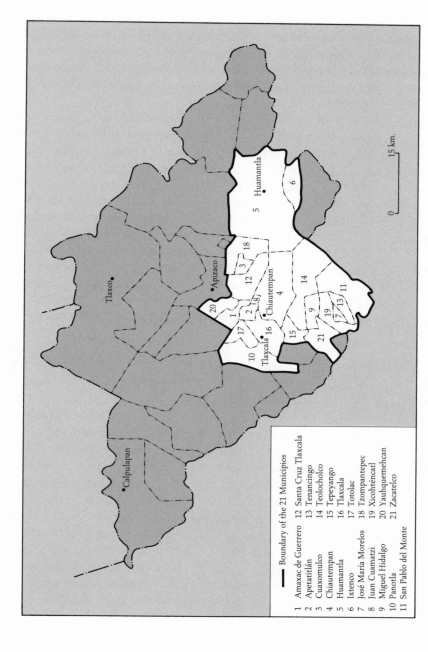

MAP 1. Municipios Surrounding La Malintzi Volcano

after the normative system has been thoroughly understood. Another lesson is that, unless anthropologists are thoroughly grounded in psychology, it is more appropriate that the epistemological approach be implemented in cooperation with trained psychologists. Had Nutini had the benefit of such cooperation twenty-five years ago, the psychological data base of this monograph would be of much better quality.

Searching for a model to describe and analyze bloodsucking witchcraft in rural Tlaxcala and finding none in the traditions of social and psychological functionalism, we devised our own. Whether the epistemological approach, as envisaged here or in a number of possible variations, represents an answer to the functional approach for the study of magic and religious supernaturalism, we would not even guess. But if social and psychological functionalism has not produced any alternatives or new avenues of development in a generation, it is difficult to say what the future of supernaturalism is in anthropological research. Ethnographically and ethnologically, this monograph is on solid ground, and the description and analysis of bloodsucking witchcraft in rural Tlaxcala is as exhaustive and in-depth a study as any that has seen print in two generations. The reader may totally disagree with our interpretation and analysis, but the facts, normative and structural, are there for his own interpretation and analysis.

Demographic, Historical, and Ethnographic Note

By rural Tlaxcala we do not mean to include all forty-four independent *municipios* comprising the state of Tlaxcala, but rather the twenty-one municipios surrounding La Malintzi volcano, the most prominent feature in the Tlaxcala-Pueblan Valley (Nutini and Isaac 1974:28). Since before the Spanish Conquest, this has been the heartland of the Tlaxcalan region; it includes two-thirds of the entire population of the state, which at the time of the ethnographic present of this monograph was about 350,000 (see map 1).[1] The demography, ethnohistory, and contemporary ethnography of rural Tlaxcala have been thoroughly described and analyzed in six monographs and many articles. To place the present monograph in these settings, we suggest the following publications: Nutini (1968:23–93); Nutini and Isaac (1974:275–372); Nutini and Bell (1980:197–379); Nutini (1984:372–467); Nutini (1988). These publications are concerned with the most important institutions (kinship, *compadrazgo*, folk Catholicism, and anthropomorphic supernaturalism) in which bloodsucking witchcraft is embedded, and the reader may want to consult them.

CHAPTER ONE

An Outline of Weathermaking, Nahualism, and Sorcery in Rural Tlaxcala

BETWEEN 1898 AND 1900, the American ethnologist Frederick Starr conducted three ethnographic surveys of the Indians of central and southern Mexico. During his first and third surveys Starr spent at least two months in the heartland of Tlaxcala, and, in fact, visited most of the twenty-one municipios surrounding La Malintzi volcano. Quoting his chief informant and guide—a Nahuatl-speaking Indian by the name of Quechol—Starr gives the following description of the Tlaxcalan Indians' non-Catholic supernatural practitioners:

> The great superstitions are four in number—*Tetlachiwike, Tlawelpochime, Kiatlaske* or *Tesitlaske*, and *Nahuatl*. The *Tetlachiwike* are witches. They can harm people or render them ill by touch or glance. . . . The second great superstition of the modern Aztecs is *Tlawelpochime*. These are female beings who love the blood of young infants. They are much feared and mothers take much pains to guard against them. They prefer to suck the blood from the back of the neck; they also draw it from the sides of the neck or the cheeks; they may not, however, take it from the chest or lower body. . . . The third great superstition is *Kiatlaske* or *Tesitlaske*—conductors or bringers of rain and hail. These receive their power from Malintzi. . . . The fourth great superstition of our Tlaxcalans is the *Nahuatl*. This is a male being, who is a robber and capable of indefinite self-transformation (Starr 1900:18–22).

Starr goes on to describe in some detail the main behavioral attributes of these supernatural practitioners. Most of what he describes, especially concerning bloodsucking witches, applies to the contemporary ethnographic situation, except perhaps for some terminological confusion about witches and sorcerers. These four practitioners are the most important anthropomorphic, personified supernaturals in rural Tlaxcalan society. Their basic form and attributes can be traced to pre-Hispanic times, but they were interestingly syncretized by the infusion of elements of European witchcraft and sorcery and African sorcery throughout the seventeenth century. Since then, they have remained a constant feature in the non-Catholic complex of beliefs and practices of the region. In 1959, when an ethnographic survey of the Tlaxcala-Pueblan Valley was conducted (Nutini and Isaac 1974:27–148), these four practitioners were universally present, not only in the communities surrounding La Malintzi but in those on the eastern slopes of the Sierra Nevada as well. The situation has since changed, but the beliefs and practices concerning them remain rooted in the average community, despite the significant changes in modernization and secularization that the region has undergone. Inasmuch as these four supernatural practitioners constitute a fairly integrated complex in the native belief system, it is necessary to describe briefly the other three before analyzing bloodsucking witches.[1]

WEATHERMEN OR CONJURERS

Weathermen, rainmakers, or conjurers are known in rural Tlaxcala as *tiemperos, graniceros,* or *conjuradores* in Spanish, and as *tezitlazcs, quiatlazcs, tezitlazques,* or *quiatlazques* in Nahuatl (henceforth *tezitlazcs*). The tezitlazcs are individuals endowed with supernatural powers destined to control the natural elements in their several manifestations: to stop hail, temper the force of torrential rain, ask for rain during the dry season, hasten the coming of rain at the beginning of the rainy season, divert the course of whirlwinds, and change the direction of wind storms. These varied activities of the tezitlazcs fall under the general category of *conjurar o atajar el mal tiempo* (to conjure or stop bad weather), and they are performed on a public communal basis. Most communities in rural Tlaxcala have from as few as three to as many as eight tezitlazcs, two of which are regarded as the "official" weathermen, which generally leads to competition and rivalry with the non-official weathermen. The official tezitlazcs, always the most prestigious and reliable in the community, receive for their services some kind of compensation, which may range from donations of food, drink, and/or corn from specific individuals and families, to communal payments in cash. In the most traditional communities, the tezitlazcs are paid a flat annual salary—which may range from 500 to 2,500 pesos—generally given by the *fiscales* (administrative officials) out of their weekly collection of alms, or every household in the community may be assessed a certain amount ranging from 3 to 10 pesos. In the more secularized communities, the tezitlazcs are recompensed on a more or less voluntary basis by individuals, households, or even larger residential groups, in the form of donations of money or contributions in kind. As official servants of the community, through the year the tezitlazcs must be constantly alert in order to detect quickly, or even anticipate, the capricious behavior of the natural elements; as such, they may be regarded as primitive meteorologists. If they do not perform according to the expectations of the community, they are quickly replaced by other tezitlazcs. In addition to their public-communal functions, the tezitlazcs also perform as individual, private practitioners. Every tezitlazc has a number of "contracts" with particular *milpa* (cultivated plot of land) owners for the individual protection of their land. For these services, the tezitlazcs receive a flat annual sum which may vary from 10 to 25 pesos (12.50 pesos per dollar), depending on the size of the plot.

Tezitlazcs are always male, and they are recruited in basically two ways: there are those who are born with immanent powers to conjure the natural elements, and there are those who must learn their craft by strenuous apprenticeship. The former are less numerous than the latter, and they are also considered more efficient and reliable. What is common to both types of tezitlazcs is a direct and intimate relationship to La Malintzi and El Cuatlapanga (the legendary spirits and owners of the mountain) through or from whom their powers are transmitted or derived. When those born with immanent powers reach early middle age (forty or so), La Malintzi appears to them in a dream and makes them fully aware of the nature, extent, and practice of their knowledge.[2] La Malintzi then summons the newly called tezitlazc to her place of abode, a huge cavern in the heart of the mountain, in order to instruct him in the proper and beneficial use of his craft. How immanent powers come to be vested in particular individuals is not known even by the tezitlazcs, who are quick to point out that this is not an attribute of La Malintzi herself, whose only role is to make them aware of their craft and make sure that they use it for the benefit of people. On the other hand, any man who reaches the age of forty-five or so may become a tezitlazc by learning the craft of conjuring from an established tezitlazc with the consent and approval of El Cuatlapanga, for, if by then La Malintzi has not appeared to him in a dream, he realizes that he does not possess immanent powers. The prospective tezitlazc reveals his desire to an established practitioner who cannot refuse to take the applicant under his guidance, but he makes clear to him that only El Cuatlapanga can accept or reject him.

Unlike La Malintzi, El Cuatlapanga does have knowledge of and power over natural elements, which he can bestow upon whomever he wishes. In any event, the established tezitlazc journeys to El Cuatlapanga's residence (also a large cave deep down under the prominent hill of the same name on the western slopes of La Malintzi) to plead the case of the applicant. But as one tezitlazc informant slyly put it, "The truth is that *I* really decide whether a candidate is accepted or rejected, for El Cuatlapanga trusts his servants, and I can always influence the pleading." If the applicant is rejected, no hard feelings result between applicant and tezitlazc, for the latter is always careful to tell the former that it was El Cuatlapanga's decision. If he is accepted, there immediately begins an intensive indoctrination period of two years, which includes not only learning the weather conjuring craft but fasting for days at a time in the solitude of the mountain and learning about the various ancillary functions and activities of being a tezitlazc. At the end of the two years of training, preferably during a full-moon night, master and student journey to El Cuatlapanga's residence, where the new tezitlazc is fully empowered by El Cuatlapanga to conjure the natural elements. From then on he can practice his craft independently of his mentor, and he acquires the right to visit El Cuatlapanga whenever he wishes. But the bond between the two generally remains close, especially in cases when master and student are kinsmen. In fact, quite often non-immanent tezitlazcs have transmitted the craft from father to son for four or five generations. But this is not the case with immanent tezitlazcs, whose knowledge dies with them, as they are not allowed to teach others; were they to defy this adjunction, La Malintzi would strike them down. The inherent superiority and efficacy of immanent tezitlazcs emanates from their close relationship with La Malintzi, who in the native belief system is regarded as a benevolent supernatural always predisposed to help man, whereas El Cuatlapanga, even though he may have the inherent power of controlling the natural elements, is regarded as a capricious and unreliable supernatural, and his dictates do not always work for the benefit of man.

The tezitlazc's craft includes a large roster of prayers, rites, ceremonies, and activities which may have a propitiatory, intensifying, or protective character. Among these the most important are: the use of noise (bells, rockets, wooden rattles); incantations, litanies, and supplications to La Malintzi, El Cuatlapanga, El Peñon, the patron saint of the community, San Lorenzo, San Isidro, San Miguel Arcángel, and San Juan Bautista; fasting, ritual flogging, and the induction of dreams; harnessing the inherent weather-controlling properties possessed by hummingbirds, toads, and snakes; the manipulation of sacred objects and talismans endowed with special powers such as black crosses, palm crosses, *copal* (incense), human bones and skulls, coyote bones, stone idols, clay figurines, human hair, holy water, and so on; the calling of collective participation in the form of ritual walking, pilgrimages, and processions; et cetera. For example, in the case of protecting a milpa against the natural elements, the tezitlazc builds a sacred fence (*tlatepantil*) by burying clay figurines or coyote bones on the four corners of the cultivated plot, in the middle of which he sets up a black cross accompanied by an incense burner; these activities are accompanied by prescribed prayers and ritual incantations.

In addition to the tezitlazcs' main functions and activities concerning the control of natural elements, they perform as prayer leaders (*rezadores*) for a variety of occasions such as wakes, funeral rites, rosaries connected with *mayordomias*, baptisms, and so on. The role of tezitlazcs as rezadores is greatly enhanced when there is no resident priest. Moreover, tezitlazcs officiate on some important ritual and ceremonial occasions, such as the erection of crosses at particular spots, erection of burial crosses, *limpias* (symbolic cleansing of a sick person), setting the foundations of a new house, when the first pair of earrings is given to a baby girl, when a person finds a twin fruit and vegetable, et cetera. In summary, tezitlazcs are highly visible and public individuals in the average rural Tlaxcalan community. The tezitlazcs' manifold and useful roles make them respected members of the community, for despite the supernatural powers they are supposed to have, the people at large consider them incapable of harming their fellowmen. There are variations in detail from community to community, but the basic elements presented here constitute a high common denominator on the structure and roles of the tezitlazcs.

NAHUALES OR TRANSFORMING TRICKSTERS

Probably the most universal non-Catholic practitioner, not only in rural Tlaxcala but in the entire Tlaxcala-Pueblan Valley, is the *nahual*, which has often been described as a "transforming witch" (Foster 1944:89; Saler 1964:306). This gloss is not appropriate (for rural Tlaxcala as for most of Mesoamerica), given the fact that the term "witch" connotes something inherently evil and dreadful, which is most certainly not the case with the concept of *nahual*. A better gloss would be that of "transforming trickster," as we shall see below. There is no Spanish term for this concept, and the people employ exclusively the term *nahual* (*nahuales*, in the plural), which is a corruption of the Nahuatl term *nahualli*. Be this as it may, nahuales are individuals endowed with supernatural powers to transform themselves into animals, most commonly donkeys, turkeys, and dogs, but also coyotes, cats, and foxes. Nahuales can be either male (*nahual*) or female (*nahuala*), and their powers of animal transformation are always learned. Nahuales are always more numerous than nahualas in the average community (notice that we are using the term nahuales to mean both masculine-plural and the plural of both genders). Quite commonly the power is handed down from father to son, and the people believe that there are long lines of nahuales. There are variations from community to community concerning the belief and practice of nahualism, and what follows is a fairly accurate common denominator for rural Tlaxcala.

A prospective nahual can learn the animal-transforming power in two ways. He may directly approach a man whom he suspects of being a nahual and ask him to teach him the craft. If the nahual accepts, the period of indoctrination begins immediately and may last for as long as two years. If he does not want to accept the applicant, he will firmly deny that he is a nahual. The second way of becoming a nahual is by catching a practitioner in his animal form and forcing him to teach the craft to his captor, under the threat of being clubbed to death. This method implies, as discussed below, that there are ways of immobilizing nahuales in their animal form. The process of recruitment is the same for male as for female nahuales, but there are two significant provisos. There is always a concordance of gender—that is, a male must learn his craft from a nahual, while a female must learn it from a nahuala. Moreover, there are no lines of nahualas, for they can never pass on their craft from mother to daughter, but they can choose a kinswoman, usually a younger one, as their successor. In all other respects, however, there are no differences between nahual and nahuala.

Nobody knows where the transforming power of nahuales comes from. The only certainty is that it is not derived from higher supernaturals or principles, either pagan or Catholic. The people believe that it is a craft that goes back to times immemorial and that it is always passed on by word of mouth from master to apprentice. Nahuales know each other instinctively, and not infrequently they get together for purposes of training neophytes and exchanging information. Their conventicles take place between midnight and 4:00 A.M. in the thickness of the forest on the upper slopes of La Malintzi. Participant nahuales, who may often come from all the communities of the region, must arrive in their animal form. Obviously nobody knows for certain about the powers of transformation themselves or the mechanisms involved. But the average informant is surprisingly well versed on these matters. First of all, the more powerful the nahual, the more different animal transformations he can achieve. The most powerful nahuales can transform themselves into as many as five animals, always including the burro and turkey; neophytes however, generally start with the power of transforming themselves into either turkeys or dogs. Nobody may become a nahual or nahuala before the age of thirty, and people believe that most bachelors and spinsters over forty end up as nahuales. The act of transformation cannot be undertaken in the presence of ordinary men, and the literally hundreds of informants who have had experiences with nahuales uniformly affirm that, in order to effect a transformation, a nahual either hypnotizes people or gets beyond their range of vision. Moreover, since nahuales operate at night, it is often difficult to determine what goes on. Be this as it may, the man-into-animal transformation must always be effected in the privacy of the nahual's house or in other secluded spots, while the animal-into-man transformation can be effected automatically wherever the nahual may find itself. The former involves a series of well-defined rites and incantations, without which the transformation is not possible, and among which the most frequently reported are the recitation of magical formulas over the *tlecuil* (hearth), followed by either jumping three times over a pile of live ashes in the north-south and east-west directions, or by going around the *temazcal* three times clockwise and counterclockwise. The latter, on the other hand, involves nothing more than an act of will on the part of the nahual.

The basic behavioral attributes of nahuales can be categorized as follows: he (or she) is a thief, a deceiver, a prankster, and a trickster. As a thief and deceiver, the nahual's main motivation to action is laziness and lack of determination; as a prankster and trickster, the nahual embodies the social shiftiness and unreliability which characterizes him in the popular consciousness. It appears, however, that the nahuales' mainspring to action is lucre. This is clearly expressed in the often-repeated assertion that when a nahual transmits the craft to his son, "it is the only possible way that such an unreliable person can provide his son with an adequate means of making a living," which, in fact, the people regard as the son's inheritance. In any event, nahuales transform themselves into animals for the following main purposes: to steal crops, domestic animals, construction materials, clothing and household utensils, and, in fact, everything except money, for in their animal form nahuales are frightened and lose control by the touch of metals; to deceive people who have done them wrong (they do this by hypnotizing people and putting into their heads all kinds of wild or silly ideas, so that when they wake up they are made to look foolish); to abuse sexually men and women, married or single (they hypnotize their victims, and, after they have satisfied their sexual appetite, they return them home so that the next morning they do not realize what has happened). Again by the use of hypnosis, nahuales constantly play tricks and pranks on people they dislike or simply for the fun of it, such as making individuals undress in the middle of the street so that they are found in the nude, beating up people at night, sending them on impossible errands, hiding things, and so on. (Three or four of the most educated informants actually used the term "hypnotized." What they meant by the gloss is not entirely certain, but probably they had in mind the popular connotation of putting people to sleep and making them lose control. To describe this power of nahuales, most informants used phrases such as "they put people to sleep," "they make people lose their will," and "they control people with their sight.") Despite these bothersome and undesirable traits, nahuales are not in any way malevolent, for in their stealing and pranks they can only go so far, and their powers do not ever permit them to kill ordinary men.

What is the attitude and behavior of the people at large toward nahuales? Except under exceptional circumstances, no one knows for certain who is a nahual. People often suspect their identity, but they are never confronted with the fact unless the nahual is in his animal form. The average rural Tlaxcalan community has at least two or three nahuales, but it is rare when one is caught in his or her animal form. (Nahualism suspicions and accusations have interesting sociological dimensions. These are beyond the scope of this monograph, but, more than any other aspect of anthropomorphic supernaturalism, they reflect the dynamics of social structure.) Suffice it to say that, despite the awesome powers of animal transformation that the people attribute to nahuales, they are not unduly afraid of them, nor do they in any way regard them as basically evil or loathsome individuals. Rather, the people think of nahuales as a kind of pest that needs to be properly controlled. Psychologically, the people at large have an ambivalent attitude toward nahuales: they admire their powers of animal transformation as an easy way of making a living and having fun, on the one hand, whereas they regard them as basically lazy and unworthy individuals who must be taught a lesson whenever possible, on the other. The former attitude always tempers the latter, and on the occasions when a nahual is caught in his animal form he receives a beating but almost always escapes with his life. Under such conditions, there are several methods of protection against the power of nahuales, all of them having to do with their inherent fright of metals. To protect oneself against the nahuales' pranks and sexual abuse, a knife or a pair of scissors is placed by the bed or *petate* (straw mat), or some small metal object (coin or nail) is attached to a garment or one's sheet at night. To protect one's property, domestic animals, or crops, a needle or small safety pin is attached to the lintel of the house or the fence surrounding corrals, pigsties, or chickencoops, and, in the case of a cultivated plot, an old metal pot is set on a pole in the middle of the milpa.

There are rather elaborate procedures for stopping and catching nahuales (*marcarles el alto*). Upon seeing or sensing a nahual in his animal form, a man quickly draws a cross on the ground, sticks a knife or machete at its center, and places his hat on top of it. Following this action, the nahual is immobilized and his captor—and other people with him, if he is not alone—may proceed to interrogate him. In this position, the nahual cannot use hypnosis upon his captor or captors, and he is therefore required to reveal his name. If he does so quickly, still in his animal form, the nahual is let go after a beating. If he resists, the nahual is severely beaten, and, on very rare occasions, even killed.

When the latter takes place, next morning the human body of the nahual is found on the spot, and this evidence verifies that the man was indeed a nahual. The interaction between nahuales and ordinary men in the many different situations of confrontation or capture in which they may find themselves is significant and always entails interesting psychological interpretations on the part of ordinary men concerning the animal-into-man transformation of nahuales and their detection. Succinctly, interpretations involve how ordinary men can distinguish a nahual in his animal form from an ordinary animal, the dialogues that take place between the nahual and his captor, and the conditions and states of mind that underlie these events. In situations such as nahualism in rural Tlaxcala it is almost impossible to separate the psychological from the sociological matrices in any adequate explanation of supernaturalism. Nahualism in Mesoamerica is probably one of the most interesting concepts that may serve as the basis for the construction of a sociopsychological theory of anthropomorphic supernaturalism.

SORCERERS AND SORCERY

Sorcerers are known as *hechiceros* in Spanish, and as *tetlachihuics, tetlachihuiques,* or *tetlahuachimics* in Nahuatl. Very rarely people may employ the alternative term *brujo* (witch in Spanish; in two out of sixty-four rural Tlaxcalan communities for which we have information on this topic) to refer to a sorcerer; almost invariably the reference term is *tetlachihuic,* and henceforth this term will be used. The tetlachihuics are individuals endowed with supernatural powers to do good or evil, induce or cure illness, control the progression or regression of illness, alter the anatomy of people, manipulate and bend the will of men and women, cause sudden or slow death, and, in general, alter or influence the natural order of things by the performance of magical rites and ceremonies, recitation of special prayers and formulas, incantations, use of talismans, and the manipulation of many plants and animals endowed with particular properties. In other words, the tetlachihuic is a practitioner of both white and black magic, which he undertakes by employing sympathetic, homeopathic or imitative, and contagious methods. Tetlachihuics are either males (*hechiceros*) or females (*hechiceras*); people very seldom use the Spanish reference terms, instead preferring the Nahuatl term which does not involve contrast in gender. Male sorcerers, however, by far outnumber female sorcerers, and the average community seldom has more than one female sorcerer among the four or five tetlachihuics who are commonly present.[3] Sorcery in rural Tlaxcala is quite uniform; there are variations from community to community, but these differences are rather minimal and concern mostly the methods and implements employed by the tetlachihuics in their good or evil deeds. What follows then, is a fairly accurate outline of pan-rural Tlaxcalan sorcery.

Tetlachihuics are normal individuals except for the supernatural powers they possess. There are no specific signs by which one can distinguish or detect a tetlachihuic from ordinary people, nor are there any particular somatic or be-havorial characteristics that point to their craft. There is nothing inherent or hereditary about the tetlachihuics' craft, for their power and knowledge is al-ways learned from other tetlachihuics. However, tetlachihuics are born with certain inclinations or dispositions which manifest themselves when children reach the age of fifteen or sixteen. This is not manifested in specific forms of behavior but rather in something extraordinary that the child can do, such as breaking eggs or glassware with his tremendously strong sight (*tlapaltizoliztli, vista fuertísima*) or hearing people's talk at a distance of 500 meters or more. When the parents of the child discover this latent predisposition, they have two alternatives. First, in the majority of cases, his parents will be terribly disturbed and even terrified, for they know that it is the sign of a prospective tetlachihuic, but they do not want the child to become one. They immediately put the child through a series of ritual *limpias*, generally officiated by a tezitlazc, which is supposed to neutralize the latent predisposition of the child and render him completely normal. The limpias are repeated until the tezitlazc determines that the child is totally clean, which sometimes may take an entire week.

Second, upon the initial manifestation of a child's predisposition, his parents do nothing, either because they are paralyzed by fright or because they in fact want the child to become a tetlachihuic when he grows up. In the former case, the parents will try to hide the child's strong sight or fine sense of hearing from the people at large. This does not mean that children who do not undergo a series of ritual limpias will necessarily become tetlachihuics, for some will and some will not, but what is quite certain is that the child will retain for the rest of his life the strong sight, fine hearing, or other sense attributes connected with the latent predisposition. These people are known in rural Tlaxcalan soci-ety as *metepalca* or *yotlezahuitl* ("gente de mala suerte o de mal agüero," people of bad luck or bad omen). In the latter case, the parents of the child will find a tetlachihuic willing to accept the prospective neophyte for future indoc-trination. By the payment of a certain amount of money, the parents of the child strike a bargain with the tetlachihuic by which the latter promises to take the child as a student upon reaching the age of twenty-five. Until the child reaches that age, the tetlachihuic advises the child and his parents to hide or play down the child's latent predisposition and, most certainly, to keep the bargain a secret. Some of the children who are not ritually cleansed will on their own attach themselves to a tetlachihuic when they reach the prescribed age. The tetlachihuic's craft can also be passed from father to son, providing that the latter exhibits the appropriate predisposition. If he does not, the father will search for a close kinsman, generally a nephew, who does, and failing this, he searches for an unrelated young man known to be a yotlezahuitl. It is interesting to note that, as in the case of nahuales, female tetlachihuics cannot pass on their craft to their daughters, and a girl yotlezahuitl who wants to become a sorcerer, must always learn the craft from an unrelated female tetlachihuic. The period of indoctrination lasts from six to eight years, and seldom can a student tetlachihuic be on his own before the age of thirty-two.

It is not known for certain where the power of the tetlachihuics comes from, but again, as in the case of nahuales, the people clearly assert that it does not derive or emanate from any particular pagan or Catholic supernatural. The people suspect that the tetlachuic's craft is handed down verbally from master to student or that it is written in secret books that tetlachihuics guard carefully, and that they give to their chosen disciples when they die. On the other hand, the people are quite certain about the inherent, latent predisposition which is the necessary condition to become a tetlachihuic. The state or condition of yotlezahuitl is something over which the child has no control; it is implanted there at birth by evil, personified supernaturals, and it can only be eradicated by repeated ritual manipulations or limpias. All this makes sense only if one takes into consideration the almost Zoroastrian belief of the people in the constant struggle that goes on between the good supernaturals propitious to human existence (personified by God and the Christian Saints, La Malintzi, and to a certain extent El Cuatlapanga) and the evil anthropomorphic supernaturals antagonistic to human well-being (personified by the Christian Devil, Matlalcihua, La Llorona, and Cocolitzingo). Be this as it may, the people firmly believe that tetlachihuics are one of the human expressions of this supernatural struggle; therefore they may use their powers for good or evil in their relationship to ordinary man, depending on the context in which they are approached and the behavior of specific individuals toward them. Tetlachihuics are public individuals—that is, they are known by the community at large, which regards them as practitioners of a certain craft and accessible to the average person. As such, tetlachihuics are supernatural practitioners hired to do either good or evil, generally when everything has failed in the normal course of affairs. Thus, a person consults or hires a tetlachihuic when all else has failed and neither *curandero* (curer) nor physician has been able to alleviate or cure him of a certain illness, when a man or woman has failed to win the favors of a beloved by the normal means of courtship, or when a man is powerless to take revenge upon an enemy on social, economic, or religious grounds. On these and many other occasions, the people refer to tetlachihuics as instruments of inducing illness, curing illness, causing death, predisposing people toward them, and so on. The conception of the tetlachihuic as an instrument of last resort by no means exhausts the utilization of his supernatural powers, for there are many individuals in communities toward the Indian end of the ethnocultural continuum who consult the tetlachihuics normally before they have taken advantage of other means available to them to cause or cure illness or to influence people's will, activities which fall under what may be called the normal course of everyday life.[4]

As supernatural practitioners for hire, the people think of tetlachihuics as useful members of the community performing needed services regardless of their good or evil nature, since the powers of a tetlachihuic can be counteracted by those of another. It is as individuals per se that tetlachihuics are greatly feared by the people, for they are considered extremely spiteful, vengeful, and all too ready to take offense and use their powers to harm people. Thus, the people may be afraid of tetlachihuics and even hate them intensely, but they are always treated with respect and deference so as not to elicit any feelings of dislike or antagonism on their part. If the people need the tetlachihuics' services they do not hesitate to consult them, but they feel well advised to keep away from them unless they are bound by their services. On the other hand, the tetlachihuics are well aware that the use of their powers must be limited, for they know that, if they transgress certain limits, they may be put to death by enraged members of the community, as Nutini ascertained on two occasions in 1961 and 1963.

Motivated by spite and vengeance, the tetlachihuics' most common procedure is to induce a certain illness that neither curandero nor physician can alleviate or cure, and in extreme cases they can cause the sudden death of an enemy. If the illness is diagnosed in time as the evildoing of a tetlachihuic, the people concerned may hire another tetlachihuic to counteract the action. In this sense, tetlachihuics are often pitting their powers against each other. And yet, tetlachihuics constitute a closely knit fraternity united by an oath of protection and mutual aid against ordinary men. As supernatural practitioners, tetlachihuics are bound by a kind of gentlemen's-agreement ideology which precludes their personal confrontation, in the same fashion as lawyers in our society may be totally committed opponents in court but the best of friends outside it.

In many communities there are special kinds of tetlachihuics known as *tecuates*, who specialize in breaking bones, and, predictably, most orthopedic injuries are attributed to them. However, the greatest amount of the tetlachihuics' activity consists of hiring themselves out to particular individuals. The people in general consult or hire tetlachihuics for many reasons and purposes, as has been noted, but they do it mainly on four occasions: to counteract the action of another tetlachihuic—that is, to cure or arrest supernaturally induced illness; to cure ordinary illness when all else has failed; to cause an enemy to become seriously ill, and in extreme cases of personal vengeance to provoke his death; and to achieve success in love, sex, and the acquisition of a desirable marriage partner. In fact, "amatory magic" may be one of the busiest departments of the tetlachihuic's practice, and in this respect he may be regarded as a dispenser of love amulets and talismans not only to adults and young adults but to teenagers as well. What transpires between tetlachihuic and client is highly privileged and secret; people go to extremes not to be seen consulting tetlachihuics, with the result that most consultations take place very late at night or very early in the morning. It is, of course, to both the client's and the tetlachihuic's advantage to keep transactions secret, especially in cases of causing sudden death; but the tetlachihuic warns the client to keep the secret under the threat of his vengeance. This injunction is always complied with, for the people believe that tetlachihuics can hear everything that is said about them for a kilometer around.

Every consultation, cure, and evil action effected by tetlachihuics has a fairly standard price, which varies remarkably little from community to community and remained much the same from 1961 to 1965.[5] For example, the dispensation of a love charm may cost from 20 to 30 pesos, the curing of a supernaturally induced illness from 200 to 400 pesos, and the causing of a person's death from 1,000 to 1,500 pesos. Tetlachihuics always require payments in advance, and nobody would be foolish enough to demand the money back if the required action was not successful.

Finally, a few remarks about the methods and procedures employed by tetlachihuics. These include a large roster which can be succinctly subsumed under the following categories:

1. The use of sympathetic techniques: the classical manufacture of effigies of people to be harmed; the ritual manipulation of images, such as sticking pins into it, burning it in a special kind of fire, interring it in certain enchanted places, subjecting it to specific incantations, and so on; and the use of photographs in very much the same fashion as effigies, but usually for curing and benevolent purposes.

2. The employment of homeopathic or imitative techniques which include the following: the symbolic replication of people's behavior such as copulation, the spasms of death, or any other bodily action of particular individuals to be alleviated or harmed; the recitation of prayers and magical formulas connected with specific psychological and bodily states; and incantations performed in specific spots such as caves and ravines on the upper slopes of La Malintzi.

3. The performance of contagious rites and incantations involving a person's excrement, nails, hair, or anything that has been in intimate contact with him or her; the casting of magical spells on the house, *temazcal,* or any other place intimately associated with a given person; the ritual manipulation of footprints or anything that has been stepped on by a person; and the use of exorcism and intrusion, mostly for curing purposes.[6]

4. The prescription of a wide range of potions and poultices made of various mixtures of vegetable, animal, and mineral substances: *copal, ocoxochitl* (a parasitic plant), *zoapatl* (local analgesic herb), the roots of the *capulin* tree, the dry roots of the century plant, certain varieties of mushrooms, balm-gentle, and many other plants and herbs; human excrement, urine, hair, nails, saliva, semen, and blood; ground human bones, ground coyote bones, coyote excrement, hummingbird and grasshopper powder, dried toads and lizards, and snake rattles; sulphur, finely ground obsidian, lime, quicksilver, and finely ground pre-Hispanic clay figurine heads. These prescriptions are either given to clients to administer or are administered surreptitiously by the tetlachihuic.

5. The magical manipulation of a number of animals endowed with particular properties, either recently dead or in dessicated form, such as toads, snakes, lizards, hummingbirds, buzzards, coyotes, crows, skunks, et cetera. After these animals are subjected to prescribed incantations, they are either buried in or near the house of the persons which they are supposed to affect or hidden among their possessions.

6. Finally, tetlachihuics can effect many bodily and psychological changes by the direct application of their powerful *tlapaltizoliztli.* This is done either with the consent of interested people in the case of curing or counteracting the action of another tetlachihuic, or secretly and inadvertently when they are causing harm.

Most of the above methods and techniques may, of course, be applied to the good or evil deeds comprising the tetlachihuics' craft. Moreover, practically every method and technique has a specific occasion and range of application. In conclusion, it may be noted that the widespread distinction in Mesoamerica between hot (*caliente*) and cold (*frío*) foods is extended in rural Tlaxcala to bodily and psychological states. In this context, the tetlachihuics' craft is mainly concerned with the confrontation and contraposition of hot and cold states. As in the case of nahualism, sorcery in rural Tlaxcala has sociological implications concerning the tetlachihuic-client relationship and the suspicions and accusations of the tetlachihuics' abuse of their power, some examples of which will be given in the following chapters.

The main reason for including the foregoing outline of weathermaking, nahualism, and sorcery in rural Tlaxcala is that, together with bloodsucking witchcraft, they constitute a rather integrated complex. The ideology underlying these different manifestations of magic supernaturalism is deeply rooted in the cosmological belief system of rural Tlaxcala, which makes no distinction between what is pagan and what is Catholic. But here we are more concerned with the structural discharge of anthropomorphic supernaturalism, and something had to be said about the three manifestations accompanying bloodsucking witchcraft. Tezitlazc, nahual, tetlachihuic, and bloodsucking witch are markedly distinct practitioners, but in different degrees and spheres of action they are bound together by the possession of supernatural powers, which, in the conception of the people, set them apart from ordinary men, regardless of their knowledgability, their public status, and the degree of fear or acceptance they inspire. Moreover, these four supernaturals are bound together by certain rules of etiquette which preclude their confrontation. Even the tezitlazc, the least endowed with supernatural powers and most restricted in their application, is never affected by the pranks, evildoings, or abominable deeds attributed to the other three. In fact, the corpus of these four anthropomorphic practitioners constitutes a mediating entity between man and the cosmogonic supernaturals: part men and part deities, they inhabit or participate in two different worlds; they serve either as the intermediaries, for good or evil, between man and the higher personages governing his destiny, or they enact a social structure binding the two worlds of existence.

CHAPTER TWO

The Belief System and Structural Context of Bloodsucking Witchcraft in Rural Tlaxcala

DEFINITION OF THE BLOODSUCKING WITCH AND HER BASIC ATTRIBUTES

Witchcraft in rural Tlaxcala revolves essentially around the practice of sucking blood from infants, as well as the more rare but similar attacks on children and adults; hence, we have described the phenomenon as "bloodsucking witchcraft." Witches are known as *brujos* (male) and *brujas* (female) in Spanish, and as *tlahuelpuchis, tlahuelpoches,* or *tlahualpochitzi* in Nahuatl. The Spanish reference terms are very seldom employed; the most commonly used Nahuatl term is *tlahuelpuchi,* and we shall henceforth refer to witches by this term. Moreover, the Nahuatl plural of tlahuelpuchi is *tlahuelpochime,* but in order to avoid confusion the Spanish plural, tlahuelpuchis, will be used. Tlahuelpuchis are individuals endowed with supernatural powers to transform themselves into a variety of animals in order to suck the blood of infants, and occasionally to attack and harm children and adults. Despite their specialized activities, tlahuelpuchis are in rather intimate contact with ordinary people; married couples in rural Tlaxcala feel under constant threat of the blood of their infants being sucked. Ideologically, tlahuelpuchis epitomize everything inherently dreadful, loathsome, abhorrent, and hateful, and they personify the exclusively evil and malevolent aspects of the supernatural struggle that constantly affects humanity.

The tlahuelpuchis can transform themselves into donkeys, dogs, cats, chickens, ducks, turkeys, buzzards, crows, fleas, ants, and other small animals and insects. Tlahuelpuchis prefer to transform themselves into fowl, and the turkey (*totolli, huexolotl*) is by far the most common choice. In fact, in about 75 percent of the more than 100 legends and 300 accounts of tlahuelpuchis collected between 1959 and 1966, the transforming animal is the turkey. Tlahuelpuchis, however, have the power to transform themselves into any of the above animals, and the form that they choose depends on the circumstances, as we shall see below. Their powers of animal transformation make tlahuelpuchis structurally similar to nahuales, but this similarity is only superficial: tlahuelpuchis are inherently evil, whereas nahuales are primarily thieves and tricksters; tlahuelpuchis are born with their powers, whereas nahuales must learn theirs; tlahuelpuchis are greatly feared and hated, whereas nahuales are merely regarded as pests and may even be admired. Functionally, tlahuelpuchis are closer to tetlachihuics in the enactment of the forces of good and evil and in being dreaded individuals; structurally they differ in their motivation to action and in knowability. In fact, there is an interesting relationship among nahual, tetlachihuic, and tlahuelpuchi, which points to a common origin in the pre-Hispanic situation.[1]

Tlahuelpuchis are either male or female. Since there is no contrast in gender in the Nahuatl term tlahuelpuchi, generally the only times that the people employ the Spanish terms *brujo* or *bruja* is in order to distinguish the sex of the witch. The great majority of tlahuelpuchis are women; this information was elicited directly from informants and is corroborated in the content of hundreds of legends and accounts. Furthermore, female tlahuelpuchis are universally regarded as more powerful, evil, and bloodthirsty than male tlahuelpuchis. As one moves from the social structure of ordinary men to that of the tlahuelpuchis, there is a complete inversion in the male-female relationship; the female completely dominates the male and has the greater power of decision-making. In fact, one of the most telling signs of being a tlahuelpuchi is the domineering and overly possessive role of the wife occasionally observed among married couples. Unlike the position of tezitlazcs, tetlachihuics, and even suspected nahuales within the structure of the community with respect to their knowability and numbers, it is impossible even to guess the number of tlahuelpuchis who are active in any given community, for, except on the rarest occasions, they are not confronted in their human form. In addition, bloodsucking witchcraft is truly a pan-rural Tlaxcala phenomenon in that, in regard to their evil doings, tlahuelpuchis are impervious to community membership, and people tend chauvinistically to regard tlahuelpuchis as being from other communities rather than their own. At the regional level, the small communities of Olintla and Hueytochco (the former in the valley and the latter in the middle slopes of La Malintzi) are famous and universally regarded by the people as the place of residence of innumerable tlahuelpuchis. Thus, the following description and analysis applies to the region as a whole with little extra-community variation.

Tlahuelpuchis are the most secretive, surreptitious, ethereal, and difficult to identify of all anthropomorphic supernaturals in rural Tlaxcala. There are few overt signs distinguishing tlahuelpuchis from ordinary men and women; with the exception of tezitlazcs, nahuales, and tetlachihuics, who are well aware of their activities but are bound never to reveal their identities, the people at large can only guess at and vaguely suspect their identities. Even the suspicion of being a tlahuelpuchi is seldom verbalized in public, for, unless people are absolutely certain, they risk the reprisal of the tlahuelpuchis, given the fact that, like the tetlachihuics, they are supposed to sense and hear everything that is said about them. That is why the formal accusation of a tlahuelpuchi is extremely rare and brings immediate death to the person in question. Despite their secretiveness and surreptitiousness, the people know a good deal about tlahuelpuchis, their nature, how they operate, and how they can be counteracted. Tlahuelpuchis are born with their immanent evil powers, something over which they have no control. If a person is born a tlahuelpuchi, she or he remains one for life, and there is no force on earth that can eradicate the powers of the tlahuelpuchi. The usual way of expressing this finality about tlahuelpuchis is the people's saying that "las tlahuelpuchis nacen con una maldición que ni Dios ni el diablo pueden borrar" (tlahuelpuchis are born with a curse that neither God nor the devil can erase). Paradoxically enough, it is this finality about the fate of tlahuelpuchis, as well as the lack of control over their destiny, that somehow tempers the inherent abhorrence of the people for their evildoings.

The ultimate explanation of the origin of the tlahuelpuchis' powers is destiny or fate, and informants invariably commiserated with the tlahuelpuchis' luck. There is no locus from which the powers of tlahuelpuchis emanate or are derived, but the people believe that they are kindred spirits to the Christian Devil, Matlalcihua, La Llorona, and other evildoers. In other words, the people regard tlahuelpuchis as independent agents, unrelated to higher evil supernaturals for the discharge of their powers. Rather, tlahuelpuchis are seen as the colleagues in evildoing of these supernaturals, to whom they may have access to be sure, but their essentially human nature makes them much closer to ordinary people. On the other hand, tlahuelpuchis are regarded as occupying a position of subordination with respect to the higher evildoers, often doing their bidding for particular acts of mischief. For example, in all transactions such as "selling one's soul to the devil" or "making a compact with the devil for money," tlahuelpuchis in their animal form serve as intermediaries. Fundamentally, the people conceive of tlahuelpuchis as the recipients of a raw deal, the possessors of something that they did not want; therefore, it is unthinkable that they should want to pass it on to someone else. Thus, the condition of being a tlahuelpuchi is confined to a single individual's life, and tlahuelpuchis cannot transmit, induce, or teach their powers to another individual. There are therefore no lines of tlahuelpuchis and no master-student relationships; their powers inexorably die with them. In general, the people exhibit a considerable degree of anxiety about the vagaries of destiny or fate, for they believe that anyone can be cast at birth in the role of tlahuelpuchi and that there are no known means to counteract this action.

Nothing at birth identifies or sets apart tlahuelpuchis from ordinary infants. Tlahuelpuchis are in every way normal until they have reached puberty, when their inherent nature is suddenly manifested. For both male and female tlahuelpuchis, this event is always dramatic. In the case of female tlahuelpuchis, the power of animal transformation comes automatically with the setting of the first menses, and the young girl is almost instantly transformed into a full-fledged tlahuelpuchi. Until the day she dies, there is no growth or decay of her powers, evildoing propensities, or radius of action. These developments are the same for a male tlahuelpuchi, except that the event marking the awareness of his nature does not come at a fixed point, nor is it connected with any bodily changes. Rather, a superlative case of *espanto* or losing his soul for three days marks the activation of his powers. In any event, at this point female and male tlahuelpuchis not only become aware of their powers of animal transformation, but they are imprinted for life with an insatiable and uncontrollable desire to drink the blood of human beings, especially of infants. This event is a great trauma for the girls and boys in question; it affects not only themselves but also their nearest kinsmen, such as parents and older siblings and, later in life, their spouses. The main reason why people at large know a good deal about these inner matters concerning tlahuelpuchis is that it is practically impossible to keep their secret from at least some of their closest relatives. Sooner rather than later the tlahuelpuchi's immediate kinsmen become aware of her or his powers and activities, and this is a cause of much unhappiness. The tlahuelpuchi's relatives who are in on the secret try by all means to restrict it, but it generally becomes known to all members of the household, for reasons that will become clear below. The tremendous sense of shame, desperation, and hopelessness among the members of the household is the principal reason for their success in maintaining the secret identity of the tlahuelpuchi.

Under normal circumstances, tlahuelpuchis cannot harm or suck the blood of kinsmen, but they would feel compelled to do so if the relatives were about to reveal their identities. In fact, the tlahuelpuchis' relatives often cover up for them; not infrequently, they bail them out of difficult situations. Tlahuelpuchis cannot marry their own kind, and they must search for spouses among ordinary men and women. The normal spouse is, in fact, an important adjunct to the tlahuelpuchi's activities, for without him or her the tlahuelpuchi cannot operate with complete safety. The normal spouse becomes her or his unwilling accomplice, for, when she or he finds out about it, they are already married and bound by secrecy under the threat of death. Many times informants stated that tlahuelpuchis can be killed with no undesirable effects only by people not re-lated to them, or at least not related as siblings, parents, or spouses. Were a tlahuelpuchi to be killed by anyone in these categories, it would be to no avail, for the powers and loathsome inclinations of the tlahuelpuchi would automati-cally be transferred to the killer. In essence, then, the primary relatives of a tlahuelpuchi are burdened with her for as long as she lives. They must do their best to protect her and see to it that the secret of her identity does not become public, for this would bring great social opprobrium and religious ostracism. (Since the great majority of tlahuelpuchis are females, they will henceforth be referred to in this gender to avoid cumbersome expressions.)

THE TLAHUELPUCHIS' POWERS OF ANIMAL TRANSFORMATION

The tlahuelpuchis' power of animal transformation is quite similar to that of nahuales, but there are some significant differences. All tlahuelpuchis can trans-form themselves into any of the animals mentioned above. The greater power of the female tlahuelpuchi as compared with the male consists only in the ability to effect more frequent transformations and to have a wider radius of action. Like nahuales, tlahuelpuchis cannot transform themselves into animals, and vice versa, in the presence of ordinary men. To achieve a transformation, they employ the same means—either hypnotizing people or getting beyond their range of vision. But unlike nahuales, the human-into-animal transforma-tion can be effected automatically, at any time and in any place that the tlahuel-puchi may find herself. This greater versatility of tlahuelpuchis affords them better protection in their nocturnal, or even diurnal, foragings in search of victims. However, once a month, tlahuelpuchis must undergo rites similar to those of nahuales every time they effect a human-into-animal transformation.

On the last Saturday of every month, tlahuelpuchis must perform the follow-ing rites in the privacy of their homes. After midnight, the tlahuelpuchi retires to the kitchen, which in her house must always be a separate room or a well-enclosed and thatched hut. She lights a fire made of capulin wood, copal, cen-tury plant roots, and dry zoapatl leaves. Each of these ingredients has certain supernatural powers which are activated by the tlahuelpuchi as she is lighting the fire and chanting magical formulas and incantations. Once the fire is crack-ling, the tlahuelpuchi walks over the fire three times in the north-south and east-west directions. She then sits on the fire facing north and her lower legs and feet separate from her body. At this point she transforms herself into an animal—generally a dog—and arranges her lower legs and feet in the form of a cross with the feet pointing to the east and west. Then she goes out into the night. Upon leaving the house, the tlahuelpuchi transforms herself into a turkey, buzzard, or chicken and searches for an infant to suck. If by daybreak she has not been able to suck the blood of a human being (infant, child, or adult), the tlahuelpuchi dies at sunrise. Usually, however, she finds an infant to suck, for people often forget to activate the methods of counteracting the bloodsucking power of the tlahuelpuchi. The tlahuelpuchi returns to her house, sits again on the fire, and in her human form fits the lower legs and feet to her body, accompanied by the appropriate chanting of formulas and incantations. It is of the utmost importance that, while the tlahuelpuchi is away, her lower legs and feet are kept absolutely still, for otherwise she cannot effectively use her powers. This duty falls to one of the tlahuelpuchi's primary relatives (a parent or sibling if she is unmarried, and her husband if she is married), who must also sweep the fire after the tlahuelpuchi rejoins her lower legs and feet. This monthly rite of intensification may be considered a kind of recharging of the supernatural batteries of the tlahuelpuchi, which for an entire month, allows her to effect the human-into-animal transformation by a mere act of will (as is the case for the animal-into-human transformation).

The power of tlahuelpuchis is limited in this way: they cannot change the natural attributes of the animals into which they transform themselves. In other words, they cannot make crows fly faster than they usually fly, or chickens run faster than dogs, or donkeys fly. There is, however, one notable exception. Tlahuelpuchis can make the turkey fly, which partly accounts for the turkey being the most common transforming animal. The transforming animal tlahuelpuchis choose depends, of course, on the circumstances and the specific predicaments in which they may find themselves. For example, the radius of action of tlahuelpuchis may be as much as 30 kilometers; in traveling such long distances, they generally transform themselves into buzzards or crows. In their diurnal operations, they may use the form of donkeys, chickens, or dogs, given their ubiquitous presence in the average household. If they have spotted a house where there is a potential victim but the door is locked, they transform themselves into an ant or flea in order to get in through the keyhole or under the door. In their nocturnal or diurnal operations, tlahuelpuchis may transform themselves into a series of animals in order to evade or escape ordinary men.

At this point one may ask, what is the difference between tlahuelpuchis and nahuales in their animal form? At night it is impossible to confuse these two supernaturals, for tlahuelpuchis emanate a certain luminosity which informants variously describe as an augmented version of the phosphorescent light emitted by fireflies, a kind of intermittent spark that hovers over the animal, or an opaque, small ball of fire which seems to roll with the tlahuelpuchi. In addition, tlahuelpuchis exude a faint odor of blood, which is significantly stronger after they have sucked a victim. Nahuales, on the other hand, do not have any telltale indications of their nature; they walk, run, or fly like ordinary animals, except that they seem to elevate themselves from the ground when walking or running. Nahuales do not operate during the day, whereas tlahuelpuchis do so occasionally. Since the faint odor of blood is the only thing that may give them away, it is extremely difficult to detect and kill tlahuelpuchis during the day, unless they are caught *in flagrante delicto*. One of the favorite tricks of tlahuel-puchis when they are being chased in their nocturnal foragings is to transform themselves into a flea, ant, or any other miniscule insect in order to escape certain death. The telltale luminosity of the tlahuelpuchi does not disappear, but it is practically impossible for ordinary men to find such tiny animals at night, so that the tlahuelpuchi lies low until her pursuers get tired of searching and go home. Unlike nahuales, tlahuelpuchis in their animal form do not talk to ordinary men, for once they have been identified it means death if they cannot escape. Moreover, the tlahuelpuchis' hypnotizing power does not work well in the presence of more than one man or woman in a fully awake state. In conclusion, despite this disadvantage and their telltale odor, what makes the capture of tlahuelpuchis more difficult than the capture of nahuales is the former's ability to transform themselves into tiny animals.

THE INCIDENCE OF BLOODSUCKING AND THE TLAHUELPUCHIS' RELATIONSHIP TO THE OTHER ANTHROPOMORPHIC SUPERNATURALS

In addition to sucking the blood of a human being on the occasion of the monthly rites described above, the people believe that tlahuelpuchis experience their uncontrollable thirst for blood at least once a month, and as many as four times a month in the case of the most bloodthirsty tlahuelpuchis. Moreover, the tlahuelpuchis' craving for blood increases greatly during rainy and cold weather, and informants are quick to add that the greatest number of infants are sucked by tlahuelpuchis during June, July, and August, and December, January, and February, the rainiest or coldest months of the year. There is hardly a *paraje* (circumscribed, inhabited areas of land, quite often associated with kinship units) in the dozens of communities where Nutini has worked which does not experience during these months at least one bloodsucking a year. Individual bloodsucking events are taken as a matter of course, but there are also occasional bloodsucking epidemics (*rachas*), which may take the lives of several children in a single night and which terrify the people for days. Tlahuelpuchis generally operate at night, but occasionally their hankering for blood cannot wait until nightfall, and they must venture into the light of the day. But the most usual hours for the tlahuelpuchis' foragings are between midnight and four in the morning, when it is easiest for them to suck the blood of victims.

As noted earlier, tlahuelpuchis can suck the blood of any human being, but their overwhelming choice is the blood of infants, not only because it is easier but also because it is tastier and more invigorating to them than the blood of children or adults. Tlahuelpuchis can detect infants by their characteristic odor hundreds of meters away and thus can identify from outside the particular houses that harbor their most desired victims. Of bloodsucking victims examined from 1960 to 1966, there were dozens of infants but only one child of seven and no adults. Tlahuelpuchis will attack a child or an adult only when they cannot possibly find an infant. Moreover, they are very reluctant to attack children and adults because hypnosis, a requisite in the bloodsucking process itself, is less efficacious than with infants, and the victims may wake up in the middle of the operation and alert the entire household. In the rare cases of children or adults being sucked by tlahuelpuchis, they are either caught napping during the day or are old men not in the possession of all their mental faculties, with whom tlahuelpuchis dare take risks compelled by their uncontrollable urge. Finally, as far as bloodsucking witchcraft is concerned, by infant it is meant a person of either sex between the ages of three and ten months. Informants could not explain why tlahuelpuchis never suck infants younger than two months old, except to say that the blood of very young infants is not yet palatable or invigorating to the tlahuelpuchi. Tlahuelpuchis also do not suck the blood of infants older than ten months, unless they find themselves in the predicament described above. The rationale for this practice is that, after infants begin to ingest foods other than milk, their blood is again not as palatable or invigorating to the tlahuelpuchi. This preference is corroborated by the fact that, of the dozens of sucked infants examined, all except one fell within these age limits. There is no concordance of gender, and tlahuelpuchis can suck the blood of either male or female infants. As the reader may have already surmised, the tlahuelpuchis' bloodsucking practices constitute largely a tight, self-fulfilling system.

Tlahuelpuchis are extremely jealous and quick to take offense of each other. All tlahuelpuchis instinctively know each other in their human or animal form, no matter from how far away they come. They are bound by an oath not to harm each other's primary relatives, to protect each other in case of capture or suspicion of danger, and to let each other know anything that may affect their malevolent activities. Tlahuelpuchis are solitary individuals, and they do not have a social structure of their own as do nahuales. There are no conventicles or get-togethers of any kind, and they operate essentially alone. Once in a while two or three tlahuelpuchis may get together for reasons of protection, but there is nothing organized about these sporadic meetings. What is very clear, however, is that they fiercely guard their foraging territories, over which they have exclusive rights. In other words, tlahuelpuchis do not permit trespass on each other's territories, except for reasons of vengeance against adults and with specific permission of the owner—but never for bloodsucking purposes. Serious fights among tlahuelpuchis arise from bloodsucking trespassing, many of which end with the death of one of the participants. Since their animal transforming powers are canceled out, they fight in their human form. If one of the tlahuelpuchis dies, the other is bound by *noblesse oblige* to return the body to her house secretly, so that her family will not come under suspicion because of her disappearance, and the people will regard the death as natural.

It has been established that the relationship among the four main anthropomorphic supernaturals in rural Tlaxcala is characterized by non-confrontation, secrecy, and acquiescence in each other's craft or practice. These rules of non-interference are ultimately rationalized by the people in terms of the supernatural powers that they possess, for, in one way or another, these powers are the expression of the good-and-evil struggle that goes on constantly but that human beings cannot fundamentally change. Thus, anthropomorphic supernaturals feel toward each other the same fatalistic attitude that ordinary people exhibit toward them. In the same fashion that ordinary men may loathe, dread, fear, or dislike those individuals endowed with supernatural powers but cannot help commiserating with their fate or use of their powers, tezitlazcs, nahuales, tetlachihuics, and tlahuelpuchis are bound to each other by the same sentiments. It would be unthinkable for these four supernaturals to use their powers to harm, interfere, or molest each other in any way. Ordinary men and women understand this behavior, for after all, supernaturals are made in the image of man and not vice versa. Therefore, no person would ever use or take advantage of the powers of one anthropomorphic supernatural to counteract the powers of another, for that would mean tampering with the fixed order of the universe. But ordinary people set tezitlazc against tezitlazc, tetlachihuic against tetlachihuic, and they themselves battle against nahuales and tlahuelpuchis, for such confrontations are nothing more than the expression of the ideological imperative of the struggle between good and evil. In fact, were it possible to set nahual against nahual or tlahuelpuchi against tlahuelpuchi, people would not hesitate to do so. Hence, the fundamental behavioral principle binding man and the supernatural: one does not tamper with the established order, but, in the confrontation between good and evil, anything is permitted among men and supernaturals of the same status. This theme is a recurrent one in traditional rural Tlaxcalan society; it affects most cultural domains and quite often explains seeming behavioral contradictions.

TLAHUELPUCHIS AND ORDINARY MEN: THE LOGIC OF INTERACTION

Of more interest to the main concern here is the behavior and attitudes of tlahuelpuchis toward ordinary men and women. In addition to their bloodsucking compulsion, for which tlahuelpuchis are not necessarily blamed by ordinary people, tlahuelpuchis are also volitionally responsible for harm and violence done to people. In this respect, tlahuelpuchis are not different from tetlachihuics or even nahuales, who take advantage of their supernatural powers in order to harm people for disdain or offenses received, spite or envy, or simply because they do not like particular individuals. Unlike nahuales, who can only take revenge by playing tricks on people, tlahuelpuchis can kill their offenders or enemies. By using their hypnotizing powers, the most powerful tlahuelpuchis get into the houses of their victims at night, make them get up and walk to a place of danger such as a steep *barranca* (ravine), a tall bridge, or a high wall or building, and make them jump to their death. Whenever individuals die of accidents of this nature, the people almost invariably attribute it to the tlahuelpuchi, who is the only anthropomorphic supernatural endowed with the power to kill in this fashion. Another less drastic method employed by tlahuelpuchis to harm their enemies is to hurt them economically. The tlahuelpuchi may transform herself into a donkey and trample over an enemy's young milpa, or in the form of a coyote she may kill the enemy's domestic animals. What is most interesting is that the people never mistake the provenance of certain kinds of death, accidents, illnesses, economic disasters, loss of property, and other undesirable events, for they know exactly what nahuales, tetlachihuics, and tlahuelpuchis can do and under what circumstances, as these are the only individuals endowed with supernatural powers who can do such things. From this perspective, anthropomorphic supernaturalism in rural Tlaxcala is a neat, compartmentalized, and logical system of the "witchcraft-explains-unfortunate-events" type (Evans-Pritchard 1937:64–83).

It should be pointed out, however, that the actions of these supernaturals are a contextual matter and that not all deaths, accidents, illnesses, disasters, and other unwelcome events that affect individuals and groups are attributed to them. What we are saying is that there is a clear division of labor in attributing unfortunate events. Thus, deaths that have to do with accidents that the people consider outside the "normal" course of events are invariably attributed to tlahuelpuchis, whereas deaths due to illnesses that the people regard as "abnormal" (that is, that neither doctors nor curers have been able to treat, or that have been contracted under suspicious circumstances) are generally attributed to the action of tetlachihuics. Loss of property is generally attributed to thieving nahuales, whereas damage to crops and domestic animals can be attributed either to nahuales or tlahuelpuchis, depending on the circumstances. Compartmentalized as it is, anthropomorphic supernaturalism in rural Tlaxcala is not nearly as causal-effective as witchcraft and sorcery are among the Azande in their single-minded compulsion to explain unfortunate and undesirable events by the action of supernatural forces. The epistemological system of the Azande does not appear to distinguish operationally (immediately) between "natural" and "supernatural" action, whereas in rural Tlaxcala (and probably in most witchcraft-sorcery systems) there are rather intricate, often capricious, operational mechanisms that determine whether an action is "natural" or "supernatural" — that is, an action in the normal course of events but often attributed to the Christian God or to fate or destiny, or an action attributable to any of the anthropomorphic supernaturals.

The logic of the operational system is not unlike that of the classification of hot and cold foods and states so prevalent in many parts of Mesoamerica, in which intrinsic physical properties and contextual-ideological states are inextricably interrelated. The key to the system involves the interdigitation of some obvious physical-observable properties and events (such as the circumstances, time, and place in which a man fell down a ravine in order for his death to be attributed to a tlahuelpuchi) and contextual ideological and psychological states and considerations (such as the personality characteristics of the dead man, his social standing in the community, and the esteem or dislike that he elicited from the people at large). We cannot at this point go into the epistemological processes that the people go through in assigning natural or supernatural origin to a given action; suffice it to say that they are consistent, discriminating, and uniform. Although informants were mostly unable to verbalize the criteria of discrimination, it was possible to infer the logic of the assignment contextually and by circumlocution.

THE STRUCTURAL CONTEXTS OF THE BLOODSUCKING EVENT AND ITS PHYSICAL MANIFESTATION

There are three contexts in which tlahuelpuchis suck the blood of human beings: children and adults during the day; infants during the day; and infants at night.

1. It has been established that the sucking of children and adults is extremely rare, motivated by the tlahuelpuchi's uncontrolled urge when she cannot find an infant. The tlahuelpuchi approaches the victim, usually in her human form, and, with one pretext or another, draws him away from the house without being seen. If the victim is a child, it is easier for the tlahuel-

puchi to hypnotize the boy or girl in order to suck its blood. If the victim is an adult, it is usually a cranky old man or woman whom the tlahuelpuchi manages to lure surreptitiously away from the house. In order to approach the house of the victim, the tlahuelpuchi usually undergoes a series of animal transformations, which, after she has sucked the victim, enable her to get away unnoticed. When children or adults are sucked by the tlahuelpuchi, their bodies are always found in the milpa, near ravines, or in wooded areas. Informants universally asserted that this occurrence is very rare, and most of them had never seen the bodies of children or adults sucked by the tlahuelpuchi. Nevertheless, the corpses of sucked children or adults appear frequently in the legends about bloodsucking witchcraft.

2. The frequency of infants sucked by tlahuelpuchis during the day is in the proportion of 1 to 12 to those sucked at night. We arrived at this figure on the basis of 47 corpses examined between 1960 and 1966, 4 of which were infants sucked during the day. The relative infrequency of this type has already been explained. But how does it actually happen? Usually the sucking takes place between 10 A.M. and 3 P.M., the busiest time of the day for all adults in the household, when infants are most likely to be alone. Moreover, tlahuelpuchis suck infants in their cribs or wherever they may be resting; they cannot remove them from the house. Given the fact that infants are quickly hypnotized by tlahuelpuchis, the event is easily managed. In the ubiquitous form of a donkey, dog, chicken, or turkey, the tlahuelpuchi stalks her victim for the propitious moment to enter the house and perform her evil deed. Once the tlahuelpuchi has sucked the infant, she places the corpse on the floor or by the door as she goes out. Again, by the use of her powers of multiple animal transformations, the tlahuelpuchi manages to get away undetected. Many male and female informants asserted that often half an hour or as much as an hour had elapsed between the last time they saw their infants alive and the time the tlahuelpuchi sucked them. Informants universally agreed that the relative infrequency of bloodsucking witchcraft during the day led people to slacken the measures that prevent or counteract the power of tlahuelpuchis.

3. Given the fact that nighttime bloodsucking witchcraft is overwhelmingly more common than daytime sucking, it is quite natural that the people at large know more about the activities of tlahuelpuchis at night. Between midnight and four in the morning tlahuelpuchis roam the countryside in search of victims, and on cold rainy nights the inhabitants of the average rural Tlaxcalan community do not venture into the night if they can avoid it. The tlahuelpuchi's preferred time to strike is near four in the morning, when most people are sound asleep. If the tlahuelpuchi comes from a distant place, she usually flies in the form of a crow or buzzard; if she comes from a nearby place, she

generally walks as a dog, cat, or coyote. When the tlahuelpuchi approaches the house of an intended victim, she invariably transforms herself into a turkey. Why the turkey is such a preferred animal, we were never able to elicit from informants, nor was it possible to deduce it from the analysis of legends.[2] Be this as it may, the tlahuelpuchi flies over the house twice in the form of an oblique cross. If she can get into the house as a turkey—that is, through a window or a door ajar—she does so; but, if everything is tightly closed and locked, she transforms herself into a tiny animal and gets into the house through the keyhole or under the door. In the latter case, once the tlahuelpuchi is inside, she must again transform herself into a turkey, for it is in this animal form that she must hypnotize her victim and those around her. The term "hypnotize" has been used to describe a technique employed by both nahuales and tlahuelpuchis. Let us clarify that, in the case of nahuales, the term is more or less employed in its usually understood meaning, for the people believe that nahuales can put people "to sleep" and under their control by the use of their powerful eyes. This is not so with tlahuelpuchis, in the sense that they do not use their eyes. Rather, the people believe that the tlahuelpuchi releases a kind of vapor or mist (*vaho*) which induces in the victim and those around it a state of heavy drowsiness (*sopor*), from which they fall into normal sleep after the tlahuelpuchi leaves without realizing what happened. Many informants stated that they know the details of this technique because it is not effective against people with tremendously strong sight or tlapaltizoliztli (informants also used the expression "con aires muy fuertes," with very strong airs). In other words, when a tlahuelpuchi gets into the house of a yotlezahuitl (that is, a person endowed with tlapaltizoliztli) a battle of wills ensues between the two, and eventually the former retreats because she is not able to put the latter into a soporific state. In this context, tlahuelpuchis are described by yotlezahuitls as turkey- or fowl-like animals surrounded by an intense aureola of light. In any event, once the infant and those in the room are immobilized, the tlahuelpuchi must again assume her human form, for it is only as such that she can suck her victim. If the infant is sleeping by himself in a crib or petate, after the tlahuelpuchi has sucked him, she will leave him on the floor by the inside of the door; but, if the infant is sleeping next to his mother or in her arms (a common practice among rural Tlaxcalan women), the tlahuelpuchi will suck him in that position, in order to avoid awakening anybody in the room. As the tlahuelpuchi goes out of the room, she leaves the door open or ajar. Again, we were not able to discover the reason for this action, either from informants or in legendary accounts. If there is no danger of being detected, the tlahuelpuchi will walk for a while in order to enjoy her feast; otherwise, she will make use of her array of animal transformations to return safely home as quickly as possible.

Of great importance to the self-fulfilling aspects of bloodsucking witchcraft are the telltale signs or physical marks left by tlahuelpuchis on the corpses of infants. Informants universally agreed that the corpses of infants sucked by tlahuelpuchis exhibited the following characteristics: "Moretones y ronchas en el pecho, en la espalda cerca del cuello, y a veces en las orejas y el cuello. Manchas moradas o medias rojizas, como cuando uno se mayuga, en el pecho y a veces en la cara" (bruises and ecchymoses on the chest, on the back near the neck, and sometimes on the ears and neck. Purple or rather reddish spots, as when one suffers a contusion, on the chest and sometimes on the face). This description was corroborated by Nutini's examination of the forty-seven corpses of infants mentioned earlier, thirty-nine of which exhibited the telltale signs and physical marks mentioned by informants and described in his fieldnotes as the kind of black-and-blue or yellowish marks that result from bruises. In addition, in most of the corpses he observed a faint or sometimes fairly intense bluish or purplish color on the face and neck. It may be added that nine of the examined corpses had been dead for less than five hours and showed no sign of rigor mortis setting in, whereas the rest had been dead for periods varying from five hours to a day, and some were ready to be buried. Moreover, a fair number of informants stated that occasionally tlahuelpuchis bite their victims on the lips, nose, and ears, seriously deforming these organs; also, it was not infrequent for the mothers of the sucked infants to exhibit bruises and black-and-blue marks on their breasts. None of the forty-seven corpses showed any evidence of having been bitten, for all the infants had their lips, noses, and ears intact; bruises on the mothers were corroborated in the case of sixteen of the infants' mothers, who were also examined in the process of investigating the death of the victims. All these women exhibited a slight or pronounced irritation of their areolas, black-and-blue marks in the upper and lower cup of their right or left breast, or both.[3]

In 1954, the government of the state of Tlaxcala passed an ordinance requiring municipal presidents to refer all cases of death by bloodsucking witchcraft to the medical authorities (Salubridad Estatal) in Tlaxcala City for examination. For decades it had been the standard practice in the municipios on the slopes of La Malintzi to enter *chupado(a) por la bruja* (sucked by the witch) as the cause of death in the required *acta de defunción* (death certificate), whenever an infant had died with the physical marks and in the circumstances described above. In 1953, however, the chief archivist of the state discovered the large number of infant deaths attributed to *chupado(a) por la bruja*. (All municipios in the state of Tlaxcala are required to keep two sets of books [*registros*] where all deaths, births, and marriages that occur throughout the year are recorded. One set of books remains in the municipal offices while the other is forwarded to the state archives at the beginning of every year.) Intrigued and suspicious of the physical cause of death, government authorities passed the ordinance. It did little good, however, for municipal authorities never really complied with the ordinance, either resenting unnecessary state intervention or afraid of being laughed at for their beliefs and practices. They either stopped writing sucked by the witch as the cause of death or simply did not bother to report infant deaths of this nature.

Finally, at least in the more conservative communities, the wake and burial of an infant sucked by the tlahuelpuchi are not the same as for an infant or child who has died of natural death: an oblique cross of pine wood ashes is made under the table where the coffin usually lies, no music is played on the way to the cemetery as in the case of a normal child, a special cleansing of the body by a tezitlazc is required, and so on. All these rites and ceremonies are designed to purify the body of the infant from his contact with the tlahuelpuchi and to mark his special status among the dead. Comparable cleansing rites are undergone by the mother of the infant in order to rid her of any possible impure contact with the tlahuelpuchi.

PROTECTION AGAINST WITCHCRAFT AND THE CONFRONTATION OF ORDINARY MEN AND TLAHUELPUCHIS IN THEIR ANIMAL FORMS

There are several ways of protecting infants against being sucked by tlahuel-puchis and of ensuring adults against falling under their control. A rather specific complex for immobilizing and killing tlahuelpuchis exists. In contrast to nahuales, there are no known ways of protecting one's property against the vengeance of tlahuelpuchis, be it the burning or trampling of milpas, the slaughter of domestic animals, or the destruction of *cuezcomates* (storage bins). Despite the nature and limitations of their actions, tlahuelpuchis are inherently more powerful than nahuales, and thus the various means and techniques of protection against them are not always effective. Both nahuales and tlahuelpuchis are by nature afraid of metals; the former will always be stopped or neutralized by a metal object, but the latter is frequently able to counteract its effect. The same can be said about most of the means and techniques employed against tlahuelpuchis: sometimes they work, sometimes they do not. Informants universally agreed that it is very important to protect infants against tlahuelpuchis soon after they are born until they are about twelve months old, when they begin to ingest regularly foods other than milk. People often forget, however, to activate the traditional means of deterring tlahuelpuchis, especially at night. Thus, it appears that the majority of infants sucked by tlahuelpuchis were not protected by any of the traditional techniques.

Analysis of the forty-seven–corpse sample indicates that only eighteen were protected, and investigation of these cases revealed that people are sometimes skeptical about the deterring power of the means employed. The result is a considerable amount of anxiety, especially when the word gets around (*se corre la voz*) that a tlahuelpuchi is operating in the neighborhood, paraje, or section. These periodic alarms begin when the number of infants sucked by tlahuelpuchis exceeds what is normally accepted by the people or when there are out-of-season suckings — that is, when it is not rainy or cold. At these times, the people are extremely careful, and, despite their occasional skepticism, they exhaust the techniques of protection. Regardless of the efficacy of deterring techniques, informants uniformly stated that most of the time it was too much trouble to remember nightly protection. Moreover, mothers whose infants had not been protected when they were sucked, exhibited strong feelings of guilt, and, to a lesser degree, so did their fathers. When an occasional epidemic of bloodsucking witchcraft afflicts a paraje or section, fear and anxiety rise to a peak of collective near-hysteria. For a week or ten days the people exhaust the means and techniques of protection, adults take turns staying awake at night, and women closely supervise their infants during the day. But this vigilance usually subsides after the second week, and rather quickly things return to normal. The self-fulfilling fact of no more infant deaths in the interim accounts for the quick return to normality. In the average community, epidemics (rachas) do not generally take place more often than once or twice every ten years, but their terrifying events are long remembered.

Adults are most careless about their own protection against falling under the control of tlahuelpuchis, even though this failure may mean death by accident. Since people obviously do not know whether they have offended or antagonized a tlahuelpuchi and there are not too many accidents in the average Tlaxcalan community, the average person considers himself safe and does not overworry about activating his or her defenses. The most common and effective means of warding off tlahuelpuchis is to rub periodically a clove of raw garlic against the back of one's scapular (which most rural Tlaxcalans wear from childhood) or to insert between the front and back cloth of the scapular a thin onion skin. These precautions protect the wearer day and night, and it would be impossible for tlahuelpuchis to attack successfully. Individuals who must be out at night, especially for reasons of labor migration, seldom forget to intensify this means of protection. Alternative means of adult protection against tlahuelpuchis are: to make a cross with two safety pins attached to an undergarment; to wear a blessed cross or Saint Christopher's medal; and to attach a pin or needle to the inside of one's hat. At least until 1966, even the most sophisticated labor migrant or secularized individual in the average rural Tlaxcalan community did not regularly walk at night without at least one of these means of protection against tlahuelpuchis.

The means and techniques of protection of infants against tlahuelpuchis, either at night or during the day, are more complex and varied. It goes without saying that whatever means of protection is employed, it extends to all the adults and children within the room at night. When the word is out that a tlahuelpuchi is operating in the vicinity or has been sighted nearby, the array of physical objects or things employed to deter her remain untouched, but, once people consider that the danger has passed, they remove these objects or things; henceforth, one or more may or may not be activated at nightfall. Every household puts its faith in a particular technique, but the most commonly used are the following: a piece of bright metal, a knife, a machete, or a box of needles or pins under the crib or next to the petate where the infant is sleeping; a pair of open scissors under the crib or next to the petate; a cross made of silver coins at the head of the crib or petate; a metal cross at the head or petate; pieces of tortillas strewn under the crib or around the petate; a dirty pair of shorts or a soiled diaper at the foot of the crib or petate; a mirror on the pillow or anywhere close to the body of the infant; a cross made of safety pins attached to the infant's outer garment; two blessed silver medals attached to a garment on the chest and back of the infant; a bucket of water near the door or where the infant is sleeping; an upside down hat with four needles pinned to the brim in the form of a cross placed next to where the infant is sleeping; and so on. Particularly effective means of protection for male and female infants include mirrors for boys and scissors for girls, or a metal cross for the former and silver medals for the latter.

None of these means of protection is 100 percent effective, for informants universally believe that, if the tlahuelpuchi tries hard enough or is desperate enough, she will be able to counteract their deterrent power. Only two things can offer certain protection against infants being sucked by tlahuelpuchis: garlic and onion. Thus, two or three cloves of garlic wrapped in pieces of tortillas placed under the swaddling band of the infant, or several pieces of onion wrapped in pieces of tortillas strewn under the crib or around the petate, are the only foolproof means of protection. These precautions are always taken when the people are alerted by the rumor of a tlahuelpuchi operating in the vicinity and after an epidemic takes place. But in normal times people tend to forget; they regard this method as rather tedious to practice nightly. In any event, tlahuelpuchis are able to smell garlic and onion from a distance away and would never enter a house where they are to be found in the sleeping quarters. The other deterrants, however, are not always effective. Depending on the availability of other infants to suck, the intensity of her uncontrollable desire, or other circumstances, the tlahuelpuchi may decide that an attack is worth the unpleasant consequences of fighting the power of protective substances or things. When that happens, people believe that a veritable battle of supernatural powers takes place between the tlahuelpuchi and deterrents and that this battle somehow embodies or reflects the forces of good working for humankind.

There is a close relationship between the availability of infants to be sucked (in itself a reflection of the effectiveness of protective techniques) and the visibility of tlahuelpuchis at night: the harder it is to locate easy victims, the more chances the tlahuelpuchi takes to find a prey, thereby making her more vulnerable to being identified and killed. It is in this context that most confrontations between ordinary men and tlahuelpuchis in their animal form take place. Few adults in the average rural Tlaxcalan community have not seen the tlahuelpuchi at night in her animal forms, especially as a turkey. Tlahuelpuchis are sighted or directly confronted in two contexts. The first is when the tlahuelpuchi as a turkey ready to strike is on or near the house of the victim, is perched on a tree or stalking the house, or is in the act of flying over the house just before entering. What always gives her away is the luminosity, phosphorescence, or fireball invariably associated with tlahuelpuchis in their animal forms, and it is in this context that most tlahuelpuchis are killed. In the second context, the tlahuelpuchi, after her feast of blood, walks in her human form enjoying her evil deed and unaware of the proximity of ordinary men in the streets, paths, or in the open country. Upon sighting humans, the tlahuelpuchi immediately reveals her presence by assuming an animal form, since the last thing she wants is to reveal her human identity. In trying to escape, the tlahuelpuchi makes use of her power of multiple transformation in eluding her pursuers, especially by transforming herself into a tiny animal; almost invariably, she manages to get away.

Under the circumstances just described, there are three principal techniques for immobilizing and killing a tlahuelpuchi in her animal form: take one's pants off, turn one of the legs inside out, and throw them to the tlahuelpuchi; make a knot in three corners of a white handkerchief, wrap it around a stone, and throw it to the tlahuelpuchi; take off one's hat, put it upside down on the ground, and drive a knife or machete through it. If these actions touch the tlahuelpuchi or fall within 10 meters of her, she is automatically immobilized. The most commonly used technique is that of the pants, for people do not always carry knives or machetes, and it takes more time to tie knots in a handkerchief. Once the tlahuelpuchi in her animal form has been sighted, a chase ensues, and in many accounts it takes hours either to kill her or to lose her. Immediate death follows the tlahuelpuchi's immobilization, usually by clubbing or stoning, for it is considered extremely unclean to touch her. No dialogue ever takes place between the tlahuelpuchi and her killers, who leave immediately after their deed. The next day, nothing remains of the animal, for it is the duty of other tlahuelpuchis to pick it up and take it to the doorstep of the dead tlahuelpuchi, where she will be buried secretly under the temazcal by one her kinsmen. The killing of tlahuelpuchis is not exactly rare but is less common than the beating of nahuales, who are easier to immobilize. Some individuals are especially adept at spotting and killing tlahuelpuchis, and they are much in demand when the word is out that a tlahuelpuchi is on the prowl in a certain area or after an epidemic. Whenever a man or men have killed a tlahuelpuchi, they must undergo a limpia or *hojeada* (symbolic brushing of a person with capulin branches) in the temazcal. Finally, it is interesting to note that tlahuelpuchis cannot harm animals in any way, and animals in turn do not notice or are not aware of tlahuelpuchis in their animal forms.

WITCHCRAFT ACCUSATIONS AND THE CONFRONTATION OF ORDINARY MEN AND TLAHUELPUCHIS IN THEIR HUMAN FORMS

So far we have discussed the tlahuelpuchi per se, her attributes and behavior, and her relationship to ordinary humans in her animal forms. Before concluding, it is important to discuss the relationship of tlahuelpuchis in their human form to the community at large. This discussion can be brief because there is relatively little to say, in the sense that the social structure obtaining between ordinary men and tlahuelpuchis occurs primarily in the context of animal transformations, the bloodsucking process itself, and the ideology of danger and protection. But ordinary men also conceive of tlahuelpuchis as humans, although interaction may take place only rarely. Be this as it may, the people at large have a fair idea of what tlahuelpuchis are as human beings, and they are able to verbalize what they feel about them. Although the concept of the tlahuelpuchi embodies what is most dreadful, loathsome, and abhorrent in the domain of social and supernatural relations, ordinary men fear and hate tlahuelpuchis with a serenity tempered by a measure of compassion for their inexorable fate, for which they are never held responsible. Except during the rare bloodsucking epidemics, there is no panic or overemotional manifestations of fear or anxiety about tlahuelpuchis; rather, they are taken as one of the manifestations of the inevitable evil which is part of the natural world of existence. Thus, when an infant is sucked by the tlahuelpuchi, those concerned may feel guilty about possibly not having exhausted the means of protection, but they take the event stoically and without undue outbursts of emotion. This attitude applies also to the other anthropomorphic supernaturals discussed here, and to whatever harmful, malevolent, or undesirable activities they may be associated with. In fact, in rural Tlaxcalan society, the relationship between humans and anthropomorphic supernaturals is marked by a rather high degree of equanimity, inevitability, emotional control, and, it may be added, *noblesse oblige* in the game of combating evil. Rural Tlaxcalan society is not ridden with fear and anxiety about witchcraft and sorcery, as parts of the foregoing description may lead readers to believe. On the contrary, the people regard anthropomorphic supernaturals, and the good or evil powers that they wield, as part of the natural world with which they must learn to cope.

In such an environment, there is no clearcut line of demarcation between what is natural and what is supernatural, thereby minimizing fear and anxiety about things and behavior that are not entirely understood. In this universe an almost Zoroastrian struggle between good and evil takes place. But unlike the Christian universe, it is not fixed. Rather, there is a degree of randomness and contingency, which is amply counterbalanced by what the people refer to as destiny or fate. In such a universe, the only thing people can do to make social existence safe and agreeable is to propitiate through rites and ceremonies those supernaturals favorably disposed to human existence and to combat the manifestations of evil supernaturals by any means available. Thus, rural Tlaxcalans undertake a great many religious rites and ceremonies directed toward Christian supernaturals, as well as toward a few pagan supernaturals, in order to predispose them toward individual and collective well-being. They also employ a variety of methods and techniques to fight the evil powers of anthropomorphic supernaturals, embodied mainly in tlahuelpuchis and tetlachihuics. This is the primarily utilitarian, pragmatic, and ritualistic focus of religion and magic in rural Tlaxcala.

It has been stated that it is almost impossible to determine with certainty the human attributes of tlahuelpuchis. Nevertheless, the people conceive of tlahuelpuchis ideally as endowed with certain characteristic attributes. First of all, regardless of the inherent evil and abhorrence that tlahuelpuchis connote, they are not considered as particularly more vicious, jealous, easily offended, or vengeful than tetlachihuics, or, for that matter, than many ordinary people. Tlahuelpuchis are not the personification or embodiment of bad or antisocial character traits, since they are not responsible for their bloodsucking compulsion. Except that tlahuelpuchis are regarded as irascible (*geniudas*) and very domineering and possessive, their principal physical attributes are as follows: They are fat women, for blood is considered to be a particularly rich nutrient; they generally limp, for after so many monthly separations of their lower legs and feet, they cannot be affixed to the rest of the body properly; they have squinty eyes and long beaked noses; their voices are thin and squeaky; and a faint odor of blood never leaves them, which they may try to hide by selling various kinds of meats. In addition, tlahuelpuchis never keep garlic and onions in their houses, nor do they ever allow strangers into their kitchens. Despite the fact that males and females are tlahuelpuchis, not a single informant was able to verbalize the physical and behavioral characteristics of the former. The predominance of female over male tlahuelpuchis only partly explains this inability, for it involves the question of what constitutes conscious and unconscious social behavior, something we shall touch upon presently.

Finally, the structure of witchcraft accusations and the direct confrontation of ordinary men and tlahuelpuchis in their human form must be considered. This is a very rare event. In fact, only a handful among hundreds of informants in direct interviews had personally witnessed or participated in witchcraft accusations leading to the killing of the tlahuelpuchi, and less than 50 percent had heard of such proceedings. In the context of in-depth interviews, informants never expressed their suspicions of particular individuals as tlahuelpuchis, much less made intimations as to their identity. The only common instances of suspicion and accusation are collective ones, in the sense that informants frequently expressed the fact that the most famous, effective, and tricky tlahuelpuchis are from Olintla and Hueytochco. But this kind of scapegoatism, as far as we know, has never been translated into actual violence or death against these two communities as a whole. In a generation of working in rural Tlaxcala, Nutini has been able to verify the killing of one tlahuelpuchi, and in two other cases (July 1965 and January 1972) he had it from reliable sources that accusations led to the killing of the tlahuelpuchis.

In August of 1961, while Nutini was working in the municipio of San Diego Tlalocan, a most trusted informant on bloodsucking witchcraft came to tell him excitedly one afternoon that a woman had been accused of being a tlahuelpuchi in a community of a nearby municipio; she had been killed the night before, and her cadaver was at the bottom of a ravine. The informant had been told of this by a *compadre* (ritual kinsman) in that community, with whom he had business deals. He agreed to accompany Nutini to examine the body of the tlahuelpuchi, and after a great deal of persuasion they convinced his compadre to tell them exactly where the corpse was. The body of the tlahuelpuchi lay totally naked on the ground; most of her bones were broken, and her body was a formless mass of bruises and wounds. Her eyes had been plucked from the sockets, her ears, nose, tongue, and lips had been totally severed, and her ten fingers had been cut clean. Nutini wanted to inquire about the episode in situ, but the informant firmly insisted that it was impossible; he correctly pointed out that they were not entirely safe. But it was important to confirm that tlahuelpuchis in their human form were indeed put to death. Subsequent investigation clarified the terrible nature of the bloodsucking witchcraft accusations that had led to the killing of the tlahuelpuchi. First of all, when a person has been singled out as a tlahuelpuchi—that is, when a considerable number of people verbalize her name—she is swiftly put to death. The mob quickly runs to the house of the tlahuelpuchi, immobilizes her by one of the methods described above so that she cannot transform herself into an animal, and on the spot she is clubbed and/or stoned to death. Once she is dead, two men with knives symbolically kill her again by depriving her of her physical sense organs. The two chosen men drag the naked body of the tlahuelpuchi to a deserted spot where she is left to rot, for she cannot be buried. The executioners must undergo a series of eight consecutive limpias to cleanse themselves from the polluting contact with the tlahuelpuchi. Some informants indicated that the execution of tlahuelpuchis may be more common than is thought, for people must obviously try to keep the affair as secret as possible since it is against the law to kill anyone. But it is clear that such executions take place under extreme conditions, and decades go by without one taking place in a community.

On the basis of only one execution, it was obviously impossible to verify empirically the physical and behavorial characteristics of tlahuelpuchis—that is, whether those persons put to death comply with what the people at large believe them to be. But what about the sociological context and psychological mood accompanying such executions? Here again we are on firmer ground; despite the lack of direct knowledge of most informants, the following picture emerged. The accusation is something completely spontaneous, which may be initiated by a single person or a group of individuals. This quickly gathers momentum, and, in a matter of an hour, the executing mob has agreed on the killing of the person singled out as the tlahuelpuchi. Without any warning, they break into the house of the designated culprit. The relatives of the tlahuelpuchi are generally paralyzed and do not put up any resistance or utter even a word in her defense. After the deed has been committed, the perpetrators, the relatives of the victim, and, in fact, the neighborhood or community as a whole are bound to keep it a secret. They usually succeed; sometimes word gets to the state authorities, but it is reasonably certain that the state police have never been able to charge or arrest anybody for killing a tlahuelpuchi. All informants who were able to provide information on this topic universally agreed that the execution of tlahuelpuchis always takes place during a serious epidemic in the midst of the panic and hysteria generated by this event. An epidemic is defined as the bloodsucking of three, four, five, or sometimes more infants, either in a single night or over a period of two or three nights, and within the confines of a paraje, neighborhood, or section.

In normal times, as was indicated, nobody dares to verbalize suspicion of the identity of a tlahuelpuchi, and this fact acts as a powerful deterrent against the indiscriminate use of witchcraft accusations. It is quite possible that the individual who casts the first accusation during an epidemic, thereby becoming the nucleus of the consensus, may be motivated by vengeance or personal spite. An epidemic provides the circumstances in which he can succeed in an accusation that, under normal circumstances, would be disastrous to him, because he would not be able to generate the appropriate consensus, people would pay no attention to him, and he would leave himself totally open to the self-fulfilling wrath of the tlahuelpuchi. After the execution of a tlahuelpuchi, things quickly return to normal and the people consciously try to forget the terrifying event. It is not so for the household members of the victim, who may suffer for years under the stigma of having harbored a tlahuelpuchi. They are subject to religious ostracism and social discrimination stemming from their association with the loathsome and polluting qualities that tlahuelpuchis are supposed to possess. Although the people understand and commiserate with the members of the household for such terrible luck and bad fortune, they avoid persons who have had such long and intimate contact with the tlahuelpuchi. The rarity of tlahuelpuchi executions may be functionally interpreted as an object lesson in reinforcing the self-fulfilling premises of bloodsucking witchcraft.

CONCLUDING REMARKS: THE SELF-FULFILLING, IDEOLOGICAL CONTEXT OF BLOODSUCKING WITCHCRAFT

It should be clear that this account is put together entirely from the viewpoint of informants who had had mostly indirect but some direct experience with the execution of a tlahuelpuchi and who are obviously expressing the ideological and behavorial expectations of this not necessarily central aspect of bloodsucking witchcraft. Thus, since the informants who provided accounts of executions and the social and psychological frameworks in which they take place obviously believe that tlahuelpuchis exist, it is evident that their information is based much more on the normative-ideological knowledge of bloodsucking witchcraft than on actual empirical evidence. That the few informants who had actually participated in the execution of a tlahuelpuchi gave an accurate description of what had transpired is reasonably certain, but rather what we are trying to emphasize is that their actions and behavior were essentially determined by the normative-ideological knowledge of the system. This framework is compatible with the normal self-fulfilling components possessed by all witchcraft systems. But, how are we to interpret the behavior and action, or rather lack of it, of the kinsmen of the executed tlahuelpuchi? Or, why do the tlahuelpuchi's kinsmen accept the execution so passively and are invariably so unable to do anything on her behalf when they may doubt that she is indeed a bloodsucking witch? Answers to these questions are even more tentative and are again recon-structed through the screen of informants who may or may not have been in the position of the tlahuelpuchi's kinsmen.

First, the constraints of the ideological belief system of bloodsucking witch-craft are so strong that, even if the to-be-executed victim's kinsmen suspect that she is not a tlahuelpuchi and that the consensus to kill her was generated by exogenous motives, they go along and are too paralyzed to put up any resistance, verbally or physically. It is for this reason that the rare executions are so effectively accomplished with a minimum of social and psychological friction and conflict. This kind of constraint is clearly implied in the following statement of one of our most knowledgeable informants: "Los pobres parientes de la tlahuelpuchi ni se oponen ni pueden hacer nada, ya que se dan cuenta de que nadie se atrevería a darle muerte rápida si no tuvieramos la seguridad completa de que sí era tlahuelpuchi" (the poor kinsmen of the tlahuelpuchi can neither put up any resistance nor do anything, as they realize that no one would dare put her to death quickly if we were not completely certain that she was indeed a tlahuelpuchi). Second, the problem is simplified for the tlahuel-puchi's kinsmen by the fact that there seems to be a high degree of congruence between the ideology of the system and the physical and psychological rep-resentation of the tlahuelpuchi. In other words, those rare individuals who are executed as tlahuelpuchis comply with the physical and psychological stipula-tions of how they are supposed to look and act, as specified above. This fit with ideology is probably the most powerful factor in overriding the skepticism of the tlahuelpuchi's kinsmen. Third, the execution of a tlahuelpuchi takes place so suddenly, so swiftly, and in such a way that it leaves the kinsmen literally paralyzed psychologically, whether the tlahuelpuchi lives alone or with a num-ber of relatives, and regardless of the ideology of the system which stipulates that a husband or near relative must assist the tlahuelpuchi with the monthly ceremony of intensification. Once the execution has been accomplished, all con-cerned are bound to secrecy under the threat of serious social and physical con-sequences. It may be that some of the executed tlahuelpuchi's kinsmen may still harbor doubts and resentment, but they would not be foolish enough to express them overtly unless they were prepared to suffer serious individual and com-munal reprisals.

The foregoing account of bloodsucking witchcraft in rural Tlaxcala is based on information elicited directly from hundreds of informants in the context of in-depth, structured, and open-ended interviews. This information represents the personal knowledge of informants concerning the tlahuelpuchi complex, what they believe to be the general knowledge of the people at large, their direct involvement with tlahuelpuchis in their animal forms, and their direct or indirect experience with infants sucked by tlahuelpuchis. Moreover, this account is buttressed by Nutini's own empirical observation of most of the manifestations of bloodsucking witchcraft, including forty-seven—corpse sample of infants sucked by the tlahuelpuchi over a six-year period, a household census of six communities in one municipio to determine the incidence of sucked infants, and other statistical data analyzed below. Except for passing references, all the legendary and semilegendary information concerning bloodsucking witchcraft has been left out. What we have in mind here are more than 100 legends collected over the years, in which the tlahuelpuchi is the central character of the account. These legendary accounts concern tlahuelpuchis in many kinds of situations, interacting with ordinary people in both their animal and human forms, interacting with higher supernaturals such as the Christian devil, Matlalcihua, La Malintzi, El Cuatlapanga, and generally illustrating a moral point or the relationship between man and the supernatural. In addition, included in semilegendary accounts is that information about the tlahuelpuchi provided sporadically by informants but of which they had no direct or indirect experience: it took place many years ago, in another community, far away from their communities, they were told about it, or they could not vouch for the information. All these semilegendary accounts were prefaced by phrases such as "many years ago . . . ," "they say that in . . . ," or "it is said that those from . . . ," which was easy to differentiate from the informants' own factual knowledge and experience.

Legendary and semilegendary information has not been included in the foregoing description because it is not directly pertinent to the problem at hand, and its lengthy analysis will be presented elsewhere. However, a few remarks are in order. This corpus of information is valuable mostly in illuminating the ideological underpinnings of the tlahuelpuchi complex in particular and anthropomorphic supernaturalism in general, but it does not alter the basic structure presented above. Furthermore, it helps to understand the general conception of the universe of rural Tlaxcalans and the symbolic mechanisms binding together man and the supernatural. But, on the other hand, legendary and semilegendary accounts diminish the self-fulfilling dimensions of the tlahuelpuchi complex by vulgarizing the confrontations of ordinary men with tlahuelpuchis: animals talk back, man-into-animal and animal-into-man transformations take place in front of humans, tlahuelpuchis make alliances with ordinary men. Be this as it may, since legends and legendary accounts are not primary data, not even for the informants themselves, they can safely be ignored in this analysis.

Throughout this chapter, we have repeatedly referred to the tlahuelpuchi complex as a self-fulfilling system. A self-fulfilling system is defined as a well-organized and logical system in which ideology and physical parts are inextricably interrelated, so that something is true structurally if there is a high degree of concomitance between the former and the latter. Given the high degree of concomitance between what people believe regarding the tlahuelpuchi complex and the physical manifestations associated with it, the system is predictably efficacious, despite occasional breakdowns. Epistemologically, then, the fact that the bloodsucking event itself, the physical antecedents to it, and the actors' perception of its aftereffects unfold according to the stated ideology is not only psychologically reinforcing, but at the same time lead the experiencing actors immediately involved to color and interpret what *really* happened, along the entire chain of events, in terms of their a priori knowledge of the system, in terms of what is supposed to have taken place as handed down by tradition. Hence the apparent efficacy of the system, and the very subtle breakdown or transposition of the causal chain of events which leads people to believe firmly in the action of the tlahuelpuchi. This, of course, is the very nature of any witchcraft or sorcery system. What is noteworthy about the bloodsucking system of rural Tlaxcala is the specificity and neatness of the system's ideology and physical manifestation, which in most similar systems generally remains blurred and nebulous and sometimes can be inferred only with significant difficulty and risk of distortion (cf. Kluckhohn 1944).

The Syncretic and Historical Development of Anthropomorphic Supernaturalism in Mesoamerica

MAGIC AND RELIGION AND THE ORIGIN OF ANTHROPOMORPHIC SUPERNATURALISM IN RURAL TLAXCALA

One of the outstanding features of the anthropomorphic supernatural complex described in Chapters 2 and 3 is that all four supernaturals are of pre-Hispanic origin. This is not to say that they have survived in their pristine or even basic form since the time of the Spanish Conquest. To the contrary, they have been somewhat syncretized, and they are today combinations of pre-Hispanic elements, form, and behavior which have been amalgamated with essentially Spanish or European counterparts and some African elements. The tezitlazc and nahual do not have equivalents in the Spanish witchcraft-sorcery complex, but the tetlachihuic and tlahuelpuchi correspond roughly to the European concepts of sorcerer and witch, respectively. Knowledge of the origin and development of these four anthropomorphic supernaturals is important to an understanding of their contemporary structure and functions.

The study of the original sources dealing with the pre-Hispanic religion of the Central Mexican Highlands, pertaining mostly to the Nahuatl-speaking peoples, indicates that the position of magic (primarily the practice of witchcraft and sorcery) vis-à-vis formal or even folk religion was not unlike that prevailing in the same general domain of Spanish and European culture (Sahagún 1956; Durán 1967; Mendieta 1945; Motolinía 1903; Ricard 1947). In other words, magic was to a large extent an independent realm of behavior and action with respect to formal or folk religion, although magic and religion merged at certain junctures because they shared a common ideological system. Thus, in the same way that witches in Spanish Catholicism had a close connection with the Christian devil and derived their power or performed their evil-doings as acolytes of this supernatural, so did special kinds of witches or evildoers in pre-Hispanic Indian religion relative to various gods in the polytheistic pantheon (Sahagún 1956:I, 353–68). Unfortunately, the available sources are not detailed enough to reconstruct the nature of the relationship between magic and religion. For example, Sahagún (1956:III, 117, IV, 307–15), the best source on these matters, does not provide enough information about a host of anthropomorphic and non-anthropomorphic supernaturals that are known to have existed side by side with the formal or folk manifestations of the vast polytheistic pantheon. This inadequacy is clearly evident in Motolinía (1903: 35–66) and in the Spanish-Nahuatl and Nahuatl-Spanish dictionary of Fray Alonso de Molina (1944), originally published in 1571, which contains a large number of glosses for witch, sorcerer, weathermaker, transforming witch or trickster, conjurer, diviner, enchanter, charmer, soothsayer, astrologer, deceiver, and assorted demons and spirits. All these terms for anthropomorphic, animistic, and ethereal supernaturals point to a high degree of diversification in the realm of magic, but how this broad supernatural complex fitted in with the structure and ideology of formal polytheism is not exactly known.

We can assume, however, that the realm of magic in pre-Hispanic religion was not only differentiated in terms of anthropomorphic and non-anthropomorphic supernaturals, but, in one way or another, magic was not an integral part of the mainstream of religious beliefs and practices; it existed, rather, as a subsidiary, parallel system. In Mesoamerica, the position of witchcraft and sorcery vis-à-vis religion was perhaps never the same as in many modern or contemporary tribal or primitive societies in Africa, Oceania, and other parts of the world, where no clear operational distinction emerges between magic and religion, and where witchcraft, sorcery, and related supernaturalism are an intrinsic aspect of the social structure. Although it would be difficult to prove, it seems that this state of affairs goes back to the beginning of the Classic period, and it makes sense in the light of the rise of a very diversified polytheistic pantheon, a specialized priesthood, and the concept of the state. Under such circumstances, the relationship of magic and religion, in the context described above, is an invariant evolutionary development in the rise of civilization, be it in Nuclear America, the Near East, India, or China.

In an interesting, potentially useful, but superficial analysis of Spanish and pre-Hispanic elements of witchcraft and sorcery, Madsen (1960:121–23, 127–30) describes some of these independent, parallel, and convergent elements that accompanied the general process of syncretism structured by the confrontation of Indian religion and Catholicism starting immediately after the Conquest. Madsen confines himself to describing the combination of some elements and forms from these two religious traditions; then, skipping more than three centuries, he tells us that many contemporary religious and magical practices are syncretic, without bothering to analyze how this came about.

ANTHROPOMORPHIC SUPERNATURALISM IN PRE-HISPANIC
MESOAMERICA: A CRITIQUE OF LÓPEZ AUSTIN'S RECONSTRUCTION

Alfredo López Austin is one of the most perceptive contemporary students of Mesoamerican pre-Hispanic magic and religion. Although he does not employ the term anthropomorphic supernaturalism to refer to a number of magical practitioners and their craft, he clearly refers to individuals endowed with supernatural powers that fall essentially into the categories of witchcraft and sorcery. In a number of publications, López Austin (1966; 1967; 1973) discusses the standard sources of the sixteenth century (Las Casas 1966; Códice Ramírez 1944; Durán 1952; Florentine Codex 1963; Molina 1944; Motolinía 1941; Sahagún 1956; etc.) and seventeenth century (Ponce de León 1953; Ruiz de Alarcón 1953; Serna 1953; Torquemada 1944; etc.) in an attempt to analyze and classify the highly diversified world of pre-Hispanic anthropomorphic supernaturalism. It is not clear whether the sixteenth- and seventeenth-century sources are confused, deficient, or both, or whether pre-Hispanic anthropomorphic supernaturalism itself was not so coherent and integrated a system as the polytheistic religious system of Mesoamerica. López Austin's analysis does not definitively settle this question. On the basis of our own reading of the sources, we regard pre-Hispanic anthropomorphic supernaturalism as a rather more organized system, ancillary to and structurally more or less independent of polytheism, but underlined by the same ideology and cosmogony.

The Interrelationship of Magic and Religion

López Austin (1967:87–88) implies a greater structural integration of magic and religion in pre-Hispanic times than we are willing to admit. Partly, this slight disagreement is due to a conceptual stand, but mostly to a matter of focusing. Magic (essentially anthropomorphic supernaturalism) and religion are underlain by the same ideologic and cosmogonic system, and, from this viewpoint, no significant difference emerges between these two supernatural orders. Indeed, López Austin (1966:102–3) provides ample evidence that the polytheistic gods and anthropomorphic practitioners are governed by the same moral and behavioral principles and reflect a single domain and that often the practitioners are harbingers and human impersonators of the former. The same is true, however, in the contemporary religion of rural Tlaxcala and several regions of Mesoamerica, in which anthropomorphic supernaturalism and the

Catholic folk religion are structurally two different systems but are ideologically and cosmologically integrated (Nutini and Isaac 1977:84–90). Moreover, we suggest that the same obtains in probably the majority of supernatural systems of societies that have attained a state organization and a priestly hierarchy. Thus, witchcraft and sorcery in medieval and modern Europe are only intelligible within the context of Christian theology and the organization of the Church; and much the same can be said about Greek and Roman witchcraft and sorcery and the ideology, cosmology, and organization of Indo-European polytheism. But the ideological and cosmological integration of magic and religion in the majority of state and priestly organized societies entails at the same time the structural differentiation of these two supernatural domains. In this vein, the structural discharge of magic and religion are kept separate — that is, the activities, functions, rites, and ceremonies of these supernatural domains take place in different contexts and involve different kinds of personnel and supernatural practitioners. Thus, while both ancient Roman polytheism and Christianity (at least until about two centuries ago) not only believed in witchcraft and sorcery but regarded them as a part of the social and supernatural worlds, Roman and Catholic priests were thought of or regarded as witches or sorcerers, and their structural and behavioral domains of action involving themselves and the collectivity were always kept separate.

(Although the great majority of the Christian faithful may no longer believe in witchcraft and sorcery, these supernatural practices, for all we know, may still be part of the theology of different branches of Christianity. For example, it was not uncommon as late as the second half of the eighteenth century for individuals to be brought before the Inquisition for maintaining that witchcraft and sorcery did not exist. In practical terms, however, it can be said that the theological and individual belief in witchcraft and sorcery in Europe began to decline rapidly when the last witches were burnt at the stake in the first half of the eighteenth century. European witchcraft and sorcery are not intelligible without the structural separation of magic and religion; magic and religion coexist within the strong Manichean ideology that has always pervaded Christianity.)

It is this ideological and cosmological monism and the accompanying structural pluralism of magic and religion that we wish to maintain as prevalent in pre-Hispanic times. Despite the unitary ideological and cosmological meaning of pre-Hispanic magic and religion, it is unlikely that these two supernatural activities involved any significant ritual and ceremonial overlapping; nor, for example, is it likely that the organized priesthood functioned coterminously in capacities structurally denoted by the forty "magos del mundo nahuatl" (magicians of the Nahuatl world) described by López Austin (1967:88–112), or at least not in those that can clearly be classified as witches and sorcerers. This interpretation is implied by López Austin (1967:113), when he says that the pre-Hispanic priest in the century or so after the Conquest "perdió prestigio paulatinamente hasta quedar al nivel de un brujo y muy pronto se confudió con éste" (gradually lost prestige and sunk to the level of a witch [we would say sorcerer] and very quickly they became one and the same). On the basis of the available sources, the structural differentiation-integration of magic and religion in pre-Hispanic times cannot be definitively determined, but we tend to think that it is closer to the high differentiation entailed by Christianity than to the almost total integration exhibited in many primitive societies described in the ethnographic literature.

López Austin's Classification of Anthropomorphic Supernaturals

López Austin (1967:87–113) identifies more than forty anthropomorphic practitioners, which he classifies into seven categories, most of which, with the exception of the *titici* (essentially curers), may be regarded as variants of either witches or sorcerers—that is, individuals endowed with manifold supernatural powers manifested in a large number of contexts and occasions. The categories of *magos no profesionales* (non-professional magicians) and *pseudomagos* (pseudomagicians) are discussed mostly in the decaying context of the post-Conquest period; most of them cannot be classified as witches or sorcerers, and they denote essentially the individual rather than the collective and publicly oriented practice of magic. The remaining categories are: *los tlatlacatecolo* (literally, owl-men; essentially practitioners of black magic against man); *los hombres con personalidad sobrenatural* (men with supernatural personalities); *los dominadores de los meteoros* (literally, the controllers of meteors; essentially weathermen); and *los tlaciuhque* (astrologers, diviners).

Los dominadores de los meteoros and los tlaciuhque are clearcut categories that must be classified as variants of the sorcerer. The former have survived almost unchanged until today, and their weather-controlling and curing and ritual powers are embodied in the present-day tezitlazcs in rural Tlaxcala. Los tlaciuhque, essentially as diviners, astrologers, and fortune tellers of several kinds and employing a number of manipulative techniques, have disappeared from rural Tlaxcala, but they have survived in several parts of Mesoamerica where maize, reed, and other forms of divination, casting of lots, and fortune-telling still exist. At least one supernatural practitioner (the *tlachixqui* or *tlaciuhqui*) must be regarded as a kind of weatherman—and thus must not be classified as a tlaciuhque but as a *dominador de meteoros*. Moreover, some of the manipulative, curative, and interpretative techniques of several of the tlaciuhque have survived and are embodied in the contemporary tezitlazc, as described in this monograph. For example, the procedures of the tezitlazc to bring the soul back to the body in case of soul loss are similar to those of the *atlan teittaqui* in order to return the *tonalli* (soul, guardian spirit) to the body; also, a generation or so ago, the tezitlazcs in rural Tlaxcala were regarded by the people as interpreters of dreams, in the same way as the *temiquiximati* were, as reported in the sources for the pre-Hispanic situation discussed by López Austin (1967:107). Thus, insofar as practically all dominadores de los meteoros (2) and tlaciuhque (12) can be classified as kinds of sorcerers, they probably had the following fundamental attributes: they were public figures, their supernatural powers were essentially learned and manipulative, and they were basically for hire. In López Austin's analysis, these characteristics are evident for some of the practitioners, but it is also evident that the sources contain many gaps, are at times confusing, and admit of alternative interpretations.

It is López Austin's two main categories of anthropomorphic supernaturals, los tlatlacatecolo and los hombres con personalidad sobrenatural, that present some difficulties of analysis and classification. At first glance, the former look like sorcerers, and the latter look like witches. This is not so, however, for both categories contain supernaturals that may be classified either as witches or sorcerers, and, in at least one case, as neither. Let us take first los hombres con personalidad sobrenatural. Under this rubric there are two supernaturals: the *nahualli* and the *teutlipan moquetzani* (he who represents a god). We do not think that the latter can be classified as an anthropomorphic supernatural. Rather, the teutlipan moquetzani, regardless of the magic components that he evoked, must be regarded as an integral part of the ritual and ceremonial organization of pre-Hispanic polytheism, which embodied functions and activities that had little or nothing to do with witchcraft and sorcery. A better term for this personage is "ritual impersonator," for he was probably an individual endowed with certain physical characteristics, elected to the role by the people, and probably devoid of manipulative supernatural powers. The nahualli, on the other hand, is definitely a kind of transforming witch but was a much more complex supernatural than was described by the sources. López Austin (1967: 97) rightly points out that the information is not sufficient to answer a number of significant questions regarding its behavior and place in the pre-Hispanic belief system. There is no doubt that the nahualli is a composite term that stands for a number of supernaturals with varied powers, attributes, and spheres of action. The contemporary nahual, described in this monograph as a transforming trickster, is obviously a survival of one of the variants of the pre-Hispanic nahualli but embodies a composite of attributes of several of the variants. Be this as it may, the nahualli in its many manifestations was probably not a public figure, was born with its powers of animal transformation, and was basically independent of ordinary people.

OUR MODIFIED CLASSIFICATION OF THE TLATLACATECOLO

The largest category of anthropomorphic supernaturals described by López Austin (1967:88–95), the tlatlacatecolo, is confusing and the most difficult to understand. From our standpoint, the category is not significant, for it includes in one classification both sorcerers and witches, some of which have basically different supernatural powers and social behavior. As discussed below, it is in these cases that we must make a clear determination of the criteria according to which anthropomorphic supernaturals must be classified. Briefly, they are: the inherent or learned origin or provenance of their supernatural powers; the essentially public or fundamentally secret nature of their human identities; the immanent or manipulative working of their supernatural powers; and their basic independence of ordinary people or their amenability to be hired for good or evil. From this viewpoint, the tlatlacatecolo must be subdivided into the following categories.

1. The *tepan mizoni, el que pinta las paredes de las casas, tetlepanquetzqui, nomotzale (pixe, teyolpachoani), temacpalitoti (nomacpalitoti, tepopotza cua-huique), cihuanotzqui (xochihua, cihuatlatole),* and *el que trueca sentimientos* are fundamentally sorcerers. In other words, most of these diversified super-naturals were probably endowed with the following attributes: their powers were essentially learned, they were on the whole public individuals, their pow-ers were manipulative, and most of them were for hire. Again, the sources are confused and incomplete, but there is enough evidence to affirm tentatively that the anthropomorphic supernaturals in this category are kinds of sorcerers. Since the majority of the tlatlacatecolo fall into this category, the very alterna-tive, generic names by which they are known—*teipitzani* (he who blows harm-ful spells on people), *tetlachihuiani* (he who enchants people), *tococoliani* (he who makes people ill), et cetera—indicate that they are sorcerers. That some of these supernaturals could be hired by the people is evident in Sahagún's de-scription of the nomotzaleque as "asesinos a sueldo" (assassins for hire), de-spite López Austin's (1967:93) interpretation of Sahagún's informants, to the effect that the magic manipulation was undertaken against themselves in order to acquire courage and not against enemies. The intent is clear, however, in the implication that the nomotzaleque were public individuals that people con-tracted for malevolent purposes. This raises the following questions: were the supernatural practitioners in this category specialists exclusively in inflicting

evil and injury on people, as generally defined by the tlatlacatecolo, or were they also specialists in the craft of white magic? If the former is the case, which were the supernaturals who counteracted the black magic of the tlatlacatecolo? The tlaciuhque? The titici? These are questions that the sources cannot answer, but we are of the opinion that the tlatlacatecolo that we have classified as sorcerers were practitioners of both black and white magic, like the contemporary tetlachihuics described in this monograph. Indeed, it makes no sense to regard a supernatural as a sorcerer if it is not within its power to practice both black and white magic. Probably the strongest evidence that anthropomorphic supernaturals of this category were kinds of sorcerers is that the contemporary tetlachihuics in rural Tlaxcala embody many of their behaviors and possess several of their manipulative powers. For example, the sympathetic, contagious, and homeopathic techniques and procedures employed by the tetlepanquetzqui, nomotzale, cihuanotzqui, and el que trueca sentimientos have survived and are practiced today by tetlachihuics with relatively few changes. In fact, we would say that the tetlachihuic, as a dispenser of amatory magic, has survived almost unchanged since the cihuanotzqui of pre-Hispanic times. Finally, the last piece of evidence that the anthropomorphic supernaturals in this category are sorcerers and the direct ancestors of the tetlachihuic is linguistic: the terms tetlachihuiani (one of the alternate, generic names of the tlatlacatecolo) and tetlachihuic denote in essence practitioners of the same supernatural activity—namely, those who enchant people.

2. The *teyollocuani* (he who eats the hearts of people), *tecotzcuani* (he who eats the calves of people), *mometzcopinqui* (she whose legs are torn off), *tlahuipuchtli* (luminous incensory), and *moyohualitoani* (he who is ready to make love at night) are unquestionably witches and, more precisely, possibly transforming witches. These five anthropomorphic supernaturals were probably endowed with the following attributes: they were born with their malevolent powers, they were essentially secretive individuals, their powers were basically immanent, and they were independent from ordinary people. Once more the pre-Hispanic sources are not clear, but the evidence, with one exception, is strong to support our contention that the supernaturals in this category were witches. We have in mind the case of the *tecotzecuanime*, described by Sahagún's informants in a way that indicates that they were public individuals for hire, thereby making this supernatural a sorcerer in our terminological classification (López Austin 1967:92). On the other hand, it may well be the case that the teyollocuani and the tecotzcuani were two different supernaturals and that the former was indeed a witch while the latter was a sorcerer. But there is no doubt that the other three supernaturals in this category are witches, and the stringent evidence is again ethnographic. The contemporary tlahuelpuchi in

rural Tlaxcala embodies all the attributes and behavior of the mometzcopinqui, tlahuipuchtli, and moyohualitoani: as part of the rites of animal transformation, her legs are separated or disarticulated from the rest of the body in the fashion denoted by the linguistic meaning of the first; the luminosity that she emanates in her animal form is closely reminiscent of the linguistic meaning of the second; the sexual connotation of the third is embodied in the contemporary nahual rather than in the tlahuelpuchi, but there is no contradiction here since we have defined the former as a kind of witch. The pre-Hispanic tlahuipuchtli and the contemporary tlahuelpuchi are linguistic cognates, as several of our rural Tlaxcalan informants gave its meaning as "luz que se mueve" (moving light), "luminosidad andante" (moving luminosity), and "bola de fuego que se mueve" (moving ball of fire), denoting the light or luminosity that emanates from both the pre-Hispanic and contemporary supernatural in its animal form. Moreover, in 1959 Nutini recorded the term tlahuepuchtli for a kind of bloodsucking witch-animal in the community of Xaltepuxtla near Huauchinango in the Sierra de Puebla. In summary, then, there is no question that the contemporary tlahuelpuchi in rural Tlaxcala is a composite anthropomorphic supernatural that embodies many of the attributes and behavior of the pre-Hispanic supernaturals included in this category.

3. Finally, *el que ve fijamente las cosas* and *el que toca las cosas* are not anthropomorphic supernaturals—that is, they are neither witches nor sorcerers nor magos (magicians), as López Austin calls them. Rather, these are individuals born with certain extraordinary attributes, not powers, because they cannot essentially manipulate them in any specific way. From our viewpoint, if any individual endowed with some extraordinary or supernatural attributes or powers cannot manipulate them in any discernible way, he or she is neither a sorcerer nor perhaps a witch—that is, he does not have the ability to practice black or white magic. In other words, the attributes or powers associated with the two supernaturals in this category are inherent but beyond their control; their volition has nothing to do with whatever good or evil they may cause. (In a sense this is the case with the bloodsucking compulsion of the contemporary tlahuelpuchi—for which the people make due allowances, as has been discussed—but she can also cause evil at will.) It is very likely that the two categories of individuals described as magos are really versions of the evil eye (*mal de ojo*); that is, they are individuals born with the ability to influence the physical world by sight or touch. They cause injury to people and objects by these two means—for instance, by breaking objects, causing children to become ill, causing adults to wither away, and so on. The evil eye has a rather wide distribution in the Old World, and we now know it to have existed in the New World. The *tlatzini* and *tlamatocani*, as López Austin (1967:91) calls these two

pre-Hispanic individuals, have their contemporary counterparts in rural Tlax-cala as embodied in those individuals born with *tlapaltizoliztli* (very strong sight) and the attribute of *xoxal* associated with twinning. The former has been discussed as an example of the evil eye, and we need only to say that its attribute of breaking eggs and glassware and influencing other physical objects is similar to the action of the tlatzini. Twins in rural Tlaxcala are thought to possess "de nación" (by nature) certain supernatural attributes, according to which "uno pone y el otro quita" (one inflicts and the other takes away). One of the twins may adversely affect a living person (for example, cause a constant pain in the part of the body that has come into contact with him or cause a symptom of the evil eye). Removal of the pain or neutralization of the evil eye can be effected by only the good twin, "el que quite"; however, he need not be the brother of the bad twin, but just any good twin, that is, any twin "que quite." To bring about relief, the good twin must rub the affected part of the body with his own saliva. This attribute of twins to cause or remove injury is called xoxal, and it may obviously be either good or bad. It is evident that the tlapaltizoliztli associated with the evil eye and the twins' attribute of xoxal are syncretic versions of the attributes and behavior of the pre-Hispanic tlatzini and tlamatocani, a kind of convergence that still has a good deal of force even in secularized rural Tlaxcalan communities.

SOME ADDITIONAL REMARKS ON LÓPEZ AUSTIN'S RECONSTRUCTION

López Austin's (1967:1966) description and partial analysis of pre-Hispanic anthropomorphic supernaturals and associated personages endowed with some extraordinary attributes or practitioners of extraordinary activities is of high caliber, and, he cannot, of course, be faulted for the shortcomings of the sources. Still, for comparative purposes, it makes more sense to classify and analyze the majority of the forty supernaturals discussed by López Austin in terms of witches and sorcerers. If nothing else, it helps to understand their basic structure, the nature of their supernatural powers, and their relationship to the social structure of ordinary people. There are three additional points that are significant.

First, it is not clear within the context of López Austin's (1967) principal publication on the subject, whether the typology of the forty pre-Hispanic magos is his own or is drawn primarily from the sources themselves. On the basis of our own knowledge of the sources used by López Austin, it is our impression that the seven categories of supernaturals that he presents are in part elicited from the sources and are in part the result of his own analysis. In other words, the typology is essentially emic, and what we have done is simply to endow it with the etic dimensions that are necessary for the comparative and syncretic analysis underlying this chapter.

Second, López Austin employs the Spanish term brujo(a) (witch) and hechicero (sorcerer) as content-free glosses to refer to the forty magos of the pre-Hispanic magic system, and, in the context of his description, he often uses them interchangeably. Although this usage may be standard and acceptable in vernacular Spanish (and in English, for that matter), it is not acceptable in scientific anthropological vocabulary. This terminological confusion tends to obscure or distort whatever emic distinctions may exist in a given situation, and certainly it does not help in arriving at etic generalizations.

Third, we are not entirely convinced of the adequacy of using Colonial sources in the reconstruction of specific pre-Hispanic anthropomorphic supernaturals or in complementing the original sixteenth-century sources, as López Austin (1967:92, 93, 95, 103, etc.) often does. The work of scholars such as Ponce de León (1953), Ruiz de Alarcón (1953), and Serna (1953) for the Nahuatl-speaking area of the Central Mexican Highlands, and that of Balsalobre (1953), Feria (1953), and Sánchez de Aguilar (1953) for other regions of Mexico is very useful. But these sources were written between 100 and 135 years after the Conquest, and what they have to say about anthropomorphic supernaturalism denotes a situation that had undergone considerable change and decay of a once vigorous system. Because they are ethnographically sketchy, the value of these sources are as attestations of the syncretic and/or acculturative process that anthropomorphic supernaturalism had most assuredly undergone in five generations after the Conquest, rather than as material for the reconstruction of the pre-Hispanic situation. In other words, by the middle of the seventeenth century the supernaturals in question had already undergone significant transformations (both through changes in the socioreligious structure of Indian society and by the interaction with European and African elements of witchcraft and sorcery), so as to render risky any extrapolation to the pre-Hispanic situation, at least in a reasonably exacting analysis. For example, Ruiz de Alarcón, according to López Austin (1967:92), gives *texoxqui* (he who enchants people) and *tetlachihuiani* (he who bewitches people) as synonyms for the pre-Hispanic teyollocuani and tecotzcuani. If we grant that the pre-Hispanic teyollocuani was a witch, then, for reasons and in a context that would be impossible to specify, this kind of witch had evolved in the belief system into a sorcerer as possibly denoted by the pre-Hispanic term tecotzcuani. Again, we consider two possibilities: Ruiz de Alarcón's (1953:24–28) informants were correctly expressing some sort of syncretic coalescing (but more likely a natural depletion and contraction of a belief system whose social structure had been fundamentally altered) of the concepts of witch and sorcerer, out of a situation in which they were kept conceptually separate; or Ruiz de Alarcón misinterpreted his informants, and indeed the conceptual separation between witch and sorcerer was still there. At any rate, the same can probably be said about the pre-Hispanic sources and those who interpreted them, but in assessing them we do not at least have to contend with any syncretic or acculturative dimensions.

ETHNOGRAPHIC ANALYSIS AND THE PRE-HISPANIC SITUATION

From another standpoint, the foregoing remarks may be regarded as an illustration of how contemporary ethnographic analysis may be useful in extrapolating the nature and structure of pre-Hispanic anthropomorphic supernaturalism. Such an extrapolation is possible because contemporary ethnography, unlike the Colonial sources on magic and religion, is anchored to a social structure and belief system that permits the gauging of elements and comparison of supernaturals. Thus, when the structure and behavior of the nahual and the tlahuelpuchi are compared, inferences can be drawn to pre-Hispanic counterparts from which they were syncretized and derived. But between the pre-Hispanic anthropomorphic supernaturals described in the original sources and those of contemporary ethnography there is a gap of more than 400 years for which the documentation is generally sketchy; extrapolating about the original entities in question on this basis may be dangerous.

By comparing, not extrapolating, the structure of anthropomorphic supernaturalism in rural Tlaxcala today and its counterpart in pre-Hispanic times, it is immediately apparent that the system has shrunk six and a half times: from a total number of twenty-six specialized supernaturals (López Austin's numbers 1, 4–13, 16, 17, and 18–29) to the four described and analyzed in this monograph. What is interesting is that much of the diversified specialization of the pre-Hispanic supernaturals has survived and is embodied in the four contemporary supernaturals, as we have demonstrated in the foregoing pages. To be sure, a significant number of practices and attributes of the pre-Hispanic supernaturals have disappeared. For example, seashell divination and the regular interpretation of dreams (López Austin's supernaturals numbers 24 and 29) are no longer practiced in rural Tlaxcala, and determining when they stopped would be practically impossible. This decrease is no doubt a function of the transcendental changes undergone by Indian culture and society during the first 100 years after the Conquest. But as the pre-Hispanic anthropomorphic system shrunk and many of the attributes and much of the behavior of particular supernaturals disappeared, new elements were introduced from the Spanish complex of witchcraft and sorcery, as well as some from Africa, especially beginning during the last decade of the sixteenth century and throughout most of the seventeenth century; thereafter, syncretism was probably rapid. In summary, the four anthropomorphic supernaturals of contemporary rural Tlaxcala are composite models of the twenty-six supernaturals described by López Austin (1967:88–107) that have been analyzed essentially as variants of the witch and sorcerer.

As we have indicated, the structure and general position of contemporary anthropomorphic supernaturalism in rural Tlaxcala cannot be fully understood without reference to the obvious process of syncretism that the four supernaturals discussed in this monograph have undergone throughout Colonial and Republican times. To be sure, syncretism of the four supernaturals differed in fashion and extent for Spanish and African elements of witchcraft and sorcery. However, they can be arranged in degrees of syncretism, depending primarily on the elements of the Spanish and African witchcraft-sorcery complex that found their way into the syncretic matrix roughly over a period of a century. After the end of the seventeenth century, there were undoubtedly some syncretic developments, but by then the basic complex of anthropomorphic supernaturalism described in this monograph had been essentially structured. On the whole, the documentary information for a thorough analysis of the syncretic development of anthropomorphic supernaturalism in Mesoamerica is not good. However, it is sufficient to give a possible outline of its main features and the socioreligious matrix in which it took place, not only for rural Tlaxcala but for the Nahuatl-speaking areas of the Central Mexican Highlands. This is especially the case for the eighteenth century, for there is little in the published sources after 1700 that can be used as reliable data for the above purposes until two centuries later in the work of Frederick Starr (1900).

THE LINGUISTIC STRUCTURE OF ANTHROPOMORPHIC SUPERNATURALISM: EXTRAPOLATING FROM THE PRE-HISPANIC SITUATION

Independently of López Austin's (1966, 1967, 1974) work, and on the basis of almost the same sources (Sahagún 1956; Motolinía 1903, 1941; Durán 1952; Mendieta 1945; Tezozomoc 1943; Molina 1944; and others), we have ascertained the pre-Hispanic origin and partly outlined the syncretic components of anthropomorphic supernaturalism in rural Tlaxcala and have arrived at rather similar results. From the viewpoint of this monograph, the account would be incomplete without a brief discussion of the Spanish-Nahuatl and Nahuatl-Spanish dictionary by Molina (1944). This dictionary gives the whole range of diversification of anthropomorphic supernaturalism. For example, all four rural Tlaxcalan supernaturals are given at least two or three glosses: *"quiauhtlaz-*

qui," "teciuhtlazqui," "teciuhtlacani," for weatherman, *tiempero,* or *tezitlazc; "naualli," "tlamati,"* for transforming trickster or *nahual; "tetlachiui," "tecotzcuani," "texoxqui," "tectlaxihuani,"* for sorcerer, *hechicero,* or *tetlachihuic; "tlauipuchin," "teyollocuani," "naualli,"* for witch, *bruja,* or *tlahuelpuchi.* In fact, the number of glosses for *"bruxa"* (witch) and *"hechizero"* (sorcerer) is more than fifteen, and in several cases the glosses are given specific meaning: *tetlachiui* "hechizero que hechiza a alguno" (sorcerer who bewitches someone); *atlanteittani* "hechizero que mira en agua" (sorcerer who looks into water); *tlapouhqui* "hechizero que echa suertes" (sorcerer who foretells the future). On the other hand, much of the diversification and specialization of anthropomorphic and non-anthropomorphic supernaturalism are lost in the Spanish glosses, and this is especially true with respect to more than a dozen Nahuatl terms which are glossed simply as *"bruxa"* and *"hechizero."* In this context, a careful study of Molina's dictionary may illuminate the structure of anthropomorphic and non-anthropomorphic supernaturalism among the Nahuatl-speaking Indians of ancient Mexico. Particularly for our purposes here, the analysis of the Spanish meanings for the three main Nahuatl glosses for *"bruxa"* has yielded some results.

If we look at the nature of the nahual and tlahuelpuchi, it is immediately apparent that they share a number of attributes in common (primarily their animal transforming powers and the secret, non-public nature of their human identity) which points to a common origin but with a rather significant and diversified number of acquired elements. These elements were of Spanish witchcraft origin, and they were part of the whole complex of European witchcraft and sorcery that constituted the syncretic counterpart of what is glossed in Nahuatl under the terms *bruxa* and *hechizero* in Molina's dictionary. Be this as it may, it is quite clear that *"naualli"* denoted primarily what Molina understood as denoted by the Spanish term *bruxa* at the time, whereas *teyellocuani* (bloodsucking witch) and *tlauipuchin* (another kind of witch) did not have specific Spanish counterparts; Molina simply glossed them as specialized witches, but it is possible that the former was not a witch. The point is that Molina was obviously hampered by the great diversification of Nahuatl anthropomorphic supernaturals which he did not know how to denote in Spanish. In this light, it seems probable that *tyelloquani* (despite its linguistic meaning), was not a witch (see page 87 for a discussion of the *teyollocuani-tecotzcuani*) but some sort of sorcerer or enchanter, given the meaning of the gloss *teyolloqualiztlitlatolli* "palabras de encantador que matan y quitan la vida" (enchanter's words which kill and take away life). Whatever supernatural was denoted by *teyellocuani* probably disappeared from rural Tlaxcala by the middle of the seventeenth century, whereas the supernaturals denoted by the terms *naualli* and *tlauipuchin*, as well as those denoted by the terms *teciuhtlazqui*, *quiauhtlazqui*, and *tetlachiui* have survived relatively unchanged linguistically, and with their essentially pre-Hispanic form and content. The contemporary nahual and tlahuelpuchi represent, of course, syncretized anthropomorphic supernaturals partaking of both the European concept of the witch and the pre-Hispanic naualli and tlauipuchin. It goes without saying that the same applies to the tetlachihuic, as a syncretized product of the pre-Hispanic *tetlachiui* and the Spanish concept of the sorcerer plus a significant number of African elements. The tezitlazc, on the other hand, is the most characteristically pre-Hispanic of the four rural Tlaxcalan supernaturals, and, although he has undergone some modifications, the tezitlazc should not strictly be regarded as a syncretic entity, for, so far as we know, its pre-Hispanic form did not have a specific Spanish counterpart.

It should be noted, however, that the linguistic analysis of glosses of anthropomorphic and non-anthropomorphic supernaturals must not be overemphasized. It is impossible to make strict inferences from the linguistic structure of a gloss to what it denotes magically and socially. Thus, the fact that, say, the contemporary tlahuelpuchi is a cognate and the direct linguistic descendant of the pre-Hispanic *tlauipuchin* does not necessarily mean that the former supernatural today has the same form and content that the latter supernatural had 450 years ago. Indeed, if there were a strict correlation between linguistic and sociomagical structure, the gloss *teyollocuani* should obviously have survived for the contemporary bloodsucking witch, for it is the closest denotation of the tlahuelpuchi. Why, instead, did "*tlauipuchin*" survive as the gloss for the contemporary bloodsucking witch? The answer will most likely never be known, nor is it really a significant question. The self-contained specialization of the *naualli* and the *quiauhtlazqui* and *teciuhtlazqui* as a specific kind of witch and as kinds of conjurers, respectively, presents no difficulty in inferring that these supernaturals have survived rather unchanged not only linguistically but sociomagically as well. (It should be noted that Molina glosses both "*quiauhtlazqui*" and "*teciuhtlazqui*" as conjurers against hail, that is, *granicero* in Spanish, when the correct linguistic meaning of the former is conjurer against rain, that is, *lluviero—sic pro tiempero—*in Spanish.) It is the high diversification of glosses denoting the pre-Hispanic categories of witch and sorcerer that makes it difficult and risky to undertake meaningful linguistic and sociomagical inferences to the contemporary situation. In the present context, the linguistic analysis of glosses is useful as it helps to understand the nature and form of particular supernaturals that cluster into meaningful sociomagical categories at a specific point in time, but not as to how and why they change through time. Like all the primary sources on pre-Hispanic anthropomorphic supernaturalism, Molina's dictionary shows that this magical complex was not clearly structured, at least in the linguistic consciousness and to the extent that it was elicited from informants by this scholar.

We have not made an exhaustive study of Molina's dictionary for anthropomorphic and non-anthropomorphic supernaturals. The following is a partial list of Spanish-Nahuatl and Nahuatl-Spanish glosses (generally nuclear) that illustrates the extent and diversification of the pre-Hispanic complex.

SPANISH	NAHUATL
Adivino (diviner)	ticitl, tlapouhqui, tetlempantlatoani, tonalpouhqui
Agorero (augurer)	tonalpouhqui
Astrologo (astrologer)	ylhuicatlamatilizmatini
Bruxa (witch)	naualli, teyolloquani (*chupa sangore*), tlauipuchin (*otra*)
Conjurador (conjurer)	teciuhtlazqui (*de granizo*), tecamocentlaliani, tecamononotzani (*contra alguno*)
Curador (*medico*) (curer, physician)	tepati, tepatiani, ticitl
Encantador (enchanter)	temacpalitoti, tecochtlazqui (*para urtar*), texochiuiani (*robar muger*), moyouahtoani (*idolo*)
Granizero (weatherman)	teciuhtlazqui, quiauhtlazqui
Hechizero (sorcerer)	tetlachiuiani, tetlachiui, texoxqui, tetlanonochilia, teyolloquani, tecotzcuani, teotlaxihuani, teixcuapani, naualli, atlanteittani (*que mira en agua*)
Nigromantico (necromancer)	naualli

NAHUATL	SPANISH
Naualli	bruxa (witch)
Quiauhtlazqui	conjurador de pluvia (rain conjurer)
Ticitl	agorero (augurer), echador de suertes (fortuneteller)
Teciuhtlazqui	conjurador de granizo (hail conjurer)
Teciuhtlacani	conjurador de granizo (hail conjurer)
Tetempantlatoani	el que echa juizios de lo que podra acaecer (he who foretells the future)

NAHUATL	SPANISH
Teyolloquani	bruxa que chupa la sangre (bloodsucking witch)
Tecamocentlaliani	conjurador contra alguno (conjurer against someone)
Tecohtlazqui	encantador (*para robar*) (enchanter in order to steal)
Tecotzquani	hechizero (sorcerer)
Teotlaxiliani	hechizero (sorcerer)
Tonalpouhqui	adivino o agorero que echa suertes (diviner or augurer who foretells the future)
Tlapouhqui	hechizero o agorero que echa suertes (sorcerer or augurer who foretells the future)
Texoxqui	hechizero (sorcerer)
Teixcuepani	engañador (deceiver), embaucador (impostor), burlador (trickster), hechizero (sorcerer)
Tetlanonochilia	hechizero (sorcerer)
Tetlachiui	hechizero que hechiza a algunos (sorcerer who bewitches others)
Tetlachiuiani	hechizero que hechiza a algunos
Tetlachiuique	hechizeros (sorcerers)
Ylhuicatlamatlizmati	astrologo (astrologer)

Finally, let us compare the list of forty pre-Hispanic anthropomorphic and non-anthropomorphic supernaturals given by López Austin (1967) with Molina's list presented above. Counting the supernaturals that López Austin describes in Spanish, there are twenty-one that are not glossed in Spanish in Molina's dictionary. But there are almost as many Nahuatl glosses in Molina that are not mentioned by López Austin among the forty supernaturals (including many alternatives and specializations) together with the many terms by which his main categories were known. An exhaustive survey of Molina's dictionary would not only establish the presence of all the glosses denoting the vast array of anthropomorphic, non-anthropomorphic, and anthropomorphic-like supernaturals discussed by López Austin, but many more glosses having to do with the pre-Hispanic magical system. If nothing else, the study of Molina's dictionary would reveal an even greater complexity and diversification of the magical system than what López Austin and other modern scholars have been able to establish by culling the sources on the pre-Hispanic culture and society of the Central Mexican Highlands. Since Molina's dictionary and the principal primary ethnographic sources (Sahagún 1956; Durán 1952; Motolinía 1941; Florentine Codex 1963; Códice Ramírez 1944; etc.) were gathered roughly

between 1530 and 1570—that is, within a generation and a half after the Conquest—their comparative study is really the only corpus of data that fairly
accurately reflects the great complexity and diversification of the pre-Hispanic
magical system. This corpus of data also reveals that, despite the excellence of
these early scholars, there was probably a significant loss in the translation
(linguistically and culturally) of pre-Hispanic concepts to Spanish counterparts.

THE SOCIAL AND RELIGIOUS CONTEXTS OF SYNCRETISM:
PRE-HISPANIC AND SPANISH INPUTS AND COMPONENTS

It is during the second half of the seventeenth century and the first two decades
of the eighteenth century that the contemporary complex of anthropomorphic
supernaturalism in rural Tlaxcala acquired its basic syncretic form. We have
some direct and specific historical evidence to support this contention—mainly,
a document that Nutini found in the parochial archive of San Diego Tlalocan,
dated 1653. This document is a letter by the visiting priest of San Diego Tlalocan to the Bishop of Puebla, complaining about the independence of the people
of the community in carrying out many ritual and ceremonial aspects of the
cult. The visiting priest also complains that the Indians openly practiced a large
number of superstitions and that they entertained heretical and idolatrous beliefs totally incompatible with Catholic doctrine. Quite perceptively, the visiting priest goes on to say that he had been able to detect many beliefs and
practices that were of distinct Spanish heretical origin, which had managed to
reach the rural areas of the province. Specifically, the visiting priest mentions
several "superstitions," as he calls them, among which are all four rural Tlaxcalan anthropomorphic supernaturals, with slightly different spellings, but unmistakably the same: "*quiatlalpizque*," "*nahualli*," "*tetlahuachin*," "*tlahue-
pochin.*" With the exception of the "*quiatlalpizque*," who is also specifically
described as *rezador* (prayer leader) and an important cargo in the *ayuntamiento religioso* (Nutini 1976), the other three supernaturals are described as
despicable and abhorrent individuals with satanic powers that the people often
consult for unfathomable purposes or to defend themselves against their evildoings. This description leaves no doubt that the visiting priest is talking about
the contemporary nahual, tetlachihuic, and tlahuelpuchi. The information contained in this document is important for two reasons. First, it shows that the
terminology of all four contemporary supernaturals had survived (among a
host of other similar supernaturals) some 130 years of intensive campaigns of
Catholic conversion and catechization, although it is not clear in what form
or with what structural attributes. Second, the document is explicit about
the Spanish elements of witchcraft and sorcery (although the visiting priest

does not use these terms) that had been diffusing to the rural areas of Tlaxcala since the turn of the seventeenth century, initiating thereby the process of syncretism.

It is now appropriate to ask, what were the factors and under what conditions did the syncretic amalgamation of pre-Hispanic and Spanish elements of witchcraft and sorcery acquire more or less their present form? Shortly after the middle of the seventeenth century, the religion of the Tlaxcalan Indians was a thoroughly syncretic entity, in which diverse elements of Spanish and pre-Hispanic origin had combined into an inextricable whole. Under the guidance of the Franciscan friars, a series of Spanish religious institutions, such as the cult of the saints (especially of the community patron saint), the system of *hermandades* (brotherhoods), *cofradías* (sodalities), and *mayordomías* (stewardships), and the main moral and theological tenents of Catholicism were introduced. These institutions and beliefs interacted with a large roster of pre-Hispanic beliefs, practices, and institutions, which shared with Catholicism a degree of structural or ideological similarity. Among the most salient pre-Hispanic religious institutions were a highly specialized and diversified polytheistic pantheon (structurally resembling the also specialized and diversified Catholic pantheon of saints, angels, and other lesser supernaturals), the *telpochalli* (men's houses), the *calmecac* (priestly houses), military organizations, and practices such as a form of baptism, confession, and others (Carrasco 1961). For nearly 100 years the Franciscans were in complete control of the Indian population, and it was during this time that the two key stages of the developmental cycle of the syncretic process occurred (Nutini 1976). By the time the Franciscans were completely removed from the Indian communities in the third decade of the seventeenth century, the religion of the Tlaxcalan Indians was essentially Catholic but was permeated with structural and ideological attributes and elements of the by now organically forgotten pre-Hispanic religion. By the second half of the seventeenth century, Tlaxcalan Indian religion was firmly centered on the cult of the saints, the mayordomía system, and the ayuntamiento religioso, which became the central institutions of Indian folk Catholicism. This situation persisted for more than 250 years, for by the end of the seventeenth century Tlaxcalan Indian religion had acquired its contemporary form. The process of syncretism (acculturation is a better concept from now on) did not stop, of course, but appears to have continued until the beginning of this century. But the basic syncretic cycle had been completed by the end of the seventeenth century, and the next two centuries witnessed only a series of much less important cycles and epicycles, which did not fundamentally alter the original syncretic synthesis. Witchcraft and sorcery are even more telling in this respect, in the sense that the syncretism found today in rural Tlaxcala is the product of pre-Hispanic anthropomorphic supernaturalism and Spanish (European), and to some degree African, practices and concepts introduced when the Franciscans began to lose control in rural Tlaxcala and when the central institutions of community religion were beginning to crystallize (Nutini and Bell 1980:312– 20). How did this new syncretic synthesis come into existence?

The Franciscan friars in Tlaxcala were in complete charge of the conversion and catechization of the Indians throughout the sixteenth century and until the middle of the second decade of the seventeenth century. The Franciscans began to lose control of their Indian flocks soon after the turn of the seventeenth century, in the sense that secular priests, jealous of the Franciscans' monopoly, began trying to establish themselves as religious leaders of Indian communities. This problem became especially acute by the turn of the century, when a number of secular priests arrived from Spain and increasing numbers were being trained in the seminaries of New Spain. There is also no question that the efforts to unseat the friars from their control over the Indians was helped by the *encomendero* (Indian grantee) class and other Spanish colonists. These elements of Colonial society had always regarded the friars with suspicion, feeling that the friars served as an obstacle to their economic interests by preventing a more thorough exploitation of the Indian population. Without minimizing the fact that the friars by the end of the sixteenth century had become concerned with power for its own sake and had become involved in serious internal dissensions, throughout the sixteenth century they had protected the Indians against undue exploitation, and, by their genuine interest and identification with the Indian population, they had softened many of the most unpleasant aspects of the early stages of the conquest and colonization of New Spain. At any rate, it was in the context of this change in religious leadership from regular orders to secular priesthood that the final syncretic stage of the religious mainstream took place. At the same time, the stage was set for the initiation of a new syncretic synthesis, out of elements ancillary to the pre-Hispanic Tlaxcalan religion such as witchcraft, sorcery, tutelary mountain owners, and fertility and intensification rites, which were by then largely separate from and/or parallel to the mainstream of folk Catholicism.

The friars were in charge of ministering to the religious needs of Indian communities created by conversion and indoctrination, but they also functioned as administrators and organizers of a variety of social and religious activities at the community level. The friars were careful to protect the Indians from excessive influences from the outside world, and they actively opposed the settlement of Spaniards and other non-Indian elements of Colonial society in the communities under their charge. The friars also participated actively in local community projects and advised community officials on the conduct of relations with the outside world. In short, the friars were effective leaders who extended their influence far beyond their strictly religious ministry. All of this changed as the friars surrendered their control of the Indian communities to the secular priests, a control which was lost completely by approximately 1635. During these three decades the spiritual leadership and church administration of Indian communities passed into the hands of secular priests and clerics who did not have the interests of the Indians at heart, who had little knowledge of Indian affairs, and who were often motivated more by economic gain than by the spiritual needs of their flocks. One important factor is that the secular priests were less numerous than the friars had been at the end of the sixteenth century. By about 1640, the new secular leaders numbered about one-fourth less than the total number of friars four decades earlier. If we add that the secular priests were not nearly so conscientious as the friars in their weekly or twice weekly visits and general duties and obligations toward their *iglesias de visita* (congregations), the quality and quantity of the religious life and continuous indoctrination of the Tlaxcalan Indians unquestionably suffered significantly by the middle of the seventeenth century (Nutini and Bell 1980:320–24).

It is in this setting that the syncretic process of witchcraft and sorcery in Tlaxcala was initiated. When the friars were in complete control, and probably during the earliest stage of losing control, the Indian communities were well protected from outside interferences, largely isolated, and minimally affected by the diffusion of customs and practices from the larger Colonial society. But as the friars lost control and the secular priests asserted themselves as the new spiritual leaders, the Indian communities were left more and more to their own devices, owing essentially to the basic disinterest of the new visiting priests, who often did not minister to their flocks more than once a month. When the friars had finally disappeared, local Indian communities were significantly more in contact with the outside world and to some degree on their way to regional integration. The demise of the friars coincided with a new, outward-looking attitude of the Indian congregations, which, after more than a century of isolation, began to open themselves to the outside world. To some degree, Indian congregations became open communities, subject to the influence of a number of customs, practices, and beliefs from which hitherto they had been protected by the zeal of the friars and by their somewhat self-imposed isolation from the wider Colonial society in the cities and towns, composed by then of a wide spectrum of Spaniards, Creoles, Mestizos, Mulattoes, and other ethnic groups (Nutini and Bell 1980:324–31). In this context, all supernatural beliefs and practices that had remained outside of the original syncretic synthesis (which was by then crystallizing into an organic entity) or that had been dormant or practiced sub rosa because of the watchful control of the friars began to interact with a rather large complex of beliefs and practices concerning witchcraft, sorcery, and other non-Catholic activities of Spanish and, to a lesser extent, African origin.[1] The initial syncretic stage of the developmental cycle of witchcraft, sorcery, and related supernaturalism began by 1620 and ran its full course in approximately 100 years, for by about 1720 we can say that the complex of anthropomorphic and non-anthropomorphic supernaturalism in rural Tlaxcala had acquired its present form. In this developmental cycle, one of the least known components is the presence of elements of African sorcery, which probably had a maximum degree of influence on the syncretic matrix during the last two decades of the seventeenth century. Although we have barely studied this component, it must be explored carefully in a definitive analysis of witchcraft and sorcery in Mesoamerica (Aguirre Beltrán 1946, 1963). Just as the basic religious complex, centered on the cult of the saints, the mayordomía system, and the ayuntamiento religioso had remained constant since it crystallized as a syncretic synthesis by the late seventeenth century, the syncretic synthesis of rural Tlaxcalan anthropomorphic supernaturalism had experienced few if any significant changes since the early eighteenth century.

The fundamental nature of all four anthropomorphic supernaturals in rural Tlaxcala is essentially pre-Hispanic—that is, it conforms to certain non-Spanish patterns in both structure and ideology. Although the behavior of these supernaturals may at times resemble that of the traditional European witch and sorcerer, their position within the world view is not the same: they are underlain by an ideology that contains practically no Catholic elements. Moreover, the position of these supernaturals with respect to ordinary men is not that of witches, sorcerers, or other practitioners in traditional European society; the situation is instead one in which there is no clear-cut demarcation between what is natural and what is supernatural, what is sacred and what is profane, characteristic of traditional Indian society. The syncretism that these supernaturals have undergone, has not basically altered their pre-Hispanic position in the supernatural system and the social structure of ordinary men. The syncretic process, thus, has been asymmetrical on the pre-Hispanic side. In the syncretism of Indian religion, on the other hand, the process has also been asymmetrical but on the side of Catholicism. This is understandable in light of the fact that forced acceptance and strong social and political pressures were brought to bear against the Indians to convert and be indoctrinated in the practice of Catholicism, whereas the syncretism involved in anthropomorphic supernaturalism, as a more subtle, peripheral, and less visible phenomenon, escaped most of these pressures and developed in a freer form.

At one extreme we have the tezitlazc, with no Spanish counterpart, and therefore a direct descendant of the pre-Hispanic teciuhtlazqui. But even this supernatural has been syncretized to the extent that it has acquired the role of rezador and employs techniques which are of Spanish or non-Indian origin such as the ringing of bells, the use of rockets, and so on. The nahual does not have a Spanish counterpart either, but it has been more syncretized than the tezitlazc because it partakes of several attributes of the European witch. But it is the tetlachihuic and tlahuelpuchi that are the most syncretized supernaturals, for they correspond closely to the European concepts of sorcerer and witch. Perhaps the majority of the methods and procedures employed by the tetlachihuic are of European and African origin, especially in the case of sympathetic and homeopathic techniques. More or less the same can be said of the tlahuelpuchi; not only does she exhibit several behavior patterns of the European witch, but most of the techniques to stop her, such as the use of metals, scissors, crosses, and so on, are also of European origin. However, we must not overemphasize the syncretic nature of the tetlachihuic and tlahuelpuchi, for even they, in the final analysis, are significantly more pre-Hispanic than European. The problem is complicated, of course, by the presence of many parallel and convergent elements which makes it difficult to determine what is pre-Hispanic and what is European. For example, there is no doubt about the European origin of the use of odoriferous substances such as garlic and onions as a deterrent against witches, but there are several characteristics and attributes of the pre-Hispanic forms of the tetlachihuic and tlahuelpuchi that are shared by the European sorcerer and witch. A clear case of convergence is the sticking of a knife in the ground in order to immobilize a witch, which is definitely of European origin, and the use of an obsidian knife in the same fashion, which is clearly of pre-Hispanic origin (López Austin 1966:112; Pedro Carrasco, personal communication). Thus, the syncretism exhibited by anthropomorphic supernaturals in rural Tlaxcala today is heightened by the significant degree of structural parallelism and convergence between the pre-Hispanic and European and, to some extent, African magical traditions (Aguirre Beltrán 1940:209–16). It is the ideological domain that rural Tlaxcalan supernaturals have retained their fundamental pre-Hispanic nature and have been the least syncretized.

THE SYNCRETIC AMALGAMATION OF THE PRE-HISPANIC,
EUROPEAN, AND AFRICAN TRADITIONS

Given the particular social, political, and religious conditions that Tlaxcala experienced from the Conquest to the first two decades of the seventeenth century, it is unlikely that any significant syncretic changes in the anthropomorphic supernatural system took place during the first 100 years. There were many changes, to be sure, but they were the result of basic transformations in

Tlaxcalan culture and society, and, more specifically, of the magico-religious system as the result of forced conversion to Catholicism. The most important consequence of these transformations was the contraction and decay of anthropomorphic supernaturalism, since it was no longer anchored to an established theological, cosmological, and organizational system of religion as it had been in pre-Hispanic times. Many of the magical practices that had been openly conducted went underground as a result of the active campaigns of the Franciscan friars and other personnel of the Catholic Church to eradicate any pagan elements that could not possibly be accommodated within the practice of Christianity. On the other hand, the magical practices of an essentially secretive, non-public nature went on relatively unchanged insofar as they were on the whole independent of pre-Hispanic organized religion. What we are saying is that sorcery practices probably suffered the most changes compared with the more stable witchcraft system, which by its very nature occupies a more or less fixed ancillary position vis-à-vis organized religion.

The one significant exception to this generalization is the general category of sorcerers designated by López Austin (1967:99) as the *dominadores de los meteoros* or weathermen, the tezitlazcs of contemporary rural Tlaxcala. These basically benevolent supernatural practitioners in pre-Hispanic times, whose public practices and activities involved controlling the weather and curing, probably rather quickly managed to be incorporated into the framework of the evolving local religious hierarchies; and this, of course, is the origin of the *quiatlalpizque*, described as a *rezador* for San Diego Tlalocan in the 1653 document mentioned above. It should be noted, however, that this added role of the forerunner of the tezitlazc does not necessarily constitute a case of syncretism, for the roles of rezador and weatherman appeared to have been kept separate, and this has remained so until today. It is evident, nonetheless, that the useful, benevolent, and highly desired crafts of weathermaking enabled them not only to survive rather unchanged but to come to occupy a significant position in the local ayuntamiento religioso. In a nutshell, the evolution of the anthropomorphic supernatural system during the first one hundred years after the Conquest represents a process of adaptation to the drastic transformation of Tlaxcalan culture and society, from an independent politico-polytheistic system to the folk Catholic system of communities within the framework of colonialism.

The Process of Contraction and Decay (1519–1620)

But how did the process of contraction and decay really proceed? Unfortunately, there is no documentation for the sixteenth century that would enable us to give a precise description of these changes. At a guess, the process was probably as follows. First, as the organizational framework of polytheism was destroyed by the friars and the civil arm of the Spanish government, knowledge of the old religion (essentially its theology and cosmology) began to fade from the people's consciousness, as did the knowledge of the magical system that was somehow ancillary to it. Thus, the highly diversified anthropomorphic supernatural system contracted and decayed; specific supernaturals disappeared completely because the cosmological and theological bases in which they were embedded were no longer there or had been greatly altered; and many of the functions, roles, and activities of specialized supernaturals became concentrated in an increasingly fewer number of them. In this process of shrinking, the most likely candidates for ultimate disappearance were the pre-Hispanic super-naturals that were more connected with the cosmology and practice of poly-theism, or in one way or another symbolically denoted specific gods or their activities, such as the *moyohualitoani* (he who is ready to make love at night), *cihuanotzqui* (he who calls women), *paini* (the messenger), *matlapouhqui* (he who counts through the forearms), *temicnamictiani* (interpreter of dreams), and so on (López Austin 1967:88–107). On the other hand, the practitioners who survived either intact (that is, with the diversified integrity that they had in pre-Hispanic times) or whose roles and activities contracted and became embodied in an increasingly smaller number were basically the anthropomor-phic supernaturals that were the most useful, those whose symbolic, psycho-logical, and sociological content were not affected by forced conversion, whose nature was the most public or the most secretive but independent of the old religion, and whose socioreligious or magical functions had no counterpart in the new religion. To some extent, this hypothesis is corroborated by the three main sources on anthropomorphic supernaturalism for the Central Mexican Highlands during the first half of the seventeenth century (1620–1656): Serna (1953:69–95, 202–13, 267–90) for the valleys of Mexico and Toluca; Ponce de León (1953:375–79) for what is now the state of Hidalgo; and Ruiz de Alarcón (1953:24–32, 49–50, 138–41) for several regions of what are now the states of Guerrero, Morelos, and Puebla. If we assume that mid-seventeenth century Tlaxcala was not significantly different from these Nahuatl-speaking regions of the Central Highlands (and there is no reason to assume otherwise), we can see the significance of these sources. A number of specific anthropomorphic super-naturals are discussed by Serna (1953), Ponce de León (1953), and Ruiz de Alarcón (1953), but the moyohualitoani, cihuanotzqui, paini, matlapouhqui, temicnamictiani, and several other pre-Hispanic supernaturals in this category mentioned above are not present. It is possible that for a number of reasons these scholars were not able to record them, but we rather tend to think that by then they had totally disappeared as independent entities. On the other hand, all the anthropomorphic supernaturals discussed by Serna, Ponce de

León, and Ruiz de Alarcón belong to the second category and fit the classical configuration of the sorcerer and witch.

Second, to the extent that magic cannot be significantly differentiated from the pre-Hispanic polytheistic system, the decay of anthropomorphic supernaturalism during the first one hundred years after the Conquest is tied to the evolution of the priest, as suggested by López Austin (1967:113). Quickly stripped of its social, ritualistic, and ceremonial functions and activities, the rather large priestly class of the old polytheism went underground to escape the imposition of the new religion. It is quite likely that priests became the depositories of certain kinds of magical knowledge that they formerly practiced independently of their main ritual and ceremonial roles such as divination, astrology, and so on—practices that we largely ignore because of the incomplete understanding of the relationship between magic and organized polytheism. Again, there is no information on the transformation and evolution of the priesthood in the post-Conquest period of the sixteenth century. Although priests might, in one way or another, have been incorporated into the nascent ayuntamiento religioso fostered by the Franciscan friars at the local level (Nutini and Bell 1980: 305–20), it seems unlikely. We tend instead to think that the priestly class was mostly obliterated, and what priests remained became essentially practitioners of sorcery—that is, they emphasized magical roles that they may have had in the pre-Hispanic situation and acquired new ones, such as those of weathermen and specialized fortune-tellers. It is also unlikely that the priests-turned-sorcerers were able to retain the high social status that they had had in pre-Hispanic times, given the general leveling of the *pipiltin-macehualtin* (noble-commoner) distinctions at the village level throughout the sixteenth and seventeenth centuries. Finally, it is inconceivable that priests became witches, for it does not make sense to us that an anthropomorphic supernatural would change from an essentially public status to a basically secretive one. Moreover, as discussed, the witchcraft complex, however contracted, survived throughout the sixteenth century relatively unchanged and in a rather stable form.

Third, there is no evidence that throughout the sixteenth century magic in general, and anthropomorphic supernaturalism in particular, underwent a process of syncretism similar to the one undergone by religion in Tlaxcala and many other regions of Mesoamerica. Pre-Hispanic polytheism and Catholicism interacted along the full organizational, theological, ritualistic, and ceremonial spectrum, and by the end of the sixteenth century the religion of Tlaxcalan Indian communities was well on its way to a thoroughly syncretic synthesis (Nutini and Bell 1980:329–31). The same process did not happen in the realm of anthropomorphic supernaturalism because there was no significant European-Spanish counterpart to the pre-Hispanic magical system; nor were there

any significant African elements that could have affected a syncretic or acculturative situation. The reasons for this somewhat peculiar situation have been
discussed, namely, the isolation and close control maintained by the friars in
local communities. Whether this can be generalized to other regions of Mesoamerica converted and catechized by the mendicant orders we do not know,
but probably it can. In any event, the changes of contraction and decay that
pre-Hispanic magic in general and anthropomorphic supernaturalism in particular underwent for the first 100 years after the Conquest were not due to
syncretism, acculturation, or diffusion. Rather, they were internal changes
brought about by the demise of the old polytheistic religion, adaptation of
Tlaxcalan culture and society to the Colonial situation, and the increasing dis-
tancing between magic and religion.

Reinvigoration, Diffusion, and Growth (1620–1720)

It was in the second one hundred years after the onset of Colonial times that
anthropomorphic supernaturalism in rural Tlaxcala became the syncretic complex that still exists today. By the end of this period, anthropomorphic supernaturalism had acquired its intrinsic configuration, for as far as it can be determined, it remained essentially the same until a generation ago, or at least until
Starr (1900) described it for the first time at the turn of the twentieth century.
Moreover, there is no available published documentation for the Central Mexican Highlands for the eighteenth and nineteenth centuries that might throw
some light on this supernatural complex in rural Tlaxcala. In a sense this could
be interpreted as the crystallization of anthropomorphic supernaturalism as an
ancillary and largely sub rosa system to the folk religion of rural Tlaxcala,
which by the end of the seventeenth century had also become fully syncretized.
One way or another, it can be assumed that by the second decade of the eighteenth century, anthropomorphic supernaturalism and the folk-supernatural
complex had become stable and largely static components of the global magico-
religious system of rural Tlaxcala.

Let us take the four contemporary anthropomorphic supernaturals in rural
Tlaxcala and determine their antecedents and syncretic components throughout the period in question. The tezitlazc and the nahual are the most straight-
forward, and their development can be most easily understood. The reason for
this is simple: strictly speaking, these supernaturals do not have Spanish counterparts. This is especially true with the tezitlazc, and slightly less with the
nahual as a transforming trickster. For the period shortly before 1640, Serna
(1953:69, 77–81) provides us with a general picture of the tezitlazc for the
community of San Mateo Texcaliacac near Tenancingo (Valley of Toluca, Sierra
de Calimaya). (Ponce de León [1953:379] gives a similar but shorter description

of the tezitlazc for roughly the same period, in which the weatherman in the region of Tzumpahuacan is known locally by the term *teciuhpauhque.*) Serna's description is astonishingly similar to the position of the tezitlazc in the average rural Tlaxcalan community today with respect to its functions, activities, incidence per locality, and so on. Only the details have changed, and these modifications are not due to any significant transformations but rather to added functions and activities that probably came to enrich the basic configuration of the tezitlazc. Whatever transformations the tezitlazc underwent from the Conquest to the time of Serna's description may be conceptualized as a process of contraction and adaptation: contraction of functions, activities, and roles through which it emerges as an integrated anthropomorphic supernatural out of the differentiated *dominadores de los meteoros* (López Austin 1967:99–100) of pre-Hispanic times; adaptation of the emerging supernatural practitioner (with manifold functions of weatherman, prayer leader, and curer of sorts) to the constraints of Catholic religion.

The case of the nahual is not so clear as that of the tezitlazc. As a transforming trickster, the contemporary nahual partakes of some of the attributes of the witch, but at the same time it is something else that does not connote the loathsome and abhorrent characteristics and activities generally associated with the witch. Whether the pre-Hispanic nahualli was a trickster of sorts it is not certain, for the documented evidence is inconclusive. On the whole, however, López Austin's (1967:95–99) description of this anthropomorphic supernatural must be accepted as basically correct, except perhaps that its craft could either be benevolent or malevolent to human existence—that is, that he could function either as a practitioner of white or black magic at will. If this is the case, the nahualli described by Serna (1953:90–91, 203–6)—information largely repeated from Ruiz de Alarcón (1953:24, 27–28)—had undergone some significant transformations, mostly along the lines of specialization and contraction; that is, this supernatural no longer had the manifold functions and activities that it had in its original setting. Again, it is difficult to say how complete the information of these two scholars was, and it is quite possible that the nahualli may have retained other functions and activities that they do not describe. It is possible, however, that the picture of the nahualli given by Serna and Ruiz de Alarcón for the first half of the seventeenth century is accurate and that this supernatural had indeed contracted and become more specialized.

But did the nahualli undergo changes other than those due to the processes of contraction and specialization mentioned above during this 100-year period? Was it affected by any kind of diffusion, acculturation, or syncretism? We do not think so, but Ruiz de Alarcón (1953:27–28) suggests otherwise. He describes the differences between the *brujos nahualles* (as he calls witches) of

Mexico and Spain and, in passing, presents some interesting comparisons. Ruiz de Alarcón (1953:27) goes on to say that the powers of animal transformation and evildoing are acquired by the nahualli at birth, by its parents making a "pacto con el demonio" (compact with the Christian devil). We think that Ruiz de Alarcón was simply projecting his own European conception of some of the attributes of the witch. Although our contention cannot be proved, Ruiz de Alarcón's description would gain credence if some of its elements had survived until the present. At least for rural Tlaxcala, nothing of the sort has survived, and nahualism has nothing to do with the devil or any other Christian supernaturals (see Aguirre Beltrán 1963:111). Finally, when we compare Serna's and Ruiz de Alarcón's descriptions of the nahualli and the contemporary nahual in rural Tlaxcala, the differences are minimal, and the basic attributes and ideology of the animal-transforming complex are the same. As contrasted with the tezitlazc, however, the evolution of the nahual from the Conquest to the present has little to do with the processes of acculturation undergone by the folk Catholicism that came to dominate the religious life of rural Tlaxcala. As an essentially public supernatural, the tezitlazc came to be partly incorporated into the fabric of the evolving folk religion; such an incorporation was impossible with the nahual because of its secretive nature and actions independent of ordinary people. It should be pointed out, however, that the nahual and, by extension, the tlahuelpuchi today represent more of a process of convergence than meets the eye. This suggestion is made by Aguirre Beltrán (1963:110–14) when he equates nahual and *familiar* and points out a number of similarities between European and pre-Hispanic witches. If this process of convergence did not necessarily take place at the local Indian level, it most certainly obtained at the wider, Mestizo level throughout Colonial times.

In conclusion, the nahual and, especially, the tezitlazc in rural Tlaxcala exhibit a remarkable degree of continuity from the Conquest to the present. Their general form, their attributes, and their position within the fabric of local culture and society have not changed essentially in 450 years. The ideology of these anthropomorphic supernaturals has remained constant, and, although their structure has changed in terms of contraction, expansion, and adaptation, their basic configuration has remained the same. The tezitlazc today may have incorporated non-indigenous new roles but it still remains basically a weatherman, whereas the nahual may employ some non-indigenous elements in its craft but it remains essentially a transforming trickster.

As prototypes of the sorcerer and witch, respectively, the contemporary tetlachihuic and tlahuelpuchi present quite a different problem. Basically these two supernaturals have been strongly subjected to all the processes that were mini-

mally and mildly significant in the evolution of the tezitlazc and nahual: syncretism, acculturation, and diffusion. Another important variable is that the
tetlachihuic and tlahuelpuchi did have specific counterparts in the European
sorcerer and witch. In addition, there were magical elements of African origin
that diffused from the large black slave populations that were brought to the
coastal regions of the Gulf of Mexico and to many provinces of Central Mexico
(primarily in the archbishopric of Mexico and the bishopric of Tlaxcala-Puebla)
beginning in the middle of the sixteenth century and continuing without interruption until the middle of the seventeenth century (Aguirre Beltrán 1946:
199–222). These elements affected primarily the evolution of the sorcery complex but hardly affected the practice of witchcraft. On the other hand, there
were specific European witchcraft elements that either reinforced already existing practices in the native system or added a new dimension to it. In the
discussion of López Austin's (1966, 1967) reconstruction of pre-Hispanic anthropomorphic supernaturalism, we segregated the general category of the tlatlacatecolo into sorcerers and witches. This large roster of specialized sorcerers
and witches appeared to have dwindled significantly by the early decades of the
seventeenth century, as has already been discussed. It is out of this diminished
sorcery-witchcraft complex that the roles of the contemporary tetlachihuic and
tlahuelpuchi in rural Tlaxcala are further contracted but, at the same time,
amplified by the acquisition of roles from other supernaturals and by a process
of syncretism that contributes significant new elements and practices of European origin. With the rather scanty historical documentation available, we can
give a brief outline of the processes and elements involved.

Of all four anthropomorphic supernaturals in rural Tlaxcala it is the tetlachihuic that has unquestionably undergone the greatest range of changes since
the Conquest, and these changes can be traced mostly to the second century of
Colonial times. Unfortunately, the process of syncretism that took place can
only be inferred, for, other than the sources cited above, we have found very
little that would enable us to give a definitive account of this process. But that
there was a significant process of syncretism cannot be doubted, and it began
when European elements of sorcery began to filter down to local communities,
probably at the beginning of the seventeenth century. Two kinds of elements
and practices of European origin came to interact and amalgamate with counterparts of pre-Hispanic origin: (1) new ones that found an appropriate niche
in the organization of black and white magic; (2) those that came to reinforce
already existing ones in the native magic system. In the first category are
potions, poultices, ritual incantations, imitative techniques, and the use of
ritual prayers that came to enrich the manipulative complex of Tlaxcalan sorcer-

ers, which had become significantly depleted since pre-Hispanic times. Again, we are extrapolating from the contemporary situation, for it is evident that many of the practices and manipulations of the contemporary tetlachihuic are of definite European origin but smoothly integrated into the aboriginal system. As an example of the second practice of European origin, amatory magic immediately comes to mind. There is no question that amatory magic was present both in Europe and in Mesoamerica and the sources reinforced each other in the role of the emerging tetlachihuic as a dispenser of amulets and talismans with the power to bend the desired person's will (Aguirre Beltrán 1963:165).

The exact provenance of these eventually syncretized elements and practices is hard to determine, but they probably came from the increasing contact of local Indian populations with the urban centers of the region, particularly with the city of Puebla, where we know that there was a well-established barrio of Tlaxcalan Indians by the end of the sixteenth century and that this Indian population shuttled back and forth to the city from Tlaxcalan communities (Marín Tamayo 1960). We also know that between 1590 and 1630 a number of Spaniards and Mestizo men and women from both Puebla and Tlaxcala were brought before the Inquisition on charges of sorcery. In the depositions of several of these inquisitorial trials it is stated that the accused practitioners of sorcery consorted with the lowest elements of the city of Puebla, that several were itinerant vendors in rural Tlaxcala, and that they constituted a serious danger to the spiritual life of the Indians (Solange Behocaray de Alberro, personal communication). The conditions at the time were propitious for this kind of diffusion and eventual syncretism of Spanish and Indian elements of sorcery and related practices. With the Franciscan friars out or on the way out of rigid control over Indian communities, and with the lack of control and often the indifference of the replacing secular clergy for their local flocks, these European magical elements must surely have found easy acceptance and internalization in countless Tlaxcalan communities. It goes without saying that similar conditions were present in several other regions of Mesoamerica in the seventeenth century and that they eventually resulted in variants of the anthropomorphic supernaturalism present in rural Tlaxcala today.

Another significant contribution to the general configuration of the tetlachihuic's craft came from black slaves of African origin (Szewczyk n.d.:137–53). By the early decades of the seventeenth century there were large numbers of black slaves settled in the coastal areas of central Veracruz and as far inland as the cities of Orizaba and Jalapa. A number of blacks also settled in the city of Puebla, Tepeaca, and possibly other cities and towns in the eastern Central Highlands. It is probably from these populations that several sorcery elements and practices diffused to rural Tlaxcala (Aguirre Beltrán 1946:209–14). We also know of another possible source of diffusion: several black slaves from Tlaxcala were brought before the Inquisition in the city of Puebla on charges of sorcery similar to those leveled against Spaniards, Mestizos, and Mulattoes (Solange Behocaray de Alberro, personal communication). Again, there is no question that the contemporary craft of the tetlachihuic in rural Tlaxcala exhibits a number of elements and practices that are of distinct African origin (Aguirre Beltrán 1946:162–66; 1963:55–72). What is not known, unfortunately, is whether these African elements and practices came to enrich or to reinforce already existing elements and practices in the pre-Hispanic complex. It is uncertain, for example, whether many of the sympathetic, homeopathic, and contagious practices exhibited in the contemporary tetlachihuic's craft were used by pre-Hispanic sorcerers. Of these possibilities, sympathetic techniques are the ones most probably used, as in the case of the *tepan mizoni* (he who bleeds on people) when it let its malevolent blood drop on the effigy of a person to be injured (López Austin 1967:91). Whatever the preexisting practices, it is important to realize that the sympathetic, homeopathic, and contagious techniques of African provenance came to invigorate a sorcery system that had contracted and had probably lost a significant amount of its original strength and diversity. Contemporary practices of the tetlachihuic in rural Tlaxcala — such as the ritual manipulation of images, the symbolic replication of people's behavior, and the performance of contagious rites and incantations — are very similar in structure and function to those of the black population of Haiti described by Herskovits (1964:219–50). It is thus clear that, regardless of what the pre-Hispanic sorcery complex of the Central Mexican Highlands included in the way of ritual and manipulative techniques, the sympathetic-homeo-pathic-contagious complex of African origin outlined here is of more recent origin and has permanently colored the practice of sorcery in rural Tlaxcala.

What can be said about the actual contraction and the specific anthropomorphic supernaturals that were present in the seventeenth century after more than one hundred years of Spanish domination? Again, the only reliable and concrete information is the work of the three scholars cited above, but analysis of this work is illuminating. What they have to say for a number of communities and regions in the Central Highlands from approximately 1620 to about 1660 can probably be generalized for the Nahuatl area throughout the seventeenth century. First, it is difficult to determine how exhaustive these sources are, and even Ruiz de Alarcón (1953), the most detailed of the three, presents us perhaps with little more than an outline of the range of actual supernaturals in operation at the time. In light of the difficulty, even today, of eliciting reliable information on anthropomorphic supernaturalism, it is likely that there were more supernaturals in the average Nahuatl community in the Central Highlands than these scholars recorded.

Second, of the general categories of pre-Hispanic supernaturals that López Austin (1967:88–95, 101–7) designates as tlatlacatecolo and tlaciuhque, there are approximately sixteen that can be categorized as sorcerers—that is, as practitioners who, discounting those that fell under the general category of weathermen, were in one way or another public individuals for hire or consultation for a variety of supernatural activities and occasions. By the middle of the seventeenth century only three are mentioned by Serna (1953:69, 92, 211): and Ruiz de Alarcón (1953:27, 30, 50) repeats one of Serna's (tetlachihuiani) and adds three more—*matlapouhqui, tlaolximiani,* and *tlachixqui.* Linguistically, the names of these supernaturals had changed significantly in 100 years, and only three (tonalpouhqui, matlapouhqui, and tlaolximiani) retained their original spelling. The linguistic structure of the other supernaturals, however, fairly clearly denotes the activity of the practitioners, and from this viewpoint can be seen the contracted continuity of sorcery from the more diversified context of the pre-Hispanic tlatlacatecolo and teciuhque.

Third, it is, of course, impossible to tell whether these seven kinds of sorcerers were present in all or most communities in the Central Highlands throughout the seventeenth century. But neither can we generalize about the distribution of the forty magos described by López Austin (1967) for pre-Hispanic times, because the information upon which this reconstruction is based comes from several Nahuatl-speaking areas and the picture is therefore a composite. In any event, it is our contention that the modern tetlachihuic in rural Tlaxcala represents a further contraction of the situation described by the above cited scholars and that probably by the first two decades of the eighteenth century it had acquired the form in which we know it today.

The tlahuelpuchi had also undergone a significant process of syncretism, and, in overall changes and transformations since the Conquest, it ranks a close second behind the tetlachihuic. As in the case of the tetlachihuic, the process of syncretism of the tlahuelpuchi can only be inferred, and all the constraints already discussed apply here also. It must be added, however, that for the tlahuelpuchi it is even more difficult to envisage the process of syncretism throughout the seventeenth century that permanently marked the configuration of this supernatural and, by extension, even riskier to extrapolate from the contemporary situation. But there are certain generalizations that can be made about the evolution of the witch, from the contemporary structure of the tlahuelpuchi. When we analyze the context, form, and ideology of the tlahuelpuchi in rural Tlaxcala today, we are struck by the fact that it is a very specialized anthropomorphic supernatural. Primarily, it is a bloodsucking witch; it does have other attributes and functions in a number of contexts, but in the people's consciousness it is essentially a malevolent, abhorrent supernatural whose principal function is to suck the blood of infants. Analysis of the concept of the witch in pre-Hispanic times shows that it was a more diversified supernatural, as exemplified by the four practitioners among the tlatlacatecolo classified as witches. These supernaturals are, to be sure, conceived of as cannibals specialized in eating different parts of the body, but they also undertake activities having to do with sexual seduction, stealing, and other evil activities. Some of these elements and activities are latently present in the contemporary tlahuelpuchi, and others are part of the configuration of the nahual but devoid of their essentially malevolent characteristics. Perhaps more significantly, the pre-Hispanic ancestors of the tlahuelpuchi appeared not to have been thought of as inherently hateful, abhorrent, and dreadful, and as the personification of evil that the tlahuelpuchi is today. Why this was not so is impossible to determine for certain. The sources are not detailed enough on the intrinsic nature of witchcraft and its relationship to organized polytheism, but this apparent trait of the complex was probably related to the pronounced emphasis on ritual cannibalism and obsession with human sacrifices. Given these antecedents, it seems that the origin of today's totally negative and repellent conception of the tlahuelpuchi is of European origin and probably constitutes the single most important syncretic element in its contemporary configuration. The European conception of the witch, as an evil and hateful creature whose powers derived primarily from the Christian devil, found a willing receptacle in the syncretic emerging of the tlahuelpuchi; in time it came to be strongly magnified, as human sacrifices and ritual cannibalism disappeared and this supernatural became a bloodsucking witch preying on infants, the most vulnerable of human beings.

We do not detect anything of particularly African origin in the contemporary tlahuelpuchi, and the process of syncretism that went on involved the interaction of only the pre-Hispanic and European witchcraft complexes. The analysis of the tlahuelpuchi in contemporary rutal Tlaxcala shows a number of elements and traits of European origin. We say European, and not exclusively Spanish, because the concept of the witch seems to have been quite generalized and uniform throughout Western Europe by the sixteenth century. For example, elements and practices such as the tlahuelpuchi's limited conventicles, the deterrent effect of odoriferous substances, the insatiable compulsion of the tlahuelpuchi to suck the blood of human beings at least once a month, and so on, are definitely of European origin. Indeed, we can make a good case for regarding the contemporary tlahuelpuchi, considered exclusively as a bloodsucking witch, as a syncretic complex in which the witchcraft cannibalism of pre-Hispanic times was reinforced by a kind of European vampirism, in which the basic structural attributes of the witch are contracted and molded on the basis of the specialized configuration of the vampire. In such a syncretic situation, the structural contexts in interaction change and amalgamate, while the ideology of the emerging tlahuelpuchi remains essentially indigenous and its position within the total configuration of anthropomorphic supernaturalism remains essentially pre-Hispanic.

Just as in the case of the tetlachihuic, the emerging tlahuelpuchi experienced a significant process of contraction out of the diversified pre-Hispanic context during the first one hundred years of Colonial life. Of the four supernaturals in the general category of tlatlacatecolo (López Austin 1967:92–95) classified as variants of the witch for pre-Hispanic times, only one, the *teyollocuane* or *teyollocuani* or texoxqui mentioned by Serna (1953:92) and Ruiz de Alarcón (1953:27), had apparently survived as an independent practitioner by the first half of the seventeenth century. Ruiz de Alarcón (1953:27), however, does mention the brujos nahualles, but we have rather regarded them as forerunners of the nahual—that is, as kinds of witches that are essentially non-malevolent tricksters. The fact that, of the four tlatlacatecolo classified as witches, only the teyollocuani survived as an independent practitioner is significant, for it embodies and personifies the bloody and cannibalistic activities out of which the modern tlahuelpuchi must have emerged. At the same time, the tlahuelpuchi inherited the basic properties of at least two of the other three tlatlacatecolo witches: from the mometzcopinqui the separation of the lower limbs as a rite of intensification; and from the tlahuipuchtli (to which the tlahuelpuchi is most closely related linguistically) the luminosity that it exhibits in its animal form. As was indicated, the sexual connotations of the fourth supernatural in this category, the moyohualitoani, became rather embodied in the emerging nahual. Thus, just as in the case of the tetlachihuic, the tlahuelpuchi evolved from pre-Hispanic times to the present by a process of contraction in terms of specialization, but coupled with increasing role diversification by drawing from most pre-Hispanic variants of the witch as well as by syncretic borrowings.

Crystallization of the Syncretic Process
In the foregoing paragraphs we discussed the seventeenth century as a key period in understanding the historical evolution of anthropomorphic supernaturalism in rural Tlaxcala and as the period in which the syncretic process that affected this complex had its strongest effect. In a number of contexts it was emphasized that by the first two decades of the eighteenth century the four anthropomorphic supernaturals had been configurated and that they retained

their basic structure and functions until after the onset of the twentieth century, when the processes of modernization and secularization began to have a differential effect on rural Tlaxcalan communities. In the intervening two hundred years, there were changes and transformations, to be sure, but a thorough analysis of the contemporary ethnography of anthropomorphic supernaturalism indicates that they were not very significant.

There is a final piece of ethnohistorical evidence that demonstrates the continuity of anthropomorphic supernaturalism in particular, and magico-religious beliefs and practices in general, since the middle of the seventeenth century: a large number of rites, ceremonies, and activities described by the scholars cited above are still practiced in rural Tlaxcala, in many cases almost identically. This continuity confirms the seventeenth century as the key period when the contemporary magico-religious system of rural Tlaxcala (and, by extension, many other regions of the Central Mexican Highlands) was syncretically forged. The most notable of these features are the following: the ceremony of smearing the four corners of the building with turkey blood upon the handseling of a new house (Serna 1953:77); the childbirth ceremony of blessing the fire (*tecuixtli-liztli*) (Serna 1953:77); beliefs and practices about the phases of the moon and the belly button and placenta upon childbirth (Serna 1953:214); beliefs and practices about twinning and the *temazcal* (Serna 1953:216–17); rites and ceremonies concerning the agricultural cycle (Ponce de León 1953:375); cleansing rites to counteract the effects of *espanto* (Ponce de León 1953:379); the use of clay figurines in the *cuezcomate* as an intensifying element (Ruiz de Alarcón 1953:32); ceremonies undertaken to return the soul to the body (Ruiz de Alarcón 1953:138–41); and so on. The continuity of these beliefs and practices also indicates that this magico-religious complex was widely, and probably quite uniformly, distributed throughout the Nahuatl area in the seventeenth century.

In conclusion, the four anthropomorphic supernaturals of rural Tlaxcala today represent a contracted complex that evolved out of a highly diversified pre-Hispanic complex. But each of these four contemporary supernaturals is a composite manifold that includes elements, attributes, and practices from at least three pre-Hispanic counterparts, so that a significant part of pre-Hispanic anthropomorphic supernaturalism has survived. The two most important processes by which anthropomorphic supernaturalism evolved have been diffusion and syncretism: diffusion mainly from an African complex brought to the New World by black slaves; and syncretism between the witchcraft-sorcery complexes of European and pre-Hispanic origins. The process of diffusion affects almost exclusively the tetlachihuic, whereas the process of syncretism affects primarily the tlahuelpuchi, nahual, and tetlachihuic; the tezitlazc is little affected by these processes. Thus, the changes that these four supernaturals have undergone since the Conquest may be scaled as follows: The least changed is the tezitlazc, and whatever changes it underwent were mainly by diffusion of specific manipulative techniques of European origin. The next least changed is the nahual, and the changes this supernatural experienced are both by diffusion of specific manipulative techniques and some syncretic witchcraft components, both of European origin. The tlahuelpuchi has changed significantly more than the nahual but in the same fashion, especially in the syncretic confluence of witchcraft cannibalism of pre-Hispanic origin and European vampirism. The tetlachihuic is the supernatural that has changed the most, by the diffusion of manipulative techniques of African origin as well as by syncretic interaction with European techniques and elements.

Finally, it should be emphasized that the process of syncretism that has affected the evolution of anthropomorphic supernaturalism in rural Tlaxcala since the Conquest has been skewed. The process of syncretism that shaped the formation of folk Catholicism in rural Tlaxcala affected both the structure and ideology of the religious system that had fully crystallized by the end of the seventeenth century and has remained constant since then (Nutini and Bell 1980:297–331). In such a context, the folk religion of rural Tlaxcala today is essentially Catholic but laden with pre-Hispanic elements, both in structure and ideology. The situation is more or less the opposite with respect to anthropomorphic supernaturalism in particular and the magical system in general, in which syncretism took place primarily in the structural domain, whereas the ideological domain, the belief system, remained relatively untouched. Thus, anthropomorphic supernaturalism in rural Tlaxcala is only structurally syncretic, essentially pre-Hispanic, but laden with a number of Catholic, European, and African elements.

The Comparative Distribution and Definition of Witchcraft and Sorcery in Mesoamerica

DISTRIBUTIONAL OUTLINE OF WITCHCRAFT AND SORCERY IN THE NAHUATL-SPEAKING AREAS AND MESOAMERICA AT LARGE

The distribution of anthropomorphic supernaturalism in Mesoamerica poses some problems of immediate significance. The first problem that we are faced with is a lack of adequate comparative information. Neither a single monograph on a specific complex nor a general survey of Mesoamerican non-Catholic supernaturalism has been written. A few articles (Foster 1944; Wisdom 1952; Kaplan 1956; Nash 1960; Saler 1964) contain good piecemeal information on specific supernatural complexes, including witchcraft, sorcery, nahualism, and related phenomena. In addition, the average monographic publication (that is, the so-called village study) includes a few paragraphs, sometimes an entire section, on the structure or nature of non-Catholic supernaturalism, and with a few exceptions (Parsons 1936; Madsen 1960; Vogt 1969), adequate descriptions and analysis of local non-Catholic supernatural practices. Also, a number of popular accounts of anthropomorphic supernaturalism are not considered in this analysis (see Castiglioni 1972; Olavarrieta Marenco 1977; Barba de Piña Chan 1980; Scheffler 1983). Mesoamerican ethnography indicates that in the great majority of Indian communities and in many rural Mestizo communities, non-Catholic beliefs and practices, including various forms and manifestations of the four supernaturals discussed in this monograph, are still an important functional aspect of local culture and society. Mesoamerican ethnography does not offer a comprehensive picture of the depth, extent, and variation of the sometimes large rosters of anthropomorphic and non-anthropomorphic supernaturals, their social and psychological context, and the way in which they are ideologically related to the mainstream of Catholicism and the social structure. However, with the information available, it is possible to give a distributional outline of witchcraft, sorcery, nahualism, and weathermaking.

In the Tlaxcala-Pueblan Valley, the anthropomorphic supernatural complex described in this monograph is nearly universal. There are variations, to be sure, but in both Indian and rural Mestizo communities, we find the presence of at least two supernaturals. In the Tlaxcalan part of the valley, about 75 percent of the communities exhibit beliefs and practices concerning all four supernaturals, whereas 25 percent exhibit them concerning only three, and in a handful of the most secularized communities, exhibit them concerning only two. The nahual and tetlachihuic are found in nearly all rural Tlaxcalan communities, whereas the tlahuelpuchi and tezitlazc are present in perhaps 75 percent of the settlements. In the Pueblan part of the valley, the situation is slightly different in that both Indian and rural Mestizo communities are on the whole more secularized than those in Tlaxcala. The distribution of supernaturals per community is pretty much the same, but the percentages given above are also slightly less for the Pueblan part of the valley. But regardless of degree and intensity of distribution, what remains constant throughout the entire Tlaxcala-Pueblan Valley is the basic structure and nature of all four supernaturals and their ideological position with respect of the folk religion.

As we move from the Tlaxcala-Pueblan Valley to other Nahuatl and Nahuat-speaking areas of central Mexico, the Sierra de Puebla manifests anthropomorphic supernaturalism closest to that of rural Tlaxcala. However, there are a few significant differences. First, the tezitlazc does not exist as a separate supernatural; rather, sorcerers play the role of weathermen and have more or less the same powers to conjure the natural elements as the tezitlazc has in rural Tlaxcala. The other three supernaturals have essentially the same nature and attributes as those described here. The *nahual* is known by the same term, whereas the *tetlachihuic* and the *tlahuelpuchi* are known respectively by the following terms: *tlachihke, tetlachihke,* or *tlamatique; tlahuelpoche* or *tlamaine*. It is interesting to note that all these terms for sorcerer and witch have fairly similar Nahuatl glosses in Molina's 1944 dictionary. Second, the non-Catholic supernatural complex of the Sierra de Puebla is significantly more animistic than that of the Tlaxcala-Pueblan Valley—that is, there is more emphasis on non-anthropomorphic supernaturalism. Soul loss, many varieties of *mal aire* or *yeyecatl,* and a host of active, non-material spirits are the most constant and significant supernaturals in the community life of the Sierra de Puebla (Montoya Briones 1964: 153–79), whereas anthropomorphic supernaturals are not so distinct and clearly delineated as in the Tlaxcala-Pueblan Valley, nor are they so high in incidence and intensity. The Tlaxcala-Pueblan Valley is significantly more secularized than the Sierra de Puebla and yet the richness, elaboration, and neatness of both anthropomorphic and non-anthropomorphic supernaturalism is greater in the former than in the latter. In a way, this is a baffling phenomenon for which we have no explanation, but it probably has to do with the always marginal position, in both pre-Hispanic and post-Conquest times, of Sierra de Puebla in relation to the heartland of the Nahuatl-speaking peoples of central Mexico (Nutini and Isaac 1974:361–66). (Shortly after this manuscript was submitted for publication, an excellent book by Signorini and Lupo [1989] on magic supernaturalism in a Sierra de Puebla community was published. The reader is urged to consult this work.)

The Córdoba-Orizaba region and its environs, from the southeastern slopes of the Citlaltepetl (Orizaba) volcano to the Sierra de Zongolica and toward the coastal plains of Veracruz, is another important Nahuatl-speaking area. Here again, we find the presence of substantially the same complex described in this monograph but with an even less elaborate form and richness than that in the Sierra de Puebla. The omnipresent *nahual* is known by the same term; the *tetlachihuic* is known by the terms *tuxtlachic* or *tetlachinec*; while the *tlahuelpuchi* is known as *tlahulpochi* or *tlahuapochin*. What was said about the Sierra de Puebla in comparison with the Tlaxcala-Pueblan Valley also applies here, and it needs to be explained. For example, even in wholly Indian, almost entirely Nahuatl monolingual communities in the Sierra de Zongolica or on the slopes of Citlaltepetl, one does not find the precise and neat picture of anthropomorphic supernaturalism embedded in a complex and diversified legendary system (Nutini and Forbes n.d.) that one finds in rural Tlaxcala.

So far the three Nahuatl and Nahuat areas where Nutini has personally conducted several regional surveys have been discussed. Passing to the Nahuatl areas of the Valley of Mexico and Morelos, we must rely almost exclusively on public ethnographic sources. In the Valley of Mexico and its environs, the situation appears to be essentially the same as that described for the Tlaxcala-Pueblan Valley but with a degree of intensity and elaboration roughly the same as that of the Córdoba-Orizaba region. One significant difference here is that, with the exception of the term *nahual* for transforming trickster or witch, the other Nahuatl terms for weatherman, sorcerer, and witch have nearly disappeared. Madsen (1960:202) mentions the term *tlacique* for what he calls the vampire witch, evidently the *tlahuelpuchi* of the Tlaxcala-Pueblan Valley. In the community of Chiautla near Texcoco, Nutini encountered nearly the same term, *tlaciuhque*, but it was employed locally for sorcerer or *tetlachihuic* in rural Tlaxcala. This leads us to believe that Madsen is mistaken, and his *tlacique* (*tachihke* in the Sierra de Puebla) is really the Nahuatl term for *tetlachihuic*, not *tlahuelpuchi*. We assume, of course, that the structure of anthropomorphic supernaturalism is essentially the same in the Valley of Mexico and in the Tlaxcala-Pueblan Valley, which is a reasonable assumption, to say the least, given the same pre-Hispanic background and a similar Colonial development for the two regions. Again, as in the Nahuatl and Nahuat areas described above, in the Valley of Mexico the tezitlazc seems to have disappeared as an independent, individualized supernatural and is embodied in the concept of the sorcerer. Be this as it may, Madsen's monograph on the community of San Francisco Tacospa (1960:193–207) is the only source containing fairly detailed information about witchcraft and sorcery in the region. Madsen describes what are essentially the concepts of nahual, tetlachihuic, and tlahuelpuchi as they are found in rural Tlaxcala, but in an otherwise informative chapter on these supernaturals, he does not distinguish between sorcerer and witch, and even the nahual is not clearly described. In fact, there is a significant degree of confusion among these three supernaturals, and there is not enough information to judge whether the people are unclear about the nature of these entities or Madsen simply did not analyze the situation correctly. However, an attentive, between-the-lines reading of Madsen's description leaves no doubts that anthropomorphic supernaturalism in Tecospa, regardless of the terminological difference, is fundamentally the same as that of the Tlaxcala-Pueblan Valley; it is less neatly structured, to be sure, but has the same basic attributes. As far as we can tell, it is impossible to generalize for the entire Valley of Mexico and its environs on the basis of Tecospa, but if this community constitutes an adequate common regional denominator, then the Valley of Mexico is not too different from the Tlaxcala-Pueblan Valley in the intensity and distribution of anthropomorphic supernaturalism. In the Morelos area, on the other hand, the information on the subject is apparently poorer, and we can only generalize on the basis of Tepoztlán. Lewis (1951:279–81) ascertains the presence of sorcery, witchcraft, and nahualism, but barely tells us about the nature of sorcerers, witches, and nahuales. In the absence of more pertinent information, insofar as we are aware, we can tentatively say that the nature of anthropomorphic supernaturalism in Morelos is basically the same as that of the Valley of Mexico.

We do not have any information about the last important Nahuatl-speaking region, namely, the state of Guerrero; but here again we can assume that it is not significantly different from the regions discussed above. In summary then, the distribution of anthropomorphic supernaturalism in the Nahuatl and Nahuat-speaking areas of central Mexico exhibit a rather high common denominator. This is of course a natural development, given the fact that the distribution of pre-Hispanic populations has not changed since the Conquest, and it is in the general domain of religion and the supernatural that the peoples of central Mexico exhibited the highest degree of uniformity. Nonetheless, it is of historical interest to account for regional variations such as why, in the Tlaxcala-Pueblan Valley (one of the most acculturated of the Nahuatl-speaking regions), the linguistic, cultural, and magical nature and structure of anthropomorphic supernaturalism has survived with the highest numbers of pre-Hispanic elements.

Beyond the Nahuatl and Nahuat-speaking areas of central Mexico the complex of anthropomorphic supernaturals described in this monograph has a wide distribution in Mesoamerica. The nahual is the most universally distributed supernatural in most community studies (Tax 1952; Adams and Rubel 1967; Madsen 1967; Tranfo 1974; Scheffler 1983) and a number of specialized articles (Foster 1944; Villa Rojas 1947; Saler 1964) present a series of slight variations of the general theme of the transforming trickster or witch. Foster's (1944) study of nahualism in Mexico and Guatemala is a very good account of this concept and the only specialized article dealing both ethnographically and ethnohistorically with a non-Catholic supernatural. The practitioners embodied in the rural Tlaxcalan tezitlazc, weathermen, are the least commonly distributed independent individualized supernaturals in Mesoamerica. Just as in the case of the Nahuatl- and Nahuat-speaking regions outside the Tlaxcala-Pueblan Valley, the powers of conjuring the natural elements and other associated practices are more often embodied either in rather Catholic practices (ringing bells, praying to San Lorenzo and San Isidro, firing rockets, and so on) or in other more inclusive practitioners such as sorcerers or shamans.

In between the nahual and the tezitlazc we find a distributional melange of sorcery and witchcraft and its varied practitioners. In all regions of Mexico and Guatemala and in practically every Indian community and a considerable number of rural Mestizo communities we find the presence of a significant variety of sorcerers and witches, sometimes known by the local Indian language term, and often by the Spanish terms *hechicero(a)* and *brujo(a)*. Comparative knowledge about these two supernaturals is the weakest. There is a fundamental confusion concerning the concepts of sorcerer and witch that renders the comparative study of these concepts very difficult. Whether one holds that sorcery and witchcraft are discrete concepts standing for different phenomena or that they are merely convenient labels for denoting basically similar or impossible to disentangle psycho-social phenomena, the published literature for Mesoamerica is never clear, detailed, or systematic enough for the reader to assess the local nature of the sorcerer and/or witch. In a considerable number of cases the terms *sorcerer* and *witch* are used interchangeably (Madsen 1969; Harvey and Kelly 1969); in others (Ravicz and Romney 1969; Weitlaner 1969) a conceptual attempt is made to distinguish sorcery from witchcraft, but it is not followed through substantively. In the majority of cases there is nothing but confusion. In summary, one is never sure whether the confusion and lack of discreteness of sorcerer and witch is the result of local emic categories or of the indiscriminate etic categories that anthropologists bring to bear upon a particular situation. Thus, it seems that a comparative study of sorcery and witchcraft in Mesoamerica must start with at least an operational definition of these concepts, which will permit the establishment of the basis for comparison. In any event, sorcery and witchcraft are common in Mesoamerican Indian and rural Mestizo communities. Whether as individualized, discrete supernatural practitioners or as embodying miscellaneous beliefs and practices, they play a significant role in the life of the community.

A SAMPLE ANALYSIS OF THE MESOAMERICAN LITERATURE ON WITCHCRAFT AND SORCERY

The published literature on anthropomorphic supernaturalism in Mesoamerica, witchcraft and sorcery if you will, is unquestionably deficient. It suffers from a lack of good descriptions and comprehensive analyses that would lay bare the nature, distribution, and fundamental attributes of a rather extensive complex of supernaturals that are known to be present in Mesoamerican Indian communities and sometimes in Mestizo communities. For example, volumes 7 and 8 of the *Handbook of Middle American Indians* (Wauchope 1971) contain very little information describing and analyzing witchcraft, sorcery, and related phenomena of the societies of this vast and diversified area. The social anthropology volume (6) of the *Handbook of Middle American Indians* contains twenty-five specialized articles including "Lacquer" and "Play: Games, Gossip, and Humor" but none on witchcraft and sorcery.

There are only a handful of analytical and comparative articles on the nature and practice of witchcraft, sorcery, and related phenomena in Mesoamerica. The specialized articles are not comprehensive, but their authors cannot be criticized too much, for the articles are essentially based on the published literature on the general subject of magic—that is, the category that covers a wide spectrum of phenomena in Mesoamerica ranging from witchcraft, sorcery, nahualism, and weathermaking to shamanism, curing, soul loss, the etiology of folk illnesses, and several other magical beliefs and practices. With a few notable exceptions, this corpus of literature ranges from fair to inadequate, and it is often confusing about the configuration of supernatural beings and practices. Moreover, the belief system that supports or underlies this fairly extensive array of persons, things, and activities is seldom spelled out. With two or three exceptions, there is no systematic description and analysis of witch or sorcerer in a particular community setting, let alone what these concepts mean or how they can be comparatively construed. The material on almost all the categories described above appears to be mostly anecdotal, and no one attempts to tie several of the beliefs and practices into a coherent whole, although some of them evidently belong together in some sort of system. Granting that magical beliefs and practices in the folk societies of Mesoamerica do not have the neatness, circumscription, and explicit ties to other social systems (mainly religion and kinship) that they have in tribal societies, Mesoamericanists have taken this too literally and have thereby missed a significant opportunity to explain the role and function of magic in non-tribal settings.

We have read most of the monographic and article literature on Mesoamerica that contains information on anthropomorphic supernaturalism. There are about a hundred monographs and articles in this category, but none of the sources, published roughly between 1930 and 1980, constitutes an exhaustive self-contained analysis of either witchcraft or sorcery. With the exception of some twenty articles, most of the information is presented as part of wider ethnographic studies. We have taken as a sample twenty-one of these sources, containing perhaps one-fourth of the meaningful information on the topic and covering a period of nearly forty years (1936–1973). Of these, five are of a general or comparative nature: Adams and Rubel (1967), Foster (1944), Mendelson (1967), Mendoza (1952), and Wisdom (1952). The other sixteen sources are ethnographic. Of these, three are self-contained articles: Johnson (1939), Nash (1960), and Saler (1964); thirteen sources are parts of monographs: Beals (1946), Carrasco (1952) Fuente (1949), Guiteras (1961), Ichon (1973), Lewis (1951), Madsen (1960), Montoya (1964), Parsons (1936), Redfield and Villa Rojas (1962), Reina (1966), Villa Rojas (1945), Wisdom (1961). Let us briefly discuss what these sources tell us about the beliefs and practices of witchcraft and sorcery in Mesoamerica.

Unquestionably, the ablest and most complete of the comparative articles is Foster's (1944). He gives a good account of nahualism in Mexico and Guatemala, and his analysis is particularly interesting in dealing with the pre-Hispanic and historical antecedents of the concept. He also presents the distribution of nahualism in Mesoamerica and warns us to be careful in distinguishing between nahual and tonal. Foster's description and analysis remains the best single description of one of the most widely distributed anthropomorphic supernaturals in Mesoamerica. Mendoza's (1952) article is little more than a catalogue of the distribution of the witch in Mexico, but it usefully confirms the wide-ranging presence of this supernatural in Mesoamerica. What Mendoza does not make clear is the significant degree of diversification that the witch exhibits throughout countless Indian and Mestizo communities. The article by Wisdom (1952) in *Heritage of Conquest: The Ethnology of Middle America* is disappointing, inasmuch as this book was supposed to be a compendium of what was known about the area up to 1950. Wisdom has a number of interesting things to say about witchcraft and sorcery, but no comprehensive picture of these supernaturals emerges in the review article. Much the same can be said about the article by Mendelson (1967) for the *Handbook of Middle American Indians*.

All three ethnographic articles make some significant contribution to the clarification of witchcraft and sorcery in a particular setting. Nash's (1960) article analyzes the concept of witchcraft, including nahualism and curing, in Amatenango, a Tzeltal community. He discusses insightfully the concept of witchcraft as a social process and some of the implications of this practice within the fabric of the community. The article by Johnson (1939) is a generally able discussion of Mazatec witchcraft and one of the very few fairly comprehensive studies of a particular anthropomorphic supernatural. But Saler's (1964) work is undoubtedly the best contemporary article on anthropomorphic supernaturalism. His discussion of nahualism, curing, witchcraft, and sorcery for the village of Santiago El Palmar in Guatemala gives a clear and fairly comprehensive picture of this communal complex and at the same time it contributes to the comparative understanding of particular supernaturals.

Of the thirteen monographs in the sample containing information on witchcraft, sorcery, and related phenomena, the majority are generally community studies. The exceptions are Carrasco (1952), Guiteras (1961), and Ichon (1973), all monographs concerned with religion and related matters. Carrasco and Guiteras are disappointing, for in their excellent descriptions and analyses there is little on witchcraft and sorcery of local or comparative value. Ichon, however, has a number of interesting things to say about these concepts within the context of Totonac religion in the Sierra de Puebla. His forte is a good analysis of the cosmology and belief system that underlies some of the practices of anthropomorphic supernaturalism. His is a welcome contribution, but Ichon is remiss in delineating both the nature of witchcraft and sorcery in action and the structural description of the various practitioners involved.

The remaining ten community studies either directly and specifically deal with the complex of witchcraft and sorcery or contain varying kinds of information ranging from passing remarks to specifically discussed points. None, however, deals systematically with this magical complex and its attendant components; rather, they are discussed as ancillary to the folk religion, to the conduct of social relations, and to the folk practices of illness and death. The casual reader might easily conclude that witchcraft and sorcery are structurally insignificant and constitute an unimportant aspect of religion or play an insignificant role in the life of the community in Mesoamerican Indian and sometimes in Mestizo societies. These would be mistaken conclusions and would perhaps reflect deficient ethnographic reporting.

Of these ten community studies, two stand out because of good descriptions and some analysis of anthropomorphic supernaturalism: Madsen (1960) and

Parsons (1936). In an informative chapter on witchcraft, sorcery, and nahual-ism, Madsen manages to convey the general attributes and behavior of a num-ber of supernatural practitioners which may perhaps have counterparts in all Nahuatl-speaking regions of the Central Highlands. In many ways, Parsons's description of witchcraft and sorcery in the Zapotec community of Mitla is probably the best in the literature and the most exhaustive and insightful. This is ironic, since this monograph is one of the earliest community studies in Mesoamerica. But as good as Parsons's description is, her analysis is confusing. She does not envisage the structural and behavioral implications of distinguish-ing witchcraft and sorcery in action. But unlike Madsen's, Parsons's description leaves no doubt that the people themselves do distinguish between sorcerer and witch, and a situation not unlike that of rural Tlaxcala clearly obtains. The other eight monographs present varying kinds of intensive and extensive infor-mation on witchcraft and sorcery, but from these accounts the reader cannot piece together a coherent picture of the belief and practice of anthropomorphic supernaturalism, let alone place it within the context of religion and the social structure. To be sure, each of these sources makes a significant point concerning witchcraft and/or sorcery or nahualism, or presents a fairly clear account of a supernatural in isolation. Thus, Fuente (1949) gives a good description of the context of sorcery and its implications for interpersonal relationships; Lewis (1951) distinguishes between sorcerer and witch but does not pursue the impli-cation to its logical conclusion; Beals (1946) presents a competent account of witchcraft that is really sorcery, distinguished solely by the exception that sorcerers can transform themselves into animals, a distinction which Beals never explains; and so on. What does not emerge from these invariably frag-mentary accounts is a sense that the ethnographer really immersed himself or herself into the nature of the phenomena at hand.

In conclusion, what has been achieved by Mesoamerican ethnology concern-ing anthropomorphic supernaturalism? On the basis of the above sample, a rather meager picture emerges. One can piece together the general distribution of the main supernaturals in the area, essentially the four discussed for rural Tlaxcala or variations of them. An outline, often confused and blurred, of the main attributes and general behavioral characteristics of witches, sorcerers, shamans, curers, transforming witches (or tricksters), and weathermen also emerges. The pre-Hispanic nature and origin of most anthropomorphic super-naturals are quite evident, and there are often good guesses about the European contribution to witchcraft and sorcery and the syncretic process that took place. What does not emerge from the sources is a systematic view of witchcraft and sorcery, the body of cosmogonic and magical beliefs that support and underlie the practices, and the position of anthropomorphic supernaturalism within the context of religion and the social structure. Finally, it should be noted that a few anthropologists, not included in the sample, have done significant work which has brightened the picture presented in the foregoing paragraphs. Among these, the work of Aguirre Beltrán (1963) contributing to our understanding of the diffusion of African elements and complexes to Mesoamerican anthropomorphic supernaturalism, and of Vogt (1969), for his good description of sorcery in Zinacantan is outstanding.

ATTRIBUTIONAL AND DEFINITIONAL DISTINCTIONS BETWEEN SORCERER AND WITCH

Given the deficiency of the published literature and the distribution of anthropomorphic supernaturalism in Mesoamerica, a clarification of the concepts of witchcraft and sorcery is a sine qua non. Essentially, since all the work that has been done in Mesoamerica concerning witchcraft and sorcery has been exclusively descriptive, there has been no need to refine the merely emic categories that ethnographers have employed in little more than mentioning the sometimes complex nature of both anthropomorphic and non-anthropomorphic supernaturalism. A cursory analysis of the ethnographic literature shows that a good deal of what passes for witchcraft is really sorcery, for, in one degree or another, what has been said for the Tlaxcala-Pueblan Valley probably applies to most regions of Mesoamerica. This attitude also reflects the a priori bias held by those anthropologists who have worked in the area against the conceptual possibility of distinguishing operationally between witchcraft and sorcery. The problem is compounded by the anthropologists' indiscriminate acceptance of the terminological confusion which generally obtains at the community level because of the interchangeable use of the terms *hechicero* and *brujo*, or perhaps more often because of the designation of a number of diverse supernatural practitioners by the term *brujo*. For example, when the sources mention bloodsucking witches (probably the most widely distributed anthropomorphic supernaturalism in northern Mesoamerica after the nahual [Mendoza 1952]), there is little doubt that they are essentially describing various forms of the tlahuelpuchi of the Tlaxcala-Pueblan Valley. But when the same term is applied to various forms of nahuales and to practitioners which can be hired to cause good or evil, then the situation gets hopelessly confused and in need of clarification. We have refrained from making specific citations, for not a single source has dealt with the problem conceptually. Therefore, it will not be amiss to say something about this vexing problem in the light of the four supernaturals discussed in this monograph.

The reader can verify for himself the individualized structure and attributional neatness of the tezitlazc, nahual, tetlachihuic, and tlahuelpuchi in rural Tlaxcala. Whether this represents a unique situation in Mesoamerica we do not know, for the comparative information needed to make a definitive judgment is not available. It is very likely, however, that the structure and neatness are also present in other regions of Mesoamerica. The discreteness of these supernaturals is not confined to their precise Nahuatl terminological referents but to their basic attributes and behavior patterns as well. Each of these supernaturals has its own sphere of action and particular modes of behavior, even where two of them resemble one another significantly in some specific domain. Thus, nahuales as well as tlahuelpuchis have the power of animal transformation, but only the latter can kill, whereas the former can only play tricks on people and cause a certain degree of unpleasantness; or, tlahuelpuchis as well as tetlachihuics can kill ordinary people, but they do it in distinctly different ways to leave no doubt concerning the provenance of death. Anthropomorphic supernaturalism in rural Tlaxcala exhibits the same characteristics that Evans-Pritchard (1938:19–26) describes for the same phenomenon among the Azande, namely, a clear emic distinction between sorcerer and witch. It is evident that the tezitlazc and tetlachihuic are variant types of the sorcerer, whereas the nahual and tlahuelpuchi are different manifestations of the witch. This assertion needs clarification. We agree with Middleton and Winter (1969:2–3) that Evans-Pritchard's distinction is of vital importance for the comparative study of anthropomorphic supernaturalism, and we disagree with Douglas who maintains that the terms for witch and sorcerer should be used as content-free labels that must be specified for each individual case (Simmons 1971:144). In the case of Mesoamerican anthropomorphic supernaturalism, this distinction is highly needed, for it forces ethnographers to be more precise in their observations and to avoid the indiscriminate use of these terms, which to some extent imposes upon the ethnographic situation an a priori etic category of their own. Moreover, since pre-Hispanic Mesoamerica exhibited a high degree of uniformity in the domain of magic and religion and all of its regions were more or less subjected to the same process of conversion to and catechization in Catholicism, it is certainly more conceptually advantageous to assume (in the absence of detailed ethnographic reports) that most regions of Mesoamerica are basically similar to the Tlaxcala-Pueblan Valley in the structure of anthropomorphic supernaturalism.

The analysis of the four supernaturals under consideration immediately brings to the fore the basic criteria by which they can be classified as either sorcerers or witches. These criteria are:

1. *The inherent (innate) or learned source of their power.* Although heredity does not seem to play a significant role in the witchcraft and sorcery systems throughout the world, supernatural powers can be transmitted by learning from generation to generation. Yet learned powers are often conditioned by congenital characteristics, such as the tetlachihuic's tlapaltizoliztli or the homosexuality or epilepsy that is often a prerequisite for becoming a shaman in countless societies in the New World. In the case of the tlahuelpuchi, the bloodsucking compulsion is a curse that fate inflicts upon individuals at random, therefore, hereditary transmission is totally out of the question. But the ethnographic literature includes a number of instances in which kinsmen, generally in the prevailing line of descent, inherit the powers of the witch. It seems to us, however, that in such cases the concept of the witch is ideologically conceived as a diversified system of evildoing, most often involving lucre, vengeance, and lust directed against ordinary men. To some extent, in rural Tlaxcala this applies to the nahual as a witch of sorts. Thus, the discriminating factor in the congenital or hereditary nature of the witch's power is the degree of compulsion, wickedness, and antisocial qualities with which this supernatural is ideologically conceived by the functioning social group. In any event, this is the least important of the four criteria. Nonetheless, there seems to be a strong correlation between the innate power of the witch and the learned powers of the sorcerer.

2. *The essentially public or fundamentally secret nature of their human identities.* It is quite likely that, for obvious reasons, sorcerers may keep a low profile in the conduct of daily life and are not as visible as other public individuals in the magico-religious system. By contrast, the secretiveness of witches comes from their ethereal and nebulous nature and from the fact that ordinary men cannot approach or contact them, given their basically evil nature. There are degrees of secretiveness, to be sure, but by no stretch of the imagination can witches be regarded as public or as individuals knowable by ordinary men at large. As a corollary of this basic attribute, there are no accusations of sorcery qua public supernatural practice but only conflicts between private individuals. When in the exercise of his supernatural powers a sorcerer transgresses what the social group regards as tolerable, punishment, including death, is meted out by those directly affected by the action of the culprit. In other words, since the sorcerer is known, what could be construed as an accusation is really nothing but the private and direct confrontation between a supernatural practitioner and an ordinary man or men. Witchcraft accusations, on the other hand, are sociologically and psychologically factual entailing specific outcomes. Fundamentally, witchcraft accusations consist in determining publicly the human identity of evil and hateful supernatural practitioners according to a well-

established ideological blueprint. Witchcraft accusations involve the collective confrontation of the operational social group, or a significant segment of it, and a witch or witches, leading to the punishment and usually the death of the latter. This confrontation generates or conditions the varied sociological and psychological consequences and functions which have been well documented in the ethnographic and historical literature. Thus, collective actions under particular conditions of social and psychological stress generally entail witchcraft accusations. Nothing comparable obtains in the sorcery complex, for it is the secrecy of witchcraft that functions as the social and psychological escape valve. In summary, the public or secret nature of an anthropomorphic supernatural constitutes its most distinguishable attribute.

3. *The immanent or manipulative working of their power.* By immanent we mean two things: a general core of behavior or compulsion that defines the basic configuration of the witch; and the activation of certain powers at will for the performance of specific evildoings. By manipulative we mean essentially the activation of a usually large roster of magic formulas, incantations, and physical actions that sorcerers bring to bear upon a particular case of either black or white magic. Since the powers associated with sorcerers are always learned, sorcerers can control only manipulative powers. However, it is possible that in addition to their immanent (congenital) powers, witches may learn manipulative techniques as a complement to their evildoings. This is true of the tlahuelpuchi in rural Tlaxcala and a rather common occurrence in the ethnographic literature.

4. *Their basic independence of ordinary men or their amenability to being hired for good or evil.* This criterion is really a corollary of 2 and 3. It is meant to emphasize the ethereal, nebulous, and vague nature of the witch, on the one hand, and the clearly ascertainable and well-delineated physical and social presence of the sorcerer, on the other. While this criterion is essentially subsidiary, it is nonetheless the most visible and generally the starting point in investigating anthropomorphic supernaturalism. It is therefore important that the ethnographer keeps clearly segregated what informants tell him about a particular supernatural practitioner (mainly the ideological configuration of the witch) and what informants can ascertain and the ethnographer can verify (mainly the social and physical presence of the sorcerer).

These discriminating criteria for classifying sorcerers and witches are seldom absolute in every detail. It is highly probable, however, that they have significant worldwide validity as a standard in the classification of anthropomorphic supernaturals. It certainly applies to the European witchcraft-sorcery complex and to the syncretic system that developed in Mesoamerica by interacting with pre-Hispanic anthropomorphic supernaturalism. Thus, to take the two main criteria discussed above, there are no witch's apprentices but there are indeed sorcerer's apprentices (as in Dukas's musical composition) in the Western tradition; whereas ordinary men do not interact with witches until they are caught (accused) and confronted, sorcerers most certainly participate in the social structure of ordinary men. Pretty much the same obtains in the magic system that developed in Mesoamerica after the Conquest. It is possible that these classificatory and attributional distinctions for witchcraft and sorcery do not work for many ethnographic areas of the world, but we are quite certain that they work for the present area of concern.

Returning to rural Tlaxcala, the tetlachihuic and the tlahuelpuchi correspond respectively to the classic definition of sorcerer and witch. The tetlachihuic always learns his powers from practicing white or black magic; he is a public and fairly visible individual; he cures and causes illness, transformations, and death by the manipulation of substances, prayers, and particular modes of behavior; and he is for hire by average ordinary men. The tlahuelpuchi is the exact opposite: she is a fundamentally secret entity as a human being, and no one is completely certain about her identity; the workings of her evil powers are immanent but also activated by an individual act of will; and obviously, she cannot be for hire. The other two supernaturals are not as clear cut, but there is a strong attributional correlation to classify them as either sorcerer or witch. The tezitlazc is a public figure, is for hire, and he employs manipulative techniques similar to those of the tetlachihuic. The only departure from the tetlachihuic is that some tezitlazcs are born with their powers to conjure the natural elements rather than learning them. The nahual is more or less similar to the tlahuelpuchi. The nahual's identity as a human being is basically secret, the workings of his powers are immanent, and he most certainly is not for hire. The only fundamental attribute that distinguishes the nahual from the tlahuelpuchi is the fact that the former always acquires his powers by learning. We have essentially left out of this set of criteria the intrinsic good or evil nature of the supernaturals' actions because it is either conditioned by inherent factors, as in the case of the tlahuelpuchi who can do nothing against the vagaries of fate, or it is a question of individual will, as in the case of the tetlachihuic. It is only when the good or evil nature of a supernatural's actions enters the picture that one is free to call that supernatural by another term, such as calling the nahual a transforming trickster rather than a transforming witch.

With three exceptions (Parsons 1936; Saler 1964; Vogt 1969), literature on Mesoamerican witchcraft and sorcery does not permit even the sketchiest analysis along the lines presented above. This is not a question of mere terminological quibbling about what supernaturals are to be called sorcerers or witches, or whether gradations may exist between these opposites, but a question of significant conceptual importance, without which one cannot make meaningful social or psychological assignments. It is therefore important that more adequate data come forth before the meaningful comparison of Mesoamerican anthropomorphic supernaturalism can be undertaken. To put this point across has been the principal aim of this rather extended discussion. We can now return to bloodsucking witchcraft in rural Tlaxcala.

CHAPTER FIVE

Anatomy of a Bloodsucking Witchcraft Epidemic

AT EIGHT O'CLOCK in the morning of Friday, 9 December 1960, Don Julián Tecolotzin came to see Nutini in the *cabecera* of the municipio of San Diego Tlalocan, where he had been working since late September of that year. Don Julián was a resident of San Pedro Xolotla, one of the main dependent communities of the municipio, located about two and a half miles from the cabecera. Nutini had met Don Julián during the summer of 1959 while he was conducting an ethnographic survey of the Tlaxcala-Pueblan Valley, and in time Don Julián, who was seventy-three then, and who died at the ripe old age of ninety-seven at the end of 1983, became one of his most trusted and inexhaustible informants. In a great state of excitement Don Julián proceeded to tell Nutini that in the adjoining parajes of Meztitlán, Chicomoxtoc, and Aztlán seven infants had been sucked by the tlahuelpuchi that night and that all of them had appeared dead early that morning. Being a resident of Chicomoxtoc himself, Don Julián described in detail the state of fear, apprehension, and even hysteria that had quickly spread throughout the population of the parajes in less than an hour after two infants had been found dead in nearby households. By seven o'clock the parajes were in a state of great agitation, and Don Julián decided to come to tell Nutini about it, for he had asked Don Julián to report to him any infants sucked by the tlahuelpuchi or anything connected with it. In fact, in late November, Don Julián had led Nutini to the examination of a sucked infant. They left immediately for Xolotla and arrived shortly before nine o'clock.

THE ETHNOGRAPHIC SETTING OF THE EPIDEMIC

Meztitlán, Chicomoxtoc, and Aztlán are the largest parajes in San Pedro Xolotla. They are located between a large *barranca* (ravine) and a parallel street in the southeastern part of the community. The parajes cover an approximately rectangular area of some 200 by 750 meters. Some houses are located along the barranca, some along the street, but most are dispersed throughout the area. Some houses are built in small clusters of three or four but most are separated from one another by thirty or forty meters. About two-thirds of the houses are of the *solar* type, that is, a quadrangular compound surrounded by a wall, wherein all rooms have access to an interior yard, and quite often the wall forms a part of the house itself. The other third are single construction houses, sometimes with two rooms, with a separate kitchen adjoining the main building. The three parajes are inhabited by four kinship groups: one each in Meztitlán and in Aztlán and two in Chicomoxtoc. The parajes are the locality referents for the kinship groups with which they are intimately associated. The total population of the parajes at the time (or to be exact, four months later when a census was taken) was 347 people, constituting 51 households. Of these households, 30 consisted of independent nuclear families, while 21 were extended family households. The average nuclear family household had 5.2 members, while the average extended family household had 8.7. Of the total number of households, 39 had children five years old or younger, and 13 of them had infants of less than one year old. San Pedro Xolotla is well known regionally for its textile production, and the three parajes are especially noted for their rug (*tapete*) production. Thus, the economy of these parajes is a combination of textile production (the average household has from six to eight looms) and labor migration. In fact, practically every household harbors weekly or daily labor migrants to Mexico City or to the factories in the Tlaxcala-Pueblan Valley, and all the households manufacture some kind of *sarape* (woolen blanket), rug, *tilma* (woolen cape), or several other articles. We say this because it is important to impress upon the reader that, although 75 percent of the inhabitants of these three parajes still spoke Nahuatl in 1965, they constituted in many ways an open community with many contacts with the outside world. This should be kept in mind in the ensuing analysis. Finally, the parajes of Meztitlán, Chicomoxtoc, and Aztlán harbor the main kinship groups that constitute the core of one of the barrios into which the municipio of San Diego Tlalocan is divided. Consequently a fair number of social and religious ties exists among them, and they are in intimate spatial contact daily. All these social, economic, and territorial facts constitute the matrix underlying the bloodsucking witchcraft epidemic that we are about to describe.

Word about the sucked infants and the households where it had happened, spread very quickly; by the time Don Julián and Nutini arrived in the parajes, everybody knew the main facts about the terrible event. It had been an unusually cold night for that early in the season, but the morning was already warming up, and the sun shone brilliantly in an intensely blue sky. But such a splendid day did not help much. The people were withdrawn and, with fear in their eyes, milled about their houses. They could hear cries everywhere, not only from the women of the affected households, but from kinswomen from nearby households who had gathered to commiserate with those who had been affected. The children had gone to school as usual, but grownup folk were not working at their looms as they should have been since six o'clock. None of the two dozen or so daily labor migrants who generally left their homes before seven o'clock had gone to work. The daily activities had been almost completely paralyzed, and the thoughts and actions of the people were totally focused on the night's events. As Don Julián and Nutini walked about the parajes, they could hear the different theories, opinions, and explanations that the people were already beginning to formulate regarding the epidemic. They were stopped several times and asked by men and women alike their opinions, their advice about what they should do, and precautions that they could take in the future to avert similar events. At the same time, the people expressed their great state of tension and anxiety by commiserating and feeling sorry for themselves, by asking themselves what they had done to deserve such a terrible blow, and by answering themselves to the effect that they could not think of the supernatural cause of the epidemic, for they had complied with their mayordomias, had propitiated the saints properly, and they were not aware that they had offended "los muchos buenos y malos espíritus y personajes que nos ayudan o acechan constantemente" (the many good and bad spirits and personages who help us or are constantly waylaying us), as an elderly man put it. Solicitude was a natural reaction toward Don Julián and Nutini, for the former was probably the most respected *tiaxca* (elder) in Xolotla, and the latter was fairly well known in the parajes and regarded as a knowledgeable and educated person by the people at large, since Don Julián always referred to him as "una persona muy importante" (a very important person).

The people's response was the most extraordinary manifestation of the collective "thought" of a large group of people that Nutini has ever witnessed, and which he never again experienced in the subsequent twenty-seven years of fieldwork in rural Tlaxcala. It was as if the latent ideological underpinning of the people's supernatural belief system, seldom manifested or expressed in the normal course of affairs, was somehow unleashed verbally, not only to relieve tension, but as a conscious effort to understand and to cope with the terrible events that had befallen that intimate group of people. During the course of the following five days, Nutini was to learn more about the supernatural belief system of a sector of rural Tlaxcala and about its motivation to ritual and ceremonial action than in many subsequent years of fieldwork.

A PHYSICIAN EXAMINES THE SUCKED INFANTS

By eleven o'clock, Don Julián and Nutini had visited all seven affected households, examined the corpses of the infants, and briefly interviewed their parents and other members of the household. Nutini then suggested to Don Julián that it would be a good idea to have the infants examined by a physician and that he would take it upon himself to fetch one from Tlaxcala City or Santa Ana Chiautempan. At the beginning Don Julián strongly rejected his advice, saying that physicians knew nothing about infants being sucked by the tlahuelpuchi and that in the end the doctor would only laugh at them for their beliefs and be of no help at all. But Nutini finally managed to convince him that the physician could not do any harm, and he just might be of some service. Don Julián got together with several of the elders of the parajes and, in council, convinced the members of the affected households to allow a doctor to examine the corpses.

By 2:30 in the afternoon Nutini had gone to Tlaxcala City to fetch the chief medical officer of the state of Tlaxcala, with whom he had arranged to share information concerning bloodsucking witchcraft. Unfortunately the doctor was out of town, but Nutini managed to interest his deputy in coming to Xolotla and examining the corpses.

The deputy medical officer was a young fellow, no more than four or five years out of medical school, who had occupied his post for about a year, but he did know about bloodsucking witchcraft in rural Tlaxcala. Nutini asked him bluntly and specifically to diagnose the cause of death of the seven infants and the circumstance under which he thought they had occurred, which under no circumstances was he to verbalize to the parents of the infants and to other concerned people. Nutini also asked him to refrain from making any comments regarding the tlahuelpuchi or from in any way making disparaging remarks or from questioning the belief in bloodsucking witchcraft. He was extremely cooperative. Being quite well briefed by his chief regarding the phenomenon at hand, knowing that it would do little good to tell those concerned the physical nature of the deaths or to offer any advice regarding future incidence, and contravening in no way his code of ethics as a physician, he agreed to the following plan. The physician would examine the cadavers or corpses carefully and later discuss with Nutini the causes, circumstances, and his general medical opinion concerning the death of the infants. He would tell those concerned the approximate time of death and would express vague uncertainty about the cause of death. If asked for advice, he would offer none, except to suggest that they should do what they thought best for such circumstances, and that he would think of something later. The young physician was a bright fellow who understood the ethnographic aims perfectly. He did not want in any way to influence or bias the subsequent sociological investigation of the epidemic by anything that might be said or done. He understood also that, if anything practical was to be gained from the medical viewpoint of preventing infant death, it was certainly more logical and advantageous to know in detail the sociological dimensions of the phenomenon and the belief system which underlay it.

The physician and Nutini arrived in Xolotla by six o'clock, and again through the good offices of Don Julián, they proceeded to examine the corpses of the infants. By nine o'clock they had finished with the seven cases, and Nutini drove the physician back to Tlaxcala City. The examination took place without any incidents. As Nutini had expected, parents and other adult members of the affected households asked few questions, but in each case, the physician told those concerned what had been agreed upon beforehand, which seemed to have quelled the apprehension that the people obviously felt concerning the examination of the corpses by an outsider. The examination of each of the seven corpses was witnessed by large numbers of neighboring kinsmen congregating in the house, anxiously talking to Don Julián and Nutini, while the physician examined the corpse in a separate room. Before leaving Xolotla to fetch the physician, Nutini had asked Don Julián to make sure that the corpses were not touched—that is, that preparations for the wake (*velorio*) be postponed until after the physician's examination. It was a measure of Don Julián's great influence that everyone scrupulously complied; the corpses had been placed on a clean petate on top of a table and covered with a white cloth. It became clear later that the main reason the people of the parajes allowed the physician to examine the corpses was to convince an important outside authority that the tlahuelpuchi was no superstition, "como mucha gente de afuera cree" (as many outsiders believe), but something very real, not at all a figment of their imaginations. They expected to accomplish this by having the physician examine the abnormal physical marks on the corpses and challenging him to explain the extraordinary event of seven infants dying in a single night under the same circumstances and with roughly the same telltale signs: a logical argument indeed, from the standpoint of their belief system, but lacking sufficient knowledge of modern medicine.

On the way back to Tlaxcala City the physician diagnosed the cause of death for all seven infants and the circumstances under which they probably took place. We shall discuss the medical and etiological aspects of the epidemic in chapter 8. Suffice it to say here that Nutini and the physician agreed to discuss the epidemic and exchange detailed information in a few weeks, once Nutini had thoroughly investigated the many ramifications of the phenomenon. On his way back from Tlaxcala City, he picked up at his headquarters in the cabecera the necessary things that he needed for five or six days, for he had arranged to stay with Don Julián in his house for this period of time to be able to observe subsequent developments with the greatest possible minuteness and intimacy.

THE IDEOLOGICAL, RITUAL, CEREMONIAL, AND PSYCHOLOGICAL CONTEXTS OF THE EPIDEMIC

Nutini was back in Don Julián's house by 11:30 that evening to continue the most intensive and rewarding five days of fieldwork of his career. (Throughout this period, Don Julián was his constant companion and colleague, helping him to gather information, clarifying data as a resourceful informant, and above all, facilitating his entry into various kinds of situations and events.) Most of the ritual, ceremonial, and protective activities surrounding the epidemic focused, obviously enough, on the affected households, among which Nutini rotated, spending most of the time. The members of the households readily accepted Nutini, for Don Julián had asked them to cooperate fully with him, and to regard him as a member of the households because he had nothing but their interest at heart.

The first order of business was the structured, in-depth interviews of the parents of the infants, of those who were sleeping in the same room when the infants had been sucked by the tlahuelpuchi, and in general, of all members of the affected households. Nutini quickly prepared an open-ended questionnaire asking the estimated time when the infant had been found dead, who had found him and under what circumstances, whether there had been any ostensible signs of the presence of the tlahuelpuchi, what were the sleeping arrangements, whether there was any observed unusual event, where the infant had been placed before the mother went to sleep, and several other questions that he had thought about regarding the general circumstances under which bloodsucking witchcraft takes place; all were based on his observation of two previous cases and a considerable amount of recorded information. It took part of that night and the next two days to create the questionnaire, as we shall soon analyze.

The parajes presented an eerie and unusual aspect. Although it was past midnight when Don Julián and Nutini started to make the rounds of the affected households, every house of the parajes had lighted candles or kerosene lamps; electricity was not installed in Xolotla until 1964. In front of a number of houses, sizeable groups of men and teenagers congregated around bonfires drinking coffee or *atole* (corn-gruel drink), and men with heavy sticks patrolled the footpaths connecting the houses or stationed themselves under large trees. Inside the houses only small children slept, under the watchful supervision of the women. The pungent odor of garlic and onion could instantly be detected upon entering every household, an unmistakable indication that the people were not taking any chances against the tlahuelpuchi striking again by activating the only surefire deterrent. The tension, fear, and anxiety had not subsided. This was most clearly expressed in the desire of the people to huddle together to seek the comfort and reassurance of physical proximity and in the almost constant chatting and remembering of their experiences concerning the tlahuelpuchi.

Several weeks had passed before Nutini could reflect calmly and order in his mind the unfolding of this extraordinary event. In his field diary of 27 January 1961 he wrote the following:

> The most propitious circumstances for the investigation and gathering of data concerning the ethos and ideological system of a social group is under the strain and tension of unforeseen, out of the ordinary, and feared events and occasions. Under such conditions, the people seem to let their ideological guard down, and many deep-seated beliefs and tendencies (which are normally kept latent, and to some degree at the subconscious level, by a series of cultural screens and by the exigencies of societal living, especially in situations of rapid culture change) swiftly come to the surface, where they can be examined within the actual context of the social structure. The extraordinariness of the situation will bias or distort the manifest ethos and ideology, but this can always be corrected by the counterbalancing effect of the ethos and ideology in action, that is, under normal conditions and constraints, which are much easier to observe and record.

This piece of intuition has served him well throughout more than a generation in the field.

By two o'clock in the morning Don Julián and Nutini had visited all the affected households; by then the corpses had been cleansed or were being prepared for the wake; or, the wake was already in progress. Each corpse had been placed in a simple wooden coffin on top of a table, underneath which an oblique cross of pine wood ashes had been made, according to the traditional practice involving those who have been sucked by the tlahuelpuchi. The people believe that pine wood has the special property of warding off evil spirits and purifying the environment when something evil or dreadful has taken place, such as an infant being sucked by the tlahuelpuchi or a person being affected by the evil eye or the bad wind; but it was impossible to elicit a verbal explanation of the shape of the cross. Symbolically, however, the oblique cross is a homologous inversion of the tlahuelpuchi's characteristic rite over the house of the victim that marks the different status of the dead infant.

Two well-known tezitlazcs from the community of Teoxintla in a nearby municipio had been hired by the affected households to undertake the ritual cleansing of the dead infants, their mothers, and the rooms where the blood-sucking had taken place. The cleansing rites had started immediately after the physician had left the parajes, and Nutini had had the opportunity to witness two identical ceremonies performed by the hired tezitlazcs. The table for the coffin was set aside, and the completely naked corpse of the infant was placed on top of the oblique cross. The head of the infant rested on the intersection of the two arms of the cross with the body along the longer arm. A *copalcaxitl* (incense burner) was placed at the foot of the cross and the tezitlazc undertook the cleansing rite. Picking up the burning copalcaxitl, he went around the cross three times clockwise and three times counterclockwise while reciting litanies in Nahuatl and invoking the protection of San Lorenzo, San Juan Bautista, La Malintzi, and El Cuatlapanga. He then returned the copalcaxitl to the foot of the cross, and with a tied bunch of *capulin* branches, *ocoxochitl* leaves, and dry roots of the century plant he cleansed the body of the infant from feet to head and from hand to hand three times, this time invoking for the infant the protection of Our Lord, the Holy Virgin, and the patron saint of Xolotla. Then the corpse was picked up by non-kinsmen and placed on the coffin, and the table was returned to the top of the oblique cross. The tezitlazc cleansed the mother of the dead infant in the following fashion. She was placed against one of the walls of the room with her arms spread apart in the form of a cross, and the tezitlazc brushed the same cleansing brush that was used for the dead infant against the body of the mother three times from feet to hand and from hand to hand in complete silence. He then asked the mother to bare her breasts and rubbed them lightly with *zoapatl* leaves that he produced from a leather pouch on his belt. The tezitlazc returned the zoapatl leaves to his pouch and asked the mother to kiss the foot of the oblique cross underneath the table. These cleansing rites are done in view of a large number of household members, kinsmen, and non-kinsmen. The presence of non-kinsmen is a requirement, for according to local custom, kinsmen cannot handle their own dead. Finally, the tezitlazc proceeded to cleanse the room where the infant had been sucked by the tlahuelpuchi by brushing the doors, windows, walls, floor, and ceiling with the cleansing brush and again reciting litanies and prayers in Nahuatl.

The last event of the cleansing rites was the burial of the cleansing bunch in a hole next to the *temazcal* that the tezitlazc dug while saying a prayer in Nahuatl and facing north. For his performance, which lasted approximately half an hour, the tezitlazc charged thirty pesos. After Nutini had witnessed the second cleansing he asked Don Julián why the tezitlazc had buried the cleansing bunch but had returned to his pouch the zoapatl leaves with which he had rubbed the breasts of the mother. Don Julián was not certain, but he suspected that those zoapatl leaves had to be placed in a particular place by the tezitlazc so that the responsible tlahuelpuchi would pick them up and destroy them. Don Julián did not know why. He went on to say, however, that although the tezitlazcs were invariably people with good supernatural powers, they were bound to evil supernaturals by a covenant of mutual aid and secrecy. Nutini was never able to find out why the tlahuelpuchi needed an element that had been in contact with the breasts of the mother of one of her victims.

The wake of the infants attracted large numbers of people, not only from the parajes of Meztitlán, Chicomoxtoc, and Aztlán but from Xolotla as a whole. The affected households were jammed with people, many of whom had to stay in the courtyard and adjoining kitchen. They were served coffee, atole, tamales, and bread while they engaged in animated conversation that incessantly revolved around the supernatural and extraordinary occurrences, and they asked one another for any reason or logic that could explain the epidemic. It was nearly three in the morning when they arrived at the household of one of Don Julián's collateral kinsmen, whose infant grandson had been one of the victims. It took Nutini about an hour to interview the members of the household, especially the mother and father of the victim, using the open-ended questionnaire that he had prepared beforehand. At four o'clock people were still around, and for more than two hours he interviewed collectively more than a dozen middle-aged and old men present in the house, with an occasional comment from a few elderly women. By then, the fear and anxiety of the people had subsided considerably, perhaps due to the therapeutic effect of incessant verbal expression. Apprehension persisted, but to a large extent fear and anxiety had given way to resignation and acceptance of the inevitable—namely, that it is a random and contingent universe in which there is no certain way to prevent the intervention of evil supernaturals. In such a determined universe, the psychological states of fear, anxiety, dread, ambivalence and so on accompanying death, unexpected or unfortunate events, and the vagaries of the supernatural are never of long duration; sooner rather than later, people return to their normal selves. From this viewpoint, the modal personality of the average rural Tlaxcalan has a fundamental tendency toward quick volitional transition to a normal state of affairs—that is, to the social and psychological recognition and acceptance of destiny or fate—when something disturbs what they regard as the normal but precarious course of things.

That night innumerable legends, stories, and accounts of supernatural events and occurrences were told by the participants about Catholic and non-Catholic supernaturals, including the entire roster of anthropomorphic supernaturals discussed in this monograph as well as several animistic spirits and practices. Again and again the conversation turned to the foremost questions in their minds: why, how, and from where had such an epidemic of bloodsucking witchcraft befallen them? Repeatedly, they asked themselves what they had done to deserve such fate and always came back to the same conclusion—namely, that they had done nothing that they could sincerely regard as an offense against the supernaturals that required such cruel action. On the contrary, they enumerated their public and private celebrations concerning the proper cult of the saints, the sumptuous discharge of their mayordomias, the many *compadrazgos* that they had contracted, their occasional supplications to La Malintzi and El Cuatlapanga, their due respect to the known tetlachihuics, and so on. It became clear that they regarded the human-supernatural relationship as a kind of covenant in which humans and the supernatural are arranged in an established order where each has rights and obligations, and as long as both sides comply with their parts, the world will run fairly smoothly, given the fact that the world of human affairs is the best of a bad job. In such a state of affairs, some sort of connection exists between Catholic supernaturals (regarded as exclusively benevolent and always well disposed toward human existence) and several pagan supernaturals (especially the tlahuelpuchi, la Llorona, and Matlalcihua, regarded as malevolent and almost always ready to harm humans) in which compliance with obligations toward the former is supposed to ensure protection of humans against the latter. In their quandary, they invoke the logic of unappealable destiny or fate, which ultimately sanctions resignation and acceptance (Nutini 1975).

Not being able to determine the *why* of the epidemic, people turned to the *how* and *from where*—that is, to the motivation and provenance of the perpetrator or perpetrators of the evil deed. In retrospect, it seems strange that the possibility that the tlahuelpuchi had been from Xolotla let alone from the parajes of Meztitlán, Chicomoxtoc, and Aztlán was never verbalized, for in the majority of cases subsequently investigated, the suspicion that the responsible tlahuelpuchi was a local individual was expressed by the affected family or interested parties, although specific names were never mentioned. The only possible explanations for this were the extraordinary magnitude of the event and the fact that the people believe that tlahuelpuchis do not attack kinsmen if they can help it, and the parajes constituted a fairly closely integrated body of kinship groups. Be this as it may, practically every participant had a theory or opinion about the provenance of the tlahuelpuchis. Some believed that the tlahuelpuchis were from Olintla, others believed they were from Hueytochco, and still others cited both of these communities. In subsequent days, several other possibilities were mentioned, mainly that the tlahuelpuchis were from communities in neighboring municipios or even from a nearby community in Xolotla's own municipio. Interestingly, for many years Xolotla had been having a good deal of friction over disputed arable lands and the usufruct of communal lands with all these communities. However, beyond the fact that it seemed natural to blame one's enemies or litigants for one's misfortunes, no other sociological generalization can be drawn from this complex; on the basis of the extremely rare personification of tlahuelpuchis, bloodsucking witchcraft in rural Tlaxcala cannot be construed as having either the primary sociological function of serving as a mechanism for social control, or the direct collective function of expressing hostilities in socially acceptable ways. What became quite clear at the end of five days of almost constant observation and interviewing was the consensus that three tlahuelpuchis had participated in the sucking of the seven infants, for the people could not conceive of a tlahuelpuchi wanting to suck the blood of more than three children in a single night. By the following Sunday, when the ambience of the parajes had more or less returned to normal and the people had ceased to speculate about the reason, manner, and provenance of the epidemic, they continued to wonder and were still unable to understand how it could have been possible that seven children had been sucked in one night. For years to come, this amazing event would be a favorite topic of speculation, indeed, with every reason, since nothing of that magnitude had ever happened in the region as far as the oldest people could remember.

It was past 6:30 in the morning of Saturday the tenth when Nutini and Don Julián returned to the house to get a few hours of sleep. Don Julián woke Nutini at ten o'clock to tell him that the burials of the infants were ready to begin. Between 10:30 and 2:00 in the afternoon all seven infants were buried in the municipal cemetery two miles away. Two of the infants belonging to closely related families were buried together, whereas the other five were buried separately. As prescribed by custom, no music was played on the way to the cemetery, and the fifty or so people accompanying each of the infants made the trek in complete silence, in ominous contrast to the music, rockets, and singing which accompany the burial of all other infants and children. The priest was not called to say the traditional responses while the bodies were being lowered into the ground, and one could feel the great urgency of all concerned to get the burial ceremonies over as quickly as possible. All the rites were done in utter silence, except when the erection-of-the-burial-cross *padrino* (godfather) and/or *madrina* (godmother) commended the soul of the infant to God while planting the burial cross at the foot of the tomb. When the people returned from the cemetery, the traditional burial banquet was being prepared and was served shortly thereafter. By six o'clock, the ceremonial meal had been eaten, and the last vestiges of the death of the seven infants had been removed from the households. All the clothing and other intimate possessions which had belonged to the infants were gathered together and burnt behind the house. Then the erection-of-the-burial-cross padrino gathered the pine wood ashes of the oblique cross and buried them in a hole next to the temazcal. There was to be no *octava de cruz* (visit to the tomb by the padrino and madrina after the eighth day of burial), no flowers were ever to be placed on the tomb of the sucked infant, he was not to be remembered on the family altar for All Saints Day and All Souls Day, and his family and kinsmen were to avoid thinking about him as if he had never existed. Such is the fate of all infants sucked by the tlahuelpuchi.

That night the people stayed up late, and pairs of men continued to patrol the footpaths and milpas of the parajes and stationed themselves in strategic places. The odor of garlic and onion was still in the air, and one could clearly notice that many of the traditional means of deterrence against the tlahuelpuchi had been activated in the average household. When Don Julián and Nutini went to bed at about two o'clock, things were quiet but the tension could still be felt. On Sunday morning the people resumed their normal activities. During the day, the women of the affected households, accompanied by varied numbers of kinswomen, walked to the parochial church in the cabecera. They bore flower offerings to San Diego de Alcalá and the Virgen de los Remedios, and they asked for protection against further attacks by the tlahuelpuchi. That evening, rosaries were said in many households of the parajes, led by Xolotla's own tezitlazcs. Don Julián asked one of the tezitlazcs whether it was possible to build a sacred fence, or *tlatepantil*, around the parajes for protection against the tlahuelpuchis, as is done for protection against the natural elements. The tezitlazc answered that it was impossible, asserting that he did not have deterrent powers against personified evildoers, causing Don Julián later to reiterate that tezitlazcs had some connection with tlahuelpuchis that they could not betray. That evening the people were more visibly relaxed but exhuasted after three days of intense emotional and physical activities and psychological tension. Men no longer patrolled the parajes, and by midnight everybody had retired. During the following two days things gradually went back to normal; Wednesday morning, when Nutini left Don Julián's household to return to the cabecera, it was difficult to tell that such a terrible event had affected the parajes. The careful observation of several households on Sunday night revealed that the level of activating deterrent techniques against the tlahuelpuchi was also back to normal. Three days later, the parajes presented a quiet, undisturbed aspect, but by then, with his sensitized perception of the psychological ambience, Nutini could still detect a conscious effort to control tension and anxiety by a nonchalant attitude toward the epidemic. Sunday, Monday, and Tuesday were days of arduous and intense interviewing and observation. Nutini expanded his original open-ended questionnaire and twice again interviewed in depth the personnel of the seven affected households. At the same time, it was important to observe the changing verbal behavior of the people as tension, fear, and anxiety receded and their ideological guard went back to normal. Never again in his career would Nutini gather such a singly integrated and complete body of behavioral and ideological facts comprising a circumscribed ethnographic domain. What follows is a description of each individual case, and the structural and temporal contexts in which the seven victims were sucked by the tlahuelpuchi.

THE STRUCTURAL AND TEMPORAL CONTEXT OF THE BLOODSUCKING EVENTS

Household 1: This was a nuclear-family household occupying a single-construction house with two rooms (a general-purpose room and a bedroom) and separate *zacate* (grass walled hut) kitchen, and was composed of the following personnel: Pedro Tlahuicole, 29, head of the household and father of the victim: María Cortés, 25, mother of the victim; a son, 5, and a daughter, 3; and Juan, the victim, five months old. Juan exhibited the classic bruises, acchymoses, and purple spots on his chest and in the back near the neck, and his face and neck had a rather pronounced purplish color. María's breasts were normal, that is, there were no irritation or black-and-blue marks in her areolas. Juan had not been protected that night by any of the traditional deterrents against the tlahuelpuchi. All the members of the household slept in the same room: Pedro and María in a large petate, the two children in a smaller petate, and Juan in a large wooden box, a rather common substitute for the crib in rural Tlaxcala. The sleeping room had a window and a door with access to the general-purpose room, which had a door to the outside. The door connecting the two rooms always remained open; the outside door was always closed and secured by a stick at night, but when Juan was found dead by his father early in the morning the door was ajar. That night the children went to bed early; Juan was sound asleep by nine o'clock. Slightly past midnight, Juan woke up and María put him to the breast. Under questioning, she insisted vehemently that after nursing Juan she put him back in the box. Both Pedro and María stated that after they last saw Juan alive, they went soundly to sleep ("con un sueño muy pesado"). Upon being questioned, they stated that nothing unusual had happened between midnight and the time they got up, except that each woke up with a strong headache and feeling very drowsy. Shortly before six, Pedro got up and found Juan dead inside the receiving room next to the outside door. He called María, who was still dozing, and she went into near hysterics. Crying desperately, María went to her nearby kinsmen and gave the word of alarm. Both Pedro and María were well versed in the lore of the tlahuelpuchi, but they had not had direct experience with the complex, for, as far as they knew, the tlahuelpuchi had never before tried anything on their infants, either when they were living patrilocally or since they had separated from the extended family household a year and a half earlier. However, Pedro stated that before he got married his extended family household had a similar experience when one of his elder brother's infants had been sucked by the tlahuelpuchi. He emphasized that the general circumstances and the telltale signs on the infant were remarkably similar in the two suckings.

Household 2: This was a nuclear-family household occupying a single-construction house with two rooms and attached kitchen, and was composed of the following personnel: Javier Patlahuatzin, 35, head of the household and father of the victim; Pilar Teyohualmiqui, 33, mother of the victim; a son, 10, and three daughters, 9, 6, and 2; and Ramiro, the victim, eight months old. Ramiro exhibited all the classic telltale signs of having been sucked by the tlahuelpuchi. Pilar's breasts were normal. Ramiro had been protected that night by a cross made of safety pins attached to his shirt. All the members of the household slept in the same room: Javier and his son in a petate, the three daughters in another petate, and Pilar and Ramiro in another. The sleeping room has a window, a door to the outside, and it is not directly connected to the general purpose room. The window and door of the sleeping room were always locked from the inside when the family retired for the night, but when Ramiro was found dead early in the morning the door was slightly ajar. That night Pilar and the children had retired about 10:30. She had nursed Ramiro and gone to sleep by eleven o'clock. Javier, a labor migrant in the second shift at a nearby textile factory, arrived slightly before one in the morning, and after a short talk with Pilar, they fell asleep. That was the last time that Javier and Pilar saw Ramiro alive. Upon being questioned, Pilar insisted that the last time she put Ramiro to the breast was before eleven o'clock. Moreover, Javier and Pilar stated that nothing unusual had happened that night, except that upon arriving on the outskirts of Xolotla walking from the factory, Javier had seen the telltale ball of fire of a tlahuelpuchi. He did not consider this unusual, for occasionally he saw the moving light of the tlahuelpuchi on his nightly walks from work. But upon arriving home, he asked Pilar to make the safety-pin cross on Ramiro's shirt as a precautionary measure. Javier woke up with a strong headache next morning, and Pilar had deep chest pains. Pilar got up at 6:30, and seeing the door ajar, she quickly went outside and found Ramiro dead on the ground to the left of the door. Javier and the children were awakened by Pilar's screaming, and soon afterward neighboring kinsmen began to congregate in the house. Pilar became completely hysterical and had to be restrained by her mother-in-law and a co-sister-in-law (*concuña*), who live in a nearby house. Pilar was unusual, in that almost all mothers manage to control themselves and to maintain their presence of mind when confronted with their infants having been sucked by the tlahuelpuchi. Further, Pilar claimed to know little about the tlahuelpuchi complex. Pilar's reaction was both intriguing and suspicious, for Javier, whom Nutini knew fairly well, claimed not only to know a great deal about tlahuelpuchis but often talked about the times he had seen them and participated in chasing them. The case of Pilar presented some interesting dimensions which will be analyzed below.

Household 3: This was a nuclear-family household occupying a single-construction house with three rooms and separate zacate kitchen, and was composed of the following personnel: Luis Alvarado, 43, head of the household and father of the victim; Margarita Olmedo, 43, mother of the victim; three sons, 18, 12, and 7; and two daughters, 15 and 4; and Paula, the victim, seven months old. Paula exhibited to a rather abnormal degree all the classic telltale signs of having been sucked by the tlahuelpuchi, for her face, neck, and chest were almost covered with bruises, acchymoses, and purple spots. In fact, Paula exhibited the most pronounced telltale signs of the forty-seven sucked infants that Nutini had the opportunity to examine. Moreover, the areola in Margarita's left breast also exhibited rather pronounced black-and-blue marks. Paula had not been protected that night by any of the methods against the tlahuelpuchi. The sleeping arrangements were as follows: in the middle room, the two elder sons slept together in one petate and Luis slept with his youngest son in another; in the next room, the two daughters slept together in one petate and Margarita and Paula slept in another. The two adjacent sleeping rooms had windows and are connected by a door; the middle room has an outside door, but it is not connected directly to the general-purpose room; the windows and outside door are always locked at night. That night the younger children were asleep by ten o'clock, but Luis, Margarita, and the oldest son and daughter stayed up until about one o'clock in the morning, in the loom shack in the back of the house, working on an order of ten sarapes that had to be delivered next day. They ate coffee and bread after quitting work, and by 1:30 they had all retired. When Margarita laid down on the petate Paula woke up and was put to the breast. Margarita insisted that after some ten minutes of nursing, she placed Paula away from her before she went to sleep. Upon being questioned, Luis, Margarita, and the two eldest children said that they had been very tired and had fallen asleep quickly. The eldest children woke up normally, but Luis and Margarita had splitting headaches and nausea. Manuel, the oldest son, got up first about 6:30. He went into the adjacent room to wake up his mother and saw Paula lying on the floor a yard or so from her mother's petate. Margarita woke up, and immediately upon seeing Paula away from the petate, she realized that Paula had been sucked by the tlahuelpuchi. According to Luis, her reaction was composed and resigned, as was his, for this was the second time that they had lost an infant to the tlahuelpuchi. The first took place 16 years before, when their secondborn, a female, had been sucked by the tlahuelpuchi, but in that case, she had been left on the ground inside the open door of the room that Luis and Margarita occupied while they were residing patrilocally in his father's household.

Household 4: This was a nuclear-family household occupying a solar type of house with four rooms and a kitchen, and composed of the following personnel: Felipe Diaz, 38, head of the household and father of the victim; Altagracia Acxotecatl, 39, mother of the victim; a son, 11, and a daughter, 7; and Julián, the victim, three and a half months old. Julián exhibited all the telltale signs of having been sucked by the tlahuelpuchi. Altagracia's breasts were normal. That night Julián had been protected against the tlahuelpuchi by a pair of open scissors placed next to the crib. The sleeping arrangements were as follows: the two children slept on a large petate in a room by themselves; in an adjoining room Felipe and Altagracia slept in a large petate and Julián was in a crib nearby. The adjoining rooms had no windows and were not directly connected, but they had separate doors directly to the courtyard of the solar. The doors of the sleeping rooms were closed from the inside at night, more for protection against the cold than for security. That night the children went to sleep at the usual time—that is, about ten o'clock. Felipe and Altagracia went to bed shortly thereafter, for next day Felipe had to get up before five to take an order of sarapes to Puebla. At about one in the morning Julián awoke and Altagracia put him to the breast. Felipe was awakened by the proceedings, but he went back to sleep in a short while. Altagracia stated that after nursing Julián she kept him with her in the petate, but although she was very tired, she could not go back to sleep. As she was finally falling asleep ("como entre sueños"), she saw an intense luminosity coming from under the door which vaguely materialized into some sort of bird, which in retrospect, she thought was either a turkey or a buzzard. She instinctively hugged Julián and pressed him against her body to protect him, but she remembered nothing more and she fell intensely asleep. Felipe stated that after being awakened by Julián he also fell deeply asleep; he slept so deeply that he got up only with great effort, knowing that he was already late to catch the six o'clock bus from the cabecera. He noticed the door of the room almost completely open, and as he rose to get a clean pair of pants from the table next to the door, he saw Julián lying on the ground next to the crib some two yards toward the farther end of the room. It took Felipe sometime to awaken Altagracia, who got up drowsily and, upon seeing her dead infant, vomited on the spot. Both Felipe and Altagracia stated that they had splitting headaches when they woke up, and that the headaches did not go away until late the next day, after the pine wood ashes of the oblique cross had been buried by the erection-of-the-burial-cross padrino. Felipe claimed to know relatively little about the tlahuelpuchi complex, but he fell within the boundaries of what was *normal* to know by the average inhabitant of Xolotla. Altagracia, by contrast, said that she knew a good deal about the workings of the tlahuelpuchi, and that she had experienced two other suckings while she was single and living in her extended family household with two elder married brothers (Altagracia married rather late, at the age of 26). The case of Altagracia, together with case number six, is extremely interesting and will be analyzed below.

Household 5: This was an extended-family household occupying a solar type of house with five rooms and two kitchens, and was composed of the following personnel: Macario Tlahuicole, 26, father of the victim; Justa Quetzalxochitl, 24, mother of the victim; a daughter, 2; Lorenzo, the victim, nine months old; Macario's father, 57, the head of the household; his wife, 56; and two unmarried daughters, 18 and 16; Macario's elder brother, 33; his wife, 35; and three sons, 6, 4, and 3. Lorenzo exhibited the classic telltale signs of having been sucked by the tlahuelpuchi; in addition, his two cheeks and the right side of the neck were faintly scratched. Justa's breasts were normal. That night Lorenzo had not been protected against the tlahuelpuchi by any of the known methods. Macario's father and his nuclear family occupied two rooms next to the receiving room in front of the compound. Macario, his married brother, and their respective nuclear families occupied two separate rooms at the end of the solar's courtyard. Macario's room had no windows and a single door to the courtyard. He slept in a large petate with Justa, their daughter slept in a small petate a yard or so from Macario's side, and Lorenzo slept in a small petate next to Justa. After Macario and Justa retired for the night, they always closed the door of their room. That night their child and infant were asleep by nine o'clock, but Macario and Justa stayed up dying wool in the courtyard until about midnight, when they had coffee, then went to sleep. Justa stated that perhaps two hours later Lorenzo woke up screaming and that she put him to the breast to calm him down. For nearly a month Lorenzo had slept the night through, and Macario was mad at being wakened. It took him a little while to go back to sleep, but Justa could not fall asleep for a long time. After nursing Lorenzo, Justa kept him in her arms and did not remember putting him in his own petate. Both Macario and Justa stated that nothing unusual had happened after Lorenzo woke up, but that the next morning they were so drowsy that it had been difficult for them to get up when they were called excitedly by Macario's father; also, for the entire day they had had a bad headache. Macario's father was always the first to get up to check the looms for the day's work. That morning he rose at 5:30, and although it had not yet dawned, the night was clear enough for him to see something lying in the courtyard in front of Macario's door, which was slightly ajar. Getting closer, he recognized the dead Lorenzo and immediately awakened the parents. When asked, none of the other adult members of the household reported anything unusual that night or morning. Macario and Justa were desolate but accepted stoically the death of their infant, according to custom. Macario's father and mother were very angry at Macario and Justa when they learned that Lorenzo had not been protected against the tlahuelpuchi that night. Macario's father stated that, as far as he could remember, there had never been a sucking in his family because his parents had been very careful to protect infants and that as long as there were infants in the household, there was always a handy piece of onion for that purpose. He angrily expressed the universal admonition that "los jóvenes siempre lo saben todo y ahí tiene las consecuencias" (the young always know everything and there you have the consequences).

Household 6: This was an extended-family household occupying a solar type of house with six rooms and three kitchens, and was composed of the following personnel: Filemón Teyohualmiqui, 34, father of the victim; Francisca Sandoval, 33, mother of the victim; two sons, 9 and 4; a daughter, 6; and Cristina, the victim, seven months old; Filemón's father, 62, the head of household; his wife, 58; an unmarried son and unmarried daughter, 20, and 17; Filemón's elder brother, 38; his wife, 37, two sons, 14 and 5; and two daughters, 12 and 10; Filemón's younger brother, 27; his wife, 23; and a daughter, 2. Cristina exhibited all the telltale signs of having been sucked by the tlahuelpuchi, and her chest was significantly scratched. It was also noticed that her fingernails were quite long and unkempt. Francisca's breasts were normal. That night Cristina had not been protected against the tlahuelpuchi by any of the methods. Filemón's solar type of house was large and all rooms were geometrically distributed around the almost perfectly square courtyard. The two rooms in the back opposite to the entrance were occupied by Filemón's father and mother and their two unmarried children. Filemón's married brothers and their respective nuclear families each occupied one of the two rooms on the left hand side of the courtyard as one entered the solar. Filemón and his nuclear family occupied the room below the receiving room on the right hand side of the courtyard. Filemón's room had a glass window open to the outside of the solar—a rather unusual feature in this type of house—and a single door to the courtyard. Filemón slept in a large petate with his two sons, Francisca and her daughter slept in another, and Cristina slept in a small petate next to her mother. The children went to bed at the usual time that night, and by ten o'clock they were asleep. Filemón and Francisca stayed up until midnight, making *madeja* (skein) and carding wool respectively. About that time, Filemón's elder brother returned from Mexico City, where he had gone to deliver an order of sarapes, and he was invited to have coffee. Before retiring Francisca woke up Cristina to nurse her. She said that by the time she put Cristina back in her own petate, Filemón was sound asleep and snoring and that she quickly fell asleep, for they were both very tired. Asked about whether anything unusual happened that night, Francisca stated that perhaps two or three hours after falling asleep she halfway woke up and remembered seeing a rather intense light moving about in the window. She tried to get up but she couldn't, for her body felt very heavy and her legs did not respond. Some time later, still half-asleep, she experienced something like fog filling the room and remembered fuzzily a blue and red chicken-like bird materializing out of the mist, then she quickly fell into a deep sleep. Filemón stated that he experienced nothing unusual that night, but his father said that when he got up sometime during the night to relieve himself in the back of the courtyard, he saw a bright light hovering near the wall of the solar. He immediately thought of the tlahuelpuchi, he reported in retrospect, and quickly got into his room, secured the door, and woke up his wife. They commented that something bad was going to happen for sure ("de seguro que algo malo iba a suceder"), but they did not get up. The other members of the household did not notice or experience anything unusual that night. Filemón got up shortly after six o'clock and immediately noticed that the door was ajar; opening it completely, he saw Cristina on the floor next to the wall side of her petate. When he realized that she was dead, he shook Francisca to get up, but it took her several minutes to become completely awake. By that time the entire household were in Filemón's room, and seeing her dead infant, Francisca burst into loud cries. But she quickly calmed down and even had the presence of mind to express her desire for the selection of the erection-of-the-burial-cross padrino. Days after, Filemón said that for at least a week after he was sort of drowsy and in the state of *tzipitictoc* (in a constant state of irritation), whereas Francisca said that for three days she had nausea and headaches. All adult members of Filemón's household exhibited good knowledge of the tlahuelpuchi complex, and they had an unusual degree of experience, for this was the fourth time that the tlahuelpuchi had sucked infants in the more than forty years that Filemón's father, starting as a *xocoyote* (lastborn son), had lived in the same house with his own father and elder married brothers.

Household 7: This was an extended-family household occupying a solar type of house with four rooms and a kitchen, and composed of the following personnel: Enedino Alvarado, 31, father of the victim; Guadalupe Tzontlimatl, 31, mother of the victim; a son and a daughter, 5 and 3; and Petra, the victim, five months old; Enedino's father, 59, the head of the household; an unmarried son, 22; and two unmarried daughters, 19 and 13; Enedino's younger brother, 28; his wife, 23; and a son, 3. Petra exhibited all the telltale signs of having been sucked by the tlahuelpuchi, and her cheeks were slightly scratched. Guadalupe had black-and-blue marks on the areola and lower part of her right breast. That night Petra had been protected against the tlahuelpuchi by two silver medals attached to the shirt on her chest and back. Enedino's father and his unmarried son and two daughters occupied the room on the left side of the courtyard as one entered the solar. Enedino's younger brother and his nuclear family occupied the room below the receiving room on the right side of the courtyard; Enedino and his nuclear family occupied the room at the back of the courtyard. Enedino and Guadalupe slept in a large petate, his two children slept in another, and Petra slept in a crib next to the wall. That night the children did not go to sleep until about eleven o'clock, shortly after Guadalupe returned with them from Apizaco where she had gone late that afternoon to deliver an order of sarapes because Enedino had been ill with a bad case of influenza for the past two days. She had left Petra with her concuña (Enedino's younger brother's wife) while she was away. She nursed Petra, put her to bed in the crib, and prepared Enedino's medicine. Shortly after midnight they were sound asleep; Enedino was under the influence of the warm medicine, and Guadalupe was very tired. Under questioning, Enedino stated that he did not remember anything until he was brusquely awakened by Guadalupe next morning, whereas Guadalupe said that she vaguely remembered Petra's cries sometime during the night but that she felt so heavy and drowsy that she went back into a deep sleep. Guadalupe awoke shortly before six o'clock and immediately noticed that the door was ajar. She got up quickly, opened the door completely, and saw Petra on the ground next to the wall on the left side of the door. None of the other members of the household experienced anything unusual during the night, except that Enedino's younger unmarried brother noticed that the door of the solar was open when he came out of the room he shared with his father and sisters when he heard Guadalupe's loud cries. Both Enedino and Guadalupe stated that they had headaches and did not feel good for four days after that morning. Enedino's father stated in retrospect that he had had a sort of premonition that it was about time for the tlahuelpuchi to strike again, for his immediate family had not experienced a sucking since he was about fifteen years old. That, in his view, represented a good deal of luck, for which he was thankful, and he attributed it to his faithful compliance with all the ritual and ceremonial obligations toward the supernatural powers. Indeed, Enedino's father was expressing the people's overwhelming concern about the bloodsucking witchcraft epidemic.

CONFORMITY TO THE BELIEF SYSTEM AND THE EXTRAORDINARY
FEATURES OF THE EPIDEMIC

The foregoing describes the main structural and temporal features which marked the most serious epidemic of bloodsucking witchcraft on record. It was an extraordinary and terrifying event. More than a decade later, in communities far away from Xolotla, people still remembered it as the greatest epidemic that they had ever heard of. To a remarkable extent, the epidemic conformed to the belief system that the average rural Tlaxcalan, probably since childhood, had internalized about the tlahuelpuchi complex: all the sucked infants fell between the three to nine months age limit; in varying degrees, all the infants exhibited the telltale signs of having been sucked by the tlahuelpuchi; the suckings took place past midnight but before dawn; the doors of the rooms where the suckings took place were left either open or ajar; the infants had been found dead either next to the door or next to the petate or crib; and so on. Even the deviations or discrepancies in a few facts or events of the epidemic fell within the range allowed by the self-fulfilling tlahuelpuchi complex: only three infants had scratches on their cheeks, necks, and/or chests; two mothers exhibited irritated breast areolas; three infants were protected against the tlahuelpuchi whereas four were not; and so on. All these facts indicated the great consistency and internal logic of bloodsucking witchcraft in rural Tlaxcala. Moreover, the epidemic produced in the parents of the sucked infants a series of what might be termed psychosomatic ailments that were elicited or became apparent within the context of direct or indirect interviewing.

In two ways, however, the epidemic was atypical. First, the fourteen bloodsucking witchcraft epidemics that were recorded over a period of more than seventy years fell within the range of three to five infants sucked by the tlahuelpuchi within a night or over two to four consecutive nights, and for territorial segments similar or slightly larger than the parajes of Meztitlán, Chicomoxtoc, and Aztlán. If to this we add the fact that seven infants were sucked out of a possible total of thirteen infants under one year of age for the three parajes, then the epidemic was totally extraordinary and the possibility that it would happen again was very remote. Second, no one from the three parajes was accused of being one of the responsible tlahuelpuchis, leading to an immediate death. According to the belief system underlying bloodsucking witchcraft, the tremendous magnitude of the epidemic most certainly warranted the execution of a tlahuelpuchi. Why this did not happen Nutini was unable to answer with certainty, but he suggested that it may have been the tightly knit kinship structure of the parajes that prevented it, for the people believe that tlahuelpuchis, if they can possibly help it, do not suck the blood of kinsmen. However, other sociological and psychological factors that we do not control might make intelligible the fact that not all epidemics lead to accusations and to the execution of tlahuelpuchis. This also indicates that even the most logical and internally consistent belief system involves discrepancies and departures from the stated ideological order. Since witchcraft accusations leading to executions are extremely rare and sociologically not very significant, we can dispense with the further analysis of this point.

CHAPTER SIX

The Empirical Evidence of Bloodsucking Witchcraft: Methodology and Systematic Presentation

WE CAN DETERMINE how the self-fulfilling bloodsucking witchcraft system works by analyzing the interrelationship between the system's ideological imperatives and its manifest physical components leading to the death of infants. The ideological and structural reality of bloodsucking witchcraft in rural Tlaxcala cannot be questioned, for it is not only a highly consistent system, but it is buttressed by a high degree of interrelationship between what is ideologically expected and what is physically experienced by the people. Moreover, there is always enough leeway between what the people expect and what they actually experience so that any specific discrepancy can always be reinterpreted as a reinforcement of the underlying belief system: the ideology of bloodsucking witchcraft in rural Tlaxcala was still powerful enough in 1965 to be able to reinterpret any "rational" or "scientific" explanation of the death of infants sucked by the tlahuelpuchi. Thus, when on several occasions traditional informants were confronted with a possible immediate scientific cause of infants' deaths, they invariably retorted that that might very well be so, but only because of the way the tlahuelpuchi sucked the blood of her victims.

From this viewpoint, then, the perception and epistemology of a traditional rural Tlaxcalan perhaps as late as 1970, was essentially the same as that of the Azande. When an Azande man breaks a leg by stumbling on a leaf-covered stump, he does not disagree that a particular chain of events was the immediate cause of the injury, but he does maintain that this particular sequence of events was due to witchcraft (Evans-Pritchard 1937:63–84). The principle of multiple causation and the non-objectification of causality seem to be universal attributes of witchcraft throughout the world. Witchcraft is always embedded in an ideological explanatory system that stipulates that, since the action of witchcraft transcends experience, it cannot be rejected simply because it contradicts what the people regard as the "natural" course of events. Thus, the principle remains the same; what varies from society to society are the different elements in the chain of causation that are not objectively ascertained, that is, secondary causes.

However, when the epistemology of witchcraft begins to change, generally due to changes brought about by prolonged contact with other explanatory systems, mainly technology and science, one of the first things to be questioned is the direct outcome of witchcraft's action, whereas the belief system underlying the practice may linger on for considerably long periods of time. Thus, during the past twenty-five years, rural Tlaxcalans have become increasingly aware of modern medical practices, and this has led to serious questions and doubts about witchcraft, while the basic complex of beliefs and practices surrounding bloodsucking witchcraft remained fairly well organized in the minds of the people.[1] It is therefore appropriate that we begin the discussion with the analysis of the practice's central feature, namely, the efficacy of the tlahuelpuchi to kill. Before this can be done properly, two tasks are necessary: a discussion of the methodology and procedures employed in the collection and recording of the data, and the systematic presentation of the empirical evidence surrounding bloodsucking witchcraft.

ORGANIZATION OF THE FIELD SITUATION: THE FORTY-SEVEN CASE SAMPLE

During the summer of 1959, Nutini conducted an ethnographic survey of the Tlaxcala-Pueblan Valley (see map 2). He surveyed twenty-seven communities and spent on average two to five days in each one of them. One of the several results of the survey established the widespread incidence of bloodsucking witchcraft at the community and regional levels. A year later, Nutini began a two-year period of intensive fieldwork in the municipio of San Diego Tlalocan, and by then the tlahuelpuchi complex was fairly well known to him. But it was not until November 1960 that he was able first to examine an infant sucked by the tlahuelpuchi, due to the exigencies and time limitations of the survey. Although he could hardly have failed to appreciate the significance of bloodsucking witchcraft, it would have remained one of many topics of investigation that the ethnographer normally encounters in the field, had it not been for two fortuitous events: his acquaintance with the chief medical officer of the state of Tlaxcala, and San Pedro Xolotla's bloodsucking epidemic. The chief medical officer not only provided Nutini with a working hypothesis about the nature of bloodsucking witchcraft, but also specified a series of steps to follow in the

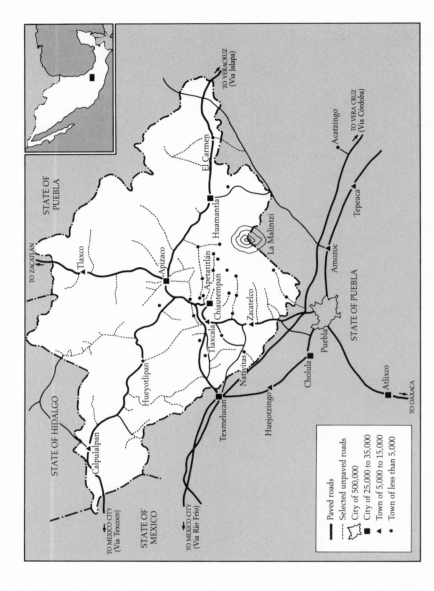

MAP 2. Highway and Road Network

examination of sucked infants, which, he indicated, would be encountered fairly often in the course of research. Moreover, the medical officer insightfully suggested that, after investigating the circumstances surrounding the death of sucked infants, Nutini should concentrate on the parents of the victim and keep them under observation for one or two weeks, thereby hinting at the psychosomatic aftereffects they often developed. The three extended conversations with the chief medical officer in mid-October were a veritable crash course on the diagnosis and etiology of bloodsucking witchcraft. Slightly over a month and a half later, the Xolotla epidemic took place. In early November, Nutini asked Don Julián, as well as five of his most trusted informants, to report to him the death of any sucked infants. Thus, he had already investigated the death of two infants before the epidemic took place. But it was the drama, extraordinariness, and sheer intensity of the Xolotla epidemic that coalesced his interest in bloodsucking witchcraft and led to its systematic investigation throughout 1961 and for four subsequent summers.

Don Julián led Nutini to the first case of bloodsucking witchcraft in Xolotla on 27 November; five days later Nutini investigated the second case in San Diego Tlalocan, his headquarters and the headtown of the municipio (see table 6.1). These two cases served in effect as a trial run for the preliminary preparation of the basic questionnaire and observational procedures which acquired their final form during the Xolotla epidemic. He would use the questionnaire in standardized form for all cases of bloodsucking witchcraft during the following six years. In fact, the investigation of cases 1 and 2 had to be completed after the epidemic, for several questions had not been developed when they occurred. The questionnaire, observational procedures, and sequential format were based primarily on the knowledge about bloodsucking witchcraft of the chief medical officer, and on the experience that he gained through the investigation of the seven cases of the Xolotla epidemic. All subsequent cases were investigated in the same fashion, and they constitute the single most systematic corpus of data that he has collected. The questionnaire contained some thirty-five open-ended questions that have been collapsed into twenty in the presentation of this monograph (see tables 6.1 to 6.20).

A few words must be said about each of the tables. All cases were numbered from 1 to 47: (6.1) the date of occurrence; (6.2) the name of the community, section, and/or *paraje*; (6.3) the age of the victim in months approximated to the lowest month, except in one case in which the victim was seven years old; (6.4) the sex of the victim; (6.5) the birth order of the victim; (6.6) the age of the victim's parents; (6.7) the social and physical composition of the household; (6.8) the number of people who slept in the victim's room; (6.9) the approximate time of finding the victim's body; (6.10) who found the body of the victim; (6.11) the exact location where the victim's body was found; (6.12) the time elapsed between the approximate death of the victim and Nutini's or a physician's examination of the body; (6.13) the physical marks on the victim's body; (6.14) the physical marks on the mother's body; (6.15) the victim's protection against the tlahuelpuchi; (6.16) any unusual events surrounding the sucking; (6.17) the parents' aftereffects due to the sucking; (6.18) previous suckings in the victim's nuclear family; (6.19) previous suckings in the victim's household; (6.20) language spoken in the household and degree of acculturation.

After the Xolotla epidemic Nutini could not spend more than a fraction of his time on the investigation of bloodsucking witchcraft, for the main thrust of the research was the kinship system and social organization of the municipio of San Diego Tlalocan, a sociopolitical unit involving six separate settlements and more than ten thousand people. Early in January he gathered two of his most reliable and respected informants from each of the six settlements in the municipio and asked them to report immediately to him any deaths due to the tlahuelpuchi. As the year progressed, Nutini was able to expand his network of informants who were willing to report the death of sucked infants to communities in nearby municipios. Thus, by the time he left the field at the end of December 1961 he had cases from four communities in San Diego Tlalocan and three communities in nearby municipios (see table 1). Had Nutini not relied on this technique, it would have been impossible to investigate as many cases as he did. Over a period of twelve months (27 November 1960 to 3 December 1961) he was led to thirty-six cases of bloodsucking witchcraft. Using local informants was an efficient method which demanded not too much of his time and led to quick results: the victims were examined shortly after they had died (see table 6.12), and he arrived to investigate the bloodsucking event and its aftereffects well recommended and with most of the obstacles smoothed out. The period of observation of the members of the victim's household, which could last up to three weeks and involve four or five interviews, was routinely conducted and standardized. In nine of the eleven cases investigated during the summers of 1962, 1964, 1965, and 1966 (see table 6.1), the same procedure was followed, but the aftereffects of the bloodsucking event were recorded in a slightly less systematic fashion. These cases took place in communities quite far apart, and given the exigencies and time limitations of summer fieldwork, it was impossible to undertake as many postsucking observations of the victim's household. But this did not matter very much, for at the end of 1961 the patterning, consistency, and regularity of the bloodsucking event had become entirely apparent. During the following summers, the only reason for investigating more cases was to gain a wider regional distribution. In summary, the mean average data-gathering time per case was about ten hours: four hours for the sucking event itself, and six hours of postsucking interviewing and observation.

As the reader will recall, the seven cases of the Xolotla epidemic (numbers 3 to 9 in table 6.1) were examined by a physician within approximately eighteen hours after the death of the infants. The physician diagnosed the cause of death in all seven cases and stated the likely circumstances under which they had occurred. Four more cases were examined by a physician: three throughout 1961 (numbers 21, 31, and 36) and one during the summer of 1965 (number 44). In these eleven cases the physician either positively diagnosed the cause of death (9), or stated that short of an autopsy it was impossible for him to determine for certain the cause of death (2). It would have been ideal to have had all sucked infants examined by a physician, but this was impossible, given the exigencies of the field situation, for none of the communities involved had a resident doctor. A physician had to be fetched from one of the four cities in the state of Tlaxcala or from the city of Puebla some twenty to thirty miles away. It was difficult to have even eleven cases medically examined before the infants were buried within the next thirty to thirty-six hours. In addition, the majority of the victims' parents and kinsmen would have refused such an examination. In any event, the eleven cases constituted slightly less than 25 percent of all recorded sucked infants, and this certainly gave Nutini an adequate medical sample on which to base the victims' physical causes of death. Moreover, the chief medical officer and his assistant (the physician who examined the victims of the Xolotla epidemic) instructed Nutini carefully in detecting the marks on the body of the victim that were characteristic of the most common cause of death, which will be discussed below.

ADDITIONAL ETHNOGRAPHIC, QUANTITATIVE, AND CENSUS DATA

The quantitative data on which this monograph is based include not only the forty-seven cases of bloodsucking witchcraft, but other data as well. During the summers of 1967 and 1968, seven more cases were reported to Nutini; five occurred in communities in the 47-case sample, and two occurred in communities outside the sample. Nutini visited the households where the suckings took place but did not collect complete information or make observations in depth. Thus, they are not included in the sample, but the bloodsucking events were pretty much the same. No new insights were gained. From 1969 to 1976 eight more cases were reported to Nutini, but they were not formally investigated; two of them involved households of *compadres,* and he felt obliged to visit the victims' parents and attend the funeral and ceremonial banquet. In fact, since the summer of 1966 he has felt that nothing would be gained by the observation of more cases. The majority of these fifteen cases were reported by Nutini's network of compadres (who by 1976 numbered more than fifty couples throughout rural Tlaxcala) who knew of his interest in bloodsucking witchcraft.

Of more significance for establishing the incidence of bloodsucking witchcraft was the census information gathered during the months of March, April, May, and June 1961. During these months, Nutini conducted a household census of the entire municipio of San Diego Tlalocan with the assistance of four local informants. It involved a total of 1,636 households inhabited by 2,559 nuclear families: 1,534 nuclear families composed 611 extended-family households, whereas 1,025 were independent nuclear-family households. The printed census forms contained 25 questions on kinship, residence, economics, and language, but on the back of the form he instructed the census-takers to ask two more questions on bloodsucking witchcraft: what was the total number of infant deaths due to the tlahuelpuchi in the memory of the oldest members of the household, and what were the sexes of the victims. The main purposes of asking these two questions were to determine the male-female ratio of the victims and any changes in the incidence of bloodsucking witchcraft which might have occurred during the four generations recorded by the census forms. The results of the census were as follows: No information was obtained for 564 households; members refused to answer the two questions.[2] The breakdown of the 1,072 households which answered the questions give the following results: 487 were extended-family households and 585 nuclear-family households. Of the extended-family households, 3 had 6 infants sucked by the tlahuelpuchi, 11 households had 5 infants sucked, 37 had 4, 98 had 3, 146 had 2, 154 had 1, and 38 had none. Of the nuclear-family households, 21 had 3 infants sucked by the tlahuelpuchi, 49 had 2, 230 had 1, and 285 had none. The total number of infants sucked by the tlahuelpuchi in these 1,072 nuclear- and extended-family households was 1,352 (391 and 961, respectively), of which 439 victims were male and 913 female.

An exhaustive analysis of these results would not add anything significant to the practice and incidence of bloodsucking witchcraft in rural Tlaxcala, but a few generalizations are in order. First, these statistical facts indicate unequivocally that bloodsucking witchcraft is widespread in rural Tlaxcala, since, at least until 1965, the extremely high incidence of the phenomenon in the municipio of San Diego Tlalocan was the rule rather than the exception in all the municipios on the western slopes of La Malintzi volcano. Second, given the fact that until 1962 nearly 50 percent of all children born in San Diego Tlalocan died before the age of five, bloodsucking witchcraft accounted for about 20 percent of infant mortality. This estimate is based on the study of municipal-death registers, which have been kept fairly complete since 1883. Third, the incidence of bloodsucking witchcraft had remained fairly constant for at least three generations before 1965—that is, since approximately the 1880s: the mean average number of sucked infants per nuclear family and household had not changed significantly until the last time data was collected systematically on the subject. Since 1978, however, we suspect that the number of sucked infants may have been reduced by more than two thirds. Fourth, the difference in the number of sucked infants between nuclear- and extended-family households has two reasons: the mean average extended family is composed of 2.5 nuclear families and has a total membership of more than twice the mean average nuclear-family household; the average extended family may have a genealogical depth varying from two to four generations, whereas the nuclear-family household never includes more than two generations. Of course, the situation becomes more complicated when one takes into consideration the developmental cycle of the extended family, but the foregoing reasons clearly explain the differences. Finally, the disproportionate male-female ratio of sucked infants will be discussed below.

DEMOGRAPHIC PARAMETERS AND VITAL STATISTICS

The social and psychological facts surrounding bloodsucking witchcraft, with special reference to the bloodsucking event, can now be discussed. We shall analyze independently each of the twenty tables which summarily present the most salient factors of the phenomena. This procedure is better suited to expanding several aspects of bloodsucking witchcraft which cannot be subsumed under a tabular presentation and to discussing anomalous features which depart from the stated ideology with significant consequences for the interrelationship of social and psychological components.

Table 6.1 lists in chronological order the total number of bloodsucking cases that were investigated in depth and for which we have complete information. Is the sample representative of absolute and seasonal incidence of bloodsucking witchcraft for rural Tlaxcala as a whole? The answer is yes on both counts. First, thirty-six cases (1–36) were investigated within the context of an annual cycle (November 1960–December 1961). Twenty-seven of these cases were from four of the six communities comprising the municipio of San Diego Tlalocan. When one compares this figure with the total number of cases covering approximately a seventy-year period for the entire municipio, this sample can be regarded not only as representative but as indicating the constancy of bloodsucking witchcraft from the turn of the century until 1970, at least for San Diego Tlalocan.[3] This is posited, of course, on the assumption that Nutini

Table 6.1 Occurrence of the Bloodsucking Event

Case no.	Date	Case no.	Date	Case no.	Date
1	27 Nov 60	17	16 Feb 61	33	22 Aug 61
2	2 Dec 60	18	17 Feb 61	34	23 Oct 61
3	9 Dec 60	19	22 Feb 61	35	11 Nov 61
4	9 Dec 60	20	12 Mar 61	36	3 Dec 61
5	9 Dec 60	21	21 Mar 61	37	25 Jul 62
6	9 Dec 60	22	4 May 61	38	27 Jul 62
7	9 Dec 60	23	18 May 61	39	29 Aug 64
8	9 Dec 60	24	28 Jun 61	40	29 Aug 64
9	9 Dec 60	25	29 Jun 61	41	31 Aug 64
10	5 Jan 61	26	2 Jul 61	42	5 Sep 64
11	12 Jan 61	27	19 Jul 61	43	17 Jun 65
12	19 Jan 61	28	20 Jul 61	44	29 Jul 65
13	26 Jan 61	29	31 Jul 61	45	30 Aug 65
14	26 Jan 61	30	2 Aug 61	46	3 Jul 66
15	28 Jan 61	31	7 Aug 61	47	17 Aug 66
16	7 Feb 61	32	13 Aug 61		

examined most infants sucked by the tlahuelpuchi throughout the year. This assumption is reasonable, for his informants reported religiously the cases that took place in their neighborhoods, and probably no more than two or three cases escaped their attention. Moreover, San Diego Tlalocan is representative of the municipios surrounding La Malintzi volcano in most respects—variations in degrees of acculturation, and religious traditionalism, and diversification of subsistence and occupation. By contrast, the nine cases examined during the same period in communities of two municipios bordering San Diego Tlalocan, together with the eleven cases (37–47) examined in subsequent summers, are obviously not a representative sample. Rather, these twenty cases must be interpreted as a strong indicator of the regional distribution of bloodsucking witchcraft and as establishing the practice as a uniform phenomenon throughout rural Tlaxcala.

Second, and much more significant for the present analysis, is the seasonal variation of bloodsucking witchcraft. According to the ideology of the practice, the tlahuelpuchis' craving for blood increases greatly during the coldest and rainiest months of the year. This ideological aspect of bloodsucking witchcraft is amply corroborated (see table 6.1). Taking the total number of cases, we can see that forty cases took place during the coldest months (December, January, and February) and the rainiest months (June, July, and August) of the year. The seven remaining cases (1, 20, 21, 22, 23, 34, and 35) are not exceptions, but rather the validation of the ideological belief that tlahuelpuchis must, in fact, suck the blood of infants at least once a month to stay alive. When we break down the incidence of the forty "seasonal" cases, nineteen cases took place during the coldest months, whereas twenty-one took place during the rainiest months; that pattern is statistically highly significant, especially if we compare the latter to the seven out-of-season cases: cold weather is the most significant variable in the incidence of bloodsucking witchcraft, for the rainiest months are also the coldest after December, January, and February. This is explicitly recognized by rural Tlaxcalans who often verbalize the greatest degree of anxiety about tlahuelpuchis by statements such as "el frío parece aumentor su maldad" (the cold seems to increase her wickedness), or "durante el invierno hay que proteger más a las creaturas" (during winter infants must be more protected). Symbolically, fire and heat are the natural environment of tlahuelpuchis, and rural Tlaxcalans believe that cold and water act as disturbing stimulants leading to greater bloodsucking activity. Finally, cases 37 to 47 are all seasonal suckings, but they are not representative, for they were not collected as part of the entire yearly cycle in any of the five communities where they occurred.

There are four communities belonging to the municipio of San Diego Tlalocan (Xolotla, Tlalocan, Omeyocan, and Mictlán), three communities in two municipios bordering San Diego Tlalocan (Topitla, Malinalco, and Meztitlán), and three communities in two municipios on the southernmost part of the western slopes of La Malintzi volcano (Ozomatlán, Coatlán, and Tlacopan). The geographical distribution of these communities extends from the north central to the southernmost part of rural Tlaxcala (see map 1.1), and their altitude varies from 7,400 feet (the bottom of the valley) to 8,700 feet on the slopes of La Malintzi volcano (the highest limit of human habitation). From this viewpoint, the communities where incidents occurred are representative of the area; but even if they were not, it would not matter, for geographical considerations do not seem to play a significant role in bloodsucking witchcraft. Demographically, the communities vary in size from about four thousand (Tlalocan) to one thousand (Omeyocan) inhabitants, while the eight communities in between vary from approximately two thousand to twelve hundred inhabitants; but size is not a significant variable either. No significant variations in the incidence and structure of bloodsucking witchcraft among the ten communities in the sample which may be attributed solely to demographic or geographical variables exist (see table 6.2). Minor differences occur in the ideology and physical manifestation of bloodsucking witchcraft, but overall, the complex remains constant throughout rural Tlaxcala. However, some variations can be attributed to language and degree of acculturation, both at the community and household levels, as will be discussed below.

The ideology of bloodsucking witchcraft is again fully validated in its physical manifestation if we examine the age of the sucked infants at the time of death (see table 6.3). Disregarding case 35 (because rural Tlaxcalans believe that the tlahuelpuchi sucks the blood of children and adults only in extremely rare occasions), only case 34 falls outside the ideologically stipulated sucking age—that is, between three and 10 months. The greatest number of suckings occur at ages four (9 cases) and seven (8 cases) months, but no statistically significant correlation emerges from the analysis of the information in table 6.3. Moreover, we cannot offer any explanation for the fact that there are almost twice as many infants sucked at ages four and seven months than at any other age. Nothing of interest may be added, ideologically or physically. With respect to the former, it would be most extraordinary indeed if rural Tlaxcalans could specify the minuteness of their ideology more than they actually do; with respect to the latter, we are not medically trained, and any significant discriminatory factors in age at the infants' deaths unfortunately escaped us. The significance of the infants' ages, however, will emerge when specific cases

Table 6.2 Distribution of Bloodsucking Cases by Community

Case no.	Community	Case no.	Community
1	San Pedro Xolotla	25	San Antonio Omeyocan
2	San Diego Tlalocan	26	San Cristobal Mictlán
3	San Pedro Xolotla	27	San Diego Tlalocan
4	San Pedro Xolotla	28	San Pedro Xolotla
5	San Pedro Xolotla	29	Santa Clara Topitla
6	San Pedro Xolotla	30	San Lorenzo Malinalco
7	San Pedro Xolotla	31	San Lorenzo Malinalco
8	San Pedro Xolotla	32	San Diego Tlalocan
9	San Pedro Xolotla	33	San Juan Meztitlán
10	San Diego Tlalocan	34	San Antonio Omeyocan
11	San Antonio Omeyocan	35	San Diego Tlalocan
12	San Antonio Omeyocan	36	Santa Clara Topitla
13	San Cristobal Mictlán	37	San Pedro Xolotla
14	San Cristobal Mictlán	38	San Diego Tlalocan
15	San Cristobal Mictlán	39	Santa Elena Ozomatlán
16	San Diego Tlalocan	40	Santa Elena Ozomatlán
17	Santa Clara Topitla	41	Santa Elena Ozomatlán
18	Santa Clara Topitla	42	Santa Elena Ozomatlán
19	San Cristobal Mictlán	43	San Esteban Coatlán
20	San Lorenzo Malinalco	44	San Esteban Coatlán
21	San Pedro Xolotla	45	San Esteban Coatlán
22	San Lorenzo Malinalco	46	Santa Cruz Tlacopan
23	San Diego Tlalocan	47	Santa Cruz Tlacopan
24	San Antonio Omeyocan		

Table 6.3 Age of the Victim at the Time of Death[a]

Case no.	Age in Months	Case no.	Age in Months	Case no.	Age in Months
1	6	17	3	33	8
2	4	18	7	34	12
3	5	19	9	35	7 years
4	8	20	10	36	4
5	7	21	3	37	7
6	4	22	9	38	6
7	9	23	4	39	7
8	7	24	8	40	4
9	5	25	7	41	4
10	10	26	7	42	3
11	3	27	5	43	8
12	8	28	4	44	6
13	6	29	9	45	5
14	10	30	10	46	7
15	5	31	3	47	4
16	4	32	9		

[a]The age of the victim in months approximated to the lowest month, except in one case in which the victim was seven years old.

are analyzed in the context of several other attributes of the bloodsucking event.

There are almost exactly twice as many female (31) as male (16) victims in the sample (see table 6.4).[4] There is no specification in the ideology of blood-sucking witchcraft about the sex of victims. Tlahuelpuchis do not discriminate between male and female infants as desirable sucking subjects or as being easier or more difficult to approach. Yet the ratio appears to have been a constant for the past three generations as attested by the 439 males and 913 females sucked by the tlahuelpuchi during the past 70 years or so. But is the sex of the victim significant, and what is the explanation of such a disparate ratio? We are not certain about the answers, but some light will be shed on the subject when the medical causes of the victims' deaths are analyzed below. Suffice it to say here that rural Tlaxcalans themselves provide a clue when they affirm that more attention is given to males than to females in protecting them against the tlahuelpuchi by the traditional means. This affirmation is not corroborated by the sample, however, for table 6.15 shows that of the 18 infants that were protected against the tlahuelpuchi only 5 were males whereas 13 were females. Rather, the answer lies on the fact that in rural Tlaxcala child-rearing practices are significantly biased towards the psychological care and physical well-being of male infants, a process that is generally extended until children reach the age of five or six.

Table 6.4 Sex of the Victim

Case no.	Sex	Case no.	Sex	Case no.	Sex
1	Female	17	Male	33	Female
2	Female	18	Female	34	Female
3	Male	19	Female	35	Male
4	Male	20	Male	36	Female
5	Female	21	Male	37	Female
6	Male	22	Female	38	Female
7	Male	23	Female	39	Female
8	Female	24	Female	40	Male
9	Female	25	Female	41	Female
10	Female	26	Female	42	Male
11	Male	27	Female	43	Female
12	Female	28	Female	44	Female
13	Male	29	Female	45	Male
14	Female	30	Male	46	Female
15	Female	31	Female	47	Male
16	Female	32	Male		

The birth order of the victims was one of the questions which did not originally occur to Nutini, and it was suggested by the physician who examined the seven corpses of the Xolotla epidemic. At that time, he correctly predicted that there would be few firstborn infants sucked by the tlahuelpuchi, but we do not know whether he made this prediction on the basis of the seven infants he examined (cases 3–9), all of which were at least thirdborn, or on the basis of a general knowledge of the practice. Either way, Nutini felt at the time that it was important to record the birth order of sucked infants, for it could lead to significant correlations involving child rearing practices, the age of parents, care in protecting infants against the tlahuelpuchi, degree of household acculturation, and so on. The distribution of birth orders alone does not entail any statistically significant correlations and seems to be somewhat random, except that suckings appear to cluster between birth orders second and fifth, which may not be significant (see table 6.5). But the birth order of victims acquires considerable significance when correlated with several other variables. This is particularly the case for the four cases in which the victims were firstborn. It is simple enough to say that primiparae are much more careful with their infants than are women giving birth a second time, third, or *n*th time. But this does not tell the whole story. In fact, unravelling the bloodsucking practice situation is much more complicated.

By itself, the data in table 6.6 is not necessarily significant, but together with that in tables 6.5, 6.7, 6.18, and 6.19, they acquire correlational signifi-

Table 6.5 Birth Order of the Victim

Case no.	Birth Order	Case no.	Birth Order	Case no.	Birth Order
1	2nd	17	2nd	33	2nd
2	3rd	18	1st	34	3rd
3	3rd	19	2nd	35	4th
4	6th	20	8th	36	5th
5	8th	21	2nd	37	4th
6	5th	22	3rd	38	3rd
7	3rd	23	1st	39	2nd
8	6th	24	7th	40	6th
9	5th	25	4th	41	5th
10	3rd	26	2nd	42	2nd
11	2nd	27	1st	43	5th
12	4th	28	2nd	44	4th
13	2nd	29	5th	45	2nd
14	2nd	30	6th	46	9th
15	10th	31	1st	47	7th
16	3rd	32	3rd		

cance for the etiological analysis of bloodsucking witchcraft. But a quick look at what table 6.6 tells us in isolation will not be amiss. First, although in ten cases the husband is younger than the wife by as much as three years, in the majority of cases either husband and wife are of the same age or, more commonly, the husband is older than the wife by as much as eight years. This is quite consistent with the marriage structure of rural Tlaxcala (Nutini 1984:Part I). Second, the average marrying age in the sample is between twenty-one and twenty-five for men and eighteen and twenty-two for women, again consistent with the marriage structure of the area. Third, analysis of table 6.6, plus some additional information for the years 1965, 1966, and 1967, well establishes the reproductive career of the average rural Tlaxcalan women: she gives birth for the first time within fifteen months after marriage; from then on she gives birth every two and a half years until the end of her reproductive age, which generally comes at forty-three to forty-six. It must be noted in this connection that until 1965 infant mortality in rural Tlaxcala was extremely high, and out of 10 children born, 4.5 died before the age of five. In San Diego Tlalocan, from 1960 to 1967, infant mortality dropped from approximately 50 to 40 percent, but from 1967 to 1977 it decreased rapidly, and stands now (1985) at less than 20 percent (that is, out of 10 live births more than 8 reach the age of five). In this respect, San Diego Tlalocan is fully representative of rural Tlaxcala as a whole. As far as we have been able to determine, the most significant variables in explaining this rather dramatic drop in infant mortality are not only

Table 6.6 Age of Victims' Parents

Case no.	Age of Parents	Case no.	Age of Parents	Case no.	Age of Parents
1	Fa: 28; Mo: 27	17	Fa: 23; Mo: 19	33	Fa: 27; Mo: 27
2	Fa: 31; Mo: 27	18	Fa: 22; Mo: 18	34	Fa: 34; Mo: 31
3	Fa: 29; Mo: 25	19	Fa: 32; Mo: 28	35	Fa: 41; Mo: 39
4	Fa: 35; Mo: 33	20	Fa: 47; Mo: 39	36	Fa: 34; Mo: 30
5	Fa: 43; Mo: 42	21	Fa: 28; Mo: 24	37	Fa: 29; Mo: 28
6	Fa: 38; Mo: 39	22	Fa: 33; Mo: 29	38	Fa: 28; Mo: 30
7	Fa: 26; Mo: 24	23	Fa: 23; Mo: 21	39	Fa: 23; Mo: 21
8	Fa: 34; Mo: 33	24	Fa: 48; Mo: 41	40	Fa: 49; Mo: 44
9	Fa: 31; Mo: 31	25	Fa: 30; Mo: 29	41	Fa: 39; Mo: 38
10	Fa: 32; Mo: 30	26	Fa: 26; Mo: 27	42	Fa: 26; Mo: 24
11	Fa: 24; Mo: 25	27	Fa: 22; Mo: 25	43	Fa: 37; Mo: 40
12	Fa: 36; Mo: 31	28	Fa: 22; Mo: 21	44	Fa: 30; Mo: 31
13	Fa: 29; Mo: 22	29	Fa: 37; Mo: 34	45	Fa: 26; Mo: 25
14	Fa: 25; Mo: 20	30	Fa: 35; Mo: 36	46	Fa: 43; Mo: 41
15	Fa: 51; Mo: 44	31	Fa: 24; Mo: 25	47	Fa: 46; Mo: 39
16	Fa: 27; Mo: 29	32	Fa: 40; Mo: 31		

improved medical practices, but better housing and more balanced diets for infants and children. Perinatal death is practically unknown in rural Tlaxcala, and it may very well be that which is denoted by bloodsucking witchcraft accounts for the majority of infant mortality before the age of one year. In rural Tlaxcala, practically all of the infant mortality occurs between ages one and five, with the greatest number of deaths clustering between ages one and a half and two and a half. The most common causes of death are respiratory diseases.

COMPOSITION OF THE HOUSEHOLD AND SLEEPING ARRANGEMENTS AT THE TIME OF THE SUCKING

Table 6.7 indicates the social and physical composition of the victims' households. Solar or compound houses predominate, and this expresses nothing more than that rural Tlaxcala on the whole was still traditional (1965) in this realm of material culture, for this type of construction goes back to Colonial times. Single-construction houses are inhabited by two types of domestic groups: nuclear families which have recently separated from ancestral extended-family households, and are thus in the second stage of their developmental cycle; and nuclear families representing the most secularized segment of the population. Recently separated nuclear families will in time develop solar houses by the addition of rooms in the traditional quadrangular pattern and the construction of a wall around the compound, thereby completing the sociophysical cycle of the household. Secularized nuclear families will generally develop urban-style houses, for they represent the segment of the population most susceptible to modernizing influences from the outside. Extended-family households outnumber nuclear-family households in the sample, but this is not a good indicator of the incidence of the former in rural Tlaxcala because the majority of the bloodsucking cases came from San Diego Tlalocan, which had a much higher incidence of extended-family arrangements than the average municipio. In 1965, the mean average incidence of the extended family in rural Tlaxcala was between 30 and 33 percent, whereas in San Diego Tlalocan it was nearly 70 percent. There is a clear correlation between extended families and solar houses, on the one hand, and between nuclear families and single-construction houses on the other. This is the result of the prevalent patri-neolocal rule of residence, ultimogeniture, and the developmental cycle of the domestic group, which entails the single-construction house growing into a

Table 6.7 Social and Physical Composition of the Victims' Households[a]

Case no.	Household Structure	Case no.	Household Structure
1	ext-fam; solar	25	nuc-fam; solar
2	nuc-fam; sing-const	26	ext-fam; solar
3	nuc-fam; sing-const	27	ext-fam; solar
4	nuc-fam; sing-const	28	ext-fam; solar
5	nuc-fam; sing-const	29	nuc-fam; sing-const
6	nuc-fam; solar	30	nuc-fam; sing-const
7	ext-fam; solar	31	ext-fam; solar
8	ext-fam; solar	32	nuc-fam; sing-const
9	ext-fam; solar	33	ext-fam; solar
10	ext-fam; solar	34	nuc-fam; sing-const
11	ext-fam; solar	35	nuc-fam; solar
12	nuc-fam; sing-const	36	nuc-fam; sing-const
13	nuc-fam; sing-const	37	nuc-fam; sing-const
14	nuc-fam; solar	38	ext-fam; solar
15	ext-fam; solar	39	ext-fam; solar
16	nuc-fam; sing-const	40	ext-fam; solar
17	ext-fam; solar	41	nuc-fam; solar
18	ext-fam; solar	42	ext-fam; solar
19	nuc-fam; sing-const	43	nuc-fam; sing-const
20	ext-fam; solar	44	nuc-fam; sing-const
21	nuc-fam; solar	45	ext-fam; sing-const
22	nuc-fam; sing-const	46	ext-fam; solar
23	ext-fam; solar	47	ext-fam; solar
24	ext-fam; solar		

[a]Under this rubric were included the compound house (solar) and single-construction house, and whether they were inhabited by nuclear or extended families. The number of people living in the household and the spatial arrangements within it were important to the analysis of the phenomenon at hand.

Table 6.8 Kinsmen Sleeping in Victim's Room at the
Time of Death[a]

Case no.	Category and Number of Kinsmen (Ego = Victim)
1	Fa, Mo, and one sibling age 2
2	Fa, Mo, FaMo, and one sibling age 4
3	Fa, Mo, and two siblings ages 5 and 3
4	Fa, Mo, and four siblings ages 10, 9, 6, and 2
5	Mo, and two siblings ages 15 and 4
6	Fa, Mo
7	Fa, Mo, and one sibling age 2
8	Fa, Mo, and three siblings ages 9, 6, and 4
9	Fa, Mo, and two siblings ages 5 and 3
10	Fa, Mo, and one sibling age 7
11	Fa, Mo, Fa yg Si, and one sibling age 2
12	Fa, Mo, and three siblings ages 13, 8, and 3
13	Fa, Mo, FaFaBr, and one sibling age 4
14	Fa, Mo
15	Fa, Mo, and five siblings ages 17, 15, 10, 8, and 3
16	Fa, Mo, and two siblings ages 3 and 1
17	Fa, Mo
18	Fa, Mo, Fa yg Si
19	Fa, Mo, MoSi (Fa's Co-Wi), and one sibling age 5
20	Mo, and two siblings ages 16 and 9
21	Mo, FaSi, and one sibling age 2
22	Fa, Mo, and one sibling age 4
23	Fa, Mo
24	Fa, Mo, and three siblings ages 8, 5, and 3
25	Mo, and two siblings ages 6 and 2

solar at midpoint in the cycle. There are seven exceptions to this generalization (cases 6, 14, 21, 25, 35, 41, and 45), but they can be explained by the contingencies that the developmental cycle of the domestic group encounters in its three- to four-generational span, such as the untimely death of married adults, social friction among married couples of the same extended family, and economic pressures. By themselves, the social and physical compositions of the victims' households give the general personnel and space parameters in which bloodsucking witchcraft takes place, but they acquire direct correlational significance in connection with several other variables.

In the investigation of most cases, immediately after the examination of the victim's body, Nutini proceeded with the census and physical arrangements of the household. He paid special attention to the sleeping arrangements in the victim's room; but only part of the information can be presented in tabular form. Let us discuss the personnel arrangements first. It is a general practice in rural Tlaxcala that nuclear families occupy an independent sleeping room. This

Table 6.8 *Continued*

Case no.	Category and Number of Kinsmen (Ego = Victim)
26	Mo, FaMo, and one sibling age 2
27	Fa, Mo
28	Mo, FaMo
29	Fa, Mo, and three siblings ages 13, 7, and 4
30	Fa, Mo, and two siblings ages 7 and 4
31	Fa, Mo, Fa yg Br, and Fa yg Si
32	Fa, Mo, and one sibling age 13
33	Mo, Fa yg Br
34	Fa, Mo, FaFaFa, and one sibling age 5
35	Mo, FaMo, and one sibling age 11
36	Fa, Mo, MoBr, and two siblings ages 9 and 3
37	Mo, and two siblings ages 8 and 3
38	Fa, Mo, FaBr, and one sibling age 7
39	Fa, Mo, and MoSi
40	Mo, FaSi, and two siblings ages 14 and 8
41	Fa, Mo, FaFaBr, and two siblings ages 6 and 4
42	Fa, Mo
43	Fa, Mo, MoMo, and three siblings ages 9, 6, and 2
44	Mo, and two siblings ages 5 and 2
45	Fa, Mo, and MoSi
46	Mo, FaMo, and three siblings ages 17, 14, and 11
47	Fa, Mo, and four siblings ages 16, 10, 7, and 3

[a]Here are also included the sleeping arrangements (beds, cribs, petates, etc.), who slept with whom and where, the spatial arrangement of persons and furniture, and access to the room (doors, windows, etc.).

usually presents no problems in solar houses, but in single-construction houses it is fairly common that lineal or collateral kinsmen may sleep in the same room with the couple and their children. Table 6.8 shows that there are twenty-seven "normal" sleeping arrangements in the sample and twenty cases in which a rather wide variety of kinsmen are attached to the sleeping room. Of the normal arrangements, five cases (5, 20, 25, 37, and 44) had only the mother sleeping in the room at the time of the victim's death while the father was away at work or for some reason out of the house that particular night. Of the arrangements including lineal and collateral kinsmen, six more cases (26, 28, 33, 35, 40, and 46) had only the mother sleeping in the room of the victim while the father was absent for the same reasons given above. Thus, the most significant fact of table 6.8 is that victim and mother slept in the same room at the time of death in all forty-seven cases. This acquires statistical significance when we take into consideration that mothers often have their infants spend the night in another room with mothers-in-law or sisters-in-law, in extended-family households, or with attached female kinsmen in nuclear-family households. There are several reasons for this practice, the most common ones being the almost constant attention that mothers-in-law and unmarried sisters-in-law lavish upon the infants of the household, exhaustion on the part of the mother, and illness. Moreover, after breast-feeding infants for the night, mothers seldom waste an opportunity to have them in another room of the house.

Of the arrangements involving lineal and collateral kinsmen, fifteen cases are connected to patrilineal kinsmen whereas only five are connected to matrilineal kinsmen. This is simply an expression of the sometimes strong patrilineal bias of rural Tlaxcalan society. The categories of kinsmen in these anomalous sleeping arrangements generally include matrilineally attached mothers or siblings (cases 19, 36, 39, 43, and 45), while in extended-family households, and occasionally in nuclear-family households, there is a wider variety of attached patrilineal kinsmen: younger and elder siblings, parents, grandparents, uncles, aunts, granduncles, and grandaunts. Regardless of the variety of personnel sleeping in the victim's room at the time of death, what must be kept in mind is the large number of children and adults quartered in the same room, varying from three to eight persons, including the victim. Thus, the bloodsucking event usually takes place within a narrow and cluttered space, despite the fact that sleeping rooms in the average rural Tlaxcalan house are invariably large. The personnel structure of this context is very significant to the analysis of the bloodsucking event, for it forces us to examine a series of social, ideological, and physical variables before dealing with the difficult question of the victims' *actual* cause of death. Among other things, it leads to the examination of the culturally defined behavior patterns so intimately associated with every aspect of the bloodsucking event.

The physical arrangements of the rooms where victims died is well exemplified by the description of the seven cases of the Xolotla epidemic. Of course, these cases do not exhaust the various arrangements, but they can be considered variations on the same theme. Moreover, the minutiae of variation are not necessarily significant for the statistical analysis. Nonetheless, a few generalizations are in order. First, the majority of rural Tlaxcalans as late as 1965 slept in petates. Only during the past ten years have beds become common. In fact, one of the criteria for classifying households according to degree of acculturation was the use of beds. All the households in which beds were found are classified either as Transitional-Mestizo or Mestizo-Secularized. Thus, table 6.20 indicates that the members of only thirteen households of the sample slept in beds, which was slightly over-representative for rural Tlaxcala as a whole. Beds occupy much more room than petates, which are always rolled during the day and at night are generally positioned against the walls. Moreover, whether rural Tlaxcalans use beds or petates, adults as well as children seldom sleep alone; it is not unusual for as many as five children or three adults to occupy a single bed or petate. The physical proximity in a sleeping room may often even exasperate the average rural Tlaxcalan adult. Until they can walk, however, infants always sleep alone in a small petate or crib or with their mothers in a separate petate. About half of the infants sleep in cribs, which are either made to order by local carpenters or are simply wooden boxes conditioned for that purpose. Second, sleeping rooms are generally rectangular, and the arrangement of beds and/or petates is well patterned: the married couple, infants, and children up to the age of three or four at one end of the room and children over four at the other end, usually leaving an empty space of four to nine feet in the middle. The most common variant of this arrangement involves lineal or collateral kinsmen attached to the room, who almost always sleep with the children. The infant's crib or petate is generally placed no more than a few feet from the mother's bed or petate and quite often right next to it. If infants wake up at night or have to be fed, mothers simply reach for them without having to get up. Third, sleeping rooms in the average household do not have much furniture, except perhaps a table, a few chairs, and a small wardrobe (*ropero*). As it is, sleeping rooms are cramped, and the most prized personal possessions and items of furniture of the family are kept in another room. Thus, it is in large extended-family households, especially those with separate expense budgets, that space is at a premium; there is seldom more than one room per nuclear family, and everything that the nuclear family owns must be crowded into the sleeping room. By contrast, single-construction houses occupied by nuclear families are the most spacious, for they generally have two rooms and a kitchen. Fourth, sleeping rooms in solar houses are invariably constructed around a central courtyard with direct access to it. The door is located in the middle of the long side of the rectangle, and it is always closed after the people retire for the night. The majority of sleeping rooms in solar houses, however, do not have a window facing the outside of the compound. In single-construction houses, either the sleeping room is connected to the general purpose room through an inside door, or both rooms have doors to the outside. In most houses of this type, however, the sleeping room does have a small window facing the back. Urban-style houses, having a more elaborate ground plan and sometimes two stories, were uncommon in rural Tlaxcala at the time the data was gathered, and they are not represented in the sample. We have gone into considerable detail into the description of the room of the victim where the sucking took place, for it bears directly on several aspects of the event (see tables 6.10, 6.11, and 6.16), and it is important for the reader to have a clear conception of this social and physical space.

Table 6.9 Approximate Time of Finding the Victim's Body[a]

Case no.	Approx. Time	Case no.	Approx. Time	Case no.	Approx. Time
1	05.30	17	05.00	33	06.00
2	05.00	18	06.45	34	11.00
3	05.45	19	04.00	35	07.00
4	06.30	20	05.45	36	04.30
5	06.30	21	13.30	37	07.30
6	06.15	22	12.30	38	03.30
7	05.30	23	14.00	39	06.30
8	06.15	24	05.30	40	06.15
9	05.45	25	05.45	41	05.00
10	04.30	26	05.00	42	05.30
11	05.15	27	07.30	43	06.30
12	04.30	28	06.00	44	07.30
13	05.00	29	05.30	45	05.00
14	07.15	30	05.00	46	06.15
15	06.00	31	05.45	47	05.45
16	05.15	32	05.30		

[a]This was done with fifteen to thirty minutes of approximation, for although few households have clocks, their schedules (getting up, going to work, preparing food, etc.) are highly patterned.

TEMPORAL, SPATIAL, AND PERSONNEL PARAMETERS
OF THE BLOODSUCKING EVENT

Table 6.9 shows the approximate time of finding the victim's body. This is another physical affirmation of the ideological efficacy of bloodsucking witchcraft, for in all cases, with one exception (38), the bodies were found within the periods of the night or day that tlahuelpuchis are most active because they deem them either the easiest or the most propitious to suck the blood of infants. The time of the finding was easy to elicit from parents or other members of the household, since there was usually a patterned activity to which it could be referred: getting up to go to work, to prepare food, to work on the looms, to go to school, and so on. On the other hand, in eleven cases the discovery of the body was related to more out-of-the-ordinary events such as getting up early in the morning to relieve oneself, being awakened by the loud cries of the children, coming out of a nightmare, or simply awakening for some reason at an unusual hour. In any event, despite the familiarity of most adult rural Tlaxcalans with the bloodsucking witchcraft complex, the discovery of the victim's body was always a shock and occasionally a traumatic experience, not only for the finder but for the immediate kinsmen of the victim as well; this quite clearly marked the exact time of the event. It was most important to establish

Table 6.10 Person Who Found the Victim's Body (Ego = Victim)[a]

Case no.	Found by	Case no.	Found by	Case no.	Found by
1	FaFa	17	Fa ol Br	33	Fa yg Br
2	FaMo	18	Fa yg Si	34	FaFaFa
3	Fa	19	MoSi	35	FaMo
4	Mo	20	Br (16)	36	MoBr
5	Br (18)	21	Mo	37	Neighbor
6	Fa	22	Mo	38	FaBr
7	FaFa	23	FaMo	39	MoSi
8	Fa	24	Fa	40	Si (14)
9	Mo	25	FaMo	41	FaFaBr
10	Fa	26	Mo	42	Fa
11	Fa yg Si	27	FaMo	43	MoMo
12	Fa	28	FaMo	44	Neighbor
13	FaFaBr	29	Br (13)	45	Fa
14	Fa	30	Fa	46	Si (17)
15	FaMo	31	Fa yg Br	47	Br (16)
16	Fa	32	Fa		

[a]This also includes the circumstances leading to the discovery, his or her immediate reaction, and any action taken with respect to the body.

as accurately as possible the time of death to calculate the time elapsed between the death of the victim and the examination of the corpse.

Table 6.10 indicates the person who found the victim's body. Although the victims were found by a wide variety of kinsmen, it is interesting to note that in only eight cases (1, 7, 15, 17, 23, 27, 37, and 44) the person did not sleep in the victim's room for the night. The bodies were accidentally found by the father's father or mother or, in two cases, by neighbors. In six cases (5, 20, 29, 40, 46, and 47) the victim was found by siblings ranging in age from 13 to 18 who were getting up to go to school or to perform some chore around the house. In the majority of cases (33), the body was found by either parents or lineal or collateral kinsmen who that night slept in the victim's room and who often literally stumbled on the body by virtue of getting up first. Strikingly, in only five cases it was the mother who found the victim's body, and this includes two (cases 21 and 22) of the four suckings that took place during the day. In all cases, including those where the victim was found by young siblings, the sight of the body in the location and position prescribed by the ideology of blood-sucking witchcraft immediately called to mind the action of the tlahuelpuchi. Despite the fact that this information was elicited ex post facto, it attests to the intimate acquaintance of rural Tlaxcalans with the bloodsucking event, even among fairly young children. Whoever finds the victim's body may experience

Table 6.11 Location and Position of the Victim's Body
Upon Discovery[a]

Case no.	Location and Position of the Victim's Body
1	On the courtyard outside door ajar
2	On the floor two yards from her *petate*
3	Inside the receiving room next to outside door
4	Outside the room to the left of door ajar
5	On the floor a yard from her mother's *petate*
6	On the floor two yards from his crib
7	On the courtyard outside door ajar
8	Door ajar. On the floor next to her *petate*
9	Outside door ajar next to the courtyard wall
10	On the floor to the right of door ajar
11	On the floor to the left of open door
12	Door open. On the floor next to her parent's *petate*
13	Door ajar. On the floor next to FaFaBr's *petate*
14	On the courtyard outside door ajar
15	On the floor next to the door ajar
16	On the floor next to her parents' bed
17	On the left of open door next to courtyard wall
18	In her crib faceup
19	On the floor inside door ajar
20	In the middle of the courtyard
21	In his *petate* faceup
22	In her crib completely covered with blankets
23	In her *petate* faceup
24	Inside the door ajar next to the wall
25	On the floor two yards from her mother's *petate*

shock, but the discovery seldom gave rise to hysterical behavior, which occurred in only three cases (4, 26, and 39). Again, this is significant and has important psychological implications, for in two of the three cases the mother herself found the body. Rural Tlaxcalans are generally self-controlled and seldom given to emotional outbursts concerning death, which they accept fatalistically in whatever form it comes. Upon discovery, the victim's body is not supposed to be touched except by his or her father or mother. Thus, if siblings, kinsmen, or non-related persons discover the body, they must notify the parents immediately. After notifying the parents and the household, the finder must alert the neighbors concerning the sucking so that they may prepare for further attacks from the tlahuelpuchi. Shortly after the discovery of the body and the shock of realizing that the infant has been sucked by the tlahuelpuchi, the victim's father or mother must secure the help of non-related neighbors (generally adult women) to cleanse preliminarily the body of the victim, to place him or her on top of a table in the main room, and to light a couple of candles at

Table 6.11 *Continued*

Case no.	Location and Position of the Victim's Body
26	On the floor inside door ajar
27	On the floor next to her parents' bed
28	On the floor next to FaMo's *petate*
29	On the floor two yards from her *petate*
30	On the floor next to his mother's side of the *petate*
31	On the floor to the left of door ajar
32	Door ajar. On the floor next to his parents' bed
33	On the floor next to her mother's side of the *petate*
34	In her crib faceup
35	On his bed together with his brother (11)
36	On the floor next to door ajar
37	On the ground in front of door ajar
38	Door ajar. On the floor next to FaBr's bed
39	On the courtyard next to door ajar
40	On the floor next to FaSi's bed
41	Outside the entrance to the *solar*
42	On the ground next to the *solar*'s main entrance
43	On the floor to the left of door ajar
44	On the ground next to the house well
45	Door ajar. On the floor three yards from his parents' bed
46	On her *petate* faceup
47	Door ajar. On the ground next to the *solar*'s wall

[a]Includes the position of the body, its clothing, and its spatial relationship to doors, windows, etc.

the head and the foot of the victim until they can begin to prepare for the wake once the coffin has arrived. Parents ask neighbors to do this because in most rural Tlaxcalan communities there is either great reluctance of kinsmen to handle their own dead for burial or a prohibition against it.

Table 6.11 briefly describes one of the most characteristic diagnostic attributes of having been sucked by the tlahuelpuchi: the locations and positions of the victims' bodies upon discovery. There are only seven exceptions (cases 18, 21, 22, 23, 34, 35, and 46) to the following manner or location stipulated by the ideology of bloodsucking witchcraft: the door of the room should be ajar, open, or slightly open; the victim should be positioned inside, outside, in front, to the left, or to the right of the door; the victim should be located on the floor of the room, on the ground of the courtyard, on the floor next to the mother's bed or petate, or on the floor next to the victim's petate or crib. Moreover, these seven cases include the four suckings which took place during the day, and the sucking of the seven-year-old boy. The latter is definitely anomalous, whereas in the former the ideology of bloodsucking witchcraft does not specify the position in which the victim is left by the tlahuelpuchi after the sucking. But since, during the day, the tlahuelpuchi sucks infants in their cribs or petates and cannot remove them from their rooms, cases 21, 22, 23, and 34 may be interpreted to accord with the ideology of bloodsucking witchcraft. If we thus disregard the case of the seven-year-old boy, we see that only two cases (18 and 46) of forty-three night suckings depart from the prescribed pattern. This is one of the most striking examples of the strict concordance sometimes obtaining between what is ideologically prescribed and what is empirically observed in the bloodsucking witchcraft complex. It should be pointed out, however, that in all "normal" night suckings there is a gradation of concordance, centered primarily on the fact that upon leaving the room the tlahuelpuchi leaves the door open or ajar. All those persons who had discovered sucked infants invariably stated when questioned that it was the position or location of the bodies with respect to their cribs, petates, or the petates of their mothers and doors open or ajar that had immediately triggered the thought or even certainty that the infant had been sucked by the tlahuelpuchi. The information presented in table 6.11 is of central importance in explaining one of the key psychological aspects of bloodsucking witchcraft.

Table 6.12 shows the hours elapsed between the approximate time of the victim's death and the examination of the body by Nutini or a physician. The procedure in this calculation was basically to place the time of death at one to three hours before the body was found. Why one to three hours? In some cases this was little more than a guess, but in a considerable number of cases it was possible to estimate the one to three hours (plus or minus half an hour) quite accurately on the basis of clues provided by members of the household, the time the body was found, and certain physical signs. In only five cases (14, 36, 39, 44, and 46) the corpses were examined more than twenty-four hours after death, whereas in thirteen cases the examination took place within ten to eighteen hours. Thus, in the majority of cases the examination of the corpse and the preliminary interview of household members took place less than ten hours after the bloodsucking event; in fact, on several occasions Nutini was called to the household not much more than an hour after the victim's body had been found. Since the great majority of suckings took place very early in the morning, and the preparation of the corpse for the wake is not generally undertaken until the late afternoon or early evening, Nutini was able to examine the corpse before it had been unduly handled. Incidentally, it should be noted that the chief medical officer of the state of Tlaxcala and his deputy instructed Nutini in how to examine the corpses with respect to the setting of rigor mortis. Indeed, experience confirmed what they had stated at the beginning of the research:

Table 6.12 Hours Elapsed Between Approximate Time of Death and Examination of the Victim's Body[a][b]

Case no.	Hours	Case no.	Hours	Case no.	Hours
1	10	17	7	33	4
2	14	18	12	34	6
3	5	19	9	35	5
4	5	20	6	36	28
5	5	21	7	37	4
6	6	22	16	38	4
7	6	23	3	39	37
8	6	24	9	40	14
9	6	25	5	41	7
10	4	26	6	42	9
11	16	27	3	43	12
12	18	28	4	44	27
13	15	29	7	45	6
14	25	30	11	46	36
15	13	31	13	47	10
16	17	32	3		

[a]The times elapsed were computed with reference to Nutini's examination of the victims' bodies. In seven cases (3 to 9), a physician again examined the victims' bodies between nine and ten hours later, whereas in four cases (12, 16, 22, 31) a physician and Nutini together examined the victims' bodies.

[b]In the cases examined by a physician, Nutini simply accepted his estimated time of death, whereas in the cases he examined alone the time of death was placed at one to three hours before the body was found, depending on the circumstances surrounding the death.

the tissues and muscles of infants are so flaccid and delicate that rigor mortis is hardly perceptible. Only in infant corpses examined more than twenty-four hours after death was it possible to detect anything slightly resembling the rigor mortis found in adult corpses that had been dead for six to eight hours. It should be emphasized, however, that neither rigor mortis nor any other medical criterion had anything to do with calculating the approximate time of the victim's death; this was done solely on the basis of the criteria given above. Yet, the value of the acknowledgedly unsystematic medical data that was collected becomes important to the analysis of the physical aspects of bloodsucking witchcraft, as we shall see below. The chief medical officer was eminently correct to insist that Nutini should observe and record several medical aspects of the bloodsucking event, even though he was not medically trained.

PHYSICAL MARKS LEFT ON THE VICTIM'S AND MOTHER'S BODIES
AND PROTECTION AGAINST THE TLAHUELPUCHI

We come now to what is probably the most characteristic physical sign for reaching the diagnosis that a victim has been sucked by the tlahuelpuchi—

Table 6.13 Physical Marks on the Victim's Body[a]

Case no.	Marks on the Victim's Body
1	Bruises, acchymoses, and purplish spots on the chest and back. Face and neck slightly purplish
2	Acchymoses and purple spots on chest and neck
3	Bruises, acchymoses, and purple spots on the chest and back near the neck. Face and neck slightly purplish
4	Bruises, acchymoses, and purple spots on the chest and neck. Face slightly purplish
5	Serious bruises, acchymoses, and purple spots on the chest, back, and neck. Face and neck quite purplish
6	Bruises, acchymoses, and purple spots on the chest and neck. Face slightly purplish
7	Bruises, acchymoses, and purple spots on the chest and back. Cheeks and neck slightly scratched and purple
8	Bruises, acchymoses, and purple spots on the chest and back. Chest significantly scratched. Face and neck purple
9	Bruises, acchymoses, and purple spots on the chest, neck, and back. Cheeks slightly scratched. Face and neck purplish
10	None
11	Bruises, acchymoses, and purple spots on the chest and back. Face slightly purplish
12	Bruises, acchymoses, and purple spots on the chest, neck, and back. Face and neck purplish
13	Purplish spots on the chest and back. Face and neck purplish
14	Acchymoses and purplish spots on the chest and neck. Ears and cheeks slightly scratched
15	Slightly bruised chest. Purplish face and neck. Scratched nose
16	Acchymoses and purplish spots on the chest and neck
17	Bruises and acchymoses on the chest and neck. Chest slightly scratched
18	Very purplish face and neck
19	Serious bruises, acchymoses, and purple spots on the chest, neck, and back. Cheeks and neck scratched. Face very purple
20	Serious bruises, acchymoses, and purple spots on the chest, neck, and back. Badly scratched face and neck
21	None

namely, the physical marks left on the victim's body after the sucking. Table 6.13 shows that in only eight cases there were no marks left on the victim's body, and this includes three of the four day suckings in addition to the seven-year-old boy. Thus, in only four of the forty-three normal night suckings the tlahuelpuchi did not leave any marks on the victim's body. The marks on all

Table 6.13 *Continued*

Case no.	Marks on the Victim's Body
22	Slightly scratched face and neck
23	None
24	Bruises and acchymoses on the chest and neck. Slightly purplish face
25	Purplish face and neck. Scratched ears and neck
26	Bruises and purplish spots on the chest. Slightly purplish face and neck
27	Very purplish face and neck. Face slightly scratched
28	Bruises, acchymoses, and purple spots on the chest and back. Very purplish color on the face
29	Very purplish-yellowish face and chest. Scratched cheeks
30	None
31	Very purplish face and neck. Face and neck quite scratched
32	Dry blood around nose and mouth. Purplish face and neck
33	Face and neck quite scratched. Face quite purplish
34	None
35	None
36	Scratched checks and neck. Purplish-yellowish chest and back
37	None
38	Bruises, acchymoses, and purplish spots on the back, neck, and chest
39	Bruises and acchymoses on the chest and neck. Ears, neck, and face badly scratched. Slightly purplish face
40	Bruises, acchymoses, and purple spots on the chest, neck, and back. Ears slightly scratched
41	Dry blood around the nose and mouth
42	Bruises and acchymoses on the chest and neck. Face and neck very purplish
43	Dry blood around ears and nose. Purplish face and neck
44	None
45	Bruises and acchymoses on the chest and neck. Very purplish face and neck
46	Bruises, acchymoses, and purple spots on the chest, back, and neck
47	Dry blood around the nose and mouth. Acchymoses on the chest and back

[a]There was never any difficulty in the examination of the body, and it was done carefully according to the instructions of the chief medical officer. Nutini also noted the garments that the infant wore and examined the crib or petate where he or she normally slept.

thirty-nine corpses fall squarely within the range of those stipulated by the ideology of bloodsucking witchcraft: bruises, acchymoses, and purple spots on the chest, back, or neck. In addition, scratches on the face or chest of the victim, which appeared in several cases, also fall within the compass of the tlahuelpuchi belief system. It is only the degree and intensity of the marks which vary from case to case: serious, medium, slight; on the chest or back or face or neck, or in two places or in all of them. In any event, the marks left on the victim's body by the tlahuelpuchi are highly patterned, as shown by table 6.13. The degree and intensity of the marks may to some extent depend upon the time elapsed between the death of the victim and the examination of the corpse according to personal communication with Drs. Aron A. Szulman and Hernando Salazar of the University of Pittsburgh Medical School. Three informants in one case, who had seen the victim's body immediately or shortly after it was found, remarked that the marks and coloration of the face and chest seemed to be more pronounced by the time the corpse was being prepared for the wake, which appears to confirm the opinion of the above physicians. In addition, Nutini was generally able to examine the clothes the infant wore at the time of the sucking, but this procedure by itself did not yield any meaningful clues. The examination of the victim's crib or petate, on the other hand, was illuminating, for in seven cases (10, 21, 23, 34, 41, 44, and 47) the mattress or blankets where the victim had lain were covered with vomit or blood. This evidence became very important in explaining the variants in the physical death of victims and the people's rationalizations of departures from the bloodsucking witchcraft ideology.

The physical marks left on the victim's mother's body by the tlahuelpuchi are another symptom of bloodsucking witchcraft, but not as important as those left on the victim's body. Table 6.14 shows that marks were left on the mother in only sixteen cases of the sample—that is, in one-third of the total. It should be stressed, however, that this does not necessarily constitute a departure from the expectations imposed by the ideology of bloodsucking witchcraft, for informants were quite explicit about stating that the tlahuelpuchi only occasionally left marks on the mother's body due to the exigencies of the sucking itself. Again, the marks left on the mother's body are highly patterned and concentrated exclusively on the breasts. Notice, however, that in all cases, either the pronounced or the slight black-and-blue marks were observed in the right or in the left breast, never in both. Evidently, the tlahuelpuchi leaves marks on the mother's right or left breast in night suckings only, but the significance of this pecularity will become apparent below. Notice also that in twelve of the sixteen cases the marks were on the left breast. The importance of this fact escaped Nutini until the summer of 1974 when, quite by accident, he discovered that it was a generalized pattern among rural Tlaxcalan mothers to put their infants to the breast during the night as they reclined on the left side of their bodies. In about half of the cases it was possible to examine the mothers physically immediately after the examination of the victim's body and of the room where the sucking had taken place. But in many cases the women did not want to be examined, and Nutini had to go back a second or third time within the next twenty-four hours. In the end, however, he persuaded reluctant women to agree to the examination, generally by securing the help of their husbands or elder members of the household. He made them bare the upper part of the body and carefully examined the breasts, neck, and arms. In five cases it was not necessary to ask to examine the mothers, for this operation was performed while they were being ritually cleansed by a tezitlazc. In two of these cases (5 and 19) the mothers exhibited pronounced telltale black-and-blue marks, and the cleansing procedures were significantly more elaborate than in the cases where the mothers did not exhibit any marks: the tezitlazc rubbed the breast of the woman several times with the cleansing bunch before producing the zoapatl leaves, which he did not return to his pouch but burned on the spot with a match; he made the woman lie flat on the ground of the room where the sucking had taken place and rub herself slightly against (*restregarse*) the floor several times. The tezitlazc (in the cleansing of case 19) explained that when the tlahuelpuchi leaves marks on the body of the mother, it is particularly important to bring the marks into contact with something else that had been touched by the tlahuelpuchi—namely, the floor that she had walked on upon entering the room to suck the infant. Symbolically, of course, this ritual is nothing more than an allopathic technique to counteract and erase contact with an unclean, malevolent entity. It is interesting to note that allopathic rituals are quite generalized in magic and religion in rural Tlaxcala, and their origin is probably pre-Hispanic.

Table 6.15 indicates whether the infant was protected against the tlahuelpuchi and specifies the methods employed. Eighteen infants were protected against the tlahuelpuchi at the time of death. This figure is quite consonant with the ideology of protection against the tlahuelpuchi at night or during the day: the techniques may work on some occasions but not on others, and the only sure means of protection is the use of garlic and onion. Given these beliefs, the people are rather careless about the matter unless the people are confronted with a bloodsucking epidemic; table 6.15 shows that only slightly more than one-third of the infants were protected. The table also shows that the most common means of protection involve metal, not so much because parents believe that it is the most effective element in counteracting the efficacy of the tlahuelpuchi, but because, as many informants explicitly stated, metal objects are always at hand and easy to place as protective agents. In fact, of the many methods of protection involving substances other than metal, only four are present in the sample (cases 12, 32, 37, and 41). Moreover, table 6.15 shows that in fourteen cases the prescribed means of protection for males (a mirror or a metal cross) and females (a pair of open scissors or silver medals) were

Table 6.14 Physical Marks on the Victim's Mother's Body[a]

Case no.	Marks on the Mother's Body
1	None
2	None
3	None
4	None
5	Pronounced black-and-blue marks on the left breast
6	None
7	None
8	None
9	Black-and-blue marks on the areola and lower part of the right breast
10	None
11	None
12	Slight black-and-blue marks on the lower cup of the left breast
13	None
14	None
15	Black-and-blue marks on the areola and lower cup of the left breast
16	None
17	None
18	None
19	Pronounced black-and-blue marks on the areola and lower cup of the right breast
20	Black-and-blue marks on the upper and lower cups of the right breast
21	None
22	None
23	None
24	Slight black-and-blue marks on the areola of the left breast
25	Black-and-blue marks on the areola and lower cup of the left breast

followed. On the whole, the protection suggested by the ideology of bloodsucking witchcraft is fairly well complied with in practice. Of more significance for the present analysis, however, are the observed expressions of guilty feelings by the parents of the victims who had not been protected at the time of death, especially of mothers in those cases where the means of protection could not be visually detected by examining the clothes of the infant and the surrounding area where the sucking had taken place. When asked if the infant had been protected, many mothers and a considerable number of fathers were reluctant to admit that the infant had not been protected that night. Moreover, there were a few women who did not want to answer and completely avoided the matter. These cases are highly significant and will be analyzed below. The guilty

Table 6.14 *Continued*

Case no.	Marks on the Mother's Body
26	None
27	None
28	None
29	Black-and-blue marks on the upper and lower cups of the left breast
30	None
31	None
32	None
33	None
34	None
35	None
36	Slight black-and-blue marks on lower cup of the right breast
37	None
38	None
39	Pronounced black-and-blue marks on the areola and upper and lower cups of the left breast
40	Slight black-and-blue marks on the lower left breast
41	Black-and-blue marks on the areola and upper and lower cups of the left breast
42	None
43	Black-and-blue marks on the areola and lower cup of the left breast
44	None
45	None
46	Slight black-and-blue marks on the lower cup of the left breast
47	Black-and-blue marks on the areola and upper and lower cups of the left breast

[a]Permission to perform this examination was not always readily forthcoming, but all the women eventually acquiesced. Nutini examined the upper part of the body, especially the breasts, neck, and arms.

feelings exhibited by parents after the sucking are an integral part of the observed aftereffects of this event, and they will be discussed in connection with table 6.17.

UNUSUAL EVENTS AND HAPPENINGS SURROUNDING
THE BLOODSUCKING EVENT

Table 6.16 details the most salient, unusual events surrounding the victim's sucking. These were the most difficult, impressionistic, and least reliable data gathered on the structure and temporal unfolding of the bloodsucking event, usually the result of the ex post facto nature of the elicited facts. What does

Table 6.15 Victim's Protection Against the Tlahuelpuchi[a]

Case no.	Method of Protection
1	None
2	An open pair of scissors next to her petate
3	None
4	A cross made of safety pins attached to his shirt
5	None
6	An open pair of scissors under his crib
7	None
8	None
9	Two silver medals on her chest and back
10	A small mirror next to her petate
11	None
12	Pieces of tortilla strewn around her petate
13	None
14	None
15	None
16	An open pair of scissors under her crib
17	None
18	None
19	None
20	None
21	None
22	None
23	Two silver medals on her chest and back
24	A cross made of silver coins at the head of her petate
25	Two silver medals on her chest and back
26	None

this mean substantively? First, that it was sometimes impossible to determine whether an informant was lying outright, exaggerating an event or happening that would have been considered "normal" in a different context, imagining under the influence of the self-fulfilling nature of the bloodsucking witchcraft complex, or reporting what he genuinely experienced or thought he had experienced. Second, in many cases conflicting evidence about whatever unusual events took place during the night of the sucking was elicited not only from household members at large but from those who had slept in the victim's room. In other cases, it was evident that informants were in such a state of bewilderment that they unconsciously verbalized as fact what the ideology of the complex stipulated. Third, it became clear that the more impressionistic and unreliable data was elicited immediately or shortly after the examination of the victim's body, whereas the more reliable and coherent accounts were elicited after many hours had elapsed, sometimes days afterward. Thus, table 6.16 represents what may be considered the most subjective and, to some extent, indi-

Table 6.15 *Continued*

Case no.	Method of Protection
27	None
28	None
29	None
30	None
31	None
32	A mirror under his crib. A bucket of water next to the door
33	None
34	None
35	None
36	A metal cross at the head of his petate
37	Pieces of tortilla strewn around under her crib
38	None
39	None
40	A metal cross under his crib
41	A dirty pair of shorts at the head of her crib
42	None
43	Two silver medals on her chest and back
44	An open pair of scissors at the head of her petate
45	None
46	A box of pins at the head of her petate
47	None

[a]In some cases it was easy to see the means of protection, for it was either something attached to the garments of the victim or something on, under, or near the crib or petate. When there was nothing visible, Nutini asked the parents of the victim. In several cases the reluctance to admit that the victim had been unprotected was apparent.

rectly verifiable information on the difficult and elusive domain of unusual events. In only eight cases no unusual events surrounded the victim's sucking, or, better stated, there were no warranted happenings elicited from any member of the affected households, which predictably enough included two of the day suckings and the anomalous case of the seven-year-old boy (cases 21, 23, and 35). The unusual events or happenings reported by various informants are basically of two kinds: the mother and/or father of the victim experienced during the night or exhibited upon waking up some physical or psychological state which included severe or mild nausea, headaches, drowsiness, vomiting, nightmares, deep sleep, and difficulty in waking up (fourteen cases); and the victim's parents, other members of the household, or neighbors experienced one of the telltale signs of the tlahuelpuchi (luminosity, ball of fire, vaho) or stated flatly that they had seen her near the house (nineteen cases). The parents of the victim reported a combination of both kinds of happenings in six cases (4, 6, 8, 24, 29, and 46).

Table 6.16 Unusual Events Surrounding the Victim's Sucking[a]

Case no.	Unusual Events Surrounding the Sucking
1	FaFa sighted the tlahuelpuchi flying over the house when he returned from work at about 03.00
2	Both Fa and Mo woke up very drowsy, and could hardly react when they were told of the sucking by FaMo
3	Both Fa and Mo woke up with a strong headache and very drowsy
4	Fa saw the telltale ball of fire of the tlahuelpuchi upon returning from work at 00.45. Fa and Mo woke up with a strong headache and Mo with deep chest pains
5	Both Fa and Mo woke up with splitting headaches and nauseu
6	As she was falling asleep Mo saw an intense luminosity on the window in the form of a turkey or buzzard. Both Fa and Mo woke up with great difficulty and with splitting headaches
7	Both Fa and Mo woke up drowsily, with difficulty, and with a bad headache
8	Mo half work up and saw a rather intense light moving about in the window, followed by a fog-like substance filling the room, in the midst of which she saw a chicken-like bird before falling deeply asleep. Fa got up during the night to relieve himself and saw a bright light hovering near the wall of the *solar*. Fa and Mo woke up with nausea and headaches
9	Fa and Mo fell heavily and drowsily asleep and could not wake up upon hearing victim's cries
10	At 01.00 Fa and Mo fell suddenly asleep, and Mo woke up at 04.30 with an attack of nausea
11	Fa younger Si saw a luminous bird perched on a tree outside the solar when she got up at 03.00 to relieve herself
12	Fa and Mo woke up with a strong headache and vomited after finding the victim's body
13	None
14	None
15	FaMo saw the intense luminosity of a tlahuelpuchi outside the solar when she got up at 04.00 or 04.30 to relieve herself
16	Mo distinctly remembers having tried to stay awake when an intense luminosity invaded the room
17	Fa saw the luminosity of the tlahuelpuchi disappearing into a ravine as he approached his paraje upon returning from work at about 02.00
18	Fa younger Si saw a light under the door but shortly after fell deeply asleep
19	MoSi saw a turkey-like bird flying over the house when she got up about 02.00 to relieve herself
20	Fa younger Br said that he tried to stop a tlahuelpuchi about 300 yards from the house upon returning from work at about 02.00
21	None
22	At about 12.00 a neighbor saw a dog that was not supposed to be there stalking the house of the victim
23	None

Table 6.16 *Continued*

Case no.	Unusual Events Surrounding the Sucking
24	Fa and Mo woke up very drowsy and could hardly get up. Mo woke up in the middle of the night and almost immediately felt a kind of vapor that paralyzed her; in a matter of minutes she was again fast asleep
25	Mo got up with strong attack of nausea when she was awakened by FaMo
26	None
27	FaFa saw a ball of fire near the back of courtyard when he got up to relieve himself at about 05.00
28	FaMo saw an evanescent luminosity flying from the house when she got up about 05.30
29	Mo was very drowsy, and it took several minutes to be awakened by Fa. Mo had a nightmare in which she went to relieve herself in the milpa and was attacked by a dog emanating a bright light
30	None
31	FaFaBr saw the tlahuelpuchi near the house upon returning from work at 05.00
32	Fa and Mo had terrible nightmares, and Fa woke up frightened (*sobresaltado*) to find the victim dead
33	Fa younger Br vaguely saw a ball of fire trying to get into the room under the door but suddenly fell deeply asleep
34	FaFaFa saw a turkey come out of the room where the victim was asleep about half an hour before he found the body
35	None
36	Fa woke up with a splitting headache while Mo had a bad case of nausea when she got up
37	Mo was so drowsy that she could hardly be awakened by the neighbor who found the body of the victim
38	FaFa saw the tlahuelpuchi that night and pursued it in a nearby paraje at about 02.00
39	Fa and Mo were so soundly asleep that they had to be slapped to consciousness by MoSi upon discovering the victim's body
40	A neighbor saw the tlahuelpuchi perched on a tree near the victim's house at about 04.00
41	Fa and Mo got up with a bad case of nausea and they were so weak that they could hardly walk
42	None
43	MoMo saw a flying ball of fire just before the dawn when she got up to make tortillas
44	Mo was totally drowsy, and it took the neighbor who found the victim's body about 15 minutes to wake her up completely
45	Fa woke up in the middle of the night and then was engulfed by a mist-like substance that gradually put him into a deep sleep, while Mo actually stated that she consciously and semi-consciously fought the tlahuelpuchi's vaho but finally succumbed to its power and fell into a deep sleep

Table 6.16 *Continued*

Case no.	Unusual Events Surrounding the Sucking
46	Mo had a terrible nightmare in which she saw the tlahuelpuchi sucking the blood of several children. Both Fa and Mo woke up very drowsily and the daughter who found the victim's body had a hard time in getting them up
47	Fa and Mo were totally nauseated upon being awakened by the son who found the victim's body

[a]This was the most difficult and least reliable information to obtain. It involved the interview not only of the victim's parents but of all the members of the household, especially those in the victim's room that night or those who had been close to him or her if the sucking took place during the day. Sometimes it took several interviews to get at these impressionistic and often ex post facto data.

In the investigation of the first fifteen cases occurring by the end of January 1961, Nutini approached the subject of witchcraft right after finishing the physical examination of the different elements of the sucking. By then, it became apparent that he was getting a torrent of information from various members of the household that, in retrospect, was primarily a reaffirmation of the ideology of the tlahuelpuchi complex and not what they had experienced or imagined they had experienced. Nutini had the distinct impression that every adult in the household wanted to validate the efficacy to kill of the tlahuelpuchi and to convice him of the efficacy. Psychologically, it was as if something was being threatened and had to be defended. It is interesting to note that the most vocal members of the households were women, who, upon being interviewed privately or with the household as a group, verbalized something concerning the telltale signs of the tlahuelpuchi that night—dreams in which she had materialized or her outright sighting. Regardless of the respondent's sex, the affirmations of household members sounded much more like rationalizations than the verbalization of imagined or actually experienced events or states of consciousness: they were not *really* lying but unconsciously transposing ideology and experience according to culturally patterned behavior. So patent was the ex post facto nature of their verbalizations that it was virtually impossible to separate the real or imagined events of the night, the patterned ideology of the tlahuelpuchi complex, and past experience of suckings. The best way to explain and encapsulate the experience of these interviews is to invoke Freud's theory of displacement, which, in the context of bloodsucking witchcraft, has a double edge: releasing the mother of the victim from the responsibility of his or her death and assuaging the "collective guilt" of the household for the sucking. Thus, unable to gauge the objective validity of the information pouring in about the supposed presence of the tlahuelpuchi in or near the house during the night of the sucking, and largely aware of the main psychological parameters affecting the members of the household within twenty-four hours after the victim's death, Nutini decided to wait until after the burial, often two or three days, to gather the data summarized in table 6.16; in all subsequent cases he waited to gather information.

This was a good decision, for the interviewed members of the household were more coherent and controlled in their affirmations of the unusual events of the night surrounding the tlahuelpuchi's visit than immediately afterward. This may be explained simply enough in terms of the psychological stress caused by suckings, despite their common occurrence. But there is more to it than the lessening of stress, for even when household members were interviewed about the night of the sucking several days afterward, there was still a tendency to transpose ideology and experience. In other words, the psychological tensions disappear as the household goes back to the routine of normal living, but the collective guilt is still there, acting as a mechanism of displacement and motivating unconsciously a reinterpretation of experience according to the bloodsucking ideology—in fact, forcing individuals literally to imagine or transcend events or psychological states with or without experiential reality. Indeed, the belief on the tlahuelpuchi is solidly founded on the mechanism of displacement, operating latently and manifesting itself according to an elaborate self-fulfilling and culturally patterned complex every time an infant is sucked. From this viewpoint, then, in all forty-seven cases Nutini elicited (or more accurately, household members forced on him) at least two accounts involving the telltale signs of the tlahuelpuchi: dreams in which she appeared in a variety of forms or animals, or movements of things which made informants suspect her powers of animal transformation at work. Why then does table 6.16 show that in only twenty-five cases (19 plus 6) household members experienced something unusual connected with the tlahuelpuchi? Primarily because Nutini could associate these experiential happenings directly with the suckings, whereas in twenty-two cases this was not possible, and the elicited information constituted nothing more than ex post facto rationalizations unconsciously fabricated.

But how did Nutini discriminate between genuinely connected and spurious elicitations? To some extent he judged intuitively, but experience taught him some discriminatory criteria; moreover, in many cases it was evident that informants were rationalizing on the bases of their own past experience. These were usually verbalized in expressions such as: "ahora que me acuerdo, me desperté en la noche y ví algo luminoso en la ventana" (now that I remember, I saw a luminosity in the window when I woke up during the night); "como cuando le chuparon la creatura a mi hija María, me pareció ver una bola de fuego que se escurría en la milpa al regresar de la fábrica" (upon returning from the factory, it seemed I saw a ball of fire gliding in the mila, like when my daughter María's infant was sucked); "me dió la sensación de una neblina que pasaba por nuestro cuarto y se metia al cuarto de Pedro por debajo de la puerta" (I had the sensation that a mist went through our room and under the door got into Pedro's room); and "mi comadrita Pilar parece que vió un huajolote rondando cerca de la casa un rato antes de que se chuparan a la creatura" (my *comadrita* [ritual kinswoman] Pilar seemed to have seen a turkey prowling near the house sometime before the infant was sucked). All these verbalizations (and many more in which the tlahuelpuchi, her multiple manifestations, and her telltale signs are said to have been experienced by various members of the household) must be interpreted as an unconscious reinforcement of the complex not related to the actual sucking. By contrast, the flat assertions of household members directly related to the sucking that he deemed important to the physical explanation of infant deaths are indicated in table 6.16. It makes no difference to discriminate between what these informants experienced and what they imagined they had experienced; indeed, undertaking such a task is impossible, given the epistemologically reinforcing and self-fulfilling nature of all witchcraft systems. In fact, probably nothing short of administering sodium pentathol to informants would have clarified the distinction between real and imagined experience. Thus, we are left with the task of elucidating the psychological matrix in which the transposition of ideology and experience takes place.

Finally, in the fourteen cases in which the victim's parents experienced or exhibited unusual physical or psychological states, the task of determining the objective reality of the states was an altogether different matter. Disregarding, of course, the objective verification of dreams or nightmares (cases 29, 32, and 46), we could easily verify the nausea, drowsiness, vomiting, or headaches usually exhibited by parents upon waking up. Probably, in only two cases they were not genuine but feigned or exaggerated. It was often evident that, upon being interviewed for the first time, mothers and/or fathers were under stress, and this manifested itself physically in verbalized expressions such as: "me siento como atontada," (I feel stunned); "siento el estomago lleno de bilis y con ganas de vomitar" (I feel my stomach is full of bile and I want to vomit); or "no puedo ni pensar del dolor de cabeza" (my headache is so strong that I cannot even think). These states were the continuation of the waking-up process or had developed shortly after the victim's body was found. Under such circumstances, it was easy to reconstruct and to some extent verify other physical and psychological states affecting the parents. In fact, the elicitation of this information led directly to the content of the following table.

AFTEREFFECTS DUE TO THE SUCKING: ESPANTO, ATAQUE DE ESPÍRITUS, CHIPILERÍA, AND TZIPITICTOC

Table 6.17 details the aftereffects on the victim's parents due to the sucking. In only eleven cases there were no manifested aftereffects, and these include the four day suckings as well as the death of the seven-year-old boy (cases 21, 22, 23, 34, and 35). Again, this clearly indicates that they are anomalous cases within the general structure of bloodsucking witchcraft. In thirty-six cases the mother and/or father developed a series of what may be termed psychosomatic ailments, which persisted for as short as four days or as long as three weeks. In varying degrees of intensity, these ailments included primarily headaches and nausea, and secondarily stomach and chest pains. In addition, several kinds of disturbances or states of an outright psychological nature developed: one case each of *espanto* (fright) and *ataque de espíritus* (attack of spirits) (40 and 44), seven cases of *chipilería*, and twelve cases of *tzipitictoc*. The psychosomatic ailments were often little more than the continuation of the waking-up state of parents or were developed immediately after the discovery of the victim's body. There were, however, several cases in which these ailments were developed much later: by the time the infant's body was placed in the coffin, after the limpia, or after the burial. Whether developed immediately or later, there were no structural differences in the ailments, and the behavior of parents showed no significant deviations. But before we can discuss this matter, it is important to describe the behavioral manifestations of espanto, ataque de espíritus, chipilería, and tzipitictoc.

These psychological disturbances in rural Tlaxcala (and with significant variations in many regions of Mesoamerica) may be regarded as folk illnesses—that is, unlike illnesses commonly known to modern medicine, they contain varying supernatural or semisupernatural elements. The disturbances are thought to be produced either by the general concept of *mal aire* or by other causes having to do with the presence or direct action of several animal or anthropomorphic supernaturals in a variety of contexts. Although there are many folk illnesses that are not primarily psychological, all do contain some physically manifested psychological component, which is the distinguishing factor separating them from ordinary illnesses.

Espanto is essentially regarded as a sudden seizure or nightmare (*pesadilla*) which may last from fifteen to thirty minutes. It may take possession of a person at any time and cause him to lose consciousness. No physical pain is involved, and when victims regain consciousness, it takes them an hour or two to regain complete possession of themselves. It attacks children as well as adults, but it is much more common among the latter. Although the sample

Table 6.17 Aftereffects on the Victim's Parents Due to the Sucking[a]

Case no.	Aftereffects on the Parents Due to the Sucking
1	Fa and Mo had continuous headaches for five days after the burial of the victim
2	Mo had nausea for a week and Fa had a continuous strong headache for five days
3	None
4	Fa and Mo had persistent headaches for five days. Fa was *chipil* for a week
5	Mo had chest pains for a week and Fa was *chipil* for a week
6	Both Fa and Mo suffered strong and persistent headaches for nearly two weeks
7	Fa and Mo suffered from strong nausea for four days after the burial of the victim
8	Mo had *tzipitictoc* for two weeks, and Fa had nausea and strong headaches for four days
9	Fa and Mo had headaches for four days after the sucking
10	Fa and Mo had intermittent headaches and attacks of nausea for two weeks
11	Mo had continuous strong headaches for a week
12	Mo had *tzipitictoc* for a week, Fa strong headaches for more than a week
13	Fa developed continuous stomach pains for a week, and Mo strong headaches for five days
14	Both Fa and Mo had strong headaches for six days
15	Mo had strong headaches for about a week
16	None
17	Fa and Mo had periodic attacks of nausea, and Fa was *chipil* for a week
18	Fa was *chipil* and cried constantly for more than a week
19	Mo had *tzipitictoc* for two weeks, and Fa strong headaches for more than a week
20	None
21	None
22	None
23	None
24	Mo developed *tzipitictoc* right after the burial of the victim and lasted for two weeks
25	Fa had strong headaches for five days, and Mo developed chest pains which lasted for a week
26	Mo had strong headaches and chest pains for more than a week
27	Fa was *chipil* for more than a week after the burial of the victim

shows that only one woman suffered espanto, it appears to be a much more common aftereffect of bloodsucking witchcraft. This was pointed out by several informants, which led to the interview of several women who had suffered it. Moreover, espanto in this context attacks only women. In the case from the sample (40), the woman in question was observed quite closely; during the

Table 6.17 *Continued*

Case no.	Aftereffects on the Parents Due to the Sucking
28	Mo had strong chest pains for more than a week
29	Mo developed *tzipitictoc* right after the burial of the victim and lasted for two weeks, while Fa had nausea for five days
30	None
31	Mo had *tzipitictoc* for more than a week, and Fa had strong headaches for a week
32	Fa had nausea for five days, and Mo had strong intermittent headaches for two weeks
33	Mo had *tzipitictoc* for two weeks, and Fa has nausea for five days
34	None
35	None
36	Mo had *tzipitictoc* and Fa strong headaches for more than two weeks
37	Mo had *tzipitictoc* for two weeks
38	Fa had *chipil* for nearly two weeks, and Mo had nausea and strong headaches for six days
39	Fa and Mo developed strong headaches and nausea immediately after the burial of the victim and they persisted for nearly two weeks
40	Fa was *chipil* for a week, and Mo was in a constant state of fright (*espanto*) for two weeks, at the end of which a *limpia* (ritual cleansing) was necessary to restore her to her normal self
41	Mo had strong headaches for two weeks
42	Mo developed chest pains right after the burial of the victim, and they lasted for two weeks
43	Mo had *tzipitictoc* for two weeks, and Fa developed strong chest pains for a week
44	Mo had *tzipitictoc* for two weeks, and she suffered a serious *ataque de espíritus* (attack of spirits) three days after the burial of the victim
45	Mo had *tzipitictoc* for two weeks, and Fa had intermittent headaches and nausea for two weeks
46	None
47	None

[a]The immediate aftereffects on the parents were easy to ascertain, for at least one of them invariably described freely how he or she felt when asked. But the persistent aftereffects, which could last up to three weeks, involved the repeated observation of the couple; in some cases Nutini went back to the household as many as five times after the sucking.

first five days of the two weeks that she was in a state of espanto she had daily seizures which lasted as long as half an hour. The seizures came in the late afternoon and were followed by attacks of vomiting and screaming, and it took the woman at least an hour and a half to regain her composure and become coherent again. Between seizures she walked about the house in a state of bewilderment, babbling, uttering complaints at times about her fate, about how she had been unable to protect her infant son, and about how she had been totally unable to take care of her household duties.[5] The seizures came unexpectedly, and the woman simply collapsed into unconsciousness wherever she was. This went on for two weeks until the members of the household, in council, decided that it was time for another limpia. The ritual cleansing was performed by the same tezitlazc who had officiated at the sucking limpia. The rites performed during this occasion are essentially the same as those which have already been described, except that the cleansing bunch is given to the woman, who has to bury it secretly somewhere in the milpa. Right after the limpia the seizures stopped, and the woman quickly went back to normal. It must be noted here that rural Tlaxcalans believe that when the mother puts up a strong resistance against being put to sleep by the action of the tlahuelpuchi's vaho, she will develop the psychological disturbances denoted by espanto and ataque de espíritus, and it is therefore necessary to perform the appropriate allopathic rituals to rid the mother of this malevolent influence produced by contact with the tlahuelpuchi.

Ataque de espíritus is an aggravated case of espanto, but the seizures, in which the individual is in a state of unconsciousness, are much longer and may last for as long as four or five hours. Moreover, these attacks may be repeated for several days. This psychological disturbance has two main origins: it is caused by a tetlachihuic for reasons of personal revenge or by being hired by a third person; or it is induced by visual or tactile contact with unclean, malevolent, or dangerous entities such as the tlahuelpuchi, Matlalcihua, or the Feathered Serpent. The former must always be countered by the power of another tetlachihuic, whereas in the latter instance the ataque de espíritus is cured by one or several limpias involving the same ritual manipulations that have been described. To resolve an ataque de espíritus, the limpia must take place right after the victim comes out of the state of unconsciousness and is repeated until the attacks come to an end. In the case from the sample (44) the woman had two attacks; the first, three days after the burial of her infant daughter, and the second, two days later. Again, Nutini was present on both occasions and observed closely the limpias. In each attack the woman was unconscious for more than three hours. When she came out of an attack, she reacted calmly but as if she had been heavily drugged, and remained in the same state throughout the limpias. After the first, she quickly became morose and irritable, but minutes after the second she was fully collected and behaved as if nothing had happened. In fact, Nutini had the distinct impression that she was deliberately suppressing whatever recollection she had of her recent behavior.

We do not know why there were only two cases of espanto and ataque de espíritus recorded in the sample, but it is certain that this is not representative of their incidence. Seven women (not in the sample) who had experienced one of these psychological disturbances after the sucking of their infants were interviewed. The most important fact to come out of these interviews (corroborated by the two cases in the sample) was that all the victims were mature women, varying in age from thirty to forty-six, and consequently in their fourth to tenth childbirths when the attacks took place. This was independently confirmed by various informants, but we cannot definitely explain why espanto and ataque de espíritus occur only in women after their fourth childbirth. Suffice it to say now that both of these psychological aftereffects are extreme manifestations of the disturbances experienced by women after a sucking, which are latently there in the majority of cases but are expressed in more subdued and less dramatic forms.

Less dramatic than espanto and ataque de espíritus but more serious than psychosomatic ailments such as nausea or strong headaches, chipilería and tzipitictoc are common aftereffects of bloodsucking witchcraft. These psychological disturbances have a rather wide range of distribution and semantic content in rural Tlaxcala; in addition, they take place in the following contexts: husbands experience them during the first four to eight weeks after their wives' first pregnancy; and in a less pronounced form during their wives' second and third pregnancies;[6] chipilería and tzipitictoc are two of the most clearly manifested symptoms and telltale signs of individuals (adults, children, and infants) under the effect of the malevolent magic of tetlachihuics; and they often take place as an aftereffect of several folk psychological illnesses such as mal de ojo, insulto, and bilis (bile). In all four contexts, chipilería and tzipitictoc exhibit a core of semantic content and manifested symptoms, but there are significant variations from one context to another. For example, where husbands are experiencing their wives' first pregnancy, the symptomatic accent is on their being belligerent, *antojosos* (always hankering for something), and very prone to contract any type of illness; whereas, in the case of individuals under attack by tetlachihuics, the symptomatic emphasis is on physical pain in different parts of the body and a state of deep moroseness. Here, however, we are exclusively concerned with the manifestations of chipilería and tzipitictoc within the bloodsucking context.

The difference between chipilería and tzipitictoc is one of degree and not of kind—that is, the latter is always more serious than the former. Moreover, in many communities in rural Tlaxcala the two terms are used interchangeably with the same meaning. The main reason for keeping them separate is not their differing degrees of intensity but rather that, at least in the present context, chipilería always affects males (husbands) and tzipitictoc always affects females (wives), and the people themselves adhere strictly to this terminological usage; or, in the words of several informants, "los hombres se ponen chipil, mientras que las mujeres sufren de tzipitictoc" (men become chipil while women suffer from tzipitictoc). This is fully corroborated by the data in table 6.17, in which all seven cases of chipilería affected husbands and all 12 cases of tzipitictoc affected wives. In other words, this general psychological disturbance is always stronger in females and often lasts longer as well.

The symptoms and observable behavior of chipilería manifest in the cases of table 6.17 are the following: total lack of interest in household affairs; moroseness and difficulty in performing even the simplest physical tasks; loss of energy and considerable lack of concentration; paleness and loss of appetite; proneness to crying at the slightest contradiction or for no reason at all; insomnia or difficulty in sleeping; and occasionally slight fainting spells (*vahidos, desmayos*). This behavior is well summarized by the head of the household in case 27: "Cuando el padre de una creatura chupada por lo tlahuelpuchi se pone chipil, ambula por la casa todo mustio, triste, llorón, sin saber que hacer y como si no estuviera presente" (when the father of an infant sucked by the tlahuelpuchi becomes chipil, he wanders about the house withered, sad, crying, not knowing what to do, and as if he were not there). Of the observed cases of chipilería, five lasted a week, one more than a week, and one nearly two weeks. By contrast, the twelve cases of tzipitictoc not only lasted longer (one case lasted a week, another more than a week, and the rest two weeks or more) but the symptoms described above were on the average significantly stronger and more disturbing to members of the household, and the women developed a number of side effects: rash, moderate to high fever, earache, and occasional fainting spells were much more pronounced. Indeed, tzipitictoc was so strong in the case of five women that they spent a good deal of time in bed under the watchful supervision of females of the household or other kinswomen. Finally, unlike espanto and ataque de espíritus, chipilería and tzipitictoc cannot be cured by a limpia, and they must run their undetermined course. The intensity of the ailments, however, may be attenuated by drinking *tecitos* (teas) made of zoapatl, *ruda*, chamomile, and other folk herbs. When chipilería and tzipitictoc strike, there is always more concern with the latter, for not only is it more serious, but it disrupts much more the normal running of the household.

There is a striking similarity between the way the concepts of chipilería and tzipitictoc are employed in rural Tlaxcala and the way the term *psychosomatic* is used in contemporary Western society. Psychosomatic may be defined as a situation in which there takes place psychological etiology accompanied by physical symptomology; the "cause" is psychological, although there may be organic, physical manifestations of illness. This is basically the meaning that chipilería and tzipitictoc have for rural Tlaxcalans, not only in the contexts described above but also in two other contexts, involving nahualism and love magic. Rural Tlaxcalans are well aware that the symptoms of chipilería and tzipitictoc in all of their contexts involve a significant element of psychological causation, induced either by anthropomorphic supernaturals clearly conceived or readily identified or by supernatural principles that they cannot easily conceive or clearly verbalize. Thus, when infants, children, and adults are afflicted by chipilería or tzipitictoc rural Tlaxcalans always take cognizance of an important psychological factor not contemplated in the etiology of "normal" illness. This is well expressed by informants when they said, "cuando un hombre se pone chipil o una mujer sufre de tzipitictoc, sus malestares y sufrimientos más se los imaginan que son de causa real" (when a man becomes chipil and a woman suffers from tzipitictoc, their misery and sufferings are more imagined than real), or "la chipilería y el tzipitictoc son estados de ánimo que no tienen causa aparente y son más bien en parte producto de la sugestión y en parte perdida de control del alma" (chipilería and tzipitictoc are states of being that do not have an apparent cause, and they are rather partly the product of induced suggestion and partly loss of control over the soul). Notice here that when traditional rural Tlaxcalans employ the term *alma* (soul) and *espíritu* (spirit) they primarily refer to "mind" as opposed to "body."

PHYSICAL AFTEREFFECTS AND INDIVIDUAL AND COLLECTIVE GUILT

Rural Tlaxcalans do not regard the aftereffects which include headaches, nausea, stomach and chest pains (occurring in the thirty-six cases, either by themselves or in addition to one or more of the four psychological disturbances discussed above) as psychosomatic in the same way they regard chipilería and tzipitictoc, but the aftereffects have been so termed because they are indubitably triggered by the psychological disturbances produced by the sucking. Analytically, of course, all observed aftereffects are essentially psychosomatic in origin, and it is only the more serious disturbances produced by espanto, ataque de espíritus, chipilería, and/or tzipitictoc that makes these ailments stand out with respect to headaches, nausea, and stomach and chest pains. Those aftereffects, however, are more "naturally" regarded in the sense that, in various combinations and varied proportions, they affect both parents of infants sucked by the tlahuelpuchi in the majority of cases. Rural Tlaxcalans rather expect that the parents of a sucked infant will suffer from headaches, nausea, and/or stomach and chest pains and are at a loss to explain their provenance. In fact, rural Tlaxcalans seldom bother to reflect upon them and simply explain them away as being the result of the grief and pain of having lost an infant. In contrast, the psychosomatic nature of chipilería and tzipitictoc, and to some extent of espanto and ataque de espíritus, are not regarded as "natural" but rather as reflecting the weakness of spirit (*debilidad de espíritu*) and lack of will (*falta de voluntad*) of the persons affected. It should be noted in this context that strength of spirit and stoutness of will not only deter against the occurrence of psychosomatic disturbances but also make it more difficult for anthropomorphic supernaturals to perform their evil deeds against persons who have those qualities. A yotlezahuitl is a good example of such a person.

Unlike their beliefs about espanto and ataque de espíritus, which are cured by limpias, and about chipilería and tzipitictoc, which can be attenuated by potions, rural Tlaxcalans believe that not only there is nothing that can effectively be done to eliminate headaches, nausea, and stomach and chest pains, but that affected parents should not try anything. There is a deep-seated attitude that, were they to try something, they would only be enhancing the possibility of suffering any of the four more serious psychological disturbances. The people adhere faithfully to this injunction, and they let the ailments run their courses, knowing that they cannot last for more than a few weeks. One informant went so far as to say that these physical disturbances were a small price for careless parents to pay for having let an infant be sucked by the tlahuelpuchi. Finally, analysis of table 6.17 shows that, in duration and intensity, headaches, nausea, and stomach and chest pains are generally worse for women than for men.

Perhaps the most striking aspect in the analysis of the physical and psychological aftereffects of bloodsucking witchcraft is the guilt complex that pervades the behavior of the victim's parents. Even as early as June 1961, when twenty-five cases had been investigated, the only conclusion that could be reached was that the aftereffects were determined by individual and collective guilt—that is, not only that of the victim's parents but that of the entire household. Indeed, it was not difficult to reach this conclusion, for the entire process of observation and interviewing in practically every case was conducted in an environment of psychological withdrawal and, to some extent, physical depression; guilt was verbally expressed or indirectly manifested by the victim's parents and most adult members of the household. This is corroborated by many specific behaviors in the foregoing description. But what is this individual and collective guilt an expression of, and what is its social function? Let us take up the problem of individual guilt first.

Table 6.15 shows that there were only eighteen infants protected against the tlahuelpuchi, or 38 percent of all the victims. Two questions immediately come to mind: Does the protection of infants against the tlahuelpuchi during the night of the sucking have anything to do with the guilt manifested afterward; and do the parents of unprotected victims feel guiltier than those of protected victims? The answers are yes to the first question and no the second. It has already been noted that parents who had not protected their infants during the night of the sucking were often reluctant to answer or avoided altogether the matter of protection. Thus, from the immediately observable viewpoint it appears that the parents of unprotected victims manifest more outward signs of guilt than those of protected victims. But given the ideological uncertainty of infant protection against the tlahuelpuchi, the difference is only superficial. If we compare the data in tables 6.15 and 6.17, no correlation emerges between the cases of unprotected infants and the seriousness of aftereffects in their parents or vice versa. Therefore, one can neither maintain that the parents of unprotected infants feel guiltier than those of protected infants, nor that physical and psychological aftereffects are a direct expression of the degree of guilt experienced by parents. Rather, the guilt felt by parents is a manifestation of individual psychology culturally expressed according to the ideology of blood-sucking witchcraft. In other words, individual guilt is a powerful reinforcement of the tlahuelpuchi complex; guilt not only validates and objectifies the underlying ideology but at the same time allows for the individual expression of pain, regret, and even a sense of purgation for actions done or left undone. This is a very important point in explaining (perhaps reconstructing is a better way of putting it) the physical death of infants sucked by the tlahuelpuchi. We say this because it was the close observation of the exceptional guilt of women in several cases of the sample that made it possible to piece together a coherent picture of the different ways that infants die. In the same context, exceptional cases were very illuminating in conceptualizing the possible psychological states of parents, but especially of women, during the sucking and after it took place.

Very often, Nutini observed that collective guilt, especially in nuclear-family households, extended beyond the domestic group to lineal and collateral kinsmen. Thus, either within the context of the household or beyond it, observable guilt extended to the following kinsmen: invariably to the parents of the victim's father (given patri-neolocal residence and the patrilineal bias of rural Tlaxcalan society); occasionally to the parents of the victim's mother; almost invariably to all adult members of the household (that is, over twenty or so years of age); quite often to lineal and collateral kinsmen residing within close proximity; and occasionally to propinquous neighbors. These various categories of kinsmen, especially the victim's father's parents, not only experienced a serious sense of loss, but they closely identified themselves with the parents of the victim and verbally expressed guilt by sayings such as: "todos tenemos la culpa cuando la tlahuelpuchi se chupa a una creatura" (we are all guilty when the tlahuelpuchi sucks an infant); "deberíamos haber tenido más cuidado de parar a la tlahuelpuchi a tiempo" (we should have been more careful to stop the tlahuelpuchi in time); "deberíamos haber enseñado mejor a nuestros hijos a proteger a sus creaturas de la tlahuelpuchi" (we should have taught our children better to protect their infants against the tlahuelpuchi); and "el por qué la tlahuelpuchi ataca nunca se puede saber, pero algo malo debemos haber hecho en la familia para que así sucediera" (why the tlahuelpuchi attacks can never be known, but we must have done something bad in the family for that to have happened). These statements clearly exemplify the responsibility that the domestic groups and close non-residential kinsmen assume for the death of the victim; at the same time, however, they give us a significant insight into the nature and origin of the collective guilt—hence, of its social function.

On the one hand, guilt stems from things and actions left undone to counteract the efficacy of the tlahuelpuchi according to the stated ideology, despite the uncertainty involved in the options. This, of course, is homologous and analogous to the individual guilt manifested by the victim's parents as exemplified above, including its reinforcing effect on the tlahuelpuchi complex. On the other hand, collective guilt is deeply rooted in the belief that certain pagan supernaturals and the entire roster of Catholic supernaturals will punish the group and bring it misfortune when what is ritually and ceremonially due to them is not complied with by either a specific individual or the group as a whole. The family group thus reasons that they must have done something or left something undone to offend the supernaturals that they worship, fear, or respect in a variety of forms and contexts, for, as they have been analyzed elsewhere (Nutini and Isaac 1977:84–90), rural Tlaxcalans do not make an ideological distinction between the Catholic and pagan supernatural realms. Hence, the social function of individual and collective guilt is to reinforce the tlahuelpuchi complex as an explanation of bloodsucking witchcraft in the absence of a "scientific" or objectified account of why infants die under the conditions specified above. Moreover, collective guilt functions as a latent explanation of why a particular family suffered the consequences of bloodsucking witchcraft by forcing the members of that group to reflect upon what they have done wrong or failed to do. The effects of guilt do not apparently persist: the third week after the sucking, the domestic group and neighborhood were so far back to normal that another sucking could take place, involving the same cycle of events, as if nothing had happened before. Such a case was not empirically observed, but it was possible to infer as much from many structured accounts. How this quick return to normality can be explained is not entirely certain, but we might venture to say that the high incidence of bloodsucking witchcraft allows rural Tlaxcalans no other choice, and this is strongly reinforced by the high degree of congruence between the ideology of the system and its physical and psychological manifestations.

LANGUAGE, DEGREE OF ACCULTURATION, AND THE INCIDENCE OF BLOODSUCKING WITCHCRAFT

Table 6.18 shows that in fourteen cases there had been previous suckings in the victim's independent or dependent nuclear family—that is, since the nuclear family had come into existence, regardless of whether the sucking had taken place in a household previous to the one the nuclear family occupied at the time of the interview. A correlation of table 6.5 and 6.18 shows that there are only two cases (2 and 21) with three or less previous births. In fact, in case 21, the firstborn and secondborn of that couple were sucked by the tlahuelpuchi. This is unusual, for firstborn infants are rarely sucked; two infants in a row is even more unusual. In any event, it is quite predictable that as the number of births increases so does the probability of infants being sucked. This is shown by the fact that in four cases (15, 20, 24, and 46) with more than one sucked infant, the birth orders were tenth, eighth, seventh, and ninth respectively. In contrast, there are six cases (4, 6, 8, 9, 21, and 41) in which no infants had been sucked after five or six offspring, something universally acknowledged as late as 1967 to be rather unusual. It may therefore be generalized that up to the point of the last case of the sample, the average couple in rural Tlaxcala had one infant sucked by the tlahuelpuchi by the time their fifth or sixth offspring had been born. There is no correlation between the degree of knowledge of nuclear family members about the tlahuelpuchi complex and direct acquaintance with sucked infants. Thus, there were no significantly detectable differences between nuclear families which had experienced previous suckings and those which had not. This, of course, is easily explained by the widespread knowledge of the bloodsucking witchcraft ideology, which the average rural Tlaxcalan begins to internalize in early childhood. Individual competence on bloodsucking witch-craft within the nuclear family is determined by specific circumstances in the process of growing up and by the peculiar conditions under which particular instances of witchcraft took place, either enhancing or inhibiting what individuals knew about the tlahuelpuchi complex. Under such conditions, it was impossible to determine the specific variables at work, nor was it crucial to the explanation of the phenomenon at hand.

Table 6.19 indicates previous suckings in the victim's household. Here, of course, because we are dealing with the household since it was constituted as a domestic group, we are concerned with both nuclear- and extended-family

Table 6.18 Previous Suckings in the Victim's Nuclear Family[a]

Case no.	Suckings	Case no.	Suckings	Case no.	Suckings
1	none	17	none	33	none
2	1	18	none	34	none
3	none	19	none	35	none
4	none	20	2	36	1
5	1	21	1	37	none
6	none	22	none	38	none
7	none	23	none	39	none
8	none	24	2	40	1
9	none	25	none	41	none
10	none	26	none	42	none
11	none	27	none	43	1
12	1	28	none	44	1
13	none	29	none	45	none
14	none	30	1	46	3
15	2	31	none	47	1
16	none	32	none		

[a]The main reason for asking this was to establish some index of the degree of direct acquaintanceship of the victim's parents with the bloodsucking complex. Nutini also elicited information on the degree of competence the parents had on the tlahuelpuchi.

households. Under such circumstances, the number of sucked infants is more difficult to analyze because it was harder to reconstruct the developmental changes of extended-family households. Nonetheless, table 6.19 shows that there are only sixteen cases in which there had not been previous suckings in the household, whereas in the other thirty-one the number was as high as four (15, 20, and 24) or five (46). Of the sixteen households reporting no previously sucked infants only two (7 and 17) are extended-family households and must be considered exceptions, whereas the others are nuclear-family households which may have been part of extended families but, for the most part, are still in the process of growth. Whatever the significance of these statistical facts, table 6.19 unquestionably indicates the high incidence of bloodsucking witchcraft in rural Tlaxcala independently of the census data discussed above, and considering that most of the households of the sample have an average life span of two and a half generations. Thus, it can be generalized that the average rural Tlaxcalan household had at least one, often two, and as many as five infants sucked by the tlahuelpuchi between approximately the turn of the century and 1965. Information was also collected on how previous suckings had taken place and any unusual events surrounding them. In at least four cases, the eldest members of the household (individuals over eighty years of age) were able to report on suckings which had taken place at the turn of the century. On the

Table 6.19 Previous Suckings in the Victim's Household[a]

Case no.	Suckings	Case no.	Suckings	Case no.	Suckings
1	1	17	none	33	3
2	1	18	1	34	none
3	none	19	none	35	none
4	none	20	4	36	3
5	1	21	2	37	none
6	none	22	none	38	2
7	none	23	2	39	3
8	3	24	4	40	3
9	2	25	none	41	none
10	1	26	3	42	2
11	3	27	1	43	1
12	1	28	2	44	1
13	none	29	none	45	2
14	2	30	1	46	5
15	4	31	2	47	2
16	none	32	none		

[a]This information was solicited from parents of the victim in nuclear-family households and from the parents of the father in extended-family households. The purpose was to obtain not only quantitive information on suckings but also a diachronic perspective on them.

basis of their information it can be definitely asserted that bloodsucking witch-craft in its social, physical, psychological, and ideological components remained a constant for rural Tlaxcalan society for more than three-quarters of a century.

Finally, table 6.20 indicates the language spoken and the degree of accultura-tion in the victim's household. Let us take language first. There are two Nahuatl-speaking households, thirteen Spanish-speaking, eleven Nahuatl-Spanish-speaking, and twenty-one Spanish-Nahuatl-speaking. The first two categories signify that all members of the household were monolingual in Nahuatl or Spanish respectively, while the other two categories represent vary-ing degrees of bilingualism. In Nahuatl-Spanish households, Nahuatl is the everyday language and children use it occasionally, but Spanish is spoken in communication with the outside. In Spanish-Nahuatl households, Spanish is the everyday language, adults still speak Nahuatl but rarely use it, and children have little or no knowledge of Nahuatl. Household linguistic competence and performance are not significant indicators in the analysis of bloodsucking witchcraft, but the above breakdown clearly shows that there is an even dis-tribution of cases along the linguistic spectrum. In other words, taking for granted that our sample is representative of the area, there is no significant association of bloodsucking witchcraft incidence with any of the four linguistic categories of households—and by extension, communities—in rural Tlaxcala.

Table 6.20 Language and Degree of Acculturation of
Victim's Household[a]

Case no.	Language	Degree of Acculturation
1	Spanish-Nahuatl	Indian-transitional
2	Spanish-Nahuatl	Indian-transitional
3	Spanish-Nahuatl	Indian-transitional
4	Spanish-Nahuatl	Indian-transitional
5	Spanish-Nahuatl	Indian-transitional
6	Spanish-Nahuatl	Indian-transitional
7	Spanish-Nahuatl	Indian-transitional
8	Spanish-Nahuatl	Indian-transitional
9	Spanish-Nahuatl	Indian-transitional
10	Spanish	Transitional-mestizo
11	Nahuatl-Spanish	Indian-traditional
12	Spanish	Transitional-mestizo
13	Nahuatl-Spanish	Indian-traditional
14	Spanish-Nahuatl	Indian-transitional
15	Nahuatl-Spanish	Indian-traditional
16	Spanish	Mestizo-secularized
17	Spanish	Transitional-mestizo
18	Spanish-Nahuatl	Indian-transitional
19	Nahuatl	Indian-traditional
20	Spanish	Transitional-mestizo
21	Nahuatl-Spanish	Indian-traditional
22	Spanish-Nahuatl	Indian-transitional
23	Spanish	Transitional-mestizo
24	Nahuatl-Spanish	Indian-traditional
25	Spanish	Transitional-mestizo

Nutini and Isaac (1974:375–96) have characterized rural Tlaxcala as an area possessing an ethnocultural continuum in which there are no sharp breaks between Indians and Mestizos. Unlike several areas of Mexico and Guatemala, in which the Indian-Mestizo dichotomy obtains in rural Tlaxcala there are no clear cultural or ethnic differences. At the community level, the distribution, participation, and access to political, social, and religious life are basically egalitarian; the community must be considered an entity with a high degree of integration, lacking in sectors with totally antagonistic interests that might divide it in one way or another. At the regional level, the situation acquires an even greater fluidity: In the urban or industrial context, whatever ethnic and cultural differences that may be envisioned at the rural community level tend to become blurred, and the rural population is perceived as a diffuse proletarian mass or simply as the lower class with respect to the city. In this dynamic, rapidly changing view of contemporary rural Tlaxcala, we locate individuals

Table 6.20 *Continued*

Case no.	Language	Degree of Acculturation
26	Nahuatl-Spanish	Indian-traditional
27	Spanish	Transitional-mestizo
28	Spanish-Nahuatl	Indian-transitional
29	Spanish	Transitional-mestizo
30	Nahuatl-Spanish	Indian-traditional
31	Spanish-Nahuatl	Indian-transitional
32	Spanish	Mestizo-secularized
33	Nahuatl-Spanish	Indian-traditional
34	Spanish-Nahuatl	Indian-transitional
35	Spanish	Mestizo-secularized
36	Spanish-Nahuatl	Indian-transitional
37	Spanish-Nahuatl	Indian-transitional
38	Spanish-Nahuatl	Indian-transitional
39	Spanish-Nahuatl	Indian-transitional
40	Nahuatl-Spanish	Indian-traditional
41	Spanish	Transitional-mestizo
42	Spanish-Nahuatl	Indian-transitional
43	Nahuatl	Indian-traditional
44	Nahuatl-Spanish	Indian-traditional
45	Nahuatl-Spanish	Indian-traditional
46	Spanish-Nahuatl	Indian-transitional
47	Spanish	Transitional-mestizo

[a]The reason for seeking these data was to establish the correlation between bloodsucking witchcraft and the degree of modernization and secularization.

and entire communities by moving along the Indian-Mestizo continuum. Thus, the population of the more than two hundred communities in the twenty-one municipios which surround La Malintzi volcano can be ordered in the following fashion: (1) Indian-traditional (12%); (2) Indian-transitional (35%); (3) transitional-Mestizo (45%); and (4) Mestizo-secularized (8%) (Nutini and White 1977:367). By extension, according to this classification, the sample contains thirteen Indian-traditional, twenty-one Indian-transitional, ten transitional-Mestizo, and three Mestizo-secularized households. Communities in rural Tlaxcala are not entirely uniform—that is, individual households in any particular community may run the entire gamut of the acculturative continuum. Under such circumstances, the fourfold classification of the forty-seven households is based on the following variables: degree of ritual and ceremonial traditionalism; degree of belief in the non-Catholic supernatural complex (witchcraft, sorcery, nahualism, and so on); comparative strength of the kinship and compadrazgo systems; and household economy and material culture (subsistence, clothing, house construction, furniture and utensils, and so on).

There is no strict correlation between degree of acculturation and the incidence of bloodsucking witchcraft. Assuming that the percentage of communities in the four acculturative stages is also representative of households in rural Tlaxcala, we can see, however, that the incidence of bloodsucking witchcraft is significantly associated with the Indian-traditional and Indian-transitional stages, in which 75 percent of the cases took place in 47 percent of the total number of households. By contrast, proportionally speaking, Mestizo-secularized and transitional-Mestizo households are, respectively, slightly and greatly underrepresented. The greater incidence of bloodsucking witchcraft in Indian-traditional and Indian-transitional communities can be explained in terms of the self-fulfilling strength of the underlying belief system, which decreases as people move from the traditional toward the secular. Yet, these figures should not be taken at face value, for the sample may not be adequate for statistical purposes. Finally, since language has been implicitly regarded as the most significant marker of the Indian-Mestizo cleavage, there is a high correlation between linguistic performance and degree of acculturation: All Nahuatl-speaking households are Indian-traditional; all Spanish-speaking households are transitional-Mestizo and Mestizo-secularized; and Indian-traditional households are mostly Nahuatl-Spanish, while Indian-transitional households are mostly Spanish-Nahuatl.

This chapter discussed the methodology employed in the collection and recording of data and the systematic presentation of the empirical evidence surrounding bloodsucking witchcraft, emphasizing the social and psychological facts surrounding the bloodsucking event. Independently, the twenty most salient variables and associated factors of the practice were analyzed, expanding many aspects directly related to its etiological and diagnostic components. We are now in the position to undertake the analysis of the foregoing variables and properties, part of which must be embedded in the etiological and diagnostic discussion, and part of which must be done independently.

CHAPTER SEVEN

Natural and Supernatural Explanations: the Logic of Witchcraft and Normative Expectations

THE EPISTEMOLOGICAL FOUNDATION OF MAGICAL EXPLANATIONS

The foregoing chapters not only established the ideology of blood-sucking witchcraft (or, if you will, the belief system in which the practice is embedded) but also presented the concrete empirical evidence of its occurrence in a forty-seven–case sample, as well as several additional pieces of evidence. At times we gave the impression that tlahuelpuchis *really* exist and that their primary activity is sucking the blood of infants because it is sometimes practically impossible to separate the people's ideological belief complex from its physical, social, and psychological manifestation when elucidating how the system works. Thus, chapter 2 presented the global belief complex on the tlahuelpuchi from the viewpoints of the native informant, and the place it has in rural Tlaxcala culture and society. Occasionally, however, it was necessary to resort to empirical evidence to demonstrate how the system works ideologically and the high consistency of its self-fulfilling nature.[1] In chapters 5 and 6 we presented empirical evidence elicited directly or indirectly from informants as well as our observation of a bloodsucking epidemic of seven cases and forty other specific cases. By contrast, we appealed at times unavoidably to the belief system to show the unfolding of the physical, social, and psychological facts and events leading to and resulting from the sucking of infants. In summary, then, we are scientifically certain that tlahuelpuchis do not exist, but the interplay of normative and empirical parameters that lead rural Tlaxcalans to believe in bloodsucking witchcraft has been made abundantly clear. This double task is solidly grounded. On the one hand, the belief system was elicited systematically and with a high degree of reliability from a representative sample of rural Tlaxcalans. On the other hand, the structural manifestation of the complex has also been systematically gathered with a significant degree of controls for a representative sample of cases.

What distinguishes this study from most studies of witchcraft is its reliance on empirical evidence that is subject to a considerable degree of verification according to established scientific canons. The great majority of witchcraft studies are primarily ideological statements, which may lay bare the belief system in which the practice is embedded, but which lack the empirical evidence of specific cases to ascertain how things *really* work, thereby leading to the assignment of objective causality. Probably in most studies, the logic of "witch-craft-explains-unfortunate-events" need not be objectified, for non-objectified causality explains events or happenings which are mundane, non-patterned, rather common, and/or within what the people consider the normal course of things: many kinds of accidents, bad fortune, failure in some activity, and so on. In this context, the part of the belief system which stipulates that the tlahuelpuchi revenges herself on particular individuals by making them fall fatally from a bridge or a steep ravine need not be objectified, and it would not have been productive for Nutini to have investigated the three or four cases that came to his attention throughout 1961, for example. Yet the highly patterned complex of infant sucking by the tlahuelpuchi most clearly necessitated the objectification of the phenomenon—that is, the systematic study of cases, without which we cannot possibly understand the social, physical, and psychological nature of the practice.

The two classic studies of witchcraft among the Azande and Navaho are illustrative, and a brief recapitulation will put the reader in context. Evans-Pritchard (1937), on the one hand, is primarily concerned with the perception of Zande witchcraft in its sociological context, but he says a lot about the ideational and psychological matrix in which magic supernaturalism takes place. He provides a great amount of descriptive material that lays bare the structure of witchcraft in action, but he does not attempt to objectify causality in terms of the interplay of belief and practice. However, the seeds are there for the examination of the interplay between natural and supernatural causation that all witchcraft systems entail. Kluckhohn (1944), on the other hand, insightfully conveys the psychological matrix in which Navaho witchcraft is sociologically discharged, but he does not examine the fundamental epistemological question of natural-supernatural inference either. Given the particular position of witchcraft in Navaho culture (that is, its secretiveness, vagueness, lack of clear ideological configuration, and a practically non-existent physical manifestation), Kluckhohn can hardly be expected to demonstrate the empirical structure of witchcraft and must confine himself to its psychological configuration (Kluckhohn 1944:13–24). In neither case is witchcraft explained to the extent that the articulation of and concordance between its normative and empirical structure is objectivized—that is, links in the causal chain are not objectively established. This is not to say that the efficacy of witchcraft has not been demonstrated but that no clear and exclusive chain of events can be regarded as the antecedents of witchcraft's efficacy. This tradition, thrust upon the analysis of witchcraft and sorcery by the work of Evans-Pritchard and Kluckhohn, has remained unchanged for forty years. Moreover, British anthropologists have overwhelmingly emphasized the sociological aspects and functions of witchcraft (see Lienhardt 1951; Nadel 1952; Marwick 1952; Wilson 1951; Mayer 1954; Forde 1958; Fortune 1963; Reynolds 1963; Turner 1964; Middleton 1967; Middleton and Winter 1969; Mair 1969; Douglas 1970; Marwick 1970), whereas only a few American anthropologists have thoroughly explored some psycholgoical aspects of the phenomenon (see Norbeck 1961; Spiro 1967; Levine 1969). This has been a serious shortcoming.

Granting that the stipulation of causal antecedents underlying the efficacy of witchcraft is not necessary in most cases, one must objectify causality when dealing with such concrete, self-contained phenomena as bloodsucking witchcraft in rural Tlaxcala if one wishes to explain the social and psychological matrix in which it takes place. Granting also that we are now on less firm ground than we were in establishing the concordance between ideological expectations and empirical observation, we must clarify what the objectification of causality means conceptually and what its consequences are for the study of witchcraft in general as well as for the particular case at hand.

Fundamentally, witchcraft works because, as Evans-Pritchard insightfully perceived, its practitioners do not distinguish behaviorally between natural and supernatural causes in the act (or if they do, the distinction is nebulous). Thus, normative expectations lead to or unfold in people's actual experiences, and this validates, or verifies in the native mind, the efficacy of witchcraft. This epistemic framework does not obtain in all instances of the phenomenon, but it certainly constitutes a folk model. Whenever expectations are not validated by experience, the system is flexible enough to adduce secondary antecedents in explaining deviation. Every witchcraft system in the literature that is reasonably well described has loopholes allowing for alternate interpretations that either reinforce the normative complex or do not diminish the self-fulfilling nature of the practice. When this psychological framework is highly patterned within the cultural matrix, the logic of witchcraft becomes very efficient. This has been amply demonstrated in the foregoing pages. In this sense, then, witchcraft studies explain the efficacy of the practice and the sociological matrix in which it takes place, unless, of course, like Castaneda (1968), one assumes the existence of supernatural causes or entities, or mystical psychological states.

The empirical matrix of witchcraft, however, is seldom complete enough to enable the investigator to reconstruct the causal chain leading to a particular outcome, such as the sucking by the tlahuelpuchi and subsequent death of infants; or if it is, there are some key unspecified missing links.

In the context of empirical research the objectification of causality means two things: *On the one hand, it means the carefully controlled specification of causal antecedents leading to a discrete and highly patterned witchcraft event, independent of the normative expectations of the people, and within the boundaries of concretely specified time and space; on the other hand, it means the specification of the psychological matrix in which the event unfolds before and after the witchcraft act, especially as it concerns primary actors and their extensions.* The social context of the witchcraft event is not mentioned because the socially patterned behavior is specified in the ideology of witchcraft; what is observed empirically before and after the witchcraft act is, to be sure, conditioned by the normative structure, but it is not its necessary cause.

By applying this strategy of objectifying causality we can determine not only the missing link in the causal chain (or establish an empirical link permitting objective entailment), but what is more important, establish the immediate psychological conditions that underlie the people's transposition of natural and supernatural causality. This modus operandi has guided this study. An adequate explanation of witchcraft, then, entails not only the elucidation of the ideological and social parameters which account for its efficacy within a certain cultural milieu, but also the unravelling of psychological mechanisms involved in the inferential process of the people affected. Examples of the social functions and the need of witchcraft and sorcery have been well represented in the ethnographic and historical literature; this study is one more example of the rather homogeneous structure of these phenomena: the sociocultural context changes from case to case, but the operational principles remain the same. This study, however, aims to contribute to the understanding of the rules of inference which underlie the practice of witchcraft as people change from supernatural explanations to naturalistic explanations.

THE OBJECTIFICATION OF CAUSALITY AND THE TRANSPOSITION OF CAUSATION

It is clear from the foregoing discussion that the interplay of natural and supernatural causes is at the heart of explaining how witchcraft works. Moreover, the tasks of determining why and how people confuse natural and supernatural causation or do not contextually distinguish immediately between the two are essentially psychological endeavors. Thus, the objectification of causality has nothing to do with assigning functions; rather, it has to do with establishing the psychological matrix in which witchcraft takes place. Traditionally, witchcraft and sorcery have been explained to be the extent that they fulfill or discharge certain positive or negative social needs within the operational social group; or witchcraft has been regarded as the psychological response to particularly determined situations of stress. As long as anthropologists have confined themselves mainly to these parameters, they have produced good descriptions of how witchcraft works and have determined its social and psychological needs. Their explanations, however, have been circular in that they have not been able to establish the psychological matrices in which normative expectations are given concrete physical manifestations, Spiro (1967) being a notable exception.

A particular case of witchcraft is not explained until the supernatural causation entailed by its underlying belief system is shown to have occurred according to a specific chain of natural events resulting in a specific physical outcome. It is this transposition of natural and supernatural causation that must be explained on psychological grounds, for there is no reason to assume that the process of logical inference of the mostly non-European societies where witchcraft is still a functioning aspect of the social structure is fundamentally different from that of science. If the transposition of natural and supernatural causes could be explained on sociocultural grounds, there would be no need to appeal to psychology. But a sociocultural explanation is impossible, for it is the culturally determined ideology of witchcraft that validates the transposition and makes the practice efficacious. Lest we are misunderstood, we do not maintain that supernatural and ideological facts cannot be used scientifically, for then no studies of magic and religion would have a place in a scientific anthropology. We are only saying that value-laden supernatural and ideological facts must be used in the object-language and not in the meta-language in the process of causal inference. Two points must be made.

First, the objectification of causality as defined above should not be confused with the determination of how people who believe in witchcraft manage the non sequitur from supernatural cause to natural effect, as in the case of blood-sucking witchcraft in rural Tlaxcala; nor should it be confused with the determination of how people for whom witchcraft is a central and overwhelming element in their ideological system manage sometimes to confuse natural and supernatural causation, sometimes to combine them into certain kinds of explanations, or sometimes even to ignore the natural-supernatural distinction whenever the occasion requires it, as in the case of the Azande (Evans-Pritchard 1937:74–83). The objectification of causality is an operation designed to establish the natural chain of events leading to a specific physical outcome underlined by the individual psychological matrix of the primary actors involved in the witchcraft episode. The explanation of the transposition, confusion, and/or combination of natural and supernatural causation, always involved in witchcraft, entails the psychological determination of that which is culturally shared by the operational group, obviously the expression of the underlying ideological system. Thus, in the case of bloodsucking witchcraft in rural Tlaxcala, the objectification of causality means the specification of its antecedents and consequences, reconstructed and partially observed independently of the belief system underlying the tlahuelpuchi complex, as summarized in tables 6.1 to 6.20. This operation, as we will demonstrate in chapters 8 and 9, is conditioned by the primary actors' perception of the antecedents leading to and the consequences resulting from the sucking event. We maintain that the perceptive distortion, exaggeration, and/or self-fulfilling interpretation of the facts and events surrounding the bloodsucking event can be explained only by reference to the psychology of those directly involved. The transposition, confusion, and/or combination of natural and supernatural causes, on the other hand, mean the elucidation of why and how rural Tlaxcalans are able to employ these two modes of thinking in their explanation of both discrete and highly patterned witchcraft events (the sucking of infants) and the random and unstructured witchcraft acts (the willful killing of adults) attributed to the tlahuelpuchi. This task must necessarily delve, along the lines pioneered by Evans-Pritchard among the Azande, into the epistemology of how rural Tlaxcalans perceive the external world. Thus, the transposition of causation may be defined as *the epistemic task of establishing why peoples at different levels of evolutionary development (primitive, folk, modern) make inferences from supernatural inputs to natural outcomes, and vice versa, as well as what psychological consequences follow, given the configuration of the* imago mundi *as a reflection of their state of knowledge.*

Second, the two analytical tasks delineated above are not equally applicable to all witchcraft systems as exhibited in the ethnographic literature. Some situations would admit only the objectification of causality, others only the transposition of causation, whereas still others would admit both. Theoretically, of course, it should be possible to engage in both analytical operations; practically, the probability of success depends on the availability of hard data and the position of witchcraft within the total social structure—by which we mean essentially that, since the data on witchcraft and sorcery are unquestionably the hardest and most time-consuming to gather, the usual periods of time that anthropologists spend in the field are almost always too short to collect the appropriate corpus of information to implement the analytical tasks envisaged here.[2] Under such conditions, most anthropologists who have written on witchcraft barely had time to collect the facts of the belief system underlying the practice on which to base their functional analyses (see Lienhardt 1951; Wilson 1951; Nadel 1952; Ruel 1965; Nash 1961; LaFontaine 1965; Middleton 1969; Brain 1970; Spiro 1967). There are many examples in the anthropological literature (see Douglas 1970; Marwich 1970; Middleton 1967; Middleton and Winter 1969) which indicates that either the objectification of causality and the transposition of causation could have been undertaken or both could have been.

CENTRALITY AND THE EXTENSION OF WITCHCRAFT IN CONTEMPORARY SOCIETIES

The ontological problem of witchcraft presents an altogether different set of considerations. The position of witchcraft within the global sociocultural framework is the ultimate determinant concerning the analytical appropriateness and explanatory adequacy of establishing the objectification of causality and the transposition of causation. As we indicated, there are essentially three types of societies in the world today which admit of the partial explanation of witchcraft in terms of the epistemological-psychological framework envisaged here. Let us discuss them in some detail and determine what the implications of our approach mean for each case.

In Societies Under the Influence of Science and Technology

At one extreme are those societies in which witchcraft is practiced minimally, is considered largely spurious, occupies an insignificant corner in the predominant belief system, and has essentially no place in the organization of religion. Thus has it been in Western societies, at least for the past hundred years and possibly since shortly after the last witches were burned at the stake in the middle of the eighteenth century. The rise of modern science has relegated supernatural causation to the realm of religiously related phenomena such as miracles, mysticism, and the like; even deeply religious people do not confuse or ignore the distinction between natural and supernatural causation in the conduct of everyday life and in the explanation of the world immediately around them—thereby rendering largely inoperative the logic of "witchcraft-explains-unfortunate-events." Hence, it would be a waste of time to determine the transposition of causation in the analysis of whatever passes for witchcraft in Western and Westernlike societies. But even in such societies there are segments of the population, albeit small and insignificant, who believe that some phenomena do not conform to natural law. One could include under this category religious fundamentalists (Christian Scientists are a good example) and a whole host of practitioners of the so-called "occult sciences," among whom it would be entirely appropriate to undertake the objectification of causality to lay bare how their process of inference differs from that of the "scientific" majority. Two additional points are in order in this connection. On the one hand, modern scientific societies in the Western European mold and many societies throughout the world under the influence of science and technology are too fragmented and diversified to be the subject of any meaningful study of witchcraft and related phenomena; essentially, what we are suggesting here is the psychological analysis of religion, which obviously involves the contextual objectification of causality. But it seems that within the global ideology of science it is quite feasible to isolate operational social groups for which supernatural causes entail natural effects (for example, largely spurious practitioners of witchcraft and sorcery in urban environments, practitioners of divination and fortune-telling, and the like). On the other hand, it is assumed here that the logic of all situations in which people believe that supernatural inputs produce natural outcomes is not different from that of witchcraft. It is therefore important to explore, psychologically and sociologically, why people under the influence of science and largely governed by it in their everyday life still compartmentalize causality and expect natural outcomes out of supernatural inputs.

In Tribal Societies
At the opposite extreme, are societies in which witchcraft is an integral part of the social structure, its position is central in the belief system and imago mundi of the people, and it is often difficult to distinguish from religion. There are differences, to be sure, among the societies classified in this category, but they all have in common the fact that witchcraft is a reality of everyday life and in varying degrees controls a significant segment of social behavior. In this category are included most of the traditional tribal societies described in the ethnographic literature, many tribal societies in the process of becoming folk societies in the context of the new national states organized out of a colonial past (mostly in Africa and Oceania), and perhaps a few folk societies of long standing. In such societies, science has had little or no influence, there is largely no conception of natural law, and witchcraft entails the transposition, confusion, and/or combination of supernatural and natural causation to an inordinate degree. This logic and this mode of inference make themselves felt in many domains of the social structure. Indeed, witchcraft in these societies is not an *extraordinary* phenomenon and largely becomes an everyday occurrence, vulgarized to the extent that it competes as a system of explanation with whatever naturalistic modes of inference may be available. Thus, the transposition of causation is a necessary condition for the proper understanding and explanation of witchcraft, whereas the objectification of causality, with perhaps

notable exceptions, cannot be undertaken meaningfully. Why is the latter not possible? Simply because the efficacy of witchcraft is so pervasive, actually or potentially, that witchcraft events and outcomes become "natural" occurrences in everyday life, which need not be specified in the belief system. In other words, when a witchcraft event occurs, the expectation of its occurrence is not posited on a fully specified normative system but on the intrinsic and unappealable efficacy of witchcraft.

Not all societies in this category are mirror images of the Azande with respect to witchcraft, and by extension, mirror images of Dobu (Fortune 1963), with respect to sorcery. Rather, there is a wide spectrum with respect to the intension of witchcraft as a domain in the social structure and its centrality in the belief system. Azande witchcraft seems to be exceptional in its intensity and centrality, if for no other reason, because it is the best-reported system. But it appears that the range of variation in this category has to do mainly with the extension of witchcraft throughout the social structure rather than with the intensity of belief and practice. Thus, positioning the Azande at one extreme in which witchcraft extends and ramifies efficaciously to all significant domains of the social structure except volitional actions (Evans-Pritchard 1937: 21–134), we find at the other extreme in this category a society such as the Mapuche, among whom witchcraft is confined to a limited and circumscribed domain of the social structure—namely, that of the personified, evil, and treacherous *wekufu* beings who cause well-specified misfortunes (Cooper 1946; Faron 1964:66–77). Between these two extremes there is a wide variety of societies—such as the Bakweri (Ardner 1970), Banyang (Ruel 1970), Cebuano (Lieban 1967), Cewa (Marwick 1952), Mandari (Buxton 1969), Nandi (Huntingford 1969), Safwa (Harwood 1970), Tswana (Schapera 1952), Navaho (Kluckhohn 1944), Ukaguru (Beildelman 1969), Wambugwe (Gray 1969), Yako (Forde 1958) and Zuni (Parsons 1927)—in which witchcraft is neither as extensive as among the Azande nor as circumscribed as among the Mapuche, but pervasive enough to affect a number of domains in the social structure and extensive chunks of individual and collective behavior. Despite differences in extensiveness, all societies in this category share a fundamentally similarly structured belief system and imago mundi of witchcraft and what it can accomplish in action. We would say, however, that even the most intensive and extensive witchcraft system may include normative expectations in a particularly circumscribed domain that are specific enough to correlate with particularly observed or reconstructed physical events, which constitutes the basic operation in the objectification of causality.

There is another dimension of the witchcraft system of societies in this category that seems important—namely, whether the nature of the practice and its practitioners is essentially secret or public. Here again there is a significant degree of variation, and, as has been mentioned, the Navaho and the Azande stand at the opposite ends of the spectrum.

Among the Navaho, on the one hand, witchcraft is something that the people may discuss among themselves but loathe to talk about with strangers (Kluckhohn 1944:13–14). Every aspect of witchcraft is shrouded in secrecy and surreptitiousness: its paraphernalia, its craft, its practitioners, and its general position and efficacy in the social structure. Indeed, Kluckhohn's monograph is probably the purest ideological construct ever assembled from a functioning society—that is, a belief system collected or put together almost exclusively from the verbalization of informants. Among the Azande, on the other hand, practically everything about witchcraft is public, above board, and in the everyday consciousness of the people. We dare say that many students of witchcraft who have read Evans-Pritchard's monograph have told themselves "how I wished that things had been as easy to investigate among the people that I studied." We remember feeling just that when we read Evans-Pritchard for the first time. This is misleading, however, for the mere fact that people were so willing to talk openly about every aspect of witchcraft and associated phenomena did not mean that the underlying belief system was specified by informants to the degree that enabled Evans-Pritchard to reconstruct so well the sociological matrix in which death, misfortune, accidents, and many other events and occurrences are explained by the Azande. Evans-Pritchard produced such a peerless description and analysis of witchcraft because he did not leave a stone unturned in complementing the elicitation of the belief system with a thorough and detailed account of the observable and directly verified physical manifestation of witchcraft, sorcery, magic, and oracles. Indeed, as Evans-Pritchard (1937:113–25; 329–22) himself implies and occasionally admits, the publicness of witchcraft among the Azande is not given at this level of the belief system (which is often vague, poorly specified, and occasionally contradictory) but at the level of its physical manifestation in terms of its paraphernalia, detection, prevention, personnel, and the ubiquity of its sphere of action. Roberts says that whether there were actual practicing witches in Navaho society at the time of Kluckhohn's study (roughly between 1930 and 1940) has never been determined. Certainly Kluckhohn did not know anyone who admitted to being a witch. If there were practicing witches, they must have been extremely rare. In Kluckhohn's own terminology, Navaho witchcraft must have been entirely projective.

At this juncture, something should be said about the nature of the secret-public contrast in witchcraft. First, we do not mean to characterize a particular witchcraft system as entirely secret or public. This is seldom, if ever, the case.

Rather, these are relative terms that denote the basic configuration of the witch-craft system, for there are always components that are either secret or public, as the case may be. Second, the terms *secret* and *public* denote respectively the closed, covert, and projective and the open, overt, and manifest aspects and components of witchcraft systems. Again, these are relative terms, for the secret-closed-covert-projective or public-open-overt-manifest denotative clus-ters probably never apply to a global witchcraft system. The most significant cleavage of those clusters obtains between witchcraft's practitioners and the craft itself, but it may obtain in a number of other domains in the actual practice of witchcraft. Third, it is important to discriminate between the secret and public nature of witches but also between self-confessed and readily iden-tified (by gossip, common knowledge, or other means) witches. Conceptually, there is a great deal of difference between the self-confessed witches of Salem, Massachusetts and the readily identifiable witches of the Wambugwe of north-ern Tanganyika (Gray 1969:168–70), and it does not take much imagination to realize that they cannot be lumped together in the same analytical scheme.

Between the public nature of Azande witchcraft and the secrecy of Navaho witchcraft there are innumerable societies, in all three categories discussed here, in which witchcraft is neither as public as among the Azande nor as secret as among the Navaho. If we could arrange all societies in the ethnographic literature with sufficient information on witchcraft on a continuum, it would be possible to predict that they cluster significantly toward the secrecy limit. Our reading of the literature indicates that there are few societies which ap-proach witchcraft as publicly in most aspects as the Azandes', whereas there is a significant number of systems which approach witchcraft as secretly as the Navaho. The problem, of course, is more complex than meets the eye in a cross-cultural survey. The problem hinges primarily on the essentially public or secret nature of witches, and not necessarily on the secret or public nature of witchcraft's paraphernalia, physical components, and social manifestations. That is why Navaho witchcraft is something of an exception, for the probable majority of witchcraft systems in the literature involve the essential secrecy of the witches themselves, but the ideological, social, and physical manifestations of witchcraft, in varying degrees, are more or less open to the standard tech-niques of investigation of anthropologists. Based on these considerations, we employed the essentially secret nature of witches as one of the criteria in distin-guishing between witchcraft and sorcery.

In Folk Societies

Finally, there is a third and increasingly larger category of societies in which witchcraft occupies an intermediate position between the essentially spurious nature of the practice in the first category and the integral and pervasive nature of the practice in the second category. In these societies witchcraft practices which are often pervasive enough to be referred to as systems are not uniform and differences which may at times be significant do obtain. What all these societies share is that witchcraft is still a functioning aspect of the social structure, albeit often in circumscribed domains, and generally exhibits ideological and structural roots in older, well-structured systems. These societies are mostly historically ascertainable entities in which witchcraft is the product of syncretism, acculturation, or diffusion. Included in this category are most folk societies throughout the world, some tribal societies in the process of becoming folk societies, and perhaps a few marginal subsocieties of industrial and developing nations. Essentially, however, we are dealing in this category with folk societies of long standing or societies out of an immediate tribal past, largely as the result of the last stage of European colonialism (roughly from the middle of the nineteenth to the middle of the twentieth centuries). Typical examples of folk societies of long standing are those that were structured in the New World due to conquest and colonization by Spain. Folk societies of longer standing can be found in Asia and southeast Asia due to the spread of the great cultural traditions of India and China. Most of the folk societies out of an immediate tribal past are to be found in Africa and Oceania, societies that are mainly the direct outcome of English and French colonialism. In most cases, witchcraft in folk societies of long standing achieved the intermediate position of this category centuries ago, whereas in the case of folk societies in the process of formation, the witchcraft system probably has not yet achieved a stable synthesis, and probably never will.

Regardless of historical, syncretic, and acculturative considerations, and regardless of when these societies achieved a witchcraft system distinct from that of most tribal societies, the facts of science and technology are of primary importance in assessing and explaining the practice in its contemporary setting. For perhaps more than a hundred years, many of these societies in one way or another have been under the influence of scientific technology; more recently, they have been influenced by science through education, medical practices, and the different means of communication. The influence of science and technology, especially during the past two generations, has inevitably altered the concept of witchcraft that these societies traditionally had, and as a consequence, the position of witchcraft within the global social structure has altered. This is evident in the example of rural Tlaxcala; if this also is representative of most societies in this category throughout the world, then one can generalize with some reliability, at least about Latin American folk societies. We can reconstruct a number of changes that witchcraft in rural Tlaxcala has undergone in this century to the extent that, two generations ago (by approximately 1930), the non-bloodsucking aspects of witchcraft were in practice more extensive and, together with the tlahuelpuchi complex, constituted a wider and more pervasive system within the global context of rural Tlaxcalan culture and society than they do today. Indeed, it is possible that rural Tlaxcalan witchcraft at the turn of the century was not that different from, say, that of many African societies reported in the ethnographic literature during the past 30 years. Thus, science and technology have in many ways, contexts, and forms influenced the witchcraft systems of folk societies which not too long ago could have been classified as essentially the same as those of tribal societies. Science and technology have brought changes not only in the ideology and practice of witchcraft in folk societies, but they have also often seriously altered the position of witchcraft within the total social structure leading to its increasing curtailment.

In no other sociocultural domain is the term *folk* more adequately applied than to the occasionally integrated domain of religion, magic, sorcery, and witchcraft, at least in Latin America, but probably in other areas of the world as well. These societies are the result of long processes of syncretism, acculturation, or diffusion in which the supernatural system was forged by the confrontation, often antagonistic, of two and sometimes three different cultural traditions. In such a situation, the witchcraft systems of folk societies have become complex amalgams, well integrated, but occupying rather ambivalent positions in the total social structure. This ambivalence is due mostly to the influence of science and technology, which has variously changed the traditional balance between the natural and the supernatural that obtained in folk societies, probably until the turn of the century. These have been the latest inputs into the slow, continuous process of change that folk societies have been undergoing during the past century.

What, then, is the position of witchcraft in folk societies in this category? Allowing for a certain degree of variation, we can say that folk societies exhibit a high common denominator in the natural-supernatural balance, and the following picture emerges. Although witchcraft may sometimes be regarded as an unstructured and diffused ensemble of beliefs and practices, more often it constitutes a system, generally tied to or forming part of another well-delineated cultural domain. Witchcraft in these societies is in one way or another connected to the religious system, often constituting an integrated ideological whole. This is certainly true of the majority of folk societies in Latin America and probably of most other areas of the world as well. Since folk societies by their very nature are syncretic, acculturative, or diffused amalgams of tribal and literate traditions, their witchcraft systems involve various combinations of ideological and structural elements operating ancillarily to religion. It could be asked to what other cultural domains may witchcraft be tied or intimately associated with? Ontologically, perhaps to none, but operationally, witchcraft is often more closely related to kinship and the social structure than to religion, and it may occasionally have some economic and even political implications. Witchcraft in folk societies generally does not have significant economic and political functions, and its kinship and wider social structural implications are considerably less than those in tribal societies. Given the rather marginal position of witchcraft in the global social structure, and the incipient or fairly strong influence of science and technology, the sphere of efficacy of witchcraft is closer to that of religion and confined to well-circumscribed domains in which the transposition of causation seldom obtains. If it does obtain, it cannot be regarded as an overwhelming mode of explanation, as it is in tribal societies, but rather as a partial interference with natural causation. Thus, what generally obtains in folk societies is that witchcraft shares entirely or partially with religion an ideology and imago mundi that is essentially local and mostly tribal in origin, whereas its sphere of action extends to circumscribed structural domains that contain significant practices and paraphernalia of foreign literate origin.

In folk societies where witchcraft constitutes an amorphous and sometimes vague ensemble of beliefs and practices it is most difficult to conceptualize this institution, for witchcraft almost invariably represents a conglomerate of acculturative or diffused elements which have been peripherally displaced by the predominant religion and the influence of science and technology. Such situations approach the rather spurious position of witchcraft in our first category and, at least from an anthropological standpoint, it seems hardly worthwhile to engage in either the objectification of causality or the transposition of causation. By contrast, in folk societies where witchcraft constitutes a system or partial system, as in rural Tlaxcala and probably in most folk societies of Latin America, the situation is significantly different. In such societies, witchcraft is generally a thoroughly syncretic system of beliefs and practices—still occupying a rather central place in the supernatural ideology and imago mundi of the people—which the predominant religion and the influence of science and technology have not yet been strong enough to relegate to a peripheral position. Thus, while witchcraft and religion constitute two different systems, the ideological centrality of the former is strong enough to be efficacious in circumscribed and well-delineated domains. The ideological centrality of witchcraft is counterbalanced by its structural periphery within the global social structure, and this is obviously the reason why witchcraft does not have any significant or noticeable economic and political functions in folk societies. Rather, the efficacy of witchcraft is most noticeable in small domains having to do with the explanation of particular events, happenings, or complexes of a social, physical, or psychological nature. Under such circumstances, it is necessary to undertake the objectification of causality to understand the psychological matrix in which supernatural causes produce natural effects; and, if one is fortunate enough to gather the necessary corpora of data, one can undertake the transposition of causation to determine to what extent the influence of science and technology or other naturalistic modes of explanation are undermining and changing the logic of magic.

As in tribal societies, the public versus the secret nature of witchcraft and its practitioners is also important in folk societies. With respect to the secret or public nature of witchcraft's paraphernalia, its physical manifestation, and its practitioners, folk societies are not essentially different from tribal societies: they both cluster toward the secrecy limit of the continuum with regard to witchcraft's practitioners, but its paraphernalia and physical manifestation are in varying degrees public. The secrecy of witches, however, is very likely higher in folk societies than in tribal societies. Our reading of the ethnographic literature indicates that witchcraft accusations are much more common in tribal societies than in folk societies, and this for us is a clear indication that the secrecy of witches in the latter is higher than in the former. In one respect the witchcraft systems of folk societies are perhaps significantly different from those of tribal societies—namely, in the public and specific nature of the underlying ideological system, which in the latter is seldom spelled out in detail. In our view this has two salient aspects.

On the one hand, the ideology of witchcraft in folk societies is the result of syncretic syntheses, usually of long standing, in which at least one of the cultural traditions in confrontation had a religion that involved an elaborate cosmology and theology in which witchcraft was anchored. Under such conditions, the ideological system specifies the normative behavior, actions, and participation of the practitioners of witchcraft and its accompanying paraphernalia and physical manifestation in the same fashion as the underlying cosmology and theology of the old religion normatively governed the gods.

On the other hand, and of more importance to the discussion here, the specificity and detailed extension of the ideology of witchcraft in folk societies stems from the explanatory dimensions that it has in circumscribed domains. In tribal societies and in societies in general where witchcraft is an integral part of the social structure in operation, magical explanations are posited on the often universal logic of witchcraft, which must assume the unquestioning and deep-seated belief that supernatural causes do produce natural effects. This is not the case in folk societies and perhaps other societies where there are alternative naturalistic modes of explanation. In such situations, the efficacy of witchcraft is also grounded in the notion that supernatural causes produce natural effects, but conditioned by the concordance of ideological expectations and physical manifestations in well-circumscribed domains in which the logic of magic and the logic of naturalism are not regarded by the people as alternative modes of explanation. Thus, in order for this concordance to obtain, the normative expectations of witchcraft must be well specified; in some rather unusual instances, the expectations must be minutely specified, as in the tlahuelpuchi complex in rural Tlaxcala. In conclusion then, witchcraft in tribal societies is not drastically different from that in folk societies. In both it is underlain by the same perceptual and behavioral principles but manifested in different ontological contexts while conditioned primarily by its centrality to religion and by the influence of science and technology.

SUMMARY REMARKS

We can summarize the substantive and perceptual discussion as follows. Ontologically, contemporary witchcraft runs the gamut from societies in which it is little more than a spurious conglomerate of disparate elements to societies in which it is a well-structured system occupying a central place in the magico-religious domain. The centrality and extension of witchcraft varies greatly in societies throughout the world, but the concept has enough unitary meaning to enable anthropologists to discuss a number of beliefs and practices under the same rubric of "witchcraft." Epistemologically, there is also a significant degree of variation. Witchcraft ranges from societies in which beliefs and practices are little more than a form of atavism that may mask universal forms of behavior and expression under certain specifiable conditions to societies in which witchcraft is a full-fledged explanatory system competing with naturalistic modes of explanation. The explanatory dimensions of witchcraft depend of course on its centrality (intension) to the magico-religious system, on its extension throughout the social structure at large, and more recently, on the influence of science and technology. But the average witchcraft system in societies throughout the world today seems to be efficacious in rather circumscribed domains where natural causation is suspended in favor of supernatural causation and naturalistic modes of explanation prevail in most other cultural domains. Finally, disregarding the spurious category of possible magical efficacy, we turn to the two main analytical tasks elucidated in this chapter: the transposition of causation is necessary to understand and explain the efficacy of witchcraft in predominantly tribal societies, whereas the objectification of causality may or may not be possible for specified domains; in predominantly so-called folk societies only the objectification of causality is a necessary requirement, whereas the transposition of causation may or may not be undertaken, depending on the degree of influence of science and technology.

Throughout this chapter the theoretical orientation that guided the general organization of this monograph was put in perspective. It was necessary to place the study of witchcraft in a contemporary context to determine the most appropriate and economic mode of analysis. At the same time our aim was to make clear that witchcraft in folk societies constitutes a problem significantly different from that in tribal societies and its study entails analytical approaches other than those in tribal societies. Although functional (social or psychological) explanations of witchcraft may still be useful, the analysis of witchcraft in folk societies and others in this category demands an essentially psychological approach buttressed by epistemological considerations, as pioneered by Evans-Pritchard fifty years ago.

CHAPTER EIGHT

The Diagnostic and Etiological Analysis of Bloodsucking Witchcraft

CHAPTERS 2 AND 5 presented the ideology and belief system of blood-sucking witchcraft in rural Tlaxcala as well as the social matrix in which it takes place. The sociopsychological ambience in which the tlahuelpuchi is supposed to kill her victims was also discussed and placed in the context of family structure and the organization of the household, occasionally giving the impression of a certain ontological reality attributed to this anthropomorphic supernatural. Chapter 6 presented the data about the circumstances immediately preceding the bloodsucking event, positioned with respect to the subsequent behavior of the primary actors involved. Thus, by interrelating the ideological expectations with the observation and partial reconstruction of the physical events of bloodsucking witchcraft, we outlined the epistemological process that, in chapter 7, we called the objectification of causality.

We can now present a scientific natural explanation of bloodsucking witchcraft and reconstruct the chain of events that allows rural Tlaxcalans the transposition of natural and supernatural entailment. Within the narrow boundaries of witchcraft, two main themes are analyzed: the interplay between ideology and structure—that is, how the ideology of the system is borne out in its structural discharge; and the physical explanation of infant mortality—and the most probable causes of death of those believed to have been sucked by the witch. Within the controlled ambience of the nuclear and extended family, the household, and the neighborhood it is demonstrated how actors conform to the injunctions and constraints of the ideology of bloodsucking witchcraft; out of ensuing physical and psychological behavior and actions, the death of infants is explained.

IDEOLOGICAL IMPERATIVES, BELIEF CONSTRAINTS, AND THE
STRUCTURAL UNFOLDING OF THE TLAHUELPUCHI COMPLEX

A survey of the literature on witchcraft and sorcery for the culture areas of the world indicates that nothing approaching the objectification of causality has been achieved. In perhaps the majority of well-authenticated witchcraft systems there was no need to undertake this operation, but in many cases it was necessary to conceptualize people's rules of inference leading to the assignment of physical causes in the context of the supernatural-natural chain of events. The evidence of more than three dozen monographs in which witchcraft events are described in sufficient detail and within the framework of a distinct ideology leads us to believe that the objectification of causality could have been partially achieved. The main reason no attempt to elucidate the chain of events leading to witchcraft acts has been made has probably been the pervasive notion that the interplay of social facts is enough to generate explanations for any system in action. There are exceptions, of course, and the Evans-Pritchard 1937 study of Azande witchcraft and sorcery is the most outstanding, whereas a few studies are observations of individual practitioners, but not necessarily while they were in action. The shortcoming of this position is that, whatever social or psychological functional assignments have been made about witchcraft, they may not necessarily reflect reality, but rather mask a physical reality that is still in need of explanation.

Objectification, Transposition, and Feedback Effect in the Bloodsucking Event
We began writing this monograph in late 1970. By late 1982 we had completed the first eight chapters. The manuscript was then set aside until now (1986). Concern with the physical unfolding and behavioral underpinnings of the bloodsucking event were serendipitously thrust upon us by the peculiar structure of the tlahuelpuchi complex in rural Tlaxcala, and we cannot claim any logical plan or well thought-out strategy that enabled us to gather the corpus of data presented in chapter 6. Indeed, the full realization of the physical components of the bloodsucking complex and its full etiological implications were late in coming. It was not until recently that we understood what it means to approach the phenomenon from the viewpoint of the objectification of causality, and the advantages that this method entails for functional assignment. When Nutini was advised by the chief medical officer of the state of Tlaxcala to approach the study of infants sucked by the tlahuelpuchi from an essentially medical standpoint, little did he realize the much wider sociopsychological implications that his systematic commitment entailed. Nonetheless, it was the

fortuitous gathering of the hard data on bloodsucking witchcraft throughout 1961 that made us realize the importance of interpreting the ideology of a witchcraft system in the light of a systematically gathered corpus of facts surrounding the discharge of a circumscribed or spatially bounded witchcraft event or complex.

Granting that perhaps the majority of witchcraft systems appear to be unsusceptible to the data gathering and analysis undertaken in this monograph one might ask why we insist upon detailing and bringing to logical conclusions those aspects of witchcraft that have been conceptualized as the objectification of causality and the transposition of causation. The answer is twofold. First, because the objectification of causality leads to verifiable functional assignments and to physical explanations that are obviously not specified in the ideology of witchcraft. Perhaps a more important reason for objectifying causality is to demonstrate the feedback effect that obtains between the ideology and belief system and the structural discharge of witchcraft in action, which is basic to understanding why and under what conditions the logic of witchcraft is efficacious. Second, the transposition of causation lays bare the mechanisms that permit the actors in a system to explain certain occurrences as supernatural inputs producing natural outcomes. The data base for undertaking this operation is inadequate, but the transposition of causation is at the heart of understanding supernaturalism (in both magic and religion) and how it becomes compartmentalized with the rise of scientific/technological modes of explanation. Let us explain with an example how the objectification of causality demonstrates the feedback effect of witchcraft.

During the summer of 1959 and the two months before the bloodsucking witchcraft epidemic of San Pedro Xolotla, the general ideology and specific belief system of the tlahuelpuchi complex had been elicited from at least a dozen informants in four communities. On the basis of that information alone, chapter 2 could have been written. Subsequent information, gathered throughout 1961 and five subsequent summers, added a few details and came to confirm the pan-Tlaxcalan incidence of bloodsucking witchcraft. As directly verbalized by informants and exemplified by specifically recounted examples of suckings, the tlahuelpuchi complex, consistent and self-contained as it appeared, was not entirely intelligible. It was not until the witchcraft epidemic and at least another dozen or so cases of infant deaths had been examined systematically that all the pieces of the puzzle fitted into place. The conclusions reached, as detailed in this chapter, are the following. The ideology of the witchcraft system elicited from informants: (1) presented a normative pattern that was consistent by itself; (2) allowed for a reconstruction of what *really* happened when infants were sucked by the tlahuelpuchi; (3) made intelligible a significant part of the behavior of the main participant actors; (4) accounted for many of the physical elements involved and for some of the accompanying elements of time and space; and (5) made it possible to assign social functions, and to some extent envisaged the psychological, normative components of the complex. To put it differently, the verbalized ideology and belief system gave a consistent, structured gestalt of how and under what circumstances infants died as the result of being sucked by the putative entity known as the tlahuelpuchi which explained the very high incidence of infant mortality in rural Tlaxcala and indicated the self-fulfilling nature of the system. Had Nutini at this point lost interest in bloodsucking witchcraft by not pursuing the examination of cases, this monograph would have been just another study of witchcraft, no more explanatory than any other study in the anthropological and historical literature.

This traditional position, however, does not allow for the verification of the causes of infant death, at least not in the sense that this term is understood scientifically, nor does it allow for the verification of functional assignment, if this operation is to be more than a circular argument. More significantly, verbalized ideology-belief configurations cannot be sufficient grounds for the assignment of psychological functions which must be posited on observed behavior. Thus, the objectification of causality is more than the complement entailed by the analysis of the ideology and belief system of bloodsucking witchcraft. Rather, it entails the necessary grounds for immediate social and psychological assignment and verification: what the ideology and belief system puts in context and configures is verified and explanations emerge when the facts and chain of events of actual cases unfold and are analyzed in the context of controlled time and space.

Alternative Structural-Ideological Modes of Conceptualizing Witchcraft
The ideology of bloodsucking witchcraft in rural Tlaxcala stipulates that the tlahuelpuchi exists, that she is the embodiment of certain principles, that she has certain behavioral proclivities that compel her to act in a prescribed fashion, and that her ultimate objective is to suck the blood of infants to survive. In turn the belief system sets up the constraints of determinate conditions of time, space, and context under which the bloodsucking event takes place while it conjointly prescribes the behavior of primary actors necessary to combat the powers of the sucking nemesis. In the syntagmatic context of investigating a witchcraft system, the elicitation of the ideology and belief system comes first, even though anthropologists may have earlier and unsystematically witnessed several witchcraft events. In the more common course of research, the anthropologist in the field initially becomes acquainted with witchcraft through verbal elicitations rather than through experiencing events or cases of witchcraft. In

either situation, however, three alternative modes of conceptualizing witchcraft may arise in investigating it.

First, after a relatively short period of time (perhaps three or four months), the anthropologist may realize that the witchcraft system in question is essentially or, more often, principally projective—that is, there are few if any physical structural manifestations that can be observed or even reconstructed (rites, ceremonies, conventicles, magical manipulations, incantations, use of physical substances, and so on). It might also be the case that even combating witchcraft, or warding against it on behalf of the group by certain practitioners, is so secretive that it precludes any physical investigation. In both cases, there is nothing concrete for the anthropologist to investigate; he or she must do the best of an incomplete job confined to the analysis of a projective or ontologically unverifiable ideological and belief system. This is evidently what Kluckhohn (1944) did in his treatment of Navaho witchcraft, and he probably set the limits of what anthropologists can do with secretive or projective systems.

Second, the anthropologist may find that witchcraft, with different degrees of openness and secrecy, constitutes a general system (probably mechanism is a better gloss) of explanation of unfortunate events à la the Azande, so well captured by Evans-Pritchard. In this context witchcraft is to different extents vulgarized, and few or no witchcraft events or occurrences are concrete and circumscribed enough to investigate the time and space matrix in which they unfold. In these circumstances the ambience and discharge of witchcraft is open enough for the anthropologist to infer and sometimes even to observe many of its manifestations in the form of magical manipulations, some of its paraphernalia, and perhaps occasional rites. Most of the witchcraft studies in the literature fall into this category, and social and psychological functions of witchcraft have been assigned on the basis of partly observed or reconstructed facts and events beyond the elicited ideology.

Third, the anthropologist may encounter a witchcraft system whose structural and physical realization are not only open but single-directed in terms of concrete, circumscribed events, although it may also contain another compartment in which occurrences are general and non-patterned. This is the case of bloodsucking witchcraft in rural Tlaxcala, and we intuit that similar cases are significantly more common than the literature suggests. It is in such cases that the analysis of witchcraft systems provides the best conditions for understanding the natural-supernatural logic of inference, and more generally, the persistence of supernatural modes of explanation, however compartmentalized, in the presence of natural modes of explanation.

When traditional Tlaxcalans (which included almost everyone until about 1960) verbalize the tlahuelpuchi complex, they are in fact presenting an explanation of why and under what conditions infants before the age of one die, given specified circumstances. Thus, the ideology of bloodsucking witchcraft emphasizes the death of infants rather than how to prevent it, the circumstances and conditions under which infants die rather than the nature of the witch, the ambience and temporal context of the sucking rather than the otherworldly character of the perpetrator. It is almost as if by design that the accent of the ideology and belief system was placed on explaining and rationalizing the death of infants as being beyond the control of the actors involved. After having heard five or six times the neatly laid out ideology and belief system of blood-sucking witchcraft, we needed only a moderate amount of reflection to grasp the rationalizing logic of the complex and how it explains the death of infants, if it was accepted a priori, of course, that infants do in fact die as specified by the normative system.

Indeed, it was not until the physical examination of the first two cases of the sample and of the seven cases of the dramatic Xolotla epidemic that Nutini realized the full impact of the interplay between what the ideology and belief system specified and what was structurally observed: the very close fit between normative specification and physical discharge; the self-fulfilling nature of the bloodsucking complex; and the conscious or unconscious physical, verbal, and psychological manipulations of primary actors to validate the efficacy of the tlahuelpuchi to kill. It is one thing to be told that infants die under such and such circumstances as the result of the action of tlahuelpuchis, but it is quite another thing to observe, or reconstruct with a degree of probability how in fact a sequential set of events appears to validate the belief that the tlahuelpuchi causes the death of the infants. It is only at this juncture that the student of bloodsucking witchcraft in rural Tlaxcala has ostensible and demonstrable evidence that bloodsucking witchcraft is not merely projective, but that, on the contrary, it takes place in the context of causally entailed actions and events. It is on the evidence of this context, and this context alone, that witchcraft must be assessed scientifically and the functions of the institution demonstrated.

The most striking aspects of the reconstruction of presucking events—shaped by the observation of the behavior of primary actors and their verbalizations and the general ambience of the household during the days following the death of an infant—are the individual and collective ideological and physical manipulations engaged in by those directly or indirectly concerned with the sucking. The close fit between what the ideology specifies and what actually transpires (physically, socially, and psychologically) cannot be envisaged until several cases of bloodsucking witchcraft have been observed. Only then does one fully realize that such a close fit can only be the result of conscious or unconscious manipulation by primary and sometimes secondary actors. There can be no other interpretation for, for example, the inordinate number of infants found dead in places and positions specified by the tlahuelpuchi complex or for the ex post facto verbalization of parents concerning the telltale signs of the witch in the house or about to strike, or, more telling, for the sighting of the tlahuelpuchi or for the ominous feeling that she was near the house the night of the sucking. That people individually and collectively manipulate the physical, social, and psychological aspects of the sucking complex to fit the specified ideology there is no doubt, and the net effect of these actions is to reinforce the self-fulfilling efficacy of bloodsucking witchcraft. Thus, collectively, the closer to ideological specifications events and actions conform, the more the belief system on the tlahuelpuchi complex is reinforced; individually, the more cases are experienced as conforming to the complex, the stronger the belief. This, then, is the feedback effect that obtains between the ideological and structural interplay of bloodsucking witchcraft in rural Tlaxcala, and it is this central epistemological feature that makes the system so efficacious for explaining the death of infants under certain peculiar circumstances. All witchcraft systems, of course, are posited on this feedback effect; they vary mainly with respect to the intensity of the reinforcing mechanism—that is, to the extent that the actors involved can manipulate the elements of the witchcraft event. What makes bloodsucking witchcraft in rural Tlaxcala a unique case in the anthropological literature is the good fortune of having been able to observe it at such close range and with some degree of intensity.

Finally, two points need to be discussed briefly. First, the implications of the projective elements of witchcraft are significant. It has been demonstrated that bloodsucking witchcraft in rural Tlaxcala is open, explicit, well structured, and couched in a directly observed or inferred complex of rites, manipulations, and paraphernalia—that is, it is quite the opposite of a projective system. Yet the tlahuelpuchi herself is a projective construction, despite the fact that once in a very great while, and under conditions of extreme stress, a woman is accused of being a bloodsucking witch and summarily executed. More important, in a generation of fieldwork in rural Tlaxcala Nutini has never heard of either a self-confessed witch, or of the kinsmen, ritual kinsmen, or friends of a woman executed as a witch ever making accusations against her before she died. The very quick process of gathering consensus leading to the naming and execution of the tlahuelpuchi attests to the projective nature of this part of the complex. At the same time, the projective nature of the bloodsucking witch is a demonstration that, were the complex structured otherwise, it would detract from its self-fulfilling validation. Thus, were there self-confessed witches or were it possible for people to verbalize with impunity that certain women are witches,

it would seriously undermine the explanatory value of the tlahuelpuchi's efficacy to kill. Epistemologically then, witches are either easy to identify (public
individuals, self-confessed, and so on) or essentially projective to achieve their
main intended function—namely, the explanation of many kinds of unfortunate events. Ease of identification leads invariably to accusations, confrontations, and often violence or some sort of settlement (Evans-Pritchard 1937:21–
107; Marwich 1970:10–19; Middleton 1969:266–75), whereas projective
construction, as exemplified in this monograph, does not, except in cases of
extreme stress and agitation. In terms of explanatory functions, the projective
nature of the witch is a more efficient and less costly mechanism, socially and
psychologically. What we do not know, in the case of bloodsucking witchcraft
in rural Tlaxcala in particular and of witchcraft in general, is whether there is an
evolutionary transformation such as from originally open witchcraft systems
in which accusations are common to systems becoming increasingly projective.

The second point is closely related to the first, and it has to do with the
changes that the tlahuelpuchi complex has undergone since the last two decades
of the nineteenth century. While the ideological conception of the bloodsucking witch and the belief system that supports it have remained constant since
about 1880, the specialization of the tlahuelpuchi has changed. (This is the
unanimous opinion of five or six informants, who in 1961 were between ninety-
two and ninety-seven years old.) Although it would be impossible to prove
with certainty, we do nonetheless *intuit* that there have also been changes in
the basic constitution of the tlahuelpuchi—namely, that it has evolved from a
fairly open entity entailing a modicum of witchcraft accusations into the essentially projective entity that it is today. In other words, during the 1880s and
1890s the tlahuelpuchi was significantly more diversified, and her evildoings
affected several domains of daily (and nightly) life; accusations of witchcraft
took place with relative frequency, but there were most likely no self-confessed
witches even then. But why the efficacy of the tlahuelpuchi has become centered almost exclusively on infant death cannot be explained. We entertained
the hypothesis that the evolution of the tlahuelpuchi from open and diversified
to projective and specialized was directly related to a great or significant increase in infant mortality in rural Tlaxcala from the turn of the century onward; that is, witchcraft shrinks to bloodsucking witchcraft, as a more efficient
and less costly social and psychological explanation. Unfortunately, it seems
that infant mortality in rural Tlaxcala has remained proportionally constant
since before the turn of the century. Instead, the evolution of the tlahuelpuchi
is related to or has been caused by some form of modernization, probably triggered by the increasing influence of education and technology, but which cannot

be entirely pinpointed. There is little doubt, however, that the elaborate and minutely laid out belief system surrounding the tlahuelpuchi's efficacy to kill infants was concomitantly developed with her transformation from an open to an essentially projective entity throughout the past three generations.

CAUSES AND CONTEXTS OF INFANT DEATH: THE EFFICACY OF THE TLAHUELPUCHI TO KILL

By mid-January 1961 the main physical parameters of the tlahuelpuchi complex had been reconstructed, and the two main causes of death when infants are sucked by the witch had been deduced. But it was not until many years later, when the data impinging directly on the bloodsucking event had been preliminarily analyzed, that all the causes of infant death attributed to the witch were identified and clarified. In this section the possible causes of infant death attributed to the tlahuelpuchi are described, the probable events leading to the point when infants are found dead are reconstructed, and the physical contexts in which these events take place are analyzed. In terms of incidence and probability, there are five contexts in which the causes of infant death, as attributed to the tlahuelpuchi, can be established: (1) Infants die of asphyxia as their mothers breastfeed them at night and fall asleep with them to the breast; (2) Infants die of suffocation, smothered by blankets, coverings, or clothes in their cribs or petates; (3) Infants are choked to death by not being burped after they are breastfed at night. (4) Infanticide; (5) Crib death. (In ordinary speech, asphyxia and suffocation are generally used as synonyms, and dictionaries do not discriminate significantly between these two terms. In medical pathology, asphyxia is the more general term, and it includes both suffocation and choking—that is, individuals die as a result of the interruption of "the respiratory mechanisms" [Gonzales, et al. 1954:454–93]. For descriptive purposes, however, we will use asphyxia, suffocation, and choking to denote the contexts of death [1], [2], and [3] respectively. This procedure is justified since we are not writing a medical description, and the main goal is to be as precise as possible about the contexts rather than about the causes of death.)

We want to reemphasize that we are not medically trained and that we have no special knowledge of pathology. Thus, the reader should understand that the following description and analysis stem primarily from Nutini's experience in examining the infants and mothers of the forty-seven–case sample, from the knowledge he gained in conversations with the chief medical officer of the state of Tlaxcala and his assistant in 1960–1961, and from consulting a manual on pathology as the data was being analyzed. From the beginning Nutini was told by the physician who examined the seven children of the Xolotla epidemic and by the chief medical officer of the state of Tlaxcala that anything short of a fairly complete autopsy would not determine with certainty the cause of death of any infant believed to have been sucked by the tlahuelpuchi. This evidently correct opinion was emphasized by several pathologists whom we consulted. They did advise us, however, that in the case of asphyxia, suffocation, and choking the accompanying somatic telltale signs of these modes of death are often patterned and characteristic enough to warrant fairly accurate predictions concerning the causes of death. Thus, the following etiological categorization and the description of events accompanying the five causes of death are probabilistic statements made by non-professional medical practitioners, but they are based on facts patterned and scientific enough to warrant the explanation of bloodsucking witchcraft in rural Tlaxcala. In other words, the probability that the infants in the forty-seven–case sample died as the result of the five causes described above is fairly high to high, and the causes make intelligible the social and psychological matrices in which bloodsucking witchcraft occurs. Even if other causes could in fact be adduced for the death of infants, the present analysis of the tlahuelpuchi complex would not be significantly altered.

Asphyxia: Infants are Unwittingly Smothered by Their Mothers
This is by far the most important context in terms of incidence and the structure of the tlahuelpuchi complex. Indeed, it appears as if the ideology and belief system of bloodsucking witchcraft naturally evolved to fit this context of infant death. Thus, the most diagnostic and characteristic physical manifestation of having been sucked by the tlahuelpuchi—that is, the visible marks (bruises, acchymoses, purple spots, and occasionally scratches) left on the victim's body are present in thirty-nine of the forty-seven cases (see chapter 6). In addition, the people's gestalt of infant death by sucking calls to mind all the details, specified in the belief system, centered in the present context. The other four contexts that have been isolated either overlap or are tangentially similar to asphyxia in the realization of some or several of the accompanying physical signs associated with the death of infants attributed to the tlahuelpuchi. This overlapping or similarity of contextual infant death is fostered by the diagnostic physical marks on the body of infants which are similar for asphyxia and suffocation, and possibly for choking. Rural Tlaxcalans themselves are well aware of and often verbalize the fact that the physical marks on the victims, and by extension on their mothers, constitute the most certain proof that infants die as the result of being sucked by the tlahuelpuchi. Several informants directly expressed the notion that perhaps most other aspects of

the tlahuelpuchi complex could be faked, imagined, or exaggerated but not the physical marks on victims and mothers, and that these ultimately attested to the existence of the bloodsucking witch.

The analysis of the forty-seven–case sample indicates that in almost exactly two-thirds, thirty-one cases, the cause of death was asphyxia. The cases are the following: 1, 2, 3, 5, 6, 7, 9, 11, 12, 13, 15, 16, 19, 20, 24, 25, 27, 28, 29, 31, 33, 36, 38, 39, 40, 41, 42, 43, 45, 46, and 47. How high is the probability that the infants in these cases died of asphyxia? High, in our opinion, and the reason is simple. A comparison of tables 6.13 and 6.14 shows that in sixteen cases (5, 9, 12, 15, 19, 20, 24, 25, 29, 36, 39, 40, 41, 43, 46 and 47) both victim and mother exhibit the characteristic marks of the tlahuelpuchi's action. This is unmistakable evidence that the infants died as the result of asphyxia. It is almost impossible to envision any other plausible way to account for the death of these infants. In the remaining fifteen cases in this category, we could envision alternative modes of death, but the evidence is not conclusive. Yet, the telltale signs of asphyxia and suffocation are pretty much the same (we indicated that suffocation is a kind of asphyxia), so that these fifteen cases can either be regarded as due to asphyxia or suffocation but not to choking, which does not appear to exhibit the somewhat characteristically patterned bruises, acchymoses, and purple of the former two. Having narrowed down the cause of death of these cases to either asphyxia or suffocation, why did we assign all of them to the former category?[1] The reasons are partly intuitive and partly based on the analysis of related data presented in tables 6.5, 6.6, 6.7, 6.8, 6.11, 6.13, 6.14, 6.16, and 6.17. Especially relevant are the birth order of the victim, variations in the physical marks on the victim's body, unusual events surrounding the victim's sucking, and the aftereffects experienced by the parents of the victim. In addition, a significant amount of unstructured data on each of the forty-seven cases was collected that proved rather unsusceptible to tabular presentation and therefore has not been presented in this monograph in this fashion. These miscellaneous data, however, have been useful in discriminating among the five categories of infant death, and at the same time, in evaluating dubious cases and gauging the possible categorization of victims exhibiting similar somatic physical marks. The analysis of these data made it possible to make more accurate probabilistic statements concerning the categorization of infants believed to have been sucked by the tlahuelpuchi. Briefly, these unstructured data have to do mostly with the social structure of the household, the kinship behavior that it entails, verbal elicitations from adult kinsmen concerning interaction among members of the household, verbal elicitations concerning the tlahuelpuchi complex in general and the sucking at hand in particular, observations of the behavior and actions of individual members of the household for a few days after the sucking, observation of the psychological state of the parents of the victim, gossip from neighbors about the household and the interpersonal relationships of its members, and so on. These ancillary data are relevant to all five categories of infant death.

In a nutshell, infants die of asphyxia by being smothered at night when they are being breastfed. As we mentioned in chapter 6, standard practice of rural Tlaxcalan women is to breastfeed their infants at night in a reclined position on the left side of their bodies. Since, however, four out of the sixteen cases in which physical marks were recorded indicated marks in the mothers' right breast, it is assumed that at least a fourth of the women in this category were feeding their infants on the right side of their bodies at the time of death. Thus, regardless of position, mothers smother their infants during breastfeeding by stopping respiration through the mouth and nose. This unwitting action probably takes place as follows. The mother gets up or reaches for the infant in a nearby crib or petate and puts it to the breast. She may then forget about the infant, doze off, or fall asleep, unintentionally asphyxiating the infant by the weight of her body, by pressing her breast too hard on the face of the baby, or by a combination of a number of possible body movements and positions. One cannot, however, discard the possibility that as women doze off or fall asleep or cover themselves and their infants with blankets or clothes, these actions do not contribute to the process of asphyxia, or, indeed, that they do not become the primary cause of the infants' deaths. As we have indicated, regardless of whether the suckings are "seasonal," the key operational condition in which infants die is cold weather. With some exceptions, in March, April, and early May, nights in rural Tlaxcala are crisp or cold, and this factor contributes significantly to the mothers' lack of attention or laziness in minding infants while they are being breastfed. In other words, the cold makes mothers nurse their infants under the protective cover of blankets, fostering carelessness, dozing off, or falling asleep. In summary, and assuming that the forty-seven–case sample is representative of the annual variation in infant deaths attributed to the tlahuelpuchi, we believe cold weather must be regarded as the sufficient condition that contributes the most to the physical circumstances that lead to the asphyxiation of infants in rural Tlaxcala.

Table 6.3 shows that the thirty-one infants in this category were nine months or younger when they died of asphyxia, with an approximate mean average of five and a half months. The young age of the infants and their lack of energy explain their inability to cry out, to move, or in any way to convey that they were being asphyxiated, given the position in which they were being breastfed, the pressure of the mothers' breast or body, and the slumbering ambience of the occasion. Unquestionably, the most reliable data of the entire bloodsucking complex are the sixteen cases in the present category, in which both mother and infant exhibit the characteristic physical marks on their bodies. These cases not only demonstrate the high probability that most infants die of asphyxia while they are being breastfed, but also indicate that death took place while they were actually sucking on their mothers' breasts. There is no other likely explanation for the congruence of physical marks on mother and infant. The black-and-blue marks on the mothers' breasts are evidently produced by rather strong pressure against the mouth and face of the infants and they attest, together with the occasional scratches found on the victim's face or chest, to the struggle of the infants to breathe as the spasms of death set in; while the bruises, acchymoses, and purple spots on the face, neck, chest, and upper back of the infants recorded in all cases in this category unmistakably attest to death by asphyxia. It should be reiterated, however, that in the fifteen cases in which the mothers did not exhibit physical marks on their breasts, the cause of death was also asphyxia, but it did not necessarily take place in the context described above: some did and some did not. Those who did not could have suffocated in the crib or petate or while they were being held by their mothers not necessarily at the breast. The gravity of the bruises, acchymoses, and purple spots on the infants' bodies may attest to the length of the victims' struggle during the spasms of death, but pathologically it does not tell us anything about whether victims died asphyxiated, as described above, or suffocated, as described below. Again, the main reason for classifying these fifteen cases as death by asphyxiation rather than by suffociation is intuitive and supported by clues that cannot be properly quantified. Nonetheless, the fact that most infants believed to have been sucked by the tlahuelpuchi die during the slumbering hours between one o'clock in the morning and an hour or so before dawn is an important factor that must not be underestimated: it physically determines the ambience of carelessness and dream-like demeanor on the part of mothers which underlies the death of infants, and it predisposes the people to manipulate the ideological and belief systems to justify ultimate outcomes.

Do any significant correlations or associations emerge from the analysis of the quantitative data presented in tables 6.4, 6.5, 6.6, 6.7, 6.8, and 6.10 concerning the context of asphyxia? The answer is both yes and no. No, if the tables are analyzed individually, and yes, if they are analyzed together. More specifically, the data of these tables are illuminating for understanding specific cases. Nonetheless, at this point a few remarks are in order.

First, the ratio of sucked infants to the order of two females for one male is significant. As we indicated, infant- and child-rearing practices until the age of approximately six are demonstrably biased toward males. Rural Tlaxcalan mothers pay more attention to the physical needs and psychological care of their male than to their female infants and small children, often disregarding their female offspring. These rearing practices constitute an important factor in explaining the much higher incidence of female infants dying in the context of asphyxia as well as, apparently, in the other contexts of infant death. In the present context, the physical and psychological framework of mothers when they breast-feed male infants at night is definitely more attentive and controlled than when they breast-feed female infants. This assertion is posited on the detailed observation of daytime infant-caring practices, and there is no reason to doubt that the same obtains at night. The result is, of course, that in caring for and breast-feeding male infants at night mothers are more careful, less prone to doze off or fall asleep, and thereby more likely to avoid the physical actions and positions that lead to infants being asphyxiated. It is the sociological ambience of the household, however, that molds the behavior of mothers in this context. When an infant is sucked by the tlahuelpuchi, the main share of the responsibility for its death is latently and manifestly attributed to the mother, especially when the infant is male. The adults of the household, especially married adults and particularly the mother-in-law in extended-family households, blame the mother for not having been careful enough to protect the infant against the tlahuelpuchi, for not having fought hard enough against the act of sucking, and for other imaginary charges that invariably ensue once the initial shock of the event has subsided. These are the kinds of cultural and psychological pressures that make mothers more careful in handling and feeding male infants at night and which ultimately explain the disproportionate ratio of female to male infants sucked by the tlahuelpuchi.

Second, although primiparae are more careful with their infants in every aspect of their care, firstborn *are* occasionally sucked by the tlahuelpuchi (see table 6.5). The four cases in this category are female, thus corroborating our first point. More significantly, these cases, especially numbers 18 and 23, exemplify other contexts of death, as discussed below. The age of the victims' parents (table 6.6) is obviously related to the birth order of infants, and the only meaningful generalization related to this correlation is that the great majority of infants sucked by the tlahuelpuchi are born during the first half of their mothers' reproductive careers.

Third, the analysis of tables 6.7, 6.8, and 6.10 is again not necessarily significant by itself for the explanation of the context of asphyxia. Yet the personnel composition of the victim's household, the kinsmen sleeping in the victim's room at the time of death, and the identity of the person who found the victim's body constitute the main sociological factors (in the broader, household sense) in which all five contexts of death by sucking take place. More important, the associations of these data and, particularly, the analysis of individual cases are essential to understand and explain the circumstances and milieux in which infanticide takes place and to discriminate, at least to some extent, between social and psychological inputs.

Even in the coldest of societies, as Lévi-Strauss would put it, there are skeptics who doubt, question, or reject the norms, constraints, injunctions, and commands of specific ideological and belief systems. There are always individuals who refuse to believe and act like the majority of the group. In the case of the bloodsucking witchcraft system in rural Tlaxcala a generation ago, even within the traditional context of the complex, there were a significant number of skeptics concerning the existence and efficacy of the tlahuelpuchi to kill. As we indicated, about 10 percent of the adult population falls into this category; they are mostly young to middle-aged male adults, they generally have a significant history of labor migration, and they are the most educated and outward-looking sector of the population. Their skepticism ranges from mild disbelief to total denial of the tlahuelpuchi complex. What is interesting at this juncture is the verbalizations of at least a score of informants to the effect that, intentionally or unintentionally, it is the mothers who cause the death of infants at night. One of the informants, in fact, came perilously close to reconstructing the steps leading to the asphyxiation of infants. He said, "Son las mujeres las que sofocan y matan a sus creaturas cuando les dan de mamar en la noche. Después, para escapar de la golpiza de sus maridos, le hechan la culpa a la tlahuelpuchi. Y lo peor es que todo el mundo se lo cree" (Women, in fact, suffocate and kill their infants when they breast-feed them at night. Afterward, in order to avoid their husband's beating, they blame the tlahuelpuchi. And what is worse, everybody believes it.) This statement, made in mid-June of 1961, strikes at the heart of the tlahuelpuchi complex: it suggests a physical explanation, and it gives a clue to the elucidation of the socio-psychological matrix in which bloodsucking witchcraft takes place. Together with the reconstruction of the complex told to Nutini by the chief medical officer of the state of Tlaxcala, this statement became the key input that structured subsequent research on the subject and the ultimate reconstruction of actions and events. Directly related to the context of asphyxia, the above statement suggests that perhaps some of the thirty-one cases in this category may be cases of intentional or unintentional infanticide committed by mothers for a number of reasons and due directly to suffocation.

Suffocation: Infants Are Smothered by Blankets or Beddings in Their Cribs or Petates

The analysis indicates that there are probably six cases in which the infants died of suffocation: 8, 14, 16, 18, 22, and 32. As we explained above, it is impossible to discriminate between the somatic telltale marks of asphyxia and suffocation, in that the latter is a form of the former. Thus, the context of suffocation denotes essentially that infants die in their cribs or petates without any direct involvement on the part of their mothers. The reader should be aware, however, that we have left open the possibility that some of the thirty-one victims of asphyxia may have suffocated under conditions not unlike those we are about to describe. In other words, the basic physical factors discriminating between the contexts of asphyxia and suffocation are that, in the former, the mother directly stops the infant from breathing by pressing a breast or another part of her body against the face of the victim, whereas in the latter the mother has no direct bodily inputs, and the infant stops breathing as the result either of indirect actions of the mother or of causes relatively independent of any inputs on her part. Of the fifteen cases (thirty-one minus sixteen certain cases of asphyxia) discussed in the foregoing subsection, our guess is that at least three must be classified as cases of suffocation.

Briefly, infants die of suffocation as the result of their noses and mouths being obstructed by a blanket, covering, and/or any other material with which they may be carelessly protected against the cold. As in the context of asphyxia, cold weather is a significant factor, and it may directly affect the death of infants. As a general practice and particularly at night during cold weather, mothers in rural Tlaxcala bundle their infants rather tightly and cover them with blankets, sarapes, or heavy pieces of cloth or rags. Mothers are particularly careful to keep their infants at this age warm, for rural Tlaxcalan houses are generally cold, and mothers know that colds, influenza, and other respiratory diseases at this age can easily kill. Cribs are small, constraining affairs, and infants can hardly move, once they have been placed on the deep, ersatz bottom that passes for a mattress. It is often difficult to see the infant once it has been put to sleep for the night, or even during periods of sleep on cold days, due to the blankets or beddings that are heaped on it. The straw mats of infants sleeping on petates are generally placed against the wall close to their mothers' own petate. Like cribs, petates for infants present a cluttered aspect, although they are somewhat less constraining to the infant. Often, petates for infants are surrounded by piles of clothes, old blankets, and sarapes; not infrequently they are propped up by bricks, household utensils, or occasionally, low chairs. The idea of this ad hoc screen is to protect the infant against domestic animals that may enter the room during the day, or indeed, spend the night indoors. This is the physical ambience in which infants die of suffocation; what we are trying to convey is a situation in which infants suffocate due to blankets, piles of cloth, or other fabrics obstructing their respiratory tracts. The faceup position in which infants are invariably put to rest and the crowdedness that surrounds their cribs or petates are the two most significant factors accounting for this kind of infant death. The other possibility that must be considered is that, even though infants at this age do not willfully move significantly, when they do move, the constraints of space in which they are placed may lead them to positions in which the obstruction of the nose and mouth is of their own making.[2] In both of these contexts neither the mothers nor other female personnel of the nuclear- or extended-family household are in any way directly linked to, nor can they be blamed for, the death of these infants. It is only the culturally determined inefficiency of infant-rearing practices in rural Tlaxcala that can perhaps be held accountable for this kind of infant death.

In discussing asphyxia, we suggested the strong possibility that some of the cases subsumed under that category were really due to suffocation—that is, indirectly provoked by mothers as they lay in bed or on petates after breast-feeding their infants at night. It is highly likely that infants in such cases die of suffocation, not by any direct contact with their mothers' breasts or any other part of their bodies but, as in the case of crib suffocation, by blankets or clothes obstructing the infants' respiratory tracts. The most likely scenario in these cases is that, after breast-feeding, instead of returning the infants to their cribs or petates, mothers settle the infants next to them for the night, and it is in this position that the infants are suffocated by the bedding with which they are covered. Other possible variations of this general theme may involve the shifting of bodily position of both mother and infant, but the result is the same: the infant dies of suffocation, and the mother can only be indirectly blamed for it. In such cases, the responsibility of mothers lies between the carelessness of asphyxiating infants with their breasts or bodies and the well-meaning care of infants in their cribs or petates leading to suffocation. At the end of 1961 Nutini discussed all these possibilities of infant death due to asphyxia and suffocation with the chief medical officer of the state of Tlaxcala and concluded that, although the several possibilities were highly likely to be realized, it was practically impossible to verify them directly. Nutini and the official also discussed the likelihood of a correlation between the patterns and gravity of the observed physical marks on the infant's body and the various kinds of scenarios leading to what we have categorized as asphyxia and suffocation. The chief medical officer was emphatic about the absence of any positive correlation between the bruises, acchymoses, and purplish spots on the infants' chests, backs, or necks and the infants having died as the result of the obstruction of their respiratory tracts by their mothers' breasts or bodies or by blankets or any type of clothes in their mothers' beds or petates or in their own cribs or petates. Even a complete autopsy would reveal nothing, except that all infants had technically died of asphyxia. Years later, we also tried to correlate the gravity, form, and manifestation (see table 6.17) of the psychosomatic aftereffects exhibited by mothers after the sucking and the ostensible degree of responsibility (and culpability, as implied above) inherent in the various kinds of asphyxia and suffocation. Again, nothing positive came out of the operation because the individual culpability of mothers does not translate into culturally determined, after-the-sucking behavior. Lest the reader misunderstand, we are only saying that there does not seem to be a subtype of specific correlations between mothers' feelings of culpability in the death of infants and psychosomatic aftereffects. But there most certainly is congruence between all infants who die as the result of being sucked by the tlahuelpuchi and the behavior of mothers after the event, as we analyze in chapter 10.

Since one cannot entirely discriminate between the contexts of asphyxia and of suffocation in the death of infants believed to have been sucked by the tlahuelpuchi (that is, in terms of verifiable facts or observations as reported in the twenty tables which summarize the hard data of the bloodsucking event), what was said about asphyxia concerning tables 6.4, 6.5, 6.6, 6.7, 6.8, and 6.10 also applies to suffocation. This is another way of saying that, with the exception of the sixteen cases in which mother and infant exhibited telltale somatic marks, in all other cases of asphyxia and suffocation (twenty-one) it is impossible to determine with certainty the conditions and specific events that led to the death of infants. What, then, is the objective evidence for categorizing cases 8, 14, 16, 18, 22, and 32 as death by suffocation? Beyond the rather intuitional assessment of all the tables, table 6.11 contains the strongest evidence. This table summarizes the location and position of the victim's body upon discovery, and in five of the six cases (8, 16, 18, 22, and 32) they deviate significantly from the rather standard position and location in which infants are found after the sucking. Cases 18 and 22 are very telling; in our opinion, they are the most surely diagnostic of death by suffocation—that is, mothers, consciously or unconsciously, did not feel in any way constrained to manipulate the tlahuelpuchi complex to justify any physical action on their part which led to the death of their infants. To put it differently, infants are found dead in more or less the same position in which they died: mothers in no ascertainable way tampered with their bodies. Cases 8, 16, and 32, by contrast, are not as surely diagnostic, but within the range of inference that mothers did not unduly tamper with the bodies after they realized that their infants were dead. It is also possible, especially in case 8, that due to unwitting movements of the mother the infant rolled away from the petate to the location where it was found. The point is that in these three cases it is impossible to say with any degree of certainty whether the mothers tampered with the bodies of their infants. Case 14, finally, clearly indicates that the mother or someone else tampered with the body, for the dead infant was found in the courtyard outside the ajar door. This is a good indication that the mother had a direct input in the death of the infant—that is, it could just as well be categorized as a case of asphyxia. In summary, it is our considered opinion that when the position and location of the infant when it is found dead indicate that the mother most likely did not tamper with the body, it is the most probable evidence that death occurred by suffocation, as described in this subsection.

Choking: Infants Die Accidentally by the Obstruction of the Air Passages

There are probably five cases in which the infants died of choking: 10, 21, 23, 34, and 44. In most ways (that is, on the basis of the information presented in tabular form) choking is the easiest type of infant death to diagnose with a degree of certainty. Unlike asphyxia and suffocation (as sociomedically defined in this monograph), death by choking does not as a rule seem to leave on the body of the victim the telltale somatic marks described above. Texts on pathology are not explicit about choking but generally maintain that this cause of death is most often unaccompanied by the telltale marks almost invariably associated with asphyxia and suffocation (see Gonzales et al. 1954:480–82). The chief medical officer of the state of Tlaxcala and several pathologists who were consulted at the University of Pittsburgh concurred with this opinion but did not completely discard the possibility that some forms of choking may produce telltale marks similar to those described above. All seven medical doctors that were consulted on this matter, however, maintained that in the great majority of cases of choking no somatic telltale marks are detectable. The most common cases of choking occur when solid objects or materials enter and obstruct the lumen of the air passsages, thereby preventing air from reaching the lungs, such as when an adult may attempt to swallow a large piece of meat or infants or children aspirate coins, marbles, large seeds, and so on. Not infrequently, however, choking may also occur when vomitus is regurgitated and aspirated into the lungs, or even when liquids such as milk are carried down into the ramification of the bronchial tree. Since infants in rural Tlaxcala are not fed any solid food (certainly not between ages two and twelve months when all suckings normally take place), all cases of infant death categorized as choking are of the second type.

The strongest evidence for categorizing cases 10, 21, 23, 34, and 44 as death by choking are tables 6.11 and 6.13. Table 6.13, on the one hand, indicates that none of the five infants had any somatic telltale marks when their bodies were found, perhaps the surest indication that the cause of death was not asphyxia or suffocation. Table 6.11, on the other hand, is not that conclusive. It is assumed that when infants supposedly sucked by the tlahuelpuchi die as the result of actions that do not directly involve their mothers, mothers have no less need to tamper with the physical evidence (mainly moving the body of the infant to conform to the tlahuelpuchi belief system) to lessen responsibility (and unconsciously assuage culpability) for the death of their infants. In three cases (21, 23, and 34) the infants were found in their cribs or petate and in more or less the position in which they died, indicating that there was no tampering of any kind. In two cases (10 and 44), however, there was definite tampering, since the infants were found in locations that fall within the range of the belief system governing the tlahuelpuchi complex and that were impossible for infants to reach on their own. The interesting fact of the five cases of choking in the sample is that in the three non-tampering cases, death took place during the day, whereas in the two tampering cases, death took place at night. Given that these three cases constitute three-fourths of the sample's total number of infants sucked during the day, can one say that most cases of choking take place during daylight hours? The answer is a qualified yes. Probably, most cases of choking are due to regurgitated vomitus of semiliquid food (the gruels and fairly consistent concoctions that infants are fed during the day), whereas the minority of cases are due to milk getting into the infants' bronchial trees after mothers breast-feed their infants at night. Perhaps more significant for the explanation of bloodsucking witchcraft is the question, why do day suckings not seem to entail tampering with the physical evidence of the event whereas night suckings almost invariably do? Concomitantly, are there any structural or psychological reasons for this behavior of the immediate actors of the bloodsucking event? The answers again are yes, but they will be discussed in chapter 12.

Of the three main contexts of infant death attributed to the tlahuelpuchi, choking is the most removed from the direct or indirect responsibility of the mothers for the demise of infants. What, then, are the significant cultural inputs that lead to the death of infants by choking? First, rural Tlaxcalan women do not burp their infants after breast-feeding them, bottle-feeding them, or giving them semiliquid foods. Second, the standard position of the infant for rest or sleep is invariably faceup. To a large extent, this practice is forced upon mothers by the narrow, constraining boundaries of cribs, whereas on petates infants are propped all around by blankets and clothes, resulting basically in the same constraints as those in cribs and precluding the facedown position. Thus, after infants are fed, by any of the three basic methods, mothers put them to rest or sleep unburped in a faceup position. It is our contention that the antecedents of all infants who die of choking entail the above chain of events. Given these infant-rearing practices, we are surprised that more infants in the sample do not seem to have died of choking, and in this respect, the sample may not be representative for rural Tlaxcala as a whole. Another bit of information (not included in any of the tables) that strongly supports our interpretation is that in all three day suckings due to choking (cases 21, 23, and 34) vomit was found on the mattress and blankets of the cribs and petate where the infants were found dead. This evidence suggests that regurgitated semiliquid food fed to the infants is the vomit, which constituted the immediate agent of death, whereas the milk of breast-feeding does not seem to produce vomit, since the two night cases of choking did not exhibit it. Once more, we remind the reader that these and all other statements concerning the diagnostic reconstruction of the various kinds of infant death are probabilistic statements that may not be entirely accurate from a medical viewpoint but which are valid for sociopsychological analysis of the problem at hand.

Asphyxia, suffocation, and choking, as sociopsychologically defined here, essentially exhaust the medical causes of death of infants supposed to have been sucked by the tlahuelpuchi. In the foregoing subsections the most highly probable causes of infant death, the events leading to it, and the immediate ambience in which it takes place were discussed. An element common to all three contexts of death which has intrigued us since we began to analyze the data is the behavior of infants immediately before death occurred. The point here is the surprising fact that in none of the forty-seven cases investigated is there any mentioning of infants crying out or making any sort of noise while they were being sucked by the tlahuelpuchi. Translated into actual physical events, this means: Why is it that infants do not appear to alert their mothers or any kinsmen sleeping in the same room while they are being asphyxiated, suffocated, or choked? In the sixteen cases (see page 243) in which it is clear that infants were smothered by their mothers' breasts or bodies, it seems quite evident that infants could have hardly emitted any sounds while they were being asphyxiated. In all other cases of suffocation and choking, however, it seems that infants could have uttered cries and sounds to alert at least their mothers sleeping nearby. It is possible, of course, that the young age of infants and the physiology involved in these modes of death (the knowledge of which we do not command) entail that infants are hardly in the position to alert their mothers. Whatever the answer, it is likely that there are psychological factors at work concerning mothers that may tangentially be regarded as tampering with the physical ambience of infant death, and these are more appropriately discussed below.

SOME SOCIAL AND PSYCHOLOGICAL IMPLICATIONS OF
INFANT DEATH ATTRIBUTED TO BLOODSUCKING WITCHCRAFT

*Infanticide: Kinship Affiliation, Psychological Ambience,
and Context and Form*

Infanticide is only a context in which infant death takes place not, in any sense,
an interrelated set of physiological facts and physical events causing death.
Indeed, infanticide may be caused by smothering (that is, asphyxia and suffocation) or choking. Sociopsychologically, asphyxia and choking can be eliminated. Asphyxia can be eliminated because it involves apparently unwitting
body contact as the necessary condition for smothering. (Here the concern is
with willful infanticide, although the possibility of unintentional infanticide
due to negligence is considered below.) Choking can be eliminated because it is
impractical and more difficult to achieve than suffocation by smothering—that
is, fatal asphyxia. In the context under consideration, choking would entail
stuffing something solid or consistent (gauze, a piece of cloth, tortilla dough)
down the throat of the victim. Probably the two main reasons against considering infanticide by choking are lack of knowledge on the part of rural Tlaxcalan
women about how to induce it, and the conditions of tremendous stress and
psychological disconnectedness under which it would take place would preclude
employing this rather complicated method. Given these considerations, we
believe suffocation is the most likely method of willful infanticide in rural
Tlaxcala. It probably occurs by simply pressing a hand or perhaps a pillow or
any other soft material over the infant's mouth and nose. Is there any evidence
to substantiate this claim? Yes, but obviously not elicited from informants or
directly observed. Not even the most acculturated, outward-looking informants willingly talked about infanticide, let alone the method by which it was
achieved. Rather, the evidence is indirect and comes partly from the legendary
domain. (It is a well-known fact in many culture areas of the world that legends
and myths often present or reflect a mirror image or inverted view of social
reality. In the case of Mesoamerica, Taggart [1983] demonstrates how legends
and myths reflect several aspects of the social structure in operation. In this
context, we take for granted that the same obtains in rural Tlaxcala, even in
such a concrete and delicate domain as infanticide.) In five different versions of
the same legend elicited in as many communities on the southwestern slopes
of La Malintzi volcano, La Malintzi, in her primary role as a sort of cosmic
overseer, punishes a dreadful woman for killing her baby by suffocating it with
her hand. Perhaps of more importance than suggesting the possible mode of
death, all five versions of the legend also suggest the social and psychological

ambience in which infanticide takes place, the conditions leading to it, and some of the behavioral constraints governing the personnel of the household.

At this juncture, the legend itself is not important, but in a nutshell, it has the following structure. A daughter-in-law residing patrilocally kills her first-born male infant to strike back at her tyrannical mother-in-law. The attendant lions of La Malintzi in their periodic rounds of the communities find out and tell her. The daughter-in-law is forcibly brought before La Malintzi, who punishes her to roam a great desert without water or food until she is forgiven by her kinsmen. In detail, the legend describes the ambience of the household and the social and psychological contexts in which the infanticide takes place. This and a similar legend not only suggest the most likely method of perpetrating infanticide, but more specifically, they provide many insights for the reconstruction of the contexts in which infanticide takes place. In the absence of directly elicited or observed information on infanticide, the following account owes significantly to the structure of rural Tlaxcalan legendary thought.

Perhaps more than any other aspect of bloodsucking witchcraft in rural Tlaxcala, infanticide is firmly embedded in the social structure and organization of the household, with some implications for the kinship system in operations. In other words, infanticide not only exemplifies certain aspects of the social structure, but it entails a definite social function. It appears as if the tlahuelpuchi's efficacy to kill infants is manifestly used by individuals to justify infanticide as an expression of the tension, friction, and antagonism which characterize several aspects of kinship behavior in the patrilocal extended-family household. Thus, before discussing the physical and behavioral evidence of infanticide, it must first be placed within the social and psychological context of the household—to be more exact, in the context of the extended-family household, for the majority of infants believed to have been sucked by the tlahuelpuchi occur in this type of residential arrangement. There are exceptions, to be sure; case 4, discussed below, is the exception that confirms the rule, in that certain patterns of antagonistic kinship behavior obtain beyond the extended-family household. Although again we do not have any hard evidence, in rural Tlaxcalan culture men are much less likely than women to perpetrate infanticide, given the general configuration of kinship behavior in the household. Willful infanticide is perhaps exclusively centered in the mother-in-law/daughter-in-law axis of social behavior and interaction, restrictedly centered within the context of the patrilocal extended-family household, and by extension, centered within the context of the non-residential extended family. A third point concerning infanticide is that it is perpetrated primarily by daughters-in-law and secondarily by mothers-in-law. These are at least the two main types of infanticide that have been well identified.

In 1960, the majority of couples in rural Tlaxcala began their married life in patrilocal residence. Separation from the ancestral household of the husband came no earlier than two to three years later, and occasionally it could be deferred six or seven years. By the time the couple established neolocal residence, usually close to the ancestral households, at least one child, and not infrequently two or three children, had been born. In most rural Tlaxcalan communities the pattern of residence within close proximity to an ancestral household throughout two or three generations gives rise to the nonresidential extended family (Nutini 1968:149–52; Nutini 1986), which may include anywhere from three or four to a dozen nuclear- and extended-family households. Within the context of the extended family in particular and the non-residential extended family in general the most unsatisfying, antagonistic, and prone-to-friction dyadic relationship is that between mother-in-law and daughter-in-law. This aspect of the kinship behavior of rural Tlaxcala reminds one of the same pattern in traditional Chinese society; it seems to be fairly common throughout the world, but it is especially common in strongly patrilineal societies where the wife is thoroughly and permanently incorporated into her husband's household and kinship group. With the exception of a single municipio, rural Tlaxcala is a bilateral society, but it does have a rather strong patrilineal bias. It is in the incorporation of wives, first into the husband's household of orientation and then into his non-residential extended family, that this bias is most clearly exemplified. Upon marriage, women immediately become active, participating members of the household, and perhaps a year or two afterward they become an integral part of the non-residential extended family, the only really operational kinship unit in rural Tlaxcalan society. Practically and pragmatically, the wife is lost to her own household of orientation and non-residential extended family since, from the moment of marriage and for the duration of her social career, she actively participates in, is rewarded in, and has rights and obligations almost exclusively within the boundaries of her husband's social units. Symbolically, the de facto termination of membership in her household and kinship unit of orientation at marriage is embodied in the *entrega de la novia* (literally, the handing over of the bride by her kinsmen to the kinsmen of the groom) ceremony during the second day of the wedding celebration in the house of the groom. On this extremely important occasion in the life cycle of the woman, she is told that, henceforth, she belongs to her husband's household and group of kinsmen. In the exchange of ritual speeches between her immediate kinsmen and those of the groom, the bride is told in no uncertain terms that she must adjust to the new conditions, that she must honor and obey the elders of her new household, and that this is the only way in which she will be content, if not necessarily happy. As a bride and wife she may occasionally return to her ancestral household, occasionally be a helper and guest in it, and occasionally seek comfort and counseling from her primary consanguineal kinsmen. But she is essentially isolated and at the mercy of her own resources in adjusting to and coping with the problems entailed by extended-family living. In a nutshell, the wife in patrilocal residence is always in a delicate position: she faces potential frictions and confrontations that only a significant degree of diplomacy and compromise can avert. The potential for conflict is by far the greatest with the mother-in-law, and it is this dyadic relationship that shapes the general social ambience of the extended family. The position of the daughter-in-law in the single patrilineal municipio in Tlax-cala acquires extreme proportions. In the communities of this municipio, the incorporation of wives into the household and patrilineal kinship units of the husband is total: if serious friction, separation, or divorce takes place, the wife cannot go back to her ancestral household; at least in traditional times, she would not be taken in by her own parents or other close collateral patrilineal households. The situation, of course, is not as extreme in all other municipios; although in instances of separation or divorce the wife may go back to her household of orientation, her consanguines encourage her to do the utmost to avert the breakup of the family, often siding with her affines to prevent any drastic change in the established order. We do not have any statistical evidence, but unquestionably, in the vast majority of rural Tlaxcalan households the dangerous or most unpleasant potentials for disruption in patrilocal residence are not actualized, and daughters-in-law live normal, fairly integrated lives under the shadow of affines, or, at least, accommodations are made by all concerned to achieve a tolerable modus vivendi.

The crucial relationship in the extended family household is that between mother-in-law and daughter-in-law. It colors the entire kinship behavior of the household, and it may determine its successful operation as a social, economic, and religious concern. If not de jure, the mother-in-law is de facto the head of the household as the organizer of daily tasks, the overseer of social and eco-nomic expenditures, and the rallying element in the discharge of social and religious functions of the family. As the wife of the head of the household, she commands respect and rather strict obedience by younger members of the household, especially daughters and daughters-in-law. The stereotype of the domineering, high-handed mother-in-law is often realized, and when she is confronted with a high-strung, testy, and difficult-to-control daughter-in-law, the results can be disastrous. In the case of the patrilineal municipio, for exam-ple, the tension and antagonism between mother-in-law and daughter-in-law can be so great that it may drive the latter to suicide or simply to abandon her children and go the city, since she cannot go back to her kinsmen of orientation. Indeed, all four cases of suicide recorded for the 1960–1970 period were women in this category. The situation is not so drastic for the average rural Tlaxcalan community, but women do occasionally leave their husbands (taking their children with them whenever possible) due, almost always, to the intolerable relationship with the mother-in-law. As a rule, accusations of sorcery in rural Tlaxcala are not made against consanguineal and affinal kinsmen. The only exception that we are aware of is sorcery accusations made by mothers-in-law against daughters-in-law, and vice versa, which do occasionally take place under extreme conditions. In a well-documented case (Nutini 1988), a mother-in-law indirectly accused her eldest daughter-in-law of having hired a tetlachihuic to cause her a serious illness. The history of this relationship went back to the inception of patrilocal residence more than fifteen years before the accusation took place, more than ten years after the daughter-in-law had been living neolocally.

From the moment of the entrega on the second day of the wedding celebration, the daughter-in-law comes under the supervision and control of her mother-in-law. If the daughter-in-law accepts her position of subservience with humor and good grace and temporizes when the situation requires it, and the mother-in-law behaves with a measure of equanimity and does not become overbearing, there ensues a good, adequate, or tolerable relationship that ultimately affects the entire kinship behavior of the extended-family household. But if the daughter-in-law is unduly independent, disrespectful, and essentially does not accept the position of subordination into which she has been cast by tradition, or if the mother-in-law abuses her power and behaves tyrannically, the relationship becomes intolerable, fraught with tension and friction at every turn, and ultimately entirely disruptive: it confronts mother and son, father and son, and husband and wife, and it leads to the termination of the extended family sooner than traditionally prescribed. Moreover, such a disruptive and antagonistic relationship survives the separation of the nuclear family from the ancestral household, and continues to mark the bonds of the former to the latter until the death of the mother-in-law. In fact, the initially negative character of the mother-in-law/daughter-in-law relationship is probably the most disruptive factor in the smooth functioning of the non-residential extended family, socially, religiously, and economically, and it ultimately leads to the early fission and separation of component nuclear families. Again, we do not have any solid statistical information on this point, but probably between 15 and 20 percent of extended families in rural Tlaxcala live in environments made from bad to intolerable by the mother-in-law/daughter-in-law relationship, and this may be a conservative estimate. It is in this environment that infanticide takes place, practiced by daughters-in-law or mothers-in-law under conditions of extreme agitation and stress involving deep-seated feelings of resentment, hatred, and desire to hurt.

While the antagonism and resentment obtaining in the mother-in-law/ daughter-in-law relationship appear to be structurally symmetrical (that is, of equal intensity in both directions), one would expect that in practice they would be heavily biased toward the member of the dyad in the position of subordination—that is, that daughters-in-law would feel and manifest a much higher degree of antagonism and resentment toward their mothers-in-law than vice versa. This is amply corroborated ethnographically. Several dozens of daughters-in-law informants gave full vent to their hate and dislike of their mothers-in-law, living or dead, whereas mother-in-law informants were much more circumspect in expressing similar feelings toward their daughters-in-law. This is not confirmed by the forty-seven–case sample, in that only two cases (4 and 26) are categorized as infanticides, one committed by a daughter-in-law and the other by a mother-in-law. Nonetheless, we intuit that daughter-in-law infanticide is much more common than mother-in-law infanticide. This is so not only for structural reasons, but because it can be more easily accomplished by daughters-in-law. There are also clues in several of the tables that point to the same imbalance in the incidence of infanticide. It is obviously impossible to determine with certainty which cases in the sample are infanticide, for we have the strong suspicion that more than the two cases listed above are willful infanticides. But the general conditions and immediate events that lead daughters-in-law and mothers-in-law to commit infanticide can be more or less ascertained. The best way to illustrate these two variants of infanticide is to describe cases 4 and 26.

Two Cases of Possible Daughter-in-Law and Mother-in-Law Infanticide
In case 4 (number 2 of the witchcraft epidemic; see chapter 5), Javier Patlahuat-zin and his wife Pilar had been living neolocally (in a house some forty yards from Javier's father's house) for more than six years when their sixthborn son Ramiro was sucked by the tlahuelpuchi. Pilar never got along with her mother-in-law throughout the seven years she lived in patrilocal residence. Even though they were poor, she kept urging Javier to build their own house and separate from the ancestral household. Finally, with great sacrifice after the birth of their fourth infant (she died two years later), they moved to their new house. After the establishment of neolocal residence, the relationship between Pilar and her mother-in-law did not improve; indeed, in some ways it grew worse. They disagreed about everything, and the slightest disagreement was cause for a confrontation. The mother-in-law continuously meddled in the

affairs of Javier's household, and Pilar in retaliation tried to turn the other young married women in the non-residential extended family against her. There was never a time in the stormy relationship of these two women when a truce was established, when they managed to get along even superficially. Perhaps more central to the hatred and suspicion that characterized this relationship was the fact that Pilar's first infant, a son born after two miscarriages, was slightly retarded. When this became noticeable after three years or so, the mother-in-law blamed Pilar for it, which naturally exacerbated the mutual antipathy governing their relationship. Pilar's next four issues were females, and every childbirth made her mother-in-law furious and unhappy. Pilar's husband was the eldest son of her mother-in-law, who wanted very badly a male heir to perpetuate the line, a strong concern in this particular community. When finally Pilar gave birth to a son, Ramiro, the mother-in-law instantly became very attached to the baby, showering him with attention and demonstrations of affection, never wasting an opportunity to be with him in Pilar's house or to bring him to her own. Because of the strong pleadings of her husband, Pilar agreed to allow her mother-in-law to see Ramiro as much as she wanted, even to take him to her own house for an entire afternoon. But this concession did not in any way soften Pilar's attitude toward her mother-in-law, whom she continued to avoid as much as she could. For several months nothing noteworthy happened in Pilar's household, until the early evening of the day when Ramiro was sucked by the tlahuelpuchi. Javier's younger brother, Manuel (thirty-three), had been elected mayordomo of the stewardship of *Las Pastorcitas* (the little shepherdesses), the main function of which is to set up the holy manger in the local church for the Christmas celebration, in addition to hosting several social gatherings in the atrium between 16 and 24 December. This is one of the several mayordomias, quite generalized in rural Tlaxcala, in which the *mayordoma* (stewardess, the wife of the mayordomo) plays a central role, which entails a high degree of religious prestige. Manuel's wife had fallen seriously ill two days earlier, and the physician who had been brought to examine her from Tlaxcala that morning (8 December) confined her to bed for at least a week. This made it impossible for her to act as the mayordoma of Las Pastorcitas, and Pilar's mother-in-law, as the oldest woman of the non-residential extended family, called a meeting of the women for that evening. About ten young unmarried and married women, among them Pilar, attended the meeting in her mother-in-law's house, the main business of which was to nominate a replacement to function as mayordoma for the important ritual and ceremonial events soon to come. It appears that the women of the non-residential extended family had informally agreed to nominate Pilar, and one of them did so in the formal assembly of women. Pilar's mother-in-law adamantly opposed the nomination, and in the heated and violent discussion that followed the mother-in-law called Pilar lazy, unreliable, and unworthy of the high honor of leading Las Pastorcitas. Pilar, who wanted badly to perform as mayordoma, replied in kind by calling her a meddlesome old hag, dishonest, and good for nothing but making trouble for everybody. They might have come to blows (a most unbecoming behavior for women in such stations in rural Tlaxcalan society) had it not been for the other women, who separated and restrained them physically. Pilar left the house of her mother-in-law in a state of uncontrollable rage. It is our contention that during the night she willfully killed Ramiro out of spite for her mother-in-law.

Do we have any evidence for this contention, beyond the suggestions found in legendary accounts that infanticide in rural Tlaxcala does take place? The answer is yes, but the evidence is inconclusive. It was not until the end of 1961, when thirty-five cases of bloodsucking witchcraft had been recorded, that Nutini entertained the possibility of infanticide. He went back to the households in which cases 4 and 26 had taken place, and from various members of the non-residential extended family and neighbors elicited the antecedent accounts of the case of Pilar described above and of the case of mother-in-law infanticide described below. Two married women in their early thirties and an old man suggested infanticide in the most subtle way in the case of Pilar. This is a most delicate matter that the natural context of gossip cannot possibly handle. The suggestion of infanticide was conveyed by gesture, facial expression, veiled reference to the legendary account of infanticide, and, perhaps more telling, by the occasionally expressed skepticism concerning the tlahuelpuchi's efficacy to kill (that is, that it may be mothers who are directly or indirectly responsible for the death of infants). While the elicitations from the two women might be interpreted as the rather standardized reaction of women toward mothers who did not properly protect their infants against the tlahuelpuchi, with perhaps a certain amount of antagonism against Pilar in particular, the elicitation from the old man cannot be so interpreted. The old man had become a trusted informant, and four months after the bloodsucking witchcraft epidemic he had become Nutini's compadre of setting up a cross. Speaking within the boundaries of frankness and confidentiality entailed by the compadrazgo relationship, the old man was more open than the two women. Still, speaking in a veiled fashion and in an undertone, the old man nonetheless let it be known that he believed Pilar had killed Ramiro willfully. The ambience in which this information was collected was not carefully recorded, nor can it be reconstructed accurately after 25 years, but what the old man said was transcribed verbatim. It was in expressions and turns of phrases such as the following that the message was transmitted: "Ya sabe Ud. compadrito lo descuidadas que a veces son las

madres"; "nunca puede uno estar enteramente seguro de que sí fué la tlahuelpuchi la que se chupó a la creatura"; "se de varios casos en que no fué la
tlahuelpuchi la responsable de la muerte de una creatura"; "sabiamos que Pilar
odiaba a su suegra, pero no para tanto"; "la conducta de Pilar se me hizo muy
rara, pero ni quiero pensar en lo que realmente pasó." (You know as well as I
do, *compadrito*, how careless mothers can be at times; one can never be entirely certain as to whether it was really the tlahuelpuchi who sucked the infant; I know of several cases in which the tlahuelpuchi was not responsible for
the death of an infant; we knew that Pilar hated her mother-in-law, but not to
such an extent; I thought Pilar's behavior was very strange, but I do not even
want to think about what really happened.) Cultural patterns in rural Tlaxcala
society that one must avoid direct confrontation, that one must exhaust all
means available before confronting anyone indirectly, and that one does not
under normal circumstances accuse anybody of anything are deep-seated. (Accusations of witchcraft, sorcery, and incompetence in any important domain
are rare, and even confrontations in daily life are carefully avoided.) Thus, this
informant's veiled, ambiguous accusation of infanticide is as far as any normal,
average rural Tlaxcalan would go, especially in such a delicate and potentially
explosive domain. Even if this accusation were false, it at least strongly attests
to the possibility of infanticide in rural Tlaxcalan society.

Perhaps more important, is there any evidence for infanticide that can be
culled from some of the tables presenting the quantitative data on which this
study is based? Again, the answer is a highly qualified yes, but what evidence
there is should rather be considered difficult-to-verify suggestions that,
nonetheless, give us insights into the nature of infanticide. First, by themselves
and concomitantly tables 6.5, 6.8, 6.10, 6.11, 6.13, and 6.17 are suggestive of
the broad parameters of infanticide. By themselves tables 6.5 and 6.8 are the
most telling. Table 6.5 indicates that only four firstborn infants (cases 18, 23,
27, 31) were sucked by the tlahuelpuchi. Given the great care that primiparae
lavish on their infants and the constant precautions that surround infant feeding and comfort, firstborn suckings are prime suspects for infanticide. In fact,
there is a significant amount of evidence similar to that in Pilar's case that case
31 was possibly infanticide. Table 6.8 shows that in five cases (2, 26, 28, 35, 41)
the mother-in-law slept in the same room as the victim. Here, of course, it is
implied that mother-in-law infanticide, which is more difficult to suggest, took
place. The presence of the mother-in-law in the same room during the night
when the sucking took place gave her easy access to the victim; otherwise, it
would be difficult for her to commit the deed. Again, there is some evidence to
suggest that case 28 was infanticide. Lest the reader misunderstands, we are
only suggesting that the nine cases of tables 6.5 and 6.8 are the most likely

candidates for infanticide on the basis of all the information presented in tabular form and certain conditions, the absence of which would make infanticide much more difficult.

Second, a significant piece of information relevant at the present juncture and not included in the tables is that in three cases (4, 26, 39) the victims' mothers became hysterical upon finding the corpse or learning about it. This is definitely atypical behavior, for, in all other cases of the sample mothers were controlled and collected upon realizing that their infants had died. Other mothers cried, to be sure, but they did not exhibit the highly hysterical behavior of these three women, who had to be physically restrained and carefully watched for two or three days. This kind of behavior is strongly suggestive of the psychological shock brought about by the mothers' realization that infanticide had been committed either by themselves or by someone else, a realization which had undoubtedly been blocked by the culturally patterned belief system. In other words, it is quite likely that the act of infanticide itself, by either daughters-in-law or mothers-in-law, is committed in a state of psychological disassociation or fugue, as discussed in the following chapter.

Third, assuming that infanticide occurs by asphyxia (with identifiable telltale somatic marks), that perpetrators adhere as much as possible to the belief practices of the tlahuelpuchi complex, and that given motivation and opportunity daughters-in-law and mothers-in-law do not hesitate to commit infanticide to hurt each other, we should see some results from comparing tables 6.5, 6.8, 6.11, and 6.13. The sample of suspected infanticides is, of course, too small for analysis, but nonetheless suggestive. For example, of the four suspected infanticides in table 6.5 (the victims were firstborn), one can eliminate case 23 on the ground that the victim did not exhibit any somatic telltale marks and case 18 on the ground that the position of the body did not conform to the tlahuelpuchi complex; of the five suspected infanticides listed in table 6.8 (the mother-in-law slept in the victim's room) one can eliminate cases 35 and 46 for the same reasons. Finally, one would expect more aggravated psychological aftereffects, as detailed in table 6.17, in the three cases of hysteria than the average degree of gravity. The association here is a mild one, but the data are not exacting enough for this type of analysis. The reader should understand that the only purpose of treading on such quicksands is to demonstrate the ambience in which infanticide takes place, the possibilities of form that infanticide takes, the considerations involved, and the likely motivation of the participants.

For the reasons given above, it appears that mother-in-law infanticide is less common than daughter-in-law infanticide. One can express this proposition differently by viewing it from the standpoint of access and opportunity for the mother-in-law to perpetrate the act, although the structural, built-in antagonism between mother-in-law and daughter-in-law retains the same potential for infanticide. For example, in case 26, the daughter-in-law had been living patrilocally since marriage four years earlier. Unlike Pilar, this daughter-in-law was docile, tried to please her mother-in-law, and apparently suppressed her own negative feelings and temporized at all times to make things more livable. The mother-in-law, by contrast, disliked the daughter-in-law and did not pretend otherwise. She thought that the daughter-in-law was too old for her son and that he should have married a younger woman. She also kept pestering the daughter-in-law about when she was going to give borth to a son, a serious concern of mothers-in-law when the two firstborn are females. The situation can be reconstructed as one in which the mother-in-law's active role of dominance and the daughter-in-law's passive role of subservience created an explosive environment: the mother-in-law expecting complete control without any negative response; the daughter-in-law accumulating pent-up hate and aggression. The explosion came suddenly and as the result of a trivial matter. On the morning of the day before the secondborn female of this particular woman was sucked by the tlahuelpuchi, her mother-in-law ordered her to prepare enough enchiladas for a *recibimiento* (the handing over of a religious image to the incoming officials) that was to take place that evening, while she went to town to buy candles, flowers, and victuals for the occasion. When the mother-in-law returned during the early afternoon she was apparently in a vile mood. Immediately, she proceeded to scold her daughter-in-law harshly for not having finished the preparation of the enchiladas. After half an hour of being called lazy, stupid, and worthless, the daughter-in-law lost control completely. All her pent-up feelings came out and she called her mother-in-law by the nastiest names she could think. She was about to assualt her mother-in-law physically when she was restrained by two women. As she recalled, the daughter-in-law surprised herself, for she never thought she would be foolish and daring enough to stand up to her mother-in-law, and so violently at that. Beside herself, the daughter-in-law left the house, went to stay with a friend, and did not return until after the recibimiento had ended at eleven o'clock. As recounted by three women who were in the household throughout the proceedings, the mother-in-law did not explode but went on with the preparations for the recibimiento in a state of controlled rage. It is our contention that that night the mother-in-law killed her granddaughter to hurt and punish her daughter-in-law for what she regarded as an inconceivable act of aggression and disrespect for her authority.

We have already discussed the suggestive evidence for mother-in-law infanticide that can be culled from the tables. The more direct evidence for this particular case comes from the elicitation of the day's events leading to the sucking from a kinswoman and two female neighbors who were in the household from the morning until the recibimiento was over. In this case, the evidence lay not so much in what these women said as in what they did not say or refused to elaborate upon being asked leading questions suggestive of infanticide. The women were nervous throughout the entire interview, and they confined themselves to relating the events rather precisely and matter-of-factly. Their circumspection is difficult to put into words, but they gave the distinct impression that they did not want to say what they had in mind, that it would be dangerous, and that it would be better to leave matters undisturbed. While their answers were proper and impartial to both the mother-in-law and daughter-in-law, they did let it be known in a subtle manner that the mother-in-law was a virago. This is a classic example of the ethnographer knowing that his informants know much more than they are willing to tell for reasons of suspicion or fear of getting involved. But the overall impression of this interview was that the three women more than suspected the mother-in-law of infanticide. The other piece of evidence, which accounts for access and opportunity to commit the infanticide, is that on the night of the sucking the mother-in-law slept in the room of the victim. As a rule, the sleeping arrangement in extended families is that every nuclear family has its own separate bedroom. Occasionally, however, the mother-in-law may sleep in the room of her daughter-in-law for a variety of reasons: when she is particularly close to one of her grandchildren, if the daughter-in-law's husband is away, to watch over the children when both parents are away, and so on. None of these reasons is valid in the present example. When she was asked why, during the night of the sucking, she had slept in her daughter-in-law's room, the mother-in-law gave the feeble and not very convincing excuse that she had done so because her own room was in disarray due to the recibimiento that had taken place. Moreover, the mother-in-law was very nervous and curt when Nutini interviewed her in the evening of the day following the sucking, and avoided him altogether when he went back several days later. All these disparate but suggestive pieces of evidence point to the mother-in-law as the perpetrator of the infanticide.

In summary, there are two soft pieces of evidence that appear to stand out in the probabilistic diagnosis of infanticide. First, on the basis of cases 4 and 26 and miscellaneous information collected throughout the years, it appears that the sufficient condition of both mother-in-law and daughter-in-law infanticide is an immediately serious, perhaps dramatic, confrontation of these actors leading to a breakdown of the modus vivendi. How often such outcomes result in infanticide is obviously impossible to determine. Given that these drastic confrontations are fairly frequent, however, we may safely assume that infanticide occurs more often than the forty-seven–case sample indicates. Second, the hysterical reaction exhibited only by daughters-in-law when they realize that their infants are dead appears to be culturally patterned. To us, this is a suggestive indication that willful or unwitting infanticide has been committed. We cannot explain why mothers-in-law do not react in this fashion, whereas we can explain why daughters-in-law become hysterical when either they or their mothers-in-law commit infanticide, as demonstrated below.

Is there such a thing as unwitting infanticide? Can one discriminate between gradations of mothers' carelessness (and by extension of mothers-in-law or of any other female in the household involved in infant care) leading to death by asphyxia, suffocation, and choking, on the one hand, and willful infanticide, on the other? Is there in rural Tlaxcalan culture something comparable to what in a court of law in the United States would be called manslaughter? The probable answers to all three questions are yes, but we know next to nothing about the answers. It has been difficult enough to pinpoint the various kinds and forms of infant death and to suggest the broad outlines of infanticide. Unwitting infanticide is probably a widespread phenomenon in societies at all levels of cultural complexity; we know the sociocultural milieu of rural Tlaxcala well enough to say that the incidence of unwitting infanticide is probably high and for a number of causes. To say more, however, would be stretching intuitions and educated guesses too much. Rather, unwitting infanticide has been mentioned as a possible means of using the rationalizing, culturally patterned underpinnings of the tlahuelpuchi complex.

We have discussed the possibility of infanticide centered on the mother-in-law/daughter-in-law relationship, but one may ask, Are there other actors, male and female, who commit infanticide? What possible causes and antecedents may involve the same social and psychological contexts described above, in addition to other contexts that are mainly of a practical, economic and personal, psychological nature? Two examples immediately come to mind. Husbands and wives may decide that, after their seventh or eighth child has survived to the age of four or five, they can no longer feed another mouth; this is a likely context of infanticide. A jealous husband who does not think that his wife's latest issue is his own may also resort to infanticide; this is apparently rather generalized and the topic of veiled gossip in rural Tlaxcala. The array of contexts and forms of infanticide in this culture area is by definition either willful or unwitting, but what may be common to both is the use of the tlahuelpuchi complex as a rationalizing mechanism and as a subterfuge to cover up the deed. In many years of fieldwork in rural Tlaxcala, we have gathered a significant corpus of indirect evidence suggesting that the rather high incidence of infanticide in rural Tlaxcala is probably the rule rather than the exception, for we intuit that the incidence of this phenomenon has been generally underestimated in the ethnological and sociological literature, including that of the supposedly more civilized and technologically advanced societies of Western culture.

Crib Death: Infant Death Due to Unknown Causes, and the Medical Diagnosis of Victims

Let us state at the outset that we know nothing medically about crib death. Nor was it mentioned in 1960–1961 by the chief medical officer of the state of Tlaxcala as one of the possible causes of what the people regard as an infant having been sucked by the tlahuelpuchi. It was suggested in 1980 by two of the several pathologists that we consulted at the University of Pittsburgh. The fact that crib death was suggested as one of the possible causes of infant death in the present context is the sole reason for including it in this monograph. Moreover, since the three cases (30, 35, and 37) that are categorized as crib death do not entail evidence that could be interpreted medically, we never bothered to learn about this form of infant death. Apparently, even today it has not been entirely understood, and, at least in Mexico, it was unknown in 1960. Thus, although we have categorized victims under the heading of "crib death," we emphasize that any infant dying under unclear or unusual circumstances may be diagnosed as a case of bloodsucking witchcraft. We also denote some of the peculiar circumstances that do not conform to the classic tlahuelpuchi complex, which may lead the people directly involved to doubt that it was indeed a case of sucking.

Of the three cases categorized as crib death, one (35) rather clearly departs from the classic tlahuelpuchi complex, whereas the other two (30, 37) more or less adhere to its main tenets. The former is the case of the seven-year-old child found dead nearing noon. When the body of the boy was found by his paternal grandmother, opinions were divided as to whether he had been sucked by the tlahuelpuchi. A slight majority of his kinsmen and neighbors of his household maintained that he had not been sucked, but we included the case in the sample because it exemplified the range of the tlahuelpuchi complex as a rationalization and explanation of infant death. Those who did not believe that the boy had been sucked alleged that he had been sick and slightly retarded since he had ceased to be an infant, and people could notice his rather erratic behavior. But the fact that nearly half of those interviewed (more than 10 adult males and females) adhered to the standard rationalization, even for such a marginal case, attests to the functional value of the tlahuelpuchi belief as an explanatory complex. The other two cases are in the middle range of normality (except perhaps that case 37 is one of eight in which parents did not exhibit any aftereffects due to the sucking) with respect to the more or less quantitative data presented in the tables. From the purely ethnographic viewpoint, however, the informal interviewing of household members and neighbors indicates that these two cases had more than the usual one or two doubters that any case of sucking is likely to generate. In each of these cases there were three or four opinions to the effect that the infants were not sucked by the tlahuelpuchi but died of "natural" causes. Two informants in case 30 indicated in a veiled way that the mother of the victim was responsible for its death because "es una madre poco cuidadosa" (she is a careless mother). But in the following sentence, one of the women informants added, "Pero solo Dios sabe lo que en verdad pasó, y sí puede que la tlahuelpuchi se haya chupado a la creatura. No es bueno sospechar de todo, pues tarde o temprano nos tocará en carne propia." (But only God knows what really happened, and it is quite likely that the infant was sucked by the tlahuelpuchi. It is not good to be suspicious of everything, for sooner or later we ourselves will be the subjects of the same suspicion.) This is a revealing statement, which encapsulates the latent doubts about the efficacy of the tlahuelpuchi to kill. It also indicates the reluctance of most rural Tlaxcalans even to make suggestions that would lead to unpleasant confrontations, manifestly opting instead to let the tlahuelpuchi be blamed, thereby rationalizing and explaining infant death at the same time.

It is highly probable that some of the infants in this sample did suffer crib death, but it would be medically impossible to determine with certainty, even if a physician had examined all infants shortly after death occurred. Cases 30 and 37 are possible crib deaths, and that is the main reason why they were so categorized. Granting, then, that crib death (whatever this means medically) is represented in the sample but cannot be adequately discriminated, we might ask if there are other causes (illnesses, syndromes) that account for infant deaths attributed to the tlahuelpuchi. The answer is probably yes, but we do not know what they are; nor are they important here. Suffice it to say that infants die due to a number of undetermined causes, and that only if the contexts of their deaths comply with at least two, but probably three or four, of the most diagnostic beliefs of the tlahuelpuchi complex would those immediately concerned attribute the deaths to the action of this supernatural. In addition to asphyxia, suffocation, choking, and crib death infants can probably die under the conditions of time and space specified by the bloodsucking complex due to many causes that are impossible to determine accurately (but most probably die of respiratory ailments and dehydration) unless one undertook a thorough medical study of infant mortality in rural Tlaxcala. Yet the basic question that must be asked is: For what reasons or causes (beyond those discussed above for asphyxia, suffocation, choking, and infanticide entailing direct or indirect responsibility for the death of the victim) do daughters-in-law, mothers-in-law, or other members of the household decide that they must tamper with the evidence to make it look like the infant was sucked by the tlahuelpuchi? Or, asked in a different form: When and under what conditions do these immediate actors recognize or become aware of their direct or indirect responsibility for the death of infants, leading to rationalization and explanation by means of the tlahuelpuchi complex? We have answered this question for the contexts of asphyxia, suffocation, and choking, where it is clear that those who felt directly or indirectly responsible for the death of infants resorted to tampering with the evidence to make it look like a case of sucking; and, of course, we have answered it more stringently in the case of willful infanticide. In all these cases, the primary actors involved consciously or unconsciously recognize degrees of culpability (or fear) that result in the tlahuelpuchi rationalization. But what about cases where no such culpability is recognized, and the primary actors, again consciously or unconsciously, know that infants died of some natural cause entirely beyond their responsibility? In other words, can people discriminate between asphyxia, suffocation, and choking (for which they probably always feel a degree of responsibility), on the one hand, and the effect of an acute case of dehydration or a fulminating case of pneumonia (for which they probably do not feel responsible), on the other? Our answer is a tentative yes. We have some indirect evidence (from hundreds of elicitations in the forty-seven–case sample and innumerable comments on the efficacy of the tlahuelpuchi to kill) that women do discriminate between those causes of infant death for which they feel in varying degrees responsible and those for which they do not, which apparently include any natural illness that would be recognized by individuals (mostly husbands and adult male members of the household) who can potentially blame them when the infant is found dead. Furthermore, we strongly suspect that, even when women (obviously the most likely candidates to be blamed for the death of infants) who discover a dead infant realize that it died of natural causes for which they cannot, in theory, be blamed, they do in fact tamper with the evidence in order to make it look like a case of sucking, thereby making sure that they are not blamed for the occurrence (see the following chapter). Playing it safe, then, probably accounts for a considerable number of cases attributed to the action of the tlahuelpuchi, and one cannot discount the possibility that this understandable behavior took place in several cases of the sample.

Finally, this is an appropriate place to discuss the eleven cases examined by a physician. We indicated in chapter 6 that in nine of these cases the examining physician positively diagnosed the cause of death, whereas in two cases he could not do so. The diagnosed cases included all of the Xolotla epidemic (cases 3 to 9) plus cases 21 and 31, whereas the physician was not certain about the cause of death in case 36 and he had no idea of the cause of death in case 44. The diagnosis for eight cases (31 plus all of the Xolotla epidemic) was death by asphyxia (that is asphyxia and suffocation, according to our sociomedical categorization), while one case (21) was diagnosed as death by choking. In fairness to the examining physicians, all three said that their diagnoses were educated guesses, and that nothing short of an autopsy could determine the exact cause or causes of death, thereby agreeing with the standard practice of pathologists and medical examiners in the USA. The examining physician of the Xolotla epidemic did say, however, that the diagnosis of death by asphyxia in these cases, on the evidence of the somatic telltale marks on the body of the infants, had a high degree of probability of being confirmed by autopsy. It is, thus, on this medical evidence that we have centered the sociological interpretation of infant death in rural Tlaxcala when it takes place in the context of the tlahuelpuchi complex. The main outlines of this interpretation appear to be soundly based, and there is little doubt that asphyxia, suffocation, and choking are by far the main causes of these infant deaths attributed to the efficacy of bloodsucking witchcraft. It has not been our intention to engage in an exercise in medical anthropology, but only to present the sociopsychological parameters of bloodsucking witchcraft in terms of the possible causes of death for which the tlahuelpuchi complex serves as a rationalization and folk explanation. This has been the sole purpose of the extended analysis presented in this chapter. Infanticide, crib death, and the social and psychological contexts in which the former take place are probably not that different from their occurrences in industrial, Western societies, although we do not have definitive evidence.

CHAPTER NINE

Social and Psychological Manipulations and the Ex Post Facto Rationalization of the Tlahuelpuchi Complex

SELF-FULFILLING PROPERTIES and feedback effects appear to be magnified in cases where witchcraft events and occurrences are most circumscribed and self-directed. We would go so far as to maintain that the more circumscribed and self-directed the witchcraft event, the higher the self-fulfilling properties and feedback effects of the system. This is certainly the case with bloodsucking witchcraft in rural Tlaxcala, where there is such a close fit between the physical manifestation and normative expectations of the complex. What is most salient about this particular instance of witchcraft is the unusual degree of tampering with the evidence of the witchcraft event and the manipulations of primary and secondary actors in the aftermath of its occurrence. Whether this is a common phenomenon in most witchcraft systems the literature does not give us any clues. Perhaps more important, the rationalizations, manipulations, and tamperings of all actors involved are part of the perception and epistemology of bloodsucking witchcraft in rural Tlaxcala that must be conceptualized. This chapter discusses the social and psychological ambiences of the rationalizations, manipulations, and tamperings engaged in by primary and secondary actors of the tlahuelpuchi complex. It also gives a general account of the affected actions, events, and domains, together with the degree of manifested social and psychological awareness—that is, their conscious or unconscious realization.

SECONDARY ACTORS: THE HOUSEHOLD PERSONNEL AND NEIGHBORS

We demonstrated that when the tlahuelpuchi strikes and an infant dies, the entire household is affected directly and the neighborhood or non-residential

extended family is affected indirectly. The array of beliefs and practices surrounding the tlahuelpuchi is not a topic of daily preoccupation in the average
household, but it does become of central concern when she strikes. For days
after the sucking, especially the first two days following the burial of the victim, the adults of the affected household and many of their neighbors become
visibly apprehensive about other potential victims and talk endlessly about the
tlahuelpuchi and the nature and potential of this dreaded supernatural. It is not
until the aftereffects experienced by the mother or father of the victim have
completely subsided that the household returns to normality. It is during the
period immediately following the sucking, which may last from four or five
days to more than two weeks, that the household rationalizes and reinforces
the tlahuelpuchi complex by many of its primary and secondary actors manipulating the belief system of bloodsucking witchcraft socially and psychologically. This occurs irrespective of whether the household is nuclear or extended.
By extension, it also affects the personnel of the neighborhood.[1] Ontologically,
the people examine the tlahuelpuchi complex, aiming to understand the form,
meaning, and motivation of this nemesis. Time and again they verbalize the
belief system, the known alternatives, and what they know or think the complex is in other communities, and they recount innumerable stories of sucking
and cases of witchcraft. Observing and hearing the demeanor and verbal behavior of household members and neighbors, one gets the distinct impression
that they are engaged in a cathartic process of accepting and coming to grips
with the apparently (to them) inevitable reality of the tlahuelpuchi. At the
same time, the adult members of the household ask themselves what they have
done or left undone, individually and collectively, to deserve the sucking of an
infant—thereby latently expressing the belief, deep-seated in rural Tlaxcalan
culture, that catastrophes and unfortunate events do not happen without a
reason, that individuals and the local polity are directly responsible. Epistemologically, since the reality of the tlahuelpuchi is assumed, all those directly
or indirectly affected inevitably perceive events, outcomes, and behaviors as
colored by the ideology and belief system of bloodsucking witchcraft. To put it
differently, certain events and happenings preceding the sucking, the sucking
event itself, and all happenings and interpretations following the sucking (until
the entire occurrence fades from the people's concern) are in varying degrees
distorted perceptions configured by the normative belief system. They are not
necessarily fabrications so much as distortions, exaggerations, or reinterpreta-
tions of the facts surrounding the sucking event and its aftermath normatively
specified by the belief system: some normal events and occurrences (unnoticed
in the daily course of living) suddenly acquire magnified proportions, whereas
others, tangentially related to the sucking, are kaleidoscopically distorted. These

are ex post facto, collectively concerted rationalizations and manipulations engaged in by the people when the tlahuelpuchi strikes, whose main function is obviously to reinforce the belief system, resulting in the more efficient and palatable explanation and acceptance of infant death.

Kinship and the Household-Neighborhood Support Group

The social and psychological ambience of the household and neighborhood surrounding the sucking event may be characterized as caring, supportive, restrained, spontaneous but apprehensive, and fearful but resigned. Kinsmen and neighbors go out of their way to facilitate the household's return to normality, preparing food, arranging for the infant's burial, and above all, giving constant companionship and physical comfort to the primary actors of the drama— that is, the parents of the victim. Confronted with a dangerous and always unforeseen event, kinsmen and neighbors are temporarily brought together into a close-knit group, caring for and supporting one another to an extent not realized in the normal course of living in the annual cycle.[2] Thus, the sucking event not only coalesces support for and attention on the affected couple, but also generates a situation in which the affected group of kinsmen and neighbors as a whole equally receives the ensuing support and goodwill.

The psychological ambience of the household and neighborhood is well exemplified by the description of the several days following the Xolotla epidemic (see chapter 5). Individuals behave spontaneously but with apprehension of whether the tlahuelpuchi will strike again, which leads to a state of alertness that may last for several days: infants of sucking age are nightly protected against the tlahuelpuchi, household members take turns staying awake at night if there are infants of sucking age, neighbors occasionally patrol the streets and paths, and so on. People seek the comfort of close proximity to others, and there is a noticeable tendency to huddle and to touch that departs significantly from the rather detached, patterned attitudes of the average rural Tlaxcalan. The generally calm demeanor of the people gives way to a heightened state of alertness that may lead the inexperienced observer to mistake it for gaiety or extroversion which is the opposite of the usually measured and grave comportment of adult rural Tlaxcalans. There develops a pronounced desire to talk, and obviously, the most commonly verbalized topic is the world of the tlahuelpuchi and what it can do to humans. As we indicated, after the Xolotla epidemic it became clear that the bloodsucking of an infant and its aftermath are occasions of high stress and anxiety—occasions in which the people let their social and psychological guard down generally and talk freely about their fears, apprehensions, and preoccupations concerning witchcraft, sorcery, and magic and religious beliefs and expectations. Indeed, stress, anxiety, and a certain degree of psychological dislocation are the key descriptive indicators which characterize the aftermath of the sucking of an infant and the reaction elicited from parents, kinsmen, and neighbors. This generalized psychological ambience colors and, to some degree, conditions the perceptions of all actors directly or indirectly affected by the sucking event. Let us briefly describe and analyze all the domains, contexts, and occasions which are distorted, manipulated, and rationalized by the various categories of actors in the psychological and social climate following a sucking event.

The rather intensive interviewing of the postsucking period for all forty-seven cases of the sample, together with much unstructured interviewing, reveals that the behavior of most actors for several days after the tlahuelpuchi strikes is quite patterned. People's responses to questions, volunteered responses, the general tone of the answers, and the particular aspects of the sucking event that were most commonly addressed did not change much from case to case. What is more, particular categories of kinsmen and neighbors also gave and volunteered standard, fairly patterned answers and statements to queries concerning the context and efficacy of the tlahuelpuchi to kill. It is therefore appropriate to analyze the distortions, manipulations, and rationalizations of kinsmen and neighbors in terms of identifiable kinship and spatial categories of actors. These categories are embedded in the nuclear-family household, the extended-family household, the non-residential extended family, the immediate neighborhood, and the paraje. With respect to the victim (ego), they are the following: father (Fa), mother (Mo); father's father (FaFa), father's mother (FaMo); occasionally father's father's father (FaFaFa), father's father's mother (FaFaMo); teenage siblings (TS), usually over twelve years old; teenage patrilateral cousins (TP), usually over twelve; father's brother (FB), father's brother's wife (FBW); occasionally father's father's brother (FaFaBr), father's father's brother's wife (FaFaBrWi); adjacent patrilateral kinsmen (APK) (in separate households, usually headed by FaFa, FaBrs, FaFaFa, FaFaBrs); undifferentiated non-residential extended-family kinsmen (UNK); adjacent neighbors (AN) (male and female adults living in households immediately adjacent or within thirty or forty yards); paraje neighbors (PN) (male and female adults living in households within the paraje—that is, generally within a radius of 150 yards or so or within the confines of about an urban block; these are usually compadres, friends, and occasionally affines). The extended-family household, the non-residential extended family, and the immediate neighborhood and paraje as a whole reflect the patrilineal residential bias of rural Tlaxcalan society, which is extended to compadrazgo in that most relationships, contracted patrilaterally, have a significant degree of residential unity within the paraje. Rarely, there are cases of matrilocal residence (usually when nuclear families do not have sons or for economic reasons) and occasionally affines may reside in the same paraje. But these are exceptions that have little or no significance for the kinship, compadrazgo, and friendship analysis of bloodsucking witchcraft, and they are therefore ignored. Inasmuch as our data allow it, the ensuing analysis will be conducted with reference to the above categories of actors.

The following are the most common domains surrounding the bloodsucking event in which actors engage in the manipulation, rationalization, exaggeration, or distortion of the tlahuelpuchi complex: occurrence of the bloodsucking event (table 6.1); age of the victim at the time of death (table 6.3); approximate time of finding the victim's body (table 6.9); location and position of the victim's body upon discovery (table 6.11); physical marks on the victim's body (table 6.13); victim's protection against the tlahuelpuchi (table 6.15); unusual events surrounding the victim's sucking, especially sighting the tlahuelpuchi (table 6.16); aftereffects due to the sucking of the victim's parents (table 6.17); previous sucking in the victim's nuclear family and household (tables 6.18 and 6.19); fanciful stories and legendary accounts of the tlahuelpuchi's efficacy to kill. To varying degrees, the foregoing environments essentially condition the perception that the average rural Tlaxcalan has of the tlahuelpuchi as a bloodsucking witch.

The Physical Context of Exaggerations and Distortions

1. Probably the most common and one of the first verbalized pieces of evidence affirming the death of an infant due to having been sucked is about the insatiable thirst of the tlahuelpuchi for the blood of infants. Usually, all categories of kinsmen and neighbors directly or indirectly affected by the sucking talk endlessly about the uncontrollable desire of tlahuelpuchis to drink blood in order to survive, which is, of course, the cornerstone of the bloodsucking complex as an explanatory construct of infant death. Naturally, off-season suckings (that is, those which do not take place in the coldest or rainiest months; see chapter 2) elicit the strongest and most exaggerated verbalizations from all concerned. People point out the viciousness of some tlahuelpuchis, the greater reinvigorating effect of multiple monthly suckings, and the conventicles in which the tlahuelpuchis participate in order to allocate which areas to prowl and what infants to suck. One gets the firm impression that kinsmen and neighbors experience the urge to rationalize and explain the tlahuelpuchi's efficacy to kill more in off-season suckings than in seasonal suckings; the belief system, when not specific enough or subject to slightly alternative interpretations, must be more strongly reinforced when it is physically actualized. Thus, the net initial reaction to a sucking is not only to exaggerate what the tlahuelpuchi can do,

but also to attribute to her qualities and proclivities that she does not have in normal elicitations of bloodsucking witchcraft (that is, elicitations obtained in the absence of the stress produced by a sucking): possessing powers of hypnosis and animal transformation that make it nearly impossible to resist and detect her; conspiring with normal human beings for the purpose of sucking infants (something no informant would ever dare verbalize in a normal interview); having a compact with other anthropomorphic supernaturals (most often with El Cuatlapanga or El Peñon) to be more successful at her evildoing (again, an attribute never verbalized in the formal ideology and belief system); and so on. Stress and anxiety caused by the sucking obviously color the "normal" normative ontological reality of the tlahuelpuchi, and this is the main source of the manipulation of the manifest ideology and the latent exaggerations and distortions thereof. The same process, of course, obtains in most of the following domains.

Let us establish at the outset that the parents of the victim are the least communicative and least prone to answer questions or to volunteer information concerning the death of the infant throughout the entire postsucking period. Being at the center of the event, they are structurally the most direct source of information. Psychologically, however, the parents of the victim, especially mothers, become withdrawn, somewhat morose, and, not infrequently, totally uncommunicative to most people around them. This psychological state is heightened in the cases of mothers or fathers who develop serious aftereffects, when even their closest kinsmen have trouble communicating with them. Rather, all categories of kinsmen and neighbor other than parents are the most important sources of elicitation and reconstruction of the sucking event, with the exception of some instances when parents are willing to talk, especially about unusual events surrounding the sucking (the domain denoted by table 6.16); that is, on the whole parents did talk and volunteered information concerning unusual events surrounding the sucking. This general ambience of elicitation and reconstruction applies to all ten domains of manipulation, exaggeration, and distortion that we have identified.

2. The age of the infants at the time of being sucked is not distorted or manipulated to fit the normative belief system, but it does constitute another of the rationalizing, reinforcing elements of the tlahuelpuchi complex. Together with the seasonal occurrence of the sucking, the age of the victim serves initially to coalesce the perception that the tlahuelpuchi was indeed responsible for the death of the infant. The overwhelming regularity in the age of sucked infants fits perfectly with the normative belief that, unless they cannot help it, tlahuelpuchis suck only the blood of infants between the ages of three and ten months. The regularity of suckings with respect to the victim's age is a power-

ful reinforcer of bloodsucking witchcraft. It is in cases such as this that it is difficult, perhaps impossible, to determine whether an event's physical realization structures the basic configuration of the underlying ideology and belief system, or, conversely, whether the ideology and belief system (configured on the basis of other physical facts and events) makes people behave in certain ways and affects the perception of specific physical events. This difficulty is at the heart of the epistemology of witchcraft (and by extension, of any behavorial domain in which supernatural inputs are believed to produce natural outcomes), and it is our contention that unless the psychology of supernaturalism is better understood than it has been so far, the phenomenon will prove intractable to the sociological treatment overwhelmingly employed by anthropologists. Once the physical existence of the tlahuelpuchi is manifested in specific time and space, the sucking event becomes a caricature of John Stuart Mill's concomitant variations, in which causal entailment is posited on false premises (for example, if one drinks whiskey and water, gin and water, rum and water, and vodka and water, then what makes one drunk is water). At another level, this statement is tautologous, for it begs the psychological question that is always left unexplained, and no amount of sociological analysis can possibly solve the problem.

3. Unlike domains (1) and (2), the approximate time of finding the victim's body can be, and undoubtedly is, manipulated or distorted by the actors most closely related to the sucking—that is, parents, grandparents, uncles and aunts, and other members of the household at the time. It is important to recognize which aspects and elements of the sucking event can and which cannot be manipulated, distorted, or noticeably exaggerated by primary and secondary actors because rural Tlaxcalans, or at least all of the more perceptive informants, know which elements can be tampered with, and that those immune to tampering constitute harder, more reliable evidence for the existence and efficacy of the tlahuelpuchi. This, of course, is stating the obvious, for there is little or no tampering that can be done with the seasonal nature of the sucking and the age of the victim, while it is evident that the time of finding the victim's body and the position and location in which it is found can easily be altered. The same Tlaxcalan awareness applies to each of the ten domains that have been isolated, all of which can be categorized as tamperable or non-tamperable, with some of them admitting a degree of distortion or exaggeration. The point is that the discriminating perceptions of even the most traditional rural Tlaxcalans (that is, those who unquestionably adhere completely to the ideology and belief system of the tlahuelpuchi complex) exhibit cracks of doubt concerning the efficacy of bloodsucking witchcraft. In other words, in transitional societies with a modicum of technological and scientific understanding such as that of the

rural Tlaxcalans, the transposition of causation is not smooth and psychologically unquestioned—that is, at certain points in the chain of causal entailment, the passage from supernatural inputs to natural outcomes is either latently suspected or manifestly doubted. Indeed, the traditional wisdom of anthropologists—that in the witchcraft systems of so-called primitive tribal societies no distinction emerges between natural and supernatural domains, and concomitantly, between natural and supernatural causation—is highly suspect, at least to the extent that witchcraft must necessarily postulate the existence of forces and personages that do not obey the regularities of daily life. If this were not so, then one could hardly explain the occasional quick disappearance of a witchcraft or sorcery system when technological or scientific knowledge related to the witchcraft or sorcery domain becomes widely known. From this standpoint, the assertion that in some witchcraft systems there obtains a distinction between natural and supernatural causation is essentially an epiphenomenological statement, and to make sense it needs psychological analysis specifying the underlying theory of knowledge and the ontological domain of perception. Apparently, this has never been done, and consequently, we really do not know whether certain witchcraft and sorcery systems entail a natural-supernatural distinction.

The latent suspicions or manifest doubts of some traditional rural Tlaxcalans are clearly exemplified by the statements of the most knowledgeable, perceptive, and exacting informant ever interviewed. Concerning the strong attack of tzipitictoc that the mother of the victim developed after the sucking in case 19 (which took place in the household of a nephew a few yards from his own), he said: "La gente sabe muy bien que la tlahuelpuchi se chupa a las creaturas de cierta edad casi siempre cuando hace frío y en las épocas de lluvia. Lo que así sucede es de nación y no se puede cambiar. Pero muchas canijas mujeres no tienen reparo en terjiversar la forma de hacer maldad de la tlahuelpuchi para que la gente vea que no hay duda de que fué esta maldita la que se chupó a la creatura. Y me da verguenza decirle compadrito que una vez, hace más de 20 años, sorprendí a una de mis nueras que vivía con nosotros poniendo a su creatura muerta en la puerta de su cuarto. Nunca dije nada pues hasta ahora creo que la tlahuelpuchi sí se chupó a esa creatura, pero a veces tengo dudas compadrito de otras muertes que me ha tocado ver de cerca. Ud. bien sabe compadrito que la tlahuelpuchi existe y que las hay en muchos pueblos de La Malintzi, pero a veces algunas madres, especialmente las jóvenes, hacen aparecer a la tlahuelpuchi como la culpable de sus propios descuidos con sus creaturas." (People know very well that the tlahuelpuchi sucks infants of certain age almost always during the cold and rainy weather. This is a natural occurrence and cannot be changed. But many devious [tricky] women have no compunction to muddle the evildoings of the tlahuelpuchi in order for people to see that there is no doubt that it was this loathsome creature who sucked the infant. And I am ashamed to tell you, compadrito, that once, more than twenty years ago, I caught one of my live-in daughters-in-law in the act of placing her dead infant by the door of her room. I never said anything, for until today I believe the tlahuelpuchi sucked that infant, but sometimes, compadrito, I have doubts about other deaths that I have had the opportunity to observe closely. You know very well, compadrito, that the tlahuelpuchi exists and that they are to be found in many villages of La Malintzi, but some mothers, especially young ones, make it look like the tlahuelpuchi was guilty for their own lack of care with their infants.) In several ways this is a remarkable statement, unique in Nutini's experience in Tlaxcala for more than a generation. No other informant ever came as close to the heart of explaining the manipulations and tamperings that primary actors engage in when the tlahuelpuchi strikes. The statement exemplifies the discrimination between tamperable and non-tamperable elements and concomitantly suggests that mothers, as the single most central actor of the sucking event, do tamper with one of the two most diagnostic elements of the tlahuelpuchi's efficacy—namely, the position and location of the victim's body after the sucking. But not even Nutini's chief informant and most trusted compadre could bring himself to doubt the ultimate efficacy of the tlahuelpuchi to kill, as befitted a traditionalist with whom he had gone witch hunting on two occasions.[3]

Let us return to the domain of time of finding the victim's body after the sucking. There is some degree of willful or unwitting distortion of fixing the approximate time of discovering the corpse. Even though it was easy to elicit the approximate time from household members, particularly from those who discovered the corpse, it does not necessarily follow that all instances recorded in table 6.9 are accurate, especially in those cases where discovery took place before the normal time for household members to get up, usually about 6:00 A.M. That is, in perhaps all cases (twenty) in which the body was discovered at or before 5:30 A.M., there were some unwitting distortions by those who found the corpse, especially by household members, who almost invariably volunteered information which helped to fix the time of discovery as presented in table 6.9. These distortions or miscalculations may be explained as the latent, unconscious desire of all concerned to achieve the closest possible fit between the belief system and the physical realization of the event: the ex post facto period of rationalization that always ensues after a sucking and that characterizes the entire flow of actions and behaviors.

4. If the seasonal character of the sucking and the age of the victim are the cultural elements immediately signifying that the tlahuelpuchi has struck, the

location and position of the victim's body, as shown in table 6.11, are the elements psychologically triggering the belief that the bloodsucking witch has caused the death of the infant. When questioned for the first time (almost always within a day after the sucking), kinsmen and neighbors invariably began by pointing out the location and position of the victim's body as the most unmistakable evidence of who had caused the death of the infant. There is no other element of the complex that psychologically reinforces more strongly the evil deed of the tlahuelpuchi. This is corroborated by the fact that, when the corpse is found, it is not removed from the spot until all members of the household and next-door neighbors are called to see it: it is as if the finder, and all household members who came immediately upon the alarm being sounded, wanted to impress upon the entire paraje that the deed had been committed by the tlahuelpuchi, thereby reinforcing the complex. Perhaps more important, the location and position of the victim's body upon discovery epitomizes a domain fraught with outright tampering. The tampering with the evidence, however, is done exclusively by mothers or persons directly or indirectly responsible for the death of the infant. Thus, this domain is more appropriately discussed in the following subsection. It is highly unlikely that secondary actors, especially neighbors, engage in any sort of tampering in this domain. The repeated verbalization of where and how the body of the victim was found may be considered an exaggeration, but as we indicated, secondary actors would go no farther in this domain.

5. The physical marks on the victim's body, described in table 6.13, are another unmistakable sign that the infant was sucked by the tlahuelpuchi. Not knowing the pathology of the various kinds of infant death, rural Tlaxcalans attribute to the action of the tlahuelpuchi the bruises, acchymoses, and purple spots on the chest, back, and neck of the victim. More specifically, the people believe that all the physical marks left on the infant's body are made by the tlahuelpuchi's mouth literally sucking the blood of its victim through the skin of the chest, back, and neck. In addition, the people believe that in the process of sucking, the tlahuelpuchi appears to infect the body of the victim with a certain liquid or humor, which in their view accounts for the fact that, as the corpse stiffens (the slight rigor mortis experienced by infant corpses), the acchymoses and purple spots become more pronounced. After a sucking, the affected household bustles with activity and kinsmen and neighbors come and go preparing for the rites to come or simply looking on curiously. Grandparents, elderly uncles and aunts, and elderly neighbors are particularly prone to comment on the marks on the corpse as they see them change and become more pronounced several hours after the body has been discovered. Older kinsmen and neighbors make assiduous comments about the phenomenon

and marvel at whatever the tlahuelpuchi infects the body with to produce the change. Quite often, elderly people remember the effects of previous suckings they have experienced, exaggerate the changes in the marks on the infant's body, and this in turn leads them to recount legends or semilegends of the effect of the sucking on infant bodies and of the world of the tlahuelpuchi. The intention of these exaggerated, distorted accounts is evidently to reinforce the tlahuelpuchi complex throughout the stressful period after the sucking. Ironically, however, these accounts tend rather to vulgarize bloodsucking witchcraft and diminish the fit between what the ideology and belief system specify and what is actually physically realized.[4] Such an unalterable manifestation as the marks on the infant's body are bound to elicit exaggerations and distortions by the most concerned kinsmen and neighbors under conditions of stress and anxiety. This, of course, constitutes a common denominator for the ten domains we have isolated here.

The physical marks on the victim's mother's body are not included as a separate domain of manipulation and rationalization because on the one hand, they are essentially part of the complex of marks left on the victim's body, and, on the other hand, the affected mothers are reluctant to show the marks and to talk about them. Moreover, kinsmen and neighbors respect this aspect of their privacy, volunteering no information or only talking passingly about it. The explanation for this behavior appears to be that, since the belief system of the tlahuelpuchi complex does not specify marks on the mother's body, there does not seem to be any advantage in intensifying such an occurrence. Yet, there is no intent on the part of anyone to hide or to be secretive about the marks on the mother's body. Quite the contrary, kinsmen and neighbors always know whether the tlahuelpuchi left any marks on the mother's breasts, since in all cases of sucking the mother must be ritually cleansed by a tezitlazc and the event is usually witnessed by many people. Several informants did say that the marks on the mother's breasts are produced by the struggle that she offers while her infant is being sucked, and this leads us to believe that the reticence of all concerned about this aspect of the sucking is simply natural courtesy: they do not in any way wish to embarrass those mothers who did not offer stronger resistance to the tlahuelpuchi.

The Psychological Context of Manipulations and Rationalizations

6. We have discussed the guilty feelings that parents have when their infant is sucked without being protected against the tlahuelpuchi. The reluctance of parents to talk about protecting infants is understandable, even though they know that the only fully effective protection is garlic or onion, which was seen to be used only once, right after the Xolotla epidemic. Table 6.15 shows that

slightly over one-third of all infants in the sample had been protected against the tlahuelpuchi, implicitly indicating the relaxed attitude of parents at large and explicitly showing their lack of confidence in any means of protection. The sample, however, may not be representative, for in the most traditional communities, and in many transitional communities, most infants are protected by one, or sometimes by two of the means described above. Be this as it may, this aspect of bloodsucking witchcraft is probably the most uncertain; this is understandable given the serendipitous nature of infant death and the latent psychological proclivity (that all witchcraft systems have) to leave certain aspects of the system undetermined. Sociologically, however, the relative disregard of protection against the tlahuelpuchi has some significant implications, which can be interpreted as distortions or exaggerations. What we particularly have in mind here is the gossip and backbiting that takes place after the sucking of a non-protected infant. Knowing perfectly well through experience that no method of protection, except garlic and onion, is 100 percent effective, kinsmen and neighbors nonetheless mildly blame the parents of the victim for not having protected it, and they talk among themselves about the probability and possibility that the infant may not have been sucked had it been protected. The inconsistency of the argument, and the distorted behavior that it generates, can be explained by the stringent compliance that most rural Tlaxcalans exhibit in discharging the injunctions and constraints of the belief system of their magico-religious world. Once the injunctions and constraints have been complied with, their duty has been done, and what happens afterward is in the hands of God, *los poderes que nos gobiernan* (the powers who govern us, including Catholic and pagan supernaturals), and fate (*el destino*, as rural Tlaxcalan use this concept). The people therefore reason that even though they know that most methods of protection are not foolproof, perhaps if one always protected infants, the results would be much more favorable and not so many infants would be sucked by the tlahuelpuchi. Too, there is always the possibility that the protection of infants is not effective because their parents did something wrong or left something undone, thereby offending those who watch over man's destiny, as traditional rural Tlaxcalans constantly tell others and themselves. More interesting is the lack of use of garlic and onion, universally regarded as foolproof. Why are such common substances used almost invariably ex post facto, as in the Xolotla epidemic? The answer is that non-compliance with this sure-fire method of protection functionally reinforces the efficacy of the tlahuelpuchi to kill, which is, of course, the ultimate goal of the complex as an explanatory ideological construct. For whatever reasons, the parents of the victim's parents, the father's brothers and their wives, and elderly kinsmen and neighbors are the most assiduous backbiters and critics of the couple when they discover that the infant was not protected. This personnel node obviously exemplifies the network of socially conditioned friction and gossip, but it also psychologically expresses the ambivalence associated with the protection of infants against the tlahuelpuchi that leads to a degree of distortion and rationalization.

7. It is in the domain of unusual events surrounding the victim's sucking described in table 6.16 that the parents of the victim generally have something concrete to say, contrasted with their withdrawn demeanor throughout the postsucking period. Moreover, this is the domain about which practically every actor interviewed or talked to following the sucking had something concrete, vague, or tangentially related to say. This is especially the case with the victim's grandparents, uncles and aunts, and immediate neighbors. Indeed, there is no other identifiable domain of the bloodsucking event and its aftermath that is more fraught with distortions, manipulations, and rationalizations than this one, which most exemplifies the latent and manifest extents to which all actors concerned go to reinforce the tlahuelpuchi's efficacy to kill. We cannot add much more to the analysis of this domain than we already presented in chapter 6, except to say that every category of kinsmen and neighbors volunteered information on the night's event that was unmistakably designed to establish the presence of the tlahuelpuchi in the household, the commission of her evil act, or, by implication, an experienced state or something that happened in the past that implicated the bloodsucking witch in the death of the infant. As we indicated, it is often hard to discriminate between actual experiences and perceptions and outright fabrications of legendary or semilegendary recollections. This psychological ambience attests to the culturally concerted effort of all primary and secondary actors to validate the tlahuelpuchi complex, displace guilt, and assuage anxiety: in essence, the reinforcement of the principal functions of bloodsucking witchcraft.

Table 6.16 indicates that sighting the tlahuelpuchi, in her luminous or animal form, and her telltale presence in or near the house are the most common occurrences of an unusual nature surrounding the victim's sucking. These occurrences are experienced by the parents of the victim, by other household members, and occasionally, by neighbors. In general, sighting the tlahuelpuchi in or near the house in any of her telltale forms undoubtedly results in the greatest range of distortion, exaggeration, and manipulation in the entire bloodsucking complex. The phenomenon is perfectly understandable in that this aspect of the belief system is one of the most detailed and clearly specified, in addition to the projective, inherent physical properties of the tlahuelpuchi, which naturally lend themselves to preceptive illusions and manipulative distortions. Hence the torrent of information that flowed from all concerned actors after a sucking. Even in the eight cases of table 6.16 in which no unusual occurrences were reported, there were many accounts of distortions and exaggerations that we did not record because they were too far after the fact. The unusual events reported by the parents of the victim are extremely telling, and they will be analyzed below. Suffice it to say here that the luminosity or any other telltale manifestation of the tlahuelpuchi—in the house, near windows, or about to strike—were freely elicited from mothers and fathers. Indeed, they were eager to tell their perceptions (usually in the first twelve hours after the sucking, and before they generally became morose and uncommunicative), obviously to buttress the claim that the tlahuelpuchi did unquestionably strike. Yet, the psychological states experienced by parents (nightmares, drowsiness, pains) during the night or upon waking up may be regarded as the onset of the aftereffects that continue for the entire duration of the postsucking period.

8. More than 75 percent of the parents experienced aftereffects due to the sucking, as indicated in table 7.17. Chapter 7 discussed in some detail what these aftereffects are and some of their individual and collective psychosomatic implications. We will return to this domain in chapter 10, particularly its effects upon parents and their immediate environment. Here, the reaction elicited from secondary actors and how they perceive the sometimes rather dramatic effects on primary actors is briefly summarized. Even in the eleven cases in which there were no discernible or obvious aftereffects (physical or psychosomatic ailments that could be labeled) in the mother or father, these actors were withdrawn and uncommunicative, a fact that kinsmen and neighbors were quick to point out. In the case of strong headaches, nausea, chest pains, or any other physical ailment, kinsmen and neighbors (particularly women to women and men to men) are solicitous but gossipy toward the affected mothers and fathers. But it is the cases of espanto, ataque de espíritus, chipilería, and tzipitictoc that elicit the strongest reaction from all categories of secondary actors. As we indicated, these can be serious psychosomatic ailments that require ministrations by household kinsmen and, not infrequently, limpias and other manipulations by tezitlazcs. These ministrations and limpias invariably attract considerable to large numbers of kinsmen and neighbors. (In the first of four limpias that the mother of the victim of case 44 underwent, more than twenty-five adults were present while the tezitlazc performed. This was a particularly difficult case, for the mother suffered a severe ataque de espíritus.) These gatherings take place in the main room of the house in front of the household altar, and they can only be interpreted as social and psychological support for the affected mother or father as she or he undergoes the cleansing or allopathic rite. As a counterpart to this universal support from kinsmen and neighbors, there is an undercurrent of criticism and suspicion toward the affected mother

or father, as people ask one another and discuss among themselves the reason for the severity of the aftereffects; and, in the ambience of the typical imago mundi of rural Tlaxcalans, they ponder on the reasons and possible explanations for the occurrence. In the fashion described above for several domains, kinsmen and neighbors tend to exaggerate and distort the mild and serious psychosomatic ailments of the victim's parents, and in so doing, cast suspicion on their character, question their adequacy in handling infants and children, and attribute to them real or imaginary wrongdoings or omissions in their social performance as kinsmen, compadres, and friends. This ambivalence exemplifies the perennial response of rural Tlaxcalans to an ambience in which they perceive and deal with unexpected, inexplicable, and seriously unfortunate events and occurrences: supportive and solicitous of those in psychological trouble and physical danger but always prone to think the worst of people when ill fortune strikes.

9. In the context and network of gossip and exaggerations and distortions that obtains in the postsucking period, the number of previous suckings in the victim's nuclear family and household, as shown in tables 6.18 and 6.19, has considerable significance. Despite the very high incidence of bloodsucking witchcraft,[5] the kinsmen and neighbors of the victim's household do not seem to remember that they have, as individuals, experienced suckings firsthand in their own nuclear and extended families. When it comes to allocating blame and displacing supernatural responsibility, rural Tlaxcalans are experts in manipulating that most common of human proclivities: they can always see the dirt in someone else's eye, never in their own.

Another, more meaningful aspect of previous suckings in the nuclear family and household is the widespread concept of individuals or groups (households, parajes, and even entire non-residential extended families) being *metepalca*—that is, of inherent bad luck. The semantic domain of this Hispanicized Nahuatl term includes individuals and groups that the community believes to be *de nación* (by nature, since birth) unlucky and of slightly bad omen—that is, most of what they do or undertake will probably not succeed. The people believe that, for no fault of their own or their ancestors, these individuals and groups are imprinted at birth with bad luck, which is thought to be caused by fate or undetermined supernaturals for reasons unknown. Metepalca individuals and groups manifest themselves in several domains of rural Tlaxcalan culture: compadrazgo, religious sponsorship, secular sponsorship, business ventures, and so on. For example, an individual or member of his family regarded as metepalca is seldom chosen for mayordomía sponsorship and hardly as a compadre. When too many infants are sucked in a nuclear family or household, the people at large are quick to brand it as metepalca. This is probably true of households that have experienced three or more suckings (numbers 8, 15, 24, 26, 33, 36, 39, 40, and 46). Being branded as metepalca in the context of suckings is less serious than in the context of compadrazgo or religious sponsorship (when individuals and families not infrequently suffer socially and psychologically), since the former does not have many significant consequences for the social life of the paraje and community. Nonetheless, the concept of metepalca unquestionably plays a role in bloodsucking witchcraft; to a considerable extent metepalca structures the distortions and exaggerations of the paraje at large—perhaps even of a large segment of the community—against the parents and household of the victim with one too many suckings. Let us say in passing that there is fairly good evidence that the concept of metepalca is a good descriptive and operational term (that is, it may effectively configure a significant domain of behavior) for observable social and, perhaps, even psychological qualities that become individually and collectively reified as a self-fulfilling complex.

10. Finally, we will say a word about the fanciful stories and legendary and semilegendary accounts triggered by the sucking event. We indicated how the most diagnostic characteristics of the tlahuelpuchi (especially the location and position of the infant's body and the physical marks it exhibits after the sucking) elicit the accounts and the stories that vulgarize the bloodsucking witchcraft complex, but which have the immediate effect of rationalizing those junctures of the belief system that are not well specified or explaining departures from the ideology in extraordinary cases. Contextually speaking, no other domain of the postsucking period conditions more the ambience of distortion, exaggeration, and rationalization than these accounts and stories told or elicited under conditions of stress and anxiety. These outbursts of creative tampering with the ideology and belief system of the tlahuelpuchi complex come to an end as quickly as they began when the household returns to normality. Tampering with the ideology and belief system may have an immediate, positive functional value, but in the long run it is detrimental to the finely tuned balance between the belief system and its physical realization. This is especially so in a situation of rapid change, as the tlahuelpuchi complex has been experiencing it since the early 1960s. Rapid change is the main reason for considering fanciful stories and legendary and semilegendary accounts told and elicited during the trying postsucking period.

It has been possible to establish that before the early 1950s, the kinsmen and neighbors of the paraje did not tell each other these vulgarizing stories and accounts: the normal, traditional ideology and belief system of bloodsucking witchcraft was enough to sustain undue departures and extraordinary occurrences; there was less need to explain the unexplainable. Shortly after the early 1950s, the situation described here began to obtain, and the vulgarization of the tlahuelpuchi complex has increased at a rapid pace since the early 1960s. In the last three cases of bloodsucking witchcraft that were closely observed, in 1979 and 1980, the pristine ideology and belief system of bloodsucking witchcraft presented in chapter 3 was gone. In its place there was a hodgepodge of precisely the vulgarizations that have been outlined in this section, in which the tlahuelpuchi had become a sort of cross between motion-picture vampirism and the Christian devil. What is more, the tlahuelpuchi was already marginal and had been relegated to a residual status as a system, since the relatively more traditional people still thought that the tlahuelpuchi occasionally struck. To put it differently, the vulgarization of the ideology and belief system of any well-delineated structural domain is diagnostic both of rapid change having established itself and of the reaction to external forces affecting the domain. In the present example, as infant death in rural Tlaxcala diminishes (rather dramatically in the past ten to fifteen years), so does bloodsucking witchcraft, and the tlahuelpuchi becomes a residual, mixed entity, a glimmer of the traditional belief structure modified by modernizing and secularizing elements. The same process of change in the institutions of compadrazgo and the cult of the dead during the past generation has been demonstrated elsewhere (Nutini 1984, 1988).

This section presented a gestalt of the household and neighborhood when the sucking of an infant takes place. Insofar as the data permitted, we were able to configure a coherent picture of the social and psychological ambiences in which this event occurs and how it is perceived and conceptualized ex post facto by kinsmen and neighbors. The screen of distortions, exaggerations, transpositions, and rationalizations through which the tlahuelpuchi complex is perceived by all primary and secondary actors constitutes the epistemological matrix which conditions, reinforces, and validates the tlahuelpuchi's efficacy to kill and makes it an efficient system of explaining infant death.

PRIMARY ACTORS: THE DAUGHTER-IN-LAW/MOTHER-IN-LAW AXIS

While one may possibly surmise that the secondary actors of the sucking event might engage in tampering with the data, the foregoing section dealt essentially with the distorted perceptions of kinsmen and neighbors in the context of ten circumscribed domains. It also outlined the distorted perceptions of the parents of the victim for the time of finding the body, the physical marks on the victim's body, and the protection of the infant against the tlahuelpuchi, insofar as this information was elicited from primary actors, as undistinguished from secondary actors. This section deals exclusively with the actual, ascertainable tampering that is entirely centered on the parents of the victim, and by extension, on perpetrators of infanticide and household members other than the victim's parents directly or indirectly responsible for the infant's death. The pivotal element here is the mother, for two reasons. On the one hand, she is the principal, most intimately in charge of infant care; on the other, she is actually and potentially the person in the household most blamed when her infant dies as the result of being sucked by the tlahuelpuchi. As we suggested, the mother's susceptibility to blame is probably the single most efficacious element that motivates tampering with the physical manifestation of the blood-sucking event. Thus, the analysis will be conducted primarily with reference to the victim's mother, tangentially with reference to the father, and by implication with reference to the mother-in-law and other responsible household members. There are three main domains in which parents and other household members engage in outright tampering with the physical manifestation of the tlahuelpuchi complex: unusual events surrounding the victim's sucking (table 6.16); location and position of the victim's body upon discovery (table 6.11); aftereffects on the parents due to the sucking (table 6.17). There is a gradation of tampering; the second domain is by far most significant in this respect, whereas the third domain presents an altogether different set of problems that can be handled much better in chapter 10, where we discuss the global psychological implications of the sucking on parents, in particular, and on kinsmen and neighbors, in general. The ensuing analysis deals exclusively with the primary actors identified above, but it is embedded in the general context of the household and neighborhood.

The Context of Unusual Events Surrounding the Victim's Sucking
The domain of unusual events surrounding the victim's sucking may be said to constitute the psychological context that most immediately frames, and to some extent conditions, the tlahuelpuchi's presence in the household for her evildoing. In this respect, table 6.16 does not tell the entire story. On the one hand, in many of the cases (particularly numbers 6, 8, 29, 32, 45, and 46) the victim's parents vividly reported a perception or physical state unmistakably related to the presence of the tlahuelpuchi. On the other hand, there are several cases in which nothing was reported or the presence of the tlahuelpuchi was implied by other members of the household. As we made clear in chapter 6, these answers and elicitations were the spontaneous statements, made by all concerned within a few hours, or at most a day, of the sucking event, which could be sifted from non-related or rather fantastic accounts of the tlahuelpuchi's modus operandi. What is not recorded in table 6.16 are the subsequent statements elicited from parents that spanned the entire postsucking period.

Thus, there are two kinds of tampering with the evidence (perhaps a more accurate way of putting it would be, tampering with the perceptions of real or imagined physical happenings): spontaneous, immediately after-the-fact and delayed, ex post facto rationalizations. It would have been cumbersome to summarize the latter in tabular form, but both types of tampering are important, and the analysis must be undertaken with reference to both. There are also two types of tampering with respect to subject matter: sighting the tlahuelpuchi in one of her animal forms or the manifestation of her telltale presence; and physical, psychosomatic states experienced by the mother or the father. These are quite different contexts, and they have to be analyzed separately.

In all cases of the sample, it was possible to elicit delayed, ex post facto tampering with sightings or with the telltale presence of the tlahuelpuchi about to strike. In general form and configuration it was not different from the spontaneous tamperings recorded in table 6.16, and on the whole it adhered to the general configuration of the normative belief of the complex. Its fabrication was evident, moreover, in the exaggerated emphasis on demonstrating the culpability of the tlahuelpuchi and the frequent departure from normative canons, especially by either humanizing the tlahuelpuchi (that is, making her act like a social person) or associating her with other anthropomorphic supernaturals (that is, vulgarizing the complex, as it were). Thus, even though the functions of spontaneous and delayed tampering are different, their similarity of form and configuration warrants their joint consideration. Three examples from table 6.16 are pertinent at this point.

Case 6 exemplifies the telltale presence of the tlahuelpuchi, both in the form of a turkey or buzzard and in her characteristic luminosity on the window of the mother's room. This is one of the most characteristic forms in which the tlahuelpuchi, about to strike, is experienced by mothers and occasionally, by fathers. Interestingly, this form of experienced perception appears to be quite patterned, since it was elicited or volunteered by most kinsmen and neighbors in the forty-seven–case sample, and it is a common feature of legends and accounts recounted or elicited under normal conditions. The most common variations on this theme are: parents experience the tlahuelpuchi moving from the window, crawling under the door of the room, and luminously reappearing in the form of a turkey; parents literally see the tlahuelpuchi getting into the room through the keyhole of the door in the form of an insect; and most commonly, the mother and occasionally the father wake up and find themselves confronted with the luminosity of the tlahuelpuchi invading the room. The reader should realize that when these experiences were told, both as volunteered statements and elicitations, they were made in categorical terms, without hesitation, and with the intention that the listener take them literally. This is the case even with delayed statements, in which the listener could gauge the distortion, exaggeration, or plain falsity of the account only in terms of context and associated meaning.

Case 45 is a good example of a joint father-mother statement about the vaho that the tlahuelpuchi employs to immobilize people or to put them into a deep sleep to commit her evil deed. Not quite as patterned as the previous example, this aspect of the tlahuelpuchi's modus operandi is commonly verbalized by parents, kinsmen, and neighbors in the postsucking period, and it appears frequently in legends and normal accounts, with the following variations: the mist-like substance enters the room through the keyhole or from under the door; it seeps in through the window of the room or through tile roofs to invade the entire room; in the midst of the vaho the tlahuelpuchi materializes as a turkey or buzzard ready to strike; she fixes her eyes on the mother or other persons in the room and hypnotizes them into a deep sleep; and so on. There are a number of permutations of these basic themes, but the end results are the same: establishment of the tlahuelpuchi's presence in or just outside the house leading to the point when she is ready to strike, and the ostensible demonstration of the two main subterfuges with which she immobilizes people to suck infants. Then there are the delayed statements of mothers or fathers to the effect that they really tried and fought hard, usually in a slumbering semiconscious state of awareness, but ultimately succumbed to the powers of the tlahuelpuchi; and the normal statements and legendary and semilegendary accounts in which individuals manage successfully to repel the tlahuelpuchi, even to kill her in the ensuing battle of wills, or, as one of the more literate informants put it about one such case in beautiful, almost knight-errant Spanish, "y derrotó a la malvada en desigual cambate" (and he defeated the evil one against all odds).

Finally, a statement in one of the cases of the Xolotla epidemic (number 8 in the sample), also elicited jointly from the victim's mother and father, is a good example of sighting the tlahuelpuchi and experiencing her powers of immobilization. Especially in delayed-elicited statements, there were many joint or separate assertions made by mothers and fathers which corroborated the physical or the telltale presence of the tlahuelpuchi. It was impossible to establish the validity of such statements (that is, whether they were real or imaginary perceptions, arrived at independently of what the mother and the father actually experienced), and that is why they were not included in table 6.16, except in the case of Filemón Teyohualmiqui and Francisca Sandoval (see chapter 5). We are inclined to think that there was no "conspiracy" on the part of mothers and fathers to tamper with the manifestation of the tlahuelpuchi; rather, what is involved here is "cultural" tampering, the result of the deeply internalized belief system, independently verbalized by mothers and fathers with the latent, unconscious aim of displacing guilt, assuaging anxiety, and validating the bloodsucking witchcraft complex. It is this kind of tampering that is most common and, in one form and degree or another, verbalized by most involved kinsmen and neighbors.

The second kind of ascertainable unusual events are exclusively experienced by mothers and fathers, for perpetrators of infanticide and other individuals who may regard themselves as directly or indirectly responsible for the sucking of an infant do not manifest any discernible physical or psychosomatic states. If they do have them, they obviously hide them; nor did kinsmen or neighbors ever offer any clues about the possibility that mothers-in-law or other members of the household experienced such states. The initial, spontaneous physical and psychosomatic states experienced by parents sooner rather than later in the postsucking period (see table 6.16) give rise to some personal disturbance experienced by mothers and fathers. These are the states of withdrawal and moroseness that were observed in almost all cases of the sample. Some delayed manifestations were the following: inability to fall asleep and serious insomnia; recurrent nightmares; an inordinate amount of daydreaming; fear of the dark; a tendency to wander away from the house for no apparent reason; a tendency to sit alone by the hearth. Most interestingly, at least 15 mothers of the sample forthrightly stated that they wanted to go home to their own kinsmen—that is, return to their households of orientation. This was more pronounced in younger mothers—that is, those under 30, who probably justifiably felt ill treated and that their circumstance lacked warmth, and sought the closeness and understanding of their own consanguines. The physical and psychosomatic states experienced by parents are, as a rule, more pronounced in women than in men, and they last longer. Since the immediate, spontaneous physical and psychosomatic states experienced by parents give rise to the more serious aftereffects, we stop here for they will be discussed in the following chapter.

The tampering with the spontaneous, or delayed, physical and psychosomatic states experienced by primary actors (readily observed in parents but only surmised or implied in infanticide perpetrators and other responsible personnel) are easily explained; their causes can be determined with a modicum of accuracy, as we will discuss below. But the tampering with spontaneous or delayed perceptions of primary actors, and by extension of all concerned kinsmen and neighbors, is altogether a different matter. The fundamental question that must be asked is, What are the physical and psychological referents of the perceptions that rural Tlaxcalans magnify, distort, exaggerate, and rationalize about the tlahuelpuchi anteceding, during, and succeeding the sucking event? Concomitantly, What is the ontological provenance of these referents and how are they sociopsychologically and culturally reinterpreted? A third important question that comes to mind is, What are the epistemological implications of the real, imagined, and distorted perceptions of bloodsucking witchcraft for the transposition of causation? Here, we discuss the first question in some detail and briefly present the main outlines of the second question; we will analyze the third question exhaustively in chapter 12.

Even though at times we have suggested that it was not possible to determine whether a magnification or distortion of an attribute or manifestation of the tlahuelpuchi was real or imagined, it is evident that, perceptually speaking, no witchcraft system or construction can be entirely projective—a construction of images and non-related empirical perceptions composed in "someone's head." Rather, perceptions of the tlahuelpuchi and of any element in her realm of action have either a specific, clear physical or psychological referent or they constitute a combination of a fuzzy, diffused physical or psychological referent and an imagined component. By a physical referent we mean a thing, animal, or occurrence in the empirical environment that upon being perceived may trigger distortions, magnifications, or exaggerations. By a psychological referent we mean a state of consciousness produced by the reinforcing effect of stories and the general knowledge of the tlahuelpuchi complex (which all traditional rural Tlaxcalans have by the time they marry and begin to procreate) and occasionally hallucinatory or disconnected states produced by shock (upon the realization of the infant's death and the accompanying culpability), pronounced fear, and anxiety. Note, however, that physical and psychological referents not only reinforce each other in producing distortions, magnifications, and exaggerations, but they are both obviously conditioned. Furthermore, these physical and psychological referents condition in turn the spontaneous as well as delayed perceptions, not only of primary actors, but of all secondary actors immediately concerned as well. More concretely, let us discuss in some detail the possible permutation of these inputs.

In varying degrees, all witchcraft systems are perceptually embedded in physical reality: animals, plants, things, objects, events, and occurrences in the natural, empirical environment are posited to bridge the gap between normative expectations and physical realizations. In the case of the tlahuelpuchi complex, these physical referents are: the turkey, donkey, buzzard, small insects, and other animals into which the witch can transform herself; the luminosity of fireflies; the asserted actions of the witch, such as leaving the sucked infant by the ajar door; and so on. Thus, when a father returns home late during the night of a sucking and sees a turkey perched on a tree near the house or a donkey in the milpa, they may constitute perceptual referents for the ex post facto account that he tells or is elicited from him next day, magnified or distorted to the extent that he recounts the presence of a flying turkey or the telltale luminosity of the tlahuelpuchi accompanying the donkey. Similarly, the mother could have actually seen a chicken or a turkey on the window of the sleeping room as she was falling asleep, or experienced actual fog on the window or smoke filtering under the door from an incompletely extinguished fire on the hearth, which, after the fact, she recounts in the distorted and magnified fashion described for several cases of table 6.16. The contexts and physical entities that serve as perceptual referents for the validation of the tlahuelpuchi are many and varied, but they probably are not the most significant set of inputs that result in the manipulations described above. Rather, physical referents constitute the empirical underpinnings of a supernatural complex that was historically structured as bloodsucking witchcraft. In other words, physical referents are the foundation blocks of reinforcing mechanisms.

Psychological referents, in contrast, may be regarded as the most effective inputs in molding the perception of bloodsucking witchcraft. Here the manipulation and tampering—or the distortions and magnifications—consist in the mostly associated verbalization by primary actors (and marginally by secondary actors) of the ideology and belief system of the tlahuelpuchi complex, generally adhering to the normative structure but occasionally departing from it and elaborating certain details while magnifying others to fit a particular sucking situation. To put it differently, the perception of the tlahuelpuchi by the mother and father in a specific case of sucking is posited on the normative system as transmitted to them by their exposure since childhood to stories, accounts, actual suckings, and the intensive period of verbalization that ensues. By the beginning of their reproductive careers, traditional rural Tlaxcalan parents have thoroughly internalized the normative system of bloodsucking witchcraft, and most likely experienced one or more suckings first hand. This set of essentially psychological referents constitutes the single most powerful perceptual input of the tlahuelpuchi's efficacy to kill. The conditioning and reinforcing power of psychological referents so conceived cannot be underestimated, for in the absence of specific or diffused physical referents, they determine the distorted, magnified, and often skewed perceptions of the phenomenon as verbalized ex post facto. For example, some of the most elaborate verbalizations, particularly of mothers, elicited or recounted spontaneously and shortly after the sucking may not have involved immediate physical referents; the experience of the tlahuelpuchi's vaho, her telltale presence in the room as a turkey or buzzard surrounded by luminosity, the ensuing battle of wills, and so on are largely psychological referents embedded in the mothers' store of knowledge of the normative tlahuelpuchi complex.

Nutini has firsthand experience of the reinforcing and conditioning power of the normative belief system intensely verbalized. One of the several witch hunts in which he participated took place after two infants in adjoining parajes (cases 13 and 14) were sucked during the same night. The people of the parajes had been subjected to a barrage of accounts and stories for two days. The parajes' attention was obsessively concerned with the tlahuelpuchi when the word spread in the early evening that she was prowling the area. Quickly and efficiently, three hunting parties were organized, and even the usual or marginal skeptics were swept by the highly charged atmosphere of the moment and the reinforced belief that the tlahuelpuchi was indeed prowling the area in search of more infants to suck. He clearly recalls the powerful ambience created by a combination of stress, on the one hand, and the conditioning effect of days of immersion in the normative system of bloodsucking witchcraft, on the other. In retrospect, the unreal, irrational activity of running after fireflies believing that they were the telltale signs of the tlahuelpuchi was at the time almost completely drowned by the literally overwhelming, mesmerizing efficacy of the verbalized normative system. Nutini remembers participation in this particular witch hunt as a suspension of his scientific faculties, as if he had been forcibly conditioned to believe that he was indeed hunting tlahuelpuchis. Perhaps the effect may be described as some sort of temporary, non-violent brainwashing, conditioned by the ominous ambience of the postsucking period and fear of the unknown.

The reader can easily imagine how much more effective the cumulative conditioning of the normative belief system of the tlahuelpuchi complex would be, say, upon an impressionable young mother, or even upon an experienced one, realizing in the middle of the night that her infant is dead. It is our claim that the shock of apprehending that she may be directly or indirectly guilty (by commission or omission) of the death of her infant constitutes the main factor that configures the perceptual experience of the tlahuelpuchi during the night of the sucking, expressed ex post facto in variations of well-internalized culturally normative themes, as partially exemplified in table 6.16. By extension, the same, in a less dramatic and delayed fashion, obtains for all other actors directly or indirectly concerned with the sucking.

The accounts elicited from several mothers (especially in cases 4, 8, 16, 45, and 46), no more than five or six hours after the victim's body had been discovered, had a dream-like, disassociated quality that can perhaps be described as hallucinatory. For example, the statement recorded for the mother in case 16 was elicited the following day. But what she expressed less than four hours after the corpse of her infant was discovered was a somewhat garbled, rather improbable statement (normatively speaking) in which: the tlahuelpuchi had materialized in a big explosion of fire out of the floor; the tlahuelpuchi had danced in the form of a strange bird about the room; the tlahuelpuchi had held her to the bed with her beak to put her to sleep; and after fighting very hard, she had inhaled the vaho discharged by the tlahuelpuchi and passed out. Interestingly, when she was interviewed the following morning, by then withdrawn and in a rather intense state of moroseness, the mother did not remember any of this elaborate statement, and instead volunteered the statement shown in table 6.16. Roughly one-fourth of the women of the sample exhibited hallucinatory or disassociated elements. The same is true of six or seven mothers, not in the sample, who were interviewed over the years but whose cases of sucking were not systematically recorded. Invariably, however, the mothers exhibiting these psychological symptoms made the most elaborate statements of unusual events transpiring during the night of the sucking. What this means theoretically for the explanation of bloodsucking witchcraft we do not know, but it does once more suggest the power of psychological referents in shaping the perception of the tlahuelpuchi in particular and of the sucking event in general.

To summarize, the physical referents of the tlahuelpuchi complex's perceptual reality constitute the historical, necessary inputs which generate whatever tamperings are involved in bloodsucking witchcraft. In the case of parents, the actors most closely associated with the victim, physical referents usually do not play a significant role (that is, usually no fireflies are seen, no turkeys experienced, or no smoke or fog misinterpreted as vaho), while they most likely do in the recounted perceptions of secondary actors (see tables 6.16 and 6.17). Psychological referents, however, are not only more widespread, but they constitute the immediate, sufficient conditions which shape the perceptions of the tlahuelpuchi complex in its entire array: the elaborate, sometimes hallucinatory, constructions of primary actors; the less elaborate but equally validating constructions of secondary actors.

Two additional points need to be emphasized here. First, the hypothesis that the degree of tampering with the perceptions of the tlahuelpuchi complex is directly related to the guilt and culpability experienced by primary actors (as the most directly responsible for the death of infants) did occur to us in the early stages of the data analysis. Logical as it sounds, as we indicated, it must remain a hypothesis. With the data presently available, it cannot be verified, since this operation, undertaken today, would entail psychological methods that would probably no longer be effective, given the fact that bloodsucking witchcraft in rural Tlaxcala has changed drastically over the last generation. Second, the question that, given their similarity of form, What are the differential functions of spontaneous and delayed tampering with the perceptions of bloodsucking witchcraft? The answer to this question is tentative, but it should be emphasized that functional assignment in dealing with witchcraft is always risky. The functions of spontaneous tampering are essentially to displace and assuage guilt for primary actors, through their own actions or those of secondary actors, while the function of delayed tampering is mainly to validate the tlahuelpuchi complex and perpetuate it as an ad hoc explanation for infant death. To put it differently, individual guilt is expressed in spontaneous tampering, whereas collective guilt and concern is twice-removed after the facts in delayed tampering throughout the postsucking period.

The Context of the Position and Location of the Victim's Body upon Discovery
So far normative, ideological tampering with the various elements of the tlahuelpuchi complex has been discussed and analyzed; the term tampering, in this sense, was used both literally and metaphorically. Now we examine tampering exclusively in its literal, physical sense in the single domain in which it is undertaken by primary actors. While one may surmise that some sort of physical tampering takes place in connection with the approximate time of finding the victim's body and perhaps in other of the domains discussed above, the only absolutely ascertainable tampering takes place in the domain of the location and position of the victim's body upon discovery, as shown in table 6.11. There is no way to interpret the empirical facts of most of the cases of table 6.11 without assuming that humans willfully and deliberately tampered with the physical evidence when infants were sucked by the tlahuelpuchi—that is, when infants died as the result of the causes analyzed above. Whereas the position and location of some of the corpses can be explained as a natural concomitant of the conditions under which death took place, most of the cases cannot be so explained, unless one assumes the impossible—that is, that infants less than ten months old can move by themselves to positions and locations from five to a dozen or more yards away.

In more than two-thirds of the cases of the sample, as shown in table 6.11, there is no possible alternative but to conclude that mothers, mothers-in-law, other possible perpetrators of infanticide, or household members (most likely fathers, elder sisters, and elder brothers) directly or indirectly responsible for the death of the infant deliberately moved the victim's body to a position and location consonant with what the normative belief system specifies about the tlahuelpuchi's efficacy to kill. Given the fact that neither the identity of the infanticide perpetrator, whether the mother-in-law or anyone else, nor the culpability of other household personnel can be ascertained, let alone proved, and insofar as the mothers of the victims are unquestionably the most directly responsible for their infants' deaths, one must center the analysis on the mothers and regard them as the tamperers par excellence. Nonetheless, the actions of infanticide perpetrators or any responsible household members are in all probability the same as those of the mothers.

Let us first reconstruct the physical setting and events leading to the actual act of tampering. Again, we must remind the reader that this is a probabilistic reconstruction, but one that fits whatever observed and recorded facts we control. In legal terms, one could say that we are dealing with hearsay evidence, which is obviously the best one can do, given the great difficulty of obtaining harder and more direct evidence without hypnotizing the mothers of the sample, giving them sodium pentathol, or using any method (if there are any) which would have elicited from them what really transpired during the night of the sucking.

Discounting the case of the seven-year-old boy (the most anomalous in the sample), we find in table 6.11 that there are thirteen cases (2, 5, 16, 18, 21, 22, 23, 25, 27, 30, 33, 34, and 46) in which there appears to have been no tampering with the victim's body, whereas in all thirty-three other cases there was definite tampering. Let us take a closer look at this breakdown. The thirteen non-tampering cases are those in which mothers did not, consciously or unconsciously, in any fashion move the victim's body — that is, the position and location of the bodies upon discovery indicate that no one had touched them until then; in six cases (18, 21, 22, 23, 34, and 46) the bodies were found faceup in their cribs or petates, probably in the same position in which they choked after their mothers had put them to sleep (see page 244); whereas in seven cases (2, 5, 16, 25, 27, 30, and 33) the bodies most likely rolled from their mothers' beds or petates after they had been smothered to death, coming to rest in the position and location in which they were found. In cases 2 and 25, however, in which the bodies were found two yards from their mothers' petates, it is quite possible that the mothers (perhaps because of laziness or of their slumberous state) put the infants there after discovering that they were dead rather than in the normative, diagnostic position in which the tlahuelpuchi leaves the victim's body after the sucking. Given the acknowledged fact that mothers try to minimize blame directed against them by displacing it to the tlahuelpuchi, regardless of whether they feel guilty or responsible for the death of their infants, we can explain non-tampering cases as the mothers' unawareness that their infants had died until the bodies were discovered.

In two of the thirty-three cases of tampering (8 and 12), there was apparently no tampering with the body of the victim but only with the door of the room, leaving it open or ajar, one of the significant diagnostic traits of the tlahuelpuchi. In the remaining thirty-one cases of the sample (and at least another dozen of cases not systematically observed) there is a combination of tampering actions, all of which fall within the range of the tlahuelpuchi's normative belief system: the victim's body is found in the courtyard, in front of the room's door, inside or outside the open or ajar door, next to the mother's or a kinsman's petate with the door ajar, or variations of these basic positions and locations. For the reasons given above, upon discovering the dead infant (or no more than an hour later), the mother (and by extension a mother-in-law or father infanticide perpetrator, an elder sister, or any other responsible household female) consciously or unconsciously places the victim's body in the position and location in which it is discovered. It is our contention that she takes this action instinctively, without guilt or culpability (which comes later) entering into her mental frame of reference, for she knows by experience that in so doing she minimizes blame and makes sure that her husband will not punish her for any real or imagined carelessness. All potential tamperers are probably governed by the same frame of reference and the same aim of escaping blame. Perhaps only mothers-in-law, as infanticide perpetrators, do not quite fit this explanation, for if their aim is to punish daughters-in-law, the punishment would be increased by letting the latter bear the burden of the tampering if they become aware of the infant's death before discovery. Yet, it is quite likely that the mothers-in-law's own conditioning by previous suckings may compel them to tamper with the evidence themselves. It should be clear, however, that the moving of the victim's body to the position and location in which it is discovered is always the same, regardless of whoever of the actors identified above does the tampering. Moreover, the physical context and the psychological frame of reference are the same, and the aim, with the exception of the mother-in-law's, is also always the same—namely, to demonstrate with a physical action that the tlahuelpuchi did indeed kill the infant.

The reconstruction of the actions and happenings during the night, before and after the death of the infant, is important to understand the psychological ambience in which the sucking takes place and the perception of the event by the mother, father, and other actors. As we demonstrated above, this is a rather conjectural undertaking, but a necessary one to the enterprise here. It is particularly conjectural from the moment the mother realizes that her infant is dead (and by extension, from the moment a perpetrator kills the infant) until its body is found by a household member, neighbor, or herself, at which point the evidence of the bloodsucking event becomes public and verifiable. But the following reconstruction, conjectural as it is, still has a significant degree of reliability.

As discussed in chapter 6, the estimated time of the infant's death is about one to three hours before the corpse is discovered. The first question that comes to mind is, When, relative to the time of discovery and the moment death occurred, was the instant the mother realized that her infant was dead? The answer to this question is no more than a guess, and ours is that it varies significantly, but that it is probably closer to the time of discovering the body than to the actual moment of death. Rural Tlaxcalan mothers usually breast-feed their children after midnight as they settle infants for the night. Our guess is that most infants believed to have been sucked by the tlahuelpuchi die between one and three o'clock in the morning and that, usually, perhaps an hour or more elapses until their mothers realize they are dead. The second question that must be asked is, How long after realizing that the infant is dead do mothers place the body in the position and location in which it is discovered or open the door of the room or leave it ajar? This is also a difficult question to answer, and our guess is that it takes place immediately or no more than an hour afterward. The fact that in eighteen of the thirty-three cases the door was found open or ajar when the infant was discovered indicates that not much time elapsed between tampering and discovery, for early mornings in rural Tlaxcala are crisp or cold, and those sleeping in the room would awaken earlier than normal because of the cold. Perhaps more important than this timetable is the fact that the tampering is most likely done instinctively, and mothers do not ponder much on the alternatives before taking action. This is as far as one can probabilistically reconstruct the actions of the mother and the timetable of unfolding events.

Mothers were singularly uncooperative about recounting what had tran-spired during the night, when they were interviewed within a few hours after the discovery of the body or a day or more afterward. As we indicated, they would talk freely enough about the unusual events that they experienced prior to the time of the alleged sucking, but about whatever happened between the verbalized unusual event and the time the body was discovered, they would refuse to say anything, alleging that they fell into a deep sleep or could not remember anything since they last saw their infants alive, usually at the time of settling them for the night after breast-feeding them. The courtroom accu-racy of the reconstruction is not high, but it is accurate enough to demonstrate the culturally patterned nature of the events and happenings that transpire when an infant dies as the result of the people's belief that he was sucked by the tlahuelpuchi. It also provides the general parameters for understanding the social and psychological ambience of the event.

What strikes one as odd and out of place, in the immediate and delayed interviews that followed the sucking, was the support that the father of the victim afforded the mother. In all forty-seven cases of the sample, and in many cases not systematically studied, no suspicion was ever detected on the part of the father about the responsibility and culpability of the mother in the death of the infant, despite the suspicion that was manifested by many husbands in the sample when they were not the fathers of sucking victims. Moreover, there was almost a concerted effort on the part of the husband to vouch for the mother's contention that the tlahuelpuchi had indeed killed the infant: the father also asserted having experienced some unusual event, he assented to the mother's perception of the sucking event by contributing supporting details, or recounted other suckings he had experienced as a household member to buttress his wife's account. The oddity of the situation resides in the incongruity between the exaggerated expectation of the mother that she would be accused of negligence in caring for the infant (the main motivating input to tampering with the body) and the support in every respect that she receives from her husband, even though she knows from past experience, or from what she has heard in her household of orientation since childhood, that he may voice suspicion of other mothers in similar situations. We cannot entirely explain this incongruity, except perhaps to say that the experience of unrealized expectations is not as significant a psychological factor as preserving the integrity of the nuclear family. The same, of course, obtains in the wider context of secondary actors, in which, despite latent or manifest suspicions, there is generally strong support for the parents of the victim. This is what has been referred to as an almost concerted ambience validating the tlahuelpuchi complex in every sucking. It should be clear, of course, that it is primarily the mother, but occasionally the father or other household member, who is initially responsible for establishing that the death of an infant was indeed the work of the tlahuelpuchi (and not a case of natural death due to a specific illness) by tampering with the body and finding it in the normative position and location. One can see, then, that the sucking event (in its immediate antecedent and succeeding elements) is structured by the physical tampering of the mother and the psychological tampering of the father in an ambience of support and complementation, as if all concerned were afraid of lessening in any way the validation of the bloodsucking complex and its most useful function of displacing guilt and assuaging stress and anxiety.

Whatever the timetable is, from the actual death of the infant to the mother realizing that it is dead to the discovery of the body, the primary consideration that governs tampering with the position and location of the corpse is fundamentally the cause of death, for it has been assumed all along that mothers instinctively play it safe (as do perpetrators of infanticide and other responsible females for related reasons), even if they do not regard themselves as directly or indirectly responsible for the death of their infants. Thus, during day suckings, there is probably no tampering with the body either because there is not time for it or because the mother was accompanied by other people all along; in cases of choking, which invariably take place in the infant's crib or petate, the mother is most likely not alerted, or alerted too late, to do any tampering before the time of discovery; in all other cases (that is, asphyxia, suffocation, and infanticide), the mother is almost invariably alerted or wakes up with sufficient time to tamper with the body in the normative manner. We have made a few guesses about when the mother does the tampering, but whether she moves and positions the body immediately or waits until later in the morning, her actions may be described as a conditioned reflex of the cultural milieu of the household that centers about the tlahuelpuchi complex. Instinctive though we have described her actions, they are nonetheless culturally conditioned and configured since they show a rather remarkable regularity in the variations of and departures from a common normative theme.

In conclusion, as the central, most diagnostic physical element of the bloodsucking complex, the position and location of the victim's body upon discovery is the direct result of the mother's (or the mother-in-law's or any responsible person's) realization that the infant has died; the ensuing behavior is culturally conditioned and psychologically directed at displacing guilt, avoiding blame, and assuaging culpability. More than any other physical manifestation of the bloodsucking complex, the discovery of the body in the normative position and location pinpoints the action of the tlahuelpuchi, leading to noticing and verbalizing other diagnostic normative elements and to the verbalization of the reinforcing, intensifying, and validating accounts that characterize the spontaneous and delayed statements of all concerned actors during the postsucking period. (In the cases in which it is apparent that there was no tampering [thirteen in all], other physical elements are initially emphasized, but they are probably not as immediately reinforcing as the position and location of the victim's body upon discovery.) From this crucial moment onward, the feedback effect of the normative belief system comes into play, and primary and secondary actors manifestly behave according to the latent psychological conditioning of past bloodsucking experiences. As we have demonstrated in at least two contexts, this psychosocial ambience of the global phenomenon (from the discovery of the victim's body until the end of the postsucking period) comes as quickly as it goes, for probably a few years will pass before a new sucking will take place in the household. The household's quick return to normality after a few days is another anomaly that has not been explained, particularly when one realizes that when the tlahuelpuchi strikes again, the same stress and anxiety will set in just as quickly. Perhaps this can be explained by the high incidence of bloodsucking witchcraft and the pragmatic, almost detached (but ritually and ceremonially very concerned) attitude of rural Tlaxcalans toward all supernatural actions and occurrences.

CONSCIOUS OR UNCONSCIOUS BEHAVIOR: STATE OF FUGUE, ALTERED STATES, OR WHAT?

Finally, we would like to discuss a fundamental point that has underlined the analysis in this and the foregoing chapter—namely, the ontological nature of the verbal, physical, and psychological distortions, exaggerations, magnifications, manipulations, rationalizations, and tamperings (as we have variously called them) engaged in by primary and secondary actors from the moment of discovering the victim's body until the end of the postsucking period. At several junctures and occasions we asked parenthetically whether the various kinds of actions, behaviors, and statements of primary and secondary actors were psychologically conscious or unconscious, or culturally patterned and conditioned, so as to demonstrate social awareness or lack of it. This problem has been dealt with elsewhere in the context of the substantive and conceptual implications of the socially conscious-unconscious in the conduct of cultural studies (Nutini 1984:172–80). Here we want to indicate simply that it is important to distinguish between the conscious or unconscious nature of the data we work with, and also between the conscious or unconscious configuration of the concepts built after the data. There is no theory of the social unconscious, but in dealing with a phenomenon like witchcraft, with a pronounced psychological component, it is of primary importance to distinguish the conscious or unconscious provenance of the data to go beyond strictly sociofunctional explanations. Thus, even though anthropologists and sociologists have not yet operationalized what constitutes conscious and unconscious social phenomena, one can certainly distinguish data gathered subject-directed (informants are aware of the polystranded relationship of the data in question to other data) from data collected by circumlocution (informants are not aware of the implication for other levels of meaning of the data in question). (A good example of this quandary is that in any culture there are domains in which people can verbalize what they do, but not what they "should do"—that is, the latent or manifest rule or injunction behind the action; whereas in other domains they can verbalize both. When the rule or injunction is latent, the ensuing action is unconscious; when the rule or injunction is manifest, the ensuing action is conscious. This rule of thumb constitutes a partial operationalization of the socially conscious and unconscious, and it is of vital importance in dealing with phenomena that must be explained essentially in psychological terms, such as the problem of bloodsucking witchcraft as formulated in this monograph.)

Nonetheless, one can speak with some propriety about the conscious and unconscious in psychological terms, both in the commonsense usage of these concepts and in the various ways they have been used by psychologists and psychiatrists. Thus, this section briefly discusses the general conscious-unconscious social parameters that structure specific psychological configurations of behavior and action of primary and secondary actors. First, we consider the social conscious-unconscious provenance of the distortions, manipulations, and rationalizations of all concerned primary and secondary actors, and, second, we discuss the psychological nature of physical tampering centered on the mother. If nothing else, the latter operation sheds light on the specific problem of the psychological framework in which supernatural inputs "cause" or result in natural outputs in a well-delineated witchcraft event.

The Manipulations of All Concerned Primary and Secondary Actors

The understanding and explanation of the bloodsucking witchcraft system of rural Tlaxcala is a good example of how behavior acquires conceptual meaning only after the ideological (what people should do) and the structural (what people actually do under certain conditions) nature of the actions are clearly specified and positioned vis-à-vis one another. It would have been impossible to understand, let alone explain, the tlahuelpuchi complex without, on the one hand, having systematically laid out the normative beliefs system, and on the other, having carefully structured the physical manifestation of the system. Only as these two dimensions are placed in a position of interaction is the system understood, and at least a partial explanation emerges concerning the different kinds of infant death attributed to the tlahuelpuchi. In implementing these basic operations, distinguishing between what is directly elicited from informants and what is gathered by circumlocution (indirectly elicited, correlating informants' answers, changing frames of reference, and so on) and assessing whether informants are conscious (aware) or unconscious (unaware) of the implications, levels of meaning, and relatedness of their verbalizations, behaviors, and actions is a necessary condition for undertaking the study of witchcraft, sorcery, or any other system in which supernatural inputs produce natural outcomes.

The questions are, then, Are the manipulations (distortions, exaggerations, and rationalizations) of all concerned primary and secondary actors of the sucking events conscious or unconscious, or what? Concomitantly, Has it been possible to scale, in any systematic or approximate fashion, the degree of consciousness or unconsciousness of the informants' manipulations?

In response to the first question, there is essentially a gradation of consciousness-unconsciousness configured as follows. The primary and secondary actors who rationalize (essentially, verbalizing and making efforts to reinforce and validate the tlahuelpuchi complex) do so largely unconsciously—that is, neither individuals nor kinsmen and neighbors as a group are aware of the intended results, nor are they aware of the rationalization's effect on the self-fulfilling nature of the complex—for example, when a sucking occurs and kinsmen and neighbors make a patent, concerted effort to buttress the tlahuelpuchi's efficacy to kill with a barrage of statements and legendary and semilegendary accounts that characterize the postsucking period. Most individuals as well as groups of kinsmen and neighbors probably distort more consciously than they rationalize; put another way, some categories of actors can perhaps catch a glimmer of the intended results of distortion and occasionally establish connections with particular aspects of the bloodsucking complex. For example, a household member or neighbor may distort the perception of a turkey on a tree or near the house of the victim during the night of the sucking into an elaborate perception of the tlahuelpuchi maneuvering for the attack. The individual, supported by the group, probably thinks or is faintly aware that his or her verbalized distortion corroborates the presence of the witch about to strike, or that his statement lends credence to previous statements made by other actors. Those who exaggerate do not do so, for the most part, exactly consciously, but have a certain degree of awareness that their exaggerations relate to other perceptions verbalized with definite aims. Exaggerations, in a way, are the catalyst that hold together the mass of manipulations designed to validate, reinforce, and intensify the tlahuelpuchi complex in discharging the various social and psychological functions discussed above. Any exaggeration concerning most of the ten domains discussed in the preceding section are to be regarded in this fashion, whether they are verbalizations of previous suckings, fanciful stories about the tlahuelpuchi, or actions such as trying to fake protection of infants against being sucked.

In summary response to the second question, we can say that the foregoing gradation, approximate as it is, constitutes a scale of consciousness-unconsciousness in which most manipulations are much closer to the conscious than to the unconscious limit; or we may say that although there may be completely unconscious manipulations, there are no completely conscious ones. While we may construe manipulations of perceptions of the tlahuelpuchi complex as individually (psychologically) conscious or unconscious, it is better to regard them as socially conscious or unconscious, for they are definitely culturally patterned, and there is little or no intragroup (the complex of household members and neighbors) deviation. To put it differently, the various elements, happenings, and occurrences of the sucking event and its antecedents and succeeding developments constitute a domain, the perception of which is posited on the juxtaposition of normative expectations and physical realization. And the conceptualization of this domain cannot be totally understood unless one specifies the conscious-unconscious axis. From still another standpoint, the explanatory value of the conscious-unconscious axis (scaling) lies essentially in the fact that, ontologically, behavior must be regarded as an expression of different epistemological substrata—that is, any piece of observable behavior is explained only if we can determine its motivation. If we can determine why a group of individuals is consciously or unconsciously motivated, we can explain a good deal about behavior itself.

The Mother's Tampering with the Position and Location of the Victim's Body
Shifting from group, social consciousness-unconsciousness to the individual, we conclude the analysis with a single, specific type of physical tampering— namely, the position and location of the victim's body upon discovery. It has definitively been established that in most cases of bloodsucking witchcraft, the mother (and by extension suicide perpetrators and other responsible females of the household) positions and locates the body of her dead infant in accordance with the normative belief expectations of the tlahuelpuchi complex. The question is, Is the mother conscious or unconscious when after realizing that it is dead, she handles the body of her infant and places it in a position and location consonant with normative expectations, almost invariably deviating little from what the tlahuelpuchi does after she strikes? Can she remember in the morning (when the body is discovered and thereafter) what she did during the night after she realized her infant was dead? These are difficult questions to answer, and even a better corpus of data than now exists would yield only partial answers. Perhaps some psychological technique or some kind of psychiatric analysis, at present largely unsuitable to the field situation, could answer these questions definitively. Nonetheless, we try to elucidate them and give some partial answers.

The most likely scenario of what transpires during the night of the sucking in rural Tlaxcala follows. Upon realizing that her infant has been smothered to death, has choked, or has died due to causes unknown to her, the mother goes into some sort of shock; whatever happens until she is confronted with the corpse of her infant (usually found by household kinsmen, occasionally by neighbors, but very seldom by the mother herself) is nebulous to her; occurrences are blurred and consciously disconnected. This is the vivid impression of two mothers interviewed less than two hours after the body had been discovered, and many household informants described mothers after the sucking as "como aturdidas, sin hacerse entender bien, y como si no estuvieran enterament presentes" (as dazed, incoherent, and as if they were not altogether there). There is no question that mothers, whether one regards them as being in a state of consciousness or unconsciousness, are by no means normal but in some kind of altered state when they "awaken" on the morning of the sucking. Although it would be difficult to prove, it is highly likely that this altered state of the mother is triggered by the realization of her infant's death and remains with her for many hours after discovery of the victim's body. Thus, ascertaining that the infant is dead (by removing it from the breast, from under blankets or clothes, and so on), placing it by the door left open or ajar, and whatever other actions she undertakes are most likely automatic, and done in a trance-like, slumbering state. Whether she actually ponders taking such tampering actions (thinking, of course, of potential blame and possible punishment) it is obviously impossible to determine, but probably this is also instinctive and automatic. There can be no doubt, however, that the mother's actions, thoughts, and state of being are culturally conditioned and well internalized by mothers early in their reproductive careers. From this viewpoint, the psychological framework of mothers when the tlahuelpuchi strikes is constrained and configured by the competence they have of the normative belief system, which they know, if it is to be effective, cannot deviate unduly from its norms. The normative system sets the parameters of the psychological state in which the mother functions after the awful, devastating realization that her infant is dead and that she may have been entirely or partially responsible for the incident.

Essentially, the syndrome of tampering with the infant's corpse is not a black-and-white question of whether the mother is conscious or unconscious throughout the period between the realization of death and the discovery of the body (and for some time afterward) but of something else. Searching for a psychological or psychiatric explanation of this phenomenon, we came upon the concept of fugue that appears to apply most closely to the present syndrome (Doren L. Slade, personal communication). This is not a definitive answer, and there may be alternative psychological or psychiatric explanations. The concept of fugue, however, seems to explain the mother's psychological state in the present context. Hinsie and Campbell (*Psychiatric Dictionary*, 1981:309) define state of fugue as follows:

> In psychiatry today, the term means a flight, so to speak, from reality in the sense that the individual becomes more or less completely unmindful of his environment and often of himself. He enters into a phase of so-called psychological amnesia, in which he may frequently seem to possess all his mental faculties, but questioning may reveal complete or partial amnesia for certain experiences. . . . A condition in which the patient leaves his previous experience and begins to wander, or goes into a journey which has no apparent relationship to what he has been doing, and for which he has amnesia afterward.

In most cases the state of fugue is precipitated by the need to escape an intolerable situation produced by fear, shame, guilt, or perhaps other inputs. In the case of the mother realizing that her infant is dead, the shock of fear and guilt most likely precipitates the state of fugue, and it is in this altered state that she remains until at least the discovery of the corpse, if not, as is most likely, for many hours afterward. Yet, is she conscious or unconscious of her actions and thoughts while she places the body by the door, leaves the door open or ajar, and does whatever else she does until the time of discovery? We guess that she is neither; rather, she is in a kind of intermediary state, as informants well describe it, for the morning after. In a sense this is an academic question, for she appears not to remember what actions and thoughts she had while she tampered with the infant's body, at least until she returns to normality—that is, until she is no longer in a state of fugue. A more appropriate question is, does she remember five or ten days later when she is herself again what transpired during the night? Our guess is that she does, and that the experience becomes part of her culturally conditioned competence of the tlahuelpuchi complex.

As we have shown, the acceptable evidence (not deductive guesses) comes partly from direct observation and partly from the accounts of kinsmen and neighbors in which mothers in the postsucking period often exhibit the symptoms of being in a state of fugue. But the symptoms and general psychological behavior of mothers throughout this period (which may occasionally last for two weeks) is not conclusive evidence that, regardless of whether they are in a state or fugue, they are unconscious of what happened during the night of the sucking. On the one hand, the mother's reticence to talk about the night's happenings, subtle clues here and there, and the fact that very few mothers (only three in the sample, discounting the two day suckings) discover the corpse (given the close, often cramped quarters of the average household) are indications that mothers are not in a state of fugue and that they do remember, at least partially, but try to avoid being confronted with what transpired from the moment they realized their infants were dead. On the other hand, the mothers' psychosomatic symptoms, their state of disconnectedness, and their incoherence strongly suggest a state of fugue or perhaps some sort of hysterical amnesia. Whatever the case, the mothers', and by extension the fathers', behavior in the postsucking period is of primary importance in understanding bloodsucking witchcraft, and it demonstrates that witchcraft systems in general, whatever their sociological attributes and functions, cannot be fully understood without the conceptualization of its psychological dimensions. Had Nutini been aware of this a generation ago, the corpus of data on which this study is based would have been much more amenable to psychological analysis. Nonetheless, with the data now available we can still make a number of psychological inferences that take us a step farther in implementing the objectification of causality and the transposition of causation of a specific supernatural system.

This chapter analyzes in some depth the social and psychological implications of manipulating and tampering with the elements and occurrences of the tlahuelpuchi complex. The primary analytical aim has been to demonstrate that the perception of the bloodsucking witchcraft process is posited on the interplay between what is normatively expected and what is psychologically and physically experienced. Thus, the physical and psychological manipulations and tamperings that individuals and the local group (kinsmen and neighbors) engage in are latently and manifestly designed to bridge the gap that may exist or contingently arise in the discharge of the system—that is, when the tlahuelpuchi strikes and an infant dies. These are the validating, reinforcing, and intensifying mechanisms of the bloodsucking witchcraft complex, a necessary condition for proper functional assignment and the causal explanation of the system.

CHAPTER TEN

Aftereffects and the Psychological Context of the Postsucking Period

IN CHAPTERS 8 AND 9 the primary aims were to establish the tlahuel-puchi's efficacy to kill (that is, the effectiveness of the normative belief system to account for infant death under certain peculiar circumstances) and the social and general psychological conditions under which the sucking takes place. We achieved three main goals: the explanation of infant death in rural Tlaxcala, or at least part of it, as the result of unwitting or willful human actions and unknown illnesses; the efficacy of the folk explanation in terms of how the normative belief system (supernatural input) entails (non sequitur) the death of infants (physical realization, natural outcome); and the physical (material, social) and psychological constraints that determine and condition the tlahuel-puchi complex as an efficient catalyst of social and psychological functions. To put it differently, we gave a folk explanation of the system in terms of the assumption of rural Tlaxcalans that bloodsucking witches do indeed exist, but we gave a scientific explanation of why infants die under certain conditions in terms of the assumption that bloodsucking witches do not exist, and then we went on to to suggest implicitly the contexts and condition in which the folk explanation will be transformed into some form of the scientific explanation and be relegated to a mechanism of last resort.

NATURAL AND SUPERNATURAL CAUSATION: THE EVOLUTION OF WITCHCRAFT TOWARD A MECHANISM OF LAST RESORT

Let us make clear that we are well aware that, in the folk system, supernatural inputs producing natural outcomes do not entail a non sequitur; this situation obtains only if one does not believe in the existence of bloodsucking witches, or of supernaturals in general. Lest the reader misunderstand, we do not assume that there is incontrovertible evidence that tlahuelpuchis do not exist in rural Tlaxcala (or for that matter, supernaturals of any kind in any part of the world). Evidently, this is one of the limits of knowledge, a question that is several thousand years old and still unsolved (L. Keith Brown, personal communication). It may even be true that, as systems of knowledge, witchcraft, so-called magic, and science share some elements of logic and organization. Furthermore, few, if any, social scientists or philosophers any longer argue along evolutionary lines like the one in, for example, the scheme (already nearly two hundred years old) that man has evolved from a stage of magic to one of religion and on to one of science—in our view an essentially epistemological scheme of how man's perception and conceptualization of the world has changed (differentially, we presume) since the Neolithic Revolution. Fortunately, social scientists, philosophers, and "intellectuals" in general have become wiser, for it is the rare scholar today who dares to argue from the standpoint of ultimate ontological entities or in terms of absolute epistemological schemes. The world is still very crowded with people at all three levels of the above epistemological scheme coexisting side by side, including some scientists who behave like magical practitioners. Thus, the saner segment of the social and physical scientific community takes a kind of laissez-faire attitude that may be characterized as "one man's entailment is another man's non sequitur" or "my logic is different from yours, but they need not ultimately conflict" (except perhaps in extreme situations, such as when a fundamentalist minority opposes the teaching of biological evolution in the schools, which the religious majority has accommodated within its supernatural beliefs). It also makes allowances and tries to understand the sociological, psychological, and moral reasons for the majority of humanity's belief in supernatural forces and personages. In short, the argument proceeds from a stochastic, perhaps pragmatic position that, once one has understood and explained the normative belief system (and its supporting ideology) of a witchcraft complex (or of religion or any supernatural system), one must go on to understand and explain the system scientifically—that is, in the full array of its social, physical, and psychological implications. More precisely, in dealing with such a highly normative system as witchcraft, adequate explanations and thorough understanding of the phenomena in question emerge primarily by conceptualizing the social and psychological inputs and constraints obtaining between normative expectations and physical realizations.

Perhaps this position is equally justified by the realization that there is ample evidence to demonstrate that systems such as witchcraft, in which supernatural inputs entail natural outcomes (and the assumption here is that, even the most "magical" societies, at least in certain circumscribed domains, do distinguish natural from supernatural causation and entailment), evolve and are transformed in such a way that supernatural causation becomes a mechanism of last resort. This transformation, furthermore, appears to set in and coalesce as new knowledge is learned and internalized. Since the Neolithic Revolution, when mankind began its increasingly more experimental approach to problem solving, technology and then science have been the two most important forms of knowledge that have continuously struck at the heart of the notion that supernatural inputs produce natural outcomes; by extension, they have tended to diminish the importance of the supernatural in any form as deus ex machina, thereby fostering naturalistic explanations in all domains. By Greco-Roman times, there were probably many laymen and scholars who were thoroughgoing naturalists (atheists, materialists, or whatever one may want to call them), and the concept of naturalistic explanation, without in any way appealing to supernatural intervention, was not uncommon. Christianity slowed down this early naturalistic thrust, but since the Renaissance it has increasingly shaped and structured the individual and collective lives of most people in the world. From this standpoint, the magic-religion-science evolutionary scheme does have some descriptive validity, but only if one realizes that it is not an absolute scheme and that it involves in large measure, individually and collectively, the concept of the supernatural in its many forms as a mechanism of last resort.

Magic is basically a method, not a province of behavior and action, whereas religion is essentially a collectively organized body of belief, behavior, and action. Thus, the magical method applies to specific domains, such as witchcraft, sorcery, or any supernatural domain in which, directly and intently, supernatural inputs produce natural outcomes: the tlahuelpuchi kills infants, or the manipulations of the sorcerer produces the death or serious illness of an intended victim. From this standpoint, religion differs from magic not only in organization and in the collective or individual discharge of behavior (which may or may not be distinguishing attributes), but perhaps more characteristically in the fact that religion does not involve a specific method, the application of which produces direct natural outcomes out of intended supernatural inputs. This is not to deny that in certain religious systems God, gods, or anthropomorphic supernaturals are everywhere, active in everyday life, and amenable to being propitiated into direct intervention in the natural course of affairs. Nonetheless, asking for direct supernatural intervention in religion and expecting specific results (for example, Christians constantly asking God to intervene on their behalf in the natural world for specific reasons and in concrete situations) are not the self-directed activities of witchcraft or sorcery, nor do they involve a characteristic method (prayers perhaps approaches it), traits well known to anthropologists who have dealt with magical phenomena. Rather, supernatural intervention in the natural world appears on the whole to be conceived by religious polities in a significantly more contingent fashion, more diffused and nebulous than the usually precise and less serendipitous nature of witchcraft and sorcery actions and manipulations. Indeed, the mastery of God and gods over the natural world and His and their efficacy to influence it and change it at will are always asserted; but direct, focused supernatural action on the natural world is viewed, at least individually, as contingent upon too many other considerations to be verbalized in more precise terms. This is clear, for example, in Christian expressions such as "thy will be done," "look mercifully upon thy servant," and "God works in mysterious ways," which suggest that God may be directly entreated and asked to intervene, but it is wise not to expect too much. With such uncertain imago mundi and chancy expectations, no witchcraft system would be efficient enough to survive for long, and it would soon become residual.

The last point suggests that not only witchcraft (and sorcery) evolves into a marginal, residual version, of an originally centrally located, fullfledged system which may be characterized as an epistemological mechanism of last resort; at least during the past three hundred years in the areas of Western influence, and more recently (perhaps only during this century) in most culture areas of the world, religion has also become significantly dislodged from its central, rectorial position in the sociocultural system and has become, to a significant extent, a moral, spiritual, and behavorial domain-mechanism of last resort. Just as witchcraft, as believed and practiced in the sixteenth century, is no longer part of the magico-religious framework of Western society and has become a marginal, residual activity spuriously practiced by fringe societal segments or occasionally overtly manifested in political and religious witch hunts and scapegoatism, so, too, has religion since then become to some extent marginal, devoid of much of its ritual and ceremonial underpinnings—in short, a kind of philosophy that may still govern or guide the moral and spiritual life of most societal segments but is no longer at the social, economic, and political center of cultural life.

There are exceptions to this blanket generalization (witness modern pietism, fundamentalism, and other fringe fundamentalist sects), but the majority of peoples of Western culture fit this characterization in that they are so-so Christians (who may aptly be characterized as religious when disaster strikes, in times of personal tragedy, and as death approaches: in essence Christians of last resort) or indifferent Christians, with many millions of agnostics and atheists. Compare this potpourri of indifference, shallow beliefs, and practices, almost devoid of deeply felt ritualism and ceremonialism (the essential catalyst and glue of successful religious systems) with the all-encompassing, obsessive, and controlling role of religion in every aspect of European sociocultural life until the Renaissance. Indeed, the Reformation may be regarded as the beginning of the end of Christianity as an integrated socioreligious system in which ritual, ceremonialism, and belief constituted an inseparable efficacious complex at the very center of the local policy. The individualization and intellectualization of religion begins perhaps three centuries earlier; this aspect of the evolution of Christianity is well exemplified by the theology of Saint Thomas Aquinas, who insisted that the justification of religion and the existence of God are not simply matters of faith but can be proven by rational arguments. This account is not new. In fact, the basic notion underlying this argument was variously expressed by the French Philosophers of the Enlightenment (especially Montesquieu, Condorcet, and Voltaire) and the Scottish Moral Philosophers (particularly Millar and Ferguson)—namely, that changes in religion (and all kinds of supernaturalism) are due mainly to science and technology, or, as we have reinterpreted this basic notion, to the internalization of new knowledge leading to alternative modes of explanation. This important idea may nowadays be a commonplace in various scientific and intellectual circles, yet true as it might be, it remains an idea, for there is no theory to explain why and under what conditions science and technology transform magic and religion, and more important, how magic and religion become mechanisms of last resort.

The last question is fundamental, for without a solution to it, it is impossible to understand, let alone explain, the irrational incongruences of modern science and religion and the uneasy truce that in several domains obtains between them. Nor is it possible to understand the irrationality of many aspects of modern life, despite the unquestionably liberating effect of most aspects of science and technology, which have led some scholars to question the claim of science that ontological reality and the perception of the world can only be understood in science's own terms, and that science is a unique system of knowledge that shares nothing with other belief systems of the past or present. Whatever is the case, for those of us who have seen the literal disintegration of traditional cultures and the virtual demise of well-structured magico-religious systems during the past forty years, there can be no doubt that science, technology, and education (that is, the internalization of new knowledge, however superficial, leading to alternative modes of explanation and understanding) have been the main variables that during the present century have transformed many magic and religious systems into marginal, residual mechanisms of last resort, a process that has been gathering momentum all over the world since the Second World War.

Witchcraft in Western society has evolved since the late sixteenth century (when it still occupied a rather central position in the magico-religious system, most people believed in and feared it, and individuals were burned at the stake for it) to a meaningless, spurious, and marginal activity today—a superstition, as most God-fearing Christians would call it—without ever stopping to ponder Voltaire's dictum that "one man's superstition may be another man's religion," or reflecting upon the inconsistency of affirming the existence of one supernatural and denying that of another. More immediately and with more specificity, we can document the transformation of witchcraft in rural Tlaxcala from 1900 to 1960 to 1985, during which the normative belief system and its physical realization have become increasingly marginal, until today they constitute a residual explanation of infant death under peculiar circumstances.

Similar changes could probably be documented in the witchcraft and sorcery systems of societies studied by anthropologists from thirty to sixty or more years ago, and one wonders what the systems studied by Evans-Pritchard, Fortune, Marwick, and many other anthropologists during the past three generations are like today. We are not saying that witchcraft and sorcery systems classically described by anthropologists during the first half of the twentieth century no longer exist. Undoubtedly there are still many in existence, but it is equally true that as Western science, technology, and systems of education have spread throughout the world, the witchcraft or sorcery systems of the Azande, Dobuans, Cewa, Araucanians, Navaho, and perhaps even those of the Arunta, Yanomamo, and others of our still truly primitive contemporaries have suffered and continue to suffer serious transformations, as tribes become folk societies, and as folk societies are more or less incorporated into national states. It is our claim that, in this changing panorama, in some areas proceeding at a very rapid pace, as new knowledge is internalized and alternative modes of explanation and understanding come into being, the classical, sociopsychologically integrated magical systems disintegrate and at different degrees of rapidity become mechanisms of last resort, marginal to the socioreligious system.

It is difficult to pinpoint the epistemological nature of witchcraft as a mechanism of last resort. Perhaps the best way of describing it is as an aspect of supernaturalism (all forms of magic and religion), but one in which direct, self-effected or collectively effected supernatural inputs are expected to produce natural outcomes when the individual or the polity does clearly distinguish between natural and supernatural causation. Or, magical behavior and action, latently present as religion is accommodated to or becomes restrictedly compatible with science, become manifest under conditions of fear, anxiety, stress, and the unexpected. From still another standpoint witchcraft, in particular, and magical behavior and action, in general, as mechanisms of last resort, denote the latent socially and psychologically irrational aspects of human behavior that apparently not even the rationality of science has been able to suppress, as attested to by the perversions to which science has been subjected by every conceivable ideology. Thus, one conceives the study of witchcraft, sorcery, magic, and supernaturalism in general as contributing to the understanding of man's irrationality when confronted with more efficient means of conceptualization and explanation, including science's own irrational quirks. The epistemological study of magical action and thought would undoubtedly contribute to the solution of several problems about which social scientists know very little.

It is in the context of the disintegration of witchcraft and of its becoming a mechanism of last resort that the objectification of causality and the transposition of causation are necessary operations to undertake. By specifying, as far as this operation is possible, the physical steps and psychological states in which the bloodsucking event takes place in the juxtaposing context of the normative belief system of the tlahuelpuchi complex, we were able to understand and explain the action of a specific kind of witchcraft. The claim is that in performing this operation the inferential process of witchcraft is demonstrated: it pinpoints the perception of the phenomena by the various participant actors, and it establishes how combined perceptions structure, condition, and intensify the witchcraft complex in a feedback and self-fulfilling fashion. In a more difficult enterprise, we deal in this chapter, albeit restrictedly, with some of the implications of the transposition of causation—namely, the reinforcing and conditioning psychological mechanisms of the postsucking period. We analyze the aftereffects suffered by primary actors, how they are related to several psychosomatic syndromes, and the implications of guilt and responsibility for the interpretation of infant death within the context of the household and neighborhood. We also discuss the psychological context of the behavior of secondary actors as constituting a supporting network of kinsmen and neighbors.

PRIMARY ACTORS AND THE NETWORK OF HOUSEHOLD BEHAVIOR

When the tlahuelpuchi strikes and an infant dies, the entire household is affected as well as the immediate vicinity of the neighborhood. The most affected personnel are undoubtedly the primary actors—that is, the victim's mother and father. Chapters 8 and 9 demonstrated that much of the behavior of the victim's parents is culturally conditioned but individually discharged (that is, particularistically psychological) as a reaction and response to specific occurrences and the various perceptions and interpretations of the bloodsucking witchcraft event. This is a good example of how culturally conditioned and reinforced behavior must be psychologically interpreted to be fully intelligible. So far the various contexts and domains of the individual behavior of primary actors have been positioned for the period extending from the immediately anteceding occurrences, through the sucking event, to the onset of the longer-lasting aftereffects. Now the analysis is centered on the postsucking period from the psychological perspective, but as the behavior of the victim's parents, especially the mother's, affects the kinship behavior of the household. Equally significant, the psychological states of the parents and how they affect household members must be analyzed by themselves and vis-à-vis the psychosomatic syndromes that characterize many of the bloodsucking cases. This exercise will, we hope, give us more clues about how the reinforcing and intensifying psychological inputs of the tlahuelpuchi complex work.

Substantive and Methodological Considerations Underlying the Psychological Context

Guilt, culpability, responsibility, and perhaps shame are the main descriptive psychological attributes and indicators that characterize the behavior of the victim's parents throughout the postsucking period. They are the expression of fear, anxiety, and stress, which not infrequently give rise to hysteria*, temporary amnesia, hallucination, disassociation, and serious states of agitation. Throughout the postsucking period, which, as we indicated, may last as few as four days and as long as three weeks, the victim's parents are unquestionably in a state of psychological disarray, physically and mentally unable to function normally—that is, according to patterns of everyday behavior in the household. From the moment the victim's body is discovered until the last physical, psychological, or psychosomatic symptom rather suddenly disappears, the mother and father of the sucked infant must be regarded as being in varying states of physical and psychological illness, as unable to function properly, thereby becoming the concern of household members and neighbors, who must see to it that they return to normality as quickly as possible. This is done by affording them care and concern, physical comfort, and more effectively, by giving them folk medicines, occasionally analgesics such as aspirin and *mejoral*, and in aggravated cases by calling tezitlazcs for one or more limpias. The analogy is evident: just as in a modern, urban setting those close to a person who becomes physically or psychologically ill provide him medicine and medical care, the rural Tlaxcalan household and, to some extent, the neighborhood provide physical and psychological care and therapy for the victim's parents for as long as it is necessary. (In the case of nuclear family households, kinsmen and neighbors in the immediate vicinity function in the role of household members, as in the case of an extended-family household.) One can even go further and equate the tezitlazc with the psychiatrist, in that the former does indeed minister to the psychological welfare of the victim's mother and father. It is in this ambience of a total transaction that the parents of a sucked infant experience the

---

*By hysteria we mean unmanageable affect states in extreme and lesser forms, accompanied by lesser outbursts.

often traumatic psychological and physical aftereffects, which may also be interpreted as a cathartic recuperation from the sucking, assuaging and helping to bring to an end the states of guilt and culpability produced by the event. Just as significant is the reaction of household members and kinsmen and neighbors of the immediate vicinity, who are directly or indirectly affected by the sucking. To a lesser extent, this array of secondary actors also experiences the feelings and psychological states of primary actors, and in varying degrees the behavior and actions of the secondary actors are a reflection of and a reaction to those of the primary actors. It is in this ambience that the aftereffects and psychological states of primary and secondary actors in the postsucking period take place, with significant functional value for reinforcing and intensifying the structure of the tlahuelpuchi complex. Before the general causes of these aftereffects and entailed psychological states are analyzed, three points of substantive and methodological importance directly related to the interpretation of the facts and variables at hand must be discussed.

First, the data on the psychological components of bloodsucking witchcraft are neither as complete nor as systematic as those on the physical manifestations of the complex. Again, the reason for this drawback is that at the time the great majority of the data was collected (1960–1966), Nutini was not entirely aware of the psychological implications of the tlahuelpuchi complex in general, nor of the psychological underpinnings of the postsucking period in particular. Nonetheless, as the systematic collection of data on the forty-seven cases proceeded, he did become increasingly aware of focusing on the psychological states of primary actors throughout the postsucking period. Thus, a considerable amount of data were collected in these six years that bear directly on the psychological contexts about to be discussed. The data, of course, are not as hard as those presented in several of the tables, particularly table 6.17; rather, they were open-ended and sporadic, but of sufficient quality to compare favorably with the data base on which good ethnographies are based. For example, this corpus of information contains fairly detailed observations on at least a dozen of the most atypical and "psychosomatically laden" cases of the sample throughout the entire postsucking period; perceptions and assessments of eight of the most disturbed mothers and four fathers by household members and neighbors; the detailed unfolding of most cases of the four psychosomatic ailments recorded in table 6.17, and the reaction of household members and neighbors toward the affected mothers and fathers; and so on. From 1966 until 1980, as the bloodsucking witchcraft complex progressively and rapidly changed, a traditional case was occasionally observed and recorded. It was not until 1982, when we fully realized the lacunae in the corpora of psychological data, that a concerted effort was made to gather more systematic and harder information. By then, the tlahuelpuchi complex was in frank disintegration, and it was difficult to observe traditional cases—that is, most people were no longer open about the largely residual structure of the complex. It was possible to study, however, two traditonal cases of sucking in detail and with a definite psychological focus. Furthermore, many affected parents and members of the household of the original forty-seven–case samples were interviewed, by now most of them men and women in their late middle age or early old age but surprisingly, living in basically the same nuclear- and extended-family arrangements as twenty years before. We interviewed members of nine of the original households (cases 4, 9, 21, 24, 26, 29, 36, 39, and 42) with mixed results.

On the one hand, it was impossible to recreate the open, totally unself-conscious ambience of the original interviews and observations, nor was it possible to recreate with any degree of accuracy, the experiences parents, living members of the original household, and even neighbors underwent sixteen to twenty-two years before. Most of the original parents and household members of the older generation were reticent about the events, occurrences, and general ambience of the sucking, which they remembered well enough, especially the fact that Nutini in all nine cases was almost constantly in the affected households throughout the entire postsucking periods. The remembrances and recollections were warm and anecdotal, but when we approached the serious matter of guided interviewing, most informants became jocular and defensive. The mood, clearly indicating the great changes that had taken place, was expressed in a rather patterned fashion by many informants as follows: "La tlahuelpuchi ya no vive en La Malintzi; parece que nos dejó para siempre" (The tlahuelpuchi no longer lives in La Malintzi volcano; she seems to have left us forever); "la tlahuelpuchi ya no apetece la sangre de las creaturas" (the tlahuelpuchi no longer desires the blood of infants); "la tlahuelpuchi no es más que una creencia, ya que son contadísimas las creaturas que mueren como antes" (the tlahuelpuchi is nothing more than a belief, because very few infants die as they did before [under such suspicious conditions]); "ya son pocas las gentes que creen en la tlahuelpuchi" (few people any longer believe in the tlahuelpuchi); and so on. The general tenor and ambience of these nine interviews, with at least thirty informants, demonstrated conclusively that by 1982 it would have been very difficult to reconstruct, with the kind of detail presented in this monograph, bloodsucking witchcraft according to the norm of a generation before. Indeed, only a couple of informants of household 21 could still be called traditionalists in terms of the complex's imago mundi of 1960. Although this corpus of information attempting to reconstruct and recreate the tlahuelpuchi complex of a generation ago has only limited synchronic value, it is certainly valuable for documenting the great changes that the complex has undergone since 1960.

On the other hand, these nine interviews produced much information on what has been called the vulgarization of the tlahuelpuchi complex. We were able to gather a significant corpus of material on the psychological states of primary and secondary actors throughout the postsucking period that was directly relevant to buttressing the original psychological matrix (that is, what was reliably collected in the context of the forty-seven cases), which was our intent in undertaking these interviews. Interestingly, while most informants were reluctant to talk about the tlahuelpuchi herself,[1] her efficacy to kill, or the sucking event itself, they were quite willing to recreate and reminisce about what transpired during the postsucking period and the psychological states of primary and occasionally secondary actors. We had the distinct impression that although most informants consciously wanted to forget or suppress the tlahuelpuchi complex, the occurrence of the sucking event, and the belief system that supported it, they were quite open and willing to talk about what actors felt and went through during the sometimes traumatic postsucking period. This ambience can be interpreted as a kind of verbal exorcism of an extremely bad experience that was no longer with them but latently gnawed at their inner selves. This attitude is well captured by an informant: "No me doy cuenta como fué posible que tantas creaturas hayan sido chupadas por la tlahuelpuchi. Tampoco sé como han cambiado tanto las cosas que ya son raras las chupadas. Solo sé que a lo mejor un buen día regrese la maldita, por más que nos hayamos civilizado un tanto." (I am not aware how it was possible that so many infants may have been sucked by the tlahuelpuchi. Neither do I know how things have changed so much that nowadays suckings are so rare. I only know that perhaps one of these days the evil one may return again, despite the fact that we may have become somewhat civilized.) This statement indicates the doubts that perhaps most rural Tlaxcalans still have, even in a very rapid situation of change, about an anthropomorphic supernatural that caused them so much misery, but whose ideology and belief system are no longer, or only marginally, efficacious. In other words, this transitional, deteriorating position embodies the essence of magic and supernaturalism toward mechanisms of last resort. Thus, the information gathered in these nine extensive interviews, especially of household 21, significantly augmented knowledge of the psychological matrix in which the postsucking period unfolds: it clarified several moot points, sharpened the focus of the interrelated behavior of primary and secondary actors, and, by extrapolation, it even generated a more insightful perspective on the sucking event itself and on the subjects discussed in chapters 8 and 9. This is essentially the result of a set of questions designed to get at the relationship between guilt, culpability, and responsibility and the structure of postsucking behavior. Incomplete as this body of data may be, it has enabled us to write the present chapter with more authority. Perhaps this point should have been made in a footnote, but it was incorporated into the text because we thought the reader should get a clear idea of the substantive dilemmas and problems one encounters in dealing with changing belief systems.

Second, the data presented in table 6.17 need to be explained, for they do not tell the whole story. Postponing the discussion of the four types of outright psychological illness (syndromes), we emphasize here what were called psychosomatic ailments (see chapter 6). The first point to note is that the psychosomatic ailments of headaches, nausea, and stomach and chest pains are not mutually exclusive in the nineteen cases in which the mother or father were afflicted with one or more of the four psychological illnesses. On the contrary the mother or father in these nineteen cases also suffered from headaches, nausea, or the other ailments. Indeed, it was evident that those individuals suffering chipilería and tzipitictoc were the most affected by headaches and nausea. For example, the mothers of cases 19 and 40 suffered constant strong headaches throughout the one and two weeks of their respective postsucking periods. To put it differently, psychosomatic ailments and psychological illnesses are, structurally speaking, part of the same complex; if our data were more complete, we intuit that they would correlate, in their compounded gravity, with guilt or felt responsibility associated with the different kinds of infant death attributed to the tlahuelpuchi. Second, even in the eleven cases of table 6.17 where no manifested aftereffects were recorded the mothers or fathers of the victims suffered occasional psychosomatic ailments, primarily headaches and chest pains. Here again there is some evidence that the gravity of the aftereffects correlates with guilt and felt responsibility. Information gathered independently of the intensive interviewing of the forty-seven–case sample indicates that, regardless of whether it is a day or night sucking and irrespective of the peculiar or unusual circumstances of the death of an infant (that is, regardless of the physical cause of death), all mothers and most fathers suffered postsucking psychosomatic ailments of varying degrees of gravity and intermittence. Thus, the eleven cases of table 6.17 in which "none" is entered signify only that they are those in which the aftereffects are the mildest, intermittent, and were not originally noticed. From this standpoint, the incidence of aftereffects during the postsucking period is apparently universal, and their gravity is the best indicator to gauge the seriousness of the sucking event and its effect on the behavior of all actors concerned. Third, headaches, nausea, and the other psychosomatic ailments are only one set of manifestations affecting primary actors during the postsucking period. As we indicated, there is another set of psychological manifestations primary actors may suffer throughout this period, the most common being mild or somewhat strong attacks of hysteria, temporary amnesia, lapses of disassociation, extreme agitation, and short lapses of hallucination. (It should be noted that both sets of psychosomatic and psychological manifestations are occasionally exhibited in a milder form by other members of the household. Not suprisingly, the secondary actors most commonly affected are close lineal and collateral kinsmen: the parents of the victim's father and elder siblings of the victim, as we will discuss below.) These psychological manifestations are not entered in table 6.17 because they were not originally gathered systematically, like most of the data of the other nineteen tables. They gradually emerged during the original research, and in the interviews conducted in 1982, four informants significantly augmented our knowledge of how these manifestations fitted into the general psychological pattern of the postsucking period.

Third, on several occasions throughout chapters 8 and 9 and in the foregoing section we mentioned or briefly discussed the various possible correlations between guilt, culpability, and responsibility, the five possible kinds of infant death, and the incidence and gravity of aftereffects throughout the postsucking period. Let us bring together this various piecemeal information and determine how it bears on the general psychological matrix of the postsucking period. The most serious problem in dealing with correlations and their implications — arising from the death of infants attributed to the tlahuelpuchi and the degree of guilt and culpability manifested in the gravity of aftereffects — is the quality of the data base. Nothing short of recreating the conditions of 1960 and approaching the data-gathering process within an essentially psychological framework would yield a fully adequate corpus of information. The substantive matrix now available permits us to make only a few general statements, intuitively likely, with a fairly high probability of falsifiability and potentially verifiable. So far we have been rather conservative in generalizing from the psychological data and the objectification of what really transpires during that critical period between midnight and dawn, when most suckings take place; since, even if one could recreate anew a forty-seven–case sample under the 1960 conditions, it would be almost impossible to get at the facts of these critical hours with the methods now in existence, it would not do any harm to become bolder and offer some likely hypotheses on this thorny problem.

Implicitly underlying the description and analysis of chapters 8 and 9 is the warranted assumption that, when an infant is sucked by the tlahuelpuchi, the primary actors individually and secondary actors collectively feel guilty and culpable for its death. The morality of individual and collective guilt and culpability is not pertinent at the moment, but it does entail significant consequences that are translated into ascertainable kinds of behavior for all actors concerned. From this perspective, the following generalizations can be made: (1) guilt, culpability, and responsibility are the direct result of the causes of those infant deaths attributed to the tlahuelpuchi, and manifested in manifold aftereffects during the postsucking period; (2) the greater the responsibility for the death of an infant felt by primary actors, the higher the intensity of guilt and culpability; and (3) the higher the intensity of guilt and culpability, the greater the gravity of the postsucking aftereffects. As we indicated, we are not talking about culturally determined behavior, the reason for which is obvious: such behavior would have to be specified by the belief system, which is not the case in the bloodsucking witchcraft of rural Tlaxcala; nor is it likely to be specified in any witchcraft system—that is, no witchcraft system can be so constrained as to specify such normatively minute behavior. Rather, we are dealing with individuals behaving as the result of patterned but specific constraints, arising out of the particular circumstances of infant death. Thus, although there are no culturally determined correlations and congruences entailed by the above generalizations, there most certainly are individual and, perhaps, collective ones of a psychological-behavioral nature obtaining between inputs (motivating mechanisms), in the form of states of being, and outputs (behavior), in the form of aftereffects, as occurrences unfold from the sucking event itself to the end of the postsucking period. Let us take each of the three generalizations in turn, and determine to what extent they can be verified.

We demonstrated indirectly that the several psychosomatic and psychological aftereffects experienced by the victim's parents throughout the postsucking period are the result of real or imagined feelings and states of guilt and culpability. There is no other explanation that comes to mind, and there is little more that one can say about this cornerstone of the bloodsucking witchcraft complex. It should be noted, however, that, to some extent, this is the only demonstrable entailment of feelings and states and experienced psychosomatic and psychological aftereffects, for the universal incidence of both sets of aftereffects when the tlahuelpuchi strikes indicates that they are as much the result of particular and specific constraints as of the reinforcing and intensifying effect of past suckings perceived through the screen of the normative belief system.

Let us expand what has already been said about the second generalization. As the situation has been reconstructed, the degree of responsibility for the death of an infant that has been attributed to the tlahuelpuchi is clear enough and deductively quite consistent: the concerned mothers are able (unconsciously?) to gauge their physical actions as inputs contributing to the death of their infants. In this scheme of things, the degree of felt responsibility unfolds along two axes: mothers feel much more responsibility for night suckings than for day suckings; and with respect to the physical cause of death, mothers feel the most responsibility in cases of asphyxia and the least in cases of crib death.

Given the extreme difficulty of pinpointing cases of infanticide, one can say little about the perpetrators of this form of infant death; if only there were a method of ascertaining the accompanying physical and psychological symptoms and syndromes. It is logical to assume, however, that the perpetrators, whether mothers, mothers-in-law, or other members of the household, feel totally responsible and feel unknown degrees of devastating guilt and culpability. Obviously, the best way of guessing, perhaps gauging, the degree of felt responsibility is by correlating the possible causes of death with the manifest aftereffects in their various forms. Another way of solving this question, as we have tentatively shown, is to determine the degree of tampering with the physical and sociopsychological evidence of the sucking event. Circular as this procedure is (tampering with the evidence is a direct entailment of avoiding blame, the social consequences of responsibility), it does ostensibly demonstrate the intensity of responsibility and the entailed guilt and culpability: the greater the tampering, the higher the degree of guilt and culpability. On the one hand, this explains, by accounting for opportunity, the lack of tampering in day suckings, and the high incidence of tampering in night suckings. On the other hand, it also explains the scaling of responsibility of the four main causes of infant death, as perceived by the victims' mothers. It appears that mothers quite logically assess (*become aware of* is perhaps a better expression) the extent to which they are willfully or unwittingly responsible for actions or things left undone leading or contributing in one form or another to the death of their infants, as demonstrated by the intensity of tampering and the ensuing guilt and culpability. The assumption here is that mothers know and can gauge how responsible they are when their infants die and the deaths are attributed to the action of the tlahuelpuchi. In this context, it was shown that the gradation of the mother's responsibility, from greater to lesser, is as follows: asphyxia, suffocation, choking, and crib death, as these causes of death have been sociopsychologically defined. The evidence for this claim was presented in chapter 8, and it centers on tampering with the evidence of the sucking, and how tampering correlates with unusual events surrounding the sucking and its aftereffects. It is not by any means conclusive evidence, but it does support our hypothesis.

Finally, what about the father's responsibility, since fathers often exhibit many of the same aftereffects, occasionally as strongly as mothers? This is a difficult question to answer, and only the following hypothetical reconstruction comes to mind in response. On the one hand, the father's felt responsibility, generating guilt and culpability and resulting in observable aftereffects, is part of the collective responsibility-guilt-culpability extended maximally to the household and minimally to the nonresidential extended family and paraje.

This ideological constraint is deeply rooted in the rural Tlaxcalan imago mundi which stipulates that unfortunate events in general, and supernatural unfortunate events in particular, are not necessarily random, but are the natural, moral outcome of having contravened, by commission or omission, the human-supernatural covenant—thereby exacting a payment for lessening the pool of goodwill that the local group must have in order to subsisst successsfully with the supernatural forces that govern it. From this viewpoint, bloodsucking witchcraft, as much as the cult of the saints and the mayordomía system, is part of a moral, ethical system binding on rural Tlaxcalan and an array of Catholic and pagan supernaturals. On the other hand, the father's responsibility, guilt, and culpability, patterned after the mother's, may also be regarded as being assigned through some kind of sociopsychological osmosis, since it is assumed that, unless the father is an infanticide perpetrator, no action on his part (that he is aware of, that is) precipitated any of the various forms of infant death due to the tlahuelpuchi, and since he has nothing to do with infant care. Or, as we discussed above, prone to suspect other women of some sort of foul play, the father never suspects, when his own infant dies, that his wife was in any way to be blamed, thereby supporting her to the extent of sharing her responsibility and ultimately, the joint suffering of always unpleasant aftereffects. This appears to be a classical example of what may be called transference in reverse: when disaster strikes, none of those immediately and directly affected is blameless enough not to share, and often share alike, in the responsibility, guilt, and culpability of those whose actions, directly or indirectly, precipitated the unfortunate event.

Intuitively, the most likely of the three generalizations is the direct correlation of the gravity of the aftereffects with the intensity of guilt and culpability. The seriousness of the former can only be entailed by the psychologically known efficacy of the latter. Moreover, there are hints in tables 6.13, 6.14, 6.15, 6.16, and 6.17 and their correlation, together with information not systematically presented, that leaves little doubt that the seriousness of aftereffects is directly linked to the cause of death and the tampering that goes on, hence to the triad of responsibility, guilt, and culpability. For example, some of the cases in which the aftereffects were the most serious and pronounced appear to be linked to possible infanticides and death by asphyxia and suffocation, the cases most directly linked to actions on the part of the mother; the occasional hysterical reaction (case 4) of mothers upon finding the bodies of their sucked infants are indicative of their direct input (unwitting smothering) in the death; and the apparently unconscious avoidance of mothers in finding the bodies of sucked infants (cases 4, 9, and 26, discounting two day suckings, 21 and 22) is another indication that it is with the onset of the postsucking period, when mothers sporadically or permanently recall what transpired during the night, that the generated guilt and culpability trigger the strongest aftereffects — that is, psychosomatic ailments and more serious outright psychological syndromes. Unfortunately, as we have admitted, the data (the systematic investigation of the forty-seven–case sample and miscellaneous ethnographic information) are not hard enough to establish a definitive, invariant correlation between the causes of death (entailing graduated degrees of responsibility [ostensibly demonstrated by definite degrees of tampering] generating corresponding guilt and culpability), which have tentatively been established with some reliability, and the aftereffects of the sucking, the hardest data available which has been observed and conceptualized with a significant degree of accuracy.

Guilt, Culpability, Responsibility, and the Entailment of Individual Action
Concentrating on the victim's mother, we see that responsibility for the sucking initiates the chain of entailment. This is perhaps the only attribute of the triad that is mainly culturally determined. In rural Tlaxcalan culture, mothers assume full responsibility for infant care and training, although they may occasionally be assisted by elder daughters (usually twelve years and older), and less commonly by the mother-in-law and sister-in-law in extended-family households. It is not until infants become children (which in rural Tlaxcalan culture takes place when the boys or girls acquire social personality at age three or so with the onset of fully intelligible speech), that fathers and other adult male members of the household begin to interact with them and acquire a measure of responsibility over their actions and behavior. Within the period of the life cycle when all normal suckings take place, the mother, regardless of whatever assistance she receives from other females of the household, is entirely responsible for whatever happens to her infant, and if any discomfort or harm is experienced by the infant, she is invariably blamed for it. This is a deep-seated theme in the kinship behavior of the household, and one for which rural Tlaxcalan women suffer unduly for real or imagined faults and deficiencies concerning their infant- and child-rearing practices: mothers-in-law, adult male members of the household, and even adult male members of the non-residential extended family are her most assiduous critics whenever anything goes wrong or the infant suffers in any way. Especially young mothers, thirty years old or younger, are constantly anxious and afraid, particularly because of the criticism of their mothers-in-law, of anything negative that may affect their infants or of departing noticeably from what is considered the norm in infant care. In this ambience of stress, mothers (particularly in the first half of their reproductive careers — that is, roughly from ages twenty to thirty-three) are conditioned to expect blame for anything that adversely affects the well-being of their infants.

This explains, by the way, the strong expectations of mothers that they will be blamed and punished by their husbands when the tlahuelpuchi strikes, even though they might have experienced other suckings, and they certainly knew of many suckings in which affected mothers' expectations were not realized and they received nothing but support from their husbands. As we indicated, this patterned behavior of mothers, coupled with latent expectations, is what conditions and configures the actions transpiring during the night of the sucking, the end result of which is tampering with the evidence for *really* felt responsibility or, as it were, for playing it safe.

How does responsibility trigger the chain of entailment during the night of the sucking? The context in which this process takes place has been carefully laid out, and we can therefore be brief. It is obviously the fear and anxiety of being blamed that determines the tampering with the evidence, but this state of mind, this urgent feeling, is conditioned by the mother's strong sense of responsibility with which the kinship behavior of the household has saddled her. Thus, from this viewpoint it really does not make any difference whether the mother is aware that some action of hers contributed to the demise of the infant, or, being aware that no direct action of hers precipitated the death of the infant and simply playing it safe, she tampers with the evidence just the same. Regardless of whether the mother is conscious, unconscious, or in a state of fugue, the latent structure of social responsibility is what generates the state of mind which compels her to tamper with the evidence upon discovering the dead infant. In summary, one could say that the primarily culturally determined social responsibility, always manifestly present, constitutes the necessary conditions for triggering the entailing chain of occurrences and psychological states, the first of which is unquestionably tampering with the body of the victim. The sufficient conditions for this process, however, are provided by the real or imagined responsibility of the mother generated by the impact of one of the four causes of infant death and also by the deeply ingrained habit of playing it safe. This sequence completes the first stage of the entailment chain, and its reconstruction is partly deductive and partly warranted by hints and indirect references by mothers in the after-the-fact elicitations at lucid points throughout the first part of the postsucking period. For example, in the nightmares from the night of the sucking occasionally reported by mothers, they find themselves struggling with the tlahuelpuchi, in her human or animal form, trying to get the infant away from the witch's clutches, while she blames the mother for not having been careful to protect the infant or for not fighting hard enough to defend her infant.[2] Added evidence for the reconstruction comes from the many legends whose main themes are the sucking event and what transpires between the mother, and occasionally the father, and the tlahuelpuchi in her human and animal forms: they talk to each other, and it is possible to infer the psychological states of the mother during the night of the sucking. This kind of information, as soft as it is, is at least as good as the information on which most symbolic analyses are posited.

Syntagmatically, culpability is the next entailed attribute. From the viewpoint of motivating efficacy, responsibility is no longer operative by the time the body of the victim is found. At this point, culpability appears to set in. In the diachronic sequence, culpability most likely begins to be efficacious when the victim's body is discovered and both the mother and father become fully cognizant of the death of their infant; the process of reinterpreting the perceptions of the sucking event begins; and the rationalization of the tlahuelpuchi's power to kill dominates the behavior of all actors concerned. From this juncture onward, the analysis is on firmer grounds, for the data base is more complete. We are no longer engaged in reconstructing likely events, occurrences, and psychological states but concerned with the process of interpreting and analyzing perceived entities and observed behavior and actions of individuals and groups in a fairly controlled setting, the household and its immediate vicinity. With the onset of the postsucking period, the father fully enters the picture; in varying degrees, the psychological states and syndromes which characterize this lapse of time are shared by the mother and the father. The most telling and diagnostic characteristic of the onset of culpability, which sets it apart somewhat from the largely inferred sucking event and its aftermath on the one hand, and from the postsucking period proper on the other, is the behavior and demeanor of the victim's parents. From the discovery of the victim's body at least until its burial, or the day afterward, the behavior and general demeanor of the parents is almost normal—that is, although they wake up with headaches and other psychosomatic ailments, the much more serious disturbances that characterize most postsucking periods begin to manifest themselves later. It is most likely that during this interim period culpability dominates the psychological states of primary actors.

Lest the reader misunderstand, we are adhering to the semantic distinction that exists in English between *guilt,* meaning "the feeling of deserved blame" or "the sentiment of having done something wrong," and *culpability,* meaning "the realization of deserving blame" or "having been found to contravene a rule or injunction."[3] Thus, throughout the early part of the postsucking period the victim's parents, or at least the mother, realize that they are to be blamed for the death of the infant (both in the individual [real or imagined] and collective, moral senses, since blame is a correlate of culpability as well as of guilt), but they do not yet feel guilty. Guilt is a delayed psychological state fully shared by the husband. More precisely, during the first twenty-four to forty-eight hours the primary actors feel culpable but not guilty, and they exhibit the symptoms that are usually present when they wake up the morning of the sucking, which may or may not be prolonged for the entire postsucking period: headaches, nausea, stomachaches, and chest pains. These psychosomatic ailments, as they have been called, may be considered as the physical manifestation of the parents' psychological state. Making allowances for the culturally conditioned injunctions and constraints that require rural Tlaxcalan adults to behave with poise and propriety, even under conditions of great stress, we may say that the victim's parents are in a state of controlled tension and anxiety until after the burial of the infant, when the psychosomatic ailments worsen or give way to the more serious psychological syndromes. The observation of the victim's parents and the perception that secondary actors have of them throughout the first part of the postsucking period lead us to describe them as follows: withdrawn but alert enough to respond to questions; occasionally disassociated but with enough presence of mind to go through the rites and ceremonies entailed by the ministrations of the tezitlazc, the wake, burial, and other events; disturbed but generally still functional members of the household. Short interviews with affected mothers and fathers indicate that the latter were more prone to talk coherently than the former. As in almost all aspects of the bloodsucking witchcraft complex, answers to questions were quite patterned, centered about the themes of responsibility, culpability, and merit — asking themselves what they had done to deserve the sucking of their infant. The most common statements by fathers were: "Me pregunto porqué nos tenian que chupar la creatura, si siempre hemos cumplido con nuestras obligaciones hacia Dios y nos comportamos bien con todo el mundo"; "no hay duda de que tenemos la culpa de lo que nos pasó, pero como haberlo evitado, no le sé"; "la responsabilidad es tanto mía como de mi mujer por no haber protegido bien a la creatura"; "como fué a suceder esto, sabiendo tan bien lo peligrosas que son las tlahuelpuchi en esta epoca del año." (I ask myself why our infant had to be sucked, after all, we have always complied with our obligations toward God and we behave correctly toward everybody; there is no doubt that we are to blame for what happened, but how it could have been avoided, I do not know; the responsibility is mine as well as my wife's for not having protected the infant well; how could this have happened, knowing how dangerous the tlahuelpuchis are at this time of the year.) Mothers were more laconic, and they expressed themselves in the following fashion: "Porqué tuvo que sucederme a mí"; "tengo gran parte de la culpa de la muerte de mi creatura"; "debí haber protejido a mi creatura, sabiendo lo que podría pasar." (Why did it have to happen to me; I am mostly to blame for the death of my infant; I should have protected my infant, knowing what could happen.) These statements and variations of them, uttered by many affected mothers and fathers, constitute the verbal, elicited information for the context in which primary actors acknowledge culpability for the death of infants—that is, they realize that they are, for whatever reasons, to be blamed for the occurrence.

The final contention is that guilt, as connoted above, is the last psychological state in the sucking event/postsucking period to motivate behavior in primary actors. As a corollary, the observational claim is that guilt develops gradually and that, entailed by culpability, its full impact begins shortly after all sociocultural constraints and injunctions have been discharged by all actors directly or indirectly affected by the sucking. Continuously or intermittently, the mother and the father suffer as as result either aggravated symptoms of the psychosomatic ailments already present at the onset of the postsucking period, or the psychological syndromes (folk illnesses) occasionally accompanied by intermittent hysteria, amnesia, disassociation, and hallucinations. Thus, the motivating efficacy of guilt operates throughout most of the postsucking period, and it affects the mother and father alike but with differential intensity. Statistically, the mother undoubtedly suffers the most aggravated cases of the four psychological illnesses and the most serious episodes of hysteria, amnesia, and so on. But not infrequently (one case, 38, in the sample), the father's psychosomatic and psychological symptoms and syndromes are more serious than those of the mother. From this viewpoint, table 6.17 is not an accurate reflection of reality, for cases of fathers with more aggravated syndromes and ailments than mothers, as we discovered years later, are more numerous. The reason for this rather peculiar phenomenon is not clear, but we suspect that it is some form of the couvade. Neither is table 6.17 an accurate index of the intensity and incidence of all psychosomatic and psychological ailments, syndromes, and disturbances experienced by primary actors throughout the postsucking period. Many of them, for individual cases and collectively, escaped Nutini in 1961, when most of the sample was generated. The reason for this is twofold. On the one hand, it appeared gradually (from 1962 to 1966, when only eleven cases were recorded) that he had misinterpreted some of the psychological syndromes for intermittent psychological disturbances such as disassociations or hysteria or even the various psychosomatic ailments. On the other hand, in all cases recorded and studied in 1960 and 1961, it also appeared that, although they were not trying to hide the states of primary actors, household members and neighbors nonetheless did not point out what they regarded as bouts of chipilería and tzipitictoc. By the end of 1961 Nutini had been alerted to these omissions and misunderstandings. That is why in the last eleven cases of the sample more than two-thirds of the parents (seven cases) suffered from one or more of four psychological syndromes. We estimate, thus, that more than 75 percent of all mothers and fathers of sucking victims are affected by serious to fairly serious psychological disturbances precipitated by guilt and accompanying feelings of inadequacy and shame.

Anthropologists of the old school of culture and personality appeared to have regarded guilt and shame as antinomous concepts, when they talked about guilt cultures and shame cultures. In our experience, this does not seem to be the case. Rather, guilt and shame can be associated concepts of a single psychological state; at least this is the case for the postsucking period described for rural Tlaxcalans. The functional, collective aspects of guilt in connection with the protection of infants against the tlahuelpuchi have already been discussed. Here we concentrate on individual guilt and associated states as generating specific behavior. The generative mechanics and dynamics of the concept are as follows. Mothers, and fathers by some kind of sociopsychological osmosis, experience guilt when, after the rush of ritual and ceremonial activity following the sucking, they ask themselves what they did or left undone to deserve such a fate, and they reflect upon how they could have offended the supernaturals or their fellow kinsmen, compadres, or friends to have brought such punishment upon themselves. The obstensible fact that the infant dies and the death becomes public knowledge—that is, that the parents are caught in either not having protected the infant against the tlahuelpuchi (a real possibility) or not having fought her off (an imagined possibility)—makes them feel shame. They also feel inadequate for not having been able to perform as careful parents and for not controlling their emotional states and for not maintaining poise and composure, as prescribed by the rural Tlaxcalan imago mundi. It is thus the conjoined action of these associated states that produces the physical, psychosomatic, and psychological syndromes and ailments that characterize much of the postsucking period. Throughout, the victim's parents are manifestly ill and disturbed, more than the casual observer may be led to believe, and they enter intermittently into periods of psychotic disarray. The ostensible demonstration of guilt, shame, and inadequacy are, of course, the aftereffects themselves, for which there cannot be any other explanation by this entailment. The victim's parents throughout most of the postsucking period are sufficiently disturbed so as to preclude meaningful information being elicited from them after the victim's burial. Verbal evidence for the efficacy of guilt and associated states, however, is amply provided by household members and neighbors. Kinsmen, compadres, and friends provide unmistakable statements linking guilt and associated states with the physical and psychological aftereffects. Among many dozens of direct attestations, the following are the most representative: "Ya no pueden con su culpa los pobrecitos"; "se sienten tan culpables que se enferman"; "tratamos de convencerlos de que hicieron lo posible"; "pero sabemos

muy bien que algo deben haber hecho para que sufrieran tan duro golpe";
"hacemos lo posible para que no se apachurren tanto, como es natural que lo
estén"; "en la mayoría de los casos los padres de la creatura no pueden con sus
sentimientos y a veces se enferman gravemente"; and so on. (They cannot cope
with their guilt, the poor little ones [the victim's parents]; they feel so guilty
that they become ill; we try to convince them that they did their best; but we
know very well that they must have done something to suffer such a hard
blow; we do everything possible so that they may not become too depressed,
as it is natural for them to be; in the majority of cases the infant's parents
cannot cope with their feelings, and once in a while they become seriously ill.)
These statements, made in the context of open-ended interviews, are too obvious to need any interpretation, and we can go on to describe the psychological
states of primary actors by analyzing the syndromes and disturbances that
they experience throughout the postsucking period.

The Structure of Folk Illnesses, Psychological Syndromes, and
Other Disturbances
A distinction has been made between psychosomatic ailments (headaches,
nausea, stomachaches, and chest pains), psychological (folk) illnesses, and psychological disturbances (hysteria, amnesia, disassociation, hallucination, and
extreme agitation). We have discussed in some detail the configuration of psychosomatic ailments, as they begin before the victim's body is found, and as
they continue throughout the postsucking period. Here we center the discussion on the psychological illnesses and disturbances, for which we have adequate ethnographic and direct-observation data. The observational data base,
however, is not nearly as complete as we would have liked, and we have com-
plemented it with the perceptions and descriptive impressions of household
members and neighbors at various times throughout the postsucking period.
Furthermore, since the four psychological illnesses (syndromes, as we have
occasionally called them, is a better descriptive term) exhibit some of the
symptoms of the disturbances noted above, in discussing the former we aug-
ment our operational knowledge of the latter.

Let us remind the reader that all aftereffects (psychosomatic ailments, psychological illnesses, and psychological disturbances) are psychosomatic in origin—that is, triggered by the devastating effect of the sucking on the primary
actors and generated by responsibility, culpability, and guilt. These three states
of physical-psychological disarray are by no means exclusive. Rather, mothers
and fathers experience them, sequentially and intermittently, in an inclusive
or partly inclusive fashion. Indeed, primary actors may experience headaches,
chest pains, and nausea before and after a bout of espanto, or throughout the

duration of tzipitictoc; and hysteria, temporary amnesia, or lapses of hallucination may occur in the same sequential fashion. In fact, at least two of the symptoms of espanto and ataque de espíritus may be pinpointed as nausea and hysteria, while chipilería and tzipitictoc exhibit symptoms that are essentially strong headaches, disassociation, and hallucinations. Let us, then, briefly describe the contextual incidence of the psychological disturbances that primary actors experience, which are often difficult to disentangle from the psychological folk illnesses. By the way, this entangling may have been the main reason why Nutini missed many cases of folk illnesses in 1961 that are not entered in table 6.17.

Hysteria is the most common of the psychological disturbances affecting primary actors during the postsucking period; it is more common among mothers than fathers. Men are culturally conditioned to be stronger than women, to stand fast in moments of trouble and stress, and to repress and not to show undue outbursts of emotion; therefore, hysteria among fathers is very rare. Hysteria takes place in three subcontexts. First, upon the discovery of the victim's body mothers occasionally become hysterical (case 4), especially if they themselves find the corpses. One likely hypothesis for this behavior is that it is a concomitant expression of a state of extreme responsibility for the death of the infant, as in blatant cases of neglect (smothering) or infanticide. Second, attacks of hysteria may occur at any time throughout the postsucking period, except, perhaps, before the victim's burial. These attacks are common, especially with younger mothers married less than seven years or so. It is not uncommon for an affected mother to suffer five or six hysterical episodes within a week's postsucking period. Third, attacks of hysteria almost invariably accompany cases of espanto and ataque de espíritus, and frequently occur immediately after the fainting spells accompanying cases of tzipitictoc. Since these three folk illnesses are significantly underrepresented in the sample, especially the first two, the incidence of hysteria in this subcontext may be much higher. The reader should also consider that, in at least the first twenty-two cases of the sample, it was often not possible to discriminate between isolated episodes of hysteria and those which occurred as part of espanto, ataque de espíritus, and tzipitictoc. In any event, hysteria constitutes the psychological disturbance of the highest incidence throughout the postsucking period, being the most conspicious, showy, and visible, and as such, perhaps the most symptomatic tension-realizing mechanism.

It is possible that these psychological disturbances may not have adequate scientific referents and that there is no technical definition for each of the disturbances. But the description of the entailed behavior accompanying these disturbances is ethnographically accurate, and it was observed with a significant modicum of *interscientific* reliability. From this standpoint, hysteria and disassociation are valid emic concepts to deal with the psychological components of an ethnographic situation. An attack or episode of hysteria in all three subcontexts of the postsucking period almost always takes place unexpectedly: one moment the mother seems fairly normal, and the next she is totally out of control. Except when the episodes take place after the fainting spells accompanying tzipitictoc, hysteria may occur at any time. Most often attacks of hysteria occur early in the morning or shortly after the mother gets up. The episodes may last as little as ten or fifteen minutes or as long as half an hour, and, like so many of the psychological disturbances and syndromes accompanying the bloodsucking event, they go as suddenly as they come, and the mother seems to return to some kind of normality, at least temporarily. This is an aspect of the tlahuelpuchi complex that from the very beginning struck us as odd, and for which we have no explanation, except perhaps to say that there is a modicum of patterning, which is essentially culturally determined. The most characteristic symptoms of hysteria in mothers are the following: screaming at a very high pitch; crying uncontrollably; pulling at their hair, and occasionally banging their head against the wall; lamenting loudly the deaths of their infants; blaming themselves incoherently; and running around in circles. Immediate kinsmen, and occasionally neighbors, generally try to restrain affected mothers, to soothe them, and to utter words of encouragement to the effect that it will all pass, that it was none of their fault, and that one must accept what one is handed with good grace. When the episode is over, the mother withdraws to where she can be alone and becomes morose and often unreachable for hours at a time.

Temporary amnesia is probably the most uncommon psychological disturbance experienced by affected mothers. Only two cases were observed in which the mothers literally did not remember anything about what had transpired before the burial of the victim. In both cases the amnesia lasted for almost exactly two days; it started when they awoke late one morning, and it extended until two days later, when they got up near midmorning. Informants asserted that these amnesia episodes were fairly common, certainly more than it was possible to observe. One interesting aspect of these two cases (numbers 9 and 15) is that except for the amnesia, they were among those in which the aftereffects were the mildest. In case 9 they were so mild that Nutini originally could not understand it. Another striking feature of these two cases is that they occurred at the end of the postsucking period. In fact, the roughly forty-eight hours of amnesia experienced by the mothers terminated the postsucking period, for, after they remembered that their infants had been sucked and what had transpired up to the burial, the mothers went back to normal and became functional members of the household. In case 9, the return occurred almost exactly a week after the sucking; in case 15, it occurred nine days later. Whether these cases are typical of postsucking amnesia, we are not certain. Several informants, however, asserted that bouts of amnesia may last for as little as a day or as long as three days, and that they usually terminate the postsucking period. During the lapse of amnesia, curiously enough, mothers behave almost normally, certainly more normally than during any other part of the postsucking period. The most interesting aspect of postsucking amnesia is that rual Tlaxcalans understand it, and have an explanation for it, that is essentially the same as the standard explanation of the phenomenon in psychiatric circles: when an individual is unable to cope with reality, amnesia may develop as an assuaging, temporary release mechanism. This is our interpretation of several informants' statements, the essence of which is well expressed by one of them: "A veces las madres se sienten tan culpables por la chupada de sus creaturas, que de verdad se olvidan enteramente de lo que pasó, hasta que de repente vuelven a la razón" (Sometimes mothers feel so guilty for the sucking of their infants, that they truly forget what happened, until all of a sudden return to reason).

Disassociation and extreme agitation are intermittent disturbances that may occur at any time throughout the postsucking period after the burial of the victim's body. They may occur together or by themselves in both mothers and fathers, and by definition, they are considered by affected secondary actors to be less serious than hysteria and amnesia. In addition, unlike hysteria and amnesia, which may be considered almost exclusively mothers' disturbances, disassociation and extreme agitation are experienced by fathers perhaps as much as mothers, and with the same degree of intensity. Contextually, disassociation and extreme agitation may occur either as part of the symptoms of all four folk illnesses or by themselves in the course of cases in which primary actors are not affected by folk illnesses. Among the folk illnesses, their incidence is particularly associated with chipilería and tzipitictoc, although primary actors may also exhibit them less commonly, especially after repeated attacks of espanto and ataque de espíritus. Where folk illnesses are absent they can occur, jointly or separately, at any time throughout the postsucking period without any specifically discernible pattern. In terms of specific incidence, disassociation is more common than extreme agitation, but when they occur together, disassociation almost invariably rapidly succeeds extreme agitation. The length of the bouts is probably equal in mothers and fathers. It is evident that the imago mundi of rural Tlaxcalans considers disassociation and extreme agitation permissible forms of behavior for men, whereas they very much frown upon bouts of hysteria and amnesia among men. For the reasons given above, the latter two are signs of weakness and lack of the manly, stout virtues that rural Tlaxcalan men must have. Why the two former disturbances are not considered unmanly, we do not exactly know. Our knowledge of rural Tlaxcalan culture suggests, however, that given the deep-seated emphasis on calm, collected, and quiet expressive behavior, especially for men, hysteria and amnesia (as extreme manifestations of overt, exaggerated, and showy loss of personal control) are regarded as highly unbecoming behavior for fathers, whereas disassociation and extreme agitation (as less drastic loss of personal control) are permitted as escape valves during times of anxiety and stress, even for men trying to embody the tougher image of themselves that the cultural system assigns to adult men in action.

Regardless of whether disassociation and extreme agitation occur in the context of the four folk illnesses, they have pretty much the same symptomatic configuration. Disassociation, on the one hand, denotes the state of being of mothers and fathers exhibiting the following behavior: verbal disconnectedness—that is, speaking in non sequiturs; unresponsiveness to people's questions, suggestions, or commands; withdrawing almost completely by taking walks or locking themselves up in a room; and ultimately, falling asleep for several hours. Extreme agitation, on the other hand, denotes the following behavior: walking about the house gesticulating, giving orders about things that need not be done, and making a nuisance of themselves; speaking loudly, giving unwanted opinions, and suggesting impossible things to do; and bursting into tears and hugging adults and children for comfort. As we indicated, the hyperactive behavior of extreme agitation quickly gives way to the totally passive demeanor of disassociation. Extreme agitation may last for as much as an hour, and then the affected mother or father sinks into the disassociated state, which may last for two to four hours before the affected individual falls asleep. In sequence or separately, bouts of disassociation and extreme agitation may take place several times throughout the course of the postsucking period, and informants pointed out that bouts may happen as many as six or seven times, sometimes within the extent of a week. Next to attacks of hysteria and the seizures of espanto and ataque de espíritus, the sequence of extreme agitation-disassociation is the most disruptive to the household, and kinsmen and neighbors must be particularly patient and careful since affected individuals may wander away from the house.

Hallucination is the least common of the experienced disturbances of the postsucking period. Again, hallucination falls in the same category as hysteria and amnesia—that is, it is experienced only by mothers. Thus, in terms of overall incidence, women undoubtedly suffer more psychological disturbances than men, but this is somewhat compensated for by the fact that bouts or attacks of espanto, ataque de espíritus, and chipilería may be as serious for fathers as they are for mothers. Nutini observed one case and was told about three cases of hallucination by household members. In all four cases, the mothers exhibited the following symptoms: waking up from dozing or from a deep sleep, they reported seeing luminous shadows in the form of turkeys, dogs, and coyotes hovering in the room or crawling up and down the walls; accompanied by violent screaming, they huddled in bed or against the wall in an almost fetal position; they shook for several minutes and developed fevers. The entire episode did not last more than fifteen minutes, and affected mothers, after being given a folk remedy, either fell asleep or became totally withdrawn for an hour or so before falling asleep. The remedy was one of the many tecitos (teas) that rural Tlaxcalans administer for a variety of folk ailments, in this case, made of chamomile with a leaf or two of *ocoxochitl* (a parasitic pine herb). Hallucination is undoubtedly the most atypical of psychological disturbances experienced by mothers throughout the postsucking period, but it does occasionally occur. We are at a loss to explain why it takes place within the present context, but it is evident that the hallucinations themselves bear directly on the central theme of the sucking event—namely, the most common animal-transformation forms of the tlahuelpuchi. In many ways, hallucination is the most serious of all psychological aftereffects, and we thought of the possibility of correlating its occurrence with the most manifestly disturbed mothers, concomitantly the result of the most serious cases of culpability and guilt. Unfortunately, nothing meaningful emerges from the incomplete data set.

The observed case of hallucination took place in the late evening, and it appears that this is the usual time of occurrence for all cases. Whether this single case is typical, we do not know, but the reaction of the adult members of the household (case 8) was interesting. It was nearly midnight, and Nutini was having coffee with most members of the affected mother's large extended family in the household's receiving room, when they heard the mother screaming at the top of her voice. They all ran to the next room (see chapter 5) where they found the mother having the hallucinatory spell. The father was motionless at one end of the room, while the mother was pointing to the ceiling to indicate the animals she was seeing. The mother babbled and trembled, as she rested on the floor against the opposite corner of the room, for more than twelve minutes, and then suddenly, she calmed down and became very still and quiet. Throughout the entire episode all the present household members, some inside the room and some crowding the door, remained motionless without uttering a word. (Nutini, as he entered the room with the affected mother's father-in-law, was signaled to do the same.) It was only after the mother had completely calmed down that she was lifted from the floor, hugged, and placed on her petate, while her brothers-in-law and father-in-law gathered about her uttering words of endearment and encouragement. It became apparent later that the reason for letting the mother go through the entire hallucinatory episode without talking to her, touching her, or making a move is the belief that, in that state, the affected mother is in an utterly unclean and polluted condition, as if by some kind of supernatural process (which informants were never able to explain) the tlahuelpuchi controls her and makes her presence felt through the mother and her hallucinations. As this mother's father-in-law put it, "las malditas tienen a veces tanto poder y son tan malvadas, que aun después de haberse chupado a una creatura se mofan de su madre haciendola ver fantasmas y visiones" (once in a while the evil ones have so much power and are so malevolent that, even after having sucked an infant, they sneer at the mother by making her see phantoms and visions). This and several other hinted powers and proclivities of the tlahuelpuchi makes us suspect strongly that this anthropomorphic supernatural was much more diversified at the turn of the century than it is today.

These five psychological disturbances, individually and collectively, are the most visible, intensive aftereffects because the psychosomatic ailments may not always be visible, because espanto and ataque de espíritus are rather concentrated intermittent episodes, and because chilpilería and tzipitictoc exhibit similar or the same disturbances. As the reader may surmise, these psychological disturbances are not exclusively manifested as aftereffects in cases of blood-sucking witchcraft. Far from it, since they are associated with several patterned folk contexts of rural Tlaxcalan life (mothers after a bad miscarriage, daughters-in-law in the context of the often serious breakdowns they suffer because of continuous friction with mothers-in-law, fathers in the context of aggravated cases of tzipitictoc during the first or second pregnancy of their wives, individual adults in general in the context of illnesses induced by the supernatural powers of tetlachihuics, and so on), or sporadically, they are manifested as exclusive or inclusive symptoms of manifold situations involving fear, anxiety, tension, and stress. We have presented little more than an outline of these rather highly patterned psychological disturbances, only insofar as they manifest themselves within the context of the postsucking period. A forthcoming publication will analyze in depth the structure and position of these disturbances within the general context of the array of folk illnesses in rural Tlaxcala. Suffice it to say here that—individually exhibited or as part of folk illnesses—hysteria, temporary amnesia, disassociation, extreme agitation, and hallucination, define one of the main psychological parameters of the aftereffects throughout the postsucking period.

We can now turn to the four folk, psychological illnesses, and assess their individual and collective significance for primary actors throughout the postsucking period. The illnesses have been outlined in some detail in chapter 6, and we refer the reader to this section. Let us start with the reiteration that all aftereffects are psychosomatic in the sense this term was defined in chapter 6. Thus, perhaps the only significant ontological difference between the four folk illnesses and all other psychological-psychosomatic disturbances and ailments is that the former are more culturally patterned, whereas the latter are more the expression of individual constraints and specific inputs. This is why these four syndromes were called folk illnesses—that is, to indicate that the people themselves recognize them as a patterned complex that may affect rural Tlaxcalans under specific situations and conditions. Essentially, espanto and ataque de espíritus on the one hand, and chipilería and tzipitictoc on the other, are two different categories, and we demonstrate what they signify for the general configuration of the postsucking period.

Ataque de espíritus, we repeat, is simply an aggravated case of espanto. The central feature of these illnesses is neither a general, prolonged state of being nor something specific which causes pain for a length of time, but intermittent seizures during which the affected person may be unconscious for as long as half an hour in the case of former, and for as long as five hours in the case of the latter. Although between seizures the affected person may experience bouts of screaming, vomiting, and episodes of bewilderment and babbling, the loss of consciousness is the defining characteristic of espanto and ataque de espíritus, the symptom that gives us the clue to their psychological function. First, the recognized need for a limpia when an individual suffers from espanto and ataque de espíritus, which no other psychological syndromes and disturbances require, indicates the culturally patterned way of dealing with the illnesses and the gravity of the physical and psychological effects on the victim. Second, although the belief system specifies that espanto and, especially, ataque de espíritus, are caused by a tetlachihuic or by visual or tactile contact with unclean, malevolent anthropomorphic supernaturals, the manifestation of these illnesses is structurally the direct result of shock or confrontation with an unbearable situation. The folk ideology is quite specific about espanto occurring when an individual suddenly and expectedly witnesses or is brought face to face with something or someone culturally regarded as abhorrent, loathsome, or potentially very harmful. The perceptive referent may be real or imagined, but the result is always the same: the manifestation of a physical symptom that underlies a psychological dislocation or disorder. This is the folk description of "shock" but what its scientific, etiological translation is we do not claim to know. Confrontation with an unbearable situation, however, is the realization and full impact of having broken a most stringent and important injunction or being responsible for a devastating or serious unfortunate event. The reaction to shock and confrontation with an unbearable situation may be either immediate or delayed: in the case of shock, it is usually immediate; in the case of confrontation with the unbearable, it is most often delayed. In all contexts or situations in which rural Tlaxcalans suffer from espanto and ataque de espíritus, these are the generating structures, ethnographically accurately described by observation and as specified by the underlying belief system; yet, what these two folk illnesses are medically, or what they mean psychiatrically, we do not entirely know. The descriptions, however, are sufficiently detailed for a physician or a psychiatrist to make some sense of the illnesses.

With respect to the postsucking period, the interpretation of the occurrence of espanto and ataque de espíritus is as follows. It is a delayed reaction of confronting the unbearable situation of the death of an infant attributed to the tlahuelpuchi. The reaction is delayed because of the cultural constraints that keep primary actors busy and distracted until after the burial of the victim. Although it would be difficult to prove, it is very likely that there is a direct correlation between the degree of felt responsibility, culpability, and guilt and the intensity of the attacks of espanto and ataque de espíritus. From this standpoint, these two psychological illnesses are equivalent structurally to hysteria and amnesia; that is, all four perform the same function—namely, temporary escape from reality. This being the case, one can assume that only extremely disturbed mothers (that is, those who for real or imaginary reasons feel the most culpability and guilt for the death of their infants) suffer from espanto or ataque de espíritus, whereas those less disturbed suffer only from attacks of hysteria or bouts of temporary amnesia. The difference between them, of course, is that the former set is more complex, is culturally determined, and has a definite place in the underlying belief system, whereas the latter set is more individually contingent on specific inputs, such as variations in personality makeup, upbringing, and the household-neighborhood support system.

Espanto and ataque de espíritus, then, are the strongest and most serious psychological states of disarray experienced by mothers throughout the postsucking period. As the most dramatic of the aftereffects experienced by mothers, they may be regarded as a metaphor for the frequently great psychological dislocation brought about by the sucking of an infant. Conversely, it is evident that the gravity of the accompanying symptoms is what ultimately returns the mother to normality. This is another good example of how an individual affected by a serious psychological disorder triggered by a dramatic, devastating event is brought to normality by the combined effect of culturally patterned behavior (the ritual and ceremonial activity accompanying the postsucking period, the support system of the household and neighborhood, the validating and displacing effects of the belief system, and so on) and individual constraints and ministrations (the strong self-image of strength and determination fostered by the imago mundi, the limpias effected at the right time, the role of the tezitlazc as a folk analyst, and so on) in a short period of time.

Chipilería and tzipitictoc, as the other set of folk illnesses, are less dramatic and serious than espanto and ataque de espíritus, but they are much more common. In fact, given the original difficulty in discriminating between some of the symptoms of these two folk illnesses and those of the psychological disturbances described above, it is quite likely, as noted above, that perhaps more than 75 percent of primary actors suffer some form of these illnesses throughout the postsucking period. We again refer the reader to chapter 6 for a general description of the illnesses. Unlike the first set of illnesses, chipilería and tzipitictoc are states of being that last more or less continuously from their onset until the end of the postsucking period. They affect both mothers and fathers, but the effects are almost invariably more serious for tzipitictoc than for chipilería, and in the patterned structure of the postsucking period they begin shortly after the burial of the victim. In the folk terminology, the tzipitictoc experienced by mothers exhibits stronger and more noticeable symptoms than the chipilería experienced by fathers. Interestingly, during the first, and occasionally second, pregnancy of their wives, husbands experience the more serious tzipitictoc symptoms, and when this is the case during the postsucking period (that is, when the father occasionally experiences not only tzipitictoc but overall stronger aftereffects than the mother) there is a significant homology. To put it differently, tzipitictoc in the case of pregnancy and in the postsucking period are structural inversions. If the couvade signifies a social and psychological claim on an infant that is about to be born, the stronger aftereffects of fathers, centered on the tzipitictoc, may be symbolically interpreted as a structural inversion of the couvade—that is, sharing with the mother in the highest degree the guilt and culpability for the death of the infant. This seems to be the main sociopsychological meaning of chipilería (structurally tzipitictoc) insofar as it affects fathers in the context of the postsucking period. Tzipitictoc as it affects mothers, however, may be interpreted as one more aftereffect that, together with psychosomatic ailments and disturbances, is the general matrix in which guilt and culpability are assuaged and ultimately resolved.

Chipilería and tzipitictoc, as subcategories of a rather extensive category of folk illness, share a broad culturally patterned base with espanto and ataque de espíritu: all four folk illnesses assuage and help to resolve guilt and culpability, the latter set intermittently and more dramatically, the former steadily and in a milder fashion. This is implicitly asserted in the belief system underlying the tlahuelpuchi complex, which specifies that espanto and ataque de espíritus may be alleviated by limpias, whereas chipilería and tzipitictoc must run their natural course. From a different viewpoint, it may be said that espanto and ataque de espíritus trigger the onset of the overwhelmingly motivating guilt-culpability matrix, which in the less serious cases (that is, the majority in which these two illnesses do not occur) develops gradually and as part of the overall conjoined influence of aftereffects; whereas chipilería and tzipitictoc underscore the unfolding of the aftereffects, as all three kinds blend into a manifest complex, which ultimately indicates the end of the postsucking period. Informants were unanimous in stating that the vanishing manifestations of chipilería and tzipitictoc signal the end of the postsucking period and the primary actors' return to normality, or in their place, the end of the effect of equivalent or overlapping psychosomatic ailments and syndromes. Another way of saying this is that the more idiosyncratic chipilería and tzipitictoc (as compared with the more culturally patterned espanto and ataque de espíritus), or their equivalent symptoms, account for the slower or faster termination of the postsucking period; that is, the efficacy of personal characteristics, the inputs of household members and neighbors, and other constraints play an important role in the process of terminating the period. This is clearly the basis for rural Tlaxcalans to say that, to a considerable extent, these two folk illnesses are not *de nación* (natural); rather, they show the weakness or lack of spirit or will of those affected. Again, chipilería and tzipitictoc reflect the combination of idiosyncratic and culturally patterned factors that make the postsucking period so effective in bringing to an end the motivating entailment of guilt and culpability. In the same fashion, all four psychological folk illnesses analyzed here have the same function in each of the various contexts in which they manifest themselves in rural Tlaxcalan society.

In summary, What is the function, or, perhaps more modestly, what is the meaning of the psychosomatic and psychological illnesses, disturbances, and ailments that we have analyzed in this section? Essentially, their unfolding throughout the postsucking period may be regarded as a catharsis of the responsibility, culpability, and guilt entailed by the always highly dislocating death of an infant attributed to the tlahuelpuchi. The cathartic process takes place by the conjoined action of the various psychosomatic and psychological syndromes and disturbances, their most functional and effective attribute being that they are coterminously culturally determined and idiosyncratic in bringing about the implicit goal of ending the postsucking period. The wisdom of the folk system is evident: by a combination of practices, traditionally developed to deal with an array of psychological syndromes and discharged within the caring and sympathetic context of the household and neighborhood, the serious dislocations suffered by primary actors, especially mothers, after a sucking, are successfully dealt with and almost always brought to a rapid end. Left unresolved, the guilt and culpability entailed by the death of an infant would in many cases develop, especially for mothers, into serious, long-term psychological disarray. Herein lies the wisdom of the rural Tlaxcalan folk system of dealing with psychological dislocation (and in the anthropological literature there are probably many similar cases in folk and tribal societies), the implications of which are evident for the practice of modern psychiatry. Finally, we regret that the study lacks a good foundation in medical anthropology, the rigor with which teams of anthropologists and physicians have been able to make good medical sense of folk illnesses, and the adequate translation of psychological syndromes and disturbances (see Rubel 1984). This has not been possible, but the folk descriptions and occasionally somewhat bold interpretations have brought us a little closer to understanding the folk concepts of physical and psychological illnesses in a vanishing world and how one can proceed to undertake the task of translating folk concepts and symptoms of illness into the etiology of modern medicine. To say the least, this tentative interpretation has contributed to the understanding of several folk illnesses with a wide distribution in Mesoamerican Indian and Mestizo communities. It is our contention that, unless one establishes, say, what espanto (*susto*) means ideologically (as objectified in a verbalized belief system) and epistemologically (as variously perceived and interpreted), one cannot translate the concept into a descriptive medical lexicon.

SECONDARY ACTORS AND THE NETWORK OF KINSMAN-NEIGHBOR INTERACTION

Implicit in the discussion of the foregoing sections is the network of secondary actors (household kinsmen, non-residential extended-family kinsmen, and neighbors), in the midst of which the mother and father of a sucked infant go through the various degrees of gravity of dislocating and painful aftereffects. In other words, the contextual matrix in which the primary actors' aftereffects set in, manifest themselves, and are ultimately resolved and the support system of affected mothers and fathers that is constituted by the social and psychological roles of secondary actors must now be discussed. Metaphorically, one could say that the relationship between primary and secondary actors is equivalent to that of medical patients (perhaps of psychiatric patients) and the environment in which they are treated and cured, including the role of all those who have a direct hand in making them well. Briefly, the underlying consequences and constraints of the web of support relations are explored to round up the overall structure of the aftereffects of an infant's death during the postsucking period. We also discuss the extent to which the primary actors' responsibility, culpability, and guilt are shared by secondary actors, and how these asymmetrically shared psychological states are in turn an integral part of the cathartic process that characterize the return to normality of primary actors. This endeavor allows for the opportunity to analyze the moral order that underlies the tlahuelpuchi complex, guiding and constraining several related systems as exemplified in the foregoing chapters. Let us begin with the second set of considerations leading to the first.

Collective Culpability and Guilt and the Structure of Moral Action

In several contexts we have stated that the maximum extension of personnel affected by an infant death attributed to the tlahuelpuchi (the household, the non-residential extended family, and the neighborhood) shares collectively, and in varying degrees, the culpability and guilt generated by this unfortunate event. The ultimate motivator for these psychological states is, of course, the responsibility that all maximally bound actors share for the death of the infant as a consequence of constraints imposed by the moral system regulating the interaction between humans and the various manifestations of the supernatural. This is a peculiar moral order, however, and it needs rather careful elucidation, for one may be easily misled to think of it as another version of the all-encompassing Christian moral order regulating not only the relationship between man and God but that among men and the collectivity as well. There is a rather intimate link here between magic and religion which has nothing to do with the folk Catholic moral order of rural Tlaxcalans. It has been a rather common mistake in Mesoamerican ethnology to regard these two moral orders as essentially one and the same. This notion has been detrimental to the proper conceptualization of Mesoamerican Indian and rural Mestizo religion and its relationship to anthropomorphic supernaturalism. The moral order is directly relevant here, and it must be dealt with in some detail. This problem has been discussed extensively elsewhere (Nutini and Isaac 1977:84–90; Nutini 1984: 371–76; Nutini 1988:Introduction); here, the discussion is tailored to the specific notion of how the moral order in question engenders the responsibility entailing culpability and guilt.

The ideological predominance of Catholicism in the folk, syncretic religion of rural Tlaxcala may easily lead the ethnographer to think that the region has a basically Catholic religious-ideological system with a few additions attributable primarily to the still rather strong presence of witchcraft, sorcery, nahualism, weathermaking (anthropomorphic supernaturalism), and other non-Catholic beliefs and practices. This assessment erroneously presupposes that the Catholic and non-Catholic beliefs systems are separate. Whereas this is true structurally (that is, the folk practices of Catholicism show few points of articulation with non-Catholic practices in ritual and ceremonialism), it is not true ideologically. Rather, Catholic and non-Catholic practices involving the supernatural share a belief system. In this common system one finds the same attitudes, the same general cosmogonic conceptions, the same conception of supernatural forces, and the same operational mechanisms, regardless of structural manifestations. Thus, when rural Tlaxcalans pray to a certain image, sponsor a certain mayordomía, or engage in the various rituals of folk Catholicism, they are essentially engaging in the same supernaturally directed activities as when they engage in non-Catholic practices such as warding off witchcraft, sorcery, the propitiation of pagan supernaturals, intensification rituals, and so on. From the ideological viewpoint, then, there is no clear distinction between magic and religion, even though these complexes of beliefs and practices are structurally differentiated by the people themselves.

Rural Tlaxcalans believe that the world in which they live is controlled and regulated by supernatural powers that they can reach, and with whom they can establish rapport to improve social existence. Furthermore, rural Tlaxcalans could be said to suffer from the fallacy of misplaced concreteness, for seldom do they think about the supernatural in terms of general principles or forces; almost always they think in terms of concrete, often personified, anthropomorphic deities, entities, or things. Although structurally there are several kinds of supernatural domains and levels of magico-religious integration, the entire roster of supernatural deities, entities, and things — whether Catholic (the various manifestations of Christ and the Virgin Mary, the saints, the devil, the angels, Catholic things and rituals endowed with sacred power, such as rosaries, prayers, the mass, benedictions, processions, and so on) or non-Catholic (anthropomorphic supernaturals such as bloodsucking witches, sorcerers, nahuales, weathermen, tutelary mountain owners, and places endowed with supernatural powers, talismans, soul loss, and a rather long list of objects and practices) — constitutes a global supernatural complex with a unitary ideological meaning. In this scheme of things, the people definitely distinguish between Catholic and non-Catholic, and consciously try to keep them separately, but the same fundamental ideological elements and psychological processes become operative when rural Tlaxcalans worship, propitiate, intensify, or approach both Catholic and non-Catholic supernaturals. In other words, the supernatural belief system of rural Tlaxcala is an undifferentiated ideological whole, but its levels of integration (the main cleavage being between Catholic and non-Catholic) are discharged structurally in different ways. Thus, when the average rural Tlaxcalan undertakes a *manda* (a promise to Christ, the Virgin Mary, or a saint in exchange for a favor) or consults a tetlachihuic, he is engaging in basically the same supernatural activity, his psychological framework is the same, and he expects to achieve the same results, although the Catholic and non-Catholic activities involve a series of distinctly different ritual steps.

The supernatural belief system of rural Tlaxcala has one general, predominant characteristic—namely, to make the individual and collective world of social existence safe and secure by the proper propitiation of all supernatural forces, regardless of the means employed. The relationship between humans and the supernatural, then, is characterized by pragmatic and rather selfish motives for which the individual and the group pay dearly, in the sense that the efforts involved demand a great deal of time and both economic and social resources. Regardless of their social or recreational value, nearly all religious activities and behavior are individually and collectively aimed at propitiation of the supernatural in order to achieve certain goals. From this viewpoint, the religion of rural Tlaxcala is surprisingly lacking in moral (in the ethical sense) attributes, and in this respect it differs greatly from orthdox Catholicism, which is permeated with ethical values. Almost the sole concern of religion and magical practices is rapport with the supernatural, whereas ethics—morality in the conventional sense—and appropriate behavior are almost exclusively a social concern. Thus, what individuals and the collectivity should or should not do, what is proper or improper, what is permissible or not permissible, and in general what constitutes acceptable behavior are regulated almost exclusively by the social structure. Failure to comply with ethics and conventional morality carries social and economic punishments and sanctions but not supernatural sanctions. If a person engages in antisocial behavior, he is punished by the group and not by the saints or any other supernatural; if a couple fails to marry properly, the pair is punished economically or socially by kinsmen or by a sizable segment of the community; and so on. In other words, the moral order that concerns us here centers upon the magico-religious system. It regulates exclusively the interaction between humans and the supernatural, but it has very little to do with ethics and conventional morality in regulating the social, economic, and political life of the people, individually and collectively.

This remarkable lack of moral and ethical component in the social religion of rural Tlaxcala and its overwhelming emphasis on propitiation and pragmatic self-interest are strongly reminiscent of the pre-Hispanic, polytheistic religion of the region. Indeed, rural Tlaxcalan religion today (and by extension that of much of Mesoamerica) must be characterized neither as monotheism nor as

polytheism but as monolatry, to indicate both this lack of moral-ethical over-
tones and the fact that, behaviorally, the people do not transcendentally discriminate between the Christian God and lesser Catholic supernaturals (the
Virgin Mary and the saints) and pagan supernaturals (Nutini 1988:Introduc-
tion). Clearly, many fundamental ideological beliefs regarding man, the supernatural, and their interrelationship have survived until the present. The most
effective domain of religious syncretism has, however, been the structural,
more manifest domain of Catholic ritual and ceremonialism and associated
administrative practices; whereas the magical domain, essentially anthropomorphic supernaturalism, has remained almost entirely pre-Hispanic in both
structure and function. Were this not the case it would be difficult to understand the present situation.

Nutini (1988:Chapter 10) has described and analyzed in detail the cosmogonic aspects of the belief system of rural Tlaxcala; here, we confine ourselves
to the main characteristics of the actors and things involved, and the attitude
of the people toward them. Rural Tlaxcalans conceive of supernatural forces,
deities, personages, and things as essentially benevolent. There are exceptions,
of course, the most important ones being the Christian devil (who is interestingly syncretized and has several non-Christian components), certain kinds of
witches (*tlahuelpochime*), and to some extent tutelary mountain owners such
as El Peñon. The exceptions, however, are not significant, and can generally be
ignored here. Furthermore, rural Tlaxcalans do not distinguish Catholic and
non-Catholic supernaturals in terms of goodness or predisposition to help.
This is clearly specified in the words of an old informant who said, "Aquí
siempre hemos creído que las fuerzas que gobiernan este valle de sufrimientos
están la mayor parte del tiempo dispuestas a ayudar, cualquiera que sea su
naturaleza. Hay gentes que rezan, otras que buscan las mayordomias, y otras
que consultan y se conectan con los tetlachihuics. Todo es lo mismo si se pone
el corazón en la súplica." (Here we have always believed that the forces that
govern this vale of suffering, whatever their nature, are most often predisposed
to help. There are people who pray, others search for mayordomias, and still
others consult and get close to the tetlachihuics. It is all the same if one puts
one's heart in the supplication.)

Supernatural forces, deities, and personages are conceived of by the people
as existing close to them, in a realm that is never clearly specified but often
reminiscent of the pre-Hispanic situation. There is no clear distinction between
above, or the sky, as the dwelling place of the good forces or spirits, and below,
or the depths of the mountains or the earth, as the dwelling place of the evil
forces or spirits—a distinction that has been reported for several parts of Mesoamerica. Rather, supernatural forces are supposed to inhabit diverse places but

always close to humans, and they are thought to be able to influence quickly and directly the acts of men and the outcome of future affairs. Given the pragmatic, self-seeking nature of religion in rural Tlaxcala, one would expect to find a good deal of supernatural specialization and one does, not only among Catholic supernaturals (whose roster of specialized saints must have blended well with the pre-Hispanic, polytheistic religion of the region), but among non-Catholic supernaturals as well. Thus, one not only prays to such and such a saint for such and such a favor according to specialization, but the same division of labor concerning powers and favor-granting attributes exists for non-Catholic supernaturals as well. Specific specialized non-Catholic supernatural personages (La Malintzi, El Cuatlapanga, Angelina María, La Serpiente Negra, and a few others), practitioners, and complexes are approached with a variety of supplications. What is never specified is the relationship that holds together this vast supernatural pantheon, nor is there a hierarchical order in which the multiple deities, personages, practitioners, and things can be placed and which determines how they influence each other. The only vague operational principle here seems to be a conscious effort to keep the Catholic complex more or less separate from the non-Catholic. But not even this is fundamental to the supernatural belief system, since Catholic rites and ceremonies occasionally blend with pagan ones.

In general, the people are conscious of the proximity of the supernaturals and of their power to affect human affairs. It is therefore of the utmost importance to keep them content and to show them the appropriate deference and respect. Rural Tlaxcalans exhibit a certain ambivalence in their relationship to supernaturals: on the one hand, the people fear them because they may remain indifferent to supplications and entreaties when not properly propitiated; on the other hand, the people love them and are firmly convinced that they are essentially benevolent. On the whole, the relationship of rural Tlaxcalans to the supernatural is governed more by fear than by love; it is a fear that unless the appropriate ceremonies and general behavior toward the supernaturals are forthcoming, the established order binding humans and their non-human overseers will be disrupted. Here, then, is the cornerstone of the magico-religious system in rural Tlaxcala and the most fundamental operational principle in the supernatural belief system: humans and the supernatural are arranged in an established order in which both have rights and obligations, and as long as both sides comply with their part, the world will run fairly smoothly, even though the world of human affairs is at best a bad job. This is, then, the covenant that governs the relationship of man and the supernatural, and it affects the entire spectrum of the magico-religious system. The conceptual, theological sophistication of rural Tlaxcalans is not sufficient to specify what would happen to the supernaturals (the gods, if you will) if humans disregarded them completely, but it most certainly specifies what happens to men when they do not fulfill their part in the bargain.

What, specifically, is man's part in the bargain? First, a certain attitude of mind that includes respect, deference, some love, and above all, a firm commitment to try to please the supernaturals constitutes the ideological underpinning of the human-supernatural relationship. On the whole, people adhere to it quite closely, whether out of fear, pragmatism, self-interest, or a combination of these. Second, there is a vast structural array of rites, ceremonies, and behavior which must be performed according to specified custom on the basis of a yearly calendar, seasonal variations, unexpected or regular events, and, above all, with respect to individual supernatural deities, personages, or objects. This ritual-ceremonial complex and associated behavior constitute not only the core of the rural Tlaxcalan magico-religious system, but almost its sole concern. The people feel that once they have carried out the prescribed ceremonies, everything else is either superfluous or must be taken for granted, for it is this compliance that predisposes the supernatural to help individuals and the group and that makes the world of social affairs reasonably safe. In complying with ritual and ceremonial prescriptions, individual and collective responsibilities are not entirely separate: what is left undone by individuals may influence the community as a whole since it hampers the smooth functioning of the established order, hence the pressure brought to bear upon individuals by the community, or part of it, to comply with rites and ceremonies.

Obviously, not all rites and ceremonies rank the same in the ritualistic magico-religious system of rural Tlaxcala. Rather, there is a kind of hierarchy of prescriptions, preferences, and options based upon the importance of the occasion, its individual or public nature, and the character and position of the propitiated supernatural. What is constant, however, is the primacy of ritual and ceremonial behavior or whatever other magico-religious behavior one finds in rural Tlaxcala. To reiterate, once rural Tlaxcalans have complied with their ritual obligations, everything else is much less important magico-religiously, for they feel released from further action. In the hierarchy of rites and ceremonies concerning Catholicism, for example, the folk aspects rank considerably higher than the more othodox aspects. Thus, it is much more important to the average rural Tlaxcalan to sponsor a given *cargo* and to participate in a certain procession than, for example, to go to mass, confession, and communion. Once he has done the former, he feels no compulsion to do the latter, for in his belief system he has already done what is required of him by the supernatural.

Given the foregoing human-supernatural order, we ask what are the main domains of the magico-religious system for whose ritual-ceremonial discharge rural Tlaxcalans are responsible, individually and collectively? Essentially these are the domains that have been termed the "sacred core" of local community culture and society (Nutini 1988:Conclusions)—that is, that core of institutions centered about the magico-religious system that keeps the community traditional, despite considerable modernizing inputs and trends. In order of relative importance, the domains are the following: periodic sponsorship of the various cargos in the ayuntamiento religioso; occasional sponsorship of the many positions of the extensive mayordomía system; individual and collective participation in the cult of the saints; individual and collective participation in the cult of the dead; establishment of prescriptive and preferential compadrazgo types; discharging obligations as members of the barrio organization; and propitiation and intensification of tutelary mountain owners (at several times throughout the year and in connection with the cult of the dead). This set of magico-religious domains entails a manifold complex of rites, ceremonies, and propitiatory, supplicatory, and intensifying kinds of behavior that configures the exclusive means of communication between man and the supernaturals.

This extensive complex, as it were, constitutes the offerings and symbolic food for the deities, personages, and entities of the rural Tlaxcalan pantheon, the human quid pro quo in the human-supernatural covenant, which keeps the social and physical universe of rural Tlaxcalans running reasonably smoothly. The responsibility of keeping the supernatural wheels turning falls both on the collectivity and the individual (and his family): if the local group fails to meet its part of the bargain, everybody suffers; if individuals fail to discharge their prescribed ritual, ceremonial, and propitiatory obligations, the group also suffers, for individuals' failure to comply is regarded as lessening the pool of the supernaturals' goodwill that must be constantly maintained. In turn, according to the traditional imago mundi of rural Tlaxcalans, when the deities, personages, and entities of the pantheon consider that individuals and the collectivity are remiss or are not properly compliant with their obligations, they punish the culprits by withholding supernatural support. This action on the part of the gods (and the term here is not used metaphorically, inasmuch as the supernatural pantheon of rural Tlaxcala is a monolatrous system) invariably results in an array of unfortunate events, disasters, and wants, meted out individually or collectively, as the case may be, the most common of which are: not enough rain; too much rain; hail storms; bad crops; not enough work; bad luck in business ventures; bad health; illness and death; individual (family, kinship, compadrazgo) and collective (barrio, community) dissension; outbreaks of violence or aggressive behavior; and so on. In fact, the imago mundi allows, indeed, often forces the individual and the collectivity to regard any unfortunate event as entailed by the withholding of supernatural support.

In the operational discharge of the human-supernatural covenant, two do-mains clearly stand out. On the one hand, considerable numbers of the local group (whether kinship units such as households and non-residential extended families, territorial units such as parajes or barrios, or the entire community) are constantly watchful about seeing that the collective ritual and ceremonial responsibilities toward the supernatural not only are properly met but met to the best of the group's ability. As a counterpart, traditionalists are constantly on the lookout for individual malingerers or unenthusiastic people (including married couples and households), and social and even economic pressure is brought to bear upon them, mostly through kinsmen and compadres, to comply with their individual responsibilities toward the supernaturals. On the other hand, given the dominant deterministic characteristic of the imago mundi, always at the tip of the tongue of rural Tlaxcalans, the people immediately ponder and search for an explanation as to how, by commission or omission, they offended the supernaturals to make them withdraw their support and allow such pain and unhappiness to occur when disaster strikes or unfortunate events befall an individual or the collectivity. There are hundreds of examples, in all the potentially punitive domains mentioned above, in which both affected individuals and the group tried very hard, after the fact, to determine what they did or did not do to the supernaturals to deserve such a fate; perhaps people sought to assign blame, but more likely, they sought to mend their ways for the future. It is in this ambience that guilt and culpability is engen-dered for having done something that displeased the supernatural or for having failed to comply with individual or collective ritual and ceremonial responsibili-ties. This is the main operational principle of the human-supernatural moral order, in which culpability and guilt do not usually obtain in the realm of human interaction but are entailed by failures of commission or omission in the interaction of humans and the supernatural forces that govern them.

In the essentially deterministic imago mundi of rural Tlaxcalans, the tlahuel-puchi is probably the only indeterminate supernatural in the entire roster of the pantheon of deities, personages, and entities. Through no fault of her own, she is saddled at birth with a loathsome and abhorrent proclivity that makes her the epitome of a malevolent entity endowed with supernatural powers. When the tlahuelpuchi strikes and an infant dies, the local group (as defined by the non-residential extended family and de facto most of the neighborhood) becomes the social environment in which responsibility, in the fashion defined above, triggers culpability and guilt. Immediately after the shock of the suck-ing event wears off, secondary actors, particularly household members, ponder over the situation and ask themselves individually, collectively, and on behalf of primary actors the following questions: "What did the poor little ones (the victim's parents) do for this (the death of the infant) to have happened to them? How and in what fashion did they displease the saints and all the powers that govern us? Did they fail to contract an important compadrazgo relationship? Did they refuse to become *acompañantes* (attendants in a mayordomía)? Were they remiss in cooperating with the celebration of the patron saint of the community or the barrio? Were they generous and thoughtful enough to set up the appropriate *ofrenda* (offering) in front of the family altar for *Todos Santos* (All Saints Day-All Souls Day)? Did they in any way offend or were they disrespectful to the Lady Malintzi or El Cuatlapanga? What did they actually do to have suffered so? How did we (household members, non-residential extended-family members, and neighbors, as the case may be) fail to notice what they (the victim's parents) did wrong or the mistakes they made in getting close to and serving the forces that watch over us, so that we might have corrected them and guided them? What did we do wrong, and how did we fail in the same manner and for the same occasions, thus bringing upon ourselves (the local group) the wrath and displeasure of God, the saints, and all the spirits and forces that are so close to us and so predisposed to help us and assist us?" On and on they recite the possible contexts and occasions and reasons for their (primary and secondary actors) failure to comply with their part of the bargain in the human-supernatural covenant.

Soon after the discovery of the victim's body, this ambience of doubt sets in and persists for most of the postsucking period. Most interestingly, despite the ostensible aim of this questioning period to assign blame and to serve as a corrective for future action, secondary actors, explicitly, and primary actors, implicitly, are really engaged in a verbal, reinforcing self-fulfilling exercise; for even if in their questioning they are able to pinpoint specific individual and collective failures in generating rapport with the supernatural, the efficacy of the exercise rests in the verbalization itself: it is a cathartic process structurally equivalent to the aftereffects suffered by primary actors in their own right. Just as the culpability and guilt of primary actors for their real or imagined inputs in the death of the infant set in quickly after the burial, so do the collective culpability and guilt of secondary actors triggered by real or imagined sins of commission or omission against the supernaturals and resulting in the unfortunate event set in. This morally generated culpability and guilt are the factors which shape the behavior and action of secondary actors, vis-à-vis each other and with respect to primary actors, until the resolution of the postsucking period and the return to normality of the household and neighborhood. In the ambience of the postsucking period, primary and secondary actors function respectively as patients and curers, and together grapple with the physical, psychological, and moral dislocation produced by the death of an infant attributed to the tlahuelpuchi.

Psychological Ambience and the Matrix of Support Relations Throughout the Postsucking Period

The social and psychological ambience of the household and neighborhood during the postsucking period is well exemplified by the Xolotla bloodsucking witchcraft epidemic described in chapter 5. Nutini observed closely the nine households from shortly after the victims' bodies were discovered, through the discharge of the rites of the wake and burial, until the household more or less returned to normality five and half days later. We can generalize to the entire sample that throughout this period, questioning and doubt are quickly followed by the realization of culpability and guilt that sets in and permeates the remainder of the postsucking period. The reader should realize, however, that this apparent return to normality of the household and neighborhood concerns only the fear that the tlahuelpuchi may strike again and the rationalization and reinforcing of the bloodsucking witchcraft complex. As we discussed, almost invariably the postsucking period lasts from at least another two or three days to as much as a week and a half more from the viewpoint of the primary actors' aftereffects. Just as we proceeded with primary actors in the foregoing section, we now give a syntagmatic account of the behavior and action of secondary actors from the inception to the resolution of the postsucking period.

As in the case of primary actors, there is a period of delayed action concerning the onset of collective culpability and guilt among household members, non-residential extended family members, and neighbors. This, again, is due to the discharge of the rites and ceremonies of the wake and burial, which keeps people distracted for a while. In other words, the day and a half or so transpiring between the discovery and burial of the victim's body is a period of intensive activity in the household and immediate vicinity. Two domains of behavior may be isolated for this initial period, one primarily social, the other essentially psychological.

First, the immediate kinsmen of the victim's parents must arrange for the mother's limpia, buy the coffin for the body, organize the wake, and the following day prepare for the burial and the ceremonial meal afterward. This responsibility falls on the parents of the father and other live-in kinsmen in extended-family households, and on the most immediate kinsmen (usually parents, uncles, or brothers and their wives) of the non-residential extended family in nuclear-family households, for the affected parents themselves are in no condition to do anything about these chores. Even if they are alert enough, kinsmen and neighbors spare them every effort and strain. Neighbors often lend a hand and become integrated into the operating group that takes care of the ritual and ceremonial activities that dominate the first part of the postsucking period. A kinsman or neighbor is nominated to find a tezitlazc, to engage him for the mother's initial limpia, and almost invariably, to retain him for any further limpias that the mother and father may have to undergo. The coffin is always bought by the nearest of kin of the victim's father (usually his parents or an elder brother and his wife), who also are in charge of preparing the wake, as described in chapter 5. The victim's baptismal padrinos must be notified immediately, for they are responsible for buying the burial cross. The padrinos and some of their immediate kinsmen play a leading part in the wake and in the preparation of the food for it and for the ceremonial meal next day. No food is allowed to be prepared by any member of the affected household, and everything that is consumed is prepared by the victim's padrinos, non-residential extended-family kinsmen, and neighbors. This injunction stems from the state of pollution in which the affected household is supposed to be until the tezitlazc ritually cleanses it and the body of the victim is buried. The people believe that the pollution effected by the presence of the tlahuelpuchi in the household extends to all those who inhabit it at the time. As in any other ritual or ceremonial context or occasion in the extensive magico-religious and social array of rural Tlaxcala, the support group of kinsmen and neighbors throughout this initial period functions smoothly and effectively, since all persons concerned know exactly what to do and how to behave.

Second, the first two days of the postsucking period are the most intensive with respect to questioning what the individual and the group have done or left undone in their relationship to the supernatural. This aspect of the postsucking period is rather dramatically exemplified by the description of the Xolotla epidemic, in which the kinsmen and neighbors of this paraje were baffled and disoriented by, and somewhat at a loss at the magnitude of the unfortunate event. The Xolotla epidemic is, of course, atypical, but it does give a general idea of what happens to the average paraje when one or perhaps two infants are sucked in one or two consecutive nights. Concomitantly with the questioning that goes on, kinsmen and neighbors become very much aware of the tlahuelpuchi as an anthropomorphic supernatural and her efficacy to kill, something that is relegated to the back of their societal concerns most of the time. As we have discussed, this part of the postsucking period continues for two or three days after the infant has been buried, and this rather long elapse of time constitutes the strongest reinforcing and intensifying process of the tlahuelpuchi complex, validating the overt, most significant physical function of the blood-sucking witch—namely, her efficacy to kill under certain well-specified conditions. Throughout this period of intensive psychological and introspective activity, the local group maximally affected by the sucking reflects on the nature of their magico-religious world; through questioning, recounting legends and happenings concerning the tlahuelpuchi, and probing their own supernatural performance, the kinsmen and neighbors of the paraje exorcise themselves of the demons of responsibility, and at the same time reinforce and validate a belief system that they deem beneficial as an explanatory mechanism.

Again, as with primary actors, culpability and guilt begins to sink in shortly after the burial of the sucked infant. The secondary actors' bouts of reflection, questioning, and commiseration lead to a state of culpability and guilt. This process initiates the longest part of the postsucking period, which is the most trying for all concerned, and lasts until the resolution of the aftereffects, from a few days to nearly two weeks later, depending on the gravity of the case. The behavior and actions of secondary actors are centered on the affected primary actors and their aftereffects, on the one hand, whereas individually and occasionally collectively they must cope with their own psychological dislocation, on the other. In the former context, the network of personnel is reduced, since it is constituted primarily by the affected household members and those kinsmen and neighbors in the immediate vicinity. These kinsmen and neighbors are the personnel immediately concerned with the care of the affected parents and with physical and psychological ministering to alleviate the aftereffects. The empathy generated by the sucking is such that the distinction between kinsman and neighbor disappears, and propinquity becomes as important as kinship affiliation. The reader should remember, of course, that the category of neighbor, as defined above, includes compadres, always a category of most solicitous and thoughtful personnel when unfortunate events occur. Non-residential extended-family kinsmen and neighbors residing farther away from the affected household may commiserate and offer to help, but, de facto, it is the propinquous group that almost exclusively comforts, ministers, and takes care of the physical needs of the affected parents in an organized fashion, frequently taking turns as the occasion may require. In the latter context, the entire non-residential extended family and the network of neighbors within reasonable distance tangibly constitute a fairly well-configured group—namely, those who, inversely proportionately to propinquity, feel and experience the guilt and culpability triggered by the infant's sucking. It is a temporary group, of course, which evidently lasts only until the aftereffects of primary actors are gone and the affected household returns to normality, but it does exhibit the configuration of a functional, corporate psychological entity. By this we mean that the maximal extension of personnel—kinsmen and neighbors—not only feel and appear to share the same culpability and guilt, but, they wish to do something individually and collectively to alleviate them. Indeed, they do do something, both by ministering or wanting to minister to primary actors and by engaging in the exorcising and cathartic exercises mentioned above. As a support system for primary actors and as a validating, psychological configuration of personnel, the maximal extension of secondary actors constitutes probably the most important psychosocial grouping in rural Tlaxcalan culture and society. Discontinuous in time and temporary in efficacy, an operational group of the kinsmen and neighbors of a paraje comes into being when disaster strikes, serious unfortunate events affect one or several households, or when properly activated by traditional mechanisms (for purposes of social and religious cooperation and exchange); this is without a doubt the most efficient and organized unit beyond the extended family. What in many tribal societies is achieved by corporate kinship, in rural Tlaxcala is achieved by the propinquity of kinship, compadrazgo, and friendship.

Let us discuss what this propinquous group means as a support system for primary actors in terms of categories of personnel. There is variation, of course, depending on whether the affected household harbors a nuclear family or an extended family. In an extended family, household members (mostly the father's parents, unmarried siblings, and married brothers and their wives) constitute the nucleus of the support group attending and ministering to the affected couple, which may occasionally include particularly close non-residential extended-family kinsmen (not necessarily residing close to the affected household) and next-door neighbors (frequently close compadres). In a nuclear family, especially when there are no older siblings, the role of non-residential extended-family kinsmen and neighbors is much more important. In such cases (twenty-three, almost half of the sample's cases, see table 6.7) kinsmen and neighbors from an array of various categories quickly constitute themselves into an ad hoc group. Such a group does not necessarily include the father's parents, but almost invariably it includes older married brothers and their wives, paternal uncles and their wives, and occasionally the father's grandparents. As far as neighbors are concerned, the group includes nearby compadres of the affected couple, good friends (usually prospective compadres) residing next door, and always the padrinos of the dead infant, although they may not necessarily reside in the paraje. In both cases, this support group may include as few as eight and as many as twenty male and female adults, frequently joined in the support activities by other kinsmen and neighbors on a temporary basis or for the duration of the postsucking period. This array of kinsmen and neighbors constitutes, then, the support system that helps the affected couple undergo the travails of the postsucking period and to a significant extent conditions the household's return to normality.

For as long as the postsucking period lasts—that is, until the victim's parents' aftereffects disappear and the household returns to normality—the support group not only runs the affected (nuclear family) household but is completely in charge of caring for and attending to the needs of the disturbed couple. Even if the father was not significantly affected by the infant's sucking and could possibly work, he remains at home and spends a good deal of time with his usually much more disturbed wife. Thus, the victim's mother as well as father need for the extent of the postsucking period rather constant care and affection, which we have analogously described as the care and treatment that a patient receives in a modern medical setup. Concretely, what are the functions, tasks, and activities performed by the support group as curers and guides of the affected couple? First, the couple is completely released from any household responsibility, and whatever tasks and duties they perform under normal conditions are taken over by specific individuals in the support group, who routinely take turns at discharging them: preparing food, washing clothes, taking care of the children, and so on. In fact, the affected couple are encouraged to rest and to visit kinsmen and neighbors, if at all possible. Second, the support group provides constant supervision of the mother and father, especially in the more serious cases, when there is always someone in attendance. Again, organized in some fashion, usually as pairs, the support group take turns to oversee that the mother and the father do not wander away in a disconnected state, that they are not in any physical danger, and that they get plenty of rest. Most important, enough males and females of the support group must always be at hand when the mother or father suffer from attacks or bouts of espanto, ataque de espíritus, hysteria, amnesia, or any of the serious psychological syndromes and ailments that they are likely to experience. This requires coordination, especially in cases of extreme aftereffects, and members of the support group must occasionally use much discretion and ingenuity to alleviate the father's or mother's symptoms as quickly as the situation warrants it. Third, but not least, the support group must provide the affected couple with loving concern, empathy, and a reassuring environment in which they are verbally reinforced to get well and to assuage their culpability and guilt. Not only the immediate support group, but kinsmen and neighbors who may by chance or purposely come into contact with or visit the affected couple are bound to do their best to provide the empathy and encouragement that is so important to the recuperating process. Even those ever-present doubters (about both the efficacy of the tlahuelpuchi to kill and the ex post facto rationalizations of the complex) agree that this propitious environment has significant therapeutic value for the affected couple, and they regard it as an indispensable element in the process of returning the household to normality. This is well expressed by one such informant: "La verdad es que no sé si la tlahuelpuchi se chupó a la creatura, o fué otra la causa de su muerte. Pero sí me doy cuenta de que los padres de la creatura sufren y se enferman por su muerte, y que el apoyo y cuidado de parientes, compadres, y amigos ayuda mucho a que se recuperen pronto." (The truth is that I do not know whether in fact the tlahuelpuchi sucked the infant, or something else was the cause of its death. But I do realize that the infant's parents suffer for its death and get sick, and that the support and care of kinsmen, compadres, and friends helps greatly in their prompt recovery.) As we have noted, the double-edged effect of the propitious and caring environment provided by the support group is the single most important factor for the recovery of the affected couple and the quick return to normality of the household.

Finally, what is the extent of culpability and guilt and how are they expressed? Let us reiterate first that, ontologically and epistemologically (that is, in origin, configuration, manifestation, and perception), culpability and guilt are experienced essentially the same by primary and secondary actors. There are two differences, however: on the one hand, the intensity of these psychological states is much greater in primary than in secondary actors, and, on the other, secondary actors do not exhibit the array of aftereffects almost invariably affecting primary actors, as described in the foregoing section. Conceptually, then, culpability and guilt are the same for all actors affected by the sucking event, and the differences are only in manifest intensity. Evidently, the single factor that accounts for the range of aftereffects experienced by primary actors, and their usually manifest absence in secondary actors, is the culpability and guilt engendered by the personal, immediate responsibility for the death of the infant felt by the mother and structurally shared by the father. Somewhat counterbalancing this personal, individual culpability and guilt may be the responsibility felt by the local group, especially those closest to the affected couple (the most immediate kinsmen and particularly important compadres), of having failed to make sure that all concerned complied strictly with their part in the human-supernatural covenant (ultimately the origin of the unfortunate event), which further generates collective culpability and guilt. This process, however, is not strong enough most of the time to produce the culturally determined but individually exhibited aftereffects in secondary actors that are exhibited by primary actors. How, then, are culpability and guilt latently or manifestly exhibited by secondary actors, individually and collectively, throughout the postsucking period?

First, only occasionally do secondary actors exhibit any one or two of the psychological dislocations described for primary actors. Informants report that once in a while the father or an elder brother of the victim's father becomes *chipil* or experiences psychosomatic ailments such as headaches or chest pains.

One informant reported that, in a case he knew, the mother of the victim's mother developed tzipitictoc for almost as long as the latter suffered from severe aftereffects. This example, by the way, is distinctly atypical, in that matrilateral kinsmen seldom belong to the propinquous local group as defined above, since rural Tlaxcalan postmarital residence is strongly patrivicinal. Although only six secondary actors who suffered mild or significant aftereffects were identified, it is quite possible that these psychological dislocations are more common, especially among the closest kinsmen of the father (household residents) and among the couple's most intimate compadres. This suggestion simply indicates that there is no sharp line of demarcation between the primary actors' aftereffects and similar but milder dislocations suffered by some secondary actors.

Second, the culpability and guilt of secondary actors, as defined by the non-residential extended family and neighborhood, are rather collective phenomena: the expression both of the group's responsibility for real or imagined failures of commission and omission in discharging their part in the human-supernatural covenant, and, equally significantly, of the group's inability to have prevented the same failures in the behavior and actions of primary actors, who ostensibly precipitated the sucking, an unfortunate event entailed by the supernaturals withholding, albeit temporarily, their essential support. This is verbally expressed by informants, one of whom puts it clearly, "no solo los padres de la creatura se sienten culpables, sino también todos los parientes, compadres, y amigos que vivimos cerca de ellos. Todos nos sentimos culpables y con un dejo de tristeza por la responsabilidad en nosotros mismos, y lo que podriamos haber prevenido en otros, de manera que la desgracia no hubiera sucedido." (Not only the infant's parents feel guilty, but also the kinsmen, compadres, and friends living close to them [the propinquous group as defined by kinsmen and neighbors in the parajel]. We all feel guilty [the propinquous group] and with a touch of sadness for our own responsibility, and for what we could have prevented in others [the affected couple], so that the unfortunate event would not have happened.) The collective culpability and guilt of secondary actors, with the exceptions noted above, are not expressed in the sometimes rather dramatic aftereffects exhibited by primary actors, but in a kind of social paralysis which lasts until the resolution of the primary actors' aftereffects, when the household and the paraje return to normality.

Third, it is the intimate, caring, and loving attitude of the support group, in particular, and the propinquous group, in general, toward the affected father and mother that characterizes primary and secondary actors as an undifferentiated group sharing in the responsibility, culpability, and guilt entailed by the death of an infant as attributed to the tlahuelpuchi. From this viewpoint, the aftereffects of primary actors and the role in their resolution played by secondary actors throughout the postsucking period constitutes a single process: a catharsis in which responsibility is assuaged and guilt and culpability exorcised. Conceptually, this is the central feature of the postsucking period, and it has significant implications for the comparative study of magical and medical practices. This is a theme that has surfaced on several occasions throughout this monograph—namely, that the analysis of witchcraft and sorcery, once the systems have been socially well positioned, required a psychological focus.

This chapter endeavored to present the social and psychological implications of the aftereffects suffered by primary actors and the general psychological ambience pervading the postsucking period. This, together with chapters 8 and 9, are the most innovative part of the monograph, in the sense that they tackle a series of problems that have not been dealt with in the anthropological literature on witchcraft and sorcery. This is a tentative chapter, but it does manage to put in perspective a number of issues that are at the heart of the psychological understanding of certain kinds of witchcraft (self-directed, circumscribed) and magical acts. From this perspective, they are worthy of replication by students of witchcraft better equipped than we are to grapple with the problems involved. Once again, we regret that our psychological competence is barely up to the task confronting this chapter, for the entailed problems deserve a much more exacting analysis that we have been able to provide.

CHAPTER ELEVEN

The Social and Psychological Functions of Bloodsucking Witchcraft

CHAPTERS 8, 9, AND 10 may be regarded as the structural analysis of bloodsucking witchcraft. Throughout these chapters, apart from description, the aim was to present the tlahuelpuchi complex as a system of behavior and action composed of several definable parts impinging upon each other at several levels of social and psychological efficacy. The main concern was to conceptualize the position of bloodsucking witchcraft in rural Tlaxcalan society as an explanatory system of infant death and, at the same time, to specify the role of individuals and groups in its actual discharge. This chapter is addressed to the social and psychological functional analysis of bloodsucking witchcraft in rural Tlaxcala, or more precisely, to the functional assignment and consequences of several aspects and subdomains of the tlahuelpuchi complex, as it unfolds from the sucking event to the termination of the aftereffects.

STRUCTURAL ANALYSIS AND FUNCTIONAL ASSIGNMENT

The fundamental distinction between the traditional functionalist position of Radcliffe-Brown and most of the other distinguished British anthropologists and the structuralist position of Lévi-Strauss is that the former involves a primarily empirical conception of social structure, whereas the latter involves a primarily supraempirical conception (Nutini 1965, 1968). These are relative statements, however, in that neither functionalism nor structuralism takes a clear-cut empirical or supraempirical position. Despite allegations to the contrary, for Radcliffe-Brown and perhaps all of his students, the structure of the social system is nothing more than the total ensemble of social relations enacted by the personnel of the system occupying specific positions and playing discernible roles. For Lévi-Strauss, the structure of a social system is something quite different—namely, the principles that govern the system translated into relational positions and statements of invariance obtaining among actors.

The empirical position of Radcliffe-Brown and his followers involves the interaction of structure (the web of personnel in action) and the functional assignment of teleological properties of specific parts, which result in the conceptual formation of the system. Thus, structural-functional analysis, as the name indicates, demands close conceptual interaction between definable parts standing in well-defined functional relationships to one another; otherwise there is no system (Nutini 1970:556–58). In this theoretical view of sociocultural phenomena, more often than not functional analysis becomes the primary conceptual force rather than being subordinated to structural interpretation.

Explicit in the structural approach are the idea of levels of analysis and the viewpoint that some levels must be operationally assumed in conceptualizing social empirical phenomena. One of the basic tenets of structuralism is that structure involves a more primitive set of elements or terms, and that function is always an inference from structure. This is sound scientific procedure, much in accord with the modus operandi of contemporary physical science. This does not mean, as has often been charged, that structuralist anthropologists are not concerned with function, a point discussed by Nutini (1970:557–58) elsewhere. Structuralists are indeed concerned with function, but only insofar as it is the result of the positional and relational arrangements of elements of a contextual social situation; this means that unless we want to run the risk of conjecturing, function can only be assigned after the structure has been thoroughly established.

But what is the immediate relevance of the empirical position of functionalism as it differs from the mainly supraempirical position of structuralism? Before answering this question, a few remarks are in order. First, the analysis of bloodsucking witchcraft in rural Tlaxcala is neither Radcliffe-Brownian nor Lévi-Straussian, but involves certain elements of both the functionalist and structuralist positions. This monograph follows Radcliffe-Brown to the extent that bloodsucking witchcraft is structured basically as a general ensemble of actions and behaviors discharged by actors occupying definite positions and playing various discernible roles. Yet we follow Lévi-Strauss in assigning primacy to structure over function—which is tantamount to saying that whenever functional interpretations are made, they are not a sine que non for the efficacy and accuracy of the analysis.

Second, the general organization of the material follows traditional functional analysis, but to the degree that it has been possible to deal with the deep organizational features of bloodsucking witchcraft (the entailment of responsibility, culpability, and guilt, and in general the psychological assignment of particular domains of the bloodsucking complexes), the analysis has come closer to the structural position of searching for metalinguistic modes of interpretation and explanation. This has been the case insofar as we have demonstrated the efficacy and feedback that obtains between the normative belief system (the ideological order) and the physical, social, and psychological discharge (the structural order) of the tlahuelpuchi complex.

Third, to some extent we have transcended the unidimensionality inherent in functionalism. One can see the immediate relevance of the functionalist-structuralist opposition to the analysis of bloodsucking witchcraft. It has to do primarily with the inability to transcend the paradigmatic conception of structure involved in functional analysis, which has led us to retain several of its organizational features in order to achieve a measure in the structural analysis. The analysis tries to combine what is best in the functional position with some of the aspects of structuralism that lend themselves to being integrated into a still somewhat paradigmatic position.

The main reason for combining functional and structural analysis is our inability to implement the latter fully. Under these conditions, functional assignment has a more important place in a strictly structural study. What is achieved by functional assignment is also achieved in structural analysis, not by the attribution of a priori, teleological properties of circular validation, but by the residual interpretation of regulating principles which govern the positions and relations of invariance obtaining in a social system. Thus, as a denotative term, function is equally important in both the functionalist and the structuralist approaches; the only difference is that in the former it is a circular, largely teleological operation, whereas in the latter it is an inference from structural components in action.

At the model level the concept of function is totally irrelevant, for this domain has to do exclusively with the principles governing a social system. At the paradigmatic level, however, the concept of function is important, for it enables us to analyze action and behavior as a result of the efficacy of the model over the paradigmatic level (or, as conceptualized here, of the ideological order over the structural order). Thus, we are using the concept of function in its traditional, empirical, paradigmatic sense but without its tautological implications. In this conceptual environment, the notion of function does not play an explanatory role as it does in functional theory; this role is played by the causal relationship (entailment) between the ideological and structural orders.

Finally, we would like to mention how the derivative, subsidiary conception of function applies to the substantive results of this study. Throughout the structural analysis, we have had two explicit aims in the discussion of bloodsucking witchcraft in its manifold aspects: the elucidation of action and behavior connected with well-defined actors and groups of actors; and the establishment of principles of behavior and modes of grouping that govern the system as a whole and its various domains—namely, the victim's parents, the household, the non-residential extended family, and the neighborhood. The analysis has not been concerned overtly with function; whenever we have used the term, it has been incidental and to a large extent synonymous with working or operation. Nonetheless, the notion of function has been used to denote the empirical configurations that result from the efficacy of the ideological order over the structural order and their feedback effect. Hence, in the structural analysis we have referred to the activities rather than to the functions of bloodsucking witchcraft and its various domains.

The concept of function, however, means more than just the statement of activities of a structural complex. What we have in mind is a more abstract, interlocked account of activities that will give not only an insight into the structure that produces them but a certain unitary meaning to the system and its parts. In this sense, function can be a conceptual entity that has unifying meaning rather than explanatory dimensions. Thus, when the function or functional properties of such and such an aspect of bloodsucking witchcraft are discussed, they denote primarily an integrated abstraction of the activities that characterize them.

SOCIAL FUNCTIONS: PERSONNEL NETWORK AND THE CONTEXT OF ACTION

As we understand Wallace (1966:167–215), in his discussion of the functions of religion, he does not fall into the circular trap in assessing the significance of functional assignment. In fact, by a different route, Wallace (1966:168–171) arrives at the conclusion, as maintained here, that function is not an explanatory construct, but that it can still be useful for anthropological analysis. As he put it, "Thus although answers to functional questions of the form 'What is the function of religious behavior?' do not lead to causal understanding of how religious behavior came to be, there is another form for functional questions about religion: 'What is religious behavior a function of?' Here religious behavior is treated as the effect of some other kind of behavior, and the explanation is causal with respect to religion" (Wallace 1966:179). Although we have qualms about affirming flatly that conceiving of function as an effect of some putative cause endows the concept with a measure of explanation, Wallace's conception of the proper role of function in structural studies certainly is interesting and profitable. With modification, this is essentially the form functional assignment has taken in dealing with bloodsucking witchcraft—namely, that by inverting the direction of entailment, a measure of descriptive explanation can be generated. Specifically, by undertaking Wallace's inversion, one can determine the relational and positional properties of the actors of the system and its discernible domains, which generate the observed behavior and action. Thus, one does not ask what are the functions of bloodsucking witchcraft, or of any of its manifest domains; rather, one asks what effects are entailed by the whole or any of its parts, given certain conditions and the positional and relational structure of the actors involved. Basically, what we want to answer is why the actors of bloodsucking witchcraft behave and act the way they do when the central feature of the system is activated.

The Distinction Between Primary and Secondary Functions
In the kind of analysis envisaged here, it is necessary to distinguish between primary or dominant functions and secondary, derived, or contextual functions. With respect to the compadrazgo system of rural Tlaxcala, for example, Nutini (1984:323–27) distinguishes between primary social functions and secondary economic and political functions, in which the economic sphere is not an independent domain by itself, but the social and religious spheres of the institution have significant economic and political functions. Thus, in rural Tlaxcalan communities there is no political life independent of religion, kinship, and compadrazgo, hence no primary political domain independent of these institutions. In such a situation, one cannot possibly speak of any primary political functions within the community's social structure, but one can certainly speak of the secondary political functions of religion, kinship, and compadrazgo.

Given the above considerations, we may nominally define primary function as complying with the following conditions: it is efficacious across the entire configuration of an institution, unit, or well-delineated domain; the behavior and action of the actors involved are the effect of other behavior and action not part of the structural configuration of the institution, unit, or domain—that is, the assigned function is a consequent and not an antecedent; substantively, the function's domain of efficacy must be equivalent, in extension and intension, to other domains of the social structure in operation—that is, the efficacy of the normative belief system is not fragmented; and the ontological configuration of the function is most often latent—that is, socially unconscious. By contrast, we may define secondary function as follows: it is efficacious only within a segment, large or small, of an institution, unit, or domain; the behavior and action of the actors involved are determined by primary behavior and action—that is, as a subordinate aspect of the latter in the circumscribed segment; substantively, the function's domain or extent of efficacy is never exclusive—that is, it is shared by comparable segments in equivalent primary functional institutions, units, or domains; and the ontological configuration of the function is most often manifest, and may be verbalized by the average actor in action. The first three properties or attributes of primary and secondary functions respectively are more or less self-explanatory, but not the fourth. It has been our experience in rural Tlaxcala that primary functions are almost always latent, whereas secondary functions are most often manifest.

On several occasions it was stressed that bloodsucking witchcraft in rural Tlaxcala today does not occupy a central position in the magico-religious system, although three generations ago it could have been significantly different, more diversified, and closer to the position witchcraft has in many of the traditional tribal societies described by anthropologists beginning in the early 1930s. Nonetheless, the lack of centrality of the tlahuelpuchi complex is counterbalanced by the role it plays in a rather self-contained domain and by the neatness and directness in the interplay between its normative belief system and its physical, social and psychological realization. Given these constraints, one would expect that this particular kind of witchcraft system would have few if any primary functions. This is indeed the case with bloodsucking witchcraft in rural Tlaxcala, in which, with one exception, all the social and psychological functions that may be assigned are secondary.

The Absence of Primary Social Functions and Its Homologous Equivalence
In the cosmological order of rural Tlaxcalans, all four anthropomorphic supernaturals discussed in this monograph are an expression of the constant confrontation between good and evil that characterizes the physical and social worlds of interaction. In this strongly Manichaean world, the tlahuelpuchi is to some extent an oddity, in that she is indeterminate (explained nebulously by the people by appealing to destiny or fate, a concept that does not fit well into their deterministic universe). At the same time, the belief system implies that she is one of the several instruments or means by which benevolent supernatural powers punish the individual and the collectivity when they do not comply with their part in the covenant. The tlahuelpuchi, then, unlike the other three anthropomorphic supernaturals, does not essentially reflect any social concerns in the structure of the local group; rather, it reflects the workings of a supernatural order in its dealings with human beings. What is envisaged here is that witchcraft in rural Tlaxcala is basically an instrument of a pantheon of gods—it may be socially and psychologically used by individuals and the collectivity for certain ends but does not entail the manifestation of processes at the heart of the social structure in operation. How can one explain this particular position of witchcraft in a folk society? The answer has to do mainly with the articu-

lation of witchcraft within the total magico-religious system. In the tribal societies described best by British and British-trained social anthropologists, it is quite evident that, at the cosomological and teleological levels, and perhaps even at the level of actual ritual and ceremonial discharge, the distinction between magic and religion does not obtain, or if it does, the distinction is minimal. Being thus at the center of the magico-religious system, witchcraft and sorcery are permanently, efficaciously at the heart of the social structure in operation. This is not true of rural Tlaxcalan society, or probably of most folk societies anchored to any of the great religions. In rural Tlaxcalan witchcraft at the turn of the century, and especially in bloodsucking witchcraft today, the distinction between magic and religion is significantly more evident than in the tribal societies. More conclusively, witchcraft and sorcery are not an integral part of the magico-religious core, nor are they in the same plane of its cosmological and teleological configuration. Under such conditions, contemporary bloodsucking witchcraft, occupying a peripheral position, has only secondary social functions. Moreover, when one considers that rural Tlaxcalan society has several formal and folk mechanisms for conflict and dispute resolution, the primary social functions of bloodsucking witchcraft are further diminished, and by contrast, its psychological functions become more visible.

Lest we are misunderstood by the historically minded reader, the assertion is that the position of witchcraft vis-à-vis the monolatrous religious system of rural Tlaxcala since the turn of the century is essentially similar to that of witchcraft vis-à-vis Christianity in Europe throughout most of the sixteenth and seventeenth centuries, when some of the greatest witch hunts in European history took place. Despite the self-confessed witches, witch finders, extensive accusations, and collective hysteria that accompanied the great witch hunts of those centuries in Great Britain and on the Continent, the position of European witchcraft at that time was closer to that in a folk society such as rural Tlaxcala than to that in the societies of the Azande, Cewa, Lugbara, Dobu, and other classic anthropological examples. There are three reasons for this contention. First, the epistemological position of witchcraft in sixteenth- and seventeenth-century Europe and among our primitive contemporaries is different. Among the latter, the line of demarcation between natural and supernatural causation is tenuous, or nonexistent, as some anthropologists maintain. In the former, there was already a significant thrust toward the concept of natural law, even among the lower and middle sectors of the social system, and most of the daily lives of people in those sectors were conducted without any direct supernatural intervention. Second, in tribal societies the magical system of witchcraft is on a par with whatever animistic, anthropomorphic, or polytheistic elements the magico-religious core might include, and the universe of social interaction

entails a significant to high degree of direct, immediate supernatural intervention. In sixteenth- and seventeenth-century Europe, by contrast, witchcraft
was anchored to a monotheistic system, to some extent an expression of the
Manichaean streak of Christianity, and the world of social and physical interaction did not usually entail direct, immediate supernatural intervention, even
though at that time miracles, as conceived by most Christian denominations,
were more common than today. Third, witchcraft in tribal societies is still an
integral part of the social structure, and within the global societal context,
witchcraft has important primary functions of various kinds. By the sixteenth
century, and certainly in the seventeenth century, witchcraft and sorcery in
Europe were already somewhat marginal phenomena, outbreaks of which were
sporadic and the result of undue social, economic, and religious stress and
anxiety. In other words, witchcraft at that time was already at the incipient
stage of evolving toward a mechanism of last resort, as we have defined the
concept. In conclusion, witch hunts, until the early part of the eighteenth
century, were occurrences under particular conditions of social stress, and despite the fact that tens of thousands of people were accused and many executed,
they were structurally more similar to a rural Tlaxcalan bloodsucking witchcraft epidemic, when a tlahuelpuchi may be instantly accused and executed,
than they were to the regular incidence of witchcraft and constant accusations,
say, among the Azande or Cewa. To lump together the witch hunts of sixteenth-
and seventeenth-century Europe with the witchcraft systems of primitive contemporaries is simply a facile generalization (see Thomas 1970:47–49; Macfarlane 1977:81–99).

It is evident that individual and collective witchcraft accusations constitute
the necessary conditions for the presence of primary social functions. This is
implicitly asserted in the anthropological literature on witchcraft and sorcery
(see Douglas 1970; Evans-Pritchard 1937; Mair 1969; Middleton and Winter
1969). A witchcraft system without accusations is an essentially projective
complex, such as that of the Navaho (Kluckhohn 1944), or that of rural Tlaxcala, in which the rare execution of witches entails not so much an accusation
as the spontaneous consensus of a group of people under great stress and anxiety. Witchcraft accusations are, in a way, the ostensible link between the normative belief system and the social structure at large: they are, in a Pickwickian
sense, the generators of primary social functions which affect individuals immediately and the collectivity in time. It is the collective efficacy of witchcraft
accusations that is most salient in the discharge of primary social functions. In
the case of essentially projective witchcraft systems and single-directed systems such as bloodsucking witchcraft in rural Tlaxcala, the social functions of

the institution are almost invariably secondary or derived, which are nonetheless useful to identify to obtain a clearer view of the personnel in action.

We have suggested that witchcraft and bloodsucking witchcraft accusations in rural Tlaxcala were more common at the turn of the century. At that time the witchcraft system appears to have been more diversified—that is, a larger array of misfortunes could have been attributed to the tlahuelpuchi. This point should not be overemphasized, for there is every indication that, since perhaps even before pre-Hispanic times, witchcraft and sorcery accusations were never of the magnitude that has been reported, say, for Africa; hence, witchcraft and sorcery in Mesoamerica never had the primary social functions that anthropologists have described for several culture areas of the world. The reason for this is the Manichaean streak that Catholicism infused into the native polytheistic system (syncretized into the monolatrous system), in which the concepts of witchcraft and sorcery are ancillary aspects of the magico-religious system playing a kind of mediating role between the supernatural and human worlds of existence. Under these conditions witchcraft and sorcery accusations do take place, but they are rather minimal and of a special kind. In any event, today as at the turn of the century the occasional collective accusations of witchcraft (little more than a mild kind of scapegoatism), the rare execution of bloodsucking witches, and the fairly common accusations of sorcery have the following configuration and position within the magico-religious system.

First, by design or through the vagaries of fate the tetlachihuic and tlahuelpuchi occupy an intermediary, ambivalent position between the social structure of humans and the configuration of the higher benevolent supernaturals. As we have analyzed these anthropomorphic supernaturals, they are to a considerable extent pawns in the human-supernatural game governed by the normative covenant: the pain they cause and the misfortunes they provoke are two of the instruments of retribution meted out by the supernatural powers when individuals and the collectivity are remiss or do not comply with their part of the bargain.

Second, those very rare occasions when a bloodsucking witch is accused and immediately executed and those occasions when a sorcerer as a practitioner of black magic oversteps the boundaries of his powers and is swiftly put to death are considered by the polity as object lessons; not only do they reaffirm the existence and powers of the tlahuelpuchi and tetlachihuic, but perhaps more significantly, they demonstrate that not even supernaturals are outside the deterministic universe of social and physical existence.

Third, the sorcerer and bloodsucking witch are regarded as agents, and not as the collective representation of fears, insecurities, or inherent anxieties of individuals and the collectivity. In this ambience, the tlahuelpuchi herself cannot coalesce or provoke any social action, whereas in cases of sorcery accusations, the tetlachihuic (when he behaves within the proper boundaries assigned to him by the normative belief system), although feared and carefully avoided, is regarded as little more than an instrument through whom supernatural powers allow the efficacy of benevolent or malevolent magic.

In the normal course of social existence rural Tlaxcalans do not engage in witchcraft accusations, and when they make sorcery accusations, they confront individuals, whereas the sorcerer remains neutral, like a physician attending a patient. Thus, in traditional rural Tlaxcalan society sorcery is a specialization; the specialists are the tetlachihuics (always well known and identified), and average, normal people do not possess the knowledge to effect the white and black magic that sorcery entails. In the several dozen cases of sorcery brought to Nutini's attention from 1960 to 1966, the perpetrator sorcerer was identified in less than 50 percent of the cases, and when he was, nothing happened to him; indeed, identification rather helped to enhance his malevolent or benevolent powers. The person who contracted the sorcerer and the object of the sorcerer's action were always identified, which did not always lead to confrontation, however, because of the deep-seated theme of compromise and accommodation in rural Tlaxcalan society. In this sense, then, sorcery accusations bring individuals and occasionally nuclear families into conflict but never any sizable segment of the local group. Moreover, individuals do not accuse other individuals of sorcery itself, but only of having contracted a sorcerer to perform his malevolent art on them.

The Secondary Functions of Bloodsucking Witchcraft
We have given two main reasons for the absence of primary social functions in the bloodsucking witchcraft system of rural Tlaxcala: accusations generating a web of social interaction, as the necessary condition for the presence of primary functions, do not obtain, at least as a permanent feature of the social system; and witchcraft in general, and witchcraft accusations in particular, are less salient, often absent, since there are superordinate and secular mechanisms and institutions for enforcing social control and transacting and arbitrating conflict and disputes. The first reason has been sufficiently analyzed, but the second needs further elaboration.

The main point to elucidate is, of course, the analogous equivalents that enforce social control and conflict resolution. The institutionalized mechanisms are of two kinds: supernatural sanctions; and the legal, kinship, and compadrazgo framework of control compliance. Supernatural sanctions take care of the social control obtaining between individuals and the collectivity and the array of supernatural powers governing them, as we have already discussed. From this viewpoint, the consequences of bloodsucking witchcraft may, in the metalanguage, be regarded as a function of enforcing the human-supernatural covenant—that is, by punishing individuals and the group when they do not do what they are supposed to do to generate enough supernatural goodwill. Natural sanctions may in turn be decomposed into two kinds: the legal recourse vested in the local secular authorities, and the folk mechanism of control vested in the kinship and compadrazgo systems. Thus, disputes, conflicts, and disagreements are adjudicated and resolved either by a local authority empowered by the state or by a local elder, or the folk constraints of kinship and compadrazgo affiliation. The latter takes the form of gossip, social and economic pressures, and outright withholding of cooperation and exchange. These, then, are the mechanisms that enforce social control in rural Tlaxcalan society at all meaningful levels of social action. Ironically, whatever pass for accusations in rural Tlaxcalan social life are really made against malingerers, uncooperative folk, and deviants in the conduct of interpersonal relations and in the propitiation of the supernatural in all its forms. Hence, the social functions of witchcraft are only secondary or derived.

In summary, bloodsucking witchcraft in rural Tlaxcala has no functions of social control, neither directly enforcing compliance with custom and tradition, nor resolving conflict and disputes in socially acceptable ways. All social functions of bloodsucking witchcraft are secondary, and of the consequent kind— that is, they are the expression of antecedent behavioral and structural conditions. The secondary social functions of bloodsucking witchcraft have to do rather with both coalescing personnel for meaningful social action and setting the social parameters for the discharge of its psychological functions. In encapsulated form, the following are the secondary social functions of bloodsucking witchcraft in rural Tlaxcala:

1. Bloodsucking witchcraft, as the most dramatic and collectively disturbing form of punishment meted out by the supernatural powers, enforces compliance with the constraints and sacred obligations in the human-supernatural covenant to the highest degree. (There are several other contexts in which sanctions befall individuals and the collectivity in the form of misfortunes, illness, economic setbacks, and so on, but the sucking of an infant is the most effective enforcer of the covenant.)

2. The sucking event and subsequent aftereffects constitute an intense socializing period effecting man's compliance with sacred obligations toward the supernatural. The postsucking period is truly an object lesson concerning what happens when the individual and the collectivity cut corners, malinger,

or do not comply with their ritual and ceremonial obligations in generating the goodwill of supernatural forces.

3. As a corollary, the aftereffects in particular and the postsucking period in general force the local group (the household, the non-residential extended family, and the neighborhood) to reflect on the nature of man's relationship to the supernatural forces. Throughout this period, the local group bound by the sucking event takes stock of itself, and through individual and collective introspection, assesses its sacred condition and prospects for the future.

4. The postsucking period is one of the five sporadic and fixed (in the annual cycle) contexts and occasions in which social relations are sacralized and the local group de facto becomes a temporary corporate group. Less extensively affecting than the Christmas Cycle, Holy Week, and Todos Santos (which may encompass the entire community), the postsucking period compensates in intensity what it lacks in dispersion by the high quality of interpersonal relations: throughout, the kinsmen and neighbors of the paraje become an integrated psychosocial group.

5. The onset of the postsucking period activates the household support group, the structural equivalents of which come into being for only two other occasions in the life and annual cycles: marriage and the sponsorship of religious cargos. The household support group (which includes outside members, kinsmen and neighbors, in cases of nuclear-family households) is directly responsible for the physical, social, and psychological well-being of the affected couple; this group constitutes the functional support system of the affected mother and father throughout the duration of the aftereffects.

6. Throughout the postsucking period, the kinsmen (the non-residential extended family) and neighbors of the paraje become a second-line support group for the affected couple and household. This group may be regarded as the functional personnel receptacle in which the social and psychological consequences of bloodsucking witchcraft are discharged: it represents the maximal extension of social and psychological responsibility delimiting the local group.

PSYCHOLOGICAL FUNCTIONS: EXPLANATORY, RATIONALIZING AND INTENSIFYING DIMENSIONS

Of all the functions of bloodsucking witchcraft in rural Tlaxcala, only one may be regarded as primary—namely, the explanatory psychological function of the tlahuelpuchi complex. For this reason alone one could say that the psychological functions of bloodsucking witchcraft are more important than its social functions. Substantively and theoretically, moreover, we have framed this particular case of witchcraft in such a way that its psychological matrix, functions, and activities loom larger than superficially meet the eye. Just as with the social functions of the complex, the foregoing structural analysis also reveals the positional and relational contexts of the psychological functions, which, for the convenience of the reader, have been put together in a single section.

The Primary Function of Bloodsucking Witchcraft

It is interesting to notice that it was Evans-Pritchard, the quintessential social anthropologist, who first conceptualized the essentially psychological, most universal function of witchcraft, which in combination with a number of social functions (centered on various forms of social control) has become the staple mode of analysis in dealing with this phenomenon and other magical domains. Yet the notion that witchcraft explains unfortunate events also has a sociological component—namely, that it configures the perception of the social group— and it is probably in this context that this sociopsychological conception of the subjective reality of witchcraft is most useful.

It has been a basic premise of this study that, even in the most "primitive" traditional witchcraft system, given certain conditions, the social group does distinguish between natural and supernatural causation, although it may not immediately appear to the participant actors of a witchcraft event that there is such a distinction, or, in other words, that perceptually there is psychological reality to the distinction. The ostensible demonstration of this position is that in the presence of alternative forms of knowledge (mostly science, technology, and education) and their action through varying periods of time, witchcraft systems become increasingly less efficacious, and in the end, they are transformed into mechanisms of last resort. Regardless of whatever social or psychological functions witchcraft may have, an epistemological perceptual approach offers the best possibility of solving the most significant, hitherto untapped problems of witchcraft and magical thought.

In a nutshell, the primary psychological function of bloodsucking witchcraft in rural Tlaxcala is to explain infant death during the first year after birth. Blaming the subjective reality of the tlahuelpuchi for the inordinate number of infants who die during this period satisfies the natural desire to explain the kind of death that the people conceive as untimely, unreasonable, and out of proportion with what they acknowledge as their responsbility for acts of omission or commission against the supernatural powers after the fact (that is, as the result of the intense period of introspection during the postsucking period). The significance of this psychological function is enhanced for two reasons. First, all secondary psychological functions of the tlahuelpuchi complex are anchored to or are a corollary of its primary functions, since the behavior and action of all involved actors unfolds from the sucking event itself until the termination of the aftereffects. It is throughout this highly patterned and institutionalized period that all psychological functions of bloodsucking witchcraft are discharged. Second, the explanatory power of bloodsucking witchcraft is very high, and more than any analyzed witchcraft system in the literature, it exemplifies the single-directed efficacy of magical explanations. We have made the educated guess that bloodsucking witchcraft in rural Tlaxcala accounts for roughly 20 percent of all infants and children who die before the age of five. If we consider that by far the highest incident of infant and child mortality occurs between ages two and four, infant mortality as attributed to the tlahuelpuchi accounts for the majority of infant death before the age of one.

The primary psychological function of bloodsucking witchcraft may be regarded as an antecedent function—that is, it entails a relationship between normative expectations and social and physical realization in subjectively explaining the death of infants under specified conditions. As a corollary, the same obtains in most secondary psychological functions anchored to this primary function. We have shown that bloodsucking witchcraft (more precisely, its normative belief system) entails several beneficial consequences for the local group. From this standpoint, given the facts of infant death, one could say that the tlahuelpuchi complex is a positive contribution to the social system in the absence of other modes of explanation. Notice, however, that functional assignment, social and psychological, is posited on the normative belief system and not on the structural realization of the system. When the normative belief system changes, and ultimately becomes residual, whatever social or psychological functions remain are the consequence of a new system anchored to a new structural matrix as the result of changes brought about by the internalization of other forms of knowledge. It is in this context that the tlahuelpuchi complex during the past generation has increasingly become a mechanism of last resort. Notice also, that the structural analysis of chapters 8, 9, and 10 does not deal with the normative belief system by itself but as one of the terms of the equation in which normative expectations and physical and sociopsychological realization generate the explanation that the bloodsucking witchcraft complex has to offer.

Let us return to the notion that witchcraft systems change and in time become mechanisms of last resort. Implicit in several of the contributions to *Witchcraft and Sorcery in East Africa* (Middleton and Winter 1963) is a homeostatic notion of witchcraft and sorcery that is typical of most functionalists. For example, Winter (1963:290) says that "it must not be assumed that witchcraft beliefs would disappear given improved medical facilities." Perhaps we ought not make that assumption, but in relatively long periods, and under the effect of variables such as education and technology, witchcraft, even in the most traditional societies, will change and ultimately become residual. In the generation or more since the research on these East African societies was done, as national states have come into being, the Amba, Lugbara, Gusii, Bunyoro, and many other tribes in this culture area have been increasingly subjected to modernizing influence. With the accelerated pace of sociocultural change in the modern world, even today (1989), the witchcraft and sorcery system of these incipient folk societies have surely undergone significant changes. This process of change in rural Tlaxcala can be documented for more than a hundred years; witchcraft and sorcery, although never approaching the magico-religious and societal integration that they have in traditional African societies, have nonetheless been transformed from well articulated systems to almost residual mechanisms. The same process of change will undoubtedly take place in African societies at different times and on different cultural scales. In conceptualizing this particular problem of change, there are two sets of variables that must be considered: on the one hand, the kind of magico-religious system (animism, polytheism, monolatrism, monotheism) to which witchcraft and sorcery are anchored, as we have illustrated; and on the other hand, the action of external variables (education, diffusion of knowledge and information, science, technology, and so on) and the degree of intensity with which they are being presented to and are being internalized by recipient social systems. In this scenario with witchcraft changing toward a mechanism of last resort, the notion of the system as explaining unfortunate events appears to be one of the aspects most susceptible to and affected by rapid transformation. This is what has happened in rural Tlaxcala during the past four generations, and we are reasonably certain that, with modifications, the approach in conceptualizing this particular case of magico-religious change can be replicated in many sociocultural contexts in the modern world. In this scheme of magico-religious change, social functions are the first to disappear, whereas psychological functions appear to retain a modicum of efficacy in the long haul but are ultimately modified by the constraints and requirements of the new modernizing situation.

The Secondary Functions of Bloodsucking Witchcraft
Given the foregoing focus on the transformation that bloodsucking witchcraft in rural Tlaxcala has been undergoing for several generations, we can say that its psychological functions appear to have been the more stable than its social functions, which have more noticeably dwindled in importance. As the traditional imago mundi of rural Tlaxcalans during the past generation has yielded to an increasingly secular view of the world in which the tlahuelpuchi complex no longer functions effectively as a means of retribution in the human-super-

natural covenant, the psychological functions and underpinnings of the phenomenon are still more or less in place—adjusted, to be sure, to the new socioeconomic conditions and modernizing influences of the outside world—but
sporadically manifested in situations of inordinate anxiety and stress. To put it
differently, the psychological functions of bloodsucking witchcraft are still an
integral part, albeit in an attenuated form, of the reduced scope of the phenomena as they evolve toward a mechanism of last resort. From this viewpoint,
although in a much less pervasive and regular fashion, the psycholgoical functions of bloodsucking witchcraft are the same in 1988 as they were in 1960,
under quite different socioeconomic conditions. Here again are the secondary
psychological functions of bloodsucking witchcraft in rural Tlaxcala:

1. Above all, bloodsucking witchcraft is a tension- and anxiety-releasing
and -reducing mechanism. When one or more infants die for no reason apparent to the household and the local group, blaming the tlahuelpuchi releases the
individual and the collectivity from undue pressure and stress so that all actors
involved, after undergoing certain culturally prescribed actions and steps, can
go back to normal with a tolerable degree of pain and discomfort. (In many
ways, most of the remaining secondary psychological functions of bloodsucking witchcraft may be regarded as corollaries or subsidiaries of this all-encompassing function.)

2. Bloodsucking witchcraft assuages individual and collective guilt and
culpability from the time of the infant's sucking until the termination of the
aftereffects. Individually, primarily in the case of the infant's mother, this is
accomplished partly by the spontaneous tamperings and partly by the psychosomatic and psychological dislocations that the individual undergoes during the
postsucking period. Collectively, the local group bound by the sucking accom-
plishes the same assuaging, and it comes to term with itself by introspection
and the realizations that only so much guilt and culpability can be assuaged
and that everyone must share a modicum of responsibility. (It must be clearly
understood that primary actors [almost exclusively the mother, and excluding
possible infanticide perpetrators] generate their own guilt and culpability out
of direct responsibility for the infant's death, whereas secondary actors generate guilt and culpability as a result of their responsibility toward supernatural
forces.)

3. Blaming the tlahuelpuchi further assuages individual and, to some extent, collective guilt and culpability by displacing direct responsibility for the
death of infants. It is the displacing mechanism, culturally defined, that allows
the mother to tamper with the physical and psychological evidence to make the
infant's death look like the work of this loathsome anthropomorphic supernat-

ural, in accordance with the complex's normative expectations. Without such a mechanism of displacement, the mother, or any other household member directly responsible for the death of an infant, would have a much harder time psychologically and would face harsher social sanctions.

4. The aftereffects suffered by primary actors may be regarded quite literally as a catharsis: a rather prolonged period of purification terminating in a clean slate reasonably exempt from responsibility, culpability, and guilt. The ministrations of secondary actors to primary actors and the processes of introspection and reflection concerning their relationship to the supernatural powers and their vulnerable place in the world may be regarded as a process of self-exorcism resulting in group solidarity, based on the knowledge that responsibility among themselves and toward the supernatural can never be entirely displaced. (The concept of sin is weak or non-existent in rural Tlaxcalan society, but its functional equivalent, social and supernatural responsibility, are very strong. The entailed correlates of social and supernatural responsibility are, of course, culpability and guilt.)

5. The entire postsucking period constitutes an intense, rather subtle period of psychological intensification, validation, and reinforcing of the bloodsucking witchcraft complex, both as an expression and as a consequence of the societal moral order. In a real sense, the local group (from housewife to neighborhood) becomes a psychosocial entity with a rather single-minded purpose of instilling in the individual the psychological desirability of behaving with circumspection in discharging human and supernatural responsibility.

6. Due to more than any social, collective consideration, the postsucking period may be regarded as the activation of the local group's "collective consciousness," and all actors directly or indirectly affected act and behave as if motivated by the same psychological springs. It is in this highly cohesive psychological ambience that the primary actors undergo the cathartic process and the local group as a whole exorcises itself.

7. Scapegoatism as a psychological function of bloodsucking witchcraft consists of verbalizing that perpetrator tlahuelpuchis are from another community, or come collectively from the upper and lower communities (with respect to La Malintzi) of Olintla and Hueytochco. This verbalized scapegoatism does not appear to translate into concrete action—that is accusations leading to some sort of social or physical violence.

8. It can also be said that bloodsucking witchcraft provides for the expression of hostilities in socially accepted ways, thereby relieving psychological tensions and anxieties. As far as this obtains between the parents of the sucked infant, this psychological function is accounted for by (1), (2), and (3) above. Rather,

what is entailed here is the perpetration of infanticide by any possible actors as a drastic action of retribution and vengeance.[1]

9. Given the very limited incidence of bloodsucking witchcraft accusations, we can see that the tlahuelpuchi complex does nonetheless provide guidelines for identification leading to the execution of telltale individuals. This is another way of saying that bloodsucking witchcraft provides identity for the culturally dissatisfied and alienated.

One of the results of putting together and analyzing the social and psychological functions of bloodsucking witchcraft in rural Tlaxcala is to present a gestalt of the system in action. This procedure gives a general idea of how the system has been changing since before the turn of the century. Although the secondary psychological functions have remained more or less constant, the secondary social functions have lessened, whereas the explanatory, major function of the complex shows significant strain and has been diminishing significantly during the past generation, beginning in the early 1960s. From the methodological standpoint, the rather intimate complementing of the social and psychological functions of the system attests to the vitality of bloodsucking witchcraft at the time of the ethnographic present of this monograph and for a few years afterward. Above all, this exercise of bringing together all the functions of the bloodsucking witchcraft system and establishing some of their interrelationships is aimed at demonstrating how functional assignment is a by-product of structural analysis.

CHAPTER TWELVE

An Epistemological Approach to the Study of Magic and Religious Supernaturalism

THROUGHOUT THE ANALYSIS of this monograph (chapters 7 to 11), we have endeavored to present the reader with an interpretation of bloodsucking witchcraft in rural Tlaxcala from an epistemological perspective substantiated by an ontological reality oscillating between the normative belief system of the institution and its physical, social, and psychological manifestation. Conceptualized from this standpoint, bloodsucking witchcraft may be regarded essentially as an explanatory construct—a theory about a particular ontological domain, in other words. Hence, our concern is with focusing the analysis on the people's gestalt of the phenomenon and the inferences that they make from perceptions configured by the normative belief system. This chapter is an account of the reasons for and utility of approaching the study of so-called magical phenomena from an epistemological standpoint. It also offers some suggestions concerning how an epistemological approach may be systematized and applied to other domains involving the direct interplay of normative expectations and structural realization. Toward achieving these aims, two topics are discussed: the imago mundi of rural Tlaxcalans, their underlying ideology and belief system, and how these constructs and perceptions of the world around them affect or mold their processes of inference and causal entailment; and the bloodsucking witchcraft complex conceived as a theory of knowledge of how supernatural inputs produce natural outcomes.

A PERCEPTUAL AND INFERENTIAL ANALYSIS OF MAGIC AND RELIGIOUS SUPERNATURALISM

A recent monograph on the cult of the dead in rural Tlaxcala describes and analyzes the imago mundi and the ideology and belief system of this society as it functioned a generation ago—that is, at the same time as the ethnographic present of this monograph (Nutini 1988:Chapters 10 and 11). The imago mundi was described, and to some extent analyzed, in standard ethnographic fashion, but the ideology and belief system were analyzed in a more systematic fashion, since they were scaled from more abstract to less abstract, from general ideological "what ought to be" conceptions of the social and physical universes to specific rules and commands implementing circumscribed beliefs. The latter are domains positioned and configured (vis-à-vis the social structure in operation) so as to measure the efficacy that obtains between the ideological and structural orders. In exemplifying the epistemological approach underlying this monograph, we use the imago mundi and ideology and belief system of traditional rural Tlaxcala as descriptively and systematically present in Todos Santos, but in little more than outline form. With reference to the tlahuelpuchi complex we indicate the logic of the approach and the lines along which it can be operationalized.

The Fundamental Tenets of the Imago Mundi of Rural Tlaxcalans

The imago mundi of rural Tlaxcalans as an acculturative and syncretic entity rather faithfully reflects these basic components of the sociocultural system. It is constituted of an array of elements of pre-Hispanic origin which have survived relatively intact (as have many structural elementals), of elements of the Spanish Colonial era rather interestingly syncretized and acculturated, and of elements of modern, machine-age provenance (which have become salient since shortly before the turn of the century). The historical analysis of how this worldview coalesced into an integrated, efficiently configured whole, has been done elsewhere (Nutini 1988:Chapters 3 and 4). Suffice it to say that the imago mundi of rural Tlaxcalans is quite uniform, and its ideational configuration molds all traditional domains of the social structure in action. This ideational order is presented as a series of entailing statements, scaled to a significant degree according to inclusivity, intensity and extensity.

The researchers of rural Tlaxcalan culture and society a generation ago could have been easily misled into thinking of the region and its people as being much more modernized and secularized than was the case. This is an important point to consider in understanding and conceptualizing the perceptual and inferential processes in changing primitive and folk societies. Material culture and the most visible components of a sociocultural system generally are not the best criteria for determining or gauging the modernization-secularization threshold at any given point, most often because they are susceptible to external pressures and constraints. When work began in Tlaxcala, Nutini did not expect to find a witchcraft and sorcery system that entailed (what he later discovered) perceptual and inferential modes quite at variance with those that the technological and material content of the culture at work seemed to entail, or more accurately, that the situation warranted. To put it differently, he did not expect to find a witchcraft system in which the people persistently believed that supernatural inputs produced natural outcomes, since in almost all other domains of the sociocultural system rural Tlaxcalans envisaged the distinction between natural and supernatural content and action, and the majority of people made inferences not noticeably different from those of educated or fairly educated Mexicans who had been subjected to the influence of science and technology for significant periods of time. Nutini did not realize until seven or eight years later that the transposition of causation was still, at least in the circumscribed domain of witchcraft and sorcery, much under the influence of a non-European, non-scientific imago mundi significantly influenced by a magical system with many pre-Hispanic inputs. It is to determine the extent of the influence of the imago mundi on the processes of perception and inference of rural Tlaxcalans in 1960 that we want to explore.

Implicitly throughout this monograph, and explicitly in the book on the cult of the dead (Nutini 1988), the imago mundi of rural Tlaxcalans has been described and analyzed as lacking in chance and serendipity. The universe in which the social and material life of the people unfolds may be regarded as essentially deterministic, a universe in which hardly anything happens that cannot be traced to or explained by fixed antecedents or actions. This is not an ontologically deterministic universe in Democritean or Leibnizian terms, but rather like a Kantian moral universe in which the actions of man are subject to moral laws, and that only by obeying these laws (read the rules, injunctions, and commands governing human-supernatural interaction) can humans be free to pursue their earthly interests and live in peace with the supernatural forces that rural Tlaxcalans regard as the architects of their natural order. It is in the manifold domain of human interaction with the supernatural that rural Tlaxcalans may be said to adhere faithfully to a categorical imperative. To paraphrase Kant, the universal rule which governs the human-supernatural covenant is the objectification of all the actions that individuals and the group, however extensive it may be, undertake in order to make the world of social and material affairs orderly, safe, and pleasant. Notice, however, that while all rules, injunctions, and commands that regulate the human-supernatural covenant have the form of categorical imperatives, the ultimate aim of the moral order is not in that form and may rather be regarded as supporting the pragmatic exigency of earthly existence.

Given this fundamental moral constraint, which colors or influences the entire spectrum of social and material perceptions and actions, rural Tlaxcalans view their universe as restrained, entailing few options, and lacking in situational choices and alternatives. In this boxed environment, rural Tlaxcalans exhibit little initiative, accept stoically the blows dealt by man and nature, and are instinctively and consistently pessimistic about the future of social and material actions. In this ambience there is no room for entitlement (social, material, or supernatural) and no feeling of achieving even a medium degree of control over the social or material environment (there are no vernacular expressions approaching the American saying "having the world by the tail"); there is only the conviction that some control over one's environment can be achieved by hard work and performing according to tradition—a conviction in itself the manifestation of a fixed and determined universe. Thus, moral determinism leads people not only to expect little but to a perception of the world around them as somewhat predetermined and subject to a small modicum of contingency.

The events, actions, and happenings of the social, natural, and supernatural universe unfold on a continuum that may not be regarded as deterministic in the sense of being essentially preordained, but is certainly lacking in serendipity and in the spontaneity that most Americans, for example, entertain about the events, actions, and happenings in their boundless, free, and controllable universe. From a different perspective, rural Tlaxcalans believe that there is not much room for making things happen and fatalistically accept a kind of nebulous order of things that is difficult, if not impossible, to change. There is nothing in rural Tlaxcalan culture that promotes or compels the drive to action embodied in the old Latin saying *audaces fortuna iuvant* (fortune helps the bold). On the contrary, rural Tlaxcalans are cautious and constrained in the context of action, they seldom take chances, and especially in their social and supernatural relationships, they weigh carefully the pros and cons of any decision or course of action.

This is not to say that once a decision has been made or a course of action taken rural Tlaxcalans are unduly vacillating or indecisive. Quite the contrary; knowing latently that there is a high degree of fixity in the universe, individuals and groups may stubbornly plunge ahead even when additional evidence tells them that they have made the wrong judgment. For example, in innumerable confrontations witnessed throughout the years, the men and women involved exhausted every means of settling disputes before coming to verbal abuse or physical blows. But once a dispute had degenerated that far, the fight was to the finish, and it terminated either in death or in individuals or groups becoming confirmed enemies. The restoration of "normal" relationships between individuals and groups can only be achieved by elaborate rites and ceremonies of atonement, manifestly expressing what rural Tlaxcalans consider the breaking of some latent and vaguely fixed order that is almost always attributed to supernatural forces.

Herein lie the most characteristic principles of behavior that operationally regulate much of the behavior of rural Tlaxcalans: latently convinced that the universe in which they live is fixed and ultimately optionless, they nonetheless manifestly contravene fate when their immediate perceptions tell them that they cannot retreat without losing social and individual status and prestige. The ambivalence generated by the interplay of what the imago mundi decidedly imprints upon rural Tlaxcalans and the situational proclivities of basic human emotions (pride, self-interest, losing face) is a rather constant source of conflict for most people, and it governs a significant part of their behavior. It is in this context that the fatalistic streak of rural Tlaxcalans represents a kind of escape valve, which must also be regarded as the real spring that motivates them to action and to a measure of risk taking. But how do rural Tlaxcalans perceive social and material relationships, the unfolding of events, and causal entailment in this rather fixed and constraining world?

Supernatural Intervention and the Moral Order
First, except perhaps for a few exceptional individuals (some school teachers and the self-educated), rural Tlaxcalans have no real conception of natural law as something fairly consistently involved in an explanation of the workings of and everyday course of events and happenings, unlike, for example, Mexican urbanites of long standing, for whom religion is still more than a kind of philosophy of life and for whom the supernatural may occasionally interfere in the course of everyday affairs. For rural Tlaxcalans, the direct and immediate action primarily of Christian supernaturals and secondarily of pagan ones (almost exclusively La Malintzi and El Cuatlapanga), on the one hand, and the action of supernatural practitioners (all four anthropomorphic supernaturals), on the other hand—in short divine and magical interventions—are always possible in the ordinary or extraordinary course of affairs; they can manifest themselves in any aspect of social or material life or can be invoked by individuals or groups to explain any baffling situation for which they do not have antecedents. But rural Tlaxcalans are not noticeably given to adduce supernatural explanations when some hard thinking can produce natural antecedents that would explain the situation naturally. Thus, even though rural Tlaxcalans cannot verbalize, or ostensibly indicate, a conception of the world in which actions and events occur without supernatural intervention, they somehow do not abuse this mode of explanation, except, as demonstrated in this monograph, when they are at a loss for precedents. This is another important notion (perhaps behavioral spring to action would be a better term) in the imago

mundi of rural Tlaxcalans: precedence and regularity are the visible manifestation of an orderly, fixed universe, and one cannot dispense with them in explaining past events or in making inferences concerning future happenings.

Second, rural Tlaxcalans may be said to perceive the world around them and make inferences from the standpoint of an intermediate position. Unlike societies with magical complexes in which there is a nebulous behavioral distinction between what is natural and what is supernatural, rural Tlaxcalans have a rather clear conception of when and under what circumstances divine and magical intervention produces situations in which supernatural inputs entail natural outcomes. But rural Tlaxcalans are not like most peoples in societies (such as those who have been for many generations under the influence of science and technology) in which supernatural intervention in the natural world is confined to the notion of cosmological origins by a prime mover or to the notion that the supernatural may perform miracles or occasionally help if adequately propitiated. From this middle-ground position, rural Tlaxcalans perceive the world in terms of direct divine and magical intervention occurring with both statistically higher incidence and regularity as well as being confined to certain specific domains in a much more predictable fashion than is the case with "civilized" societies. The structure of supernatural intervention, as understood and embodied in the imago mundi of rural Tlaxcalans, may be summarized as follows:

1. Neither divine nor magical intervention are random; they obey specific, determinable, and to some extent controllable circumstances, antecedents, and specific actions. Rural Tlaxcalans maintain that one can both induce beneficial and avoid detrimental supernatural intervention: one may ask God, Saint Anthony, or even La Malintzi for an individual boon (health, protection, success in a business venture) and be directly rewarded by performing or offering something in return (prayers, lighting candles, undertaking a pilgrimage); and one can avoid, or at least minimize, the bloodsucking action of the tlahuelpuchi by being vigilant, by protecting one's infants, and by being spiritually stouthearted. Thus, unlike those in "civilized" society who believe only in direct, divine supernatural intervention, rural Tlaxcalans assert the direct symmetry of the supernatural-natural equation—that is, that natural inputs produce supernatural results as well as natural ones, individual and group directed in the case of divine intervention and ancillary in the case of magical intervention (for example, an inordinate number of infants being sucked by the tlahuelpuchi in a given year is explained by a paraje or an entire community as the failure of its constituency to comply with what is considered an adequate degree of propitiation). Hence, all supernatural intervention, manifested in clear instances of

supernatural inputs producing natural outcomes, is related to and the expression of the human-supernatural covenant.

2. The human-supernatural covenant, as exemplified above, is directly or indirectly the source, monitor, and shaper of supernatural intervention. The Christian God in particular but, depending on the context and situation, all other Christian supernaturals and pagan deities and personages as well may use their supernatural powers to cause natural outcomes affecting individuals and groups. By virtue of their creational, regulatory, and protective powers upon the affairs of humans, all Christian and pagan supernaturals directly and all four anthropomorphic supernaturals indirectly, or as allowed by the will of the former, may change or alter the natural course of affairs and events. The operational principle of the human-supernatural covenant is, of course, fixed by the quid pro quo that obtains between the "divine" supernaturals and the individual and the collectivity (Nutini 1988:Chapters 9 and 10): humans, to the best of their abilities, perform ritually and ceremonially in honor of the deities, in return for which they are rewarded with the propitious conditions for a healthy and prosperous social and material life. The existence of all four anthropomorphic supernaturals, but especially of the tlahuelpuchi and tetlachihuic, which significantly affect the lives and actions of rural Tlaxcalans, is part of the permanent order of the universe, whose creation is not attributed to any of the "divine" supernaturals but rather to a vague notion of fate. Or as a native philosopher verbalized it, "Así son las cosas de este mundo y del otro adonde vamos. Poco sabemos y poco vale preguntar acerca de lo que nunca sabremos." (This is the nature of this world and of the other one toward which we are going. We know little and it is worth little to ask question about that which we shall never know.) The "divine" supernaturals are conceived of as the creators and conservators of a fixed order, watching over and caring for their creation; but anthropomorphic supernaturals, although also conceived of as part of the fixed order, exemplify power, knowledge, and proclivities in their Manichaean forces in some sort of constant struggle that goes on in the natural and supernatural worlds. The "divine" supernaturals may tolerate and even use anthropomorphic supernaturals (as one of several means of punishing individuals and groups), but they cannot remove, neutralize, or change the basic nature and proclivities of the supernaturals: praying to God or any of the saints or supplicating La Malintzi will not change the uncontrollable desire of the tlahuelpuchi to suck the blood of infants but can induce her to strike a certain household and paraje; and two tetlachihuics may engage in magical combat for inducing and counteracting death for a fee without being encumbered by supplications or entreaties to any "divine" supernatural.

3. As long as the ritual, ceremonial, and material duties and obligations of individuals and groups toward the "divine" supernaturals are complied with, the natural world of social and material affairs runs smoothly. This is perhaps the basic operational principle that has governed traditional rural Tlaxcalan society since it coalesced into a syncretic-acculturative synthesis: the combined efforts and actions of individuals and the collectivity are necessary in complying with the requirements of the human-supernatural covenant; the collective corpora of ritual, ceremonial, and material offerings to the "divine" supernatural pantheon discharged by individuals, groups, and the entire community maintains and enhances the pool of goodwill so necessary to predispose the supernatural to interfere beneficially on behalf of all. Under this complex constraint, spelled out in concrete commands and injunctions, the imago mundi of rural Tlaxcalans specifies that what is left undone by individuals and groups in keeping the "divine" supernaturals happy diminishes the stock of goodwill of the community as a necessary instrument to cope with vagaries of the natural world. Thus, the rites, ceremonies, and offerings which constitute the supernatural quid pro quo are also carefully specified, and social, religious, and even economic pressure is brought to bear against individuals and groups who do not comply with their sacred obligations or who malinger in their compliance. Looked at from the standpoint of this covenant, supernatural intervention, in the various forms of supernatural inputs producing natural outputs, is perceived and conceptualized by rural Tlaxcalans in three rather distinct contexts of ambiences.

a. The most pervasive supernatural intervention may be termed "normal" — that is, perceived by individuals and the collectivity in the standard unfolding of the annual and life cycles. Under this category rural Tlaxcalans include all the boons and good things that emanate from the dutiful compliance with the requirements of the human-supernatural covenant; and from this standpoint, this category manifests exclusively beneficial supernatural intervention. It includes the answers to individual and collective prayers and supplications to and entreaties of Christian and pagan supernaturals spanning the socioeconomic and religious spectrum. As it affects the people at large, "normal" supernatural intervention is experienced by rural Tlaxcalans as something subtle and nondramatic, so much a part of the natural course of events that is almost taken for granted. From this standpoint, rural Tlaxcalan religion approaches the kind of secular religion so characteristic of modern industrial countries.

b. Punitive supernatural intervention, by definition always detrimental to individuals and groups, is meted out by Christian and pagan supernaturals for outright failure to comply with the covenant or for malingering or niggardliness on the part of humans toward their overlords. Punitive supernatural intervention is essentially an inverse form of rationalization, in that, unlike (a), it is verbalized by the non-affected to those affected as a particular input deemed to be supernatural. When a person dies unexpectedly, when an extended family has an abnormally high degree of bad luck, when in a paraje there is an unusually high degree of bloodsucking witchcraft, and in other contexts and on other occasions the explanation of the natural outcome is attributed to the supernatural input generated by failure on the part of the affected individual, family, or larger social group to comply with the requirements of the human-supernatural covenant. The last step in this chain of events is to redress the lessening of supernatural goodwill by making culprits aware of how and in what specific domains they did not comply with their sacred obligations. This takes various forms, including polite admonition, stern warning, or social and economic coercion, all of which are variants of socioreligious control. Punitive supernatural intervention is more directly perceived by the local group; it is hence more dramatic in exemplifying the ever present possibility that "divine" supernaturals, individually or collectively, can have a direct input in the affairs of man. Interestingly, rural Tlaxcalans believe in miracles and know that they took place in the past, but they are not an operational aspect of their religious thinking.

  c. Magic supernatural intervention may be defined as the ostensible demonstration of the forces of good and evil that manifest themselves unpredictably in several domains of the life of rural Tlaxcalans. Under this category are included a rather large number of events and happenings in which specific supernatural inputs produce clearly perceived or inferred natural outcomes: the confrontation of two tetlachihuics, causing death or curing a terminal patient, the animal transformation of nahuales, the bloodsucking of infants, and many other magical acts. Essentially, magical supernatural intervention occurs in the context of witchcraft and sorcery, many instances of which are exemplified in this monograph. At the present (1960) stage of the magico-religious evolution of rural Tlaxcalan society, magical supernatural intervention is the least common and socially well internalized category of intervention. Epistemologically, however, the supernatural efficacy of witchcraft or sorcery in producing natural outcomes that affect individuals and groups is the most dramatic, direct, and clearly experienced instance of supernatural causation. The non-punitive action and efficacy of witchcraft and sorcery are perceived and understood by rural Tlaxcalans as a Manichaean exercise, allowed or uncontrolled by the "divine" supernaturals, which can be fought, sometimes diminished, but never entirely eliminated. And this point brings us to the last topic directly related to the perceptive structure of rural Tlaxcalans.

Magical Intervention and the Human-Supernatural Order

Third, the epistemological question of how people perceive and make inferences concerning magical supernatural intervention producing observable, or presumably identified, outcomes (e.g., a dead infant, happenings antecedent to a sucking, a person dying suddenly for no apparent reason) is one of the themes pervading this monograph. Chapter 9 analyzed the perceptual context of bloodsucking witchcraft and the reinforcing mechanisms, both social and psychological, which lead individuals to ascertain that the supernatural action of the tlahuelpuchi causes the death of infants. Here the context is widened to include the action of sorcery and to underline the logic of the inferential process that is involved in concluding that supernatural inputs produce natural outputs. Rural Tlaxcalans are conditioned from childhood to believe that there is such a thing as magical causation, that there are supernatural agents that affect directly their actions and lives. From childhood rural Tlaxcalans are directly exposed to inputs and outputs that the local group regards as the action of witchcraft or sorcery. These magical actions are reinforced time and again by the concentrated outbursts of verbal affirmations and elaborations of the people at large, when it has been established that a magical supernatural input produced a natural outcome that unfolded according to what is specified in the belief system. From this standpoint, the belief system of witchcraft, sorcery, and any other magical phenomena is the most powerful reinforcing mechanism for the Humean belief that whenever events, actions, and situations develop or unfold as specified, a supernatural input will produce a natural output. We conceptualized this situation, in explaining the tlahuelpuchi complex, as the interaction of what is normatively expected and what is physically, empirically experienced. Psychologically, then, every new witchcraft or sorcery event perceived to be unfolding close enough to what is specified in the belief system reinforces the efficacy of magical action. When this is not the case, and what is observed departs significantly from normative expectations, secondary reinforcing mechanisms come into play—namely, what in the case of the tlahuelpuchi system we analyzed as the exaggerations, distortions, and tamperings that accompany the sucking of an infant.

Concentrating on bloodsucking witchcraft in rural Tlaxcala, we ask what is epistemologically entailed by saying that the tlahuelpuchi causes the death of an infant? First, what is observed, and about which there is little or no disagreement among observers, is the output of the sucking—that is, the dead infant. Discriminating between whether it was a natural death or a death due to the magical action of the tlahuelpuchi is a more complicated matter. What are considered at the outset are the specifications of the belief system that the observers must directly, and those who are told by the observers must indirectly, bring to bear for a decision to be made. As the evidence radiates from the person who found the body to the household and then to the paraje, a consensus coalesces, based on the following considerations: the interrelationship between physical perceptions (tables 6.1, 6.3, 6.9, 6.10, 6.11, 6.13, 6.14, 6.18, and 6.19) and the observers' knowledge of the belief system's specifications; the psychological frames of mind of the immediate observers (personal reliability, state of agitation, steadiness, and so on); and extracontextual considerations (family illness history, household interpersonal relationships, and so on). Consensus is reached quickly, and probably within less than an hour the entire paraje or neighborhood has agreed on whether death was due to natural causes. This is particularly the case in the positive identification of the tlahuelpuchi as the causal agent of death. If there is no identification, the issue may be in doubt for as much as an hour and a half, and consensus is arrived at mostly on the basis of the absence or weak presence of circumstances consistent with the most characteristic beliefs of the system (the position of the body upon discovery, the age of the victim, etc.). The greatest weight is given to the evidence presented by those immediately related to the victim, and seldom do paraje members or neighbors challenge the perceptions of household members. In a nutshell, consensus means that, despite whatever unverbalized skepticism there may be, the death of an infant is directly, indubitably attributed to the action of the tlahuelpuchi, even though no one has ever been able to witness the actual sucking of the victim.

Second, the next stage of the extended sucking event may be characterized as the rationalization of perceptions and inferences. Ex post facto, observers of the sucking event and individuals propinquous to them engage in two types of rationalizations: the exaggeration, distortion, and even invention of perceptions (that is, real or imagined physical events or happenings that antecede the sucking) with the latent psychological function of reinforcing and indubitably affirming that a supernatural input has produced a natural outcome; and the conscious or unconscious manipulation of the infant's body by the individual directly or indirectly responsible for its death or by the person who finds the body. For several days, all individuals directly or indirectly affected by the sucking event become single-mindedly concerned with making sure that they made the correct decision in attributing the death of the infant to the tlahuelpuchi, and the rationalizing maneuvers in which they engage may be epistemologically explained as achieving this end.

Third, the final development of the sucking event is the reinforcing stage, which begins coterminously with the period or rationalization but may last for several more days. The verbalization of the tlahuelpuchi belief system, the recounting of past experiences of extraordinary suckings, the care and concern afforded to the victim's parents, and the cleansing and atonement rites performed on and in the household are rituals and social actions designed for and aimed at perpetuating the belief in the tlahuelpuchi as an explanatory system and asserting the ideological reality of the sociosupernatural order as a fixed and determined entity. Since at the ontological level the proclivity of the tlahuelpuchi to kill is an aberration of nature, the outbursts of social and ritual activity after the sucking may be regarded as the efforts of those affected by the sucking to return the state of natural affairs to operational normality. And this is the last important principle in the imago mundi of rural Tlaxcalans: when adverse supernatural intervention in the affairs of man occurs, adversity must be quickly redressed, no matter what the cost is, so that the world of natural events quickly returns to normality.

We have presented the imago mundi of rural Tlaxcalans, particularly centered on magical supernatural intervention, in terms of the perceptions and direct or indirect inferences of observers and participants in the manifold contexts when supernatural inputs produce natural outcomes. The principles which give operational form to the imago mundi are positioned both in the context of moral action and in the perceptual-inferential domain of supernatural intervention. With respect to the context of moral action, the commands and injunctions that derive from the imago mundi apply exclusively to the interaction between individuals and the collectivity and the diversified array of "divine" supernaturals (that is, those which can be propitiated and entreated). In the human-supernatural context of interaction, these commands and injunctions function, as it were, in the manner of moral categorical imperatives, which configure almost all supernaturally directed actions and activities and constitute the most stabilizing factor in maintaining the traditional framework of the community. This moral human-supernatural code does not obtain in the conduct of social relationships, which are regulated by mostly pragmatic considerations in the interplay of kinship, compadrazgo, and friendship as they affect individuals and groups. It is this discrepancy between human-supernatural and social morality that makes rural Tlaxcalans essentially nominal Christians, since the canons of ethical behavior that may be termed religious do not extend to the domain of social relationships, but are exclusively concerned with maintaining the human-supernatural covenant. The fit between the imago mundi and the perceptual and inferential domain of action is not as close as that between the imago mundi and moral action, but there is no question that the principles that govern the interactions of humans and the supernatural array do to some extent influence the perceptions people have of and the inferences people draw from specific instances of supernatural inputs producing natural outcomes. This is true, for example, of punitive supernatural intervention when "divine" supernaturals may permit the increase of the tlahuelpuchi's proclivity to kill to punish humans for not complying adequately with the requirements of the human-supernatural covenant. Finally, the perception itself of instances of supernatural inputs producing natural outcomes is to some extent conditioned by the belief that "divine" supernaturals have the power to influence, if not ultimately to change, the fixed order of things.

The book on Todos Santos (Nutini 1988) analyzes how the worldview of rural Tlaxcalans came to coalesce from disparate syncretic elements between the turn of the century and 1960. But even on the sole basis of the diachronic material discussed in this monograph, the reader should be able to discern what is pre-Hispanic, what is Spanish Catholic, and what is modern in the traditional (1960) imago mundi and how these disparate elements have molded the perceptive and causal underpinnings of the worldview of rural Tlaxcalans. It is quite evident, for example, that the notions of a rather fixed or determined universe, the function of ritual and atonement, the essentially pessimistic and closed view of the universe, and so on are pre-Hispanic and not Christian; moreover, the closed, restricted world of Colonial times, and of much of Republican times, must to some extent be the reflection of the subordinate and subservient position that rural Tlaxcalans (and all Indian populations of Mexico) had in the wider Colonial and Republican world, until things began to open up for them at the turn of the century.

THE SOCIOLOGICAL AND COMPARATIVE FOUNDATION OF WITCHCRAFT REGARDED AS A CAUSAL AND INFERENTIAL SYSTEM

It is universally agreed that Durkheim, and to some extent Lévy-Bruhl and Mauss, are the immediate ancestors of much of twentieth-century sociology and social anthropology. There can be no doubt that Durkheim represents the senescence of a scientific paradigm for the study of society which was born in classical Greece, underwent the pains of adolescence in the hands of medieval scholars like Ibn Hkaldun, and attained maturity in the theory of the French philosophers of the Enlightenment and of the Scottish moral philosophers. But as this paradigm has run its course, it has become increasingly apparent that there is another dimension in the work of Durkheim and Lévy-Bruhl that may be of more lasting significance—namely, the perceptual, almost epistemological tone in which they cast their investigations of the social system. As necessary as it was at the turn of the century to delimit the scientific boundaries of a discipline and establish it as a bona fide academic field of inquiry, Durkheim's categorical separation between psychology and sociology and his insistence that the latter be configured in terms of social facts alone were probably correct strategies that can be justified historically. The systematic separation of individual and collective behavior was unrealizable, however, and it did not work well in practice, but it did propel sociology and social anthropology into a naive sense of security that could not be sustained. Thus, it may very well be the case that the more permanent contributions of Durkheim and Lévy-Bruhl may turn out to be their basically epistemological focusing of human behavior and collective activity rather than their confining conceptualization of the social system.

On the Differences between Modern-Scientific and Traditional-Primitive Thought: Real and Imagined

Nearly twenty years ago an interesting book was published, entitled *Modes of Thought: Essays on Thinking in Western and Non-Western Societies* (Horton and Finnegan 1973), in which a number of anthropologists, sociologists, and philosophers address themselves to several problems that fall within the boundaries of what we have defined as the epistemological approach. Since then, one encounters individual articles with concerns akin to the epistemological concerns expressed in that volume, but no systematic effort has been focused on the conceptualization of real and spurious differences and similarities in distinctive groups at various stages of sociocultural evolution. It appears, however, that several intellectual strands and ontological domains that have been largely ignored in the formative stage of anthropology as a science are beginning to converge: expression as the obverse but complementary side of structure; determining epistemological differences and similarities of perception and inference on the basis of controlled ontological corpora; establishing the psychic unity of mankind in terms of logical priorities and substantive configurations. The psychological undertones and epistemological focusing that are exhibited in some of the recent literature, particularly in most articles in *Modes of Thought*, makes it appropriate to frame our remarks within the ambience of this work.

Until the writing of this chapter began, we had only read Tambiah's (1973: 199–229) contribution. Fittingly, the book is dedicated to Evans-Pritchard, who stimulated significant work along this line of inquiry. The first part of the book's title encapsulates the central theme of most of the articles but is nonetheless a misnomer. If the psychic unity of mankind is accepted (and all contributors of the volume do), then the subject is not the difference in modes of thought, but the difference in modes of perception and how the actors of isolable, functioning groups make inferences from perceptions. This is a rather misleading common denominator that pervades the entire volume. With the exception of the article by Colby and Cole (1973:63–91), the contributions are either programmatic or interpretative (introspective). Substantively, Colby and

Cole's article is the most significant, for it is concerned with the problem of memory and recall, suggesting that there may be significant differences cross-culturally in the way information is internalized and transmitted in cultures with oral and with literate traditions. It is likely that by pursuing the line of inquiry suggested by Colby and Cole we may achieve significant results in transcending the insidious, unconscious notion held by many anthropologists that there exists a scientific-primitive dichotomy. In a more recent work, Colby and Colby (1981) implicitly take an epistemological stance in analyzing the cognitive world of a Maya (Ixil of Guatemala) diviner; they demonstrate systematically that in translating the structure of magical behavior and discourse into scientific language one does not have to adduce a quasi-metaphysical stand by invoking differences in modes of thought. On the contrary, as this monograph at times explicitly demonstrates, Colby and Colby correctly assume that the translation rests on perceptual and inferential differences entailed by the Ixil magical system and modern science.

With the exception of the articles by Finnegan (1973:112–44), Ita (1973: 306–36), Jenkins (1973:337–56), and Whiteley (1973:145–61), the contributors to the volume have something significant to say about how the natives think, how so-called civilized or scientifically oriented people think, and how thinking processes of the natives and the "civilized" differ; with varying degrees of insight, many problems are broached with a distinctive epistemological orientation. Although only two contributors (Gellner and Wolfram) are professional philosophers, all seven contributors in this category (Nagashima, Barnes, Tambiah, Dukes, and Horton) function essentially as philosophers. Introspectively and programmatically, these seven scholars address themselves to the difficult task of trying to determine a framework, or to configure a theoretical perspective, to conceptualize the psychic unity of mankind as manifested in a manifoldly complex range of perceptual and inferential variability. From the premise that all human beings think alike, "modes of thought" entails the scientific task of determining the differential conceptualization of the physical and social universes as the confluence of two sets of variables: synchronic constraints (reduced essentially to the perceptual and inferential domains of cognition) elicited directly and systematically and translated into a common taxonomic vocabulary; and diachronic, long-term cultural traditions (as exemplified in the foregoing sections) that have resulted in specifically efficacious worldviews, usually configured by supernaturalism, the open or closed nature of the sociopolitical system, and diffusion.

The article by Nagashima (1973:92–111) may be regarded as supporting the position expressed in the first section of this chapter concerning the determinant role of a cultural tradition's imago mundi in shaping the conceptual systems through which the social and physical universes are viewed and acted upon. Just as significantly, Nagashima demonstrates that no cultural tradition or, more concretely, functioning social system has a monolithic imago mundi but rather that belief systems and ideologies may be manifested in several forms. This standpoint has been variously demonstrated in this monograph, and it is intimately connected with the concept of witchcraft as an element of last resort.

The contribution by Gellner (1973:162–81) is probably the most important in the volume. In contrasting the savage and the modern mind, Gellner clearly shows that this schema by no means exhausts the possibilities of conceptualizing the modes of perception and inference in the recent evolution of man as a sociocultural entity. Rather, it tends to obfuscate the intermediary stages as sociocultural systems evolve from magic to science as predominating in the imago mundi. He points out that science is not as "open" as Popper would like us to believe and is more constrained than Kuhn implies as entailed by the efficacy of the currently predominant paradigm, but he is skeptical of Kuhn's description of discovery and the scientific enterprise as disturbingly rigid. Most interesting to us is what Gellner (1973:180) has to say about beliefs and cognition: "In a traditional belief-system, cognition, the discovery or the endorsement of belief, is an event *in* the world, and this means in the social and moral world. Hence they are subject to the same kinds of obligations and sanctions as are other kinds of conduct — indeed, when, these ideas touch the entrenched clauses, they are quite specially subject to them." This is demonstrated in this monograph by the actors' perception of the bloodsucking event and by the conceptualization of the phenomenon as the interplay of what is normatively expected and what is physically experienced. Gellner need not have any qualms about pragmatically asserting that there is an external reality subject to objective validity, however. Science is different from all other conceptual schemata because it assumes an external reality which must be subject to objective validity.

Barnes (1973:182–98) is concerned primarily with a comparison of the belief system underlying science and those underlying magical complexes. He finds it difficult to identify formal differences between scientific and preliterate, magical belief systems. But there are operational differences in the belief systems underlying science and magical complexes, for although one may perhaps regard the belief in the tlahuelpuchi's efficacy to kill as a native theory of how infants die under certain specified circumstances, it is obviously nonsense to say that this construction is the same as a scientific theory: the native theory is a fixed, ultimate entity, whereas the scientific theory is an ideological statement only until falsified by independent experience (it is assumed that verification is an independent operation, the characteristically defining attribute of science which, obviously, does not obtain in supernaturalism). At this juncture both Horton and Barnes are right: the former by maintaining that the context of science presupposes alternative belief systems; the latter by suggesting that "if science is more prone to make radical responses to anomaly than other belief systems, then the reason lies more in the social structure than the behaviour of the individual actor; where the latter is significant it should be regarded itself as a consequence of the former" (Barnes 1973:191).

From a negative standpoint, Tambiah's contribution is the most important in the volume. In the Introduction, we discussed at length Tambiah's position; here we wish to reiterate that what he has to say concerning the difference between scientific conceptualization and conceptualization in preliterate societies with a strong magical complex, is essentially mistaken and not at all conducive to good scientific anthropology. Fundamentally, he confuses understanding with explaining: one understands at the belief or ideological level, but one explains at the level of well-specified and positioned empirical facts (even though beliefs [constructs, models, paradigms] to some extent influence the perception of facts). In his well-reasoned article Lukes (1973:230–48) maintains that even though truth and validity are socioculturally grounded, there are objective standards of truth and validity. He outlines the argument of his paper as follows:

> (1) There are no good reasons for supposing that all criteria of truth and validity are [as many have been tempted to suppose] context-dependent and variable; (2) there are good reasons for maintaining that some are not, that these are universal and fundamental, and that those criteria which *are* context-dependent are parasitic upon them; (3) it is only by assuming such universal and fundamental criteria that a number of crucial sociological questions about beliefs can be asked, among them questions about differences between "traditional" and "modern" or pre-"scientific" modes of thought; and therefore (4) despite many possible difficulties and pitfalls, the sociologist or anthropologist need not prohibit, indeed, he should be ready to make, cognitive and logical judgements [however provisional] with respect to the beliefs he studies. (Lukes 1973:230)

We agree wholeheartedly with this position as conducive to good social science. Horton's (1973:249–305) contribution stems from the same concerns discussed by Gellner, with whom he disagrees on some points which are beyond the scope of this discussion. On the whole, however, Horton's excellent article and his work on African traditionalism (Horton 1967) agree essentially with what Gellner has to say. In fact, all seven contributors discussed here exhibit a healthy degree of positivism. Liberal anthropologists, perhaps misguidedly disenchanted with science or perhaps because of the West's colonial past, have tended to idealize the natives, to abstain from making value judgments when the situation required it, and to assign ontological similarities in the configuration of native cultures as latently reverse cases of discrimination. This rather widespread attitude during the past generation is not only scientifically misplaced in the task of understanding other cultures but ultimately self-defeating and patronizing to the natives. It is in this light that the contribution of these seven scholars should be assessed.

Finally, Wolfram (1973:357–74) draws attention to the qualitative differences that may exist in the collective perceptions of societies—that is, she purports to know what differences qualify as "basic" and what are the criteria for such a classification. This is a theme that underlies this monograph and its efforts to conceptualize the differences and similarities between science and all kinds of supernaturalism. In other words, as it has become increasingly apparent that cultural sharing is much less monolithic than has traditionally been assumed, it becomes equally important to study the variability of modes of perception and inference intra-culturally and cross-culturally.

A Programmatic Outline of How to Implement the Epistemological Focus and Strategy

The value of the foregoing contributions rests mainly in raising interesting questions concerning the various forms of conceptualizing the social and physical universes and in formulating, albeit tentatively, strategies that may perhaps result in a new paradigm of looking at the manifold configurations of human behavior. Occasionally one reads an article along similar lines, but nothing has yet coalesced that can be considered a concerted effort toward the formulation of a new approach. In the remainder of this chapter, we venture an outline of the operations that need to be undertaken toward the formalization of the epistemological approach as envisaged in this chapter.

Briefly, the analysis of cognitive styles and structural interplay of the social and physical universes must rest on the assumptions that all humans think alike and that differences in perception and inference are to be explained as the effect of cultural traditions of long standing. The culture history and social evolution of humanity during the past five thousand years exhibit two fairly clear characteristics. On the one hand, cultural traditions come into being and develop distinct worldviews (due to initial ecological and demographic inputs and conditions and perhaps to other variables even more difficult to pinpoint) that largely determine the epistemological screens through which the social and physical universes are viewed. On the other hand, no matter how dominant the imago mundi (worldview, ideology-belief system) of a cultural tradition it is seldom if ever monolithic, it almost invariably admits compartmentalization, and it is subject to change by outside inputs and new forms of knowledge.

First, what does it mean to establish the implications of perception and inference? Primarily that, regardless of whatever form they take, and however they are formalized, the logic of entailment and making judgments about the world is constant. What varies from cultural tradition to cultural tradition, and intra-culturally in extreme cases of compartmentalization, is not the form or mode of thought but its content and context. Thus, there are no differences, logically speaking, between the cognitive operations underlying the manifold manifestations of magic and religion and the many procedures of science. But there may be a great many differences in the diversified form in which perception (including introspection) takes place along the magic-religion-science continuum. With respect to the modes of inference typically associated with isolable modes of perception, the differences may be equally great. Practically speaking, however, given the effect of diffusion and the homogenization of cultural variation during the past two centuries, we intuit that there are a manageable number of concomitant modes of perception and inference. The question is, then, What makes those bound by the predominant imago mundi of an isolable, reasonably well delimited social group perceive and infer distinctly differently from another equally delimited group? This is an extremely difficult question, and only tentative answers can be given. Thus, the first order of business in implementing the epistemological approach is the systematic gathering of a cross-culturally representative corpus of data along the evolutionary continuum on how and under what conditions ideology and belief systems determine, distort, or condition perception and inference. In fact, even in the case of the so-called modern, secular, scientific societies we do not know the range and efficacy of the predominant scientific paradigm coexisting with various forms of supernaturalism. With respect to traditional, primitive, non-literate societies the problem is empirically even more obscure. Even the best ethnographic accounts of witchcraft, sorcery, religion, and other kinds of supernaturalism do not contain systematic accounts of ideologies and belief systems.

Second, throughout this monograph the primary concern has been with how rural Tlaxcalans make inferences in a circumscribed domain—that is, how those who believe in bloodsucking witchcraft validate their belief that supernatural inputs produce natural outcomes. It is the analysis of this circumscribed domain that permits one to say something meaningful about the mode of perception of this folk segment of Mexican society. Perception and inference is a crucial juncture, and the most profitable way to frame its study, since the passage of supernatural inputs to natural outcomes is at the heart of the differences obtaining between scientific and non-scientific societies or parts of societies. The other advantage resulting from this formulation of the basic problem of the epistemological strategy is that it is squarely focused on the nature of supernaturalism. It is assumed, of course, that belief in supernatural causation may color, influence, or determine the perception of phenomena, the inferences made after them, and the causal entailments that isolable segments of society generate. Thus, all sociocultural systems, and their compartmentalized segments, may be arranged in a continuum ranging from an operationalized limiting parameter in which supernaturalism has a maximum effect (at this extreme, on the basis of the extant ethnographic literature, are included the Azande, the Dobuans, the traditional Australian aborigines, and so on) to an equally operationalized parameter in which supernaturalism has a minimum effect (here would be included all philosophically religious people and magico-religious people of last resort, including practicing scientists who believe in the supernatural). In this way of looking at the manifold perspective in the conceptualization of social and physical domains, it is not a question of gross dichotomies such as the traditional-modern or primitive-scientific segments of humanity, but a discernible continuum in which well-delineated functioning systems, and parts of them, slide into increasingly more naturalistic conceptions of the universe. Finally, the perceptions and inferential modes molded and conditioned by supernaturalism must then be analyzed in their various expressions throughout the entire societal and subcultural spectrum—on the one hand, to determine whether belief in supernatural causation in turn influences or conditions perception and inference as they take place in all other social and physical domains; and on the other hand, to determine whether there are other inputs that affect these cognitive processes.

Third is compartmentalization, which has been an underlying theme in the foregoing discussion as well as in the descriptive chapters of this monograph; this and the following step are a corollary of the two above steps, but they need to be discussed separately for practical and conceptual reasons. Fundamentally, compartmentalization may be defined as the breakdown of the perceptual and inferential structure entailed by the concomitant effect of naturalism and supernaturalism realized in identifiable domains of isolable functioning societies and subcultures. Surveying the ethnographic literature treating the range from the most primitive society to the most scientific community, we find no instance in which supernaturalism does not affect the perceptions and causal judgments of actors—that is, no occasions and domains in the social and physical lives of the people in which supernatural inputs are not believed to produce natural outcomes, and vice versa, natural inputs are not believed to produce supernatural outcomes. Evolutionarily, societies and subcultures could be arranged on a continuum according to the proportion of supernaturalism and naturalism that enter into the processes of perception and causation. At the lower, primitive extreme or limit supernaturalism undoubtedly prevails, but there is no evidence in the ethnographic literature on the basis of which one could roughly estimate the sub-breaking domains in which naturalism prevails. At the upper, scientific limit, no significant segment of Western society, no matter how scientific, is not subject to varying degrees of supernaturalism. Of crucial importance is to focus the problem from the intra-cultural perspective, and here the example of Western society during the past three hundred years or so is extremely significant. Concentrating on the present, one still finds segments of most variants of European society in which rather extreme forms of supernaturalism coexist side by side with what one would operationalize as scientific communities. Here one could also establish a gradation between these extremes. Let us take as an example extreme fundamentalist Christian sects in the United States.

Two facts are immediately apparent. First, except that the discharge of Christian Fundamentalism today does not necessarily entail the physical and ideological coercion that was present in the seventeenth century, several of these sects are not significantly different in belief and, to some degree, practice from the various forms of Christianity out of which they evolved. Fundamentalists believe in direct supernatural intervention in human affairs—that is, that God can discernably punish or reward individuals and the collectivity and in a number of ways influence noticeably or greatly the natural course of affairs. By itself, ideologically American fundamentalism can be placed on a socioevolutionary continuum of changing subcultural traditions as it moves from maximum supernaturalism to maximum naturalism. On such a scale, rural Tlaxcalans and American fundamentalists would occupy adjacent positions. Second, at the practical level of compartmentalization the differences are much more pronounced. In most domains of behavior and action, American fundamentalists behave essentially the same as non-fundamentalist Christians or even the most scientific segment of American society—that is, compartmentalization is clear cut, cause-and-effect relationships are naturalistically conceived, and supernaturalism is held in suspended judgment. To put it differently, with a few exceptions (such as Christian Scientists denying the germ theory of disease, a magical belief essentially similar to bloodsucking witchcraft in rural Tlaxcala), when their manifest beliefs collide with the prevalent, scientific worldview of the majority of the larger society, fundamentalists behave in a more or less modern and naturalistic fashion, and it is hard to distinguish them from other segments of American society. (Witness, for example, creationists justifying biblical chronology by adducing scientific or pseudoscientific arguments.) This is not the case with the primitive magico-religious systems described in the literature, or even those of folk societies such as rural Tlaxcala. Compartmentalization in these societies is not clear cut, naturalistic cause-and-effect relationships affect a much smaller proportion of the cultural array of the functional system, and supernaturalism pervades many domains that are not directly related to magic and religion.

Fourth, evidently the analysis of the foregoing steps is posited on the assumption that all systems of magico-religious supernaturalism entail the distinction between natural and supernatural causation. In fact, in most ethnographic descriptions of witchcraft and sorcery in primitive societies it is maintained that no distinction obtains between the natural and the supernatural, and that it is therefore useless to discriminate between supernatural inputs and natural outcomes. We repeat that denying the operational effect of the natural-supernatural distinction is related to confusing levels of analysis. While it may be true that at the ideological level what actors maintain, configured as specific belief complexes, may to some extent mold or influence most domains directly or indirectly related to magic and religion, it is highly unlikely that most actors' actions related to the social and physical environments are not conducted on a naturalistic basis—that is, without being underlined by supernatural inputs or considerations. The point is, of course, that no supernatural imago mundi, however dominant and pervasive, can be powerful enough to prevent naturalistic behavior from taking place in much of the daily life of any society; and, conversely, no naturalistic, scientific imago mundi can completely obliterate that residue of supernaturalism inherent in all humans, as far as it can be presently determined. Psychologically, however, one can hardly imagine a functioning social group in which the predominant supernatural imago mundi does not allow for the conduct of most of daily life without immediate thoughts or considerations that have nothing to do with magical or religious intervention of any kind.

Fifth, anthropologists who have worked in a culture area for a generation or more are sensitive to the fact that a stable, traditional social system may quickly collapse due to strong pressures from the outside world and under the steady influence of diffusion. In this context, it is safe to assume that, with various degrees of rapidity, the magico-religious systems that have been reported in the ethnographic literature during the past fifty years or so, for example, have been significantly to drastically transformed. Perhaps an efficient method of initiating the implementation of the epistemological focus and strategy would be to restudy the best-reported cases of witchcraft and sorcery to determine the extent to which the belief system and imago mundi of these societies have changed since they were originally investigated. The consideration of change, however, is incidental at this point. What must necessarily be brought to the fore is that, for perhaps more than a hundred years, traditional folk and primitive societies have been influenced by the modern, technological, and scientific external worlds. This new knowledge, when differentially internalized by folk and primitive societies, has probably been the single most important variable that has transformed not only magico-religious systems but the entire fabric of societies.

Lest the reader misunderstand, what we are saying about sociocultural change in the modern world has been said before; what is new is the notion that significant or drastic changes in the imago mundi due to modernization and secularization are irrevocably blurring and ultimately obliterating the distinction between primitive and scientific-technological societies. From a slightly different perspective what is evidently happening, as primitive societies become folk societies and folk societies become increasingly modernized and secularized, is that a homogenized, incipiently technological culture is beginning to emerge: a worldwide culture with many areal subcultures. Of more significance here is the realization of the basic premise that changes in the imago mundi, concomitantly viewed as modernization and secularization, rest on naturalism asserting itself over supernaturalism as the predominant cultural ideological paradigm, thereby restricting supernatural causation to increasingly self-contained and smaller domains.

Sixth, science-technology during the past hundred years has become the predominant paradigmatic imago mundi of the universal culture that is now in the process of formation, and it is in this sense that the old, often unjustly abused, magic-religion-science evolutionary sequence still has potential operational validity. If it is warranted to assume that the scientific-technological imago mundi has been progressively displacing the magico-religious imago mundi as the predominant paradigm in the modern world through which the physical and social universes are experienced and conceptualized, then there are two tasks that must be performed in implementing the epistemological focus and strategy.

Within the boundaries of Western society, technology and, particularly, science must be examined processually and ontologically: by determining the stages that science has undergone since approximately the beginning of the seventeenth century in displacing its magico-religious competitor as the predominant imago mundi, first in Western Europe, and subsequently in other parts of the world; and perhaps more significantly, by detailing syntagmatically the process of compartmentalization that has taken place and by specifying the content and form that the almost totally socially obliterated European magic system have taken, together with the increasingly marginal position that religion has come to occupy in the global array of organized life at most subcultural levels. This task would help significantly in establishing a model that could be processually replicated as the predominance of Western science and technology diffused. We envisage the following specific sub-tasks: establishing the progression of scientific discoveries, their diffusion, and the steady process of erosion they have produced in the Christian ideology and imago mundi (the heliocentric theory, Newton's physics, Darwinism, and so on); measuring the inputs into and impact on the Christian belief system produced by the increasingly naturalistic conceptions of humans and their place in nature (beginning in the late seventeenth century with the work of Vico, continued in the work of the French philosophers of the Enlightenment and of the Scottish moral philosophers, and brought to a conclusion by contemporary social science); assessing systematically the reaction of the collective religious hierarchies and religious polities against the bombardment of scientific ideas, almost invariably producing changes in the dogma and practice of the faith (the belief in witches is dogmatically abolished, the definition of heresy is increasingly liberalized as it becomes impossible to sanction, God conceived as a wrathful father becomes an exclusively loving God; and so on); determining in what contexts and progressions the separation between church and state further hastened the process of secularization effected by the scientific technological revolution; determining specific technological inputs which, as modernizing complexes, have syntagmatically led to even more secularization; and so on.

The same tasks detailed here within the context of Western culture and society must also be undertaken for a representative sample of nations, culture areas, and functioning societies. There is one significant difference, however, that must be clearly kept in mind. In the case of Western culture, the processes of modernization and secularization must be framed by the direct confrontation of the emerging scientific imago mundi and the sacred ideology and belief system of Christianity, for it is this struggle that produces the drastic changes in the organization of sociocultural life. In the external and manifold process of diffusion and acculturation (directly or indirectly conditioned by the expansion of western European peoples since the sixteenth century, and in the contexts of colonialism or some form of economic dominance) it is more appropriate to focus the problem other than in terms of confronting imago mundi. The scientific-technological view of the world does not necessarily collide head-on with other manifold civilized or primitive worldviews; its effect is instead somehow selectively distributed in the various cultural domains of the societies in question. It is therefore important to determine how, in what sequence, and at what degree of rapidity the scientific ideological worldview affects and modifies impinged cultural and subcultural domains. Ultimately, of course, the impinging scientific-technological imago mundi does confront local counterparts, but this is an indirect process in that the latter have already been modified by changes in many other domains.

Seventh, and finally, is a consideration of great significance. Anthropologists have been successful in conceptualizing, albeit descriptively, the structure of social systems in action, but they have been singularly unsuccessful in describing, let alone positioning, ideology and belief systems and the entailing relationship that obtains between the ideology and the belief systems. Somehow the anthropological tradition has so disregarded the analysis of ideologies and belief complexes that, even in the mechanical descriptions of societies and subsocieties, no modus operandi has emerged for placing in a position of entailment the rules, injunctions, commands, and values (the manifold complex of the "what ought to be") and the actual structure in operation. In the present context, the problem is compounded pragmatically and analytically: lack of a systematic method hinders the process of configuring exhaustive ideological and belief complexes, in turn leading to an inadequate conceptualization of the interplay between normative expectation and physical realization, the key epistemic operation in determining the form and content of social and physical perception and inference and concomitant causal entailment. Thus, the implementation of the epistemological approach requires the formulation of a method, structured in terms of levels of exclusivity and inclusivity and intensity and extensity, for the systematic and standard description and analysis of ideological and belief complexes.

The Cultural Configuration and Epistemic Structure of the Tlahuelpuchi Complex

To conclude, we present bloodsucking witchcraft in rural Tlaxcala as a construct in which supernatural inputs produce natural outcomes within a perceptual and inferential matrix in which the efficacy of the tlahuelpuchi to kill is entailed by the interaction of a highly specified normative system and the physical realization of the sucking event. The intent is not only to summarize and give a focused gestalt of the perceptual and inferential underpinnings of bloodsucking witchcraft but also to present a replicable model of an instance of magic supernaturalism within a carefully controlled environment. Furthermore, we wish to set the main substantive and methodological parameters in the quest to formalize the epistemological focus and strategy.

It has been assumed that all societies or subsocieties distinguish between natural and supernatural causation in at least a significant or circumscribed number of domains. In this context, bloodsucking witchcraft in rural Tlaxcala, as presented in this monograph for a traditional baseline (1960), may be placed somewhere in the middle of a continuum, more or less equidistant between Azande witchcraft and sorcery and the magico-religious system of "Middletown USA." Substantively, the tlahuelpuchi complex is a circumscribed, self-contained segment of magical supernaturalism that is almost ideally configured for exemplifying the epistemological focus and strategy. But, most determinately, it is the self-directness and regularity of the tlahuelpuchi's efficacy to kill that has permitted us to center the problem of magical supernaturalism on the structure of supernatural inputs producing natural outcomes. In summary, the synchronic analysis of bloodsucking witchcraft in rural Tlaxcala presented in this monograph is the first attempt to explain a concrete case of magical supernaturalism focused on a native theory of knowledge in which the people's perceptions, and the inferences they make from this perceptual milieu, is conditioned by a normative belief system discharged in a structural domain of closed social and physical events. This is the model that has been developed in this monograph. What is its substantive composition and how may it be regarded theoretically and epistemologically?

First, the corpora of facts on which the analysis of bloodsucking witchcraft in rural Tlaxcala is based were not gathered and organized with a specific or even general theoretical and methodological orientation. Three data sets are used in the analysis of this monograph. The first is the ideology and belief system of the tlahuelpuchi complex firmly embedded in the ideology and belief system of the total ensemble of rural Tlaxcalan magic and religion. This corpus of data was systematically gathered from many informants; the normative structure of bloodsucking witchcraft emerges as a rather pristine statement in terms of specified beliefs and accompanying injunctions and constraints, and the consequences that follow from them. The second set of data is the forty-seven—case sample of bloodsucking witchcraft collected over a six-year period. After several cases were observed, procedures were standardized and the facts and observations of the entire sucking event were collected and recorded in a fashion as systematic as that for any corpus of data in traditional ethnography. This set of data may be regarded as a model for the collection of information on magical domains similar to the bloodsucking event—that is, in situations in which witchcraft and sorcery events are highly patterned. The third set of data, and the least systematic, was collected after we began writing this monograph. Although it was not as reliable as the other sets, it was nonetheless useful in verifying several key points of the analysis, and coterminously, it served to expand the range of interpretation of the original data set.

Second, the analytical steps, procedures, and results of this monograph may be summarized as follows. Within the circumscribed and carefully delimited bloodsucking complex we determine and operationally define what constitute natural and supernatural causation and entailment: those infants who die under the circumstances strictly specified by the normative system are attributed to the efficacy of the tlahuelpuchi to kill, whereas those who do not die under specified circumstances are regarded has having died of identified or unidentified illness contemplated by folk or modern medical theories; in the wider context of the tlahuelpuchi's sphere of action, mishaps and unfortunate events are equally classified as natural or supernatural events by the same operational principle. Briefly stated, this operation may be conceived of as the dynamic principle of bloodsucking witchcraft: regularity and consistency in the social and physical perception of what the normative belief system stipulates verify or confirm the supernatural action of the tlahuelpuchi; and, concomitantly, in a feedback fashion, normative expectation and sociophysical realization reinforce each other by conscious physical, ritual, and symbolic manipulations, tamperings, and exaggerations. It is at this juncture that the following conceptual operations are achieved: specification of the normative chain of events that, as perceived by all actors of a sucking event, determines the efficacy of the tlahuelpuchi to kill; determination of the natural chain of events that results in infant death, independent of normative expectations and social and physical realizations; isolation of individual and collective tamperings, manipulations, exaggerations, and transpositions engaged in physically, socially, ritually, and symbolically by all actors of the sucking event; and delineation of the psychological matrix in which natural and supernatural inputs and outputs are discharged, the bloodsucking witchcraft system is rationalized and reinforced, and all actors affected by the sucking event return to normality. Directly, within the bloodsucking witchcraft system in operation, and indirectly, in the broader context of anthropomorphic supernaturalism and the folk religion, we demonstrate the nature and form of compartmentalization, to the extent that the inclusive and exclusive domains of magical efficacy are fixed or contextual.

Compartmentalization is not as crucial for the implementation of the epistemological approach in a single, ethnographic case as it is ethnologically and comparatively. Thus, the isolation and delineation of the entire array of rural Tlaxcalan domains, configured as actual or potential contexts for the realization of supernatural or natural causation, are the primary considerations. The dynamic, obverse aspect of compartmentalization, however, is discussed in the description of how, in what detail, and at what rate of speed the bloodsucking witchcraft complex has changed during the past generation. This operation concludes the analysis by specifying the demise of the tlahuelpuchi complex as a native explanatory construct, which is entailed by the reception (modernizing phase) and internalization (secularizing phase) of new knowledge (a more naturalistic view of the world brought about by some science, a significantly more technological ambience, and the influence of formal education and the various means of communication). What has the implementation of the epistemological approach produced theoretically? No theory of bloodsucking witchcraft or magical action has emerged, and from this standpoint, this monograph has not conceptually advanced what has been achieved by witchcraft studies so far. But it has managed to explain why and under what circumstances infants die and how the concept of the witch is employed in this particularly explanatory function. In other words, we have demonstrated the logic and substantive composition of the native theory in action but verified independently of the sociophysical outputs it entails. From this viewpoint, this study transcends most studies of witchcraft in which ideological and belief inputs are implied but not verified.

Third, epistemologically the enterprise may be characterized as an exercise in translating a native, folk theory of knowledge of a subcultural, magical domain into a theory of knowledge of contemporary science. Thus, we manage to give a general account, buttressed by physical observations, of the rural Tlaxcalans' perception of a magical phenomenon through the screen of the normative system and the inferences people make. Three sets of epistemological considerations are undertaken in this monograph. First, establishing the perceptual antecedents that lead people to experience the sucking event, ex post facto rationalized and elaborated according to normative expectation: the social and physical contexts in which all actors affected by the sucking event manipulate, exaggerate, distort, reinterpret, and transpose real or imagined events, ideas, and reinforced notions. Second, analyzing the perceptions of all affected actors during the postsucking period, by themselves (that is, as the referents of physical and social events and actions) and in relation to the feedback effect that obtains in the interplay of normative expectations and structural realization: the actions of the sucked infant's mother during the night, of other members of the household, of secondary actors immediately after the sucking, and so on. Third, conceptualizing the entire spectrum of physical, social, ritual, and symbolic behavior and action of the maximum extension of actors bound by the sucking event as a series of outputs entailed by the manifold array of perceptions specified temporally until the body of the victim is found, but rationalized and intensified as a consequence of and complemental to the reinforcing structure of individual and collective experience of the tlahuelpuchi complex: the psychological disturbances and psychosomatic ailments experienced by primary actors, the reaction of secondary actors, the ritual and symbolic reinforcement of the tlahuelpuchi's efficacy to kill, and so on.

The sucking event, together with the strongly verbalized belief system and the actors' past experience of the complex, constitute the epistemological matrix in which perceptions and inferences are shaped and explanations emerge.

This is the subtle, brittle environment that ultimately sanctions or makes it easier for rural Tlaxcalans to continue to believe in magical causation. Thus, emically the essence of the epistemological approach is the elucidation of the perceptions that make people infer actions and events out of the interplay of normative, what-ought-to-be constructs and physical and social experience viewed through the screens of the feedback effect of the constructs and reinforced tradition. This part of the approach has been reasonably well achieved in this monograph.

Finally, can we encapsulate the several strands of what we have termed the epistemological approach? The following is a conditional answer, and a statement of how the approach can be applied comparatively or cross-culturally. One cannot experience the external world directly, physically, and socially; because human beings are organized in social systems, their individual and collective perceptions and inferences are always conditioned by normative, what-ought-to-be constructs, the fundamental function of which is collective living through successful communication. If we accept this, then once the cultural spectrum along the socioevolutionary scale has been well understood, described, and conceptualized (as is the case after a hundred years of ethnology and ethnography), the central problem of anthropology becomes epistemologically centered: the study of modes of perception and inference as societies move along the evolutionary continuum from a limit of maximum supernaturalism to a limit of maximum naturalism. The epistemological perspective demands that the perception and conceptualization of the social and physical worlds be focused as a concomitant expression of causal entailment obtaining between the natural and supernatural domains, operationalized in all possible combinations of inputs and outputs (the direction of cause and effect).

Conclusions

THIS MONOGRAPH PRESENTS the changing and evolving aspects of bloodsucking witchcraft and ancillary components of the magical system in rural Tlaxcala: from their syncretic inception at the time of the Spanish Conquest, to their Colonial development and stabilization throughout the sixteenth and seventeenth centuries, to the beginning of their transformation at the turn of the century by the sequential effect of the processes of modernization and secularization. Although the complex remained fairly stable from 1900 to 1960, during the generation before the ethnographic present of this book bloodsucking witchcraft began to be subjected to the effects of modernization. This period may be considered as a prelude to the rapid, drastic changes that were in store during the following generation. In concluding this monograph, the following topics are discussed: (1) The structural and ideological changes that bloodsucking witchcraft has undergone from 1960 to 1986, as a concomitant expression of the processes of modernization and secularization. (2) The extent to which specific external variables and the increasing incorporation of rural Tlaxcalan society into the fabric of the nation have affected the transformation of magic supernaturalism. (3) A general statement on the conceptualization of changing witchcraft systems in particular, and magic supernaturalism in general, under the influence of diffusion and the internalization of alternative forms of knowledge.

THE TRANSFORMATION OF BLOODSUCKING WITCHCRAFT DURING THE PAST GENERATION

The reconstruction of bloodsucking witchcraft in rural Tlaxcala on the basis of living informants can be extended to approximately a hundred years ago—that is, to the 1880s. Briefly, the period from the 1880s until about 1960 may be characterized as the rather slow but steady transition from a fairly open and significantly more diversified witchcraft system to the specialized bloodsucking witchcraft system described in this monograph. Three stages may be fairly clearly isolated for this eighty-year period.

First, from approximately 1880 to shortly after the turn of the century bloodsucking was just as extensive as it has been described here, but it was one of perhaps several aspects of witchcraft probably exhibiting some domains, still fairly intact, of the highly diversified pre-Hispanic complex that survived the last syncretic stage at the turn of the seventeenth century. Witchcraft may be characterized during this period as more of an integral part of the social structure, entailing a higher incidence of accusations and less compartmentalized (that is, the natural-supernatural cleavage obtained in a higher number of circumscribed domains) than it is today.

Second, roughly from the onset of the Mexican Revolution to the middle 1930s, the diversification of witchcraft was almost obliterated, and the complex became essentially what it was at the ethnographic present of this study, bloodsucking witchcraft. Nonetheless, several changes centered on the strict configuration of the belief system underlying the antecedents and consequences of the bloodsucking event took place as witchcraft became focused almost exclusively on infant death. Thus, the vulgarization of the tlahuelpuchi's efficacy to kill was minimal (that is, mythical and legendary accounts did not portray the bloodsucking witch and its interaction with ordinary humans in ways and situations not specified by the belief system that was independently verbalized by the people), and all the injunctions and constraints of the belief system, particularly those connected with the postsucking period, were strictly complied with. There were very few skeptics, and the bloodsucking ensemble was more of an extensive closed system than described in this monograph.

Third, from the middle 1930s to the ethnographic present of this monograph, bloodsucking witchcraft underwent further changes, not as significant as those in the previous stage, but already presaging the great changes soon to come. Structurally, the system remained stable in the discharge of the antecedent and consequent complex surrounding the sucking event, and the arrangement of the personnel and the support system of the affected household remained undisturbed when the tlahuelpuchi struck. It is ideologically, in the belief system, that bloodsucking witchcraft exhibited noticeable changes. Foremost among these was the beginning of the vulgarization of specific beliefs, particularly those concerned with the transformations of the tlahuelpuchi, her relationship to ordinary humans, and her interaction with other anthropomorphic supernaturals and the Christian devil. Finally, it should be noted that changes in bloodsucking witchcraft during these three stages correlate well with the processes of modernization and secularization as they have affected rural Tlaxcala since the beginning of factory work in the area: during the first stage the process of modernization was initiated; at the end of the second stage, modernization began to trigger secularization, as a few communities began to be integrated into the national culture; and by the end of the third stage there were a significant number of communities already secularized or in the last stages of modernization (Nutini and Isaac 1974:431–44). These two processes set the stage for the transformation of bloodsucking witchcraft during the next generation, and the account below is given with reference to them.

Structural Changes and the Magical System
By as early as 1976, it would have been impossible to replicate the present study—that is, to gather a comparable corpus of data in the communities listed in Table 6.1. It is likely, however, that in the handful of traditional communities (those at a level of modernization-secularization comparable to that of communities listed in Table 6.1) remaining in rural Tlaxcala today this task may still be undertaken. Even in such an atypical situation, however, the probability is fairly high that changes have taken place that have resulted in quantitative and qualitative differences. For the average rural Tlaxcalan community (those in which secularization during the past generation has become well established or is on the verge of destroying the traditional socioreligious core), the bloodsucking witchcraft system has changed greatly or it may well be on its way to becoming a mechanism of last resort. This accelerated trend was clearly there five years ago (see chapter 10), and such is the accelerated rate of change in the average rural Tlaxcalan community that, as these lines are being written (December 1987), the situation has been noticeably transformed. Four months ago, all communities listed in Table 6.1 were surveyed for a final update to these conclusions. Even though it was not a systematic survey, selective interviewing of young, middle-aged, and old male and female informants from at least three households from each of the communities unmistakably indicates that the magico-religious system of rural Tlaxcala in general, and bloodsucking in particular, have been changing perceptibly at an almost biennial rate, probably since the early 1970s. As in the 1982 interviews, at least one household per community in the original sample was surveyed. Thus, the following account is based on the original research (1960–1966), on occasional but fairly regular observations on bloodsucking witchcraft in communities both in the original sample and others throughout rural Tlaxcala between 1967 and 1981, and on the limited surveys of 1982 and 1987. The structural changes are the more visible and may be summarized as follows.

First, since the late 1960s, there has been a steady decrease in the incidence of bloodsucking witchcraft—that is, in the number of infant deaths attributed to the tlahuelpuchi. The data base is not sufficiently exacting and systematic to indicate the rate of progression, except to say that the attribution of the death of infants to the tlahuelpuchi in 1960 was a very common occurrence in most rural Tlaxcalan communities, whereas in 1987 it has become rare. Furthermore, it appears that the most rapid rate of change occurred roughly between 1972 and 1982. During this ten-year period, the incidence and entire superstructure of the tlahuelpuchi complex was drastically transformed: from a central position in the magical life of rural Tlaxcalans, it shifted to become not an oddity, to be sure, but a rather rare event that the households concerned tried to conceal as much as they could. Gone is the openness, visibility, and access to the various aspects of the sucking event, and it became very difficult, perhaps impossible, to observe and investigate the various aspects of the practice. Those who were the children of young and middle-aged couples in 1960, now with growing families of their own, were either singularly disinterested in discussing any aspect of the tlahuelpuchi complex, or when willing to talk, they exhibited a great loss of knowledge concerning most aspects of the sucking event in particular and the practice in general. As a rule, married couples under age forty-five did not want to be confronted with questions about bloodsucking witchcraft, felt embarrassed when elicitation was attempted, and used the most commonly verbalized evasion that the tlahuelpuchi was no longer active, or at least not as active as it used to be—implicitly asserting the latent belief in the efficacy of this supernatural to kill infants. Late middle-aged and old people, by contrast, were willing to talk and could describe the events, occurrences, and overall ambience of bloodsucking witchcraft. But they also were quick to point out that for some mysterious reason the tlahuelpuchi was no longer as voracious as it used to be, phrasing their verbalizations in such a way that there was no doubt that most of them still maintained the ontological reality of the tlahuelpuchi, her proclivity to kill, and most of the superstructure built about her. Interestingly, they complained that when the tlahuelpuchi still occasionally struck, younger families no longer adhered to and complied with the actions and procedures traditionally associated with the sucking event. This is significant, because the complaints of the older generations implicitly confirm that, even among the young and early middle-aged married couples, the tlahuelpuchi complex is still alive, although structurally well on its way to disappearing.

There is no doubt that there have been great changes in the bloodsucking witchcraft system in rural Tlaxcala in a generation. The changes can be described in detail, some of their effects can be isolated, and even a few of their side effects can be determined, but there is no theory that explains this transformation. The most that can be said is that there is a causal relationship between the great decrease of infant mortality and the rapid diminution of bloodsucking witchcraft during the past twenty-five-year period. Bloodsucking witchcraft is an elusive phenomenon; it is perhaps impossible to offer meaningful quantifications of the changes in the phenomenon, except to say that at the ethnographic present of this study it accounted for an inordinate number of infant deaths, and the average community had many cases every year, whereas today (1988), the same communities may be affected by one or two suckings a year. In summary, although bloodsucking witchcraft in rural Tlaxcala has been greatly curtailed, it is still an ongoing concern; it is a minimal expression, one could say, before becoming a mechanism of last resort. Whether this situation is the result of pressure by the communities' traditional sector, the natural inertia of magico-religious systems, or both is difficult to say. Be this as it may, the following points describe the most salient domains which have experienced the greatest changes.

First, people at large no longer have the tlahuelpuchi, her evil doings, and her general attributes and modus operandi at the tip of their tongue. The fear of this anthropomorphic supernatural may still be latently strong, but the complex no longer commands center stage; when the tlahuelpuchi strikes, the outbursts of ritual events and activities that follow are minimal and simplified. The ambience of the postsucking period is short lived, subdued, and restricted to the affected household. There is none of the concern, group action, and communal affect that a traditional sucking entailed for the propinquous paraje, and the verbalizations concerning the sucking event are muted, mild, and exhibit little of the old fear and anxiety that so characteristically marked the action of the tlahuelpuchi. The traditional rationalizing and explanatory functions of blaming the death of an infant on the bloodsucking witch are still there, but the elaborate complex of social, ritual, and ceremonial action that buttressed them is no longer present. Gone also are the underpinnings of moral action and the guilt entailed by the quest of those affected for a source of the unfortunate event. As the incidence of bloodsucking witchcraft diminishes, so does the entire supporting social, psychological, and magical ensemble that constituted the most visible and elaborate structure of the institution. What remains is not only a simplified version of the manifold complexes described in chapters 10 and 12, but a system that appears disconnected and not quite integrated with the traditional social and psychological context of anthropomorphic supernaturalism. Yet, there is still that lingering, gnawing belief that, despite doubts and a more naturalistic approach to problem solving, the tlahuelpuchi may still have a hand in the demise of infants under peculiar circumstances or, perhaps equally plausibly, that, even if what *really* causes the death of infants is strongly suspected, the people at large do not wish to give up the anxiety-reducing and assuaging mechanisms and functions of blaming the tlahuelpuchi.

Second, perhaps the most striking aspect of the changing bloodsucking witchcraft system is the vulgarization of the complex. Whereas most male and female informants were reluctant or unwilling to talk about the tlahuelpuchi as a killer of infants and about the central features of this loathsome activity, they talked freely about other aspects and components of her craft and modus operandi. As the incidence of sucked infants rapidly decreased, and the traditionally precise, focused, and well-verbalized belief system became lax, diffused, and nebulously expressed, legends and myth-like accounts in which the tlahuelpuchi is the main *dramatis personae* in a variety of contexts proliferated. The themes of these legends and accounts are concerned with various situations in which the tlahuelpuchi interferes with, tries to control, and influences the affairs of ordinary humans, or she plays the role of mediator between humans and other supernaturals in the context of supplications, entreaties, and even outright bribes. Nearly all these legends and accounts greatly depart from the traditional belief system, often in outlandish ways in which the tlahuelpuchi becomes a caricature of her traditional self. Interestingly, the tlahuelpuchi acquires some of the characteristics of La Malintzi and El Cuatlapanga but with a complement of characteristic attributes of the more nebulous anthropomorphic supernaturals of traditional rural Tlaxcala such as Matlalcihua and La Llorona. With respect to La Malintzi and El Cuatlapanga, the tlahuelpuchi does not become a benefactor of individuals and groups, but she does facilitate the interaction with these supernaturals, or in her own right she may be predisposed to be kind and considerate to humans. With respect to the more nebulous anthropomorphic supernaturals, the tlahuelpuchi is much more of her old self, being nasty to individuals, stealing children, and behaving malevolently to the extent of causing death, but in ways that have nothing to do with the magic structure of traditional anthropomorphic supernaturalism: the tlahuelpuchi transforms herself into another woman, she becomes a snake, or she may even become a diviner for profit. Finally, the tlahuelpuchi also transcends the boundaries of the traditional belief system in the fashion described in chapter 2, but in greater degree and in more improbable contexts. The eighty or so legends and mythical accounts of the tlahuelpuchi gathered in 1982, and occasionally from 1978 to 1981, give the distinctive impression of a system in serious structural disarray on the evidence of its underlying belief system (that is, most of the fit between normative expectations and structural realization is gone), when compared to the state of affairs at the ethnographic present of this monograph. This hodgepodge of legendary and mythical creativity combines a number of traditional magical elements, which indicates that the overall complex of anthropomorphic supernaturalism is still there in various latent and manifest degrees of realization, but it also demonstrates how seriously the structural discharge of the bloodsucking witchcraft system has been affected.

Third, in many ways one of the strongest reasons why folk, transitional societies, or societies with some access to or under the mild influence of the scientific and technological world may have efficacious witchcraft systems is the systematic reinforcing of the normative belief complex in fashions similar or comparable to what transpires during the postsucking period for bloodsucking witchcraft and on a number of other occasions described in the foregoing chapters. By 1980 or so, the verbalized and to some extent ritual reinforcement of the tlahuelpuchi complex was gone. Today, when she strikes, the postsucking period is subdued and almost uneventful, a radical transformation from the barrage of magical accounts, the insistent questioning of reasons and motives, and the monotonous repetition of the perpetrator's modus operandi that characterized the traditional sucking event. Since the tlahuelpuchi is no longer an entity causing perceptible anxiety and apprehension, particularly during the cold and rainy seasons, the accounts of her doings, mostly at the time of the evening meal when people sat around the hearth, have almost vanished from the intimacy of family life. The legendary and mythic-like accounts that have proliferated since the onset of rapid change are not reinforcing. Rather, these accounts are verbalized as part of the storytelling of which rural Tlaxcalans are fond. What is gone are the structured contexts of reinforcement, and what remains is the empty shell of a complex that provides a good avenue for expression, particularly in that age group fifty and above.

Considering the great decrease of bloodsucking witchcraft and the accompanying changes described above, we think probably the most noticeable transformation has taken place in the structure of the postsucking period, the most elaborate component of the entire system. Informants were emphatic about the de facto demise of the support group generated by a traditional sucking, of the network of action involving the household and the propinquous group of kinsmen and compadres, and of the structured behavior involving all personnel concerned. The rites, the various complexes of behavior, and the precise deportment of affected personnel described in chapters 9 and 11 have either disappeared or been greatly simplified and become diffused. The general tenor of the household after a sucking may now be characterized by a certain degree of indifference toward the parents of the victim, and the main concern is for the quick return of the household to normality. Without intensive, direct observation of the victim's parents, particularly of the mother, it was impossible to determine the elaborate complex of guilt, culpability, and responsibility that always accompanied a traditional sucking. Several informants, however, implicitly suggested that most of the social, physical, and psychological manifestations of the postsucking period were minimal or no longer there, but whether parents, particularly the mother, exhibited measurable degrees of guilt, culpability, and responsibility they could not say.

Fourth, the last rapidly changing aspects of bloodsucking witchcraft not centered on the sucking event are the demise of the witch hunts, epidemics, and accusations. In the community of San Pedro Xolotla (where the great epidemic described in chapter 5 took place), several informants were quick to point out that, because of both mothers taking better care of their infants and the inexplicable reduction in the voracity of the tlahuelpuchi, epidemics no longer occurred. The former reason is significant. When informants were asked whether "better care of infants" meant better protection against the tlahuelpuchi or better physical and psychological care of infants, they invariably answered the latter, clearly implying what many people suspected, even in traditional times: that in one way or another mothers, and perhaps other members of the household, were directly or indirectly instrumental in infant death attributed to the tlahuelpuchi. Overall, bloodsucking witchcraft epidemics do not appear to have been part of local culture and society since the middle 1970s. The same can be said about witch hunts, although in the community of San Antonio Omeyocan they took place as late as 1978. This aspect of the tlahuelpuchi complex elicited quite a few chuckles from young informants (in their late thirties or early forties, who as children had assiduously participated in them) about the naivete of hunting witches in animal form. This is noteworthy, for it appears that the belief in the tlahuelpuchi's power of animal transformation is one of the first aspects of the system to be extensively doubted and forgotten, without entirely doubting the existence of humans that may suck the blood of infants. The last witchcraft accusation leading to the execution of a woman took place in 1973, and as far as we know, at least for the communities listed in Table 6.2, this is the end of the practice. Rather predictably, since fear of the tlahuelpuchi was largely predicated on her powers of animal transformation, the people at large are much more free today than in traditional times to point to possible candidates and occasionally even name them. This is most significant, for it indicates that the inevitable scapegoatism that accompanies witchcraft systems is, in this particular case, being adapted to new, often very different conditions as an element of last resort.

Finally, the transformation of bloodsucking witchcraft described above is not an isolated phenomenon. Rather, it is part and parcel of the structural changes that the entire anthropomorphic supernatural system has undergone during the same period, Briefly, the changing position of the tlahuelpuchi with respect to the other three anthropomorphic supernaturals in rural Tlaxcala is as follows. Nahualism has undergone transformations very similar to those de-scribed here, although it is a less elaborate and extensive complex. Naturally enough, the nahual and the tlahuelpuchi, partaking of the most characteristic attributes of the witch as a general category, have undergone similar fates as the result of the conjoined forces of modernization and secularization. By con-trast, the tezitlazc and the tetlachihuic, essentially variants of the sorcerer, have survived more successfully these processes of change by undergoing less serious transformations. Weathermaking still goes on in perhaps most commu-nities, not as intensely as a generation ago, to be sure, but in essentially the same fashion. If one considers the religious functions of the tezitlazc as a prayer leader and occasional officiant at a number of rites and ceremonies in the life and annual cycle of the community, it is evident why this magical practitioner has survived less changed and to some extent affirmed in its posi-tion as part of the folk religion. Sorcery has also fared better than witchcraft, and the tetlachihuic is still very much a going concern. This aspect of the transformation of magic supernaturalism has been analyzed in detail elsewhere (Nutini n.d.). Suffice it to say here that the tetlachihuic has changed, but it has managed quite successfully to adapt to more modern conditions, despite the deterioration of the underlying belief system, common to all forms of magic supernaturalism in rural Tlaxcala. Occasionally under a different name (hechi-cero, curandero), but in the same general contexts and with basically the same manipulative techniques of old, the tetlachihuic continues to minister to those who are willing to hire him, and the people at large still believe that he has supernatural powers to influence the natural world and cause all kinds of mis-fortunes including death. The questions that immediately come to mind are: Why have the variants of witchcraft changed so much under conditions of accelerated modernization and secularization, whereas the variants of sorcery have largely managed to survive and adapt to new conditions? and, Is this a generalized phenomenon in transitional tribal and folk societies? There are neither definitive answers nor any theoretical stand to deal with the problem. Our tentative, intuitive answers are interrelated as follows. To the first question we answer that witchcraft is by definition more projective than sorcery, and this fundamental property makes sorcery more adaptive to changing condi-tions. Moreover, under the increasing influence of science and technology it appears that sorcery, given its basically public natures, is at least transitionally more apt to accommodate to the modes of perception and inference fostered by these external forms of knowledge. Hence, the answer to the second question is yes, sorcery will outlive witchcraft in the transitional magical environment of changing tribal and folk societies. Witchcraft, to the contrary, will tend to disappear as a structured practice, both in circumscribed and general contexts, to become latent, and to surface under specific conditions of instability, anxiety, and stress affecting individuals and groups.

Ideological Changes and the Belief System

We have assumed that structural changes in any well-bounded social system are entailed by metalinguistic changes in perception and modes of inference. In other words, ideological changes and engendered beliefs underlie and to some extent determine structural changes. This is especially the case in dealing with magico-religious systems, in which belief and practice are always in a feedback relationship. There is no theory or systematic work on what this relationship is supposed to be and accomplish, and ideology has almost invariably been used unsystematically and often emptily. In the analysis of bloodsucking witchcraft, by contrast, the institution has been conceptualized as a situation in which folk explanations emerge in the feedback relationship between normative expectations and physical, social, and psychological realization. Granting that bloodsucking witchcraft is a circumscribed, small-scale system, we have nonetheless been able to ascertain and to some extent measure the feedback relationship as an invariant aspect of how the system works and explains infant death, in the absence of more naturalistic explanatory inputs. It has been demonstrated how, and under what conditions in a folk model, explanations emerge by the interaction of what is (what is empirically observed and inferred) and what ought to be (what is normatively expected). This section elucidates how and under what conditions the structural changes undergone by bloodsucking witchcraft since a generation ago have been largely determined by the demise of this interaction.

If it was difficult to substantiate the structural changes undergone by bloodsucking witchcraft syntagmatically, it was even more difficult to pinpoint the specific, often subtle, junctures and ways in which the normative system was efficacious in the foregoing process. We found it possible, nonetheless, to specify particular trends and terminal outputs in the comparison of two baselines (the ethnographic present of this monograph and 1982–1987), buttressed by some longitudinal observations in between. The results were not as exacting as we would have liked, but they do illuminate some of the problems of change in systems in which normative expectations and structural realization exhibit an intimate interrelationship.

Fundamentally, what has changed in the belief and normative system of rural Tlaxcalans is the firmness and extension of supernatural inputs producing specific natural outcomes. This operation is at the core of explaining how and why magical systems evolve and naturalism asserts itself in most of daily life, if not necessarily in most of society's institutional life. As this belief and its accompanying injunctions wane and ultimately lose efficacy, the interaction between normative expectations and structural realization no longer obtains, and the system does not explain the death of infants under peculiar circumstances. It is not possible to document the progression of this deterioration of the tlahuelpuchi belief system since a generation ago, but it is an unquestionable fact that by 1982, or perhaps a few years earlier, belief in the central feature of the bloodsucking witch was in serious disarray. From this standpoint, the structural changes described above are explained by the decreasing efficacy of the normative system: seriously doubting or no longer believing that a supernatural entity does in fact suck the blood of infants, and strongly suspecting human intervention, rural Tlaxcalans curtail in varying degrees, or no longer discharge the manifold complexes of rites, functions, and activities of the traditional system, nor do they behaviorally discharge accompanying social and psychological states. This explanation must be qualified in two ways. First, the subsidiary relationship obtaining between the individual and the group must be harnessed if one is to activate this explanatory framework—that is, it must be established how and at what rate of progression individuals question the underlying belief in the tlahuelpuchi and the normative system decreases in efficacy, leading to collective disarray. The converse relationship must also be established—namely, the feedback effect that compels the group to reinforce the belief, and how this mechanism slackens and ultimately disappears and bloodsucking witchcraft comes to an end. Second it has been severally emphasized that the phenomenon of inertial momentum may prolong the life span of a system or institution after its demise as a traditional entity (that is, in a situation in which there is a good fit between the normative system and structural realization). Thus, the normative system of bloodsucking witchcraft has not been effective, probably for more than eight years, but a modicum of structural realization still takes place—that is, the tlahuelpuchi is occasionally blamed for the death of an infant.

Rural Tlaxcala has been open to influences from the outside world in a fairly consistent and continuous manner for more than a century—that is, since the onset of the machine age and factory production in the area. Thus, as far as it has been possible to reconstruct bloodsucking witchcraft, it was never an entirely closed system ideologically in the fashion that witchcraft and sorcery systems were described as late as two decades ago, and as far as is known, may still be found in several parts of the world. We suspect that as early as the turn of the century the seeds of doubt concerning the existence of the tlahuelpuchi and her powers to kill and animal transformation had been planted. This state of affairs is implicit in elicitations from informants who were in their early twenties just before the turn of the century. At the ethnographic present of this monograph, however, such doubts were part of the traditional system for that time. In fact, the situation was to some extent quantified by stating that there were about 10 percent of skeptics at different levels of doubt. Note 1 of chapter 7 briefly discussed this important question and the progression that sets in once doubt begins to gnaw at the traditional belief system. The five-point typology presented there is an appropriate vehicle to describe and illustrate the ideological and belief changes that have taken place. But first, let us briefly encapsulate the traditional belief system as it was a generation ago.

At least in the communities listed in Table 6.2, roughly 90 percent of the people adhered to the belief system described in chapter 2. The structural realization that this belief ensemble underlay and interacted with constitutes the description and analysis of chapters 8 to 12. There were undoubtedly deviations from the injunctions and commands entailed by the belief system and the prescribed modes of interaction that governed normative expectations and structural realization, but compliance with and adherence to this belief and normative complex was extremely high, as attested by the analysis of this monograph. Most of the deviations and departures may be regarded as expressive and consisted in elaborations, emphases, and ritual innovations, whereas the heart of structural realization remained highly standardized. Bloodsucking witchcraft functioned smoothly, and even the skeptics were often drawn into the web of behavior and activities entailed by the manifold aspects of the system. This state of affairs persisted until 1966, possibly for two or three more years. From then on, the percentage of individuals at various levels of skepticism began to grow rapidly, particularly from 1973 onward. Moreover, for the twenty-year period from 1966 to 1986, rural Tlaxcalans could be differentially and approximately categorized in terms of the five-point typology.

1. The first stage of skepticism is characterized by the fact that the tlahuelpuchi is not as effective or as voracious as she used to be at a generally unspecified time. This verbalization of disbelief in the efficacy of the tlahuelpuchi to kill infants is not usually accompanied by similar doubts in other parts of the system, and consequently, it does not appear to entail perceptible changes in the structural realization of the various aspects of bloodsucking witchcraft, although psychologically one could say that a particular frame of mind which sets the stage for more insidious doubts has come into being. This ideological change appears to have an empirical referent when people inevitably begin to notice that there are not as many suckings as there used to be, a situation that probably becomes noticeable between 1966 and 1973. What age groups this syndrome appears to affect the most is difficult to say; we suspect that it may affect anybody from young married adults to old-age couples, given the fact

that it is one short step from the inherent doubts that may have affected any person in traditional times and that focused on the notion that somehow mothers and others directly responsible for the care of infants have an input in their death when it is attributed to the tlahuelpuchi.

2. The second stage is a rather serious departure from traditionalism, for skeptics begin to verbalize the notion that the tlahuelpuchi does not cause the death of infants by sucking. Strong doubts or outright denials take basically two forms. The tlahuelpuchi cannot transform herself into animals; and in normal human form, she kills the infant in the process of tasting, not drinking, a considerable quantity of blood, in what essentially amounts to a variant of European vampirism. And the tlahuelpuchi, now a normal human being except that she has the power to hypnotize people, is conceived of as a very vengeful individual who strangles or kills infants in some other fashion for wrongs done to her or for reasons of her inherent malevolence. The belief in the tlahuelpuchi is still there, but she has been deprived of some of her supernatural powers and animal attributes and fashioned into a more human figure, exemplifying some of the more loathsome human proclivities: cruelty, vengefulness, and envy. This change in the ideological and belief configuration of bloodsucking witchcraft ushers in the first significant departures in structural realization, both in the nature and attributes of the tlahuelpuchi itself and in the ensemble of behavior and action surrounding her: the various means of protecting infants against being sucked vanish; witch hunts and witchcraft accusations begin to disappear, but apparently with an increasing incidence in personalized scapegoatism; the vulgarization of the tlahuelpuchi complex proliferates; and so on. Differentially, this state of affairs manifests itself perhaps coterminously with stage 1, but by the middle 1970s it has asserted itself with full force. In this case again, skepticism affects probably the entire spectrum of age groups, except perhaps the oldest, most conservative segments of local communities.

3. The radical transition in the ideology and belief system of bloodsucking witchcraft is marked by the outright verbalization that the tlahuelpuchi does not in any way cause the death of infants, that they die of "natural" causes. This normative change strikes at the heart of the system and entails most damaging structural consequences. The gnawing doubt that human inputs, particularly those of mothers, might lead to the death of infants attributed to the tlahuelpuchi now becomes a distinct possibility, and the three main physical causes of infant death discussed in chapter 8 are often verbalized by the most skeptical individuals at this stage. Under this state of affairs, the most skeptical may even state the primary explanatory function of the tlahuelpuchi complex—namely, that mothers and other individuals directly responsible for the care of infants are relieved from blame and accountability by blaming the death

on this supernatural. This turning point in the transformation of the tlahuel-puchi complex affects men more than women, for women have a vested interest to defend, whereas men may occasionally become rather aggressive in their verbalizations about what they perceive as women's tricks, without realizing that in traditional times they themselves were instrumental in reinforcing the belief in the tlahuelpuchi's efficacy to kill. The majority of men and women, however, adopt a tolerant, relaxed attitude when infants die under peculiar circumstances, and those concerned go through the motions of the manipula-tions and exaggerations as if indeed the death of the infant had been due to the tlahuelpuchi. As discussed above, this is the inertial momentum that makes people realize the social and psychological benefits that accrue by blaming the death on the tlahuelpuchi. The most affected age groups at this stage of skepti-cism are young and middle-aged couples, but it is not unusual to find even old men and women in this category, particularly the more outward-looking seg-ments of the former—that is, men who have been highly exposed to the out-side world through labor migration and the main avenues of diffusion. Proba-bly as early as the late 1970s, most rural Tlaxcalan households were at this stage of skepticism but in various degrees that would be impossible to identify.

4. This stage is not a syntagmatic sequence of 3 but rather a corollary of it. As the tlahuelpuchi is displaced as an explanation of infant death, she does not necessarily disappear as a malevolent supernatural in other domains of action. Indeed, people who no longer believe in the tlahuelpuchi's efficacy to kill infants may continue to believe in this supernatural's powers of affecting ordinary humans adversely. At this stage, the ontological reality of witchcraft is not denied, but the belief system underlying it is simplified and much less intense, since the tlahuelpuchi is no longer conceived as a bloodsucking witch, but only as a malevolent human with some supernatural powers. By the early 1980s, probably most rural Tlaxcalans were at this level of skepticism, combining stages 3 and 4, a situation in which inertial momentum more than any other consideration maintained the minimal effectiveness of the belief system of bloodsucking witchcraft in determining structural realization.

5. The final stage of skepticism means, of course, the disintegration of bloodsucking witchcraft as an ideological and structural entity. The ontological reality of the tlahuelpuchi is denied, and the belief is attributed to ignorant people. People at this stage are evidently the most secularized segment of the communities listed in Table 6.2, although if all rural Tlaxcalan communities were considered, the number would increase significantly, since there have been entire communities going back to the ethnographic present of this mono-graph that must be classified at this stage, including most of that 10 percent of doubters mentioned in chapter 6. At this stage rural Tlaxcalans manifestly do

not believe and practice any aspect of the tlahuelpuchi system; neither do they believe and practice any form of magic supernaturalism, and all anthropomorphic things, entities, and personages described and analyzed in this monograph are regarded as superstitions that one is well advised to forget as aberrations of the past, as one rabid modernist put it. Latently, however, probably none of these fully secularized individuals or households is above engaging in some form of magical behavior and action under conditions of extreme fear, anxiety, and stress, in domains of both witchcraft and sorcery: reactivating several aspects of the dormant tlahuelpuchi complex in the context of a particularly frightening, but unlikely-to-happen bloodsucking witchcraft epidemic, as a hypothetical example; and going through the entire array of traditional sorcery in the hands of a tetlachihuic upon falling seriously ill and being unable to be cured by folk and modern medicine, in an extensively reported case (see Nutini n.d.) of a member of a fully secularized household. These are examples of witchcraft and sorcery as mechanisms of last resort, for individuals engaging in magical behavior do so when all else has failed or under frightening conditions. By the same token, individuals and groups at stages 3–4 may be said to be on the verge of a magical complex as a mechanism of last resort. Herein lies the operational distinction between a magical complex near a terminal point and as a mechanism of last resort: in the one the practice of witchcraft and sorcery is manifest, but minimal; in the other, the activation of these beliefs and practices is latent but extraordinary.

Let us briefly summarize the foregoing sequence in terms of some rough and tentative figures. Probably less than 10 percent of rural Tlaxcalans are still traditional in fully adhering to the ideology and belief system of bloodsucking witchcraft as it was discharged at the ethnographic present of this monograph. Perhaps another 15 percent are at stages 1 and 2; individuals and households appear on the surface to adhere to the traditional tlahuelpuchi complex, but the manifold aspects of bloodsucking witchcraft have changed significantly. The majority of rural Tlaxcalans may be classified as being at stages 3 and 4, with varying degrees of intensity; that is, in perhaps 60 percent of households bloodsucking witchcraft is discharged in stages of decay from low to minimal. Finally, for nearly 15 percent of all rural Tlaxcalans bloodsucking witchcraft, and all forms of magic supernaturalism, have become mechanisms of last resort.

In analyzing the ideology and belief system of bloodsucking witchcraft, one cannot separate these normative components from those of the entire magical ensemble on the one hand, and those of the folk religion on the other. Time and again throughout this monograph we have demonstrated that one must analyze the magico-religious system as underlain by a unitary ideology and normative system. From this standpoint, all major components of magic and religion have changed normatively, hence structurally, during the past generation. The change, however, has been differential, since some components or subsystems have changed more than others. For example, witchcraft has changed more than sorcery, whereas in the folk religion, the socioreligious underpinnings of the mayordomía system have proven more resistant to change than the cult of the saints per se. Fundamentally, the most damaging ideological change has been the serious deterioration of the human-supernatural covenant, which not only regulates directly the discharge of the folk religion, but has significant implications for the discharge of several aspects of magic supernaturalism: It undermines the moral structure and retribution aspects of witchcraft and sorcery, the propitiatory or mediating position of other anthropomorphic supernaturals, and the entreating aspects of tutelary mountain owners. More immediately, what has been gnawing at the magico-religious ideology and normative system is the perception that, directly and indirectly, supernatural inputs do not entail natural outputs or they entail less consistent ones, or vice versa. As we stated above, sorcery has survived less changed than witchcraft because of pragmatic reasons, and the same can be said of differential aspects of the folk religion.

The Dynamic Context of Change: Internal and External Variables
So far we have determined how, when, and where the structure and ideology of bloodsucking witchcraft in particular, and of magic supernaturalism in general, have changed during the past twenty-five years. Broadening the scope of the problem to include religious supernaturalism, we aim in this section to give some answers to why the magico-religious system of rural Tlaxcala has changed during the same period. There is probably no cultural domain more fragile than supernaturalism, particularly magic, that is so subject to transformation by the influence of science and technology as they are disseminated and diffused by education and the various forms of communication, including radio, television, and exposure in the work place. The following analysis is a modest attempt to sort out the contexts of scientific and technological efficacy that have thrown out of kilter the belief and practice of rural Tlaxcalan supernaturalism for more than a generation by seriously affecting the peoples' modes of perception.

All so-called theories of modernization assume that changes are produced in folk and tribal societies by sustained exposure to science and technology: either these are diffused to local contexts, or local personnel come under their influence through various forms of labor migration and engagement in regional and national markets. Since theories of modernization are descriptive generalizations and not really theoretical statements, they do not specify exactly how and under what conditions the many forms and variations of science and technology do in fact produce local and regional changes in the structure of society. While establishing the diachronic order of change (that is, that changes have taken place between two well-established points in time) is the first analytical task that must be performed, a theory of change based on the effects of modernization can only emerge when the precise context in which the external variables of science and technology interact with a number of specifiable internal variables centered on social, demographic, and other local conditions is demonstrated. This scheme of change has been formulated in terms of the concept of modernization (essentially the effect of external variables) and secularization (essentially the local reaction socially, economically, and religiously) with a modicum of success (see Nutini and Bell 1980:389–400). Science and technology, specified as external variables of many and various forms, affect local conditions in the form of diffusion (direct introduction of material elements and implements, ways of doing things, fashions, and so on) and direct and indirect borrowings and acquisitions (through education, labor migration, and in general by outside involvements through various institutions). The changes produced by these external variables are positively or negatively conditioned by local institutions and systems that always reinterpret the diffused, borrowed, and acquired elements with various degrees of intensity and rapidity: a process that is usually determined by the need of the elements or the lack of it, in the local social structure. We may ascertain that a particular external variable is the most instrumental element in causing a specific local change (for example, that the introduction of hybrid seeds increases local yields, or that improved medical practices or better housing reduce infant mortality), but this operation is almost never established in conjunction with other variables, in the presence of specified local conditions, and as a reaction or response to determined local necessities or constraints. Essentially, this approach emphasizes the social and psychological transformations that are produced by the sustained effect of external variables through extended periods of time, and not necessarily material transformation of specific domains, which is specifically termed "modernization." The ultimate aim is to demonstrate the massive effects of modernization on local and regional situations, which in the long run almost invariably transforms the sociocultural system beyond recognition.

Narrowing the problem to magico-religious change, we see the following framework emerge. Rural Tlaxcalans have been in contact with the outside world since before the onset of the machine age and the introduction of factory work in the area more than a century ago. But these various contacts, mostly in the economic sphere, do not appear to have influenced much the traditional imago mundi that had been forged throughout Colonial and early Republican times. As factory work increased and attained large proportions by the late 1920s, and primary school education was introduced early in that decade, modernization, already present, increased with full force and began to affect the ideology and belief system that had probably not changed much since late Colonial times. From 1930 until the ethnographic present of this monograph, the influence of the outside world through labor migration, the schools, and physical mobility increased significantly, including heavy labor migration to the United States since the Second World War years. By the time of our first contact with rural Tlaxcala in the late 1950s, the social system was already exhibiting signs of disarray in that the traditional ideology and belief system was being seriously stressed by the cumulative weight of modernizing elements. In the late 1950s, regular access to modern medicine made its appearance in rural Tlaxcala and began to affect increasing numbers of people first through local clinics and resident doctors doing required social work in rural areas, and increasingly in the several state facilities of the Mexican social security system. The process of secularization that rural Tlaxcala had been experiencing as a generalized phenomenon gathered momentum from the early 1970s, and it was intimately related to the incorporation of the region (with the exception of a handful of communities) into the stream of national culture through the combined involvement in education, the work market, commerce, and health practices.

Of course, the reinforced processes of modernization and secularization mean the transformation chronicled above, in which the belief system and normative configuration of rural Tlaxcalan society has been thrown completely out of kilter with the new structural requirements. In this scheme of things, changes in the fundamental framework of society are not directly produced by the diffusion, introduction, and internalization of new elements and complexes of elements but by the creation of a new imago mundi—a new ideology, if you will—expressed in a belief and normative system that in its own right generates fundamental institutional and systemic changes. The conjoined action of external inputs on the overall framework of the sociocultural system structures a new perceptive and inferential milieu that constitutes the dynamic activator of change. With respect to supernaturalism in general, and magic supernaturalism in particular, the changes may be encapsulated as follows.

The normative system of the folk religion is no longer effective, practice slackens, and in feedback fashion the human-supernatural covenant, no longer the central feature of the system, leads to further deterioration. Magic supernaturalism, as the normative system is less and less entailed by the belief that supernatural inputs produce natural outcomes, deteriorates, and what survives are those aspects of witchcraft and sorcery that are most pragmatic and psychologically displacing. More specifically, bloodsucking witchcraft ceases to be a folk explanatory system, as the death of infants under peculiar circumstances is explained in more or less naturalistic fashion, and certain aspects of the practice are carried on mainly by inertial momentum.

Most fundamentally, underlying the process of change in the domain of magico-religious supernaturalism is the naturalization of perceptions and inferences and the increasing tendency to rely less and less on explanations and forms of interaction which assume that supernatural inputs produce natural outcomes and vice versa. Supernatural behavior is compartmentalized, the end result of which is the practice of Catholicism in an essentially orthodox fashion, whereas the various forms of magic supernaturalism either disappear or become elements of last resort. In principle, it should be possible to formulate a theory of change in terms of a continuum of invariant constructs and to operationalize inputs and outputs in an acceptable fashion.

TOWARD A LIMITED-RANGE THEORY OF CHANGE IN FOLK SOCIETIES

One caveat must be noted first. We are not considering the distinct possibility that the direct effect of external variables may produce specific local changes. For example, it is undoubtedly the case that the new infant-rearing practices that rural Tlaxcalan mothers have been learning during the past twenty years from local clinics, in school, and through more intimate contact with the outside world constitute a determinant input in the reduction of infant death, which in turn has resulted in the consistent reduction of bloodsucking witchcraft. Although this operation is an important aspect of the descriptive analysis of change, by itself it is not conducive to the formulation of theoretical statements. Rather, a theory of change is more likely to emerge from a context in which the interaction of external outputs with internal reactions is emphasized, and the process is the inferential structure of the latter. It is this perspective that must be emphasized, for it forces us to examine the psychological and institutional mechanisms that are conjoined in the reinterpretation of foreign elements and the creation of a new perceptual and inferential matrix.

External Inputs and Internal Effects

Let us take the three most encompassing external variables almost always employed in accounting for change in local and regional environments: science, technology, and education. Decomposing them into their most significant parts, pinpointing the levels and junctures at which they are efficacious, and ascertaining their individual and conjoined effect are the first steps in implementing the present approach to change.

First, these variables are evidently neither exclusive nor entirely comparable substantively and conceptually. Thus, ascertaining their entailing effect as agents of change with respect to the internal matrix must be carefully assessed in terms of spheres of action and intensity. In the case of rural Tlaxcala during the past hundred years, one must include under "science" a number of inputs categorized under the rubrics of technology and education, occasional inputs filtering directly from the national society (which itself may be regarded as being in the process of becoming "naturalized" under the influence of science), and possibly conceptual notions acquired by village-enfranchised personnel in the context of the urban work place. In rural Tlaxcala, science has had no direct effect on the changing context of the region, and one cannot identify any circumscribed domains exhibiting specific or general changes attributed to it. Rather, science has made itself felt indirectly through the main branches of technology, education, and the general naturalistic trends that have affected the larger society. Nonetheless, indirect as the effect of science has been on the perception and noticeable degree of naturalization undergone by the people at large, one can identify trends and attitudes that bear the imprint of this way of looking at the world. This is particularly true among the young and middle aged, for whom the manifold terms of technology and education have had a significant impact during the past generation: their imago mundi has been expanded; their approach to problem solving has become more experimental; their conception of the world has definitely become more naturalistic; and perhaps most significantly, their traditional conception of a closed, largely deterministic universe has been broadened, and their view of interpersonal relationships irreversibly changed.

Second, the influence of technology and education can be more or less pinpointed, both in terms of contexts of entailment and to some extent degrees of effectiveness. Under the category of technology are included the following domains and subdomains: technology proper—that is, from the simple agricultural tools introduced more than a hundred years ago to new techniques of machine production to internal combustion vehicles; all means of communicating and transportation, including radio, television, cinema, road construction, motorized and railroad travel, and accessibility to urban areas and sources of work; access to modern medicine at the local and regional levels, and participation in the manifold structure of bureaucracy at the state and federal levels; and access to labor migration in several forms, the introduction of factory production at the local level, and the diversification of community work and production. Under the category of education are included the following domains and subdomains: formal education at the primary and secondary level; technical education in local, state institutions and in the cities of Central Mexico; professional education in several universities of Central Mexico; and informal education for male and female adults on diet, home economics, health care, house construction, agricultural extension, utilization of natural resources, and several arts and crafts; religious education imparted by local priests and the bishopric of Tlaxcala on Catholic ethics, social participation in Catholic associations, and communal activities; and a modicum of political education imparted by the ruling Institutionalized Revolutionary Party (PRI) on political participation and the political process. It is simple enough to say that the conjoined effect of this rather massive complex of technology and education, beginning at varying times during the past hundred years, has produced the drastic transformation in the perceptual and inferential structure of rural Tlaxcala; or, going a step farther, it is possible to interdigitate bundles of these domains and subdomains in terms of general inputs that have produced broad outcomes.

Third, before critical junctures at which individual and entire domains entail specific or general changes in the local context can be isolated, it is necessary to give a syntagmatic account of the inception of external inputs with reference to the recipient personnel and social sector of the population. Simple technology—that is, the introduction of several agricultural implements, including shovels and the double-bladed plow—made its appearance as early as 1870. Two decades later, the sewing machine, as an important household item, was introduced together with a number of household utensils such as crockery, metal spoons and forks, and non-earthenware pots. In the work place, moreover, substantial numbers of rural Tlaxcalans became acquainted with as well as operated the machine technology of textile production, as the earliest factories in the area began operations by 1880 or so. Before this baseline, the technology and technological involvement of rural Tlaxcalans was pre-machine age and probably had not changed much since the late seventeenth century. Can it be determined that this early, often considerable, effect had any impact on the world of rural Tlaxcalans? The answer is a qualified no. The various forms of education detailed above definitely had no impact, since the introduction of primary schools came three decades later. On the whole rural Tlaxcala was a rather closed world, in which contacts of any significance with the outside were limited to occasional travel to the city of Puebla, for the city of Tlaxcala itself, well into the twentieth century, was little more than a sleepy town. However, it is possible to reconstruct from living informants that just before the turn of the century rural Tlaxcalans were increasingly becoming aware of the modernizing and secularizing trends that the cities of Central Mexico were undergoing at the time. This awareness, as an external input, cannot be said to have entailed specific changes in the milieu of local communities, but it definitely constituted the beginning of modernization as a measurable phenomenon that must be regarded as the turning point in the changing imago mundi. It is during the years between the turn of the century and the onset of the Mexican Revolution of 1910 that the worldview of the people ceased to be exclusively locally centered, as they began to perceive particular domains through the screen of external inputs. This is a key juncture to establish, for it pinpoints the transition from a situation in which individual elements diffused from the outside were strictly reinterpreted in terms of the traditional ideology and belief system to a situation in which diffused elements began to affect the ideology and belief system themselves, leading henceforth to changes in perceptual stand.

Throughout the years following the onset of the Mexican Revolution, roughly until the early 1920s, rural Tlaxcala became increasingly drawn into the sociotechnological milieu of the Central Mexican Highlands, as the network of labor migration brought many communities into more intimate contact with cities, particularly Puebla and Mexico City. But the most significant external input of this period was the establishment of primary schools in several then essentially Indian communities. By the beginning of the 1930s, most municipal headtowns had primary schools, and by the middle of that decade, at least five secondary schools had been established in the most important municipios. In the early 1940s, the first normal school was established in Tlaxcala, and it immediately became accessible to prospective primary school teachers from rural communities. This intense period of modernization also witnessed the introduction of motorized vehicles, public motorized transportation, and the construction of a rather extensive network of paved and dirt roads that connected most communities to the state capital, the three other small cities in the state, and all large and important cities and centers of production in the Central Highlands. Throughout the first five years of the 1940s, labor migration became the single most important factor in the economic life and subsistence of rural Tlaxcala, where daily, weekly, biweekly, and seasonal migration became more important than the combined activities of subsistence agriculture, arts and craft, and other trade and commercial operations in the great majority of rural Tlaxcalan communities. Migration to the United States began in 1943, and its effect in creating community elites was a significant force in the rapid process of transformation that began at this time.

In a limited way, technical and professional education also made their appearance in the middle of the 1940s, as the first engineers, physicians, lawyers, and accountants of local origin graduated from the University of Puebla and from the National University in Mexico City. During the Second World War years, radios were introduced in rural Tlaxcala, and by the end of the decade they had become a household item. It would be almost impossible to detail the array of tools, household implements, and craft implements that made their appearance and quickly became part of daily life. But one technological innovation must be mentioned—namely, the corn mill powered by an internal combustion engine, which was introduced in rural Tlaxcala in the late 1930s, and quickly became universal. This technological item greatly influenced the household economy by reducing the daily chore of women of preparing tortillas, the basic item in the diet, by as much as two hours. No less significant, the corn mill directly acquainted women with the efficiency of technology, something up to that point experienced mostly by men. Finally, as an aspect of the explosion of labor migration and the increasingly outward-looking tendency of a very large sector of the rural Tlaxcalan population, massive bureaucratic involvement made its appearance; from then on, the people became increasingly drawn into the network of state and federal agencies that access to outside resources involved.

By the end of the Second World War, the Tlaxcalan area was well on its way to integration into the fabric of the nation. In varying degrees most people had been drawn into technological, educational, and bureaucratic networks, forging perhaps more linkages to the greater society than anthropologists, at least in Mesoamerica, have regarded as tolerable for categorizing communities and regions as being at a transitional folk stage. The conjunction of manifold technological and educational inputs by this time were already strong enough for the categorization of individuals, and perhaps four or five communities as a whole, as being at a clear stage of secularization, in which the ideology and belief and normative systems were only tenuously anchored to the old traditional system. Most communities had become open, and the closed corporateness that had characterized them manifested itself mainly in the domains of kinships, compadrazgo, and the magico-religious system, which began to show the first signs of strain. This represents the inception of that most diagnostic trait that characterizes ideologies and belief systems on the verge of fundamental transformation: compartmentalization. In the overall context of change, compartmentalization not only means the breakdown of the belief and normative system as a monolithic structure, but also that individuals and groups compromise ideologically—that is, they may adhere to the injunctions and command entailed by the normative and belief system of certain domains but not of others. In summary, this period of rural Tlaxcalan history, roughly from the end of the First World War to the end of the Second World War, constituted the most intensive and concentrated diffusion of external inputs that the area underwent in more than two centuries. The combined effects of technology, education, and a certain rudiment of science through education, in the context of a society with a high degree of physical mobility, had visibly transformed significant numbers of individuals into "compartmentalized" social beings, in turn exerting an influence on the population at large, already on the verge of compartmentalizing several domains of the socioreligious system. The traditional perceptual and inferential structure of rural Tlaxcalans, conditioned largely by the magico-religious system, was in disarray but still mainly traditional, in that the greatly mobile adhered to the injunctions and commands of the ideology, belief, and normative systems of the core of rural Tlaxcalan culture and society as they had since two generations earlier (1890).

The following twenty years—that is, until 1966 or thereabouts—witnessed the introduction of or the exposure to all other technological and educational domains listed above: cinema, television, access to modern medicine, the introduction of factory production at the local level, informal education, agricultural extension, catechizing education, and political indoctrination. By the end of this period, then, the entire array of technological and educational external inputs had been introduced in rural Tlaxcala, many of which had been well internalized by the people at large. At least formally, one could say that this short generation constituted the de jure incorporation of rural Tlaxcala into the life of the nation, whereas the period since then represents the maturation of this incorporation. From a different standpoint, this period did not witness many significant changes; it is rather a period of stabilization and adaptation throughout which rural Tlaxcalans became used to, reinterpreted, and innovated the many external inputs that for two generations had become the inevitable realities of sociocultural life. While it is the case that even before 1950 perhaps five or six communities had shed most of their past, were no longer traditional, and had been, de facto, incorporated into the fabric of the regional-national culture, this was not true of the overwhelming majority of communities which clung tenaciously to traditionalism until well into the 1960s. Several surveys conducted in rural Tlaxcala between 1959 and 1966 indicated that the traditional ideology and belief systems were still in place and that, despite a significant degree of compartmentalization, the majority of people perceived the world around them and conceived of their existential situation as largely conditioned by the traditional normative system. But the balance between the hold of tradition and the exigencies of modernity was a delicate one, and the factors favoring the latter appeared to have been primarily three: the inordinate impact of television, moderate access to modern medical practices, and the high degree of relative economic prosperity and access to well-remunerated work that characterize the period between the mid-1960s and the mid-1970s. When economic hard times began to affect not only the Tlaxcala-Pueblan valley but the Mexican nation as a whole, the impact was irreversible. Be this as it may, the modernizing-secularizing impact of this period can clearly be detected in the magico-religious system, both in its structural discharge and its ideological and normative underpinnings.

Nineteen sixty-six marked the beginning of the disintegration of traditional rural Tlaxcalan society, since the past twenty years have witnessed the transformation of the culture almost beyond recognition. The best way to characterize this short generation is compartmentalization in reverse: it is no longer a question of mapping the domains in which the traditional belief and normative system is no longer efficacious, but of identifying domains that have not been obliterated or are not in the process of being obliterated by a new ideology and belief system in the process of formation. Nothing new was introduced in or diffused to rural Tlaxcala during this terminal period, which must be characterized as subjected to the most intensive conjoined action of all the external domains and subdomains listed above. As we write these lines, the economy, material culture, and to a significant extent the political position of the majority of rural Tlaxcalan communities is almost indistinguishable from those of the provincial towns of the Tlaxcala-Pueblan valley, and from this perspective the area has essentially been incorporated into the fabric of the nation. It is in the domains of magic and religion, and in some aspects of the social structure in operation, mostly kinship and compadrazgo, that rural Tlaxcala may still be rather minimally anchored to a traditional, folk milieu, and thus characterized by an imago mundi that distinguishes it from rural and urban Mestizo sectors of the valley, which in their communal life have been nationally oriented for more than a generation. Therefore, in gauging this terminal transition, one must focus on the magico-religious system, for to a large extent it also underlies the discharge of the kinship system.

Let us focus on the transformation from another perspective and determine the conjunction of external elements that have elicited internal reactions. When one investigates the sociocultural system of rural Tlaxcala today (1987) in the regional and national contexts, one is immediately impressed by the modernity of the economic, political, and material culture of the average community, as contrasted with the social organization and magico-religious system, which at least in outward appearance look rather incongruously more traditional. This again appears to be a universal feature of folk societies entailed by the nature of their embedment in a wider society. A significant theoretical feature of this phenomenon is that changes come first in the cultural domains that folk societies more commonly share with the wider urban-national society or that are more easily influenced by it, whereas changes in the cultural domains that are peculiarly local and folk are more resistant to change. This equivalence has been expressed by the process in which modernization comes first and secularization follows and by the notion that modernization may have a long period of incubation before it translates into secularization affecting the entire societal framework. From a slightly different perspective, it is the feedback effect that comes to obtain between structural transformations (the modernizing phase) and ideological adjustments and modifications (the secularizing phase) that largely structures the new perceptual and normative imago mundi, the end results of which are further structural changes which complete the transformation of the folk society from a "sacred" entity into a "secular" entity, and from a society regulated by the ideology and belief system of kinship, magic, and religion to society regulated largely by the constraints and exigencies of the economy and the political system.

Reaction, Reinforcement, and Feedback Effect
Narrowing down the analysis to the magico-religious system, we see the following picture—specified in terms of internal reactions, feedback effects, and the emergence of a new perceptual and inferential configuration—emerge. The rather closed system, or something approaching it, that characterized magico-religious supernaturalism at the turn of the century does not appear to have changed despite some thirty years of technological diffusion and the physical opening of rural Tlaxcalan society, a situation that continued for two decades into the twentieth century. Yet the introduction of primary education and the intensification of physical mobility, mostly through labor migration, beginning immediately after the end of the armed conflict of the Mexican Revolution of 1910, marked the onset of the transformation of the rural Tlaxcalan imago mundi. For the next generation, only male children and adults were almost the exclusive cultural transmitters of external inputs, since women rarely attended school and did not participate in labor migration. The same exclusivity obtained in the incipient engagement in technical and professional education, for women did not participate until the decade of the 1960s. It was in the ambience of male culture that the initial, crucial exposure of rural Tlaxcalans to the rudiments of science, simple technology, and basic education took place, and in which the first departures from traditionalism were conditioned and perceptual changes began to emerge. Confronted in primary school with other configurations of knowledge, with somewhat foreign modes of inference, and with a wider perspective of the world, the rural Tlaxcalan boy grew up to become a labor migrant and expanded these notions and perspectives within the context of the greater world of the cities and places of work. By the late 1930s the average community had a hundred men or more in this category. The combined effect of these modernizing inputs and forces on this sector of the population may be regarded as a gnawing process that affected first the largely determinis-

tic, closed, and egocentric belief system and normative structure of the community, generating a kind of domino effect that expanded from individuals to the family, to the propinquous kinship-compadrazgo group, and on to the community at large. The people began to think and conceive of perspectives beyond the confines of the community, which had a rather immediate effect on the allocation of resources and the establishment of priorities that were not contemplated in the traditional systems: saving time; capitalizing for economic ends that were family centered and had nothing to do with the discharge of kinship and the magico-religious system; engaging in new expressive endeavors and realizations; and so on. Individually, this stage marked the onset of the secularization of Catholicism, which is almost invariably accompanied by local agnosticism in the realm of magical supernaturalism, meaning primarily two things: that witchcraft and sorcery were largely spurious; but that, nonetheless, supernatural inputs could produce natural outcomes, as in the case of miracles and direct intervention by Catholic supernaturals. In this conception of Catholicism, magical agnostics are, of course, more or less orthodox, in belief if not necessarily in practice, as communal exigencies draw them into the web of the local folk religion. As small as this sector was in the average community, its orthodox religious notions and its practical rejection of magic supernaturalism nonetheless did have a significant impact on the community at large. The great majority of people, however, remained traditional in the extended domain of magico-religious discharge and its kinship and compadrazgo underpinnings; modernization was nibbling at the edges of the system and individuals were already taking shortcuts in the discharge of social and religious duties and obligations, but the imago mundi of the sacred covenant was still in place and coloring the entire spectrum of human and supernatural interaction.

The next stage in this evolutionary sequence was the direct input of women into the changing situation, which coincided with their incorporation into the educational system, their participation in labor migration (mostly as domestic servants) and higher degree of mobility, the equal impact of television on the population at large, and access to modern medicine, which had a particularly significant effect on women and child-rearing practices. The critical mass of external inputs approached peak intensity during this stage, in terms of both specifically diffused items and complexes and forms of internalization and reinterpretation, coupled with the entire age and occupational spectrum of local society. This new element in the changing equation was decisive, for it came not only to reinforce an existing situation but to extend the effect of external inputs of all forms to every ambience of the social system, reactions to which initiated sustained feedback effects. The conservative strain of women changed rather abruptly among the young and middle aged, and they quickly began to catch up with the more avant-garde male sector of the population. From this point onward (that is, roughly from 1965), age and sex per se ceased to be good indicators for traditionalism and conservatism, since males and females who were then, say, in their mid-forties had been experiencing some fifteen years of rather intensive external influence and internal feedback reaction.

In this calm-before-the-storm period, the structural discharge of magic and religious supernaturalism was still in place, despite some noticeable changes at the edges of the system brought about by economic exigencies that could not be accommodated to the traditional belief and normative system. Thus, the traditional ideology was still powerful enough to enforce structural compliance, but the feedback effect was gathering momentum and seriously undermining the belief and normative system to the extent that structural compliance during that period may be regarded as inertial momentum, which could not be sustained given the intensified effect of external inputs. Two examples may explain this critical situation. Between 1950 and 1956 there was a significant growth in the mayordomía system, in terms of both the introduction of new sponsorships and the increasing elaboration of the cult of saints of long standing. At first sight this phenomenon looks incongruous or out of focus with the modernizing and secularizing trend of the time. But an in-depth analysis of the situation reveals the cause of the phenomenon: the growth of this fundamental institution of community structure was not a reflection of the strength of the human-supernatural covenant, but it was entailed by modernizing changes in the social structure, mainly the incipient stratification of communal life. New mayordomías were established and old ones were more lavishly discharged by members of new economic elites as a means to consolidate their position vis-à-vis the traditional egalitarianism of community life, not infrequently by the sponsorship of saints and ritual occasions that were never part of the folk religion—that is, diffused from the larger society.

The second example has to do with sorcery, and exemplifies the direct effect of external inputs on the process of creating an internal reaction tending strongly to modify a traditional belief and practice. As early as 1955, the traditional position and craft of the tetlachihuic were being expanded to include a number of contexts that went beyond the classical definition of the sorcerer. Employing sorcery methods and manipulations hundreds of years old, the rural Tlaxcalan sorcerer had been converted into a kind of itinerant curer (curandero) ministering to both traditional and new needs. This juncture involved two main considerations. On the one hand, the tetlachihuic's craft expanded, within the controlled ambience of a well-defined belief and normative system, to the broader domain of curing under quite different conditions entailing the direct efficacy of external inputs (the higher physical mobility of a transitional society, a concept of curing no longer posited mainly on a supernatural notion). On the other hand, the creation of new contexts of curing into which the tetlachihuic's craft expanded were also created by direct external inputs (illnesses that are intractable to modern medicine, folk illnesses that have been identified with a modern medical tag, and even in the extension of the concept of "psychological" illness) but in conjunction with an already established belief transformation that made the transition from tetlachihuic to curandero a normative-structural entailment exemplifying a specific change: the malevolent-benevolent constitution of the tetlachihuic was transformed into the essentially benevolent character of the curandero; or, the belief that the tetlachihuic can cause death or seriously harm by virtue of his supernatural powers was on the wane, while his beneficial supernatural powers were perpetuated in the latter.

The final stage leading to the disintegration of the traditional culture of rural Tlaxcala may be characterized as the massive effect of all external variables and inputs discussed above. The great majority of people were directly and indirectly bombarded with specific external inputs that were the result of both increasing involvement with the wider society and needs created internally by previous involvements. This final phase is, of course, still going on, for the inertial momentum of traditional culture has not yet spent itself, and one still finds many communities at various stages of disintegration. As these lines are being written perhaps more than 50 percent of rural Tlaxcalan communities are indistinguishable from the national rural culture of the Tlaxcala-Pueblan valley. In this transitional-terminal stage no imago mundi can emerge—that is, whatever belief and normative guidelines can be ascertained are really a combination of residual traditional elements accommodated to the new exigencies and constraints that the secular context has literally forced on the body politic but increasingly reflecting the technological, economic, and political milieu of the wider national culture. Literally, perhaps the majority of rural Tlaxcalans are in an ideological no-man's land, often torn between the beliefs and norms of the traditional system and the exigencies and constraints of the secular world into which they find themselves increasingly drawn.

In the traditional system, and throughout its slow evolution from the turn of the century to the decade of the 1960s, every aspect of cultural and societal living was determined, underlined, or colored by an imago mundi whose ideology, belief system, and normative configuration were centered on the human-supernatural cleavage, on the notion that supernatural forces and personages can directly and indirectly affect the outcome of individual and collective actions and behaviors, and on the cardinal principle that within the confines of a limited, scarce universe the supernatural must be kept happy and placated when the vagaries of the uncertain world of human affairs is out of control. It is this conception of man and its place in nature that took three generations to get seriously out of kilter and to become functionally inoperative during the past generation in most domains of the sociocultural life of rural Tlaxcalans. In this dynamic of change in which external inputs exact internal reactions and there obtains a feedback effect between the two, one would not expect a uniform transformation of the global sociocultural system. The cumulative result, however, is the same: the weakening and the ultimate demise of a way of perceiving and making inferences from perceptions that gave unity to an entire sociocultural system. For many rural Tlaxcalans, increasingly for the great majority, this perceptual and inferential configuration is entirely gone, or it may still have a place in the compartmentalization that the rapid transformation has entailed. In more concrete terms, the various forms and permutations of supernatural inputs producing natural outcomes have been relegated to residual, circumscribed domains. Moreover, the normative and perceptual ambience that conditions the belief that supernatural inputs produce natural outcomes no longer colors many domains of social life as in traditional times, further contributing both directly and in feedback fashion to the process of secularization across the entire sociocultural spectrum.

Finally, and to recapitulate, how is magico-religious supernaturalism changing, what will its secular form be, and what does it entail perceptually and inferentially? Religion is well on its way to the belief and practice of orthodox (Mexican) Catholicism, and in many communities there are few detectable folk elements still in place, whereas in a few communities the transition from folk to orthodox has already been achieved. Ritualism and ceremonialism, however, are proving resistant to change; even in the most orthodox communities there is still a certain emphasis on this aspect of religious practice, particularly for those occasions in the annual cycle of centuries-old tradition—namely, the Christmas cycle, Holy Week, Todos Santos, and the celebration of the patron saint of the community. These residual aspects of the folk system are still in place essentially because of expressive reasons, and are likely to color the religious life of the community for many years after orthodox practice has become fully established. But there has been a decisive compartmentalization of religion, in that it no longer colors and influences many aspects and domains of the social structure and daily life of the people. Secularization in this particular context means that most people have been released from many religious constraints (foremost among them, and in a sense underlying all others, that Catholic and pagan supernatural personages can be propitiated and entreated for the benefit of one and all without the complex and expensive array of ritualism and ceremonialism of old), and this in turn has fostered a new image of interpersonal relationships and ways of doing things that emphasize individualism and self-reliance to an extent hardly ever realized in traditional times. This new religious imago mundi has been perhaps the single most effective feedback reaction that has propelled secularization in rural Tlaxcala during the past twenty years or so.

Magic, in its four main forms of nahualism, weathermaking, sorcery, and witchcraft, has fared worse than religion in that it has become even more compartmentalized—that is, there are few domains in which the majority of people still believe that immediate supernatural inputs produce specific supernatural outcomes. In some rural Tlaxcalan communities magic supernaturalism is de facto a mechanism of last resort, whereas in the majority of communities it is approaching that limit. Bloodsucking witchcraft in particular has almost disappeared as the coherent, self-contained system that it once was, and of the four anthropomorphic supernatural complexes, it is the closest to a mechanism of last resort. The direct effect of external inputs, especially access to modern medicine and the naturalistic outlook fostered by certain aspects of formal education and television, was decisive in the great transformation suffered by bloodsucking witchcraft, since it is the internalization of this new scientific and technological knowledge that made the tlahuelpuchi complex obsolete as an explanation of certain kinds of infant death. In the overall effect of the spread of naturalism and secularization, however, the reaction exacted from bloodsucking witchcraft entailed by the above external inputs is not nearly as significant as that exacted from religion. The reason for this phenomenon is evident: any form of witchcraft is the most pristine, spectacular context in which the belief that supernatural inputs produce natural outcomes is realized, and the most likely domain to fall prey to external knowledge without wider implications, whereas religion, much more diversified in the implications of its belief and normative structure, affects many more domains as it is forced to change by the same external forms of knowledge. Thus, people no longer fundamentally believe that infants are killed by the tlahuelpuchi, but they still believe, many somewhat nebulously, that indirectly, neither as precisely nor as consistently, Catholic and some pagan supernaturals can affect and produce outcomes in the life of individuals and the community.

Preliminary Formalization of Elements in an Epistemological Approach to Change
We conclude with an attempt to formalize the notions about change that have been employed in this analysis, focusing on problems of the internalization of new knowledge when societies come under the influence of persistent and massive external influences. If acculturation and syncretism characterized the

transformation of pre-Hispanic society into Spanish folk societies in the six-teenth century, it is diffusion that characterized the transformation of rural Tlaxcalan society during the past four generations. Essentially, then, this brief discussion may be regarded as a redefinition of diffusionism in the modern, technologicial, scientific era underlying the disintegration of folk societies. From this standpoint, acculturation and syncretism are forms of diffusion — that is, they are triggered by elements and institutional complexes that involve diffusion, buttressed by the sustained contact of two more more cultural tradi-tions under a variety of conditions including conquest, colonization, political domination, symmetry and asymmetry, and so on. The difference between syncretism and acculturation and diffusion proper (as the concept has been used in the Conclusions) is that syncretism and acculturation usually involved asymmetry and some form of coercion or domination of one cultural tradition over another whereas diffusion generally did not; moreover, the changes pro-duced by syncretism and acculturation are almost invariably more massive and definitive than those produced by diffusion, the differences in cultural configu-ration being what they are. Diffusion as conceived here constitutes essentially the transmission of new knowledge between two or more adjacent cultural traditions or between two cultural traditions, one of which is embedded in the other, the classic position of the folk society. In this conception and configura-tion of change, the dynamics of change are focused on the internal reaction that colors and to some extent determines the transformation of a sociocultural system from one stage to another. It is thus the reinterpretation of diffused elements and complexes that must essentially be conceptualized to explain why change takes place.

It is not a theoretically profitable enterprise to ascertain the effect of indi-vidual inputs on either part or the total ensemble of a well-delimited sociocul-tural system. Individual inputs must be identified, to be sure, but as elements of a theory of change, they must be viewed as bundles or complexes that affect a certain area, juncture, or domain of the local situation. Although locally centered and internally focused, the first task in implementing an epistemolog-ically oriented theory of change is to ascertain the sequential action of bundles of diffused inputs, the degree of exposure to which local populations are sub-jected, and the contexts in which they are exposed. The quantification of these operations is difficult but not impossible; one can readily imagine setting up experiments, the total effect of which can give an adequate account of the inten-sity of combined inputs that have affected individual domains and institutions over specific periods of time. This is particularly true of measuring the effect of labor migration, physical mobility, primary and secondary education, and television.

The second step is the most difficult to structure and implement. It is an extension of the first step and involves establishing the interrelated, conjoined effect of external inputs on the local sociocultural system at critical stages. It is easy enough to visualize, perhaps even delimit, critical areas where the massive effect of external inputs produces reactions in the body politic, but it is not as easy to establish how various bundles of external inputs in manifold contexts are combined and reinforce each other to produce such reactions. It is of fundamental importance to determine this aspect of a theory of change, for it is the particular combination of external inputs that elicits internal reactions that are not only cumulative but affect or color other reactions across the entire societal spectrum. The main problem of conceptualizing this juncture derives from the fact that even if one could with exactness harness the lines of entailment and the ways in which a massive input of external variables affects the local situation, it is almost impossible to quantify the individual inputs of the massive ensemble in terms of how and under what circumstances they exact individual and conjunctive reactions. It would be impossible, for example, to determine the degree and extent to which certain aspects of secondary education, television viewing, and physical mobility leading to acquaintance with broader ways and usages interrelate and affect the conduct of interpersonal relations in the family and the community, determining in turn the follow-up reaction. Given this quandary, we ask, What can be done in order to implement this part of the scheme? First, one must assume that the effects of external bundles of variables are not uniform and that their effectiveness is determined as much by internal needs and considerations as by the actual exposure to local personnel. This enables one to assess the differential impact of the specific inputs of an external complex on various segments of the population, leading to an invariant gauging of what is affecting whom under specific conditions. Second, one must intuitively make certain assumptions having nothing evident to do with quantification, which, in the testing of any theory, are as good or as inadequate as the outputs that follow. In other words, even if not all parts of a theoretical construction can be quantified, some of them can be regarded as part of the axiomatic set.

The third step involves first, establishing and quantifying the local reactions to external inputs and variables, and second, the feedback effect that obtains between reactions and newer changes—that is, changes that are provoked by either new individual inputs or the intensification of already present bundles of diffused inputs. Both of these aspects can be quantified, but the former more easily than the latter. Reactions computed in terms of individuals and groups are the most visible and tangible elements that obtain in any situation of change, and they can be observed throughout relatively long periods of time—

that is, from the moment a few individuals depart detectably from established norms to the moment when the majority of the local group does the same. Identifying, assessing, and quantifying the ensuing feedback effect, by contrast, is not that simple, and it takes some ingenuity to undertake this operation. The task is not by any means impossible, particularly if one focuses on the inputs specific reactions have on adjacent domains. For example, one could focus on the use of mayordomía sponsorship for upward mobility coupled with the contraction and simplification of its ritualism and ceremonialism due to the constraints and exigencies imposed on individuals and groups by labor migration. Labor migrants and their families rather quickly learn to save time and resources in the discharge of their ritual and ceremonial duties and obligations, at the beginning in marginal and unimportant details, but increasingly in more and more significant aspects, until the point at which it is evident that the traditional normative injunctions are no longer operating. One can readily see how inimical this trend is to other domains of the socioreligious life of rural Tlaxcalans: if people dare to skimp, to cut corners, and ultimate not to discharge duties and obligations in the most sacred domain of the religious and social structure, they find it much easier to do the same in other less central and sacred domains. This is a good model of the feedback-effect reaction that, originally localized, may quickly affect a large number of domains in the social structure, further propelling the process of secularization at an increasingly rapid pace.

The fourth step constitutes the assessment of consequences—that is, the specification, measurement, and configuration of outputs of a situation that is either well on its way to a new ideological-structural configuration or to terminal disintegration as a traditional system. The case of rural Tlaxcala is, of course, concerned with the former situation but both must be discussed in the same context. Although one can conceive of alternative contexts of change, the transformations of folk societies in the national mold is almost exclusively posited on the notion of the "sacred" becoming secularized across the societal spectrum. With respect to measuring this final step, the present approach is on solid ground, for what most anthropological studies have done well is to measure how a system has been transformed between two points in time. What we intend here, however, is more than descriptively measuring this transformation; rather, we intend to establish the new perceptual and inferential configuration that comes into being, expressed in a new, secular ideology and imago mundi. Ascertaining the compartmentalization of supernatural inputs producing natural outcomes becomes a central concern in conceptualizing the new belief and normative system, which will be determined by the secular, naturalistic constraints fostered primarily by scientific and technological considerations. Here again, what we must measure and place into some relationships of invariance are the perceptual and inferential changes, the degree of compartmentalization, and the efficacy of the new belief and normative system. In the present study we have measured, albeit approximately, these three variables: the way rural Tlaxcalans in 1987 perceive bloodsucking witchcraft compared to the way they did in 1960, and the way the inferences they make from these perceptions are radically different; the degree to which compartmentalization today is greater than it was in 1960, or as it has been established, that it is de facto localized in that nebulous domain of religious expectations; and whether consequently the efficacy of the traditional belief and normative system underlying bloodsucking witchcraft in particular, and magic supernaturalism in general, has been stretched to the maximum. What this study has not managed to demonstrate is the relationship of invariance that obtains among these variables. They have not been operationalized, but they have been formalized enough for a theory of change to begin to emerge.

Given the universality of folk societies becoming part of national cultures, we think it would be ideal to have a limited-range theory of change in which explanations were of the deductive-nomonological kind. At the moment this is evidently impossible, but this goal could become a reality if something like the model here envisaged were to be tested in perhaps ten folk environments at different levels of traditionalism. There are sufficient grounds for this assertion, for the foregoing analysis lends itself well to formulating nomonological constructs. At the moment, however, what can be done is to set the foregoing elements in the following relations of invariance, primarily in terms of the direction of entailment and the logic of related parts.

The folk system must first be identified at a stage of traditionalism of long standing but beginning to be affected by individual external items. There follows a period in which external inputs progressively increase, but do not exact an internal reaction from the social system. There is a point, however, at which the quantity of external inputs begins to exert great pressure on the social system and an internal reaction materializes. It is of great significance to establish this point, and the sociocultural milieu that produced it must be exactingly determined. It is at this juncture that change begins to emerge, for up to it, whatever transformations take place must be considered as a period of adaptation. At this juncture direct external inputs produce a direct internal reaction which rapidly alters an entire domain. The critical mass of external outputs produces further reactions which spread across the societal spectrum and the social structure in operation is thrown totally out of kilter. At this point a new belief system, the expression of another imago mundi, initiates the formation of a normative system that is by now the reflection of an external reality.

What, then, constitutes an explanation of change in the transformation of folk societies, and how can a theory of change begin to take form? Measuring the transformation of a sociocultural system, or discrete parts of it, between two points in time (in the present monograph the period between 1960 and 1987) ceases to be a mere descriptive operation if the rate and progression of change can be measured intrinsically (that is, as structurally discharged) and relationally (that is, as a function of transformations in the belief and normative system), as entailed by the concomitant relationship of direct inputs from the larger society, direct internal reaction to these inputs, and the feedback effect of direct reaction throughout the sociocultural system and new outputs from the outside. The key elements of this model of change are measuring inputs and outputs, ascertaining the junctures at which this operation must be done, and precisely pinpointing the direction of entailment. In principle all these tasks can be undertaken, and some of them have been envisioned in this monograph. Thus, explaining change epistemologically in the folk context means primarily how, under what conditions—in the presence of specified intensities of diffusion, and underlined by ascertainable rates of progression—a traditional, sacred ideological-structural configuration is transformed into a modern, secular system in which naturalism prevails and supernaturalism is relegated essentially to the domain of religion. As a corollary, a limited-range theory of change in folk societies should specify their invariant position of embedment in greater societies, the formation and duration of the period of adaptation (that is, the length of modernization), and the overall configuration of the achieved integration.

To conclude, the formulation of a limited-range theory of change, applicable to folk societies is possible and, based on the evidence of this monograph, it would have the following form. Under conditions of sustained diffusion, societies embedded in a greater cultural tradition will be transformed and will ultimately disappear as distinct ethno-cultural entities at a rate of speed, substantive configuration, and degree of incorporation determined by five main postulates: (1) The higher the sacred, magico-religious content of the recipient society, the longer the cultural system will remain traditional—that is, the longer it will take modernization to trigger secularization. (2) The longer the period of sustained diffusion of material culture, fashions, and various non-supernatural complexes, the quicker the transformation of the recipient culture after modernization triggers secularization. (3) Whereas diffused inputs of any kind may effect direct transformations in the local culture, the total transformation of a system will be determined by the reaction triggered by its supernatural content: the stronger the belief that supernatural inputs produce natural outcomes, the more the complex and outlying domains will be resistant to secularization. (4) As secularization sets in, the critical mass of diffused inputs (the hierarchically arranged effect of individual items and complexes of material culture, fashions, and institutional arrays) generates pressures and constraints (the feedback effect) that propel the local sociocultural system toward uniformity: the more extensive and pervasive the process of compartmentalization (the sphere of effective supernatural action), the quicker and more generalized the secular transformation. (5) Incorporation into the greater society entails the homogenization of the folk and regional-national cultural traditions determined by the overall process of secularization: the more diversified and intense the involvement of local personnel arrays with non-traditional elements and complexes, the lower the retention of supernaturalism (as elements of last resort) in the emerging sociocultural system. Operationalizing this theory of change may be difficult, but it is a distinct possibility that should be undertaken.

Even though the main concern of this monograph is the description and explanation of a witchcraft system, it is underlain by several notions about the dynamics of evolution and transformation. Although we are confident that the explanation of bloodsucking witchcraft in rural Tlaxcala is essentially correct and replicable in many different settings, we are less confident of our analysis of change, beyond, of course, the description of the system as it has evolved from pre-Hispanic times to the present. This has been the norm in the conceptualization of sociocultural phenomena since the social sciences emerged as an academic discipline in this century. There is something seemingly intractable in the intellectual tradition of the West (a common thread that begins with the Greeks and is still present today) that makes it difficult to deal theoretically with the themes of change, evolving, and transformation. Time and again, change has been subsumed, camouflaged one could say, under the category of facile or spurious sociological laws (witness, for example, the handling of change by most functionalists) which have not explained change but have rather obscured what is involved in explaining it. We have ambitiously tackled the problem in this monograph; some of its conceptual notions appear to be on the right track, some of them are correctly positioned, but whether what has been done will lead to an operationalizable theory of change is difficult to say. One cannot be blamed for trying, and we hope to have contributed something to the solution of this vexing problem.

Notes to Chapters

INTRODUCTION

1. The population of these 21 municipios in the 1960 *Octavo Censo General de Población* was about 260,000, while the total population of the state stood at 346,699. About 50,000 comprised the four small cities of the region: Tlaxcala, the state capital (10,000), Apizaco (15,000), Chiautempan (12,000), and Huamantla (13,000). These cities are not only small but are socially, religiously, and economically tied intimately to the rural environment. In such context, the rural-urban continuum exhibits minimal differentiation.

1. AN OUTLINE OF WEATHERMAKING, NAHUALISM, AND SORCERY

1. The ethnographic data presented in this monograph were gathered in 12 of the 21 municipios that have been delimited as rural Tlaxcala. Nutini has been working in these 12 municipios for 30 years, and, more specifically, in 36 communities which include the entire spectrum of the regional ethnocultural continuum. Most of the data on blood-sucking witchcraft and related phenomena were gathered mainly throughout 1961, and during the summer field seasons of 1964, 1965, 1966, 1967, and 1968. Under these circumstances, 1965 will be regarded as the ethnographic present in this monograph. For reasons that will become apparent, all rural Tlaxcalan names of persons, kinship groups, settlements, and municipios appearing in this monograph are pseudonyms in order to safeguard the anonymity of individuals and places.

2. In a few communities this immanent call takes an alternate, more ostensible and dramatic form. The people believe that when a man, regardless of age, survives the direct impact of a thunderbolt he is destined to become a tezitlazc. Ultimately, such rare individuals become the most powerful and sought after of all tezitlazcs.

3. This figure was derived from a census of all known *tetlachihuics* in two municipios; one in 1961 and the other in 1965. The former has five dependent communities

in addition to the *cabecera* with a total population of slightly over 10,000, for which Nutini found twenty-five *tetlachihuics*; for the latter, he found nine *tetlachihuics* distributed in the *cabecera* and one dependent community with a population of nearly 4,000. In addition, the larger municipio occupied a transitional position in the ethnocultural continuum, while the smaller one was still traditionally Indian.

4. It is interesting to notice that the use of tetlachihuics as an instrument of last resort and as a normal practitioner in curing illness correlates very well with the indices of secularization and traditionalism: the more secularized the community, the higher the incidence of the latter. In fact, we have measured and scaled twenty respondents for each of five communities at different points in the ethnocultural continuum.

5. The main reason for this invariability is that there is a good deal of extra-community consultation of tetlachihuics. Unless the tetlachihuic has great prestige and is regionally known—Nutini knows five tetlachihuics in this category—the prices are more or less standardized. This bears witness to the closeness of the tetlachihuic fraternity, not only intracommunally but regionally as well.

6. Notice that sympathetic magic (1) is really a special kind of homeopathic magic (2) in Frazer's (1972:415–30) classical distinction. But we are distinguishing sympathetic from homeopathic techniques to emphasize the use of effigies or images in the magical manipulation.

2. THE BELIEF SYSTEM AND STRUCTURAL CONTEXT OF BLOODSUCKING WITCHCRAFT

1. López Austin (1967:87–117) shows that the sources on pre-Hispanic anthropomorphic supernaturalism are rather confusing. For example, if the distinction between witch and sorcerer—as exemplified in this monograph by the tlahuelpuchi and the tetlachihuic respectively—is accepted, then the gloss denoting a given anthropomorphic supernatural may be interpreted as either one: the *nahualli* may be either an inherently evil witch or transforming trickster, or a practicing sorcerer of white and black magic. It is not certain, however, whether the confusion is inherent in the pre-Hispanic anthropomorphic supernatural system, apparently ancillary to the priestly-polytheistic religion prevalent in Mesoamerica at the time, or is due to the inadequate reporting of sixteenth-century (Las Casas 1966; Florentine Codex 1963; Molina 1944; Sahagún 1956; etc.) and seventeenth-century (Ruiz de Alarcón 1953; Serna 1953; Torquemada 1944; etc.) sources. Moreover, the nahual and tlahuelpuchi are primarily manifestations of a single entity, but with forms and attributes significantly diversified. A comparison between the contemporary tetlachihuic and tlahuelpuchi indicates that the structure and functions of whatever pre-Hispanic prototypes these practitioners derived from are those associated with the sorcerer and witch.

2. It is evident, however, that the rationale for this practice of the tlahuelpuchi and belief of the people goes back to pre-Hispanic times. We have found no clues in the sources dealing with pre-Hispanic magic and religion, and it is unlikely that any exist concerning such a specific and eminently folk practice. The only suggestion that comes

to mind is the ubiquitousness of the turkey, both now and in pre-Hispanic times, and the fact that this domestic animal is the most closely associated with man. But not even this possible explanation accounts for the symbolic use of the turkey as the transforming animal.

3. From Nutini's first acquaintance with rural Tlaxcala during the summer of 1959, when the survey of the Tlaxcala-Pueblan Valley was conducted, the intensity and widespread dimensions of bloodsucking witchcraft became apparent. When in-depth fieldwork in the region began a year later, the belief system of the practice was well known to him. Moreover, in October of 1960 the chief medical officer of the state of Tlaxcala, who was well informed about the tlahuelpuchi complex, alerted him about what to look for, how to go about it, and whom he should talk to and examine in cases of infant death attributed to the tlahuelpuchi.

3. SYNCRETIC AND HISTORICAL DEVELOPMENT OF ANTHROPOMORPHIC SUPERNATURALISM

1. As New Spain emerged from the sixteenth century, there was a renaissance of witchcraft and sorcery among the non-Indian population. The reason for this is not clear, but we do know that the number of inquisitorial processes increased rather dramatically during the first quarter of the seventeenth century, and most of them had to do with sorcery and witchcraft accusations (Solange Behocaray de Alberro, personal communication). Hundreds of accusations were brought to the attention of the tribunal of the Inquisition in the city of Puebla. The implications of this development in the wider Colonial society are important for the syncretic cycle that was beginning at the local Indian level (Alberro 1988:140–67).

6. THE EMPIRICAL EVIDENCE OF BLOODSUCKING WITCHCRAFT: METHODOLOGY AND SYSTEMATIC PRESENTATION

1. It was stated that in 1960, 90 percent of the rural Tlaxcalan population believed in the entire bloodsucking witchcraft complex, never questioning the efficacy of tlahuelpuchis to kill infants. The 10 percent of doubters and skeptics had been increased to perhaps 25 percent by 1968, when Nutini last collected systematic information on the practice. We would guess that today (1983) that percentage has probably reached about 60 percent of all rural Tlaxcalans.

2. As far as it could be determined, the main reason why members of these households refused to answer was embarrassment concerning the fact that they had been careless in protecting their infants against the tlahuelpuchi. Although the ideology of bloodsucking witchcraft clearly specifies that there are only two foolproof methods of protection, parents generally feel guilty and ashamed when their unprotected infants are sucked, and this leads to refusal to talk about or discuss the incident.

3. Considering that only slightly more than two-thirds of the households (1,072) reported a total of 1,352 victims of bloodsucking witchcraft, we may think of the 27

cases for the November 1960–December 1961 cycle for the municipio as a realistic yearly average.

4. Henceforth, the forty-seven–case sample will be regarded as representative, unless otherwise indicated. Given the homogeneity and similarity of bloodsucking incidence throughout rural Tlaxcala, we feel justified in doing this, despite the seasonal incompleteness of the cases gathered during the summers of 1964, 1965, 1966, and 1967.

5. On the eighth day after the sucking in this particular case, Nutini had to leave the field to return to the United States but entrusted to the brightest of his three field assistants (a twenty-seven-year-old local school teacher) to keep a close watch on the woman and her household. Nutini instructed him on how to do this, and he was able to complete the account of what had transpired for a week afterward.

6. Throughout 1961 nine cases of husbands under the effects of chipilería and tzipitictoc were observed: four in San Diego Tlalocan, two in San Antonio Omeyocan, two in Santa Clara Topitla, and one in San Juan Meztitlán. In all cases the husband took to bed at least two and as many as four times during the first six months of their wives' first pregnancy and exhibited most of the characteristic symptoms that are described below. There is no question that, homologously, *chipilería* and, especially, *tzipitictoc* are attenuated forms of the classical couvade reported for several tribes of the tropical forest of South America.

7. NATURAL AND SUPERNATURAL EXPLANATIONS: THE LOGIC OF WITCHCRAFT AND NORMATIVE EXPECTATIONS

1. The efficacy of a witchcraft system (especially in such a restricted and single-directed system as the tlahuelpuchi complex) is primarily centered on the high degree of concordance between ideological expectations and empirical manifestations. This is clearly corroborated by the observation over a fifteen-year period of many skeptics, individuals who no longer believed tlahuelpuchis cause the death of infants. Once people cease to entertain this central feature of the system, the tlahuelpuchi complex — that is, the part having to do with the rather nebulous conception of the tlahuelpuchi as a vengeful entity destroying lives and property — is reduced to a minimum in explaining unfortunate or unexpected events. Indeed, once the seed of doubt is planted, there is a definite progression of skepticism marked by the following stages: (1) individuals begin to verbalize that the tlahuelpuchi was effective in the past but not any longer; (2) they say that the tlahuelpuchi does not cause the death of infants by sucking; (3) they state that infant deaths under the circumstances denoted by a sucking are due to "natural" causes (and at this juncture they may even verbalize some of the causes that we shall discuss below); (4) they say that tlahuelpuchis may still be effective in other domains, particularly in taking revenge by supernatural means; and (5) they say that tlahuel-puchis do not exist, "son nada más una creencia de la gente ignorante" (they are nothing more than a belief of ignorant people). We have been able to delineate the sociological parameters within which this change takes place but unable to conceptualize the psychological matrix which accompanies it.

2. To realize the depth of the data-base requirements that a truly scientific study of witchcraft and sorcery demand, it should be noted that after more than six years of actual fieldwork and observation among rural Tlaxcalans during the past twenty-five years, we still do not have the proper corpus of information to undertake the transposition of causation that is involved in bloodsucking witchcraft and several related phenomena. Partly, this is because this aspect of the analytical framework was formulated recently (1982), whereas the data base required for the implementation of the objectification of causality was conceived and formulated by Nutini shortly after the 1960 bloodsucking epidemic described in chapter 6.

8. THE DIAGNOSTIC AND ETIOLOGICAL ANALYSIS OF BLOODSUCKING WITCHCRAFT

1. It is important to impress upon the reader that the distinction between the contexts of asphyxia and suffocation were not made on medical grounds (that is, the exhibited telltale somatic signs on the body of infants) but on the grounds of sociopsychological contexts in which the infants regarded as having been sucked by the tlahuelpuchi die. We are employing the terms asphyxia and suffocation not as physical but as sociopsychological indicators.

2. The reader should contrast this physical ambience of rural Tlaxcalan infants with that of European and American infants in their almost antiseptic nurseries, spacious cribs, and flat and uncluttered immediate surroundings. The reader may wonder, as we do, whether infant care in Europe and the United States only four or five generations ago was that different from rural Tlaxcala in 1960, and how many infants died of suffocation under circumstances similar to those described here.

9. SOCIAL AND PSYCHOLOGICAL MANIPULATIONS AND THE EX POST FACTO RATIONALIZATION OF THE TLAHUELPUCHI COMPLEX

1. The concepts of *neighbor* and *neighborhood* in rural Tlaxcala are not analytically adequate. Rather, the concept of *neighbor* can be decomposed into *kinsman, compadre,* and *friend* (see Nutini 1988). In the present description, however, *neighbor* and *neighborhood* include different members of these categories to avoid cumbersome expressions. By extension, these concepts include various kinds of kinsmen of the non-residential extended family, the households of which are usually located within a discernable paraje.

2. Nutini (1988:Chapter 12) has discussed the sacralization of interpersonal relationships in rural Tlaxcalan society on at least three occasions throughout the year: The Christmas cycle (16 December–6 January), Holy Week (from Palm Sunday to the Octave of Easter), and the All Saints Day-All Souls Day cycle (28 October–9 November). By the sacralization of relationships (which may extend from the household to the community at large), he means the conscious effort of the people to be considerate of one another, generous, supportive, polite, and to set aside disagreements and antagon-

ism. These are times of renewal and intensification, when the household, kinship and compadrazgo networks, neighborhoods, and the community as a whole truly but temporarily become integrated, "sacred" entities. This is exactly what happens to the household and immediate neighborhood when the tlahuelpuchi strikes, the only difference being that in this case the catalyst in bringing people together and renewing and intensifying interpersonal relationships is fear and the presence of a common enemy.

3. On crisp, sometimes cold, summer nights, usually after a heavy downpour, the word spreads in the most traditional rural Tlaxcalan communities that the tlahuelpuchi is operating in certain parajes. The children and the young somewhat in jest, but the adults deadly seriously avail themselves of the paraphernalia for stopping witches (machetes, knives, knotted handkerchiefs, and so on) and set out for the hunt. These alarms are usually triggered after more than one sucking has taken place in rather close proximity, most often by the presence of animals (generally donkeys, dogs, or coyotes) that are not supposed to be in the vicinity or by rather large and luminous fireflies (*luciérnagas*), occasionally common during the rainy season. Nutini participated in several of these witch hunts, the first two with his chief informant. After the second hunt, the informant provided Nutini with the most detailed and complete description of the ideology and belief system of the tlahuelpuchi complex, taking until dawn and requiring more than five hours of elicitation. Although the adults participating in these hunts were earnest and intense about killing tlahuelpuchis, once they thought that they had done the job or driven the witches away, they became somewhat lighthearted and joined the children and the young in the bantering and considerable merrymaking that had been going on during the hunt. Afterwards, participants gathered in an important household of the paraje for a light repast, and much as hunters do everywhere, the most enthusiastic participants recounted the high points of the hunt and their exploits.

4. An example of a semilegendary account, as told by the head of the household in case 39, is the following: "Several years ago I had the opportunity to witness what happened to the body of a sucked infant in the household of a compadrito in one of the villages high on La Malintzi. The body of the infant was badly covered with bruises and purple spots, and his face was so distorted as if it had been squeezed by very strong hands. By noon the body was entirely yellowish-purplish and began to exude a strong odor of sulfur and rotten eggs. The people got scared and hurried with all the proceedings in order to bury the body by late afternoon. When we returned from the cemetery for the customary meal, the strong odor of sulfur and rotten eggs permeated every room of the house, and the milk in several containers had been curdled. There was an ominous stir in the house and my compadrito, seeing that people were getting scared, called a tezitlazc for a special limpia. When I returned the following day, my compadrito's household was in an uproar. During the night, the body of the infant had been removed from its grave by ripping the coffin to shreds. By noon a large company of kinsmen and neighbors from the paraje led by a tezitlazc went to the cemetery. The torn coffin was reburied and the tezitlazc performed another limpia on the spot. I returned the following day, and my compadrito and several neighbors told me that during the night the entire paraje reeked of the odor of sulfur and rotten eggs, that the people

huddled inside their houses afraid to go out, and that one could hear the rough flight of turkeys and the bray of donkeys that were not supposed to be there, a sure indication that several tlahuelpuchis had converged on the paraje. It was not until the fourth night after the sucking that the paraje returned to normality." This informant went on to elaborate on the fact that this particular tlahuelpuchi apparently had a compact with the devil, hence the odor of sulfur and rotten eggs, and that other tlahuelpuchis had rallied to her defense when the devil came to claim the soul of the dead infant that the perpetrator did not want to give up. This interpretation of the aftereffects of the sucking totally departs from the ideology and belief system of bloodsucking witchcraft, as elicited from hundreds of informants in many rural Tlaxcalan communities, under normal, controlled conditions. Thus, the vulgarization of the tlahuelpuchi belief system means essentially statements made by individuals under stress and in an ambience of anxiety in which the tlahuelpuchi appears to interact with ordinary humans in ways contradictory to her ontological nature or, as in the present example, with the Christian devil (and other anthropomorphic supernaturals), with which the tlahuelpuchi has nothing in common; nor does the tlahuelpuchi enter into partnership for any evildoing.

5. By the time one reaches the age of forty probably every individual in rural Tlaxcala has experienced a sucking in his or her nuclear family or within the context of the developmental cycle of the extended family. This probably obtained until the middle to late 1960s. Since then the situation has changed radically, but the phenomenon is an integral part of the great decrease in infant mortality during the past twenty years.

10. AFTEREFFECTS AND THE PSYCHOLOGICAL CONTEXT OF THE POSTSUCKING PERIOD

1. It is highly indicative that perhaps half of the more than thirty individual informants that were interviewed no longer used the native term, *tlahuelpuchi*, to refer to the bloodsucking witch. Rather, they used the Spanish term *bruja* (witch) to refer to it. This linguistic change suggests the great structural and ideological changes that the complex has undergone since the 1959 survey of Tlaxcala. There is good evidence that for most rural Tlaxcalans (there are four or five small communities that are still the exception) 45 years of age or older (that is, those in their early twenties a generation ago) the complex is still latently there, while among those 40 years old and younger the tlahuelpuchi complex is vaguely residual and on its way to disappearance.

2. The victim's mother in case 32 reported the terrible nightmare that she had during the night of the sucking in the following terms: "Me acuerdo venir llegando a casa a la oración, ya casi oscuro. Al acercarme veo la puerta de la casa entreabierta, y siento como que se me quería salir el corazón del pecho. Con mucho miedo, suelto el chiquihuite de hongos que traia del monte, y corro a nuestro cuarto. Habro totalmente la puerta y veo una aparición luminosa, en forma de mujer y sin piernas, como flotando sobre la cuna de mi creatura. Me abalanzo sobre ella tratando de alejarla de mi bebito, y al voltearse veo que tiene una cara horrible como de guajolote. No sé de a donde saqué fuerzas, pero comense a forcejear y luchar con la tlahuelpuchi, que ya no me quedaban dudas que era

ella, tratando de proteger a mi creatura. Rodamos por el suelo y me acuerdo haberle arrancado unos pellejos rojos que tenia en su largo cuello, y ella, tratando de immobilizarme contra el suelo y jalándome del pelo, me decia: 'defiendete cabrona; a ver si eres tan buena para proteger a tu creatura, como para salir a pasear y dejarla sola y abandonada.' Jadeante y ya sin fuerzas, veo que algo como neblina le comienza a salir de aquellos ojos malignos, y a los pocos segundos me desvanezco, como si me hubieran dado un macanazo en el cuello. No me acuerdo de nada hasta que muy temprano en la mañana me despertó mi marido diciendome que la tlahuelpuchi se habia chupado a mi Juanito." (I remember arriving home at dusk, when it was almost dark. Nearing the house I see the door ajar, and I feel as though my heart wanted to give up. With great fear, I let go of the basket of mushrooms that I was bringing from the mountain, and I run to our room. I throw the door open and I see a luminous apparition, in the shape of a woman and without legs, hovering over the crib of my infant. I lunge at her trying to get her away from my little baby, and as she turns around I see that she has a horrible, turkey-like face. I do not know how I gathered strength, but I began to struggle and fight with the tlahuelpuchi, whose identity I no longer doubted, trying to protect my infant. We roll on the floor and I remember having torn off some red skin from her long neck, and, as she was trying to immobilize me against the floor and pulling my hair, she said: "defend yourself, you bitch, let us see whether you are as good to protect your infant, as you are to go gallivanting and leave your infant alone and abandoned." Panting and without strength, I see that something like mist begins to emanate from those malevolent eyes, and a few seconds later I fainted, as if I have been dealt a blow to the neck. I do not remember anything until early in the morning my husband woke me up telling me that the tlahuelpuchi had sucked my Juanito.) There is no other likely interpretation of this nightmare but the one given in the text. It is also interesting to note that this particular household is classified as mestizo-secularized—that is, its members belonged to the most modern, outward looking sector of rural Tlaxcalan society in 1960. Among other things, this demonstrates that, at least as far as the bloodsucking witchcraft complex is concerned, even the most acculturative segment of the population at that time was still traditional. Notice also that the nightmare is really a variation of one of several themes that constitute the general configuration of unusual events experienced by primary and secondary actors. This suggests, as we have indicated in several places, the highly patterned structure of the physical and psychological manifestations of the tlahuelpuchi complex. The dozen or so nightmares recorded for mothers and the two for fathers, from the forty-seven–case sample and from cases not in the sample but having essentially the same structure, have as their central feature the struggle of the tlahuelpuchi with the mother for the safety of the infant. Notice also the father finds the body of the victim, as is quite commonly the case, and it is he who, upon finding the corpse in a suspicious or unusual position and location, initiates the consensus that it was the tlahuelpuchi who sucked the blood of the infant. This is an important fact, because it demonstrates the culturally conditioned behavior that the father, independent of the mother, lends credence to and fully supports the latter concerning the efficacy of the witch to kill.

3. There are, of course, other meanings of these glosses, but what we wish to convey here is that guilt connotes what one feels after one realizes that one deserves blame for having contravened or broken a culturally determined rule or injunction, whereas culpability connotes only the realization of being responsible for neglect or of having broken a rule or injunction but not a state of feeling for something that one has done or left undone—that is, irrespective of whether one deserves blame. In Spanish the situation is even more complicated semantically in that there is only the Latin root *culpa*, and *culpabilidad* means both "guilt" and "culpability," and *culpa* also means "blame." The advantage of English here is that of having an Anglo-Saxon and a Latin gloss, while in Spanish only context discriminates between guilt and culpability.

11. THE SOCIAL AND PSYCHOLOGICAL FUNCTIONS OF BLOODSUCKING WITCHCRAFT

1. There are indications that infanticide was more common at the turn of the century. The oldest informants suggest this, but legendary accounts also point in the same direction. This is implied, for example, in the mediation of La Malintzi in a terrible dispute between a daughter-in-law and her mother-in-law in which this tutelary mountain owner brings them together after accusations of infanticide have been made. Whether this is entirely projective we do not know, but it suggests a wider implication of the tlahuelpuchi's functions.

References Cited

Adams, Richard N., and Arthur J. Rubel
    1967   "Sickness and Social Relations." In *Handbook of Middle American Indians*, edited by Robert Wauchope. Vol. 6. Austin: University of Texas Press.

Aguirre Beltrán, Gonzalo
    1940   *El Señorío de Cuautochco*. México, D.F.: Ediciones Fuente Cultural.
    1946   *La Población Negra de México*. México: Fondo de Cultura Económica.
    1963   *Medicina y Magia. El Proceso de Aculturación en la Estructura Colonial*. México: Instituto Nacional Indigenista.

Alberro, Solange
    1988   *Inquisition et Société au Mexique: 1571–1700*. Mexico, D.F.: Centre d'Etudes Mexicaines.

Ardner, Edwin
    1970   "Witchcraft, Economics, and the Continuity of Belief." In *Witchcraft Confessions and Accusations*, edited by Mary Douglas. London: Tavistock Publications.

Balsalobre, Gonzalo de
    1953   "Relación Auténtica de las Idolatrías, Supersticiones, y Vanas Observaciones de los Indios del Obispado de Oaxaca." In *Tratado de las Idolatrías, Supersticiones, Dioses, Ritos, Hechicerías y Otras Costumbres Gentílicas de las Razas Aborígenes de México*, Jacinto de la Serna, Mexico, D.F.: Ediciones Fuente Cultural.

Barba de Piña Chan, Beatriz
    1980   *La Expansión de la Magia*. México, D.F.: Secretaría de Educación Pública, Instituto Nacional de Antropología e Historia.

Barnes, Barry
    1973   "The Comparison of Belief-Symptoms: Anomaly Versus Falsehood." In *Modes of Thought: Essays on Thinking in Western and Non-Western Societies*, edited by Robin Horton and Ruth Finnegan. London: Faber and Faber.

Beals, Ralph L.
   1946   *Cherán: A Sierra Tarascan Village.* Institute of Social Anthropology Publication No. 2. Washington, D.C.: Smithsonian Institution.
   1950   "The History of Acculturation in Mexico." In *Homenaje al Dr. Alfonso Caso.* Mexico, D.F.: Imprenta Nuevo Mundo.

Beidelman, T. O.
   1969   "Witchcraft in Ukaguru." In *Witchcraft and Sorcery in East Africa,* edited by John Middleton and E. H. Winter. London: Routledge and Kegan Paul.
   1970   "Toward More Open Theoretical Interpretations." In *Witchcraft Confessions and Accusations,* edited by Mary Douglas. London: Tavistock Publications.

Bryant, Arthur T.
   1966   *Zuw Medicine and Medicine-Men.* Capetown, South Africa.

Buxton, Jean
   1969   "Mandari Witchcraft. In *Witchcraft and Sorcery in East Africa,* edited by John Middleton and E. H. Winter. London: Routledge and Kegan Paul.

Carrasco, Pedro
   1952   *Tarascan Folk Religion: An Analysis of Economic, Social, and Religious Interactions.* Middle American Research Institute Publication 17:1–64. New Orleans: Tulane University.
   1961   "The Civil-Religious Hierarchy in Mesoamerican Communities: Pre-Spanish Background and Colonial Development." *American Anthropologist* 63:483–97.

Castaneda, Carlos
   1968   *The Teachings of Don Juan: A Yaqui Way of Knowledge.* Berkeley: University of California Press.

Castiglioni, Pedro
   1972   *Encantamiento y Magia.* México, D.F.: Fondo de Cultural Económica.

Códice, Ramírez
   1944   *Manuscripto del Siglo XVI Intitulado: Relación del Origen de los Indios que Habitan esta Nueva España, Según sus Historias,* Manuel Orozco y Berra, commentator. México: Editorial Leyenda, S.A.

Colby, Benjamin N., and L. M. Colby
   1981   *The Daykeeper: The Life and Discourse of an Ixil Diviner.* Cambridge: Harvard University Press.

Colby, Benjamin N., and Michael Cole
   1973   "Culture, Memory, and Narrative." In *Modes of Thought: Essays on Thinking in Western and Non-Western Societies,* edited by Robin Horton and Ruth Finnegan. London: Faber and Faber.

Cooper, John M.
   1946   "The Araucanians." In *The Handbook of South American Indians,* edited by Julian H. Steward. Vol. 2. Bureau of American Ethnology, Bulletin No. 143. Washington, D.C.: Government Printing Office.

Crawford, J. R.

1967 *Witchcraft and Sorcery in Rhodesia.* London: Oxford University Press.

Devons, Ely, and Max Gluckman

1964 "Conclusion." In *Closed Systems and Open Minds,* edited by Max Gluckman. Chicago: Aldine Publishing Company.

Douglas, Mary

1966 *Purity and Danger.* London: Routledge and Kegan Paul.

Douglas, Mary, ed.

1970 *Witchcraft Confessions and Accusations.* London: Tavistock Publications.

Durán, Fray Diego

1952 *Historia de las Indias de Nueva España y Islas de Tierra Firme.* (José F. Ramírez edition, with an atlas). México: Editors Nacional, S.A.

1967 *Historia de las Indias de la Nueva España e Islas de Tierra Firme.* Two volumes. México, D.F.: Editorial Porrúa.

Evans-Pritchard, E. E.

1937 *Witchcraft, Oracles, and Magic among the Azande.* Oxford: Clarendon Press.

Faron, Louis C.

1964 *Hawks of the Sun: Mapuche Morality and its Ritual Attributes.* Pittsburgh: University of Pittsburgh Press.

Feria, Pedro de

1953 "Revelación sobre la Reincidencia en sus Idolatrías de los Indios de Chiapa Después de Treinta Años de Cristianos." In *Tratado de las Idolatrías, Supersticiones, Dioses, Ritos, Hechicerías y Otras Costumbres Gentílicas de las Razas Aborígenes de México,* Jacinto de la Serna, México, D.F.: Ediciones Fuente Cultural.

Finnegan, Ruth

1973 "Literacy Versus Non-Literacy: The Great Divide?" In *Modes of Thought: Essays on Thinking in Western and Non-Western Societies,* edited by Robin Horton and Ruth Finnegan. London: Faber and Faber.

Finnegan, Ruth, and Robin Horton

1973 Introduction. In *Modes of Thought: Essays on Thinking in Western and Non-Western Societies.* London: Faber and Faber.

Florentine Codex

1963 *General History of the Things of New Spain,* translated by Arthur J. O. Anderson and Charles E. Dibble. Santa Fe, New Mexico: The School of American Research and The University of Utah.

Forde, Darryl

1958 "Spirits, Witches and Sorcerers in the Supernatural Economy of the Yako." *Journal of the Royal Anthropological Institute* 88(2):165–78.

Fortune, Reo F.

1963 *Sorcerers of Dobu.* London: Routledge and Kegan Paul.

Foster, George M.

1944 "Nagualism in Mexico and Guatemala." *Acta Americana* 2:85–103.

1960   *Culture and Conquest: America's Pre-Hispanic Heritage.* Publications in Anthropology no. 27. New York: Viking Fund.

Fuente, Julio de la
1949   *Yalalag: Una Villa Zapoteca Serrana.* Serie Científica No. 1. México, D.F.: Museo Nacional de Antropología.

Gellner, Ernest
1973   "The Savage and Modern Mind." In *Modes of Thought: Essays on Thinking in Western and Non-Western Societies,* edited by Robin Horton and Ruth Finnegan. London: Faber and Faber.

Gittins, Robert
1985   *Canonical Analysis.* New York: Springer-Verlag.

Gonzales, Thomas A., et al.
1954   *Legal Medicine: Pathology and Toxicology.* New York: Appleton Century Crofts, Inc.

Gray, Robert F.
1969   "Some Structural Aspects of Mbugwe Witchcraft." In *Witchcraft and Sorcery in East Africa,* edited by John Middleton and E. H. Winter. London: Routledge and Kegan Paul.

Greenacre, Michael J.
1984   *Theory and Applications of Correspondence Analysis.* New York: Academic Press.

Grottanelli, Vinigi L.
1981   "Witchcraft: An Allegory?" *L'Uomo* 5:176–83.

Guiteras Holmes, Galixta
1961   *Perils of the Soul: The World View of a Tzotzil Indian.* Chicago: University of Chicago Press.

Harvey, Herbert K., and Isabel Kelly
1969   "The Totonac." In *Handbook of Middle American Indians,* edited by Robert Wauchope. Vol. 8. Austin: University of Texas Press.

Harwood, Alan
1970   Witchcraft, Sorcery, and Social Categories among the Safwa. London: Oxford University Press.

Herskovitz, Melville S.
1937   "African Gods and Catholic Saints in New World Religious Beliefs." *American Anthropologist* 39:635–43.

Honingham, John J.
1976   *The Development of Anthropological Ideas.* Homewood, Illinois: The Dorsey Press.

Horton, Robin
1973   "Levy-Bruhl, Durkheim and the Scientific Revolution." In *Modes of Thought: Essays on Thinking in Western and Non-Western Societies,* edited by Robin Horton and Ruth Finnegan. London: Faber and Faber.

Horton, Robin, and Ruth Finnegan, eds.

1973   *Modes of Thought: Essays on Thinking in Western and Non-Western Societies.* London: Faber and Faber.

Huntingford, G. W. B.

1969   "Nandi Witchcraft." In *Witchcraft and Sorcery in East Africa,* edited by John Middleton and E. H. Winter. London: Routledge and Kegan Paul.

Ichon, Alain

1973   *La Religión de los Totnacas de la Sierra.* Serie de Antropología Social No. 16. México, D. F.: Instituto Nacional Indigenista.

Ita, J. M.

1973   "Frobenius, Senghor and the Image of Africa." In *Modes of Thought: Essays on Thinking in Western and Non-Western Societies,* edited by Robin Horton and Ruth Finnegan. London: Faber and Faber.

Jenkins, Hilary

1973   "Religion and Secularism: The Contemporary Significance of Newman's Thought." In *Modes of Thought: Essays on Thinking in Western and Non-Western Socities,* edited by Robin Horton and Ruth Finnegan. London: Faber and Faber.

Johnson, Jean B.

1939   "The Elements of Mazatec Witchcraft." *Ethnological Studies* 9:128–50.

Kaplan, L. H.

1956   "Tonal and Nagual in Coastal Oaxaca, Mexico." *Journal of American Folklore* 69:363–68.

Kennedy, John G.

1967   "Psychological and Social Explanations of Witchcraft." *Man,* volume 2, June.

1969   *International Journal of Social Psychiatry* 15(3):165–78.

Kluckhohn, Clyde

1944   *Navaho Witchcraft.* Papers of the Peabody Museum of American Archeology and Ethnology, no. 22. Cambridge: Peabody Museum Papers No. 22.

Kroeber, Alfred L.

1948   *Anthropology: Race, Language, Culture, Psychology, Prehistory.* New York: Harcourt, Brace and World, Inc.

Kuhn, Thomas S.

1970   *The Structure of Scientific Revolutions.* Chicago: University of Chicago Press.

LaFontaine, John

1969   "Witchcraft in Bugishau." In *Witchcraft and Sorcery in East Africa,* edited by John Middleton and E. H. Winter. London: Routledge and Kegan Paul.

Las Casas, Fray Bartolomé de

1966   *Los Indios de México y Nueva España: Antología.* México, D. F.: Editorial Porruá.

Levine, Robert A.

1969   "Witchcraft and Sorcery in a Gusii Community." In *Witchcraft and Sorcery in East Africa,* edited by John Middleton and E. H. Winter. London: Routledge and Kegan Paul.

Lévy-Bruhl, Lucien
  1966   *How the Natives Think.* New York: Washington Square Press.
Lewis, Oscar
  1951   *Life in a Mexican Village: Tepoztlan Restudied.* Urbana: University of Illinois Press.
Lieban, Richard W.
  1967   *Cebuano Sorcery: Malign Magic in the Philippines.* Berkeley: University of California Press.
Lienhardt, R. G.
  1951   "Some Notion on Witchcraft among the Dinka." *Africa* 21(4):303–18.
López, Austin, Alfredo
  1966   "Los Temacpalitotique: Brujos, Profanadores, Ladrones y Violadores." *Estudios de Cultura Náhuatl* 6:97–117.
  1967   "Cuarenta Clases de Magos del Mundo Náhuatl." *Estudios de Cultura Náhuatl* 7:87–117.
  1973   *Hombre-Dios: Religión y Política en el Mundo Náhuatl.* México, D.F.: Universidad Nacional Autónoma de México.
Lukes, Steven
  1973   "On the Social Determination of Truth." In *Modes of Thought: Essays on Thinking in Western and Non-Western Societies,* edited by Robin Horton and Ruth Finnegan. London: Faber and Faber.
MacFarlane, Alan
  1970   "Witchcraft in Tudor and Stuart England." In *Witchcraft Confessions and Accusations,* edited by Mary Douglas. London: Tavistock Publications.
Madsen, William
  1957   *Christo-Paganism: A Study of Mexican Religious Syncretism.* Middle American Research Institute Publication 19:105–80. New Orleans: Tulane University.
  1960   *The Virgin's Children: Life in an Aztec Village Today.* Austin: University of Texas Press.
  1967   "Religious Syncretism." In *Handbook of Middle American Indians,* edited by Robert Wauchope. Vol. 6. Austin: University of Texas Press.
  1969   "The Nahua." In *Handbook of Middle American Indians,* edited by Robert Wauchope. Vol. 8. Austin: University of Texas Press.
Mair, Lucy
  1969   *Witchcraft.* New York: McGraw-Hill Book Company.
  1981   "Witchcraft and Allegory." *L'Uomo* 5(1):173–75.
Marín Tamayo, Fausto
  1960   "La División Racial en Puebla de los Angeles en el Régimen Colonial." *Publicación No. 14.* Puebla, México: Instituto Poblano de Antropología.
Marwick, Max G.
  1952   "The Social Context of Cewa Witch Beliefs. *Africa* 22(2):120–35; (3):215–33.
  1965   *Sorcery in its Social Setting: A Study of the Northern Rhodesian Cewa.* Manchester: Manchester University Press.

Marwick, Max G., ed.

1970 *Witchcraft and Sorcery*. London: Penguin Books.

Mayer, Philip

1954 *Witches*. Inaugural Lecture delivered at Rhodes University.

Mendelson, Michael E.

1967 "Ritual and Mythology." In *Handbook of Middle American Indians*, edited by Robert Wauchope. Vol. 6. Austin: University of Texas Press.

Mendieta, Fray Geronimo de

1945 *Historia Eclesiástica Indiana*. Four volumes. México, D.F.: Editorial Salvador Chávez Hyahoe.

Mendoza, Virginia R.

1952 "La Bruja en México: In *Proceedings and Selected Papers of the XXIX International Congress of Americanists*, edited by Sol Tax. Chicago: University of Chicago Press.

Middleton, John

1969 "Witchcraft and Sorcery in Lugbara." In *Witchcraft and Sorcery in East Africa*, edited by John Middleton and E. H. Winter. London: Routledge and Kegan Paul.

Middleton, John, ed.

1967 *Gods and Rituals: Readings in Religious Beliefs and Practices*. New York: Garden City Press.

Middleton, John, and E. H. Winter, eds.

1969 *Witchcraft and Sorcery in East Africa*. London: Routledge and Kegan Paul.

Molina, Fray Alonso de

1944 *Vocabulario en Lengua Castellana y Mexicana*. Colección de Incunables Americanos. Volume 4. Madrid: Ediciones Cultura Hispánica.

Montoya Briones, José, de Jesús

1964 *Atla: Etnografía de un Pueblo Náhuatl*. Departamento de Investigaciones Antropológicas, Publicación No. 14. México, D.F.: Instituto Nacional de Antropología e Historia.

Motolinía, Fray Toribio de Benavente

1903 *Memoriales*. México, D.F.: Casa del Editor.

1941 *Historia de los Indios de Nueva España*. México, D.F.: Editorial Salvador Sánchez Hayhoe.

Nadel, Siegfried F.

1952 "Witchcraft in Four African Societies: An Essay in Comparison." *American Anthropologist* 54(1):18–29.

Nagashima, Noburo

1973 "A Reversed World: Or is it?" In *Modes of Thought: Essays on Thinking in Western and Non-Western Societies*, edited by Robin Horton and Ruth Finnegan. London: Faber and Faber.

Nagel, Ernest

1961 *The Structure of Science*. New York: Harcourt Brace.

Nash, Manning
    1960   "Witchcraft as Social Process in a Tzeltal Community." *América Indígena*
        20:121–26.
Norbeck, Edward
    1961   *Religion in Primitive Society.* New York: Harper and Row.
Nutini, Hugo G.
    1965   "Some Considerations on the Nature of Social Structure and Model Building:
        A Critique of Claude Lévi-Strauss and Edmund Leech." *American Anthropol-
        ogist* 67:707–31.
    1967   "A Synoptic Comparison of Mesoamerican Marriage and Family Structure."
        Southwestern Journal of Anthropology 23:383–404.
    1968   *San Bernardino Contla: Marriage and Family Structure in a Tlaxcalan Muni-
        cipio.* Pittsburgh: University of Pittsburgh Press.
    1970   "Lévi-Strauss' Conception of Science." In *Echanges et Communications:
        Melanges Offerts a Claude Lévi-Strauss,* edited by Jean Pouillon and Pierre
        Maranda. Mouton: The Hague.
    1976   "The Nature and Treatment of Kinship in Mesoamerica." Introduction to *Es-
        says in Mexican Kinship,* edited by Hugo G. Nutini, Pedro Carrasco, and
        James M. Taggart. Pittsburgh: University of Pittsburgh Press.
    1984   *Ritual Kinship: Ideological and Structural Integration of the Compadrazgo
        System in Rural Tlaxcala.* Princeton: Princeton University Press.
    1987   "Nahualismo, Control de los Elementos y Hechicería en Tlaxcala Rural." In
        La Heterodoxia Recuperada: En Torno a Angel Polerm, edited by Susana
        Glantz. México, D.F.: Fondo de Cultura Económica.
    1988   *Todos Santos in Rural Tlaxcala: A Syncretic, Expressive, and Symbolic Analy-
        sis of the Cult of the Dead.* Princeton: Princeton University Press.
    n.d.   "From Traditional Sorcery to Modern Curing in Rural Tlaxcala." In *Festschrift
        in Honor of Pedro Carrasco,* edited by Roger Joseph and Hugo G. Nutini.
Nutini, Hugo G., and Betty Bell
    1980   *Ritual Kinship: The Structural and Historical Development of the Compa-
        drazgo System in Rural Tlaxcala.* Princeton: Princeton University Press.
Nutini, Hugo G., and Jean Forbes
    n.d.   "Notes on the Ethnology of the Nahuatl-Speaking Communities of the Cór-
        doba-Orizaba Region."
Nutini, Hugo G., and Barry L. Isaac
    1974   *Los Pueblos de Habla Náhuatl de la Región de Tlaxcala y Puebla.* Serie de
        Antropología Social No. 27. México, D.F.: Instituto Nacional Indigenista.
    1977   "Ideology and the Sacro-Symbolic Functions of Compadrazgo in Santa María
        Belén Azitzimititlán, Tlaxcala, Mexico." *L'Uomo* 1(1):81–121.
Nutini, Hugo G., and Douglas R. White
    1977   "Community Variations and Network Structure in the Social Functions of
        Compadrazgo in Rural Tlaxcala, Mexico." *Ethnology* 16(4):353–84.

Olavarrieta Marenco, Marcela

1977   *Magia en los Tuxtlas, Veracruz.* Serie de Antropología Social No. 54. México, D.F.: Instituto Nacional Indigenista.

Parsons, Elsie Clews

1927   "Witchcraft among the Pueblos, Indian or Spanish?" *Man* 27:106–12; 125–28.

1936   *Mitla: Town of the Souls.* Chicago: University of Chicago Press.

Ponce de León, Pedro

1953   "Breve Relación de los Dioses y Ritos de la Gentilidad." In *Tratado de las Idolatrías, Supersticiones, Dioses, Ritos, Hechicerías y Otras Costumbres Gentílicas de las Razas Aborígenes de México,* Jacinto de la Serna, México, D.F.: Ediciones Fuente Cultural.

Psychiatric Dictionary

1981   Hinsie, Leland E., and Robert J. Campbell, eds. New York: Oxford University Press.

Ravicz, Robert, and A. Kimball Romney

1969   "The Mixtec." In *Handbook of Middle American Indians,* edited by Robert Wauchope. Vol. 7. Austin: University of Texas Press.

Redfield, Robert

1930   *Tepoztlán, a Mexican Village.* Chicago: University of Chicago Press.

Redfield, Robert, and Alfonso Villa Rojas

1962   *Chan Kom: A Maya Village.* Chicago: University of Chicago Press.

Reina, Rubén E.

1966   *The Law of the Saints: A Pokoman Pueblo and Its Community Culture.* Indianapolis: Bobbs-Merrill.

Reynolds, Bertrand

1963   *Magic, Divination and Witchcraft among the Barotse of Northern Rhodesia.* London: Berkeley.

Ricard, Robert

1947   *La Conquista Espiritual de México,* translated by Angel María Garibay. México, D.F.: Editorial Jus.

Roberts, John M.

1976   "Belief in the Evil Eye in World Perspective." In *The Evil Eye,* edited by Clarence Maloney, 223–78. New York: Columbia University Press.

Roberts, John M., Chen Chiao, and Triloki N. Pandey

1975   "Meaningful God Sets from a Chinese Personal Pantheon and a Hindu Personal Pantheon." *Ethnology* 14(2):121–48.

Roberts, John M., and Chong Pil Choe

1984   "Korean Animal Entities with Supernatural Attributes: A Study in Expressive Belief." *Arctic Anthropology* 21(2):187–99.

Roberts, John M., Saburo Morita, and L. Keith Brown

1986   "Japanese Sacred Places and Gods: Categories Elicited from a Conjugal Pair." *American Anthropologist* 88(4):807–24.

Romney, A. Kimball, Tom Smith, Howard E. Freeman, Jerome Kagan, and Robert E.
Klein
1979   "Concepts of Success and Failure." *Social Science Research* 8:302–26.

Rubel, Arthur J., et al.
1984   *Susto, a Folk Illness.* Berkeley: University of California Press.

Ruel, Malcolm
1970   "Were-Animals and the Introverted Witch." In *Witchcraft Confessions and Accusations*, edited by Mary Douglas. London: Tavistock Publications.

Ruiz de Alarcón, Hernando
1953   "Tratado de las Supersticiones y Costumbres Gentílicas que Oy Viuen Entre los Indios Naturales de esta Nueva España, Escrito en México, Año de *1629.*" In *Tratado de las Idolatrías, Supersticiones, Dioses, Ritos, Hechicerías y Otras Costumbres Gentílicas de las Razas Aborígenes de México*, Jacinto de la Serna, Méxcio, D.F.: Ediciones Fuente Cultural.

Russell, Bertrand
1945   *A History of Western Philosophy.* New York: Simon and Schuster.

Sahagún, Fray Bernardino de
1956   *Historia General de las Cosas de la Nueva España.* Four volumes. México, D.F.: Editorial Porrúa, S.A.

Saler, Benson
1964   "Nagual, Witch, and Sorcerer in a Quiche Village." *Ethnology* 3:305–28.

Sánchez de Aguilar, Pedro
1953   "Informe Contra Idolorum Cultores del Obispado de Yucatan, Año de 1639." In *Tratado de las Idolatrías, Supersticiones, Dioses, Ritos, Hechicerías y Otras Costumbres Gentílicas de las Razas Aborígenes de México*, Jacinto de la Serna, México, D.F.: Ediciones Fuente Cultural.

Schapera, Isaac
1952   "Sorcery and Witchcraft in Bechuanaland." *African Affairs* 51:41–52.

Scheffler, Lilian
1983   *Magia y Brujería en México.* México, D.F.: Panorama Editorial, S.A.

Serna, Jacinto de la
1953   "Manual de Ministros de Indios para el Conocimiento de sus Idolatrías y Extirpación de Ellas." In *Tratado de las Idolatrías, Supersticiones, Dioses, Ritos, Hechicerías y Otras Costumbres Gentílicas de las Razas Aborígines de Mexico*, Jacinto de la Serna, México, D.F.: Ediciones Fuente Cultural.

Signorini, Italo, and Alessandro Lupo
1989   *I Tre Cardini della Vita.* Palermo, Italy: Sellerio Editore.

Simmons, William S.
1971   *Eyes of the Night: Witchcraft Among a Senegalese People.* Boston: Little Brown and Company.

Smith, Watson, and John M. Roberts
1954   *Zuni Law: A Field of Values.* Papers of the Peabody Museum of American Archaeology and Ethnology, vol. 43, no. 1. Cambridge: Peabody Museum.

Spiro, Melford E.
  1952 "Ghosts, Ifaluk, and Teleological Functionalism." *American Anthropologist* 54:497–503.
  1967 *Burmese Supernaturalism: A Study in the Explanation and Reduction of Suffering.* Englewood Cliffs, New Jersey: Prentice-Hall.
Starr, Frederick
  1900 *Notes Upon the Ethnography of Southern Mexico.* Proceedings of the Davenport Academy of Natural Sciences, volumes 8 and 9.
Szewczyk, Robert
  n.d. "Settlement in Tlaxcala in the XVII Century."
Tambiah, S. J.
  1973 "Form and Meaning of Magical Acts: A Point of View." In *Modes of Thought: Essays on Thinking in Western and Non-Western Societies,* edited by Robin Horton and Ruth Finnegan. London: Faber and Faber.
Tax, Sol, ed.
  1952 *Heritage of Conquest: The Ethnology of Middle America.* Glencoe, Illinois: The Free Press.
Tezozomoc, Hernando Alvarado
  1943 *Crónica Mexicana.* México, D.F.: Imprenta Universitaria.
Thomas, Keith
  1970 "The Relevance of Social Anthropology to the Historical Study of English Witchcraft." In *Witchcraft Confessions and Accusations,* edited by Mary Douglas. London: Tavistock Publications.
Torquemada, Fray Juan de
  1944 *Los veinte i vn Libros Rituales i Monarchía Indiana, con el Origen y Guerras, de los Indios Ocidentales, de sus Poblazones, Descubrimiento, Conuersión y Otras Cosas Marauillosas de la Mesma Tierra.* Three volumes. México, D.F.: Editorial Chávez Hayhoe.
Tranfo, Luigi
  1974 *Vida y Magia en un Pueblo Otomí del Valle del Mezquital.* Serie de Antropología Social No. 34. México, D.F.: Instituto Nacional Indigenista.
Turner, Victor W.
  1964 "Witchcraft and Sorcery: Taxonomy versus Dynamics." *Africa* 34(4):314–25.
Villa Rojas, Alfonso
  1945 *The Maya of East Central Quintana Roo.* Publication No. 559. Washington, D.C.: Carnegie Institute.
  1947 "Kinship and Nagualism in a Tzeltal Community, Southeastern Mexico." *American Anthropologist* 49:578–87.
Voget, Fred W.
  1975 *A History of Ethnology.* New York: Holt, Rinehart and Winston.
Vogt, Evon Z.
  1969 *Zinacantan: A Maya Community in the Highlands of Chipas.* Cambridge: Harvard University Press.

Wallace, Anthony F. C.

1966   *Religion: An Anthropological View.* New York: Random House.

Wauchope, Robert, ed.

1971   *Handbook of Middle American Indians.* Eleven volumes. Austin: University of Texas Press.

Weller, Susan C., and Charles Buchholtz

1986   "When a Single Clustering Method Creates More than One Tree: A Re-Analysis of the Salish Language. *American Anthropologist* 88:667–74.

Weitlaner, Roberto J.

1969   "The Cuicatec." In *Handbook of Middle American Indians,* edited by Robert Wauchope. Vol. 7. Austin: University of Texas Press.

Whiteley, W. H.

1973   "Colour-Words and Colour-Values: The Evidence from Gusii." In *Modes of Thought: Essays on Thinking in Western and Non-Western Societies,* edited by Robin Horton and Ruth Finnegan. London: Faber and Faber.

Wilson, Monica

1952   "Witch Beliefs and Social Structure." *American Journal of Sociology,* Vol. 56.

1957   *Rituals of Kinship among the Nyakyosa.* London: Oxford University Press.

Winkelman, Michael J.

1987   *Magic and Religion: A Cross-Cultural Study.* Unpublished doctoral dissertation. Irvine: University of California.

Wisdom, Charles

1952   "The Supernatural World and Curing." In *Heritage of Conquest: The Ethnology of Middle America,* edited by Sol Tax. Glencoe, Illinois: The Free Press.

1961   *Los Chortis de Guatemala.* Seminario de Integración Social Guatemalteca. Publicación No. 10. Guatemala: Editorial del Ministerio de Educación.

Wolfram, Sybil

1973   "Basic Differences of Thought." In *Modes of Thought: Essays on Thinking in Western and Non-Western Societies,* edited by Robin Horton and Ruth Finnegan. London: Faber and Faber.

Index

About the Authors

HUGO G. NUTINI is University Professor of Anthropology at the University of Pittsburgh. His main theoretical interests have been anthropological theory, structuralism, sociocultural change, ethnohistory, social stratification, expressive culture, kinship, ritual kinship, and religion. On these topics he has written many articles in national and international journals. His ethnographic and ethnologic work has been done in Central Mexico, primarily among Nahuatl-speaking Indians in the states of Tlaxcala and Puebla. He is the author of eight books on this area, and he is working on a three-volume series on the Mexican aristocracy and *haute bourgeoisie*, focusing primarily on the restructuring of classes that has taken place since the Revolution of 1910. His work on the Tlaxcala-Pueblan Valley includes the following volumes: *San Bernardino Contla: Marriage and Family Structure in a Tlaxcalan Municipio*, a structural-functional analysis of the only unilineal society in Central Mexico; *Ritual Kinship: The Structure and Historical Development of the Compadrazgo System in Rural Tlaxcala* and *Ritual Kinship: Ideological and Structural Integration of the Compadrazgo System in Rural Tlaxcala*, the only exhaustive description and analysis of *compadrazgo* in the literature; *Todos Santos in Rural Tlaxcala: A Syncretic, Expressive, and Symbolic Analysis of the Cult of the Dead*, an expressive-structural analysis of household religion emphasizing folk theology, teleology, and eschatology.

JOHN M. ROBERTS was Andrew W. Mellon Professor Emeritus of Anthropology at the University of Pittsburgh when he died on April 2, 1990. He received his Ph.D. in anthropology from Yale University in 1947, and taught with distinction at the universities of Minnesota, Nebraska, Harvard, and Cornell, before he went to the University of Pittsburgh in 1971. He was a fellow at the Center for Advanced Study in the Behavioral Sciences in 1957, and in 1969–70 held the Chair of Comparative Cultures at the Naval War College. He held a number of professional offices, including the presidencies of the American Ethnological Societies (1960), the Northeastern Anthropological Association (1965–1967), the Society for Cross-Cultural Research (1974–1975), and the Association for the Anthropological Study of Play (1979–1980). He was elected to the National Academy of Sciences in 1982 and was to have served as chair of the Academy's Section 51 (Anthropology) from May 1990 to 1993.

He did extensive field research among the Ramah Navaho and the Zuni, beginning in 1945, although his most recent work was in Mexico. Much of his career, however, was spent in cross-cultural research and as a theoretician of expressive culture. In his numerous publications, he pioneered the study of several areas that have since become prominent in anthropological research. He examined intracultural diversity, beginning with *Three Navaho Households* (1951), small group culture, with *Zuni Daily Life* (1956), culture as an information processing system in "The Self-Management of Cultures" (1964), and cultural expertise in "Buttler County Eight Ball" (1979). In 1959, he published "Games and Culture" in the *American Anthropologist*, which, probably more than any other single publication, relegitimized the study of games and play in anthropology. In subsequent publications from both the cross-cultural and intracultural perspective, he and Brian Sutton-Smith developed the Conflict-Enculturation Theory of Model Involvement wherein expressive activities, including games, music, hobbies and riddles, are held to be models of "real world" cultural activities that provide both assuagement of psychological conflicts that develop during enculturation and buffered learning about those activities. From 1979 until his death, he and Hugo G. Nutini conducted intensive research on the Mexcian aristocracy, focused on its expressive culture and the changes that have taken place during three generations as the result of the realignment of classes provoked by the Revolution of 1910. Roberts was one of the most creative anthropologists of this century, with a devotion to science and a passion for knowledge. The consummate collaborator, he published on an extremely wide variety of topics and on numerous cultures, always drawing upon and drawing out the expertise of his coworkers.